Bonnie B. Strickland
Children's Medical Center
Hospital of Akron Family-Child
Learning Center (in conjunction
with Kent State University)

Ann P. Turnbull
University of Kansas-Lawrence

Developing and Implementing Individualized Education Programs

THIRD EDITION

Merrill Publishing Company
Columbus   Toronto   London   Melbourne

This book was set in Zapf Book Light.

Administrative Editor: Ann Castel
Production Coordinator: Jan Hall
Art Coordinator: Raydelle Clement
Copyeditor: Luanne Dreyer
Cover Designers: Russ Maselli, Brian Deep

Library of Congress Catalog Card Number: 89-61351
International Standard Book Number: 0-675-21142-5

Printed in the United States of America

4   5   6   7   8   9—94   93   92

To Steve and Rich, with love and thanks.

PREFACE

Every educator responsible for providing special education and related services to students with disabilities has already encountered, or will encounter, questions about how to develop and implement individualized education programs (IEPs). P.L. 94–142 at the national level, as well as legislation in almost every state, requires educators to be involved in the IEP process. The rules and regulations resulting from federal and state legislation set forth guidelines outlining what must be done. Educators, however, need assistance and training to develop skills necessary to comply with IEP requirements. To a large extent, the competencies of educators associated with IEP development and implementation will determine whether the noble ideal of providing an appropriate education to students with disabilities is, indeed, translated into educational practice. This book helps educators answer the question, How can I effectively carry out my responsibilities associated with the IEP?

The book is organized into three major parts: (1) Procedural Guidelines for IEP Development, (2) Mechanics of IEP Development, and (3) Implementation of the IEP. Part 1 includes a chapter on the six major principles of P.L. 94–142—zero rejection, non-discriminatory evaluation, IEPs, least restrictive environment, due process, and parental participation. Although legal principles and requirements are explained throughout the book, the legal requirements (P.L. 94–142) were enacted to operationalize principles of sound educational practice (e.g., individualized, nonbiased evaluation and parent involvement). Thus, the principles undergirding the IEP process and procedures are educational as well as legal. The next five chapters focus on procedural steps—from the point of referral of a child for evaluation to informing parents of evaluation results and inviting them to attend the IEP conference. Since the development of the IEP is but one step in the total process of identifying, evaluating, and providing appropriate services to students with disabilities, Part 1 helps the reader develop competencies in the educational activities that precede initial IEP development. Part 2 covers the actual development of the IEP. The first chapter in this part provides an overview of the IEP committee meeting and proposes guidelines for planning and conducting the meeting. Each subsequent chapter focuses on one of the legally required components (levels of performance, annual goals and short-term objectives, evaluation procedures, related services, and placement decisions). Special attention is given to parent and student involvement in decision making. Part 3 concludes the book with two chapters on implementing IEPs. Current implementation issues, such as coordination among service providers, transition and inservice training, are addressed in detail.

The legal requirements on which the IEP is based are drawn from both federal and state legislation. The federal legislation is P.L. 94–142, The Education of All Handicapped Children Act. Chapter 1 provides an in-depth discussion of the P.L. 94–142 regulations. Also included in Chapter 1 is a comparative description of P.L. 99–457, The Amendment to the Education of the Handicapped Act of 1986. The reader should know that, by 1991, this new legislation will extend the provisions of P.L. 94–142 to 3- 5-year-old students with disabilities. This legislation also provides strong incentives for states to provide early intervention services to infants and toddlers (birth–age 2) with disabilities and their families. Although not all educational agencies will be responsible for the actual planning and provision of early intervention services, educators should be familiar with the provisions of this legislation to ensure continuity of services between agencies responsible for these services and programs provided by the public school.

The target audience of this book is the practitioner who is responsible for IEP development and implementation. Since the composition of IEP committees is multidisciplinary, the target audience is also multidisciplinary. Preservice and inservice students in general education, special education, school psychology, counseling, supervision, and administration will find the suggestions in this book helpful in carrying out responsibilities associated with the IEP. Numerous implementation aids, such as sample notices to parents, sample IEP forms, and a variety of monitoring instruments, constitute a key feature of the book. Curriculum checklists, another implementation aid, provide a task analysis of basic competencies in five subject areas. The task analysis can greatly simplify the process of writing the goals and objectives for the IEP in the particular subject areas covered.

The noncategorical approach to programming stressed throughout the book increases the applicability of information to all segments of the disabled population. Thus the book is just as appropriate for a teacher of students with learning disabilities as for a teacher of students with physical disabilities. Another important feature is the presentation of a variety of alternatives on the various aspects of IEP development and implementation. Individuals can adapt these alternatives to their particular need and situation; no attempt is made to "sell" a single approach. Also included are evaluation questions that provide an opportunity for immediate application of the concepts and skills discussed in the chapters. These questions simulate day-to-day problems associated with IEP responsibilities. We hope that the practical and relevant nature of this book will contribute to the preparation of educators in meeting the professional responsibilities associated with the IEP.

We would like to extend recognition and appreciation to those whose contributions have added immeasurably to this book, especially, Linda Renz for her knowledge and expertise in the development of procedures and responsibilities of the special services committee; to Carol Urbiha, Calise Mossler, Beth Coley, Ruth Heruska, Jerri Moore, Joan Balde, and Ann L. Stewart, who contributed their knowledge and expertise in the development of the sample IEPs included in this book; to Stephanie White for her contribution of reporting vocational evaluation results; to the teachers and administrators of the Department of Defense Dependents for their contribution of many examples used throughout the text; and to the special education teachers of Georgia's Central Flint Cooperative Educational Service Agency, who contributed to the development of the curriculum checklists. Thank you also to our reviewers, Candice Bray, Learning Disabilities Specialist, Boston, Massachusetts; Carl R. Smith, Buena Vista College; and Jack J. Hourcade, Boise State University.

We were most fortunate to receive assistance and encouragement from Vicki Knight, the editor from Merrill Publishing Company who worked with us on this third edition. Vicki's substantive contributions and moral support enhanced the quality of our efforts. Her incredible talent for dispensing "positive reinforcement" to us added zest to many arduous working sessions. Undoubtedly, Vicki is a master motivator.

A final word of heartfelt thanks is extended to the members of our families for their support and encouragement throughout the preparation of this book.

CONTENTS

*Developing
and Implementing
Individualized
Education Programs*

THIRD EDITION

PART 1

Procedural Guidelines for IEP Development

CHAPTER 1

Public Law 94–142 and Public Law 99–457

OBJECTIVES

1. State the purpose of P.L. 94–142 and P.L. 99–457.
2. Compare and contrast the provisions of P.L. 99–457 relative to the six principles of P.L. 94–142.
3. Identify the six major principles of P.L. 94–142 and explain the specific regulations pertaining to each principle.
4. State the rights that each of the six principles of P.L. 94–142 provides for students with disabilities and their parents.
5. Demonstrate a detailed knowledge of the regulations pertaining to the IEP in the broad areas of the required content, scope, time lines for development, participants in development, parent and student participation, interagency agreements, and accountability.

The enactment of P.L. 94–142, The Education of All Handicapped Children Act, in November, 1975, marked significant procedural and programmatic changes to the educational services provided to students with disabilities. The main purpose of P.L. 94–142 was stated as follows:

> It is the purpose of this Act to assure that all handicapped children have available to them . . . a free appropriate public education which emphasizes special education and related services designed to meet their unique needs, to assure that the rights of handicapped children and their parents or guardians are protected, to assist States and localities to provide for the education of all handicapped children, and to assess and assure the effectiveness of efforts to educate handicapped children. (P.L. 94–142, sec. 601c)

The legal framework for providing a free, appropriate public education is contained in specific elements of P.L. 94–142. These elements may be summarized and discussed in the context of six encompassing principles as follows:

1. Inclusion in a program of appropriate service
2. Nondiscriminatory evaluation
3. Individualized education program
4. Least restrictive environment
5. Procedural safeguards
6. Parent participation

Each of these provisions will be discussed in this chapter as they relate to the educational services provided to school-age students.

This book focuses on the requirements of P.L. 94–142 and the development and provision of educational programs to school-age students; however, many of the provisions of P.L. 94–142 recently have been extended to preschool children ages 3 to 5 with disabilities and to infants and toddlers ages birth–2

with disabilities. The Amendments to the Education of the Handicapped Act of 1986 were enacted in October 1986 (1) to ensure the provision of a free appropriate public education to all eligible preschool students with disabilities ages 3 to 5 and (2) to make available significant federal support for the development of early intervention programs for infants and toddlers with disabilities ages birth–2, and their families. Together with P.L. 94–142, the enactment of P.L. 99–457 confirmed the legislative commitment to provide a full range of appropriate services to infants, toddlers, and students with disabilities.

Because the process of planning and delivery of services to children birth–2 and their families likely will differ significantly from that of providing services to preschool and school-aged students, this book will not address program development for this population in subsequent chapters. Nonetheless, although the degree to which departments of education will be responsible for implementation of P.L. 99–457 will differ considerably among states, educators will in future years most certainly be involved in the transition of children between programs provided through P.L. 99–457 and those provided by P.L. 94–142. Therefore, educators should be cognizant of the intent of P.L. 99–457 to ensure appropriate services to young children. To familiarize the reader with the basic provisions of P.L. 99–457, this chapter will provide a brief discussion of its coverage using the six principles of P.L. 94–142 for comparison.

The framework for the provision of early intervention services in P.L. 99–457 remains similar in many respects to that of P.L. 94–142. The cornerstone of both laws is the provision of a free appropriate program of publicly supported services to children with disabilities. In addition, the vehicle by which such services are provided is an individually designed and written program of services developed by a committee including the parents and safeguarded by a system of due process. The requirements for provision of services to school-age (including preschool) students, however, differ significantly from those for provision of services to infants and toddlers with disabilities .

INCLUSION IN A PROGRAM OF APPROPRIATE SERVICES

Definitions

The principle of inclusion, applied to educational programs, means that all students with disabilities, ages 3 to 21 must be provided with a free appropriate public education. In states where the provision of educational services to 3- to 5- and 18- to 21-year-old students is inconsistent with state law, educational agencies have been required to provide services only to students with disabilities ages 5 to 18. It should be noted here that P.L. 99–457 requires that by 1991 states not already doing so must begin serving the 3 to 5 population according to the provisions of P.L. 94–142 for school-age students. Thus, this population soon will be considered a part of the definition of *school-aged* students.

A clear definition of key terms is necessary to understand who must be included in special education and what "free appropriate public education" actually means.

First, to determine which students are included, the term *handicapped* is, for educational purposes, categorically defined by P.L. 94–142 to include the following students:

1. Students who have been evaluated according to the legislative requirements and determined to have mental retardation, impairments of hearing, deafness, speech impairments, visual impairments, serious emotional disturbances, orthopedic impairments, other health impairments, deaf-blindness, multiple impairments, or specific learning disabilities
2. Students whose impairment has a demonstrated adverse effect on educational performance
3. Students who, because of these impairments, need special education and related services. (*Federal Register*, 1977)

These criteria are important for establishing that a disability alone is not sufficient for a student to qualify for special education. Thus, if a student has a disability that does not adversely affect educational performance and/or does not require special education and related services, the student would not be considered handicapped according to P.L. 94–142 and would not be entitled to special education services (*Federal Register*, 1977). Although the language of P.L. 94–142 and its implementing regulations use the terms *impairment* and *handicapped* to define students who have a disability and are eligible for special education, the preference for terminology has changed since the mid-1970s, when this legislation was enacted. Currently, the term *disability* is preferred; thus, this book will use this term to describe the students covered by the legislation.

Other key terms define the basic entitlements of P.L. 94–142. First, the term *free appropriate public education* is defined by P.L. 94–142 as follows:

> Special education and related services which (A) have been provided at public expense, under public supervision and direction, and without charge, (B) meet the standards of the State education agency, (C) include an appropriate pre-school, elementary, or secondary school education in the State involved, and (D) are provided in conformity with the individualized education program required under section 614 (a) (5). (P.L. 94–142, sec. 602 [18]).

It is important to note that conformity with IEP requirements is an essential ingredient of a free appropriate public education.

Second, P.L. 94–142 further clarifies the meaning of free appropriate public education by defining the term *special education* as follows:

> . . . specially designed instruction at no cost to the parent to meet the unique needs of a handicapped child, including classroom instruction, instruction in physical education, home instruction and instruction in hospitals and institutions. (*Federal Register*, 1977)

Figure 1–1 provides legal definitions of each handicapping condition included in P.L. 94–142.

Third, in addition to providing appropriate educational services to all students with disabilities, the local education agency must ensure that these students receive all educationally related services required to benefit from special education. Related services are defined as follows:

> . . . transportation and such developmental, corrective, and other supportive services as are required to assist a handicapped child to benefit from special education, and includes speech pathology and audiology, psychological services, physical and occupational therapy, recreation, early identification and assessment of disabilities in children, counseling services, and medical services for diagnostic or evaluation purposes. The term also includes school health services, social work services in schools, and parent counseling and training. (*Federal Register*, 1977, p. 42473)

FIGURE 1–1
Legal Definitions of Handicapped Children

(a) The term "handicapped children" means those children evaluated as being mentally retarded, hard of hearing, deaf, speech impaired, visually handicapped, seriously emotionally disturbed, orthopedically impaired, other health impaired, deaf-blind, multihandicapped, or as having specific learning disabilities, who because of those impairments need special education and related services.

(b) The terms used in this definition are defined as follows:

(1) "Deaf" means a hearing impairment which is so severe that the child is impaired in processing linguistic information through hearing, with or without amplification, which adversely affects educational performance.

(2) "Deaf-blind" means concomitant hearing and visual impairments, the combination of which causes such severe communication and other developmental and educational problems that they cannot be accommodated in special education programs solely for deaf or blind children.

(3) "Hard of hearing" means a hearing impairment whether permanent or fluctuating, which adversely affects a child's educational performance but which is not included under the definition of "deaf" in this section.

(4) "Mentally retarded" means significantly subaverage general intellectual functioning existing concurrently with deficits in adaptive behavior and manifested during the developmental period, which adversely affects a child's educational performance.

(5) "Multihandicapped" means concomitant impairments (such as mentally retarded-blind, mentally retarded-orthopedically impaired, etc.), the combination of which causes such severe educational problems that they cannot be accommodated in special education programs solely for one of the impairments. The term does not include deaf-blind children.

(6) "Orthopedically impaired" means a severe orthopedic impairment which adversely affects a child's educational performance. The term includes impairments caused by congenital anomaly (e.g., clubfoot, absence of some member, etc.), impairments caused by disease (e.g., poliomyelitis, bone tuberculosis, etc.), and impairments from other causes (e.g., cerebral palsy, amputations, and fractures or burns which cause contractures).

(7) "Other health impaired" means

(i) having an autistic condition which is manifested by severe communication and other developmental and educational problems;[1] or

(ii) having limited strength, vitality or alertness, due to chronic or acute health problems such as a heart condition, tuberculosis, rheumatic fever, nephritis, asthma, sickle cell anemia, hemophilia, epilepsy, lead poisoning, leukemia, or diabetes, which adversely affects a child's educational performance.

(8) "Seriously emotionally disturbed" is defined as follows:

(i) The term means a condition exhibiting one or more of the following characteristics over a long period of time and to a marked degree, which adversely affects educational performance:

(A) An inability to learn which cannot be explained by intellectual, sensory, or health factors;

(B) An inability to build or maintain satisfactory interpersonal relationships with peers and teachers;

(C) Inappropriate types of behavior or feelings under normal circumstances;

(D) A general pervasive mood of unhappiness or depression; or

(E) A tendency to develop physical symptoms of fears associated with personal or school problems.

(ii) The term includes children who are schizophrenic. The term does not include children who are socially maladjusted, unless it is determined that they are seriously emotionally disturbed.

(9) "Specific learning disability" means a disorder in one or more of the basic psychological processes involved in understanding or in using language, spoken or written, which may manifest itself in an imperfect ability to listen, think, speak, read, write, spell, or to do mathematical calculations. The term includes such conditions as perceptual handicaps, brain injury, minimal brain dysfunction, dyslexia, and developmental aphasia. The term does not include children who have learning problems which are primarily the result of visual, hearing, or motor handicaps, of mental retardation, or of environmental, cultural, or economic disadvantage.

(10) "Speech impaired" means a communication disorder, such as stuttering, impaired articulation, a language impairment, or a voice impairment, which adversely affects a child's educational performance.

(11) "Visually handicapped" means a visual impairment which, even with correction, adversely affects a child's educational performance. The term includes both partially seeing and blind children.

---

[1] *Federal Register*, 1977, pp. 42478–42479; 1981, pp. 3865–3866. (The definitional change of autism from the category of "seriously emotionally disturbed" to "other health impaired" is reported in this *Federal Register*.)

It is important to note that, because related services are provided to assist a student in benefiting from special education, the student must first receive special education to be eligible for these services. Figure 1–2 provides a list of related services as defined by the *Federal Register* (1977).

Services to Preschool Students With Disabilities

As mentioned earlier, P.L. 99–457 requires extending the free appropriate public education provisions of P.L. 94–142 to preschool students with disabilities ages 3 to 5 by the year 1991. As a result of incentive grants originally included as a provision of P.L. 94–142 to serve this population, many states already require the provision of services to this population. Figure 1–3, p. 10, provides a listing of the age at which states provide services to preschool students with disabilities. The number of preschool students with disabilities served has increased 19% in the 10 years since the enactment of P.L. 94–142 (U.S. Library of Congress, 1986). According to data prepared by the U.S. Department of Education (1987), states are currently serving more than 75% of preschool students with disabilities ages 3 to 5 inclusive in the country.

As was true with the implementation of P.L. 94–142 for school-age students, the mandate to extend educational services to 3- to 5-year-old students with disabilities is accompanied by both strong incentives and strong penalties. Significant amounts of financial support are allocated to reward states who are committed to providing services to this population. However, if a state fails to provide appropriate services to all preschool students with disabilities by the year 1991, the state will not be eligible for a preschool grant and therefore will be unable (1) to count those 3- to 5-year-olds who are served to receive that portion of funds normally allocated through P.L. 94–142 or (2) to receive federal funds for any programs, projects or activities dealing exclusively with preschoolers with disabilities.

Child Find

P.L. 94–142 establishes a specific procedure for locating all children with disabilities who may be entitled to the provision of a free appropriate public education. This process is termed *child find*, and this activity initiates the inclusion principle. Each agency must conduct an annual child-find program to locate, identify, and evaluate all children with disabilities who reside in that agency's jurisdiction. Children with disabilities within specialized age and disability categories are reported by the local agency to the state education agency and, in turn, to the U.S. Office

of Education. The local education agency then becomes eligible to receive federal funds based on the number of students with disabilities served. For the purposes of funding, however, only 12% of the school-aged population can be identified as handicapped. If more than 12% are identified as handicapped, funds from local and state sources must be provided to finance the excess cost of their programs. In the 1985 to 1986 school year, approximately 11% of the total public school enrollment was served, with percentages in some states approaching or exceeding the 12% limit (U.S. Office of Special Education and Rehabilitative Services, 1987). According to this report, many educators believe that most, if not all, of the students needing special education services have been identified (Gartner & Lipsky, 1987).

Each state and local education agency has its own requirements for conducting child-find activities. Typical activities include public announcements, notices, coordination with other service agencies, referral, and preschool screening procedures.

Early Intervention Services to Infants and Toddlers with Disabilities

Just as P.L. 94–142 provides the framework by which free appropriate public education is to be provided to school-aged students (and to preschool students by 1991), P.L. 99–457 provides a framework for assisting states in developing and implementing a comprehensive, coordinated, and multidisciplinary program of early intervention services for infants and toddlers with disabilities ages birth–2 and their families. There are, however, several important differences between the educational provisions of P.L. 94–142 and the early intervention services provisions of P.L. 99–457.

First, rather than focusing on special education and related services, the term *early intervention services* is used. Early intervention services are similar in kind to the related services provisions of P.L. 94–142 listed in Figure 1–2. They include but are not limited to the following:

> Family training, counseling, and home visits; special instruction; speech pathology and audiology; occupational therapy; physical therapy; psychological services; case management services; medical services for diagnostic or evaluation purposes; early identification, screening, and assessment services, health services necessary to enable the infant or toddler to benefit from other early intervention services. (P.L. 99–457)

It is interesting to note that case management services are specifically included as an early intervention

FIGURE 1–2
Related Services in Special Education

Audiology	(a) Identification of children with hearing loss; (b) Determination of the range, nature, degree of hearing loss, including referral for medical or other professional attention for the habilitation of hearing; (c) Provision of habilitative activities, such as language habilitation, auditory training, speech reading (lip reading), hearing evaluation, and speech conservation; (d) Creation and administration of programs for prevention of hearing loss; (e) Counseling and guidance of pupils, parents, and teachers regarding hearing loss; and (f) Determination of the child's need for group and individual amplification, selecting and fitting an appropriate aid, and evaluating the effectiveness of amplification.
Counseling Services	Services provided by qualified social workers, psychologists, guidance counselors, or other qualified personnel.
Early Identification	Implementation of a formal plan for identifying a disability as early as possible in a child's life.
Medical Services	Services provided by a licensed physician to determine a child's medically related handicapping condition which results in the child's need for special education and related services.
Occupational Therapy	(a) Improving, developing, or restoring functions impaired or lost through illness, injury, or deprivation; (b) Improving ability to perform tasks for independent functioning when functions are impaired or lost; and (c) Preventing, through early intervention, initial or further impairment or loss of function.
Parent Counseling and Training	Assisting parents in understanding the special needs of their child and providing parents with information about child development.
Physical Therapy	Services provided by a qualified physical therapist.
Psychological Services	(a) Administering psychological and educational tests, and other assessment procedures; (b) Interpreting assessment results; (c) Obtaining, integrating, and interpreting information about child behavior and conditions relating to learning.

service to assist families to obtain the other early intervention services that may be required.

Second, the definition of *handicapped* is conceptualized somewhat differently in P.L. 99–457. Because early intervention services are to be provided to infants and toddlers (ages birth–2) rather than school-aged children, disabilities are defined in terms of developmental delays rather than the categorical terms of P.L. 94–142. P.L. 99–457 defines the term *handicapped* as follows:

> Individuals from birth to age two, inclusive, who need early intervention services because they (1) are experiencing developmental delays in cognitive development, physical development, language and speech development, psychosocial development, or self help skills or (2) have a diagnosed physical or mental condition which has a high probability of resulting in developmental delay. (P.L. 99–457, sec. 672)

Unlike P.L. 94–142, P.L. 99–457 indicates that the term *handicapped* may, at a state's discretion, include infants and toddlers who are "at risk" of having substantial developmental delays. Thus, children may be eligible for early intervention services even though they may not have a diagnosed physical or mental condition that may result in developmental delay or may not have been formally diagnosed as experiencing developmental delays. This deliberately vague approach is further broadened by the provision that each state has the flexibility to determine the meaning given to the term *developmentally delayed* as long as the meaning remains within the context of the five developmental areas included in the legislative definition (cognitive, physical, language and speech, psychosocial, and self-help).

Third, P.L. 99–457 reflects broader representation than P.L. 94–142. The early intervention provisions of P.L. 99–457 focus on the provision of services to

(Figure 1–2 continued)

	(d) Consulting with other staff members in planning school programs to meet the special needs of children as indicated by psychological tests, interviews, and behavioral evaluations; and
	(e) Planning and managing a program of psychological services, including psychological counseling for children and parents.
Recreation	(a) Assessment of leisure function;
	(b) Therapeutic recreation services;
	(c) Recreation programs in schools and community agencies; and
	(d) Leisure education.
School Health Services	Services provided by a qualified school nurse or other qualified person.
Social Work Services	(a) Preparing a social or developmental history on a handicapped child;
	(b) Group and individual counseling with the child and family;
	(c) Working with those problems in a child's living situation (home, school, and community) that affect the child's adjustment in school; and
	(d) Mobilizing school and community resources to enable the child to receive maximum benefit from his or her educational program.
Speech Pathology	(a) Identification of children with speech or language disorders;
	(b) Diagnosis and appraisal of specific speech or language disorders;
	(c) Referral for medical or other professional attention necessary for the habilitation of speech or language disorders;
	(d) Provisions of speech and language services for the habilitation or prevention of communicative disorders; and
	(e) Counseling and guidance of parents, children, and teachers regarding speech and language disorders.
Transportation	(a) Travel to and from school and between schools;
	(b) Travel in and around school buildings; and
	(c) Specialized equipment (such as special or adapted buses, lifts, and ramps), if required to provide special transportation for a handicapped child.

From the *Federal Register,* August 23, 1977, *42* (163).

both the child and the family rather than to the child alone. In contrast, P.L. 94–142 does not refer to families as recipients of services. Although P.L. 94–142 requires parent involvement, this involvement primarily relates to the exercise of procedural safeguards and decision-making authority. Early intervention services are designed to enhance the ability of families to meet the special needs of their infants and toddlers and to minimize the adverse effects of the disability in later years. Because of the recognized importance of the family in the development of the young handicapped child, P.L. 99–457 emphasizes this role in the identification and delivery of services by requiring identification of family needs as well as child needs and provision of services accordingly.

Fourth, ultimate responsibility for the provision of early intervention services does not necessarily lie with the state and local educational agency, as is the case with the special education provisions of P.L. 94–142. P.L. 99–457 provides for the establishment of a "lead agency" appointed by the governor of each state to be ultimately responsible for the administration, supervision, and monitoring of the program, although all agencies involved with the provision of early intervention services still are responsible for providing necessary services. While in many cases, the "lead agency" may be the state educational agency, other public agencies such as health and human services may assume this responsibility (U.S. Office of Education, 1988). Figure 1–4 indicates the public agency serving as lead agency in each state.

Regardless of which agency serves as the lead agency, a variety of disciplines and agencies may be responsible for the actual provision of services, thus creating significant coordination responsibilities. To address this issue, states must develop models of interagency coordination to define financial responsibilities of each agency for providing services and to

FIGURE 1–3
Minimum Ages Mandated by States and Territories for Providing Special Education to All Handicapped Children: July 1985

Birth	Age 2	Age 3	Age 4	Age 5	Age 6 or "School-Age"
Iowa	Virginia	Alaska	Delaware[b]	Arizona	Alabama
Maryland		California	Minnesota	Arkansas	Florida
Michigan		Connecticut	Oklahoma[c]	Colorado	Georgia
Nebraska		District of	Tennessee	Kansas	Idaho
New Jersey		Columbia		Maine	Indiana
Oregon		Hawaii		Missouri	Kentucky
South Dakota		Illinois		Nevada	Mississippi
American		Louisiana		New Mexico	Montana
Samoa		Massachusetts		New York	Vermont
Trust		New Hampshire		N. Carolina	Wyoming[e]
Territory		North Dakota		Ohio	
Guam		Rhode Island		Pennsylvania[d]	
		Texas[a]		S. Carolina	
		Washington		Utah	
		Wisconsin		W. Virginia	
		Northern		Puerto Rico	
		Marianas		Virgin	
				Islands	

[a]Mandates services for visually impaired, hearing impaired and deaf-blind from birth.

[b]Mandates services for deaf, blind, deaf-blind, and autistic children from birth; mandates services for orthopedically impaired, severely mentally handicapped, and trainable mentally handicapped from age 3.

[c]Mandates services for deaf-blind and "failure to thrive" from birth.

[d]Services mandates from 4 years 7 months.

[e]Health and social services are mandated for children from birth.

From *State EC/SE Status and State Participation in Networks* by U.S. Department of Education, Office of Special Education and Rehabilitative Services, unpublished matrix.

resolve interagency disputes. Such interagency agreements ultimately will enable coordinated delivery of services to infants and toddlers with disabilities and their families.

NONDISCRIMINATORY EVALUATION

Definition and Standards

A student with a disability must receive an individual comprehensive evaluation before placement in a special education program. Evaluation is defined by P.L. 94–142 as follows:

Procedures used . . . to determine whether a child is handicapped and the nature and extent of the special education and related services that the child needs. The term means procedures used selectively with an individual child and does not include basic tests administered to or procedures used with all children in a school, grade, or class. (*Federal Register*, 1977, p. 42494)

Evaluation, therefore, is the beginning point of planning an individualized program of services for a student with a disability. Furthermore, once identified, all students must be re-evaluated every 3 years (or more frequently if requests are made by the

FIGURE 1–4
States Included in Each Category of Lead Agency

Education	Health	Other
Alabama	Alaska	<u>Human Services/Developmental Disabilities</u>
Colorado	Hawaii	Arizona
Connecticut	Kansas	Idaho
Delaware	Massachusetts	Montana
Florida	Mississippi	New Mexico
Illinois	New York	North Dakota
Iowa	Ohio	Oregon
Louisiana	South Carolina	
Michigan	Utah	<u>Human Services/MH-MR</u>
Minnesota	Washington	Georgia
Missouri	West Virginia	Kentucky
Nebraska	Wisconsin	North Carolina
New Hampshire	Wyoming	Virginia
New Jersey		
Oklahoma		<u>Human Services</u>
South Dakota		Arkansas
Tennessee		Nevada
Vermont		
		<u>Interdepartmental Councils</u>
		Maine
		Rhode Island
		Texas
		<u>Other</u>
		DC (Department of Human Services)
		Indiana (Mental Health)
		Maryland (Governor's Office for
		Children and Youth)
		Pennsylvania (Department of
		Public Welfare)

Reprinted from *Report on the Program for Infants and Toddlers with Handicaps* by U.S. Department of Education, 1987, Washington D.C.: U.S. Goverment Printing Office.

student's teachers or parents). Evaluation procedures must meet the following standards:

  (a) Tests and other evaluation materials:
    (1) Are provided and administered in the child's native language (defined in the regulations as the language normally used by the child) or other mode of communication, unless it is clearly not feasible to do so;
    (2) Have been validated for the specific purpose for which they are used; and
    (3) Are administered by trained personnel in conformance with the instructions provided by their producer;
  (b) Tests and other evaluation materials include those tailored to assess specific areas of educational need and not merely those which are designed to provide a single general intelligence quotient;

  (c) Tests are selected and administered so as best to ensure that when a test is administered to a child with impaired sensory, manual, or speaking skills, the test results accurately reflect the child's aptitude or achievement level or whatever other factors the test purports to measure, rather than reflecting the child's impaired sensory, manual, or speaking skills (except where those skills are the factors which tests purports to measure);
  (d) No single procedure is used as the sole criterion for determining an appropriate educational program for a child; and
  (e) The evaluation is made by a multidisciplinary team or group of persons, including at least

one teacher or other specialist with knowledge in the area of suspected disability.

(f) The child is assessed in all areas related to the suspected disability, including, where appropriate, health, vision, hearing, social and emotional status, general intelligence, academic performance, communicative status, and motor abilities. (*Federal Register*, 1977, pp. 42496–97)

Interpretation of Evaluation Results

In interpreting the evaluation data, the multidisciplinary evaluation team must document and carefully consider information from a variety of sources, including tests, teacher recommendations, physical and sensory evaluations, cultural or social background, and adaptive behavior. The determination of whether a student has a disability and needs special education services is based on information obtained from this evaluation process. Despite the importance of this process and attempts to define it precisely, a number of issues related to the interpretation of evaluation results have been raised. Primary among these are the findings of several studies, which indicate that decisions based on interpretation of evaluation results often follow no discernible data-based criteria and that diagnosis instead appears to be based on social and psychological factors (Ysseldyke, Algozzine, & Epps, 1983; Ysseldyke, Thurlow, Graden, Wesson, Algozzine, & Deno, 1983) primarily aimed at corroborating and confirming initial referral information (Wang, Reynolds, & Walberg, 1986; White & Calhoun, 1987). Chapter 5, Nondiscriminatory Evaluation, will provide a more indepth discussion of these issues.

Early Intervention Programs

The basic procedural provisions of P.L. 94–142 for nondiscriminatory assessment also apply to the assessment procedures used with infants and toddlers with disabilities. There is, however, one major difference: P.L. 99–457 requires not only a timely, comprehensive and multidisciplinary evaluation of the functioning of each infant and toddler but also an evaluation of the strengths and needs of the child's family to help the family assist in the infant or toddler's development. This requirement reflects the focus of early intervention services on the needs of the family rather than solely the individual child.

Appropriate procedures and instruments must be used to measure developmental delays in (1) cognitive development, (2) physical development, (3) language and speech development, (4) psychosocial development, or (5) self-help skills. Although each state has the latitude to define the term *developmental delay*, the definition must include levels of functioning in the five developmental areas included in the definition.

The inclusion by some states of children "at risk" raises an issue of appropriate and nondiscriminatory assessment, because vague definitions of "at risk" increase the possibility of false-positive identification of handicaps. In such instances it may be determined that children need intervention when such is not the case (Fraas, 1986). Misdiagnosis of a handicap can perpetuate the view of the child as handicapped and have lasting detrimental effects. However, waiting to intervene until the adverse effect of a disability develops and is clearly apparent may create the even greater danger of preventing the provision of services necessary to minimize the effects of a disability or even to prevent the development of a disability in later years.

One advantage in the assessment of young children is that major disabilities identified at an early age (birth—2) often are diagnosed through medical procedures, which are perhaps less susceptible to the issues of race and socioeconomic bias. These considerations are significant weaknesses in the procedures currently used in most public schools to identify school-aged children with learning disabilities (Palfrey, Singer, Walker, & Butler, 1987).

INDIVIDUALIZED EDUCATION PROGRAMS

Purpose and Function

To ensure that educational programs are tailored to meet the individual needs of school-aged students with disabilities, P.L. 94–142 requires that an IEP be developed and implemented for each student. The requirements for IEPs will be set forth here and discussed in detail throughout the remainder of the book. In providing guidance related to the purpose and function of IEPs, the U.S. Department of Education (1981) summarized as follows:

1. The IEP meeting serves as a communication vehicle between parents and school personnel, and enables them, as equal participants, to jointly decide upon the student's needs, the services which will be provided to meet those needs, and what the anticipated outcomes may be.

2. The IEP process provides an opportunity for resolving any differences between the parents and the agency concerning a student's special education needs; first, through the IEP meeting, and second, if necessary, through the procedural protections that are available to the parents.

3. The IEP sets forth in writing a commitment of resources necessary to enable a student to receive needed special education and related services.
4. The IEP is a management tool that is used to ensure that each student is provided special education and related services appropriate to address identified learning needs.
5. The IEP is a compliance/monitoring document which may be used by authorized monitoring personnel from each governmental level to determine whether a student is actually receiving the free appropriate public education agreed to by the parents and the school.
6. The IEP serves as an evaluation device for use in determining the extent of the student's progress toward meeting the projected outcomes.

Content of the IEP

Each IEP must include the following components:

1. A documentation of the student's current level of educational performance
2. Annual goals or the attainments expected by the end of the school year
3. Short-term objectives, stated in instructional terms, which are the intermediate steps leading to the mastery of annual goals
4. Documentation of the particular special education that will be provided to the student
5. Documentation of the particular related services, if any, that will be provided to the student
6. An indication of the extent of time a student will participate in the regular education program
7. Projected dates for initiating services and the anticipated duration of services
8. Appropriate objective criteria, evaluation procedures, and schedules for determining mastery of short-term objectives, at least on an annual basis

In addition to these requirements, P.L. 99–457 requires that in IEPs for preschool students, instructions must be given to parents so that they can be active and knowledgeable in assisting their child's progress. Most school systems have developed standard IEP formats, which reflect these requirements and additional information considered useful in the management of the child's special education program. A sample of IEP formats is included in Appendix D.

One of the most difficult tasks for developers of IEPs is to determine how inclusive the document must be. A key element in making this determination lies in the definition of special education as "specially designed" instruction. The determination of whether instruction is "specially designed" must be made by comparing the nature of the instruction for the student with a disability to instructional practices used with typical students at the same age and grade level. If the instructional adaptations that a student with a disability requires are (1) significantly different from adaptations normally expected or made for typical students in that setting, and if (2) the adaptations are necessary to offset or reduce the adverse effect of the disability on learning and educational performance, then these adaptations should be considered "specially designed instruction" and should be included as part of the student's IEP, regardless of the instructional setting.

Specially designed instruction often occurs in regular classes, not just in resource rooms and special classes. Students placed in regular classes who require adaptation of the regular curriculum must have an IEP developed for those aspects of the curriculum that are specially designed to offset the adverse effects of the student's disability. For example, a student with a learning disability who has particular difficulty in language arts but not in other curriculum areas may require goals and objectives in language arts but not in math, science, and physical education; a student with a physical disability who uses a wheelchair but has no academic problems may need goals and objectives only in the area of physical education. In choosing the goals and objectives for the IEP, careful consideration should be given to the student's needs not only in the areas of academics but in social adjustment, adaptive behavior, physical education, and vocational development as well.

A final consideration regarding the content of the IEP relates to the extent to which special education and related services are specified on the IEP. All related services determined by the special services committee to be necessary for the student to benefit from special education must be listed on the IEP, even if the service is unavailable in the local education agency. Furthermore, the IEP represents the agency's commitment to provide the services, which may be accomplished by direct service from the local education agency, contracting from other agencies, or other arrangements. A detailed discussion of issues related to the provision of related services is included in Chapter 11.

Time Lines for Writing IEPs

A meeting to develop the IEP must be held within 30 calendar days of the determination that the student has a disability and requires special education and related services (*Federal Register*, 1977). Students must receive the required special education programs immediately after the IEP meeting, except in special circumstances such as when the IEP meeting is held over the summer or when a short delay is required to work out problems such as transportation (*Federal Register*, 1977).

IEPs must be in effect for each student receiving special education at the beginning of each school year. *In effect* generally is interpreted to mean that the IEP (1) has been developed at a meeting involving all required participants, (2) is less than 1 calendar year old, (3) is considered by the parents and school personnel to be appropriate to the student's educational needs, and (4) is implemented as written. For implementation the following year, IEPs would need to be developed at the end of the school year, during the summer months, or immediately after the new school term begins. Although the regulations specifically require meetings at least once each calendar year to review or revise each student's IEP, both parents and teachers can request more frequent meetings to ensure that the IEP is appropriate.

Participants in the IEP Meeting

According to the *Federal Register* (1977), the required participants in IEP meetings include the following individuals:

1. A representative of the public agency, other than the student's teacher, who has qualifications to provide or supervise special education
2. The student's teacher
3. One or both of the student's parents
4. The student when appropriate
5. Other individuals at the request of the parents or public agency
6. For students evaluated for the first time, either a member of the evaluation team or another individual (representative of the public agency, the student's teacher) who is knowledgeable about the evaluation procedures used with the child and the results

The potential size of the meeting is a factor in determining who, in addition to required participants, will attend the IEP meeting. Including in one meeting all individuals who have knowledge of the student may not only be impractical from a scheduling standpoint but also may be less productive than a small meeting of key individuals. Chapter 7 will provide suggestions for ensuring appropriate representation on IEP committees while maintaining a functional group size.

A strong component of P.L. 94–142 is the emphasis on involving parents in the development of the IEP. Thus, specific requirements have been established for ensuring such involvement. These include the following:

1. Notify the parents of the purpose, time, location, and participants at the meeting early enough so that they will have an opportunity to attend,
2. Schedule the meeting at a mutually agreed upon time and place.
3. Ensure that the parent understands the proceedings of the meeting, include arranging for an interpreter for parents who are deaf or whose native language is other than English.
4. Provide a copy of the student's IEP to the parent on request.

If neither parent can attend the IEP meeting, their participation may be secured through individual or conference telephone calls. An IEP meeting may be conducted with no form of parental participation only if the parents have rejected all attempts of the public agency to involve them. The agency must provide documentation of efforts to arrange a mutually convenient meeting time and place, including detailed records of telephone calls and results of the calls, copies of correspondence mailed to the parents and any responses received, and detailed records of visits to the parents' home and place of employment and the result of the visits. Parents must be provided with every opportunity to be involved in the IEP meeting.

Accountability

The IEP is the legally constituted mechanism for committing the special education and related services necessary to provide the student with an appropriate education. As such, schools can be held accountable for implementing the IEP as it is written and approved by the IEP committee. This means that all services included on the document must be provided and that the goals and objectives must be addressed as stated. The school can also be held accountable for reviewing and revising the IEP as necessary to ensure that it continues to represent an appropriate program for the student. The IEP, however, is not a performance contract constituting a guarantee that the student will necessarily accomplish all goals and objectives included on the IEP within a particular time period. Regulations governing the implementation of P.L. 94–142 do not require that the agency, teacher, or other person responsible for the student's program be held accountable if the IEP is implemented as written and the student does not achieve the growth projected on the IEP (*Federal Register*, 1977). Parents, however, have the right to request a due process hearing to present formal complaints if they do not consider the IEP to be appropriate, if they believe good faith efforts are not being made to assist the student in accomplishing the goals and objectives on the IEP, or if special education and related services are not being provided in accordance with the specifications of the IEP. In sum, then, although the IEP does not guarantee the accomplishment of the specified goals and objectives, the agency is accountable for providing the special education and related services documented on the IEP as appropriate to the needs of the student to comply with P.L. 94–142.

Individualized Family Service Plan

Just as the IEP provides the mechanism for documenting the educational needs of school-aged students (and preschool students ages 3 to 5 by 1991), the individualized family service plan (IFSP) provides the mechanism for documenting the early intervention services that an infant or toddler (birth–2) with a disability and the family require. The purpose and function of the IEP and the IFSP are similar in that both provide for communication between parties, written commitment of resources, management of services, and a vehicle for monitoring progress. The IFSP is also similar procedurally to the IEP in that it requires that the written plan be developed by a multidisciplinary team, which includes the parents, and be based on a multidisciplinary assessment of unique needs. In addition, all early intervention services necessary to address the identified needs of the infant or toddler and the family must be reflected on the IFSP.

The basic components of the IFSP are also somewhat similar to those of the IEP. They differ, however, in focus and scope. According to P.L. 99–457, the IFSP must include the following elements:

1. A statement of the toddler's or infant's present level of physical development, cognitive development, language and speech development, psychosocial development and self help skills.
2. A statement of the family's strengths and needs related to enhancing the development of the family's infant or toddler with a disability.
3. A statement of major outcomes expected to be achieved for the infant, toddlers, and the family, and the criteria, procedures and timelines used to determine the degree to which progress is being made and whether modifications or revisions of the outcomes or services are necessary.
4. A statement of specific early intervention services necessary to meet the unique needs of the infant or toddler and the family including the frequency, intensity and method of delivering services.

5. The projected dates for initiation of services and the anticipated duration of such services.
6. The names of the case manager from the profession most immediately relevant to the infant's and toddler's or family's needs who will be responsible for the implementation of the plan and coordination with other agencies and persons, and
7. The steps to be taken supporting the transition of the handicapped toddler to services provided by P.L. 94–142, to the extent such services are considered appropriate. (P.L. 99–457, sec. 677d)

The IFSP must be evaluated at least once a year with a review of the plan occurring at least every 6 months (or more often if necessary).

Despite many procedural similarities, there are a number of significant differences between the IEP and the IFSP. Figure 1–5 provides a comparison of the basic provisions of these documents.

Overall, the provisions of the IFSP are broader and more complex than those of the IEP, as follows:

1. The IFSP represents a family-centered approach to intervention rather than a child-centered approach. Focusing on the needs of the family as a whole requires a more complex and integrated system of service delivery than simply treating or teaching the child alone.
2. Services to be provided far exceed the "specially designed instruction" requirement of P.L. 94–142 and include almost any needed service that is not strictly medical.
3. Provision of early intervention services may include a multitude of public and private agencies, whereas services on the IEP are usually provided by the school. Coordination of services is thus a primary element of the IFSP.

Two other differences bear mentioning. First, although the IFSP must be developed within a reasonable time after assessment, early intervention services, unlike special education, can, under certain circumstances and with parent consent, begin before the completion of the multidisciplinary assessment and the development of the IFSP (P.L. 99–457, sec. 677c). This provision is based on the consideration that infant development is relatively rapid and that undue delay in the provision of services could be potentially harmful.

Second, because coordination is an essential and critical element of the IFSP, P.L. 99–457 specifically addresses the issue of case management by requiring that the name of the case manager be written on the IFSP. To further delineate the function of the case manager, the Committee on Education and Labor, in its report accompanying the bill that

FIGURE 1–5
Comparison of the Provisions of the IEP of P.L. 94–142 and the Individualized Family Services Plan (IFSP) of P.L. 99–457

Requirement	Provisions of the IEP Requirement (P.L. 94-142)	Provisions of the IFSP Requirement (P.L. 99-457)	Differences
Meeting of committee	An interdisciplinary team, including the parents, must develop the written document based on a comprehensive multidisciplinary evaluation.	Same	Participants of the meeting may differ.
Document present level of performance	The IEP must include a statement of the student's present level of educational functioning.	1. The IFSP must include a statement of the infant's or toddler's present level of physical development, psychosocial development, and self-help skills based on professionally acceptable objective.	IFSP requirements are more comprehensive; they specify areas in which performance levels must be stated.
		2. The IFSP must include a statement of the family's strengths and needs related to the enhancement of the infant's or toddler's development.	The IFSP also requires that the strengths and needs of the family be identified.
Goal setting	The IEP must include a statement of annual goals, including short-term instructional objectives. For preschool IEPs, instruction for parents must be included whenever appropriate and to the extent desired by the parent.	The IFSP must include a statement of the major outcomes expected to be achieved for the infant or toddler and the family.	The IFSP focuses on both the child and the family. The IEP focuses primarily on the student during school hours.

(Figure 1–5 continued)

Requirement	Provisions of the IEP Requirement (P.L. 94-142)	Provisions of the IFSP Requirement (P.L. 99-457)	Differences
Measurement of progress	The IEP must include appropriate objective criteria and evaluation procedures and schedules for determining, at least annually, whether the short-term instructional objectives are being achieved.	The IFSP must include the criteria procedures and time lines used to determine the degree to which progress toward achieving the outcomes is being made.	None
Specification of services to be provided	The IEP must include a statement of the specific special education and related services to be provided to the student and the extent to which the student will be able to participate in regular education programs. For preschool students, service-delivery models may range from part-day home-based to part- or full-day center-based models.	The IFSP must include a statement of specific early intervention services necessary to meet the unique needs of the infant or toddler and the family, including the frequency, intensity, and method of delivering service.	The IFSP focuses on family as well as child. The IFSP and IEP differ regarding service delivery models; the least restrictive environment in a school setting generally is considered to be the regular classroom. For an infant or toddler, it may be the home.
Specifications of dates of services initiation and duration	The IEP must include the projected dates for initiation of services and the anticipated duration of services.	Same	Early intervention services may, with the consent of the parents, begin before the completion of the assessment

(Figure 1–5 continued)

Requirement	Provisions of the IEP Requirement (P.L. 94-142)	Provisions of the IFSP Requirement (P.L. 99-457)	Differences
Periodic program review	Periodic review and, if necessary, revision of each student's individualized education program. A meeting must be held for this purpose at least once a year.	The IFSP must be evaluated at least once a year and the family must be provided a review of the plan at least at 6-month intervals or more often where appropriate, based on infant, toddler, and family needs.	The IFSP is more specific in time lines for review of the plan.
Coordination of services	Although P.L. 94-142 permits cooperative agreements among and within agencies, there is no specified mechanism for case management and coordination. The Amendments of 1986 require that states set forth policies and procedures for developing interagency agreements to define respective responsibilities.	The IFSP must specify the name of the case manager from the profession most relevant to the infant's or toddler's or family's needs who will be responsible for the implementation of the plan and coordination with other agencies.	The IFSP specifically requires designation of a case manager to ensure appropriate implementation and coordination of the plan. The IFSP focuses on the need of interagency agreements.
Transition between programs	No specific regulatory requirements, although most states and public agencies have specific transition procedures. The Amendments of 1986 allow grants to qualifying agencies to develop model programs that emphasize transitional services for adult students with disabilities.	The IFSP must include the steps to be taken supporting the infant's or toddler's movement to services provided under P.L. 94-142 (the IEP for school-age students) if the child requires special education and related services.	The provisions of the IFSP specifically require transitional planning. There is no requirement for transitional planning according to P.L. 94-142.

(Figure 1–5 continued)

Requirement	Provisions of the IEP Requirement (P.L. 94-142)	Provisions of the IFSP Requirement (P.L. 99-457)	Differences
Application	The IEP provisions of P.L. 94-142 apply to students with disabilities ages 3 to 21.	The IFSP provisions of P.L. 99-457 apply to infants and toddlers with disabilities ages birth-2 and to their families. The program is discretionary.	The IEP is a statutory requirement for all school-aged students with disabilities. The IFSP is a discretionary program for infants and toddlers with disabilities and their families.
Responsible agent	The state and local educational agency is responsible for implementation and monitoring of P.L. 94-142.	Designation of a "lead agency" by the governor. A state interagency coordinating council must be established to provide advice to the designated lead agency.	State educational agencies are responsible for implementation and monitoring of P.L. 94-142. The implementation of P.L. 99-457 may be any state agency appointed by the governor of that state.

became P.L. 99–457, identified specific case management services as follows:

1. coordinating performance of evaluation,
2. assisting families in identifying available service providers,
3. participating in the development of the IFSP,
4. coordinating and monitoring the delivery of available services,
5. informing families of the availability of advocacy services,
6. coordination with medical and health providers, and
7. facilitating the development of a transition plan to preschool services where appropriate.
   (U.S. House of Representatives Report 99-860, 1986)

As with the IEP, the development of the IFSP does not require that an agency or person be held accountable if an infant or toddler does not achieve the growth projected. It is expected, however, that agencies and persons responsible for the IFSP make good faith efforts toward achieving the projected outcomes.

LEAST RESTRICTIVE ENVIRONMENT

Definition

According to P.L. 94–142, the placement of school-aged children in the least restrictive environment means that, to the maximum extent appropriate, students with disabilities should be educated with children who do not have disabilities. The intent of the law is clearly evident in the regulatory guidance:

> That special classes, separate schooling or other removal of handicapped children from the regular educational environment occurs only when the nature or severity of the handicap is such that education in regular classes with the use of supplementary aids and services cannot be achieved satisfactorily. (*Federal Register*, 1977, p. 42497)

Continuum of Services

To ensure that education occurs in the least restrictive appropriate environment, the public agency must provide a continuum of alternative educational services. These alternatives include instruction in regular classes, special classes, special schools, home instruction, and instruction in hospitals and institutions. Figure 1–6 provides an indication of the degree to which various educational alternatives are currently employed to serve students with disabili-

ties. Further, schools are required to provide supplementary services to regular class placement, such as resource room or itinerant instruction. Figure 1–7 provides an example of how the concept of least restrictiveness is conceptualized, with the regular classroom generally being considered the least restrictive environment because it affords the student with a disability maximum integration with typical students. Environments become more restrictive as they limit the student's opportunity for integration with typical students. The application of the concept of least restriction also considers the student's educational needs in determining which of the placement alternatives facilitates (or least restricts) the student's opportunity for learning.

The right of students with disabilities to receive supplementary services in the regular classroom translates into a right for regular classroom teachers to receive assistance in providing specially designed instruction to the handicapped student (Hayek, 1987; Will, 1986). Supplementary services from special education teachers in the form of consultation for the classroom teacher or direct instruction for the student with a disability must be made available to classroom teachers. Thus, the regulations pertaining to the least restrictive placement provide rights to teachers, as well as students, to receive supplementary services.

Unless the IEP requires a different arrangement, students with disabilities should be educated in the same school they would attend if they had no disability. They should also participate with other students in nonacademic and extracurricular services to the maximum extent appropriate. The committee who develops the IEP for each student should specify the nonacademic and extracurricular services and activities in which the student can participate.

Placement in Private or Alternative Schools

While the legal preference regarding placement is clearly in the direction of less restrictive settings, efforts must be made to ensure that students with disabilities receive no harmful effect from placement in this environment. If a local education agency cannot provide suitable educational programs for every student, the agency may refer some students to private or state-operated programs. Another option for the local education agency is to contract with a neighboring educational agency or other public agencies, such as mental health or corrections, for service provision. When an alternative placement is necessary, the local and state education agency must ensure that the alternative program meets the spec-

FIGURE 1–6
Percentage of Handicapped Children and Youth Served in Nine Educational Environments by Handicapping Condition During School Year 1985 to 1986

Handicapping Condition	Regular Class	Resource Room	Separate Class	Public Separate School Facility	Private Separate School Facility	Public Residential Facility	Private Residential Facility	Correctional Facility	Homebound Environment
Learning disabled	15.29	61.88	21.65	0.93	0.54	0.04	0.04	0.23	0.09
Speech or language impaired	66.26	25.55	5.54	0.87	1.46	0.06	0.02	0.04	0.19
Mentally retarded	3.06	25.29	55.81	10.12	1.99	2.76	0.35	0.27	0.41
Emotionally disturbed	8.85	33.76	35.86	8.81	4.51	1.81	2.36	1.68	2.33
Hard of hearing and deaf	18.72	21.02	34.62	9.47	3.84	10.53	1.06	0.12	0.59
Multihandicapped	4.06	15.25	43.23	19.26	9.26	2.96	2.04	0.33	3.58
Orthopedically impaired	25.62	16.14	32.03	13.06	4.12	0.61	0.44	0.09	7.99
Other health impaired	25.88	18.79	25.77	5.26	2.54	3.06	0.77	0.19	17.74
Visually handicapped	31.48	24.09	19.44	10.32	2.05	10.27	0.95	0.11	1.37
Deaf-blind	6.55	17.66	23.30	11.99	3.11	27.56	8.41	8.04	1.36
All conditions	26.26	41.39	24.49	3.79	1.64	0.97	0.37	0.31	0.79

From *Tenth Annual Report to Congress on the Implementation of the Education of the Handicapped Act* (p. 30) by U.S. Department of Education, 1988, Washington, D.C.: U.S. Government Printing Office.

FIGURE 1–7
Cascade Model of Special Education Service

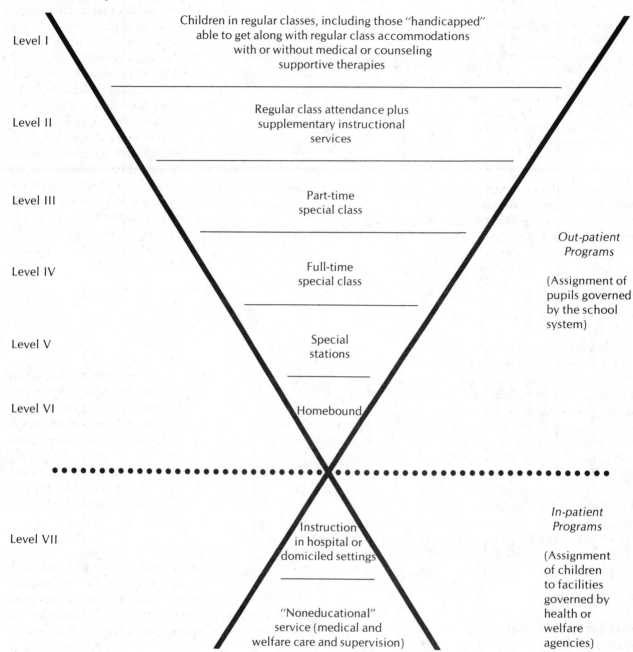

Level I — Children in regular classes, including those "handicapped" able to get along with regular class accommodations with or without medical or counseling supportive therapies

Level II — Regular class attendance plus supplementary instructional services

Level III — Part-time special class

Level IV — Full-time special class

Level V — Special stations

Level VI — Homebound

Level VII — Instruction in hospital or domiciled settings

"Noneducational" service (medical and welfare care and supervision)

Out-patient Programs

(Assignment of pupils governed by the school system)

In-patient Programs

(Assignment of children to facilities governed by health or welfare agencies)

From E. Deno, "Special Education as Developmental Capital," *Exceptional Children* 1970, 37, 229–237.

ifications of P.L. 94–142. The placement must achieve the following:

1. be located as close to the student's home as possible,
2. be based on the individualized education program,
3. meet the standards that apply to state and local education agencies,
4. afford the same rights as afforded to students with disabilities in public schools, and
5. be reviewed annually.

(*Federal Register,* 1977)

When residential placements are made by the local education agency for educational reasons, the financial obligation for the room, board, educational expenses, and nonmedical care of the student is the responsibility of the local education agency. Whenever the educational agency places a student in a private school, responsibility for ensuring the appropriateness of the educational program provided remains with the school system making the placement.

Although P.L. 94–142 is very clear regarding the legal preference for placement in the least restrictive appropriate placement, research indicates that criteria used to determine the least restrictive environment for individuals or groups of students with disabilities vary widely and may depend more on where a child lives, school-staff evaluation criteria, and systems of program funding than on the identified needs of the student (Carlberg & Kavale, 1980; Gartner & Lipsky, 1987; L. J. Walker, 1987). Findings such as these have significant implications for the development of IEPs, because regulations require that placement decisions be made on the basis of the IEP. The IEP should therefore provide a clear basis for the placement decision.

Services for Preschool Students With Disabilities

The concept of least restrictive environment applies also to preschool students with disabilities. The frame of reference, however, differs somewhat for younger students who are in the process of making the transition from a home environment to a school environment (Edmister & Ekstrand, 1987). Because the family is recognized as the primary learning environment for children under 6, a part-day home-based program may be considered less restrictive than a full-day program at school for some students. The particular model employed must be based on the needs of the individual student.

Early Intervention Services

For many infants or toddlers, the family setting is clearly the least restrictive environment. This setting is often preferred as the catalyst for the provision of early intervention services. Not all family-centered programs occur in the home, however. Infant stimulation groups, therapeutic play groups, and other early intervention services often are provided outside the home but with the participation of the parents and family group (Edmister & Ekstrand, 1987). Ultimately, the application of the concept of least restrictive environment for infants and toddlers must be determined individually, based on a model that fits most easily with the family's normal life-style. Thus, the least restrictive environment for a family with both parents employed outside the home may be a specialized day-care setting, whereas for a family with the child cared for at home, the home would be the least restrictive environment.

PROCEDURAL SAFEGUARDS

Definition

Procedural safeguards seek to ensure the fairness of educational decisions and the accountability of both the professionals and parents in making these decisions. The procedural safeguards contained in P.L. 94–142 include the due process hearing, independent educational evaluations, parent notice, parent consent, appointment of surrogate parents, confidentiality of information, and access to records. Each of these safeguards is discussed in this section.

Due Process Hearing

Due process can be viewed as a system of checks and balances concerning the identification, evaluation, and provision of services to students with disabilities.

A due process hearing may be initiated by the parents or public agency as an impartial forum for presenting complaints regarding the student's identification, evaluation, and placement, or for challenging decisions made by another party. For example, if parents and educators cannot agree on appropriate goals and objectives of the student's IEP, thus making it impossible for the required participants to approve the IEP, either party could initiate a due process hearing.

The hearing may be conducted locally by the public agency directly responsible for the student's education, or as in some states, it may be conducted directly by a hearing officer appointed by the state educational agency. The hearing officer must have no personal or professional interest that would conflict with objectivity (the officer may not be an employee of the agency). Any party (1) may be advised by counsel or by persons with expertise in the education of students with disabilities, (2) may present evidence, (3) may cross-examine witnesses, (4) may prohibit the introduction of evidence that has not been made available to the other party at least 5 days before the hearing, (5) may obtain a written or electronic verbatim record of the hearing, and (6) may obtain written findings of fact and decision. Parents have further rights to have the student (who is the subject of the hearing) present and to have the hearing open to the public. Any party dissatisfied with the findings of the hearing conducted by the public agency may initiate an appeal to the state educational agency.

The state agency is responsible for conducting an impartial review of the local hearing decision and making an independent decision, based on the review. The decision of the reviewer(s) is final, though either party may choose to bring a civil action suit in either a state or federal district court.

Time lines for hearings are set by the rules and regulations of P.L. 94–142. The public agency must reach a final decision within a 45-day period after receipt of the request for the hearing, and the state agency must reach a decision within a 30-day period. A hearing officer may grant extensions of time on the request of either party. While the proceedings of the hearing are pending, the student involved in the complaint must remain in the current educational placement unless the parents and public agency agree to a different placement. When complaints involve the student's initial admission to public school, the student must be placed in a public school program until the proceedings have been completed.

The education agency must assume the cost of the due process hearing and is responsible for informing the parents of any free or low-cost legal or advocacy services available. The local education agency is not, however, necessarily responsible for the legal fees incurred by parents unless required by a court to assume such costs. In such instances the Handicapped Children's Protection Act of 1986 provides a basis on which recovery of attorney's fees may be required (Splitt, 1987).

Since the enactment of P.L. 94–142, many issues have arisen regarding the due process hearing as an effective mechanism for resolving educational disputes. Among these are (1) the cost involved, (2) the qualifications of hearing officers, (3) the impartiality of hearing decisions, (4) reimbursement of legal fees, and (5) authority of the hearing officer to determine appropriate education and direct educational remedies (Strickland, 1982). Issues such as these may have

diminished the willingness of parents and schools to use this mechanism for dispute settlement. For this reason, or because there are actually fewer disagreements between parents and school, the number of due process hearings has decreased dramatically since the initial surge immediately following the enactment of P.L. 94–142 (Singer & Butler, 1987).

Independent Educational Evaluation

Parents may obtain an independent educational evaluation (an evaluation conducted by a licensed examiner who is not employed by the state or local education agency and does not routinely provide evaluations for these agencies) if they are dissatisfied with the evaluation obtained by the public agency. The independent evaluation must be conducted at public expense unless the public agency initiates a due process hearing to document the appropriateness of its evaluation. If the independent evaluation is conducted at public expense, the criteria under which the evaluation is obtained, including the location of the evaluation and the qualifications of the examiner must be the same as the criteria that the public agency uses when it initiates an evaluation (*Federal Register*, 1977). The school system must consider the results of the independent evaluation in any decision made regarding the appropriate education of the student.

Notice

Parents must be provided with written notice before the public agency's proposal or refusal to initiate or change the student's identification, evaluation, or educational placement. The notice must contain the following:

1. A full listing of the due process safeguards available to the parent,
2. A description of the action taken by the agency, including the rationale for choosing the particular action over other options,
3. A description of the basis of the decision, including each evaluation procedure, test, record, or report the agency considered,
4. A description of any other factors that were considered in light of the agency's proposal or refusal.

Further, the notice must be written in language that the general public can understand and must be provided in the parent's native language or other mode of communication unless it is not reasonable to do so. Essentially, the state or local education agency must ensure that the parent understands the contents of the notice.

Consent

Parental consent must be obtained before conducting the initial evaluation for placement in a program providing special education and related services and before initial placement in a special education program. Although consent is not required for continuation in special education, prior notice is required for all proposed or refused changes related to identification, evaluation, or educational placement of the student. For those instances when parents refuse to give consent, some states have laws that govern the public agency in overriding parental refusal for the student's evaluation or placement in a special education program. When there is no state law to guide the public agency in these matters, the agency has the right to initiate a due process hearing to determine if the agency's proposal regarding evaluation and placement can be allowed without parental consent. The parent must be notified of the actions of the hearing and of parental appeal rights.

Appointment of Surrogate Parents

When the public agency cannot identify the parents or discover their whereabouts, the agency has the duty to assign an individual to act as a substitute or surrogate for the parents, according to criteria set forth in the legislation. This individual is responsible for representing the student in all matters related to the provision of a free, appropriate public education and has all procedural rights afforded to the student's parents regarding the student's education.

Confidentiality of Personally Identifiable Information

The public agency must obtain parental consent before releasing personally identifiable information to anyone other than officials of the agency. Safeguards to protect the confidentiality of information include the following:

1. Each public agency shall appoint one official with overall responsibility for ensuring confidentiality.
2. Training must be provided to all persons collecting or using personally identifiable information.
3. A list must be compiled and made available for public inspection by each agency containing the names and positions of all employees within the agency who may have access to personally identifiable information.

When the agency no longer needs personally identifiable information that has been compiled, it must inform parents that they have the option to request destruction of the information. A permanent record without regard to time constraints, however, may be kept of the student's name, address, phone number, grades, attendance record, classes attended, grade level completed, and year completed.

Access to Educational Records

The state agency is responsible for providing notice to parents regarding confidentiality requirements for personally identifiable information (defined as the name of the student and/or his family, address, a personal identifier such as a social security number, and a list of personal characteristics that would make is possible to identify the student). This notice should include the following:

1. A summary of policies concerning storage, release to third party, and protection of information
2. A description of students on whom information is maintained, in addition to the methods of gathering information and potential uses of it
3. A description of the rights of parents and student as related to the personally identifiable information

Parents have the right to fully review any educational records maintained on their child by the school before an IEP meeting or due process hearing, within 45 days of any request to do so. The only exception to this right is when the agency has been advised that the parent does not have this authority under state law concerning such matters as guardianship, separation, and divorce. In addition to the right to inspect records, parents may request an explanation or interpretation of the contents, have their representative review the records, and request the records be amended because of inaccurate information or violations of privacy. If the agency refuses to amend the information, the parents must be advised of their right to initiate a due process hearing.

Early Intervention

The procedural safeguards afforded to parents of school-aged students with disabilities also apply to parents of infants and toddlers with disabilities. However, several issues currently complicate the application of the same rules to this population. Primary among these issues is the fact that many agencies, rather than educational agencies alone, may be involved in and responsible for the provision of services to infants and toddlers and their families.

Thus, the development of an effective dispute management mechanism will require that procedures be established to ensure accountability among many agencies in addition to departments of education. Such procedures may include providing the lead agency (required by P.L. 99–457) with not only administrative responsibility for ensuring the provision of services but also with sufficient control to effect and enforce procedures for interagency accountability.

PARENTAL PARTICIPATION

A strong component of P.L. 94–142 is the emphasis on providing opportunities to parents to be actively involved in decision making regarding their child's educational program.

    Each of the principles of P.L. 94–142 discussed thus far has either direct or indirect implications for parent participation. The rationale for including parent participation as a separate principle is to emphasize that every major component of P.L. 94–142 has as its basis opportunities for parents to be involved in decisions regarding their child. In fact, the due process provisions of P.L. 94–142 actually form an entitlement more for parents than for children (Singer & Butler, 1987). Thus, a school system or other public agency could (1) evaluate a child using nondiscriminatory procedures, (2) develop an individualized education program, (3) place the student in an appropriate program of services in the least restrictive environment, and (4) provide appropriate instruction. Nonetheless, without providing opportunities for parents to be involved at each step, the requirements would not be met. This section provides an overview of the potential levels of parent involvement in the education of their children. Levels of parent involvement exist on a continuum, however, just as do levels of intervention. It should not be assumed that all parents desire or need to be involved to the same degree (Allen & Hudd, 1987; Singer & Butler, 1987; Turnbull & Turnbull, 1982). The school's responsibility, however, is to encourage and to enable the active and meaningful involvement of parents in decisions regarding their children. P.L. 94–142 provides the procedural mechanism for doing so by ensuring that parents have the following opportunities:

1. Be informed about all actions proposed regarding their child.
2. Request meetings and attend all meetings at which decisions regarding their child are discussed or made.
3. Participate in long-range program planning, policy development, and serve on advisory panels regarding programs for students with disabilities.

Right to Be Fully Informed

According to P.L. 94–142, active parent participation clearly includes attendance at meetings conducted on behalf of their child. It is equally clear, however, that large number of parents, for various reasons, choose not to attend these meetings. More than 10 years after the enactment of P.L. 94–142, some school systems report fewer than 50% of parents had attended their child's most recent IEP conference (Singer & Butler, 1987). Parents of racial and ethnic minorities remain noticeably underrepresented in meetings regarding their children (Lynch & Stein, 1987). But even if parents cannot (or choose not to) attend meetings, they maintain their right to be involved. Regardless of whether parents attend meetings, the school system must ensure that parents are informed about, understand, and in many cases, consent to actions proposed by the school regarding their child.

    Regardless of whether they attend meetings or communicate regularly with the school, parents specifically have a legal right to expect the following:

1. Timely notification of meetings and attempts to schedule them at a convenient time and place so that these factors do not create obstacles for parent participation
2. An opportunity to participate in their child's education through phone calls, written correspondence, home visits, or visits to the parent's workplace
3. A full and complete explanation of the proceedings of meetings including interpreters if necessary, and to receive copies of IEPs or other documents generated at the meeting
4. To be fully informed in writing of any proposals or refusals to initiate or change any aspect of the child's education program
5. That their informed consent will be obtained before a preplacement evaluation is conducted and before their child is placed in special education
6. That they will be informed of their procedural rights (as discussed in the previous section) including their right to due process if they disagree with actions taken by the school

                           (*Federal Register*, 1977)

Thus, parents have a right to expect that they will be fully informed and that their child will receive an appropriate education, even if the parents themselves do not actively participate in the development and monitoring of that program.

Attendance at Meetings and School Activities

Although parents vary in the degree to which they feel comfortable in assuming a decision-making role in IEP conferences, federal policy clearly states that parents are expected to be equal participants with school personnel in developing, reviewing, and revising the child's IEP (Turnbull, Turnbull, & Wheat, 1982). This equal role for parents involves active participation at decision-making meetings. Thus, in addition to the involvement opportunities related to receiving information noted previously, P.L. 94–142 provides opportunities for parent participation through attendance at meetings and other activities including the following:

1. Meetings to develop, review or revise the IEP
2. Meetings conducted at the request of the parent
3. School-sponsored inservice and parent-education programs
4. Participation in related services, activities as part of the student's program of special education and related services

The school must initiate a meeting whenever an IEP is (1) developed, (2) reviewed, or (3) revised. This means that at least once a year, and more often if appropriate, the school will initiate a request for parent participation to review and revise the student's educational program. The school cannot review or make revisions to the child's IEP without conducting a meeting to which parents are invited.

In addition to the meetings initiated by the school, the parent may request a meeting with one or more school representatives regarding the child's program. The parent may request a review or revision of the IEP, challenge actions proposed or taken by the school, request services such as an independent evaluation or free or low-cost legal aid, or simply request a progress report. Thus, parents may actively participate and communicate through meetings as often as they feel necessary.

P.L. 94–142 also provides opportunities for school systems to encourage parent participation through personnel development and inservice training activities. Each school system must develop a comprehensive system of personnel development, which may include parent education and training related to the education of students with disabilities.

Finally, parents may participate directly in their child's education by participating in related service activities that are determined to be necessary for the student to benefit from special education. These might include such activities as parent counseling and training and social work services.

Development and Approval of Educational Policy

Parental participation is also secured through P.L. 94–142 by the extension of rights to parents to be involved in the development and approval of educational policy. Participation at public hearings and membership on advisory panels are examples of these rights. The state education agency is required to conduct public hearings on the annual program plan, which specifies the manner in which special education and related services will be provided to students with disabilities, before its adoption. Advance notices of hearings must be advertised through the media, and the locations and times of the hearings must allow for the attendance of interested parties. Information on the state's proposed plan is provided at the public hearings, and the participants are given the opportunity to make suggestions and comments. In the final revision of the program plan, which is submitted to the U.S. Office of Education, the state agency must include a summary of comments received at the hearing and a description of modifications made as a result of the comments. Local education agencies also are required to provide the opportunity for parents or guardians of students with disabilities to participate in the development of the local application of P.L. 94–142 funds.

A further requirement of the state education agency is the establishment of a state advisory panel on the education of students with disabilities. The membership on the panel must include at least one parent of a student with a disability. The functions of the panel include advising the state on the unmet needs, commenting publicly on the state's annual program plan, and assisting in the developing and reporting of information to the U.S. Department of Education.

Participation at public hearings and membership on advisory panels provide parents with the opportunity to influence the development of policy and procedural guidelines. In this regard, parents can provide valuable assistance to educators in attesting to barriers that prevent full implementation of P.L. 94–142 at the local school level. Parental support and advocacy can contribute to the systematic increase of state and local resources to enhance the effectiveness of educational services.

SUMMARY

The six principles of P.L. 94–142 and the extension through P.L. 99–457 of many of these principles to preschool students ages 3 to 5 and infants and toddlers ages birth to 2 provide the basis for the legislative definition of free, appropriate public education. Although these principles have been individually identified and discussed, they emerge into an integral and systematic process as students are referred, evaluated, and provided with special education services. The remainder of this text will focus only on the requirements of P.L. 94–142 for developing and implementing the individualized education program (IEP) for school-aged students with disabilities. The remaining chapters of this book offer guidance in the development and implementation of the IEP for school-aged students in meeting both the spirit and the letter of the law.

EVALUATION

1. You have been asked to plan and deliver a 1-hour workshop to classroom teachers entitled "P.L. 94–142: The Six Principles." Outline all major points you plan to cover in the presentation. Be specific.

2. A newspaper reporter is interviewing you in preparation for writing a news article on the legal requirements associated with developing and implementing IEPs. He wants the article to be as comprehensive as possible. Identify all major points you would cover in the interview, with a brief explanation of the content you would include related to each point. Remember that the article's audience is the general public.

3. You are the special education coordinator in a large school system responsible for planning educational services to children aged birth to 2, and preschool students with disabilities. Compare the entitlements provided to these populations by P.L. 99–457 with those provided to school-age students by P.L. 94–142.

CHAPTER 2

Functions of the Special Services Committee

OBJECTIVES

1. Identify the general composition of the special services committee.
2. Distinguish between the roles of permanent and changing members of the special services committee.
3. Distinguish between schoolwide and student-specific functions of the special services committee.
4. State the importance of determination of responsibilities and the development of schoolwide procedures.
5. Describe the responsibilities of the special services committee associated with the coordinating process from the point of referral of a student to IEP monitoring.
6. State the responsibility of the special services committee in advising agency officials on educational concerns identified through the coordinating and monitoring process.

The special services committee in a school is the primary mechanism for coordination of all procedures related to the identification, evaluation, and placement of students with disabilities. This committee is referred to by various names in different states, including the child study committee, multidisciplinary staffing team, educational planning committee, planning and placement committee, or special education committee. Regardless of the committee's particular title, its overall composition and function tends to be similar among states as defined by state legislation and state and local agency regulations.

P.L. 94–142 does not specifically require the formation of a committee to coordinate special education activities within the school. It does, however, indicate specific functions that must be performed to comply with the provisions of P.L. 94–142. For example, it specifies who must attend meetings regarding the development, review, and revision of IEPs, and it specifies that assessment and educational planning must be multidisciplinary. The development of schoolwide and systemwide committees is the mechanism by which schools have elected to coordinate the many aspects of P.L. 94–142. Thus, this chapter will provide a conceptual rather than a legal definition of this committee, based on its functions within the school.

COMPOSITION OF THE SPECIAL SERVICES COMMITTEE

In conceptualizing the special services committee, it is useful to think of it as a fluid body whose membership changes, depending on the function being performed. For example, a student's classroom teacher may be a member of the committee when that student's IEP is developed, reviewed, or revised but not necessarily when organizational issues such as division of special education responsibilities are discussed. Similarly, the principal may always be involved in the organizational aspects of the committee but may not normally serve on the committee when a student's IEP is developed.

Typically, membership on special services committees includes some persons as temporary members and others as permanent, or core, members. Temporary members generally are associated with one or more specific functions of the committee and usually bring in-depth knowledge and expertise related to a particular student. The most obvious of these members is the student's parent. Parents should always be full members of the special services committee when decisions are made regarding their child. Other temporary members may include classroom teachers, evaluators, related services providers such as social workers, nurses, and therapists, or parent advocates and representatives.

Permanent members generally are involved in overall special education program coordination and procedural monitoring and are likely to be involved in all cases involving individual students from referral to IEP development. These individuals often include the special education teachers in a school, the special education supervisor or coordinator, the school psychologist, diagnostician or prescriptionist, the school counselor, and sometimes the principal. The selection of the permanent or core members of the special services committee will vary depending on the philosophy and characteristics of each school. For example, in some schools the principal is required to chair the special services committee, while in other schools, she may be only minimally involved. In addition, some special services committees include representatives from all segments of the school as core members, while others include only those employed in special education. Still other schools have only one schoolwide committee, which considers all student-related issues, including compensatory education, health services and counseling, and special education. These committees typically have core members representing all factions in the school (kindergarten, primary, elementary, administration, supplemental programs, support services, and special education). This integrated group makes policy decisions related to all aspects of the school. Likewise, all student-specific activities are channeled through this committee rather than through a separate special education committee for assessment and placement. As with the traditional special education services committee, members can be added according to the function of this committee at any given time.

Considering the legal preference for mainstreaming and the current research and emphasis on maintenance of students with disabilities in regular programs (Algozzine & Ysseldyke, 1986; Gartner & Lipsky, 1987; Wang, Reynolds, & Walberg, 1986; Will, 1986), it seems essential for coordination purposes to include classroom teachers as permanent, decision-making members of the special services committee in the school. One of the most persistent problems in special education is the documented lack of knowledge of classroom teachers regarding the special education process and their lack of involvement in decision making regarding their students (Ammer, 1984; Will, 1986). The advantage of a schoolwide special services committee is that it promotes communication and an integrated approach to service delivery and encourages sharing of information between grade level, area, and supplemental and remedial specialists within the school. The disadvantage of such an approach is that it may be too time consuming because the same committee would coordinate all school policy and all student actions.

Administrative influence in the organization and functioning of the special services committee is critical. Although total school involvement in special education may be conceptually and legally preferred, it should not be assumed that administrators, classroom teachers, parents, and union representatives always wish to be actively involved in committee membership (Ammer, 1984; Halpern, 1985; Singer & Butler, 1987). Positive administrative authority, involvement, and interest in the functioning of the committee is the key to implementing an integrated approach to special education decision making (Will, 1986). Regardless of how the special services committee is organized, it has ultimate responsibility for both schoolwide and student-specific coordination. These responsibilities are discussed in the remainder of this chapter.

SCHOOLWIDE PROGRAM COORDINATION FUNCTIONS

Schoolwide procedures focus on the special education program as a whole rather than on individual students and provide the framework within which student-specific procedures are developed and maintained. These procedures ensure that each student referred to the committee because of a suspected disability is reviewed and evaluated within the framework of regulations of P.L. 94–142 and other state and local policies. To manage this function within the school, the special services committee must establish and incorporate schoolwide coordination procedures. Coordination activities should include the following:

1. Development of school-specific procedures for implementation of federal, state, and local regulations
2. Delineation of responsibilities within the school
3. Program monitoring activities
4. Program advising

Development of School-Specific Procedures

The development of school-specific procedures is essential to ensure that none of the provisions of federal, state and local regulations are overlooked at the school level. These procedures should be in writing and should clarify school compliance with all regulatory guidance and function of the overall program. Methods and schedules for development of school procedures and their specificity vary greatly among schools but should be as specific as necessary to ensure clarity to all individuals involved in the special education process. Figure 2–1 provides an example of school procedures that might be developed by a school special services committee. This example represents a very specific set of procedures and includes many locally required elements such as pre-referral procedures, school-specific forms, and procedures for assessment planning. These procedures represent one school's way of incorporating legal, regulatory, and policy requirements into an appropriate and ongoing service delivery model at the school level.

The development of schoolwide procedures is an ongoing activity. Often such procedures are developed and refined over the course of the year in regularly scheduled meetings of the special services committee. Procedures are reviewed and revised as necessary in a continuous effort to update and improve the process. Development of written schoolwide procedures have a number of advantages for

I. PRE-REFERRAL ACTIVITIES

   A. Referring teacher obtains the following forms from the counselor:

      1. "Pre-Referral Activities Checklist"
      2. "Classroom Teacher Evaluation of Student"
      3. "Pre-Referral Report"

   B. At a minimum, the following activities must be accomplished by the referring teacher before the pre-referral forms are considered complete:

      1. All items on the "Pre-Referral Report" (description, problem, strategies implemented, and results)
      2. Documentation of one parent-teacher conference
      3. Documentation of two interventions
      4. Initials and dates beside each activity completed by the teacher on the "Pre-Referral Activities Checklist" form

   C. Observations

      1. Observation by pupil personnel services staff, special educator, administrators, or other personnel may be conducted as part of the pre-referral process.
      2. For new referrals, two documented observations are required, one of which must be accomplished during the pre-referral period. The special services committee (SSC) will make the final determination as to when the observations should be documented throughout the referral-evaluation stage.
      3. Observations must occur during a time when the child's suspected disability can be observed.

   D. Pre-referral forms are submitted to the counselor and reviewed for completeness and forwarded to the SSC. If the SSC decides to accept the pre-referral as a formal referral:

      1. Formal referral is logged and placed on the next SSC agenda.
      2. Classroom teacher (referrer) is notified of the meeting date so she can make arrangements to attend the meeting and discuss the referral with the SSC core members.

(Figure 2–1 continued)

E.   Speech-language referrals

   1.   Students suspected of having articulation and/or
        language difficulties will be referred through the
        following procedures:

        a.   Referring teacher or speech therapist completes
             the following:

             i.   Appropriate sections of the "Classroom
                    Teacher Evaluation of Student"
                    checklist,
             ii.   Activities on the "Pre-Referral Form,"
                    which must include at a minimum:
                    a.   Review of student records
                    b.   Description of problem
                    c.   Documented parental
                         conference/contact
             iii.   Dating and initialing appropriate
                    sections of the "Pre-Referral
                    Activities Checklist"
             iv.   "Teacher Observation Form" (narrative
                    description of adversely affected
                    educational performance due to speech
                    or a language problem)

        b.   Completed forms are submitted to the counselor.

        c.   The counselor notifies the speech therapist that
             the pre-referral documentation has been
             received, if referral is made by a classroom
             teacher.

        d.   The speech therapist schedules and completes an
             observation of the student.

        e.   The speech therapist notifies the counselor when
             the observation has been completed, and the
             counselor schedules a review meeting.

        f.   The referring teacher is notified of the SSC
             review so she can attend and review the referral
             with the committee.

        g.   The SSC reviews the documentation and makes a
             decision as to dispensation of the referral.

(Figure 2–1 continued)

II. FORMAL REFERRAL ACTIVITIES

    A. Counselor logs the referral, adds the referral to the next SSC agenda, and notifies the referring teacher in writing of the date and time of the meeting.

    B. SSC reviews the information available and recommends the following:

        1. No further action by the SSC at this time; suggest additional classroom modifications

        2. Referral to other nonspecial education resources (i.e., reading improvement specialist, [RIS], compensatory education, social worker, English as a second language)

        3. Individual assessment needed

            a. Case manager is appointed.

            b. Case manager decides appropriate assessments, and personnel are assigned assessment-evaluation tasks.

                i.   Case manager is responsible for listing all of the assessments planned on the "Permission to Assess" form, making a copy of the form for the student's file, and ensuring the parents receive written notification including procedural safeguards.

                ii.   Case manager monitors the timely scheduling and completion of evaluation activities listed in the "Assessment Plan."

               iii. School nurse is responsible for sending and receiving developmental-social history.

                iv.   Each assessment team member documents their activity on the "Assessment Plan" by initialing and dating the completed activity.

            c. SSC reviews status of all referrals during weekly meetings to ensure members are informed of assessment-evaluation status.

            d. When all required assessments have been conducted, the case manager notifies the counselor, and the case is added to the SSC agenda for staffing.

                i.   Counselor notifies referring teacher of meeting.

(Figure 2–1 continued)

C. Parent referrals

1. Parents requesting assessment-evaluation for their child will be required to complete the "Formal Referral Form."

2. Parents must be informed of the following:

    a. The referral will be logged and will be added to the next SSC agenda for discussion, review, and recommended action by the committee.

    b. If the committee recommends individual assessments, they will be asked to give their permission for the assessments before any further action by the committee.

    c. The assessment evaluation may result in identification of handicapping conditions with recommendations for special education placement.

3. Classroom teachers will be asked to complete the "Classroom Teacher Evaluation of Student" form and "Pre-Referral Forms," compile a representative sample of the student's work, and participate in the staffing meetings.

III. SYNTHESIS OF EVALUATION RESULTS

A. Each member of the assessment team is to notify the case manager when evaluations have been completed and provide a written report of assessment to the case manager, who compiles the assessment results into one total report.

B. Case manager notifies the counselor when case is ready for staffing at the next SSC meeting.

C. Counselor adds the case to the SSC meeting agenda and notifies the classroom teacher and any other involved staff member (i.e., RIS, talented and gifted) of the date and time of the meeting.

D. SSC reviews evaluation data so that the involved school personnel agree with the evaluation results, which will be shared with the parents during the eligibility meeting.

E. Suggested dates and times with alternatives for scheduling the eligibility meeting will be discussed by the involved personnel so that individual schedules will be taken into account.

(Figure 2–1 continued)

F.   Case manager invites parents to eligibility meeting.

    1.   Telephone contact may be made with the parents to ensure their availability on the suggested date(s); however, written notice in the form of "Notice of Meeting—Invitation to Parents" must be sent to the parents.

        a.   A copy of the invitation must be placed in the student's file.

        b.   Record the dates on the "Procedural Checklist" in the student's file.

    2.   Notify the counselor of the date and time of the eligibility meeting; counselors will notify all involved personnel.

G.   If the parents notify the case manager or other school personnel that they are unable to attend the scheduled meeting (or if they do not show up for the meeting), a second attempt must be made to reschedule the meeting.

H.   The case manager is responsible for contacting all involved personnel to determine a mutually agreeable date and time (then continue with the procedures as outlined above in items D and E).

IV. ELIGIBILITY

A.   Members in attendance will be only those having an active role in the case, such as the parent(s), the classroom teacher, a special educator, other service providers (i.e., RIS, speech therapist), someone to interpret the testing information (i.e., educational prescriptionist, counselor, psychologist, medical personnel), and the school administrator(s).

B.   Meeting procedures

    1.   SSC chairperson or the case manager will introduce the participants and explain the purpose of the meeting.

    2.   The case manager will complete the "Eligibility Report," which will serve as minutes (documentation) of the meeting.

(Figure 2–1 continued)

    a.   The case manager may complete the following section of the report before the meeting:

        i.   Review of formal and informal diagnostic evaluation findings of the SSC multidisciplinary team

      ii.   Description of the student's current academic progress

    iii.   Description of the student's learning styles

3.   Participants will review all pertinent data/information and (1) determine whether the student has a handicap and (2) determine whether the student needs special education and related services.

4.   If the SSC determines the student is <u>not</u> eligible for special education and related services, the SSC will assist in designing a program to meet the individual student's needs. This may result in (1) suggesting modification to the regular educational program in the classroom, (2) resource educator assistance through non-special education programs, or (3) resource consultation from a special education teacher.

5.   If the SSC determines the student <u>is</u> handicapped and needs special education and related services, the SSC proceeds with or schedules a meeting for the development of an IEP.

6.   The SSC "Eligibility Report" is completed at the meeting, signed by all participants, and a copy of the report is given to the parents. The original is placed in the student's file.

V.   <u>IEP MEETINGS</u>

   A.   The IEP for each handicapped child shall be developed at a meeting that includes the following participants:

      1.   One or more of the child's classroom teachers

      2.   Special education teacher/speech therapist

      3.   One or both parents

(Figure 2–1 continued)

4. A member of the evaluation team, or another person knowledgeable about the evaluation procedures used with the child and familiar with the results of the evaluation. If the child is receiving related services such as occupational or physical therapy, the service provider should also be present to assist with IEP development.

5. School administrator who is qualified to supervise special education and authorized to commit school resources

6. The child, when appropriate

7. Other individuals, at the reasonable discretion of the parents or the school

B. The case manager is responsible for the following:

1. Contacting all involved school personnel to ensure their availability and participation at the IEP meeting. Suggested times and dates, with alternatives should be agreed on before contacting the parents.

2. Inviting the parents to the IEP meeting..

   a. Telephone contact may be made with the parents to ensure their availability on the suggested date(s); however, written notice in the form of "Notice of Meeting—Invitation to Parents" must be sent to the parents.

      i. A copy of the invitation must be placed in the student's file.
      ii. Record the dates on the procedural checklist in the student's file.

3. When parents confirm their attendance, the case manager notifies the counselor of the date and time of the IEP meeting; the counselor notifies all involved personnel.

4. If the parents notify the case manager or other school personnel that they cannot attend the scheduled IEP meeting (or if they do not show up for the meeting), a second attempt must be made to reschedule the meeting.

5. The case manager is responsible for contacting all involved personnel to determine a mutually agreeable date and time (then continue with the procedures as outlined above in Item B, 1 to 3).

(Figure 2–1 continued)

C.   IEP development

1.   It is permissible to develop a draft of an IEP in advance of a scheduled IEP meeting provided the draft is given to the parent with sufficient time for review before the meeting. The parent should then bring the copy of the draft to the IEP meeting with questions, comments, and proposed revisions. The draft should be revised as necessary and the IEP developed.

2.   A copy of the dated letter accompanying the draft IEP must be maintained in the file with a copy of the draft IEP.

3.   The case manager is responsible for the following:

a.   Collect suggested IEP goals and objectives from all involved school personnel, prepare the "draft IEP" to share with the parents, and ensure that required documentation is maintained in the students file.

b.   Ensure the parents are provided their copy of the IEP along with any other required support documents at the conclusion of the IEP meeting.

c.   Document the activities on the "Procedural Checklist" in the student's file, and ensure the original IEP documents are appropriately filed in the student's folder.

VI.   IEP REVIEW

A.   All IEPs will be reviewed at least annually.

1.   Special educators, classroom teachers, or parents will contact the counselor to request an IEP review, when:

a.   The child has achieved IEP goals.
b.   The child has met the criteria that indicate readiness to enter a less restrictive program.
c.   The child's current program should be modified to render it more suitable to the child's needs.

2.   The counselor will notify the SSC of requested IEP reviews and schedule them within 20 days.

(Figure 2–1 continued)

   3.   The counselor will notify the SSC of required annual reviews at least 1 month before the annual review date.

B.   Modification of program

   1.   A handicapped child's education program may be modified if:

      a.   The SSC feels there is need for new and/or different services, or

      b.   The SSC determines that the educational goals and objectives set for the child have been achieved, and the child no longer requires special education services. (See Termination of Program, item C following.)

C.   Termination of program

   1.   A handicapped child's education program may be terminated only for the following reasons:

      a.   The SSC determines that the educational goals and objectives set for the child have been achieved and the child no longer requires special education services, or

      b.   A written request for termination of services is received from the parent(s), or

      c.   The child graduates from school.

   2.   As termination of program is a major change in the IEP, parents must receive appropriate notice before any action is taken. Procedures will be as follows:

      a.   An SSC meeting, including parents, will be convened.

      b.   Assessments will be conducted to show evidence the child has achieved the goals and objectives on the IEP.

      c.   An "Eligibility Report" will be completed by the counselor during the meeting to document that the student is no longer eligible for services.

      d.   Copies of the "Eligibility Report" will be distributed as follows:

         i.   One copy to the parents
        ii.   One copy in the student's file

      e.   The cover sheet of the IEP will be completed to indicate termination of services.

(Figure 2–1 continued)

      i.   One copy to parents
     ii.   One copy in the student's file

VII. <u>TRANSFER PROCEDURES</u>

    A.   Transfer into school

        1.   The counselor will review the cumulative record of each student transferring into the school.

        2.   The following procedures apply in those cases when a student with a current IEP enrolls in the school.

           a.   The counselor notifies the SSC chairperson (administrator) of the enrollee on the same day as the enrollment.

           b.   The SSC chairperson calls a SSC meeting as soon as possible to review the current IEP.

           c.   The SSC determines which of the three available options is the most appropriate. These are:

               i.   Accept and implement the current IEP.
              ii.   Modify or revise the IEP and implement (with parental agreement).
            iii.   Initiate a current evaluation of the student to formulate an appropriate IEP.

           d.   The student will be provided special education services equivalent to those specified in the accompanying IEP (with parental agreement) until such time as the new IEP is developed and approved by the parents.

    B.   Transfer out of school

        1.   Counselor notifies SSC that a student will be transferring.

        2.   SSC meets to review the IEP to ensure that the student's present status of continuing needs is adequately reflected in documents to be shared with the receiving school.

        3.   With written documentation of parental approval, a copy of pertinent information from the student's special education file is transferred to the receiving school.

        4.   A copy of the current IEP, SSC reports, and any other evaluation reports are given to the parents to hand carry to the receiving school.

(Figure 2–1 continued)

C. Transfer within the district:

The following procedures apply in the cases of students transferring from one school to another within the district.

1. The educational needs of students being transferred to a different school are communicated to the SSC chairperson of the receiving school so that the transferring student will be scheduled to continue in special education programs and related services appropriate to her needs for the continuing or succeeding school year.

    a. To accomplish this, the sending school's SSC chairperson (administrator) will contact the receiving school's chairperson in an attempt to schedule a joint meeting between SSC members of the sending and receiving schools for the purpose of IEP review.

    b. For those students transferring from the elementary school to the high school, a joint meeting between SSC members of the sending and receiving schools should be scheduled at the end of the year for the annual review of the IEP and to develop a new IEP. The sending school's SSC chairperson (administrator) will contact the receiving school's SSC chairperson in an attempt to schedule the meeting. The following personnel will be notified to attend the meeting:

        i. Chairperson of the sending school (administrator)
        ii. Chairperson of the receiving school (administrator)
        iii. Special education provider(s) from the sending school
        iv. Special education provider(s) of the receiving school or counselor who will effect continuity at the beginning of the new school year
        v. Parent(s)
        vi. Student, if appropriate

2. The student's personal file is transferred to the SSC chairperson of the receiving school, after notification and agreement of the parent(s).

Adapted from *Procedures Developed for the Case Study Committee, Alconbury Elementary School* by Linda Renz, Department of Defense Dependents Schools, Atlantic Region, 1987.

those involved with the education of students with disabilities. They provide the following:

1. A basis for continuity and consistency in the procedures followed from referral to placement
2. An inservice mechanism for teachers new to the school as well as a reference for all school personnel
3. Documentation of procedures for compliance monitoring activities
4. A mechanism by which school personnel can share with parents and community members the procedural components of the special education program

Regardless of whether school-specific procedures are established in writing, it is essential that attention be given to this aspect of coordination. As noted earlier, P.L. 94–142 does not specifically require the formation of a special services committee. Yet, it is this group that, almost without exception, is given the authority and the responsibility for appropriate decision making regarding individual students within the school. In many instances, however, individuals who may be responsible for ensuring that procedures are appropriate and that parents are "fully informed" are not fully informed themselves regarding the procedural requirements P.L. 94–142. Many classroom teachers and administrators who have frequent contact with parents report having little knowledge regarding special education procedures (Ammer, 1984; Will, 1986). Schoolwide and committee discussion, development, and consensus provide an opportunity for informed decision making regarding the procedures followed in the school.

Delineation of Responsibilities

Equally important to the establishment of schoolwide procedures is the delineation of how those procedures will be implemented within a particular school. The implementation method differs in every school depending on its location, size, staffing, and availability and proximity of support services. Therefore, it is difficult to establish uniform personnel responsibilities. For example, some schools can use school psychologists or educational diagnosticians for a major part of student evaluations. Other more geographically isolated schools do not have such personnel readily available and thus rely heavily on the instructional staff for most assessment services while contracting for or sharing those services requiring special licensure. Even schools of similar characteristics often organize their resources differently. To maximize the efficiency of the process, special ser-

vices committees should establish how responsibility for specific tasks will be divided among staff available.

Figure 2–2 provides an example of responsibility delineation based on a matching of designated procedures within the school with staff available to perform each function. Responsibilities are assigned through discussion and consensus of the special services committee members, including representation by others to whom responsibilities may be assigned. The committee must ensure that responsibilities are distributed equitably and appropriately and that consensus is achieved. The major value of such a document stems from the discussion and consensus process involved in its development. Such a process is necessary to ensure that the delineation of responsibilities reflects the school's philosophy and characteristics. For example, Figure 2–2 assigns significant coordination responsibility to the counselor. However, to assume that the counselor in every school can or should assume these particular responsibilities is inappropriate. In addition, Figure 2–2 indicates that an administrator will chair all special services committee meetings. Again, this is not a feasible practice in all schools. Although negotiating these roles is sometimes time consuming and difficult (Singer & Butler, 1987), the process of openly and specifically addressing the issue of who should or will be responsible for special education functions is critical for the program's efficient operation.

Internal Program Monitoring

A third coordinating responsibility of the special services committee is to monitor the special education program within the school. This activity is both procedural and qualitative. From a procedural perspective, internal monitoring should serve to identify and correct problems before they become compliance issues. P.L. 94–142 requires each state educational agency to develop monitoring procedures to determine whether local schools are providing special education and related services according to the requirements of P.L. 94–142. The federal government also has established standards for monitoring the policies, procedures, and regulations of state educational agencies which ensure compliance with the provisions of P.L. 94–142 (U.S. Department of Education, 1986). Of the eighteen states monitored by federal education officials since 1985, all were found to be out of compliance with at least one requirement of federal law. The most common violation was that states had failed to develop a procedure for identifying problems in their school districts' special education programs (U.S. Department of Education, 1987).

FIGURE 2–2
Delineation of Responsibilities of the Special Services Committees

Special Services Committee Member	Responsibilities
Classroom Teacher	• Completes all activities required by the pre-referral activities forms. • Completes appropriate section of the "Formal Referral" form, when required. • Provides classroom observations, anecdotal records, or work samples when requested by special services committee (SSC). • Attends and participates in required SSC meetings. Modifies program, when necessary.
Special Educator (to include Speech Therapist)	• Completes classroom observations of students in suspected area of disability, when needed. • Serves as a member of the multidisciplinary assessment team when required. • Completes assigned evaluations in a timely manner and prepares a written report of results and forwards report to case manager. • Attends and participates in SSC meetings, when appropriate. • Serves as case manager when needed. • Provides individualized, direct instruction to students eligible for special education in the areas of reading, mathematics, written language, spelling, language development, speech therapy, etc., as indicated on the child's IEP.
Case Manager	• Maintains child's file from referral to placement. • Records events, activities, and parent contacts on checklist in student's file.

(Figure 2–2 continued)

Special Services Committee Member	Responsibilities

Case Manager (cont.)

- Coordinates, monitors, and evaluates assessments to ensure timely completion.

- Schedules SSC meeting through the counselor when assessments are complete.

- Sends written invitation to parents at least 5 days before the SSC meeting and places a copy in student's file.

- Phones to remind parents 2 days before the SSC meeting.

- Writes IEP at the scheduled IEP meeting.

- Contacts and schedules medical referrals when necessary.

- Collects all data (observation, tests, and the written reports) from assessment team members.

Counselor

- Disseminates and collects "Pre-Referral Forms."

- Reviews pre-referral documents for completeness.

- Reviews all records of students transferring into the school, documents review on appropriate form, and refers to SSC when necessary.

- Maintains formal referral log.

- Completes informal and formal assessments, when needed.

- Serves as a case manager, when needed.

- Serves as a member of the SSC or IEP committee, when required.

- Completes classroom observations of students, when needed.

(Figure 2–2 continued)

Special Services Committee Member	Responsibilities
Administration	• Chairs SSC meeting or appoints an administrative designee when necessary. • Introduces SSC members at meetings and explains purpose of meetings. • Assigns case manager. • Conducts observations of students, when needed. • Supervises special education programs and commits school resources for providing services to students with disabilities.
Pupil Appraisal Personnel	• Serves as a member of the SSC multidisciplinary assessment team when requested. • Conducts evaluations of student's strengths and weaknesses. • Obtains developmental, medical, and adaptive behavior information from parents when necessary. • Delivers a written report of findings to the SSC. • Completes classroom observations of students in their suspected area of disability, when necessary. • Provides inservice to SSC members in diagnostic and/or assessment techniques, when requested. • Participates in required SSC meetings to consult and/or provide explanation of assessment results to parents and SSC members.
Special Education Aide	• Assists special educator in delivery of instruction, under special educator's supervision.

(Figure 2–2 continued)

Special Services Committee Member	Responsibilities
Special Education Aide (cont.)	• Assists case manager in meetings, scheduling, record organization, and completing required paperwork. • May be assigned by administrator to assist a special education student in a regular classroom if the need is indicated on the student's IEP.

Related Services Personnel
  Occupational
    Therapist
  Physical Therapist
  Audiologist
  Social Worker
	• Provides classroom observations of students when requested.
	
	• Serves as a member of the multidisciplinary evaluation team when requested.
	
	• Completes assignments and submits written reports as required.
	
	• Attends staffing, eligibility, and IEP meetings as requested.
	
	• Provides direct and consultative services as required by a student's IEP.
	
	• Provides services during the pre-referral period as necessary to resolve problem before referral to special education.

Parents	• Makes available all previous school records regarding the child's educational program. • Provides information to the SSC that may be helpful in designing educational strategies or developing an individual program for the child. • Attends SSC meetings regarding the child. • Participates in IEP development. • Implements IEP goals and objectives as required by the IEP.

Adapted from *Procedures Developed for the Case Study Committee, Alconbury Elementary School* by Linda Renz, Department of Defense Dependents School, Atlantic Region, 1987, and from the *Special Education Self Study, Alconbury Elementary School,* by Linda Renz, Department of Defense Dependents Schools, Atlantic Region.

Special services committee members should be knowledgeable regarding the essential elements of compliance monitoring. These elements should provide a basis for ongoing internal program review. For example, federal and state law require that parents attend IEP meetings or that specific attempts to obtain their involvement be documented. Because the special services committee functions at the school level, it is in an ideal position to determine the effectiveness of school procedures in meeting this requirement, and if necessary, to refine those procedures to ensure that the intent of the requirement is met. By establishing a systematic mechanism for internal monitoring, program improvement becomes an ongoing and positive activity controlled by the school rather than by an outside evaluation team, as compliance monitoring is sometimes viewed.

Because state laws, state educational agency regulations, and local policy often differ and sometimes exceed the basic provisions of federal law and its regulations, members of the special services committee should have access to first-hand information regarding requirements at each rule-making level. Such access provides (1) clarification of the origin of the various requirements by which schools must operate, (2) a source of comparison between federal, state, and local requirements, and (3) original references for teachers, parents, and community members. Copies of P.L. 94–142, P.L. 99–457 (Amendments to the Education of the Handicapped Act of 1986) and their governing regulations, which are contained in various volumes of the Federal Register, can be obtained through local school systems, through all public and university libraries, or by writing to the U.S. Government Printing Office. Each state has concomitant legislation to implement federal law within the state. Like federal laws, state laws are implemented through state-developed regulations governing special education programs within that state. Copies of state laws and governing regulations also can be obtained from local school systems, public libraries, or State Departments of Education.

Local policy usually delineates how federal and state regulations will be operationalized at the school system level. It is this policy along with specific school procedures that should provide a continuous focus for program improvements and refinement. Although qualitative issues are not a major part of procedural compliance monitoring, they should be a primary focus of the special services internal monitoring function at the school level. It is often these issues which lead to problems between parents and schools rather than procedural issues. For example, the majority of due process hearings conducted in the United States focus on the belief by parents that public schools cannot or will not adequately address the educational needs of their children with disabilities (Singer & Butler, 1987). Special services committees should be sensitive to aspects of the program that, though meeting the procedural requirements of law, do not always represent best educational practice. Issues such as ensuring that classroom teachers have adequate support and services to achieve effective mainstreaming of students with disabilities, developing meaningful methods of effective home–school coordination, and monitoring student progress are all qualitative topics that the special services committee should consider.

Obviously, the special services committee cannot address all issues in the course of 1 year. The well-organized committee, however, will systematically monitor the school program to collect information for program refinement and improvement and will establish priorities that the committee will address during the year or even over a 3- to 5-year period. One excellent mechanism for program improvement is the formal accreditation process, which schools must complete periodically. This activity provides an opportunity for schools to engage in coordinated and in-depth self-study to identify program strengths and weaknesses and to generate both immediate and long-term program-improvement goals. Chapter 14 provides strategies for local monitoring, which would be appropriate for use at the school level to gain systematic information regarding program functioning.

Advising

Advising school administrators as to the nature of problems and their possible solutions is an outgrowth of the coordinating and monitoring process. When the special services committee identifies an obstacle to effective program functioning, it should immediately advise the principal (if she is not a member of the committee) and, at the principal's request, any other administrators who have the authority to help resolve the issue. For example, the recommendation for inservice training of teachers might be reported to the principal and to the director of special education, or problems associated with architectural barriers might be discussed with the principal and the director of physical facilities. The appropriate contact persons can depend on the nature of the identified problem.

The special services committee should document in written reports the precise nature of and recommended solutions to problems. The written reports can serve as a record of actions taken and as an accountability device for the committee regarding documenting good faith efforts to comply with the law.

The remaining functions of the special services committee are student specific. It should be remembered, however, that program coordination functions are inseparable from student-specific functions. The quality with which student-specific activities are performed is directly related to the efficiency of the coordination framework within which the activities exist.

STUDENT-SPECIFIC COMMITTEE FUNCTIONS

The process from the point of referral to placement in special education and related services is lengthy and complex. Figure 2–3 provides a detailed illustration of the many activities involved.

As students are referred to and move through the identification process, a mechanism for student-specific coordination is helpful for the committee. Figure 2–4 provides a sample organizational chart that can aid the committee in the specific coordination of each student referred. To complete the chart, the name of each participant who assumes the various roles listed down the left side of the form is entered in the columns provided for names. Then the task assigned to each participant may be checked to provide systematic coordination of the entire process. The tasks themselves may be defined and arranged according to the preference of the special services committee while still ensuring that all required activities are included. Many school systems maintain these documents in the students' special education file and/or in a committee referral log to monitor procedural activities regarding that student.

Figure 2–5, p. 52, provides another example of how the committee might monitor procedural activities using a special services committee referral log that enables the group to monitor required activities regarding each student referred to the committee. Such a procedure also provides quantitative data by which the committee can evaluate its functioning periodically. Numerous computerized management programs also are available for this purpose.

For purposes of discussion in this section, the student-specific functions of the special services committee will be summarized and discussed as follows:

1. Pre-referral and referral activities
2. Evaluation and eligibility determination
3. IEP development
4. IEP implementation, monitoring, and review

Pre-referral and Referral Activities

The first student-specific activity in which the special services committee is typically involved is pre-referral and referral. These activities are not specifically addressed or required by P.L. 94–142 but represent one aspect of the child-find process within a school and thus are the mechanism by which a student is first brought to the committee's attention. Many controversial issues are related to the role of referral in the identification of students with mild disabilities. These will be discussed further in Chapter 4; however, pre-referral and referral do not confirm a disability and do not, in themselves, establish that a student cannot function in a classroom setting. They are indicators that the student, for some reason, is having significant difficulty in one or more aspects of the educational program, and they are requests to look closer to rule out, or possibly to identify, the existence of a disability that may be responsible for educational difficulties.

At the point of pre-referral, the special services committee is student specific and includes the classroom teacher and usually a special education teacher, diagnostician, or consultant, and the student's parents. Some schools have specific names for these pre-referral teams including teacher assistance teams, or building level support teams. The purpose of pre-referral is to employ strategies, supplemental aids, and materials in an attempt to resolve the problem without the need for formal referral and assignment to special education. The pre-referral process is viewed as a key element in avoiding the haphazard and often unnecessary referral of children to special education programs (Nevin & Thousand, 1986; Ritchie, 1986; Shinn, Tindal, & Spira, 1987; Wang, Reynolds, & Walberg, 1986).

Although formal meetings may or may not be a function of this group, all members are actively engaged in classroom activities including the following:

1. Review of class and school records
2. Observation and/or work with the child in the classroom setting
3. Consultation between team members
4. Coordination with other support personnel as necessary
5. Development of management programs

If all pre-referral strategies fail to resolve the problem, a formal referral is made to the special services

FIGURE 2–3
Sequence and Functions of Committee Activities

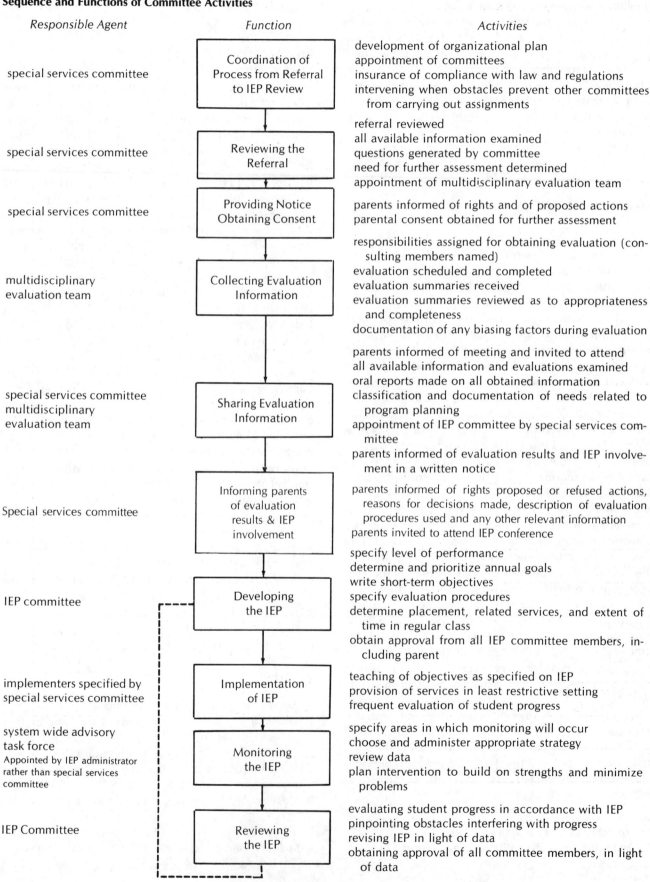

Responsible Agent	Function	Activities
special services committee	Coordination of Process from Referral to IEP Review	development of organizational plan appointment of committees insurance of compliance with law and regulations intervening when obstacles prevent other committees from carrying out assignments
special services committee	Reviewing the Referral	referral reviewed all available information examined questions generated by committee need for further assessment determined appointment of multidisciplinary evaluation team
special services committee	Providing Notice Obtaining Consent	parents informed of rights and of proposed actions parental consent obtained for further assessment
multidisciplinary evaluation team	Collecting Evaluation Information	responsibilities assigned for obtaining evaluation (consulting members named) evaluation scheduled and completed evaluation summaries received evaluation summaries reviewed as to appropriateness and completeness documentation of any biasing factors during evaluation
special services committee multidisciplinary evaluation team	Sharing Evaluation Information	parents informed of meeting and invited to attend all available information and evaluations examined oral reports made on all obtained information classification and documentation of needs related to program planning appointment of IEP committee by special services committee parents informed of evaluation results and IEP involvement in a written notice
Special services committee	Informing parents of evaluation results & IEP involvement	parents informed of rights proposed or refused actions, reasons for decisions made, description of evaluation procedures used and any other relevant information parents invited to attend IEP conference
IEP committee	Developing the IEP	specify level of performance determine and prioritize annual goals write short-term objectives specify evaluation procedures determine placement, related services, and extent of time in regular class obtain approval from all IEP committee members, including parent
implementers specified by special services committee	Implementation of IEP	teaching of objectives as specified on IEP provision of services in least restrictive setting frequent evaluation of student progress
system wide advisory task force Appointed by IEP administrator rather than special services committee	Monitoring the IEP	specify areas in which monitoring will occur choose and administer appropriate strategy review data plan intervention to build on strengths and minimize problems
IEP Committee	Reviewing the IEP	evaluating student progress in accordance with IEP pinpointing obstacles interfering with progress revising IEP in light of data obtaining approval of all committee members, in light of data

FIGURE 2–4
Committee Assignments and Responsibility

TASKS

Student Name _____

Grade _____

Date _____

ROLE	NAME	Referral	Providing Notice to Parents and Obtaining Consent	Evaluation	Informing Parents of Evaluation Results	Informing Parents of IEP Development	IEP Committee Membership	IEP Implementation	Program Monitoring	Reviewing the IEP
		1	2	3	4	5	6	7	8	9
Chairperson										
Current and/or Recent Teacher(s)										
Prospective Teacher(s)										
Child Evaluator(s)										
School Administrator										
Parent/Child Liaison										
Parent(s)										
Specialist ___ field										
Specialist ___ field										
Community Agency Representative										
Translator/Interpreter ___ language										
Recorder										
Other										

Date Task Completed _____

FIGURE 2–5
Special Services Committee Referral Log

Student Name	Teacher	Date Referral Received	Referral Decision A R O	Case Manager	Parent Notice Sent	Consent for Evaluation Received	Date Assessment Complete	Eligibility Determination Date Yes No	Notice Results to Parents	IEP Meeting Date	IEP Annual Review Date

A, accepted; O, other; R, rejected.

committee. When considering a referral, every effort should be made to ensure that the classroom teacher or other individuals involved in the pre-referral process are represented on the special services committee to present an overview of procedures tried that have not been effective (Ysseldyke, Pianta, Christenson, Wang, & Algozzine, 1983). Based on the referral question, the special services committee must establish an assessment plan and appoint a multidisciplinary team to perform the evaluation. These team members function as a part of the special services committee regarding the student being evaluated.

Evaluation and Eligibility Determination

The function of evaluation and eligibility determination is clearly one of the most important and currently one of the most controversial responsibilities of the special services committee (Algozzine & Ysseldyke, 1986; Ysseldyke, 1988). Activities of the committee associated with this function include the following:

1. Select the multidisciplinary evaluation team
2. Provide notice to parents and obtain parental consent
3. Conduct evaluation
4. Determine eligibility
5. Inform parents of evaluation results

All of these activities will be discussed at length in later chapters. A brief discussion will be provided here regarding committee functions.

Selection of the Multidisciplinary Team.   P.L. 94–142 requires that the multidisciplinary team include at least one teacher or other specialist with knowledge in the area of suspected disability and that members of the team be trained to perform the evaluation function to which they have been assigned (*Federal Register*, 1977). The size of the team will vary, depending on the referral question and the resulting assessment plan. For example, the multidisciplinary evaluation team for a student who is suspected of having a speech and language disability may consist only of the speech and language therapist to confirm that a disability exists and the classroom teacher or another individual who conducts procedures to confirm that the condition adversely affects educational performance. The multidisciplinary evaluation team for a student suspected of having an intellectual disability might consist of a psychologist to evaluate cognitive functioning and adaptive behavior, parents to be involved in the assessment of adaptive behavior and to provide background information, teachers to confirm adverse educational effects, a speech and

language therapist to evaluate speech and language function, and possibly a physician, occupational therapist, and/or a physical therapist if medical or motor problems are suspected.

Evaluation.   The multidisciplinary evaluation team must assess the student in all areas of suspected disability in conformance with the nondiscriminatory evaluation provisions of P.L. 94–142 presented in Chapter 1. The evaluation must be conducted in a timely manner. Evaluation provides in-depth information on problems identified through the pre-referral and referral process. Thus, rather than automatically administering a broad standard battery, evaluation should be designed to answer specific referral questions. The function of the special services committee is to ensure that the focus of the evaluation activity is appropriate.

Eligibility Determination.   After the multidisciplinary team has conducted the evaluation and analyzed the results, the special services committee should be presented with the results and team recommendations. At this point a decision must be made whether to classify the student as handicapped and whether to recommend placement in special education and related services. Although not required by P.L. 94–142, consideration should be given to inviting the student's parents to this meeting. Some state and local regulations may require that parents be invited to attend.

Providing Notice to Parents and Obtaining Consent.
Although parents preferably should be informed and involved throughout the pre-referral, referral, and evaluation process, P.L. 94–142 specifically requires their involvement, if not their presence, at a minimum of two points during this process. First, when the committee decides to accept the referral, parents must be formally notified and give their consent for the preplacement evaluation. Again, when the initial assessment is completed, parents must be informed of assessment results and any recommendation based on those results. At both points, notice must be provided and consent obtained according to the very specific requirements of P.L. 94–142.

When considering which individual or individuals should be assigned responsibility for meeting due process requirements by providing notice to parents and obtaining their consent for preplacement evaluation, a decision might be made on the basis of the degree of previous contact with the parents. For example, a counselor who has had extended contact with the parents may be more effective in communicating with the parents than would other team members.

If the student has not been classified as having a disability, the school must inform the parents of such action and also must alert them to any modifications in the curriculum to meet their child's needs. In cases where the student is identified as having a disability and needs special education and related services, parents also must be informed of the student's proposed classification and the involvement of the parents in the IEP process. One written notice can inform parents both of evaluation results and IEP involvement. Parents may be confused and frustrated by receiving various bits of information from a host of special services committee members; having one person assume overall responsibility for parent communication throughout the total process can enhance the clarity of the information presented.

IEP Development

If the committee indeed determines that the student has a disability that requires special education, the special services committee must ensure that an IEP is developed and effectively implemented. To accomplish this function an IEP committee is formed. Like the multidisciplinary evaluation team, the IEP team functions as part of the special services team to develop the IEP for a specific student. Committee activities associated with this function include the following:

1. Establish the IEP committee.
2. Schedule the IEP meeting.
3. Notify parents of and involve them in the IEP meeting.
4. Develop the IEP.

All of these functions provide the major focus of this book and will be discussed in depth in subsequent chapters. For the purposes of this section, a discussion of the first activity, establishing committee membership, will be reviewed.

P.L. 94–142 specifies the requirements of IEP committee membership, and thus the special services committee has legal guidelines to follow in making assignments. As discussed in Chapter 1, P.L. 94–142 requires that the committee consist of the following representatives:

1. The student's teacher (special and/or regular)
2. A school professional, other than the child's teacher, who is responsible for providing or supervising special education

3. The student's parents or parent
4. The student, if appropriate
5. The person conducting the student's evaluation or a person knowledgeable in the interpretation of evaluation data (if the student is being considered for special education placement for the first time)
6. Other individuals at the discretion and the parent or agency.

(Federal Register, 1977)

The average numbers of IEP committee members is approximately four (Goldstein, Strickland, Turnbull, & Curry, 1980; U.S. Department of Education, 1981; Vaughn, Bos, Harrell, & Lasky, 1988). Under some circumstances, the IEP committee could, at a minimum, consist of three individuals: the student's parent, the child's teacher, and a representative of the public agency. (In the case of students who are being evaluated for the first time, the teacher and the agency representative would have to be a member of the evaluation team or be knowledgeable about the evaluation procedures and results.) The IEP committee may, if necessary be much larger, depending on the needs of the student and the preference of the parent and school.

Although the contributions of all individuals with pertinent information regarding the education of the student with a disability should be considered in the development of the IEP, not all of these individuals need to be present at the IEP committee meeting. Generally, the number of participants at the meeting should be small. In establishing the preference for small meetings, the U.S. Department of Education (1981) has presented the following advantages:

1. Open, active parent involvement is facilitated.
2. Small meetings are less costly than larger meetings.
3. Small meetings are easier to arrange and to conduct.
4. Small meetings are usually more productive.

Student's Teacher. The student's teacher(s) is a required member of the IEP committee because this individual(s) alone can most accurately relate the child's classroom performance to the task of IEP development. For a student being considered for initial placement in special education, the teacher on the IEP committee may be the student's regular classroom teacher, a teacher qualified to provide special education in the child's area of suspected disability, or both. When the regular classroom teacher is included on the IEP committee, arrangements should be made to ensure the presence of at least one member of the school staff who is qualified in the student's area of suspected disability.

When a student is enrolled in both regular and special education programs, the special education teacher should attend the IEP meeting. The local education agency and the parent, however, have the option of including the regular education teacher. Such inclusion is strongly recommended for three reasons. First, inclusion of the regular classroom teacher in the development of the IEP provides a framework for comprehensive planning, a process that has heretofore been more a lofty aspiration than a real educational practice. If the student is mainstreamed, both the special education teacher and the student's regular classroom teacher will have performance information vital to the accurate development of an educational program. The classroom teacher's active contribution to the process of educational planning provides continuity in the instruction that students receive. Just as the former practice of excluding parents and students from the planning process resulted from the failure to recognize the need for such input, the exclusion of the classroom teacher omits a major source of relevant information that may not otherwise be available or considered in a systematic fashion.

Second, the classroom teacher may very well be responsible for providing "specially designed instruction" (special education) in the regular classroom. P.L. 94–142 requires that if the student's needs can be addressed in the classroom, alone or with the use of supplementary aids and materials, then the student should remain in that setting. Most students with disabilities do spend at least a portion of the day in the regular program (U.S. Department of Education, 1988). If the regular classroom teacher is responsible for a part of the mainstreamed student's day, the professional contributions and observations of this teacher are vitally important in ensuring an appropriate educational plan. The ability of this professional, moreover, to accommodate a student with a disability in the regular classroom will be enhanced.

Third, the classroom teacher's lack of knowledge of the content of a student's IEP constitutes a very legitimate basis for questioning whether the student is receiving an appropriate education. Because the concept of "appropriate education" is only vaguely defined by P.L. 94–142, the IEP provides the most tangible means of evaluating appropriateness. Most due process hearings conducted since the enactment of P.L. 94–142 have been related to issues of appropriateness of programs within the public school (National Association of State Directors of Special Education, 1978; Singer & Butler, 1987).

To date, classroom teachers have assumed little responsibility for IEP development (Ammer, 1984; Goldstein et al., 1980; Vaughn et al., 1988). However, with the current emphasis on providing necessary special instruction within the regular school environment (Council for Exceptional Children, 1987; Gartner & Lipsky, 1987; Wang, Reynolds, & Walberg, 1986; Will, 1986), it is imperative that the persons responsible for teaching the student be familiar with and involved in determining what constitutes an appropriate education for a particular child.

Such familiarity requires participation in IEP development or, at the very least, familiarity with its content. When the public agency or parent chooses not to have the regular classroom teachers represented on the IEP committee, every effort should be made to inform those teachers about the student's IEP and provide them with a copy of the IEP itself. In addition, the special education teacher should be available for consultation and assistance to the regular classroom teacher.

Agency Representative. The IEP committee must include a representative of the public agency, other than the student's teacher, who is qualified to provide or supervise the provision of special education. This individual could be a special education administrator, supervisor, principal, or a special education teacher.

The primary function of the agency representative is to ensure that the services agreed on at the IEP meeting will actually be provided and will not be vetoed at a higher administrative level within the agency. Thus, if it is evident that a student will require extensive special education and related services, the agency representative should be a person, preferably a key administrator, who has the authority to commit agency resources. If the student requires only a limited amount of special education and related services, the agency representative could be a special education teacher or perhaps a speech-language pathologist. In this instance the individual selected, while not the student's teacher, should have enough knowledge of the type of services needed to represent adequately both the interests of the student and the public agency. For example, the presence of an audiologist for a student with an emotional disturbance and normal hearing adds little to the composition of the committee, since this individual may be unfamiliar with both the services typically required for students with emotional disturbances and with the agency's options for providing these services. A more appropriate selection in this case would be a counselor or another teacher of students with emotional disturbances. It should be emphasized again that the anticipated need for extensive services necessitates the appointment of an agency representative who has the authority to commit agency resources.

In addition to committing agency resources, the agency representative also may assume the role of parent or student advocate, especially when the parents are not accompanied by a person serving this capacity. In such a role, the representative may ensure that the parent is included as an active member of the committee by ensuring that the language of the conference can be understood by all participants including the parents and the student, directing pertinent questions to parents, directing the discussion of specific subjects, and requesting clarification of statements that the parent may not fully understand (Goldstein et al., 1980). In this way parent and student participation can be encouraged and increased.

Parents. The inclusion of the student's parents as required members of the IEP committee reflects the recognition pervasive throughout P.L. 94–142 that parents have a significant role in the planning of an appropriate education for their children. Available research, however, indicates that many parents do not actively participate as members of the IEP committee (Lynch & Stein, 1987; National Association of State Directors of Special Education, 1985; Singer & Butler, 1987; K. K. Turnbull & Hughes, 1987; Vaughn et al., 1988; Weber & Stoneman, 1986). Although some parents may not wish to be involved in the development of their child's educational program, it should be recognized that parents, just as teachers, may require training regarding the significance of their role in program development. Simply assuming that parents do not wish to be involved because of their failure to attend the IEP meeting is inappropriate, because many parents do not fully realize what they choose not to be part of. In enlisting parents as team members, the significance of their involvement must be emphasized.

Student. The inclusion of the student is required when her presence is considered appropriate. In determining the appropriateness of including the student as a participant, criteria might include the parent's or student's desire to be involved; the age of the student; and the student's ability to contribute to and to benefit from such involvement. The student, having developed methods of coping and compensating for specific aspects of the disability, is in many instances the most obvious and useful source of information for a tailor-made program. Thus, although not all students with disabilities can effectively assist in the development of their IEP, school personnel should consider the potential contribu-

tions of each student and should assist parents to determine whether their child should participate.

Evaluator. Finally, a member of the evaluation team or a person knowledgeable in the interpretation of the evaluation data must be included on the IEP committee if the student is being considered for special education placement for the first time. This requirement enables continuity between the multidisciplinary evaluation team's assessment and the IEP committee's program planning. The accurate interpretation of evaluation data is crucial to both the development of an appropriate educational program and the understanding with which the resulting IEP is implemented. The individual chosen to assume this role may not necessarily be the school psychologist. Other members of the multidisciplinary team or even other individuals qualified to interpret test results (whether or not they evaluated the student in question) may serve this function. When, for example, speech is the primary disability, the individual responsible for interpreting evaluation results most likely will be a speech-language pathologist. When several disabilities are apparent, however, more than one individual may be required to interpret various evaluative data.

The IEP committee should include a person with expertise in the area of the student's suspected disability—usually the special education teacher or the public agency representative. Thus, an additional member beyond those already mentioned is not usually necessary. In some instances, however, a student may have a disability not provided for by existing public school programs. An example might be a student with a multisensory disability of deafness and blindness. To develop an appropriate IEP, an individual knowledgeable in the area of programming for multisensory disabilities should participate in the IEP development.

Other. At the discretion of the parent(s) or public agency, other members may be included as warranted. Parents may wish to have someone accompany them to the IEP to serve as an advocate for themselves and their child. This individual may be a lawyer, professional advocate, educator, social worker, or even a family friend. Often, a parent may feel somewhat intimidated at being the only nonprofessional at the meeting. Informing parents of their right to be accompanied by someone else can effectively ensure that parent interests are not overlooked.

Selection of additional participants should be based on information needed to identify the student's needs and to prescribe an appropriate educational program. Choices of possible committee members will differ with the individual student being considered. For instance, the IEP committee for a student with a hearing disability would include, along with required members of the team, the speech therapist and the audiologist. On the other hand, a committee formed for a student with cerebral palsy might include a physical therapist, a vocational rehabilitation counselor, and a physical education specialist.

Implementation and Maintenance of the IEP

The final student-specific function of the special services committee is to ensure that the IEP is implemented and appropriately maintained and reviewed. Activities associated with this function might include the following:

1. Appoint a case manager
2. Ensure the availability and provision of required services, including supplemental aids and materials
3. Coordinate among service providers
4. Maintain and review the IEP

Although ultimate responsibility for this function lies with the special services committee, one individual usually is assigned case management responsibility. This individual is usually the student's special education teacher, although some schools also assign case management responsibilities to school counselors, to educational prescriptions, and in some instances, to classroom teachers.

The case manager usually is assigned coordination responsibilities. This individual must maintain regular contact with all individuals providing services to the student to ensure continuity between programs. For example, if a speech therapist wishes to implement activities to ensure generalization of speech sounds outside the therapeutic setting, coordination with the classroom teacher, who can observe and report on the student's progress, is necessary. Likewise, a physical therapist providing services to a student with a physical disability must also coordinate with the student's teacher to ensure that skills developed in the therapeutic session will be applied in the classroom setting.

Although P.L. 94–142 does not require that a case manager be assigned, in practice the use of case managers to ensure the appropriate day-to-day maintenance of the IEP is widespread. The case manager or case management team, like other teams designated to perform specific activities, functions as part of the special services committee.

The special services committee must ensure that the full continuum of special education services required by the student's IEP is available and accessible. The U.S. Department of Education, in its *Standards and Guidelines for Compliance with Federal Requirements for Education of the Handicapped* (1986) has specifically stated that service delivery for a particular child cannot be predicated solely on (1) the configuration of the existing service delivery system, (2) availability of educational or related services, (3) availability of space, (4) the category of the student's disability, or (5) curriculum content or methods of curriculum delivery. In addition, the standards specify that services required by a student with a disability must be provided in conjunction with regular class placement wherever possible. These requirements warrant the careful attention of the special services committee, because available research indicates that these factors currently play a significant role in how and whether the services required by a student with a disability are provided (Carlberg & Kavale 1985; Singer, Butler, Palfrey, & Walker, 1986; U.S. Department of Education, 1987). If the IEP requires a resource that is unavailable or normally not provided in the setting required by the IEP, then the special services committee is responsible for working with school officials to develop these services or to provide inservice training to guarantee the provision of the services.

As part of this function, the special services committee must ensure that architectural barriers do not pose obstacles to the full participation of students with disabilities. For students with mobility impairments, the elimination of architectural barriers is necessary for the full implementation of their IEPs in the least restrictive appropriate setting. Furthermore, P.L. 94–142 requires elimination of such barriers.

A final consideration in ensuring that required services are provided relates to those students who receive all or part of their "specialized instruction" in the regular classroom. If the IEP indicates that a student with a disability can function in the regular classroom with supplemental aids and materials, then special services committees must ensure that those supplemental aids and materials are, in fact, provided. These supplemental aids and materials are as much a part of the placement decision as the location itself and are required by law (*Federal Register*, 1977). If, for instance, the IEP for a student with a physical disability requires adaptive writing equipment to carry out the objectives, the special services committee should see that a member of the IEP committee locates, stores, and distributes the necessary materials to the student and teachers.

One of the most critical but often neglected responsibilities of the special services team is coordination among the professionals involved in the education of the student with a disability. Although the majority of students spend at least part of their school day with someone other than a special education teacher, there is often little substantive communication between special education and classroom teachers regarding curriculum, instructional procedures and skill attainment (Ammer, 1984; Wang, Reynolds, & Walberg, 1986; Will, 1986). This problem is compounded when a student receives instruction in a number of programs. Lack of communication and coordination among service providers is one of the primary reasons for maintaining students in the regular program and providing services within that environment rather than in specialized settings.

Maintenance and review of the IEP ensures that, after the IEP is implemented, an appropriate education continues to be provided. One of the major criticisms of past special education practices is that students, once provided with special education, were rarely re-evaluated to check their progress. Nor was the quality of the instructional program being taught often assessed. Although greatly improved, these issues continue to be areas of concern (Carlberg & Kavale, 1980; Lipsky & Gartner, 1987). The review requirements of P.L. 94–142 are an attempt to ensure evaluation of the educational program as needed (but at least annually) and re-evaluation of the student as necessary (but at least every 3 years). Chapter 10 provides suggestions for carrying out systematic monitoring functions for individual children and their programs.

The final step in maintaining the IEP is its review. P.L. 94–142 requires review of IEPs at least once annually. The IEP committee, which originally developed the document, and the individuals assigned responsibility for implementing the IEP should be involved in the formal review process.

SUMMARY

The major consideration of this chapter has been to provide an organizational framework within which the special services committee can coordinate special education activities within the school. The functions and interrelationships of the permanent and temporary members of the special services committee, multi-disciplinary evaluation team, and IEP committee can be a confusing process for beginning teachers or for individuals entering a new school system. For any particular student, these committees are likely to have some members in common but will also have some variability. Coordination and collaboration are essential for effective IEP development and implementation. Ultimately, the special services committee must assume responsibility for the continuity of the entire process. The remaining chapters in Part 1 focus on the educational implementation of the procedural steps from referral to IEP development.

EVALUATION

1. Conduct an interview with the chairperson of a special services committee at a local school as to the composition and functions of the committee. Based on information discussed in the interview, write a job description for each committee member that outlines roles and responsibilities related specifically to the functions of the committee. Compare and contrast your interview findings with the information included in this chapter.

2. Assume you are the chairperson of a special services committee. A parent who has just been informed by the classroom teacher that her son will be referred to the committee for testing contacts you. She asks, "What exactly will your special services committee do regarding my son?" Outline the major points of your response. Role play this situation with a colleague.

3. Assume you are chairperson of a special services committee in a school system engaged in a self-study on committee decision making and duties. The superintendent asks you to draft a two-page statement on the special services committee that includes the following elements:
   a. Functions of the committee.
   b. Strategies of governance (To whom does the committee report? In what form? With what authority?)
   Draft such a statement.

CHAPTER 3   The Pre-referral Process

OBJECTIVES

1. Describe the need for a pre-referral process before referring a student to special education.
2. Define the "regular education initiative."
3. Identify four benefits of a pre-referral procedure.
4. Discuss three frameworks for implementing a pre-referral procedure in the school.
5. Discuss strategies for pre-referral interventions.

One of the major provisions of P.L. 94–142 is the stipulation that students with disabilities should be educated in the regular education program when possible.

> That special classes, separate schooling or other removal of handicapped children from the regular educational environment occurs only when the nature or severity of the handicap is such that education in regular classes with the use of supplementary aids and services, cannot be achieved satisfactorily. (*Federal Register*, 1977)

Despite this provision, educational practice typically has reflected a system in which very few supplemental aids and materials are employed or very few substantial modifications attempted before referring a student to a special education program (Ammer, 1984; Munson, 1986; Pugach, 1985; Zigmond, Levin, & Laurie, 1985). Of even greater concern is the fact that once a student is referred for evaluation, it is highly likely that the student will be identified as handicapped and be enrolled in a special education program rather than remaining in the regular program for needed assistance (Algozzine, Christenson, & Ysseldyke, 1982).

RATIONALE FOR A PRE-REFERRAL PROCESS

Need for a Pre-referral Process

For several reasons students tend to be referred to and enrolled in special education programs with little apparent intervention before referral. First, few states and school systems have operationalized requirements for substantive intervention before a student is referred to special education (Salend, 1987). In systems where requirements do exist, procedures often are designed primarily for documentation purposes rather than for the purpose of substantive intervention to maintain the student in the regular program. For example, school procedures may require that teachers provide a written description of interventions attempted before referral but may not establish a mechanism to ensure that the interventions occurred systematically. Without a clearly established pre-referral procedure, the formal referral process for special education is readily accessible and available as an alternative for any student who does not meet the educational expectations of the regular classroom.

Second, as will be discussed in Chapter 4, the referral process in many schools, though well-defined procedurally, often lacks adequate criteria to assist classroom teachers in making appropriate referral decisions or to assist special services committees in differentiating referrals to special education from those for remedial or second-language programs (Pugach, 1985). It should be noted that teachers do not always refer students with the intention of relinquishing to special education responsibility for the student's educational program. In some cases referral is an attempt to gain additional information to guide instruction in the regular classroom or to obtain compensatory education assistance within the regular program. Nonetheless, once referred, a strong possibility exists that the student will be assessed and placed in special education, regardless of the original intent of the referral (Algozzine et al., 1982; Pugach, 1985). Without specific guidelines or criteria for submitting referrals, teachers likely will continue to refer large numbers of students who may not require special education services.

Third, despite legal preference, it has become accepted practice for special education programs, rather than for regular education programs, to assume responsibility for the education of students identified as having disabilities. Special educators are often viewed, and view themselves, as possessing knowledge and skills that enable them to deal more effectively with diversity than the classroom teacher can. Classroom teachers may perceive themselves as lacking necessary skills, resources, time, and/or training and thus may often be willing, if not eager, to relinquish responsibility for these students (Gartner & Lipsky, 1987). In addition, parents seldom question the validity of placement decisions made by special educators and classroom teachers (Goldstein et al., 1980); thus, many elements of the student's educational programming tend to work together to ensure segregated placement, regardless of whether assistance could be provided in the regular program. Finally, many educators view the existing structure of the regular education program as primarily responsible for the proliferation of separate programs (Algozzine & Ysseldyke, 1986; Goodlad, 1984; W. Stainback, Stainback, Courtnage, & Jaben, 1985; Wang & Birch, 1984). The traditional regular classroom, oriented toward attaining a designated amount of material in a given amount of time, is viewed as too narrowly focused to accommodate a wide range of student differences. These educators emphasize the need to restructure the regular program to more accurately reflect the needs of an increasingly diverse student population.

The Regular Education Initiative

Prompting the increased emphasis on the process of pre-referral intervention is a movement generally referred to as the "regular education initiative." Simply stated, this movement is an attempt to focus attention on adapting the regular education program to provide appropriate and least restrictive learning environments for all students including those with disabilities (Lipsky & Gartner, 1987; S. Stainback & Stainback, 1984; Wang et al., 1986; Will, 1986). This movement has gained momentum as the number of special education programs has increased significantly since the enactment of P.L. 94–142. Many are concerned that schools are creating and maintaining a dual system of special and regular education, which can contribute to lack of coordination and accountability among services, isolation and stigmatization of students with disabilities, and students being denied the legal right to education in the regular program with students who do not have disabilities (Lipsky & Gartner, 1987; S. Stainback & Stainback, 1984; Will, 1986). Supporters of the regular education initiative advocate restructuring of the regular education program to increase its capacity for accommodating the instructional needs of students with disabilities.

The regular education initiative has been criticized by many who caution that (1) not all students can be appropriately served in regular classes

(D. Fuchs & Fuchs, 1988); (2) regular classroom teachers do not necessarily desire to or have the expertise to implement the regular education initiative (Braaten, Kauffman, Braaten, Polsgrove, & Nelson, 1988); and that (3) methodologies for implementing full-scale mainstreaming have not yet been adequately validated to ensure that they work (D. Fuchs & Fuchs, 1988).

Despite disagreement on the degree to which the regular education initiative can be fully implemented, most would agree that the regular education program is appropriate for many students with disabilities and that no student should be removed from the regular program unless an appropriate education clearly cannot be provided in that setting (Braaten et al., 1988). Based on this notion, the remainder of this chapter will focus on pre-referral procedures as a mechanism for maintaining students with disabilities in the regular education program.

Benefits of Pre-referral Procedures

Pre-referral is a process of systematic instructional intervention before referral designed to enable the student to remain in the regular education program rather than being placed in a segregated special education program.

The development of a well-conceived pre-referral process has potential benefits for all involved. First, from a legal perspective, pre-referral procedures may make the difference in whether a student can maintain membership in the regular education program in keeping with the legal entitlements of P.L. 94–142. Pre-referral procedures can ensure that the "supplementary aids and materials" required by P.L. 94–142 are employed before referral to special education. Development of pre-referral procedures has legal benefits for the school and system as well. Procedures that document a process for maintaining a student in the regular education program whenever possible may serve to demonstrate that a school or system has a mechanism for ensuring placement in the least restrictive environment. This element of compliance has been a major issue in program monitoring activities conducted by the U.S. Office of Education since the enactment of P.L. 94–142.

Second, in addition to the legal benefits of a well-defined pre-referral process, such a mechanism can help in refining vague and subjective referral and identification procedures by clearly defining the educational concerns. By defining all aspects of a problem through various interventions before referral, the number of inappropriate referrals likely will be reduced (Ortiz & Maldonado-Colon, 1986). Even for those students who are eventually referred for evaluation, pre-referral intervention can serve to clarify and define the referral question and thus can provide useful information on which to base assessment planning for the identification of a handicap (Ortiz & Maldonado-Colon, 1986). Pre-referral procedures can also benefit students with clearly established disabilities who in some cases have been referred and assigned to separate programs simply because they have a particular impairment and not because they require such segregated placement.

Third, pre-referral procedures may result in programs that are both more appropriate and cost-effective than separate programs (Affleck, Madge, Adams, & Lowenbraun, 1988; Singer & Butler, 1987; Wang et al., 1986). By combining currently separate services in a more efficient structure, staffing costs as well as significant time and expense currently devoted to the present cumbersome identification process for special education programs may be substantially reduced. This can create new resources for enhancing support for the regular program. From a systemwide perspective, cost-effectiveness is a particularly important issue because the number of poor and minority students in the schools (an inordinate percentage of the "handicapped" population) is expected to continue to increase. Unless changes are made in the existing system, the financial burden for an already inefficient special education system will be even more pronounced in coming years (Wang et al., 1986).

Fourth, pre-referral procedures may result in less fragmentation between the services a student receives in the regular program and the services received in a special education program. By re-allocating resources to the goal of maintaining students in the regular program, remedial and special education intervention can be structured in and around the regular program rather than focused on maintenance of separate programs, goals, and materials. Scheduling problems, especially at the secondary level, may be significantly reduced because many students would not leave the classroom for separate special education services.

Finally, the current emphasis on pre-referral intervention and maintenance of students with disabilities in the regular program should result in the restructuring of the regular program to broaden the range of accommodation for all students. In addition to the potential instructional benefit for all students in the regular program, such restructuring would have two distinct advantages for students with disabilities. First, modifications made to accommodate their special needs would not be so apparent, because the varying needs of all children would be accommodated. Second, research indicates that modified regular programs that provide individualized programs for students result in higher achieve-

ment levels and greater degrees of social acceptance for students with disabilities than separate programs (Affleck et al., 1988; Hagerty & Abramson, 1987; Madden & Slavin, 1983).

STRUCTURE FOR PRE-REFERRAL INTERVENTION

Despite the clear legal and educational benefits of the pre-referral process, many school districts have not developed viable implementation procedures to ensure its success (Pugach, 1985; Salend, 1987). Without a framework or procedure for making such a process operational, the pre-referral process is unlikely to reap the potential benefits discussed previously. Several alternatives exist for developing a pre-referral process, varying in specificity and structure. The options most often employed for providing pre-referral assistance to teachers include (1) teacher-assistance teams, (2) resource consultants, and (3) special education teachers.

Teacher-Assistance Teams

Some schools have established teams to develop and provide recommendations to the classroom teacher for working with specific students. These are often known as teacher-assistance teams, educational management teams, or school instructional teams. The makeup of the team varies, depending on the school, but the function is the same. That is, the team assists the classroom teacher in accommodating the students' needs in the classroom rather than referring them to special education programs. Most support team models focus on developing recommendations and strategies for the classroom teacher but do not involve direct intervention by anyone other than the classroom teacher. Such a model is depicted in Figure 3–1.

Some schools designate the special services committee as the pre-referral assistance team. Although the traditional role of this committee for pre-referral purposes has been negligible, specifically designing the membership of this committee to serve such a function could have the benefit of continuity, since it is this committee that will ultimately receive and consider the formal referral if pre-referral interventions are unsuccessful in accommodating the student's needs in the regular program.

Existing organizational units in schools might also provide a source for the development of teacher-assistance teams. For example, many schools are organized by grade levels in which the teachers of the same grade coordinate and work cooperatively

FIGURE 3–1
The Teacher-Assistance Team

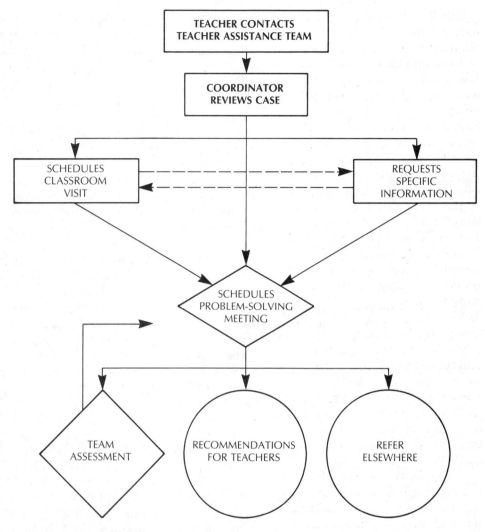

From "Teacher Assistance Teams: A Model for Within Building Problem-Solving" by J. C. Chalfant, M. V. Pysh, and R. Moultrie, 1979, *Learning Disability Quarterly, 2,* pp. 85–96. Reprinted with permission.

on issues related to curriculum and instruction in that grade. Other schools might be organized with different grade levels forming an organizational unit. These units are often referred to as "family cluster groupings" because the unit, like a family, represents a range of student ages, interests, and instructional levels. Still other schools are organized by departments or curriculum areas such as English, science, or history. An advantage of using these groups as teacher-assistance teams is that they are existing groups within the school; thus, developing an additional school structure is not necessary. An added advantage of using these groups as teacher-assistance teams is that the teachers normally work together in close proximity on a day-to-day basis and are familiar with typical grade level or grouping issues. Teachers who work together in this capacity may have more credibility with one another than do resource

teachers working as consultants to provide effective group strategies.

Some schools have established teacher teams for the sole purpose of improving classroom instructional practices through peer coaching and support. Where they exist, these teams also may serve as teacher-assistance teams to develop and implement pre-referral strategies. Teachers on such a team assist, or coach, one another in the development and use of strategies such as classroom management, individualized instruction, and other aspects of effective instruction. Coaching teams are based on the notion that teachers helping teachers is an effective method of encouraging and sustaining professional growth. These teams sometimes are difficult to initiate and maintain. With administrative support, however, as well as provisions for release time and training, and group commitment, these teams can produce an effective and ultimately efficient mechanism for addressing pre-referral issues from an overall instructional improvement perspective as well as from an intervention perspective.

The use of pre-referral teams is not always considered effective in resolving problems (Harrington & Gibson, 1986); however, evidence shows that they can provide an excellent opportunity for professional sharing, mutual support and encouragement, peer coaching, and training. Some reported disadvantages include difficulty in scheduling meeting times for team members, lack of communication and assistance in the implementation of interventions, insufficient follow-up, and extensive time and paper work requirements (Harrington & Gibson, 1986).

Resource Consultant

A resource consultation model differs from other models in that a special education consultant has as his primary responsibility providing consultative services to teachers and/or students, rather than as an added responsibility (which is often the case with teacher-assistance teams and special education teachers). Some school systems employ behavior management specialists, educational prescriptionists, and resource consulting teachers to consult with teachers and, in some models, to provide direct service and program monitoring to students in the regular program.

Although empirical research on the effectiveness of a consulting model in special education is limited, some research indicates that positive changes at the teacher, student, and system levels can be reaped from this form of special education service (West & Idol, 1987). Based on data from related fields and preliminary research in special education, it appears that a consultation model may positively affect teacher classroom behavior, reduce referrals to special education programs, and improve student performance in the regular program (West & Idol, 1987). The advantages of such a model are that trained consultants have specific expertise in communicating and collaborating with teachers and developing strategies to resolve classroom problems. Because this is their primary function, competing responsibilities, such as those of classroom teachers and special education teachers, are minimized. The success of this model, however, depends heavily on the consultation skills of the individual and may require additions to, or redesignation of, resources currently existing in most schools. This model may minimize the use of peer interaction and support as a means of resolving classroom issues because intervention may become an interaction between only one teacher and the consultant rather than a team process.

Special Education Teachers

Traditionally, special education teachers in the school have been designated as the source of pre-referral assistance for classroom teachers. This model, however, may be the least effective because it is often the least defined. Pugach (1985) noted that the degree to which a classroom teacher is likely to seek assistance before seeking special education identification depends highly on how he perceives the role of the special education teacher before referral. If the consultation role of the special education teacher is not clearly defined and visible within the school, a request for assistance is unlikely. Unfortunately, consultation responsibilities, when they are specifically assigned, may often assume low priority behind direct instruction, special services committee responsibilities, and ongoing case management responsibilities of resource teachers (Friend, 1984).

In addition, many special education teachers lack the skills and training to be effective consultants to classroom teachers. In a study of classroom teachers' perceptions of the consultation skills of special education teachers (Friend, 1984), resource teachers were judged as only moderately skilled in consultation. Such a finding is understandable, considering that many special education teachers are trained in traditional methods of small group and individualized instruction and may be unable to apply these methods within a class of 25 to 30 students. Many special education teachers are also unfamiliar with the regular classroom curriculum and materials because they employ alternative programs and materials in their special education classrooms. If classroom teachers cannot anticipate receiving valuable assistance from a specialist in the school, they are unlikely to request assistance and may proceed directly to the formal referral process.

The use of special education teachers for pre-referral purposes does have some advantages if the teacher already possesses consultation skills and if the consultation role is well-defined and sufficient consultation time is allocated. First, the teacher is a permanent member of the school staff with an existing working relationship with teachers and students, whereas a consultant is likely to be an itinerant servicing more than one school, with little flexibility in schedule and limited availability for a particular school. Second, because the special education teacher is an existing member of the staff, additional resources may not be required, although reorganization of the teacher's time and responsibilities may create such a need.

Whether a school establishes teacher assistance teams, employs consulting specialists, or uses and re-defines the role of the existing special education staff, the success of the pre-referral process depends on the support of those critical to its implementation. The willingness of the classroom teacher to request assistance and conscientiously implement the recommendations made; the skill and knowledge of content area and grade-level specialists (classroom teachers) and remedial and individual methods specialists (special education teachers); and the support and commitment of the school administration are all vital elements of an effective pre-referral process.

PRE-REFERRAL STRATEGIES

Although teachers generally report making some typical modifications for children before referral (Munson, 1986; Pugach, 1985; Zigmond, Levin, & Laurie, 1985), intervention often is described as short-lived and ineffective in resolving educational problems. Simply developing an organizational framework for pre-referral intervention is not sufficient assurance that the success of interventions will increase. To maximize the potential success of the process, specific school guidelines for establishing interventions must exist. At a minimum, guidelines must ensure that concerns are clearly defined; that intervention strategies are appropriate to the concern; that they are implemented, monitored, and evaluated consistently; and that they are as unobtrusive as possible.

Definition of the Concern

Whether a school uses teacher-assistance teams, resource-consulting teachers or existing special education teachers to provide support in the use of pre-referral strategies, the concern to be addressed must first be defined before an appropriate intervention can be developed. Information such as the specific nature of the problem, the circumstances under which it occurs, the nature of the instructional program, and what interventions have already been attempted are all important to the development of effective intervention strategies. The Student Intervention Checklist (Figure 3–2) provides a sample of preliminary information that should be gathered before initiating pre-referral interventions.

If assistance teams or individuals other than the classroom teacher participate in developing modifications, all individuals involved should participate in defining the problem. If a student review form such as the one in Figure 3–2 is used, a recorder should complete the form, based on the discussion of the group. Such a procedure has two advantages. First, a student review form provides structure to the discussion regarding the student and by so doing enables efficient, timely gathering of information. The written summary can then serve as the minutes of the meeting because the completed form represents a consensus by the group that this information provides a starting point for additional data gathering or initial intervention. Second, developing the student review form in an initial pre-referral meeting may serve to avoid the traditional problem of brief, vague, and subjective information. Team members can question, probe, and clarify information provided by the teacher to produce a document that is specific and provides an agreed on basis for further action.

In many cases, the problem must be defined or confirmed from the perspective of someone other than the classroom teacher. Systematic observation may provide important insight into the teacher's concern by identifying factors that the teacher may not have identified. Because the observer is there only to observe and is not responsible for teaching the entire class, a clear perspective of the problem may be obtained. Systematic observation can also provide a baseline for determining the later effectiveness of an intervention.

To be effective, however, observation must be designed to provide specific information related to the pre-referral problem. Though the procedures in some schools require an observation before a student can be referred to special education, the activity is often perfunctory and thus may fail to address the referral issue or provide insight into the problem. For example, if a teacher is concerned about a student's behavior in class and the observation occurs during a film or during recess, the pre-referral observation, although fulfilling a procedural requirement, may provide little helpful information on which to base an intervention. In addition, many schools have one standard observation form used to document that an observation occurred before referral. Although procedurally convenient, standard formats may fail to provide for differences in referral questions. School personnel should gather and maintain alternative observational formats to use in the definition of pre-referral issues. Observational data should be considered with all other information available to obtain a clear picture of the problem as it relates to the child, the teacher, other students, and the classroom itself. All pre-referral observational data should include information on the existing environment, teaching method and materials, and peer interactions, because it is likely that these classroom elements will provide the focus for pre-referral modification and interventions.

Selection of Appropriate Interventions

Some interventions fail not because the problem is undefined but because the intervention is inappro-

FIGURE 3–2
Student Intervention Checklist

Name _____ Age _____ Date _____

Teacher _____ Grade _____

1.   **Area(s) of Concern**
_____ academic   _____ language   _____ gross motor   _____ hearing
_____ behavior   _____ speech   _____ fine motor
_____ emotional   _____ physical   _____ vision

2.   What kinds of strategies have been employed to resolve this problem?

    A.   **Records Review and Conference**
    _____ student conference(s)   _____ review of
                                    educational records
    _____ parent conference(s)   _____ vision _____ medical _____ hearing

    B.   **Environmental Modifications**
    _____ class seating arrangement   _____ group change   _____ other
    _____ individual seating   _____ teacher change
    _____ schedule modification   _____ teacher position
                                       in class

    C.   **Instructional**
    _____ modifications in methods used with group or class
    _____ modifications in learning aids used with group or class
    _____ individual methods with regular materials
    _____ individual learning aids with regular materials
    _____ individual methods and materials different from group or class

    D.   **Management**
    _____ modification in classroom management system
    _____ use of systematic group management techniques
    _____ use of individual behavior management techniques

3.   What methods are currently employed to address the concern? _____
_____
_____
_____
_____

4.   Where does this student stand in relationship to others in class, group or grade
regarding systemwide tests, class average behavior, completion of work, etc.?

Student Behavior	Class or Group or Grade Behavior

5.   Is the concern generally associated with a particular time, subject, or person?

(Figure 3–2 continued)

6.   In what areas, under what conditions, does this student do best?

7.   Assistance Requested (observation, materials, ideas, etc.):

_____
_____
_____
_____

Assistance Provided:
Dates   Nature of Assistance   Individuals Responsible   Outcome

_____
_____
_____
_____
_____

priate to the problem. In some instances teachers may be fully aware of the problem yet initiate modifications that are admittedly inadequate in an attempt to do "something," even if the intervention stands little chance of success (Zigmond, et al., 1985). For example, if a student is presented with reading material that is too difficult, teachers may repeat directions or give further directions, neither of which enables the student to complete the task. Standard or typical modifications are those that might be made for any student and include changing the format of directions (repeating or further explanation); talking to the student, asking simple questions; extending time limits or requiring less work (Munson, 1986; Pugach, 1985; Zigmond et al., 1985). Although these modifications may be effective for many students, they may not be substantial enough for students with persistent problems.

A second consideration in ensuring the appropriateness of the intervention to the concern is the need to clarify exactly what the intervention is to be. From referral data we know little about the exact nature of day-to-day interventions made by classroom teachers, partly because interventions are often couched in vague terms such as "individualizing instruction," "talking" to students, and "behavior management" (Pugach, 1985). For an intervention to be effective, the teacher or team must define exactly

what the intervention is to be, how and when it will be applied, and how it will be evaluated. In many ways, defining pre-referral interventions may be more difficult than writing IEPs because the process exceeds developing goals and objectives; it defines specific strategies for achieving classroom objectives. Clear definition of an intervention, however, provides a basis on which to determine (1) appropriateness to the problem, (2) if the teacher can, in fact, implement the intervention effectively, (3) if additional resources will be required, and (4) how progress will be measured.

Consistent Implementation and Evaluation

Interventions may fail because they are not applied consistently or long enough. In addition they may not be systematically monitored or evaluated. In such cases the time and effort expended to develop and initiate a potentially effective intervention is essentially wasted and may result in the teacher feeling that all interventions have failed. For example, if a teacher, consultant, or team agree that a behavior management contract must be reviewed with the student daily and the teacher fails to review it for a week, the intervention is unlikely to make a positive difference in the student's behavior. This is not a failure of the student or the contract but reflects the teacher's inability to maintain the specified intervention. It is essential then, to ensure that the intervention's terms can be and are maintained over the amount of time necessary to effect student improvement.

Monitoring the intervention's application provides information on whether it is having the desired effect, whether the student is improving, or whether there is no progress at all. The mechanism for monitoring the intervention's effect should be established before the intervention begins and should continue for a specified and reasonable period of time. Chapter 10 provides strategies for monitoring students' progress toward goals and objectives on IEPs. The same strategies are useful for monitoring the effects of classroom modifications and interventions.

A final consideration in implementation is intervention evaluation. Whether successful or not, the intervention must be evaluated to provide a basis for further intervention. For example, if taping reading material in social studies clearly had no effect on a student's performance, then continuing the time, effort, and expense of this modification is unwarranted. The intervention and its effect, however, should be documented so that others will know what has not worked. If pre-referral interventions fail, precise referral information regarding attempts to address the problem can greatly enhance the referral, assessment, and identification process.

Least Intrusive Intervention

Pre-referral interventions should be as unobtrusive as possible while still addressing the problem. This means that if a student's needs can be addressed by modifying only the instructional method, rather than the materials, then such modification might be the preferred intervention. By the same token, if regular materials can be modified to accommodate a student's needs, then selecting a lower grade-level textbook for that student might be inappropriate. The concept of least intrusion is defined from the student's perspective and means that the most appropriate modifications are those that depart as little as possible from the methods and curriculum for all students in the class, while still enabling the student to benefit appropriately. Figure 3–3 illustrates this conceptual model from an instructional perspective.

The least intrusive modification may not always be the easiest to design and implement from the teacher's perspective. Less intrusive interventions often require change in teaching behavior rather than changes in the materials or curriculum employed. Therefore, modifications in group instructional techniques that are prompted by the needs of one student but that could benefit the entire class often are passed over in favor of interventions that are easier from the teacher's perspective.

Perhaps another reason why modifications requiring teacher change are somewhat limited is that teachers seldom view student problems as being due to any shortcomings in teaching methods (Ysseldyke, Christenson, Pianta, Thurlow, & Algozzine, 1982). Although modification of teaching methods can be difficult and even require further training, the result can ultimately diminish the need for special modifications for one student by broadening the accommodations for all students in the class. The remainder of this section will provide an overview of pre-referral intervention strategies beginning with the least intrusive of all, the individualized regular classroom.

Individualized Regular Classroom

The issue of appropriate accommodation of underachieving students and students with disabilities in the regular program may be symptomatic of a more pervasive and growing problem in the schools. That is, regular education programs may be too rigid and lock-step to accommodate even the limited diversity of typical students, and a complete restructuring of the regular program built on recognized principles of learning, flexibility, and individually paced instruction is necessary to effectively maximize the educational experience of all children (Stainback et al., 1986). Several recognized programs currently exist that exemplify these principles and attest to the fact that such a goal is attainable. Examples of such programs include the Adapted Learning Environments Model (ALEM) (Wang & Birch, 1984), Goal-Oriented Approach to Learning (GOAL) (Maher, 1985), the Parallel Alternative Curriculum (PAC) (McGrady, 1985), and the Integrated Classroom Model (ICM) (Affleck et al., 1988). Restructuring of this nature, however, requires system wide administrative commitment and the provision or re-allocation of resources to ensure their maintenance. Significant program modification, though clearly preferred, is not often within the authority of teacher assistance teams, consulting teachers, or special educators to dictate. While recognizing restructuring as the ultimate modification, many efforts will continue to focus on accommodation of individual students in traditional classrooms. Modifications should be considered on a continuum and should, like placement, be those that are least intrusive. It is important to remember however, that, like placement, least intrusive for one student may be most intrusive for another.

FIGURE 3–3
Least Intrusive Model of
Classroom Accommodations

Regular Program Designed to Accommodate Differences
individualized materials, instructional pacing, cooperative learning,
direct instruction, monitoring progress, corrective feedback, cuing self-management

Environmental Modifications
preferential seating, modification of noise level, scheduling,
room arrangement, adaptive equipment

Group Instructional Modifications—Regular Materials
cooperative groups, group contingency methods, modeling,
direction giving, social skills training, reinforcement,
guided practice

Group Learning Aids—Regular Materials
structured overviews, taped material, highlighted texts,
written outlines, calculators

Individual Instructional Modifications—Regular Materials
amount of material, individual or small group instruction,
time allowances, re-teaching, coaching,
peer tutors

Individual Instructional Modifications—
Different Materials
programmed materials, token economy
systems, contracts, cognitive
behavior management, individual
counseling, tutoring

Remedial Programs
compensatory education,
reading improvement,
(separate classes)

REFERRAL TO SPECIAL EDUCATION

Alternative Curriculum
special classes, life skills,
therapeutic programs

Resource Room Instruction
crisis intervention, vision training,
specific skill instruction, auditory training

Regular Class—Special Education in Classroom
individual or small group instruction, language
occupational therapy

Regular Class—Special Education Consultation
observation, task analysis, demonstration,
monitoring of contracts, provision of special materials

Less Intrusive

More Intrusive

Less Intrusive

Student and Parent Conferences

Ultimately, the least intrusive intervention will depend on the student. Thus, a good place to begin is by acknowledging the situation with the student, asking if he has any suggestions on how to help, and discussing strategies that have been helpful to others. Surprisingly, research indicates that teachers do not often confer systematically with students to identify possible methods or to share with them their own ideas about possible things the student can do to improve (Ammer, 1984; Zigmond et al., 1985). Neither is there a requirement in many schools to contact or

involve parents in discussion of strategies that may be helpful in effectively maintaining the student in the classroom with minimal modifications. Clearly, the most desirable intervention is one that requires the least modification. Thus in most cases, discussion and strategy development with students and/or their parents is a logical first strategy.

Environmental Modifications

Environmental modifications may be both the easiest and the most difficult to accomplish. Often they are overlooked as viable starting points in the pre-referral process. For example, changing a student's seating or simply changing the position of the teacher in the classroom can make a significant difference in the attending and on-task behavior of some students.

Factors such as noise levels may be somewhat more difficult to control. For many students, however, noise levels in the classroom may contribute significantly to how well they understand, attend, and perform. These noise levels can be devastating for the student with hearing impairments and/or language delays, for students for whom English is a second language, and for students who are highly distractible. Another environmental strategy might be to arrange the room so that rows have as few seats deep as possible and are in closer proximity to the front of the room than to the windows. This modification is often beneficial for the entire class. Preferential seating for a particular student within this arrangement can help to promote attention to tasks, understanding of directions, and enable individual assistance, if necessary.

Methods of Group Instruction

Following the principle of least intrusion, curricular content should not be changed unless it is apparent that the student cannot achieve minimum competency in the existing curriculum. Although it is sometimes easier to assign the student different work than to teach differently, teachers have a responsibility to present material in ways that students can understand and benefit from. Most teaching models are built on the "teacher talks—student responds" model. While this is certainly one way to present information, research indicates that alternative instructional strategies, such as cooperative grouping, peer tutoring, and problem-solving activities are more effective in enhancing the learning of all students (Madden & Slavin, 1983). These methods, though perhaps more difficult for the teacher initially, can produce desirable results and reduce the need to deal with classroom differences in ways completely different from those employed with other students.

Behavior management strategies likewise should be applied within the group whenever possible. Although these strategies are prompted by the needs of one student, a teacher may find that these strategies apply to the entire class. In situations like these, group management techniques are more appropriate and far easier to implement than several individual management plans. Group management techniques may be as straightforward as consistent enforcement of appropriate classroom rules or may involve the use of group contracts, contingency management

schemes, or cooperative grouping techniques. For a teacher who lacks group management skills, management of individuals within a group will be difficult. This is a teacher problem, however, not a student problem and should be dealt with by training the teacher rather than by referring the student to special education.

Group Teaching and Learning Aids. Pre-referral strategies also may include providing teaching and learning aids while still not changing the basic materials or content. Instructional outlines, reference dictionaries, highlighted texts, taped material, audio-visual aids, study guides, simplified maps, and note-taking guides are only a few examples of modifications that, though prepared or initiated for one or a few students, can benefit the entire class.

Individualized Instructional Methods. Small group or individualized instruction is an intervention that may not occur with the entire class but is designed specifically for one or a few students. Individualized instruction may be provided by the teacher, an aide, a volunteer, or a peer tutor. This level of intervention, though perhaps individualized for a specific student, may still be based on the regular class curriculum.

Providing a variety of response modes is another method of individualizing instruction that enables students to express their knowledge in ways designed to maximize attainment. For example, some students have difficulty composing lengthy responses to questions. If oral and/or written expression are minimized, however, the performance of these students may be greatly enhanced. Modification of work time and amount of work are also alternate response modes. For students who have fine motor difficulties or who simply work very slowly, the teacher might allow more time for completion or require less repetition of the same skill. Thus, a student might be required to complete only a representative selection of math problems rather than an entire page. Such a strategy can be employed without changing the basic instruction, material, or content in any way.

Individual behavior problems that do not respond to less intrusive measures may require individualized management plans. Before developing individual plans, however, the teacher or team should ensure that the problem is in fact an individual rather than a group problem. Development of individual plans often includes resource personnel to observe and to define the problem; design a plan that is compatible with the student, teacher, and the classroom; and monitor the plan's effectiveness. Management strategies might include individual contracts, reinforcement programs, token programs and other contingency management systems. The essential factor in behavior management is to develop a plan that can be implemented and maintained in the classroom setting.

Individualized Instructional Material. Systematic modification of the environment, group instructional techniques, and regular curriculum materials will be effective in addressing the needs of most underachieving students in a classroom. Even so, some students will continue to require student-specific interventions beyond those useful to or needed by most students. One way to enable a student to progress at his own rate and gain immediate feedback while eliminating the needs for continuous teacher attention is to use programmed material or appropriate computer software programs. The teacher, however, is still responsible for teaching and monitoring the student who is using alternative or supplemental materials.

Supplemental and Remedial Programs. Research has failed to distinguish a set of instructional strategies for students with mild disabilities that differ from those used appropriately with students enrolled in regular education remedial programs (Heller, Holtzman, & Messick, 1982). Lacking instructional justification for separate programs, remedial programs such as compensatory education can provide a theoretically less intrusive program than instruction in a special education resource room. Although the student may still leave the classroom setting for instruction, the fact that he is still enrolled in the regular education program is preferred to classifying the student as having a disability to receive essentially the same services. Efforts to accommodate students in the regular education program may result in a dramatic increase in the number of students referred to compensatory and remedial reading programs. These programs, however, also remove the student from the classroom and thus should not simply replace special education in maintaining separate programs. Students should be referred to compensatory education programs only if needs cannot be accommodated in the regular classroom.

Referral to Special Education. Although referral will be discussed in detail in the next chapter, its relevance as an appropriate educational intervention bears mentioning here. The primary intent of P.L. 94–142 is to ensure that students with disabilities who require special education are identified and appropriately educated in the least restrictive setting possible (preferably, the regular classroom unless that is clearly not feasible). Educators thus have two obligations. The first is to avoid inappropriate referrals and identification through conscientious attempts to modify the regular program to the extent necessary to accommodate student differences. Second, if modifications are unsuccessful in providing an appropriate educational opportunity for any child, the school is obliged to properly refer and evaluate that student in an attempt to design a program that does provide an opportunity for educational benefit. Although research indicates that referrals to special education may well be reduced as a result of pre-referral procedures (Chalfant, Van Dusen, & Moultrie, 1979; Nevin & Thousand, 1986), this reduction may, in some instances, reflect disillusionment with the work involved in the process and resulting discontinuance of referrals rather than the successful accommodation of students in the regular program (Harrington & Gibson, 1986). No evidence suggests that simply continuing attendance in an unmodified classroom benefits underachieving students (Madden & Slavin, 1983). Thus, maintaining a student in the regular program without attempting to address the issue is not an acceptable alternative to pre-referral intervention or, if necessary, referral to special education.

IMPLEMENTATION OF PRE-REFERRAL STRATEGIES

Student Intervention Plans

With the current focus on the pre-referral process as a mechanism for reducing referrals to special education programs, various procedures for documentation of strategies employed before referral have been developed. Three types of procedures will be discussed here. First, some procedures serve primarily a documentation function, in that they require little more than a teacher indicating in writing that strategies were attempted before referral and were unsuccessful in addressing the teacher's concern. These formats often extend the existing referral format and may even be completed at the same time as the referral. Figure 3–4 provides an example of this type of format. The advantage of this format is that it is brief and requires little, if any, additional paperwork. Unfortunately, it may come too late to encourage substantive classroom modifications before referral. Simply requiring that a teacher answer pre-referral questions on the referral form provides little insight regarding perspectives other than that of the classroom teacher and does not necessarily ensure that all attempts have been made to maintain the student in the classroom.

FIGURE 3–4
Pre-referral Checklist

Appropriate activities on this checklist must be completed before referring a student for assessment for special education services. Place the date that activities were completed in the space next to the activity. This form must accompany the referral form.

1. _____ Reviewed student educational records to determine longevity of concern and previous interventions.

2. _____ Established that student has passed vision and hearing screening or referred student for vision and hearing screening.

3. _____ Met with student to discuss concerns and possible solutions.

4. _____ Met with parents to discuss concerns and possible solutions.

5. _____ Collected and analyzed recent examples of student's classwork.

6. _____ Collected specific information from records and performance regarding student's academic skills.

7. _____ Collected specific information from the record and class regarding student's behavior.

8. _____ Brainstormed with co-teachers to obtain strategies that have worked in other similar cases.

9. _____ Identified in writing the student's specific educational problem.

10. _____ Consulted with counselor regarding student's behavior.

11. _____ Consulted with resource teachers in school to discuss concerns and obtain strategies.

12. _____ Obtained observation by another teacher or school resource to obtain information regarding concern.

13. _____ Developed and implemented instructional strategies with assistance of other educators.

14. _____ Developed and implemented a behavior management plan with other educators.

15. _____ Obtained or developed instructional learning aids to address this student's problem.

16. _____ List any other modifications, interventions, or strategies you have attempted to maintain this student in the classroom.

_____
_____
_____
_____

Teacher Signature _____ Date _____

Second, some school systems combine written teacher documentation with other procedures, such as systematic observation and required case review by teacher-assistance teams, consultants, or consulting teachers. This mechanism does ensure involvement of individuals other than the teacher to review the situation and to make recommendations for classroom accommodation. Requiring review and recommendations by someone other than the teacher does not, however, always ensure that the teacher will implement recommendations (Harrington & Gibson, 1986). One of the most often voiced complaints regarding the pre-referral process is that little direct assistance is provided to the teacher to implement the recommendations of assistance teams and consultants. If teachers view recommendations as unreasonable, unmanageable, or redundant, the likelihood of implementation may be minimal. It is therefore important to provide a mechanism not only for generating recommendations for teachers but also for ensuring that assistance in implementation and follow-up are provided when necessary.

A third way that school systems have addressed the issue of pre-referral intervention is by the development of written intervention plans, such as the Student Intervention Plan (illustrated in Figure 3–5). A process such as this focuses primarily on intervention, although documentation is an important secondary benefit. An intervention plan has as one of its benefits a potential for precision, which other pre-referral procedures may lack. Considering that many pre-referral interventions fail because they are not well-defined and systematically applied, a written plan may provide a useful mechanism by providing specificity about the intervention and its application. One disadvantage of a written plan is that it invariably creates paperwork. This disadvantage may be offset by the advantages of having a specific plan once implementation begins and the increased positive return on the investment of teacher time and effort. By documenting the exact nature of a classroom intervention and its exact outcome, a great deal of information can be gained about the student and what methods of accommodation are more and less effective. The school also gains a better understanding of the day-to-day activities of the teachers and the parameters of the modifications made for students who do not meet educational expectations in the classroom.

To achieve the desired effect of a student intervention plan (i.e., the maintenance of a child in the regular education program), the following elements should be included:

1. A clear statement of the problem, confirmed by observation, work samples, and behavior charts

2. A specific statement of the intervention
3. A monitoring plan
4. The results of the plan and revisions and recommendations

The student intervention plan may resemble the IEP in some ways, but it has at least one very distinct difference. While the IEP developed for a student with a disability is required to include goals and objectives for 1 year, it is not required to document the exact strategies used to achieve those annual goals and short-term objectives. The student intervention plan, on the other hand, must have as its primary focus the designation of strategies, aids, or materials used to accommodate the student. This process may be more difficult than writing IEPs because specific strategies for the teacher must be defined. However, the goal of maintaining students in the regular classroom deserves at least as much (and perhaps more) effort as does removing them to a special education program. A commitment to pre-referral intervention means commitment of time, energy, and resources that were previously committed to the referral, evaluation, and placement process for special education.

Resources

Although the establishment of a pre-referral process ultimately can result in a more cost-effective method for providing appropriate educational opportunities to underachieving students and students with disabilities, such a procedure nonetheless initially requires significant resources to ensure its success. Most model programs cited earlier in this chapter as providing successful models for accommodation of individual differences in the regular program use methods such as team teaching, instructional aids, and/or lower teacher–pupil ratios to support the individualized programs of the students in the classroom. These resources, however, are not typically available to the classroom teacher in most schools. Simply shifting the responsibility for underachieving students and students with disabilities to the regular classroom without allocating new resources or redistributing existing resources will undoubtedly fall short of the intended purpose of a pre-referral process. Likewise, a haphazard approach to redistribution of existing resources may fail to provide the kinds of program support necessary to ensure the success of the process.

It is likely that resoues to support the pre-referral process in the school will come from existing special education sources, rather than from new funding sources. Thus, school administrators must actively renegotiate the distribution of school resources systematically and sensitively. It should be

FIGURE 3-5
Student Intervention Plan

Student Intervention Plan

Name: Susan   **Age:** 13
Teacher: Stanley   **Grade:** 7

Primary Concern(s)	Goal	Intervention	Resources	Dates Begin/End	Interim Monitoring
Susan reads on a 4th-grade reading level, well below most other students. Does not partici-pate in content area reading. She is failing social studies.	1. Increase achievement in social studies to passing grade. 2. Increase participation in class activities.	<u>Cooperative grouping for social studies</u> 1. Teacher presentation of social studies lesson according to lesson plan. 2. Assignment of students to mixed teams. 3. Teams practice, discuss, and review. 4. Each member receives maximum of 10 points if a quiz score exceeds base quiz score by 10 points. 5. Individual contributes individual points to team score. 6. Team scores tallied. Winning team recognized by picture on school achievement board. (Base score — average of last three tests)	None	Sept. 30 Oct. 20	Weekly quizzes: Increase in score on each quiz for 5 weeks (Base: 50%) Week 1 <u>60%</u> (+10) Week 2 <u>75%</u> (+25) Week 3 <u>70%</u> (+20) Week 4 <u>70%</u> (+20) Week 5 <u>65%</u> (+15)

<u>EVALUATION</u>: Achieved goal. Other students in group "tutor" Susan on content and help with reading. Still has difficulty with reading vocabulary, but participates actively and has greater knowledge of content. Continue plan.

remembered that adding resources to one aspect of the school program will inevitably take those resources from another program within the school. For example, special education aids have traditionally been viewed as the property of special education teachers and only rarely have been specifically assigned to work in regular classrooms rather than in special education classrooms. However, with the emphasis on intervention before referral, use of instructional aids in the regular classroom is an excellent and legally permissible, if not preferable, method of pre-referral intervention. Nonetheless, redistributing resources that were once perceived as belonging solely to the special education program may meet with some resistance from special educators. The school administration therefore should ensure that redistribution is based on a systematic analysis of need and accomplished in an equitable manner.

Lack of time for planning, meeting, and collaborating with others regarding intervention strategies for underachieving students is one of the most often voiced concerns of classroom teachers and others involved in pre-referral intervention (Harrington & Gibson, 1986). An effective pre-referral process will invariably require communication and collaboration between professions within the school. Thus, alternative methods for building flexibility into the school schedule so that teachers are available to meet together regularly is essential.

Finally, the same continuum of human resources available to students in special education resource rooms should be available to enable students to be maintained in the regular program. Social workers, school counselors, nurses, and other related services personnel, as well as volunteers and instructional aids can contribute immeasurably to the success of pre-referral interventions.

Training

Many classroom teachers believe that they are inadequately prepared to address the educational needs of underachieving students in the classroom (Munson, 1986). The current emphasis on effective maintenance of underachieving students in the classroom with the overall emphasis on improving education for all students will require new and updated skills for teachers and administrators. In many instances, training must focus on renewal and refinement of principles with which teachers are already familiar, such as classroom management and efficient and effective instructional organization and presentation. During the past several years, an impressive amount of research has re-emphasized the importance of these principles in improving classroom instruction. In addition, group methods and strategies have been developed, refined, and researched to yield a number of excellent instructional practices such as cooperative grouping, peer tutoring, metacognition strategies, direct instruction, and group contingency management procedures. Application and/or refinement of these strategies and underlying principles in the classroom require a significant commitment to training by school administration.

Special education teachers also will require new skills as they assume greater responsibilities for consultation with classroom teachers and instruction of students in the classroom, rather than in the resource room. In addition to knowledge of group management and instructional techniques, special education teachers must be trained in communication and consultation skills with fellow teachers. Increased knowledge of the regular education curriculum and materials also will be essential, because special education teachers likely will be increasingly involved in adapting regular classroom curriculum materials rather than using separate programs of instruction.

Finally, school and systemwide administrators must understand, support, and actively participate in school-improvement activities. There is no question that administrative support is a critical factor in the success of all school-improvement efforts (Goodlad, 1984; Graden, Casey & Bonstrom, 1985; Idol-Maestas & Ritter, 1985; Will, 1986). Administrators should participate actively in inservice training to gain knowledge about instructional innovations that can improve the school for both teachers and students. With knowledge, the school administrator can assume responsible leadership within the school for ensuring through program supervision that training concepts are applied in the classroom. The administrator also must demonstrate support for pre-referral efforts. Participation in the pre-referral process, providing recognition for outstanding implementation of training concepts, ensuring assistance for teachers with instructional problems, providing time for consultation and training, and promoting school accomplishments within the school system administration and the community are contributions that the informed and involved administrator can add to the pre-referral process.

Parent Involvement in Pre-referral

Interestingly, P.L. 94–142 does not specifically provide for the active involvement of parents until a student has already been referred to special education and notice of and permission for comprehensive evaluation is required. Further, it is quite possible that the first meeting between the school and parents may not occur until the IEP meeting, after a student is determined to be handicapped and eligible for special education. Although notifying parents that a student is experiencing difficulty in school is a routine practice in some schools, substantive involvement of parents in strategy planning and implementation is not a commonly employed intervention (Ammer, 1984).

There are several advantages to involving parents during the pre-referral process. First, involvement at this point helps parents to understand their child's problem in educational terms that are immediate and classroom related rather than in terms of standardized assessment results, which may seem somewhat removed from the classroom setting. Parent understanding of educational concerns has important legal implications because the notice requirements of P.L. 94–142 clearly state that parents must fully understand the content of all notices regarding their child. This means that when students are referred to special education, their parents must fully understand the reasons why the school proposes such action. Involvement in interventions before referral can ensure that in the event of future referral, parents are fully aware of concerns and what interventions have been attempted.

Second, parents can have a significant positive influence on student achievement. Professionals, however, may underestimate the teaching expertise and behavior management skills normally used by parents of children with handicaps and thus may fail to include parents in developing interventions at school. Working with parents in the selection of strategies that can be implemented at school and reinforced at home is a key element for success with home school programs. Preschool programs over the years have recognized the importance of involving parents in the education of their children. As children grow older, however, substantive involvement of parents in educational planning and teaching is often less used as an instructional strategy. Many educators, especially at the secondary level, report little contact at all with parents to discuss or plan educational strategies that may enable a student to perform better in school (Ammer, 1984).

Finally, parents can provide information that is invaluable in planning intervention strategies. Information regarding homework habits, health, home responsibilities, hobbies, and interests are all relevant to designing effective strategies. The parent is the "corporate knowledge" source for any student and often is the best source of information and a logical starting point in defining an educational concern.

SUMMARY

This chapter has reviewed the regular education initiative and discussed frameworks and methods for maintaining students in the regular education program. When pre-referral strategies and interventions fail to accommodate the needs of the student in the classroom, formal referral for comprehensive evaluation is required. The next chapter will provide an in-depth discussion regarding the referral process.

EVALUATION

1. Review procedures in your school (or a typical school) to determine if pre-referral procedures currently exist. If they do exist, identify their strengths and weaknesses, and make suggestions for improvement. If procedures do not exist, review the organizational structure of the school, and provide suggestions for developing a pre-referral procedure.
2. You are the special education resource teacher in a large elementary school. You have been asked to provide an inservice training session to teachers designed to convince them that intervention before referral is beneficial for students with potential disabilities. Outline the major points of your presentation.

CHAPTER 4   Referral

OBJECTIVES

1. Identify five issues related to the referral process.
2. Describe suggested criteria for referral to special education programs.
3. Discuss school screening procedures as a mechanism for systematic identification of students with potential disabilities.
4. Discuss suggested components of the referral form and strategies for clear documentation of referral information.
5. Define and discuss the rights of parents regarding notice and consent procedures.

Referral is the mechanism that schools use to request and obtain comprehensive, formal evaluation results to determine whether a student qualifies for special education and related services. Because this procedure sets in motion the process by which students are identified as having a disability, it is imperative that professionals and others who may be responsible for referral be well informed about its purpose, requirements, procedures, and potential issues. This chapter will review current issues related to the referral process and will provide suggestions for the development and refinement of schoolwide and districtwide procedures, including systematic schoolwide screening, criteria for initiating referrals, information to be included as part of the referral, and the responsibility of the special services committee in the referral process. Because referral is essentially a proposal to initiate evaluation, the requirements for parent notification and consent will be reviewed and a rationale provided for substantive parent involvement at this point in the process.

THE REFERRAL PROCESS

How the Referral Process Typically Works

Most schools have a standard referral procedure and a standard referral form. To refer a student for evaluation and possible special education placement, a teacher or other referring individual must complete the referral form describing the educational problem and interventions that have been attempted before referral. The referral form is then submitted to the special services committee for consideration. The special services committee is responsible for review-

ing the referral and if warranted, scheduling a comprehensive evaluation. Based on the results of the comprehensive evaluation, the student may be determined to be eligible for special education services.

Several circumstances can prompt the decision to refer a student for evaluation and possible placement in a special education program. These include academic performance significantly below that of other students; behavior that differs significantly from that of other students; communication difficulties in speech and language; and physical concerns such as vision, hearing, mobility, and health. Referrals usually are made by the student's teacher but also may be made by parents and other individuals or agencies familiar with the student such as day care centers, medical facilities, and other community agencies.

Requirements of P.L. 94–142

P.L. 94–142 provides no specific guidelines for the referral process. However, several requirements of the law provide a basis for the development of referral procedures. First, the process of child find requires that each local education agency submit an application that tells how all students with disabilities, who need special education and related services, are identified, located, and evaluated (*Federal Register*, 1977). Such a provision includes the development of procedures for locating eligible students who are not in school, locating eligible students who are enrolled in other schools or facilities, and locating eligible students who are in school but not receiving necessary services. Referral is one of the several ways that a student may become known to the special services committee.

Second, referral may serve as a mechanism to fulfill the data-gathering and reporting requirements of P.L. 94–142. Educational agencies must submit comprehensive data on the number of students who receive special education services in each service-delivery area (*Federal Register*, 1977). The referral process provides a convenient method for documenting and gathering systematic data for record keeping and reporting purposes.

A third requirement of P.L. 94–142, which has recently had perhaps the greatest influence on the process of referral, is the often overlooked requirement that a student shall not be removed from the regular education environment unless the nature or severity of the concern is such that education in regular classes with the use of supplementary aids and materials cannot be achieved satisfactorily (*Federal Register*, 1977). This requirement has provided the basis for redefining referral procedures to ensure that supplementary aids and materials are made available and utilized before referring a student for comprehensive evaluation and possible special education placement.

In the absence of standard federal requirements governing the referral process, states and school districts have developed their own procedural requirements by which teachers, parents, and other agencies may initiate action to identify, locate, and evaluate students with potential disabilities. This has resulted in wide variation of practice among states and districts. For example, the state of New York has further quantified the "timeliness" provisions of P.L. 94–142 by requiring that the comprehensive evaluation must be completed within 30 days of the date of initial referral, while other states may establish a different timeline or may have no established timeline at all beyond the requirements of P.L. 94–142 (that an IEP must be in effect within 30 days from the time that the student is determined to have a disability and to need special education). States and districts also have developed a wide variety of referral forms, established various informational requirements in the preparation of referrals, established various criteria for referral, and established varying degrees of parental involvement in the referral process.

Referral procedures have been further defined in some states as a result of court orders. For example, some court orders, in an attempt to address inequities in the referral process, have further defined the process by ordering, in specific cases, such referral activities as specific training of instructional personnel, gathering of additional student data for reporting purposes, and development of prereferral requirements (*Lora v. Board of Education*, 1984). Thus, the referral process, although a generally used procedure, cannot be assumed to be uniform. This varia-

bility, although enabling states and districts to develop procedures specific to their needs, has made attempts to define and study the process somewhat difficult. The next section will review some of the issues surrounding the process of referral.

CURRENT REFERRAL ISSUES

Since the enactment of P.L. 94–142, the number of students enrolled in special education classes has increased dramatically, indicating that schools have now developed procedures for ensuring that all students with disabilities are identified, located, evaluated, and provided with an appropriate education. But whether these procedures are working adequately is the focus of much controversy. While a number of issues regarding the referral process continue to be debated, research has established some critical issues that may have a significant effect on the restructuring of the referral process.

Cost–Benefit of the Referral Process

Special education is expensive, estimated by some to range from twice to four times the cost of education for students in the regular education program (Algozzine et al., 1982). The process of referral and evaluation alone is also extremely expensive, estimated by some to be as much as $3,000 for some students. (Ysseldyke, Thurlow, et al., 1983). Considering that approximately 5% of the school population are referred annually, and of those referred, the majority receive a comprehensive evaluation (Algozzine, Christenson, & Ysseldyke, 1982; Algozzine & Ysseldyke, 1986; Pugach, 1985), cost investment in the process can be enormous. The time investment of professionals can also be inordinate, ranging from estimates of 4 to over 100 hours for some students (Ysseldyke, Thurlow, et al., 1983). Despite huge expenditures, the process is characterized by a number of problems. Teachers repeatedly indicate that the process is too time-consuming and slow, often averaging 3 to 4 months from referral to placement (Ammer, 1984; Harrington & Gibson, 1986; Pugach, 1985). In addition, the referral process is viewed as requiring inordinate amounts of paperwork, much of which is considered to be irrelevant (Pugach, 1985). Another problem relates to the perceived utility of the evaluation, once completed. Many question the value of extensive testing for instructional planning (Pugach, 1985), and evidence indicates that the data from formal assesment may be of limited value and use in determining program eligibility (Ysseldyke, Algozzine, Richey & Graden, 1982). The overwhelming cost and questionable utility of referring large numbers of students for comprehensive evaluation and special education placement has focused a great deal of recent attention on referral practices in the schools.

Lack of Referral Criteria for Students With Mild Disabilities

Students classified as having mild disabilities are reported to represent over 40% of the total number of students served in special education programs (Reschly, 1987). Even though statistically, one would expect mild disabilities to constitute the majority of disabilities among students enrolled in special education, this percentage might be viewed as disproportionately high. Lack of appropriate and specific referral criteria may be partially responsible for the large numbers of students currently referred for comprehensive evaluation and ultimately placed in programs for students with mild disabilities.

In addition, it is often difficult to identify educational characteristics that distinguish students enrolled in special education programs for mild disabilities from other underachieving students who remain in the regular classroom (Shepard, Smith, & Vojir, 1983; Shinn, Tindal, & Spira, 1987; Ysseldyke, Algozzine, Shinn, & McGue, 1982; Ysseldyke, Thurlow, et al., 1983). Of the students referred for comprehensive evaluation, the vast majority are referred because of low achievement and/or behavior problems in the regular program. Because further criteria for differentiating students with potential disabilities from other underachieving students are not clearly identified or applied at the point of referral, those students referred are usually evaluated. Of those evaluated, most are identified as having a disability and are placed in special programs.

Finally, the classification of mild disabilities is the most controversial, the least defined, and the most vulnerable to the influence of biasing variables such as environment, culture, and language. Although issues related to this classification are apparent at every level of the decision-making process, the large numbers of students determined to have mild disabilities and the overrepresentation of minority students in this classification (Heller et al., 1982) raise serious legal and ethical issues regarding referral criteria and teacher referral practices.

Impact of the Decision to Refer

The teacher's decision to refer a student to special education may be the most important decision made in the special education process. Although referral was not intended to provide the basis for placement, apparently, it may exert inordinate influence on the eligibility and placement decision. Several studies have found that most teachers submit referrals to obtain placement outside of the regular classroom (Pugach, 1985; Ysseldyke, Thurlow, et al., 1983). Research also indicates that this referral, not the results of comprehensive assessment, is most predictive of whether a student will be identified as having a disability and placed in a special education program (Algozzine et al., 1982). Therefore, once a teacher refers a student, there is a high probability that she ultimately will be classified as having a disability and will be placed in a special education program. These results are supported by evidence that eligibility decisions tend to be highly variable (Ysseldyke, Algozzine, & Thurlow, 1980), that these decisions appear not to be based on the results of assessment data presented at eligibility meetings (Ysseldyke, Algozzine, Richey, et al., 1982), and that the process of comprehensive assessment, rather than serving to adjust initial referral information, may be used primarily as a mechanism to sanction and justify referral concerns (Sarason & Doris, 1979; White & Calhoun, 1987; Ysseldyke, Thurlow, et al., 1983). Further indication of the weight of teacher referral is found in the documented but unpublicized practice in some schools of placing students in special education programs based on the referral alone, anticipating that the student will ultimately be classified as having a disability (Pugach, 1985).

Teacher Referrals as Evaluative Conclusions

The fact that the teacher's decision to refer may be the most influential element in the referral and evaluation process has stirred controversy over whether teacher opinions should be considered as legitimate evaluative conclusions (M. M. Gerber & Semmel, 1984) or whether, in keeping with current policy, teacher suspicions must be validated by traditional psychometric instruments. Some argue that, because teachers observe a range and depth of student behavior that may be greater than that of standardized tests, the teacher may be a reliable predictor of student success in a particular environment. Research also indicates that teacher referrals are consistent in that they tend to focus on the lowest achieving students. The degree to which teacher opinions and recommendations are appropriate indicators of student functioning and program eligibility will be discussed in the next chapter. However, because referral in itself has a high probability of resulting in program eligibility and placement, thorough, complete, and accurate referral information is critical.

Quality and Accuracy of Teacher Referrals

Despite the controversy over the validity of teacher opinions as appropriate evaluative conclusions, the apparent influence of the referral itself on student identification and placement has prompted questions about the adequacy of current referral practices and the accuracy and quality of information provided by the referral itself. Very little is known about classroom practices that lead to the decision to refer. Research, however, indicates that there may be reason for serious concern regarding the standard of referral information provided to justify the decision to refer a student to special education.

First, the quality of teacher referrals appears to be questionable. Referral information is reported to be generally vague, subjective, and incomplete (Pugach, 1985). Reasons for referrals are reported to be highly variable, general, and subjective, with little verification information (Ysseldyke, Christenson, et al., 1982). In addition, documentation of intensive efforts to intervene before referral appears to be sparse (Munson, 1986; Pugach, 1985; Ysseldyke, Christenson, et al., 1982).

Second, teacher referrals appear to be subject to bias (Algozzine, Schmid, & Mercer, 1981; General Accounting Office, 1981; Shinn et al., 1987). Student characteristics such as ethnic background, sex, socioeconomic background, and even attractiveness may influence the formation of negative attitudes about a student, thus increasing the likelihood of referral. The continued overrepresentation of blacks and other minorities in special education classes attests to the probability that the referral and identification process often fails to ensure that these factors are seriously considered in determining whether a student will or will not be referred to special education.

Third, referral practices are not uniform among teachers. The criteria that teachers use to determine when to refer is highly variable and appear to be related more to the tolerance level of the individual teacher than to any standard referral criteria (M. M. Gerber & Semmel, 1984; H. Walker, 1984). Because tolerance levels vary among teachers, some students who would not be referred to special education by some teachers may be referred by others. In addition, teachers have varying standards for evaluating deviance, based on the students comprising their classrooms (Shinn et al., 1987).

Finally, while few teachers tend to view student concerns as being due to shortcomings in teaching strategies, teacher attempts to intervene before referral vary greatly. Although some teachers try a number of interventions, others try none (Munson, 1986; Pugach, 1985; Ysseldyke, Christenson, et al., 1982). Thus, the accuracy of teacher perceptions regarding students problems may vary greatly.

With this knowledge, careful consideration of the development of referral procedures is critical; furthermore, procedures must be developed to ensure that teacher referral practices do not contradict the requirements of P.L. 94–142, which are intended to guard against any student being misdiagnosed and erroneously placed in special education programs. The next section will focus on establishing standard referral procedures.

ESTABLISHING REFERRAL PROCEDURES

Research indicates that schools and districts have established few guidelines beyond procedural requirements for submitting referrals (Pugach, 1985). Thus, it is hardly surprising that teachers, in an attempt to use all instructional options, refer students to special education even when they do not suspect a disability. In the absence of other instructional options, teachers may tend to define special education loosely and may well equate its function with that of remedial programs. The establishment of districtwide or schoolwide procedures is essential if the purpose of referral is to be clearly articulated and enforced. This section will provide examples of guidelines for developing schoolwide screening procedures, establishing schoolwide referral criteria, and identifying standard informational requirements for completing the referral form.

Schoolwide Screening Procedures

Considering the discretionary nature of the referral process and the documented variability in teacher referral practices, the process of locating students with potential disabilities should not be left solely to the discretion of classroom teachers or other individuals. School screening procedures, if systematically developed and enforced, can provide a method of examining the entire school population to identify those who may have disabilities that may interfere with school progress. Many schools, however, do not reap the full benefits of the screening process because existing procedures may not cover all areas adequately or ensure sufficient follow-up for those students identified through the screening process.

School screening programs routinely include vision, hearing, speech and language, and sometimes health screening. Less often included are ongoing screening programs for mild-to-moderate intellectual, academic, and behavior problems, even though the vast majority of students enrolled in special education programs fall into this category. Teacher referral is often the only way that these students are brought to the attention of the special services committee. A systematic method of identifying those students who perform significantly differently from other students may provide not only a schoolwide indication of students in difficulty but may provide an opportunity for pre-referral intervention, which may prevent the need for formal referral. Using a schoolwide screening process also enables the school administration to determine the distribution of performance for the entire school. This provides a useful measure of comparison when establishing referral procedures for students with potential disabilities.

Analysis of Systemwide Tests of Achievement. At a minimum, school screening procedures should ensure that teachers have information about students who appear to perform significantly below other students of the same age and grade. Some procedures used by schools to provide this information include listing all students who, on systemwide tests of achievement, perform below a certain percentile in reading, math, or language areas. This list, once established, might first be reviewed by grade-level teachers who are familiar with the student. For some students, test results clearly do not indicate actual educational performance. If this is the case, the names of these students should be deleted from the list. The names of remaining students should be given to the student's classroom teacher so that progress can be monitored for a period of time, perhaps 6 weeks, after which the teacher would provide a status report on the student's performance. If performance is still significantly below expectations, the teacher might implement pre-referral procedures to determine whether referral is necessary. Similar procedures may be used with student grades, attendance, suspensions, or any other variable that might indicate systematically those students within the school who may need an alternative instructional program. Records of incoming students should also be reviewed, not only for students who may be coming from special education programs but for students whose record suggests the possiblity of difficulties.

Systematic Follow-up. Screening is often viewed as an activity that occurs at a particular point in the year, usually in the fall or in the spring, and ends a few months later. After screening activities are completed, those conducting the screening usually return to the instructional aspects of their jobs. As a result, follow-up efforts may be minimal, leaving many screening concerns unresolved. Although follow-up may end almost immediately (for example, when a student is retested and passes a hearing screening), it may extend over a long period of time (for example, a student who, as a result of screening, requires audiological evaluation and amplification and perhaps even referral to special education). If screening programs are to be effective, specific requirements for extended and systematic follow-up must be included in school procedures. One way to ensure systematic follow-up to the screening process is provided in Figure 4–1. This illustration provides an example of how the results of screening might be documented and organized for follow-up.

First the criteria established for determining who passed and who failed the screening should be clearly established. As screening progresses, a list should be generated and provided to the administration designating those students who are of concern, based on the criteria used. The recommendations of the individual conducting the screening should be divided according to the level of concern and the type of follow-up required. A low level of concern might require only monitoring by the classroom teacher. For example, if a speech therapist suspects that an error in articulation may be only developmental (such as substituting "w" for "r"), the recommendation may be that the classroom teacher monitor the student's speech. The next level of concern may result in recommendation of specific activities in the classroom and rescreening at a specified time. For example, the speech therapist may be somewhat concerned about a kindergartner's language development but not sufficiently concerned to warrant referral for comprehensive evaluation. If the classroom teacher reports minimal or no educational problems, the therapist may recommend that the student participate in specific classroom language activities and that the teacher monitor progress within the classroom for a period of time. A specified date for rescreening is also established.

A third level of concern may result in a recommendation for referral for comprehensive evaluation and possible specialized speech and language services. In such a case, the therapist might observe the student in the classroom or request that the teacher provide information on any perceived adverse effect of the problem in the classroom.

The final, and most critical element of the process is to ensure that resolution is achieved in each case. The last column in Figure 4–1 provides space for the therapist (or whoever is providing the follow-up) to document what resolution was achieved

FIGURE 4–1
Results and Follow-up of Screening Concerns

Screening Procedure: _____

_____

_____

Criteria: _____

_____

_____

Name	Screening Concern	Recommendations			Resolution and Date
		Monitoring	Teacher Intervention	Referral	

and when. Such a procedure can provide program justification and a systematic method for conducting and monitoring a follow-up program. The documentation provides administrators with clearly defined needs and enables greater knowledge about screening and follow-up procedures in the schools.

Although most screening instruments are commercially produced tests of academic skills or informal samples of behavior relative to a fairly well-established list of expectancies in various areas, screening programs can be developed that reflect the curriculum of the school or district in which they are used. In addition, they can be ongoing rather than seasonal. An example is the Montevideo Individualized Prescriptive Instructional Management System (MIPIMS). This is a computerized system that monitors the progress of every student in the school within the math and reading curriculum developed for the school. The program enables an ongoing accounting of the performance of all students within the curriculum. A printout is provided every 3 weeks to each teacher to monitor performance for their own students. The program designates those students performing within the average range of the school or grade in the areas of reading and mathematics and those students performing at or below the 20th percentile (often used to designate criteria for referral to special education). If a student is not already receiving special education and performs below the 20th percentile, that student may be referred to special education. Likewise, if a student is receiving special education and performs above the 50th percentile, services may be reduced. Such a system enables systematic and ongoing screening for the entire school (Peterson, Heistad, Peterson, & Reynolds, 1985).

Establishing Criteria for Referral

Criteria for referral ideally should be established by state and local educational agencies and be included in the state plan that is approved by the U.S. Department of Education. In the absence of specific state criteria, however, districts and even individual schools, with thorough review of existing federal and state regulations and guidance, can develop their own criteria within the parameters of existing regulations.

As with all elements of referral, the criteria on which referrals are based tend to be variable. Because there have been so few guidelines established, many teachers believe (and in fact it is legally permissible) that any student may be referred for comprehensive evaluation and special education. In some schools any student who is functioning below grade level can

be referred. While this liberal criterion may ensure that no student with a potential disability is missed, it also has some potential disadvantages. First, a liberal referral policy increases the demand on an already enormously expensive process. In a school where referral is defined loosely or not at all, the referral process may be used for a number of purposes unrelated to special education, including obtaining information to assist classroom teachers in planning instruction, warning upcoming teachers that a student is experiencing educational problems, determining how a student performs on standardized tests, or providing parents with student achievement information. Second, in addition to the expense involved in evaluating large numbers of referred students, a liberal referral policy may place inordinate demands on existing assessment personnel, thus further extending the time necessary to complete the process. This means that some students who may well need special education may experience even longer delays than currently exist before receiving services. Finally, an indiscriminate referral policy may tend to increase the probability that students will be mistakenly identified as having a disability and placed in special education programs. Considering that minority students are already overrepresented in special education classes for the mildly handicapped, that teacher bias is inherent in referrals, and that once referred, the likelihood of evaluation and placement is high, schools are well advised to develop referral criteria that provide some assurance that students referred are, in fact, those truly suspected of having a disability.

An overly restrictive referral policy may present problems as well, in that narrowly and rigidly defined criteria may exclude many of the very students for whom the process was developed. Referral policy must ensure that criteria, once established, serve as flexible referral guidelines rather than as arbitrary cut-off requirements and that any student for whom adequate justification is provided can be referred for consideration by the special services committee.

If the referral process is to be confined only to those students who are suspected of having a disability and of needing a different kind of instruction than that required by typical students, the school might establish general guidelines for teachers in considering whether or not to refer a student. The three broad guidelines listed below provide a framework for establishing minimal school guidelines for referral and are based on the criteria established by P.L. 94–142 for defining students with disabilities. Guidelines might require that the teacher apply the following criteria when considering referral:

1. It is suspected that the student has a disability that may adversely affect educational performance.
2. An educational concern has been identified that is suspected to be caused by a disability.
3. It is suspected that the student may require instruction that differs from what might normally be provided as part of the regular education program with typical adaptations.

Each of these guidelines can be further developed, depending on the level of specificity required by the district or school. Further refinement can be useful in guiding the teacher or referring individual in the collection of additional information that will aid the processing of the referral.

Suspected Disability. A student should not be referred to special education unless there is reason to suspect that the student may have a disability. This means that a disability must be suspected or confirmed. P.L. 94–142 identifies allowable disabling conditions that may result in a need for special education, and these categories may provide a basis for providing guidance to teachers considering referral. These disabilities (referred to as *impairments* by P.L. 94–142) include mental retardation, hearing disabilities, deafness, speech disorders, visual disabilities, serious emotional disturbances, orthopedic disabilities, other health disabilities, deaf-blindness, multiple disabilities, and specific learning disabilities. Individual states may further delineate this list to include disabilities such as behavior disorders and autism in state laws and regulations.

One way for schools to apply these guidelines at the point of referral might be to require that the referring individual indicate the *suspected* area of disability on the referral form. To do this, a list of disabilities recognized by the state as qualifying conditions might be included on the referral form or made available to teachers and other referring individuals. Such a procedure may have several advantages. First, requiring that the referring individual gather appropriate and sufficient information to justify a suspected disability may dramatically improve the quality of referral information included on the referral form. Second, designating a suspected area of disability may serve to reduce the number of referrals made for purposes unrelated to special education by providing a reminder to the referring individual that the primary purpose of the referral process is to identify students who may have a disability. Third, designating a suspected area of disability at the time of referral can provide a basis for continuity throughout the identification process. For example, if a teacher suspects that a student may have a learning disability

and has gathered and provided information to support this suspicion, the special services committee should consider the merits of the referral in the context of a suspected learning disability. Subsequent evaluation and data gathering, if warranted, should focus on determining whether a learning disability exists according to criteria required in the particular state, and eligibility determination should be based on the cumulative data gathered and documented to support the presence or absence of a learning disability.

P.L. 94–142 clearly establishes that before a multidisciplinary evaluation can occur, an area of suspected disability must be identified to establish an appropriate evaluation team (*Federal Register,* 1977). This means that either the teacher must have sufficient information on which to base a suspicion that a disability exists, or the special services committee must be able to determine the suspected area of disability from the information provided by the referral. Considering that referrals may often fail to provide a clear basis for referral or verification of concerns (Pugach, 1985; Ysseldyke, Christenson et al., 1983), it is doubtful that the special services committee would always be in a position to adequately intuit the suspected area of disability from referral information. If a disability must be suspected for a student to be referred to special education, then it is appropriate for the teacher to identify, in a very preliminary manner, the type of disability suspected. It should be emphasized that designating a suspected area of disability constitutes only a *preliminary suspicion* that serves to provide information to and guide referral consideration by the special services committee. It should by no means be misconstrued as a diagnosis or a determination that a student has a disability and is in need of special education.

A second method of addressing the notion that a disability should be suspected to refer a student is to require consideration of the eligibility criteria established by the state for diagnosing a disability. Figure 4–2 provides an illustration of how state-established definitions and criteria for determining the existence of a learning disability can assist a teacher in the decision to refer. The school might first provide a definition of the disability area as established by the specific state in which the program is located. From this definition, the school might list the essential elements for establishing a learning disability. These elements may then be translated into sample questions for teachers who are considering referral. The teacher can then consider these questions and gather appropriate information to determine whether the problems that the student is experiencing might be caused by a learning disability.

FIGURE 4–2

Example of Teacher Referral Guidelines for Suspected Learning Disabilities Based on State-Established Definitions

STATE-ESTABLISHED DEFINITION OF SPECIFIC LEARNING DISABILITIES

A student who has a specific learning disability is one who has a severe discrepancy between ability and achievement and has been determined by a multidisciplinary team to not be achieving commensurate with her age and ability levels. The lack of achievement is found when the student is provided with learning experiences appropriate for her age and ability levels in one or more of the following areas: oral expression, listening comprehension, written expression, basic reading skills, reading comprehension, mathematical calculation, or mathematical reasoning. The term does not include students whose severe discrepancy between ability and achievement is primarily the result of a visual, hearing, or motor disability; mental retardation; emotional disturbance; or environmental, cultural, or economic disadvantage.

SUMMARY OF DEFINITION

Based on the preceding definition, a learning disability might be suspected when the student exhibits the following:

1. Is not working to potential in areas of reading, mathematics, or expressive or receptive language
2. Does not have a vision, hearing, or motor disability
3. Does not have an intellectual disability, an emotional disturbance, or significant economic disadvantage.

GUIDELINES FOR TEACHERS IN CONSIDERING REFERRAL

Before referring a student for comprehensive evaluation, consider the following questions:

1. Does the student seem to be achieving below what you would expect?
2. Did the student pass vision and hearing screening?
3. Do medical records and observations rule out a motor disability?
4. Do your observations rule out severe emotional problems?
5. Does the student show evidence of at least average intelligence?
6. Does the student have difficulty remembering, understanding, or interpreting what is seen or heard? Does the student have difficulty expressing herself in writing or speaking?

If the responses to these questions are positive, referral for further diagnosis is appropriate.

Similarly, for emotional disturbances, state-established criteria for determining the presence of a disability might require that the condition must have been demonstrated to a marked degree and over an extended period of time. If the teacher knows that a student's behavior has only recently been of concern, the student in all likelihood would not meet the state established criteria and therefore should not be referred to special education. In cases such as these, the teacher might explore other options available in the school or may attempt to justify why a referral to special education is still appropriate.

Another consideration in establishing guidelines for referrals in which a disability is suspected, but not confirmed, is the need to rule out the probability that the problem is the result of factors other than a disability. The most important of these factors are those student characteristics that are the most likely sources of potential teacher bias. The student's language, race, and socioeconomic background are factors that must be considered at every step of the identification process but must certainly be recognized and considered before a student is even suspected of having a disability. Existing referral procedures may require no more than a standard statement completed as a matter of course, usually at the time of eligibility determination, which indicates that these student characteristics are not the source of the problem. Often, there is no evidence that these issues have been substantively addressed at any point in the identification process. On the contrary, the continued overrepresentation of minority students in special education classes suggests that these factors may not have been adequately considered.

Although teacher referrals may be susceptible to bias, teachers, when properly informed, may be the most appropriate resource for considering the potential impact of student characteristics on school performance. If provided with information on how language, race, socioeconomic background, and sex of the student can influence performance and teacher attitudes, teachers should be able to consider the impact of these variables on student performance before referral. Methods for documenting that these issues have been addressed in a preliminary way by the referring individual might in some cases be as straightforward as including an indication of the student's language, race, gender, and socioeconomic background as part of the referral. If the student is, or is suspected of being, in any group at risk for referral bias, the school might require that the teacher provide a detailed explanation of why these factors are not considered to be the source of the student's difficulty. Figure 4–3 provides a sample list of questions for the teacher to consider when a student with limited English proficiency is considered for referral to special education.

Significant Educational Concern. A student should not be referred for special education unless the teacher has a significant educational concern. Unfortunately, standard criteria for determining when an educational concern is significant are lacking. Thus, teachers often apply their own classroom standards for deciding who will be referred. There are several ways that the school can provide some standard guidance for teachers in deciding when an educational concern is significant enough to warrant referral. As in establishing criteria for a suspected disability, the school might again use state-established criteria to provide guidance in determining whether educational concerns are significant enough to warrant referral. For example, some states require, in addition to having a disability, that a student perform educationally at or below a particular level to qualify for special education services. In some states, performance near the 10th percentile on individual tests of achievement in the areas of reading, math, or language may be required for a student to be eligible for special education programs. These criteria provide general guidelines for the way that the term *adverse effect* will be interpreted for the purposes of program eligibility. One way that the teacher might use this eligibility guideline in the decision to refer is to review the student's performance on systemwide tests. For example, if a student being considered for referral because of poor reading ability scores at the 50th percentile in reading on systemwide tests of achievement, chances are that the student, when assessed individually, will not meet the state-established criteria for program eligibility. The teacher must then decide whether to explore other options or whether to develop a justification for submitting a referral for special education.

Rather than using performance levels as guidelines for referral, other schools may establish procedural criteria. One procedure currently being implemented in many school districts is the requirement that formal referral cannot occur until prereferral interventions are attempted and documented. Schools have developed teacher assistance teams, consultation models, and other methods to ensure that the students ultimately referred to special education are those for whom intervention in the classroom has not been successful. These procedures not only tend to define the referred population but also have the potential benefit of reducing referrals to special education.

Finally, many school systems establish no quantitative performance criteria or procedural criteria for referral but instead provide examples or checklists

FIGURE 4–3
Guidelines for Consideration of Referral Bias

Before referring a student with limited English proficiency for evaluation and possible special education placement, the following questions should be addressed by the teacher, pre-referral team, parent, and/or others involved with the referral. A member of the school staff must meet or talk with the student's parents to obtain family and background information.

FAMILY AND BACKGROUND	Yes	No	Don't Know
1. Did the student have any difficulty learning to eat, sleep, sit, walk, or talk? If yes, explain _____	___	___	___
2. Do the parents have any significant concerns about their child at home or in the community? Does the student go about the neighborhood as independently as others? Does he or she assume responsibilities or chores at home?	___	___	___
3. Do parents have concerns about the student's school performance? If yes, What?_____	___	___	___
4. Has the student previously had problems in school? If yes, what areas?_____	___	___	___
5. Have other members of the family experienced school related problems? Explain_____	___	___	___
6. Has the student experienced any upsetting events such as death, divorce, or other family crisis? When?_____	___	___	___
7. Has the student attended more than one school in the last year? If yes, how many?____ Where?_____	___	___	___

LANGUAGE	Yes	No	Don't Know
1. Is English the usual language spoken at home? If not, what language is spoken?_____	___	___	___
2. Do any members of the family communicate in a language other than English at home? If so, who and in what language?_____	___	___	___
3. Does the student communicate in a language other than English at home? If so, what language?_____	___	___	___
4. Is the student's language similar to other family members in terms of its structure, grammatical correctness, and dialect?	___	___	___
5. Has the student been exposed to English for more than 2 years? How long?_____	___	___	___
6. Has the student ever been enrolled in a second-language or language enrichment program or other program designed to teach English? When?_____ For how long?_____ Where?_____	___	___	___

(Figure 4–3 continued)

EDUCATOR'S OBSERVATIONS	Yes	No	Don't Know

1. Are educational concerns primarily related to areas in which any student with a different language background would have difficulty? For example, vocabulary development, general information, expressive language, and/or reading comprehension? Other areas? _____ _____ _____ _____

2. Has the student attended school regularly? _____ _____ _____

3. Has the student been observed under different instructional situations (such as in a group, individually, with a parent, with a peer tutor, with an adult tutor)? In which situations does the student perform best?_____ _____ _____ _____

4. Does the student perform better in nonacademic courses such as physical education, athletics, art, and music? If so, which? _____ _____ _____ _____

5. Have other professionals observed and worked with the student in his or her native language and in English on isolated concepts to determine how quickly the student grasps new information? If yes, who_____ _____ _____ _____

6. Once a concept is understood, can the student generalize and apply it to other situations? _____ _____ _____

7. Has the student been screened in his or her native language? _____ _____ _____

8. When instructed in his or her primary language, does the student perform skills that he or she cannot perform when instructed in English? _____ _____ _____

9. Has a test of language dominance been conducted to determine preferred language? _____ _____ _____

Based on information obtained, is it possible that differential prior experiences and/or student characteristics rather than a disability may adversely affect this student's ability to achieve in the regular education program?

of educational concerns associated with various disabilities to guide the teacher in the decision to refer a student to special education. Figure 4–4 provides a list of educational concerns that may be associated with speech and language disorders. A teacher may be aware that a student has a speech problem, the presence of which, in itself, does not warrant referral. If the problem, however, appears to be associated with characteristic concerns on the checklist, the decision may be made to refer to the student.

Need for Specially Designed Instruction. A final referral guideline in deciding whether to refer a student for special education is to consider whether the student may require specially designed instruction differing from that normally provided as part of the regular program. According to the regulations governing the provision of special education, specially designed instruction may include classroom instruction, instruction in physical education, home instruction, and instruction in hospitals and institutions. It may also include speech pathology, physical therapy, occupational therapy, or any other related service, if that service is specially designed and is considered to be special education rather than a related service under state standards. Vocational education also may be considered as special education if it is specially designed to meet the unique needs of a student with a disability.

For some students, the need for specially designed instruction may be apparent. For example, if a student has a progressive physical disability such as muscular dystrophy, that student may well have been accommodated in a regular physical education class for a period of time with typical modifications that might be made for any student. As physical movement becomes more impaired, however, the student may be unable to participate in the same activities as other students. The teacher may at this time refer the student for a comprehensive evaluation with the intention of obtaining a program of specially designed instruction. Such a program might include specially designed instruction in physical education and the related services of occupational and physical therapy.

For other students, the need for specially designed instruction may not be so apparent. For example, a teacher may not know whether a student who has a learning disability requires a unique and highly specialized type of instruction. Empirical evidence does not support the notion that a defined set of instructional strategies exists that are appropriate solely for students with mild disabilities (Heller, et al., 1982). On the contrary, it appears that instructional approaches that work well with this group are the same ones that work well with many underachiev-

ing students. Thus, in deciding whether to refer a student for special education, a teacher should first attempt those instructional strategies that might be used with underachieving students in the regular education program.

It should be noted that a need for specially designed instruction does not necessarily mean that such instruction must be provided apart from the regular program. Specially designed instruction can be provided in any least restrictive, appropriate setting including the regular classroom. The trend in many schools, especially in programs for young children, is to integrate specially designed instruction, such as speech therapy, physical therapy, and occupational therapy, into the activities in the regular classroom rather than removing the student from that setting or providing isolated activities unrelated to the ongoing program in the regular classroom.

Once the teacher has decided to refer a student for comprehensive evaluation and possible special education, most states and districts require that certain information be gathered and provided on a referral form and submitted to the special services committee for consideration. The following section will discuss information that should be provided to support a referral to special education.

COMPONENTS OF THE REFERRAL FORM

Completing referral forms creates additional paperwork, which teachers and other referring individuals may regard as inordinate (and perhaps irrelevant). Thus, districts must ensure that the informational requirements of the referral form are justified and that the information is necessary for the special services committees to make an appropriate referral decision. The referral is a significant part of the student's special education record and may provide the only written documentation justifying the decision to refer a student for comprehensive evaluation and possible special education placement. Thus, the document should provide clear and defensible reasons for the decision to refer.

P.L. 94–142 establishes no specific format or informational requirements for referrals. Thus, states and districts have developed their own procedures and forms. Figures 4–5 and 4–6 provide examples of referral forms developed by two school districts. Figure 4–5 illustrates one district's preference for a checklist format, while Figure 4–6, pp. 95–97, illustrates another district's preference for an open-ended format. While districts and even individual schools may differ in the specific information required, some basic information should be considered for inclusion

FIGURE 4–4
Referral Checklist

Student: _____ Date: _____

Teacher: _____ Grade: _____

Please fill out this form and return it to the Speech/Language Pathologist. Your observations will help determine if this child's communication problem is affecting her educational performance. Thank you.

1. If the student is older (4th grade and up), are his/her language comprehension skills below average?	Yes	No	NA
2. Does the student have problems with grammar usage?	Yes	No	NA
3. Can the student recall ideas in sequence?	Yes	No	NA
4. Can the student recall facts and details?	Yes	No	NA
5. Does the student mix up the order of words in sentences?	Yes	No	NA
6. Does the student use incorrect words to name or describe things?	Yes	No	NA
7. Does the student respond inappropriately to statements and questions?	Yes	No	NA
8. Does the student have trouble understanding the meaning of words, sentences, paragraphs?	Yes	No	NA
9. Does the student have trouble following verbal instructions?	Yes	No	NA
10. Does the student use shorter sentences than the other students in your class?	Yes	No	NA
11. If this student is young, are or were his/her reading readiness skills poor?	Yes	No	NA
12. Does this student read well (verbally)?	Yes	No	NA
13. Is this student's oral reading rate slow?	Yes	No	NA
14. Is the student better in silent reading than in oral reading?	Yes	No	NA
15. Do most of this student's mispronunciations during reading occur on the articulation error sounds?	Yes	No	NA
16. Does this student have a lot of pronunciation/enunciation errors?	Yes	No	NA
17. Does this student make errors in writing (spelling) on the same sound symbols that he/she makes the verbal errors in articulation?	Yes	No	NA

(Figure 4—4 continued)

18. Is this student's intelligibility reduced (due to articulation errors) to the extent that you find it difficult to understand what he/she says at times?   Yes   No   NA

19. Does the student have problems in speech sound discrimination?   Yes   No   NA

20. Does the student ever correct his/her articulation errors by himself/herself?   Yes   No   NA

21. In comparing the child's voice to his peers (same age and **sex**), circle those that apply:
    Pitch: too low, too high
    Loudness: inadequate, excessive
    Quality: breathy, harshness or tightness, hoarse
    Resonance: denasal (nasal congestion), hypernasal

22. Is this student aware of his/her communication difficulties?   Yes   No   NA

23. Does this student appear to be a social isolate?   Yes   No   NA

24. Do the student's peers comment on his/her speech behavior?   Yes   No   NA

25. Does this student's speech problem distract you sometimes from what he/she is saying?   Yes   No   NA

26. Does this student's speech problem interfere with classroom performance?   Yes   No   NA

27. Does the student's verbal performance call attention to itself?   Yes   No   NA

28. Problems occur:
    _____ in special situations or certain periods of the day
    _____ on an ongoing basis

Additional teacher comments:
    Did a discussion with the student about his/her communication:
    ( ) Reveal an awareness and concern about the problem
    ( ) Indicate a desire to change
    ( ) Other comments: _____
    _____
    _____

_____   _____
Classroom Teacher Signature   Date

From Royal Oak Elementary School, Department of Defense Dependents Schools, Mediterranean Region, 1986.

FIGURE 4–5
Sample Referral Forms: Checklist Style

Elementary School Student ARD Referral

Date _____ School_____ Referring Person_____

Student _____ Birthdate_____ Age_____ Grade_____

1. Reason for referral. (Describe the presenting problem(s) and attach work samples.)

2. What would you like the student to be able to do that he/she does not do now?

3. What do you see as this student's strengths?

4. What interventions have been attempted?

❑ Student conference   ❑ Behavior management techniques
❑ Note/call to parent   ❑ Adjusted workload
❑ Parent conference   ❑ Alternative methods and techniques
❑ Consultation with specialists   ❑ Modifying materials and presentations
❑ Consultation with colleagues   ❑ Change of text/materials
❑ Referral to counselor   ❑ Change in grouping

5. Rate the student's level of functioning as compared to other classmates and indicate grade level, if known:

	Above Average	Average	Below Average	Estimated Grade Level
1. Listening Comprehension	❑	❑	❑	_____
2. Oral Expression	❑	❑	❑	_____
3. Basic Reading Skills	❑	❑	❑	_____
4. Reading Comprehension	❑	❑	❑	_____
5. Written Expression	❑	❑	❑	_____
6. Math Calculation	❑	❑	❑	_____
7. Math Reasoning	❑	❑	❑	_____

6. Instructional Series (Please specify book and series student is working in at the time of referral):

A. Reading _____   C. Language Arts _____

B. Mathematics _____   D. Other (if appropriate) _____

(Figure 4–5 continued)

7. Based on your observations, evaluate the student in comparison to other students in the same grade by checking problems frequently observed:

LISTENING COMPREHENSION
❑ Difficulty understanding spoken language
❑ Difficulty following verbal directions

ORAL EXPRESSION
❑ Difficulty expressing thoughts and ideas
❑ Limited speaking vocabulary

READING
❑ Difficulty with letter/word recognition
❑ Word guessing
❑ Slow, constant sounding out of words
❑ Difficulty with comprehension (factual, critical)

WRITTEN EXPRESSION
❑ Difficulty with spelling
❑ Difficulty with writing speed
❑ Difficulty completing written work
❑ Difficulty with punctuation
❑ Difficulty writing a sentence
❑ Difficulty organizing sentences and ideas into meaningful paragraphs

MATHEMATICS
❑ Difficulty with number recognition
❑ Difficulty with number concepts
❑ Difficulty with basic operations
  ❑ Addition   ❑ Multiplication
  ❑ Subtraction   ❑ Division
❑ Difficulty understanding place value
❑ Difficulty solving word problems

DISCRIMINATION
❑ Difficulty discriminating letter symbols
❑ Difficulty discriminating letter sounds

MEMORY
❑ Difficulty remembering what is seen
❑ Difficulty remembering what is heard
❑ Difficulty retaining information over a period of time

VISUAL MOTOR COORDINATION
❑ Difficulty with small motor tasks
❑ Difficulty with paper/pencil tasks
❑ Difficulty copying from the board

ATTENTION/ORGANIZATION/ACTIVITY LEVEL
❑ Difficulty beginning a task
❑ Difficulty maintaining attention
❑ Easily distracted
❑ Loses or forgets work and/or materials
❑ Difficulty with organization
❑ Late for class
❑ Difficulty completing tasks
❑ Difficulty with changes in routine
❑ Overactive
❑ Underactive

SOCIAL/EMOTIONAL
❑ Lacks motivation
❑ Lacks self control
❑ Easily frustrated
❑ Sudden changes in mood throughout day
❑ Inconsistency in performance
❑ Needs constant approval
❑ Interrupts and distracts class
❑ Unusually aggressive toward others
❑ Unusually shy or withdrawn
❑ Difficulty interpreting social cues
❑ Difficulty making and keeping friends
❑ Doesn't accept responsibility for own behavior
❑ Easily influenced by others

SPEECH
❑ Stutters
❑ Difficulty articulating speech sounds
❑ Unusual voice quality

OTHER COMMENTS:

FIGURE 4–6
Sample Referral Forms: Open-Ended Style

FORMAL REFERRAL TO CSC
(Completed by referring person)

Student's name _____ Date of birth _____
 Yr   Mo   Day

School _____ Grade _____

Teacher _____

Parents/Guardians _____ Telephone _____
 Home

Date _____ _____
 Duty

Language spoken in home: _____

PARENT NOTIFICATION
(Completed by referring person)

Date of contact_____ Contacted by: _____
 Yr   Mo   Day   *(Name of person)*

Referring individual _____ Form submitted _____
 Yr   Mo   Day

Remainder of form completed by Case Manager/Chairperson

☐ In-school referral   ☐ Out-of-school referral

Referral Accepted _____
 Yr   Mo   Day

Area(s) of suspected handicapping condition(s): _____

_____

Entered in Census _____ Student # _____
 Yr   Mo   Day

Referral rejected_____
 Yr   Mo   Day

Reason for rejection (and further recommendations):_____

_____

_____

Referring person informed of disposition_____
 Yr   Mo   Day

_____
Case Manager/Chairperson

Note: Prereferral Report Form and supporting documents must be attached.

(Figure 4–6 continued)

PREREFERRAL REPORT FORM

_____
School

_____   _____   _____
Student   Grade   Date Prereferral
                                                                                                          Process Began

_____   _____
Teacher   Class or Subject

Directions: This is a form that teachers should use throughout the prereferral process to summarize the strategies used to resolve a student's problem.

Description of Problem(s):

What strategies have been tried in the classroom to address the problem(s):

Other Educators Consulted:

Describe Parental Involvement:

_____

Did you observe any reason(s) why this student could not participate in and benefit from the regular physical education curriculum and class? *Yes* _____ *No* _____ If Yes, please specify the reason(s) below.

Vision and hearing screening results must be summarized or attached.

(Figure 4–6 continued)

SUGGESTIONS FOR PREREFERRAL ACTIVITIES

One or more of these activities may be required by the CSC:

1. Elicit information regarding student's successful and unsuccessful learning styles and settings.

2. Brainstorm with co-teachers asking for suggestions that have worked well for them in similar situations.

3. Meet with parent(s) to discuss student's current and past performances.

4. Consult with resource educator(s), e.g., RIS (reading improvement specialist), TAG (talented and gifted), special educator.

5. Collect recent examples of student's classroom work and current report card.

6. Request classroom observation by another teacher or resource educator.

7. Identify, in writing, the student's specific academic problem(s).

8. Collect specific written information relative to student's academic skill levels.

9. Collect specific information regarding social/interpersonal behaviors.

10. Consult with counselor about student's behaviors.

11. Develop a behavior management plan with assistance of resource person.

12. Develop and implement instructional strategies with assistance of resource educator.

13. Consult with school nurse.

14. Gather screening information for vision, hearing, and physical education.

15. Review student's cumulative folder for information regarding student's academic history.

The CSC may require that additional activities be conducted for all referrals.

From *Procedural Guide for Special Education* (DS Manual 2500.13), by Department of Defense Dependents Schools, 1988, Alexandria, VA: Author. **Reprinted by permission.**

on all referral forms. The elements discussed here are included in the referral form illustrated in Figure 4–7 and include establishing the purpose of referral, verifying the concern, and documenting attempts to maintain the student in the regular program. This referral developed for Joe S. will provide the basis for the sample letter of notice and consent provided to parents (Figure 4–9), the subsequent evaluation report (Figure 5–5), the sample letter to parents discussing evaluation results and IEP involvement (Figure 5–6), and an IEP (Figure 12–4).

Establishing the Purpose of Referral

The referral form should first and foremost clearly communicate in writing the reason for the referral. Unless the purpose of the referral is clearly articulated, the special services committee may have difficulty determining an appropriate course of action to follow regarding the referred student. One way to encourage clear communication of the reasons for referral is to include a statement of referral purpose. This statement might be divided into three parts including (1) suspected disability, (2) areas of concern, and (3) expected outcome. Such a statement can help the special services committee to determine whether or not to accept the referral, what priority it should be assigned if accepted, whether or not to refer the student to another program, what type of assessment should be designed, and whether or not all referral information is available to support the referral.

Suspected Disability.   The rationale for indicating the suspected disability on the referral form was discussed in the previous section. It bears reiterating, however, that such a provision can provide guidance and continuity to the action taken by the special services committee. Many school systems have discouraged the designation of a suspected area of disability, because in some instances, such a designation may be viewed as a predetermination that a disability does exist. However, if the teacher has information that led to such a suspicion, there is no reason not to provide this information to the special services committee to provide a focus for consideration of the referral. An indication that the teacher suspects a learning disability raises a questions altogether different from an indication that the teacher suspects an emotional disturbance.

Area of Concern.   A statement of the areas of educational concern identifies those areas of significant difficulty that provide the basis for the referral. Close attention should be given to this aspect of the referral to ensure accuracy, clarity, and consistency between the actual concerns of the referring teacher, the information provided on the referral form, and the action taken by the special services committee.

The purpose of the referral should identify the primary areas of concern. If there is more than one area of primary concern, both should be indicated. The teacher, however, should avoid indicating that all areas are of primary concern as a means of indicating that a student performs poorly in all areas. For most students, one or two primary problems have the secondary effect of influencing performance in other areas. For example, a student who has limited reading ability will perform poorly not only in the subject of reading but possibly also in science, social studies, and mathematics, when such areas require reading. This does not mean, however, that science, social studies, and mathematics are themselves primary areas of concern. They may be secondary concerns caused by the primary problem of poor reading ability. Inappropriate behavior also may be a secondary concern related to poor academic skills. The referring teacher is in the best position to consider which concerns are basic to the educational problems demonstrated in the classroom.

Once identified, the educational concern should be clearly stated. For example, it is not appropriate for a teacher to submit, or for the special services committee to consider, a referral that states "problems with reading." Such a statement is too vague. The statement might be further explained to indicate whether the problem is primarily with word recognition, comprehension, vocabulary development, or another aspect of reading. Likewise, indicating that a student "has problems with writing" may indicate a variety of different concerns, including problems related to handwriting, spelling, written composition, or written language. Lack of specificity in identifying the concern may result in inappropriate consideration of the referral and/or inappropriate assessment information.

The referral should reflect all concerns that the teacher considers significant to the student's inability to perform in the classroom. In some instances, teachers may tend to omit concerns that, while considered significant, may be perceived as sensitive or controversial. For example, referrals may fail to document concerns related to drug abuse, potential problems at home, or the existence of previous school-related problems. If these concerns are considered significant but are not articulated, the special services committee may fail to recognize or consider critical elements of the referral concern. If the teacher is legitimately concerned that factors such as these are significant in a student's inability to perform educationally, it is important to recognize and consider them before referral, and it is important to document

FIGURE 4–7
Completed Referral Form for Joe S.

I. STUDENT INFORMATION

A. **Name** <u>Joe S.</u> **Birth Date** <u>10-1-80</u> **Age** <u>11-3</u>
   School <u>Adams Middle School</u> **Grade** <u>5</u> **Sex** <u>Male</u>
   Parents <u>Mr. and Mrs. S.</u> **Address** <u>1016 Willow Dr.</u> **Phone** <u>(313) 261-0369</u>

B. Is there reason to believe that this student's race, sex, language, culture, or socioeconomic level may be associated with school difficulties? **Yes** <u>X</u> **No** ___ If yes, attach explanations of why these factors are not suspected to account for the student's school difficulty.

C. **Date of vision screening:** <u>June 8, 1990</u> **Results:** <u>Glasses prescribed 20/40</u>
   Date of hearing screening: <u>June 8, 1990</u> **Results:** <u>Hearing within normal limits</u>

II. PURPOSE OF REFERRAL

A. **Suspected area of disability** (Check one)

   a. _____ physical disability
   b. _____ speech and/or language disability
   c. _____ emotional disability
   d. _<u>X</u>_ intellectual disability

   e. _____ information processing disability
   f. _____ hearing disability
   g. _____ vision disability
   h. _____ do not suspect disability

B. **Area of Educational Concern**

1. Indicate those areas in which the student is functioning significantly below other students in the same grade or class.

   _____ Gross Motor   _<u>X</u>_ Reading   _<u>X</u>_ Behavior   _____ Expressive Language
   _____ Fine Motor   _<u>X</u>_ Mathematics   _____ Speech   _____ Written Language
   _____ Receptive Language _____ Other (Specify) _____

2. Provide specific examples of concerns in each area noted above:

Area	Specific Educational Concern
Reading	Reading vocabulary is approximately 2 years below grade level. Has limited skills for structural analysis. Attempts to use context clues to decode vocabulary. Comprehension is approximately 2 years below grade level. Reading difficulty affects performance in content areas.
Mathematics	Has difficulty with abstract concepts of regrouping, zeros, place value, and solving word problems. Typically does not perform these operations accurately without assistance. Has some difficulty telling time to the quarter hour and less, counting money, and measuring.
Behavior	Has difficulty establishing friendships. Behavior is immature. Frequently off-task. Day dreams, but not disruptive.

(Figure 4–7 continued)

3. Indicate other concerns that may affect educational performance.

Does not wear his glasses.

Joe's handwriting is very immature. He prints, instead of writing, in large, unevenly formed letters.

Unmotivated to perform classroom assignments or to participate in class activities.

C. Anticipated Outcome of Comprehensive Evaluation

1. _____ Consider regular class placement appropriate. Require suggestions and strategies for classroom instruction.

2. _____ Consider regular classroom instruction appropriate but anticipate need for additional instructional resources.

3. _X_ Consider alternative or supplemental instruction necessary (attach documentation of prereferral interventions).

III. VERIFICATION OF EDUCATIONAL CONCERNS

Provide examples or documentation that support the *current* educational concern(s) described. Attach copies of work samples, systemwide test results, grade cards, tests, or observations.

Informal Reading Inventory	October 10-12	Reading vocabulary at 2nd-grade basal level.
		Reading comprehension at 2nd-grade basal level.
		Structural analysis poor. Difficulty with literal and inferential meaning.
Systemwide Test (CAT)	October 25-26	7th percentile reading; 10th percentile in math.
Oral Reading Taped Sample	November 5	Oral reading at 3rd-grade level: lacks fluency and accuracy.
Mathematics Inventory	October 15	Adds and subtracts inconsistently with regrouping.
	December 5	Continues to have difficulty with concept of regrouping.
Observation of Off-Task	October 8 (Pre)	Off-task 35% of morning.
Behavior	December 6 (Post)	Off-task 25% of morning.

Is there evidence that the educational concern has existed in previous school years? Provide source of evidence.

Previous school records indicated low performance in reading and math since second grade.

Systemwide tests	grade 2	Reading: 20th percentile	Mathematics	30th percentile
	grade 3	Reading: 20th percentile	Mathematics	26th percentile
	grade 4	Reading: 15th percentile	Mathematics	20th percentile

Parents indicate that Joe has always had difficulty in school.

Joe was enrolled in a compensatory education program in the 4th grade for reading and mathematics.

(Figure 4–7 continued)

Compare this student's performance to that of other students in the class in the area(s) of concern.

Reading	25th of 25 students in class on systemwide tests. Class performance consistent with these scores. In most subjects, Joe is grouped with students of multiple abilities and performance levels. It is still difficult for him to participate in any academic activity.
Math	25th of 25 students in class.
Behavior	Joe is cooperative when working with groups of students but does not interact extensively. Cooperative groups have helped this to some extent, but other students still tend to avoid him to some extent. He is off-task more than most but interacts less than most students in the class.

IV. INTERVENTIONS ATTEMPTED

Indicate interventions attempted to address educational problem before referral. Attach pre-referral intervention plans and results if available.

Intervention	Duration	Result
Consultation	September 1990 to present	Strategies noted below have been initiated.
Peer Reading Partner	September 1990 to October	No change in reading performance.
Reading With Taped Sample	October 1990 to December	Some improvement in vocabulary using same sample but no generalization to other reading.
Extended Work Time	September 1990 to present	Increase in amount of work completed.
Modified Evaluations	September 1990 to present	Tests given verbally by teacher, modified.
Behavior Plan	October 1990 to present	On-task behavior has increased.

V. REFERRAL DECISION

After consideration of the referral information, the special services committee must document the referral decision here.

    A. __X__ **Accept the referral**. Notify parents, develop an assessment plan, and appoint a multidisciplinary assessment team.

    B. _____ **Reject the referral**

        1.___Insufficient information to support referral purpose. Require:_____

            _____

        2.___Sufficient information provided but not indicative of suspicion that a disability exists that requires special education and related services.

        3.___Refer to alternative program. (Name program.) _____

Date: __January 15, 1991__

Signature of the SSC Chairperson: *Carla Quiñones Aponté*

them if the need for referral arises. Although documentation of such concerns may lead to the conclusion that a disability is not suspected, it may lead to a more appropriate conclusion that referral to (and potential intervention by) another source is necessary.

Expected Outcome. The referral purpose should clearly communicate what information is expected to be gained from the referral. This is important because this statement guides the gathering of information and provides the basis for subsequent consideration of the referral by the special services committee. For example, if the teacher suspects a hearing impairment and expects that the referral will result in evaluation designed to confirm the presence or absence of that impairment, this gives different direction to the special services committee than if the teacher already knows there is a hearing impairment and seeks information regarding its possible effect on performance or seeks a determination on whether the student requires a program of specially designed instruction. Likewise, a parent may refer a student, expecting only to obtain achievement information. In determining a course of action to follow regarding the referral, it is helpful to understand that the expected outcome is not the identification of a disability or even assistance in program planning but simply to report student achievement levels.

Another aspect of the expected outcome has to do with anticipated placement. Teachers may tend to leave out anticipated or desired outcomes that they feel may not be viewed positively by the special services committee that is considering the referral. In a study of teacher referral practices, Pugach (1985) noted that no referral forms indicated a perceived need for one-to-one instruction, although interviews with referring teachers revealed this to be a major expected outcome of referral and evaluation. Although placement decisions are not a part of the referral process, documenting what the teacher expects can assist the special services committee in applying differential and appropriate criteria to the review of the referral. For example, if the teacher believes that the student should receive instruction in a special education class, the special services committee would expect to find supporting evidence in the referral that the student cannot function in the regular education program. If the teacher considers that the student may require specially designed instruction but wishes to maintain responsibility for such instruction, the special services committee would not expect to find such evidence. Documenting the anticipated placement on the referral form could further increase the influence that the referral already

has on determining eligibility and placement decisions. Such a procedure, however, may add a measure of accountability by requiring that referrals intended to obtain services outside the regular program include sufficient documentation of pre-referral interventions before the formal process of evaluation and identification begins.

All information provided in the referral is expected to support the referral purpose. Two methods of providing supporting information for the referral question follow. They are verification of referral concerns and documentation of interventions attempted before referral.

Verification of Referral Concerns

Research indicates that referrals often fail to provide sufficient justification for referral concerns (Pugach, 1985; Ysseldyke, Christenson, Pianta, et al., 1982). If teacher opinions are to be considered as legitimate indicators of a student's need for special education, methods must be established to ensure that teachers and other referring individuals systematically and objectively identify and describe classroom variables and factors contributing to the student's inability to perform in the classroom. Considering once again the significance of the referral in determining program eligibility, it is essential that schools develop and enforce referral standards that ensure that the educational concerns that are so significant as to cause referral for special education programs are adequately verified in the referral by classroom performance data.

Use of pre-referral procedures can assist immeasurably with verification of referral concerns. If a pre-referral process is in place in the school, developing the referral becomes a logical next step when planned interventions fail to resolve the issue of concern. Teachers who have engaged in systematic pre-referral intervention before referral are more likely to clearly understand the nature and severity of the problem than those teachers who attempt no intervention at all. In addition, verification of the problem is likely to be readily available in the form of pre-referral intervention plans or other classroom documentation. It should be noted that individuals other than the classroom teacher can and should assist in gathering information to verify referral concerns. For example, counselors might review educational records, gather information from other teachers, and interview parents to obtain information necessary to verify concerns. Remedial education teachers might document results of educational assessment in specific areas such as reading. To verify the concern, the referral should include information that confirms the current existence of a problem, provides information on the persistence of the concern over a period of time, and states the severity of the concern.

Evidence of Current Concern.   Evidence of the current concern is an element of verification that provides objective documentation to support the educational concern summarized in the purpose of the referral. Because it is an extension of the purpose, the information included should be directly related to the concerns identified in that statement. For example, if the purpose of the referral reflected a concern related to the student's aggressive behavior, the teacher would gather documentation that provides examples of the specific behavioral concern as demonstrated in the classroom. Anecdotal records, systematic observation, and records of discipline procedures administered are all examples of ways that verification of current behavior concerns can be documented. Figure 4–8 provides an example of systematic observation of off-task behavior documented to support referral for a suspected emotional disturbance. If the teacher refers a student because of poor reading ability that causes the student to fail content areas subjects, the teacher might be expected to submit copies of failed tests, a comparison of that student's grades to others in the same class or grade, and copies of systemwide tests for reading for that year. If the teacher's primary concern is speech, a taped sample of the student's speech might accompany the referral, along with an anecdotal record of how the student's speech is believed to adversely affect educational performance in the classroom. For example, if the student's ability to participate in classroom activities or to interact appropriately with peers is affected by a speech problem, incidents that illustrate this effect should be documented for referral purposes.

The information gathered to verify educational concerns depends on the nature of the problem. For academic concerns, such information might include current work samples illustrating the specific problem, test samples, results of current systemwide tests, and current or final grades. For concerns related to motor performance, observational reports from classes such as physical education, work samples, and anecdotal records describing specific concerns are appropriate.

Persistence of the Concern.   An educational concern warranting referral for comprehensive evaluation and possible special education placement should be demonstrated to be both persistent and pervasive. Such problems usually are evident over a period of time, often from year to year, and persist in all areas that the disability might adversely affect. They also exist under otherwise normal circumstances. Thus, one might expect that a behavior concern would be demonstrated in other similar situations such as in other classes, at home, and in social situations. A reading concern would be expected to be demonstrated in other areas that require reading.

A student should not be referred to special education for transient educational problems. For example, if a student suddenly becomes difficult to manage in the classroom, although there is no history of behavior problems, referral to special education may not be appropriate. It may be that the student, far from acting abnormally, is reacting very normally under unusual circumstances in his or her environment. Any number of situations may cause such behavior, including divorce, teacher–pupil conflicts, moving from one school to another, and death in the family. Poor behavior under these circumstances might be expected from any student and is not in itself a valid reason for referral.

To verify information on the persistence of an educational concern, school procedures might require information on the student's educational history. For academic problems, the student's grades in previous years, systemwide test results from previous years, and information from parents and previous teachers may be required. For behavior problems, previous records and reports from parents and previous teachers may be required.

If a student has more than one teacher, reports from other teachers are relevant as well. One potentially effective mechanism for obtaining informal information on the persistence and pervasiveness of concerns is to establish a mechanism by which teachers can routinely share information positively and productively. As practiced in one school, the faculty is invited once a week to an early morning coffee meeting in which the faculty considers and discusses individual students and groups of students from all programs in the school. Issues covered may include specific student concerns or achievements, suggested teaching strategies by teachers familiar with the student or with the type of concern described, student progress in remedial programs and other classes, or requests for advice and/or assistance from teachers who may be working with or who have worked with a particular student. The meeting is strictly to exchange information about specific students or groups of students. Other school-related issues are not discussed, and formal decisions or recommendations are not made. The school administrator attends and chairs all meetings. Names of students to be discussed at the meeting are submitted by teachers to the administrator and are provided to faculty members in advance. If a teacher has information or can provide information regarding

FIGURE 4–8
Verification of Referral Concern

Referral Concern: Demonstrates an inability to stay on task for a period of longer than 5 minutes, kissing and hugging the teacher as well as peers at inappropriate times, standing on her head, crawling under desks, lying on her back on the floor and acting "silly." Generally interfering with the activities of the fourth-grade classroom.

Behaviors: The first category includes those behaviors that have a direct effect on academic performance. These behaviors include calling out, out of seat, unwillingness to comply, interrupting the teacher, playing in seat, and crawling on the floor. Unwillingness to comply and the out-of-seat behaviors are the most labor intense for the teacher as well as disruptive to student learning. The second category of behaviors can be characterized as social behaviors having a direct effect on the student's ability to form relationships. These behaviors include baby talk, kissing and hugging teachers and children, tears, and thumb sucking. Baby talk and kissing/hugging teachers and other students seems to have the greatest detrimental effect on student's relationship with peers.

Behavior Matrix Summary

Type	Behavior	Week of 9-13 Sept					Week of 16-20 Sept				
		Mon	Tues	Wed	Thurs	Fri	Mon	Tues	Wed	Thurs	Fri
A	1	1	1	3	11	4	60	1		1	
A	2	14	11	10	11	17	47	0		95	
A	3	9	11	10	11	17	100	11	A	42	OUT
A	4	3	0	3	6	2	2	2	B	0	
A	5	9	6	5	6	11	100	42	S	12	OF
A/B	6	3	2	0	7	5	0	0	E	5	
B	7	5	5	3	5	14	3	3	N	46	ROOM
B	8	1	0	1	3	0	0	3	T	0	
B	9	0	1	1	0	1	0	0		0	
B	10	4	2	1	4	2	8	42		3	

Unweighted Total		49	39	37	64	73	320	104		204	
Type A Totals:		36	29	31	45	51	309	56		150	
Type B Totals:		10	8	6	12	17	11	48		49	

Type: Behavior:

A 1. Calling out
A 2. Out of seat
A 3. Unwilling to comply
A 4. Interrupting teacher
A 5. Playing in seat

Type: Behavior:

A/B 6. Crawling on floor
B 7. Baby talk
B 8. Kissing & hugging
B 9. Tears
B 10. Sucking thumb

Type:

A Behavior disruptive
to academic performance

B Behavior disruptive
to social interaction

any of the students on the list, he or she attends. Such a meeting of colleagues for a purpose not dedicated to school procedures and decision making can provide a useful mechanism for the teacher in deciding whether a concern is so pervasive or persistent to warrant referral to special education. The teacher might find that the student performs adequately in another class because of a particular teaching strategy or might learn from a previous teacher a successful method for managing behavior. Group meetings such as this tend to be popular with faculty for several reasons. They provide a discretionary opportunity for focused professional interaction before the school day begins. The meetings are not mandatory but tend to be well attended because the potential for sharing and gaining student-related information is viewed as worthwhile. In addition, the school administrator actively participates in the meetings and is therefore knowledgeable regarding potential referral issues.

Severity of the Concern. Referral implies that the educational concern is pronounced to the point that a student may require specially designed instruction, that is, instruction that may differ significantly from that required by other students or normally provided as part of the regular program. Thus, information that illustrates the severity of the educational problem should be included as part of the referral. A procedure that might be considered as a standard requirement to document the severity of an educational concern is the comparison of student performance to that of other students in the same grade or class. Such a requirement can serve several purposes. First, an indication of where the referred student is performing relative to other students can provide information about possible instructional grouping in the classroom. Reviewing class achievement data or observational data may also enable the teacher to further define the reasons for referral. For instance, if a teacher sees that at least two other students perform at essentially the same level as the student being considered for referral, it might be appropriate to consider what concerns the teacher about the student in question but not about the other two students. It may be that a student's classroom behavior, rather than performance alone, prompted the teacher to refer the student.

Comparing the student concerned to the performance of others may also point out the need for refining instructional strategies. If, in comparing performance, the teacher recognizes that several students appear to perform similarly to the potential referral student, the teacher may decide that referral is inappropriate and that teaching strategies for that group of students should be modified before recon-

sidering referral. Such a procedure may also serve to identify students who may need to be referred but who have been overlooked. Finally, such a procedure, completed systematically, can assist the special services committee in gathering accurate information on teacher referral decisions.

A final aspect of verification of concerns is to provide preliminary confirmation that the suspicion of a disability is not instead the result of cultural or environmental differences. Parent involvement is a very important part of this aspect of verification and one often overlooked in verifying referral concerns. Parents ideally should be substantively as well as procedurally involved in the referral process for all students. Such involvement, however, is especially important for those students at high risk of being misdiagnosed as having a disability. These include students whose language is other than English and students of racial and ethnic minorities.

Interventions Attempted and Their Results

The previous chapter focused on pre-referral procedures as a mechanism for ensuring and documenting that all attempts are made to maintain students in the regular education program before referral for comprehensive assessment and possible special education placement. P.L. 94–142 and the courts (*Lora v. Board of Education*, 1984) have been very specific in establishing this preference. If pre-referral interventions have been documented as part of a pre-referral process, this documentation should be submitted or attached as part of the referral information. If districts have not established a pre-referral process, however, then at the point of referral, a requirement for documentation of pre-referral interventions should be established. At a minimum, the referral should include a list of interventions attempted before referring the student. A more informative requirement would be to include a brief but specific description of each intervention; the dates during which each was used; the specific results of the interventions; and other individuals involved in planning, implementing or evaluating the success of the interventions. Documentation of pre-referral strategies not only addresses the legal requirements of P.L. 94–142 but also can help to establish the fact that the referral concern is specific to the student and is not due instead to factors in the environment, instructional practices, or lack of reasonable resources in the regular program. As noted previously, these are not legitimate reasons for referral to special education.

In some cases, the necessary intervention might be obvious and may clearly rest outside of the purview of the regular program. Thus, requiring that a standard set of interventions be attempted with every student before referral may be entirely inappropriate. For example, if a student clearly requires large-print material, braille, and/or Talking Books, it would be inappropriate to spend time attempting to help the student read regular-print materials before referral, simply to fulfill a requirement for documenting interventions attempted. Likewise, if a student has been diagnosed as having a severe hearing impairment but is receiving no special education, it may not be appropriate to document interventions in the classroom to avoid specially designed instruction in auditory training.

After all referral information has been gathered, the referral should be submitted to the special services committee for consideration. The next section will provide a framework for the consideration of referrals and for making referral decisions.

ENFORCEMENT OF REFERRAL PROCEDURES

If classroom teachers have been negligent in providing specific and well-documented referral data, it might also be said that special services committee members have been negligent in allowing referrals to be processed without sufficient information. At some point in the identification process, a gatekeeping or enforcement process must be seriously administered. Considering the expense of the referral and evaluation process, in addition to the well-documented implications for misdiagnosis and placement, such a gatekeeping mechanism should be established at the point of referral. Research indicates that almost all students for whom referral forms are submitted receive a comprehensive evaluation (Algozzine et al., 1982; Pugach, 1985). Indeed, in some schools every student for whom a referral form is submitted receives a comprehensive evaluation. If inappropriate referrals are to be reduced, the special services committee must exercise its authority and responsibility to carefully consider referral information, make informed decisions regarding the adequacy of referral data, and decide whether a referral warrants comprehensive assessment and ultimate consideration for special education services.

The special services committee must decide what action to take regarding each referral. Based on the information provided, two types of decisions might be made. First, if the committee agrees that the referral is complete and that sufficient evidence has been provided to support the suspicion that a disability exists and that the student may require specially designed instruction, the referral should be

accepted. In such a case, the committee should establish an evaluation plan based on the referral and, based on the evaluation needs, should establish a multidisciplinary assessment team. It is not the classroom teacher's responsibility to decide that a student does or does not have a disability. The classroom teacher is responsible for reporting, through the referral process, students who they have reason to suspect may have a disability that adversely affects educational performance. The special services committee is responsible for either confirming the possibility that a disability may exist (in which case comprehensive assessment would occur) or determining that there is not sufficient reason to suspect that a disability exists (in which case the referral would be rejected and other means of intervention pursued).

If the committee should decide that sufficient information does not exist to warrant suspicion of a disability and a possible need for specially designed instruction, the referral should be rejected with the reasons for that action clearly specified. A referral might be rejected because the referring individual failed to complete the requirements of the referral before submitting the referral form. If referral information is incomplete or insufficient to determine the purpose of referral or to support the stated purpose of referral, the referral should be returned.

In some instances, a referral might be rejected because the committee decides that, though the referral is well prepared, the necessary intervention can be provided as part of the regular education program. In such a case, the special services committee might make suggestions for accommodating the student in the regular program, recommend additional resources for the classroom teacher, or refer the student to a remedial program within the regular education program, such as compensatory education, a reading improvement program, or a school counseling program.

PROGRAMMATIC OPTIONS

It may well be that the special education referral process is inappropriately used because teachers see it as the only option for obtaining information or additional services for a student. Because of the legal mandate for appropriate education for handicapped students, and accompanying federal and state funding, it is not unusual to find at least one special education program in schools where there are no compensatory education programs or other remedial programs. If teachers have only one option, they are likely to use it. Lack of other, more appropriate options within the regular education program may result in the special education program being perceived and used as a remedial education program. If special education programs are to be used appropriately, adequate alternative remedial programs such as compensatory education, reading improvement, second language, and counseling must be made available.

School curricula must be responsive to the needs of the students enrolled in the school. If the school curriculum is so academically oriented that few options exist for underachieving students, many may be inappropriately referred to special education programs. As part of the ongoing school self-study and school-improvement activities required for accreditation, schools should review existing curricula in the context of the needs of the various student populations within the schools. At a minimum, some provisions for students who perform poorly in school but are not suspected of having disabilities must be provided. This may mean that courses at the secondary level may have to be broader in scope to accommodate the needs of those students who do not have disabilities but who, nonetheless, may not benefit from the standard curriculum. For example, all students need at least functional knowledge related to biology, though not all may master the standard high-school biology course. While this is not purely a special education concern, a regular-education curriculum which is responsive to the needs of the student population can serve to reduce the number of inappropriate referrals to special education programs.

Other alternatives for assistance within the regular program, which may not be in the form of specific curricular programs, may include a well-organized volunteer or tutorial program. Peer-tutoring programs provide effective and inexpensive individual or group instruction to those students who may benefit from further explanation or repetition of material.

Finally, providing additional options within the regular classroom means providing resources to assist the classroom teacher in accommodating a more diverse group of students. Many classroom accommodations require additional personnel or fewer students. Programs that successfully accommodate a greater degree of diversity typically have access to instructional aides, specialized training, and time to plan for individualization within the classroom. It is unreasonable to expect that a single classroom teacher, with no additional resources and a classroom of 28 to 30 students can effectively maintain individualized instructional programs for an entire class when special education class-rooms serving the same students have for years attested to the need for small groups and instructional aides.

PARENT INVOLVEMENT IN REFERRAL

Because referral is a proposal to evaluate a student with the intent of considering the student's need for specially designed instruction and possibly special education placement, the notification requirements of P.L. 94–142 apply at the point of referral. Referral is the first point in the process at which parent involvement is required, although many schools encourage involvement during the pre-referral process. Both notice of the proposal to evaluate the student and parental consent for the evaluation are requirements that must be fulfilled before the evaluation. Notice must include the following:

1. A full explanation of all of the procedural safeguards available to the parent,
2. A description of the action proposed or refused by the agency, an explanation of why the agency proposes or refuses to take the action, and a description of any options the agency considered and the reasons why those options were rejected
3. A description of each evaluation procedure, test, record, or report the agency uses as a basis for the proposal or refusal, and
4. A description of any other factors which are relevant to the school's proposal or refusal.
   (Federal Register, 1977)

P.L. 94–142 is very clear in its requirement that notice be provided in language understandable to the general public and in the native language or mode of communication of the parent. If the language of the parents is not a written language, the school must ensure and document that the notice is translated orally and that the parent understands the notice.

Consent means the following:

1. The parent has been fully informed of all information for which consent is sought, in his or her native language or other means of communication.
2. The parent understands and agrees in writing to the carrying out of the activity for which his or her consent is sought and the consent describes that activity and lists the records, if any, which will be released and to whom, and
3. The parent understands that the granting of consent is voluntary on the part of the parent and can be revoked at any time.
   (Federal Register, 1977)

Some schools comply with these requirements by mail, sending a form letter describing the action proposed or rejected (in this case evaluation); a parent consent for evaluation form to obtain consent for the preplacement evaluation; and a list of procedural safeguards. A sample letter is shown in Figure 4–9. If the material and accompanying explanation meets the requirements of law, such practice may be technically acceptable as well as being time-efficient. However, there are two major disadvantages of using this procedure alone. First, it minimizes the amount of parent involvement in the referral issues and decisions made by the special services committee and tends to further depersonalize the relationship between the home and school. Second, considering the amount of information that the school must ensure the parents receive and understand, it would be difficult to accomplish the intent of the notice requirements by mail.

A personal meeting with parents should occur at the point of referral, if not during pre-referral. This meeting will enable the special services committee to discuss the provisions of the notice with the parents, to answer any questions, and to provide information on the procedure of the evaluation process. When meeting with the parents to provide notice, the designated school representative might use the guide illustrated in Figure 4–10 to ensure that all elements of the notice requirements of P.L. 94–142 are adequately addressed.

While consent must only be obtained before the preplacement evaluation and before initial placement in special education, the notice requirements apply every time the school proposes or refuses to change the student's identification, evaluation, or placement. Thus, it is not appropriate to provide blanket notice for all referral, evaluation, and placement activities. Parents must receive full notice anytime a change is proposed or refused.

If the parents refuse to give consent for evaluation and the school considers evaluation to be essential to determine the student's needs and to provide an appropriate education, P.L. 94–142 provides that the procedures for a due process hearing may be used, unless state laws require other provisions such as obtaining court orders for overriding the parents' refusal to consent. If a hearing officer upholds the school's decision, the school can evaluate the student without the parents' consent. Considering the negative feelings such action is likely to generate, in addition to the time and expense of a due process hearing, the special services committee should consider whether the benefits of evaluation warrant the likely consequences and further alienation of the student's parents. It is possible that intensive pre-referral interventions and informal curriculum-based measures can provide sufficient information to accommodate the student's needs without formal evaluation.

FIGURE 4–9
Sample Letter to Parents Providing Notice of Proposal to Evaluate and Seeking to Obtain Consent (Based on Referral of Joe S.)

Dear Mr. and Mrs. S.:

As you know, Joe's teacher, Mrs. Snow, has been concerned about his low performance in reading and mathematics. He is not making as much progress as we had hoped for in these areas.

In reading, Joe continues to have difficulty reading the grade-level textbooks. He has difficulty learning new words because he has not developed strategies for decoding new words (such as phonetic sounds or context clues). He also has difficulty understanding the material he reads. This is partially because he must focus so much on reading the words that he cannot pay attention to their meaning. When Joe listens to other students or the teacher read, he understands the material better.

In mathematics, Joe has difficulty understanding abstract concepts such as regrouping, place value, use of zeros, and word problems. He usually can work problems presented to him on paper when reminded of the procedure to follow, but he has difficulty in determining which math operation to use in a particular situation and when different kinds of problems are included on the same page. Although he can tell time to the hour and half hour, he does not accurately tell time to the minute. Counting change is also a problem.

Joe is also reluctant to interact and form friendships with other students, although he is always cooperative and often does his best work in groups. He is therefore often left out of games and activities by other students.

Although Joe has a number of strengths, his continuing difficulties in reading and mathematics and his reluctance to interact with other students concern us. The special services committee at Adams School has reviewed the information that Mrs. Snow and the teacher assistance team have collected on Joe's school achievement. I also have observed Joe both during class and during free-time activities. Based on this information, we is suspect that Joe may have a disability that places him at a disadvantage in achieving school success. Therefore, we recommend formal evaluation of Joe's ability and achievement. Our purpose in evaluating Joe is to identify his strengths and weaknesses so that we can best know how to help him. One possible outcome of the evaluation is that we may find that Joe has a disability that affects his educational performance and requires special education services.

We would like to administer language, social-behavioral, academic achievement, and intelligence tests, which typically are not given to all students in the school. These procedures will help us identify Joe's strengths and weaknesses in each area. We will use the information to plan his educational program. We would also like to use a procedure that will help to determine whether Joe's frequent moving, differences in culture, and differences in economic status may be primarily responsible for his educational difficulties.

Before conducting the evaluation, it is very important that you are aware of all your legal rights and protections. These are summarized to you as follows:

A. In the evaluation process the following rights are assured:
   1. Joe may not receive an initial special education evaluation unless your are previously informed and voluntarily give your consent.
   2. You may withdraw your decision to give consent at any time.
   3. You are entitled to receive an explanation of all evaluation results after the evaluation is completed.
   4. You are entitled to an explanation of any action recommended or rejected by the school, based on the evaluation result.
   5. You have the right to request an independent evaluation (conducted by someone other than the school) and have the results considered in discussions regarding Joe's educational program.

(Figure 4–9 continued)

B. **If Joe is determined to have a disability and requires special education services:**
1. The school system must provide a free, and appropriate educational program with all related services necessary for Joe to benefit from his special education program.
2. Joe will be educated in regular classes with students who do not have disabilities unless his needs cannot be met in that setting. This means, for example, that Joe may not be removed from his regular class placement, unless you and school personnel agree that his instructional needs can only be met in an alternative setting.
3. You may see and/or request copies of all of Joe's educational records and ask for an explanation of any information included in the record that you do not understand. You may also ask that information be changed if you do not agree with it.
4. All records are private. Only certain individuals, besides you, are authorized to review Joe's records. You can obtain information from the school regarding the names of these individuals.

C. **If you disagree with educational recommendations regarding Joe's educational program:**

1. You have the right to request a due process hearing. This is a meeting where an objective individual listens to all sides of the disagreement and helps to make an appropriate decision on the student's behalf. At the hearing you may use the services of a lawyer or other representative, present evidence, present and cross-examine witnesses, and obtain a written outcome of the hearing decision.
2. As with all communication between parents and the school, if you cannot hear or if you communicate in a language other than English, the hearing must be conducted so that all communication is completely understandable to you.

We cannot move ahead with Joe's evaluation unless we have your written permission. If you give your consent for this evaluation to be conducted, please sign this form below. We will be waiting to hear from you. Please either return the consent form to the school office or mail it to me in the enclosed, self-addressed, stamped envelope within the next 4 days.

If you have any questions, please feel free to call me.

Sincerely,

Steven La Joie

Steven LaJoie
Counselor

I hereby give my consent for the described evaluation to be conducted with my child. I understand that my consent is voluntary and may be revoked at any time. I understand that the results of the evaluation will be treated confidentially and that I have access to a written copy and an explanation of the results of the evaluation.

_____   _____
Signature of Parent or Guardian   Date

© 1990 Bell & Howell Co. Permission granted for noncommercial reproduction.

FIGURE 4–10
Example of Notice of Action Proposed or Rejected

Student_____

Date of Notice_____

Parents_____

A. DESCRIPTION OF ACTION PROPOSED OR REJECTED

1._____Propose to evaluate the student for possible disability and need for specially designed instruction.
2._____Propose to identify the student as having a disability and being in need of specially designed instruction.
3._____Refuse to identify the student as having a disability and being in need of specially designed instruction.
4._____Propose to provide special education and related services.
5._____Refuse to provide special education and related services.

B. REASONS FOR THE PROPOSAL OR REFUSAL

1._____
2._____
3._____
4._____
5._____

C. EVALUATION PROCEDURES, TESTS, RECORDS, OR REPORTS USED AS A BASIS FOR PROPOSAL OR REFUSAL

____Grades   ____Psychological Evaluation   ____Previous Records
____Systematic Observation   ____Individual Achievement Testing   ____Motor Evaluation
____Health Concerns   ____Adaptive Behavior Assessment   ____Visual Testing
____Schoolwide Tests   ____Speech and/or Language Assessment ____Parent Interview
____Classwork   ____Audiological Assessment
____Other_____   ____Medical Evaluation
____Past School Records   ____Other_____
                                              (Explain)

(Attach copies of referral, evaluation reports, eligibility reports, or other information used as basis for proposal or refusal)

COMMENTS:_____
_____
_____
_____
_____
_____
_____
_____
_____
_____
_____

(Figure 4–10 continued)

D. OTHER OPTIONS CONSIDERED AND REASONS WHY REJECTED

      Options Considered   Reason Rejected

_____
_____
_____
_____
_____

E. PROCEDURAL SAFEGUARDS DISCUSSED

___Prior notice and parent consent
___Protection in evaluation procedures
___Independent educational evaluation
___Confidentiality of information
___Placement in the least restrictive environment
___Opportunity to examine records
___Impartial due process hearing
___Surrogate parents assigned to act on behalf of the student

A full explanation of each of these procedural safeguards should be provided to parents, along with a copy of the specific provisions of each. If notice was for initial evaluation or initial placement, a copy of the written parent consent must be attached to this form.

F. DISTRIBUTION

Date
___Copy provided to parents in SSC meeting with full description of safeguards.
___Copy provided to parents by mail with full description of procedural safeguards.
___Copy provided to parents in another conference by_____.
                                             Name

_____   _____

Signature of Individual Providing Notice   Date

SUMMARY

This chapter has identified current issues related to the referral process and provided suggestions for establishing schoolwide referral procedures and criteria. The development of consistent and specific procedures can assist teachers and other individuals in making appropriate referral decisions and in determining the type and amount of information necessary to support the referral. It should be emphasized that responsibility for appropriate referral lies with all members of the school, especially the special services committee. Although thorough referral procedures may be time-consuming for one individual (usually the classroom teacher) to accomplish alone, conceptualizing referral as a team activity in which others can participate can serve to distribute responsibility evenly and provide information from additional sources. Teacher assistance teams, parents, resource teachers, counselors, social workers, psychologists, and administrators are appropriate participants in the development of referrals.

Based on complete referral information, the special services committee must provide formal notice to the student's parents that a potential disability is suspected and that comprehensive evaluation has been recommended. After explaining all the information on which the referral is based and informing parents of their procedural rights, the parents' written permission for initial evaluation must be obtained. After notice is provided and permission for evaluation is obtained, the multidisciplinary evaluation can be scheduled.

EVALUATION

1. You have been asked to present information on the referral process in your school to the school faculty. Discuss the purpose of referral, and justify why a significant amount of information may be necessary to support referral to special education.
2. Review the referral form used in your school or another public school. Evaluate its strengths and weaknesses, and design a new form which you consider to provide sufficient information for confirming a student's educational difficulties.
3. You are responsible for informing parents that their child has been referred for a suspected intellectual disability. Consider each of the required components of notice and consent. How would you present this information to parents so that they can fully understand it?

CHAPTER 5

Nondiscriminatory Evaluation

OBJECTIVES

1. Identify and discuss two purposes of evaluation: (1) identification and classification of a disability and (2) identification of specific areas of instructional need and program planning.

2. Identify and discuss eight requirements of P.L. 94–142 for nondiscriminatory evaluation procedures.

3. Discuss three major issues related to nondiscriminatory evaluation procedures.

4. Describe a suggested procedure for planning the multidisciplinary evaluation.

5. Differentiate between the purpose and use of norm-referenced and criterion-referenced evaluation procedures, and identify the strengths and weaknesses of each.

6. Discuss three strategies for generating a written report of evaluation results.

7. Discuss requirements for reporting evaluation results to parents.

P.L. 94–142 requires that before any action is taken with respect to the initial placement of a student in a special education program, a full and individual evaluation of the student's educational needs must be conducted (*Federal Register*, 1977). Unlike for the process of referral, P.L. 94–142 regulates the evaluation process with several requirements. In this chapter, each of the evaluation requirements of P.L. 94–142 will be reviewed, issues surrounding the process discussed, and procedures for evaluation planning and selection of evaluation procedures presented.

REQUIREMENTS OF P.L. 94–142

The parameters of the evaluation process as required by P.L. 94–142 are set forth in the law's definition of evaluation, in the requirements of the tests and procedures themselves, and in requirements governing how evaluation activities will be conducted. All of these requirements are designed to ensure that the results of evaluation are accurate, fair, and appropriate.

Definition of Evaluation

P.L. 94–142, in defining evaluation, provides a clear indication of the purpose of this activity regarding special education. Evaluation is defined as follows:

> . . . procedures used to determine whether a child is handicapped and the nature and extent of the special education and related services that the child needs. . . . The term includes procedures used selectively with an individual child and does not include basic tests administered to or procedures used with all children in a school, grade, or class. (*Federal Register*, 1977)

Thus, the purpose of evaluation is twofold. It serves (1) an identification and classification purpose to determine whether a student has a disability that adversely affects educational performance and (2) an educational planning purpose to determine the kind and amount of specialized instruction the student requires. Both are required and expected outcomes of the evaluation process for a student with a potential disability.

Identification and Classification. The first function, identification and classification of a disability, implies that the student has an identifiable disorder that adversely affects educational performance. Thus, the first function of evaluation is to determine the presence and nature of the disability. P.L. 94–142 provides a list of disabilities that are included in this definition:

> . . . those students who are evaluated as being mentally retarded, hard of hearing, deaf, speech impaired, visually handicapped, seriously emotionally disturbed, orthopedically impaired, other health impaired, deaf-blind, multi-handicapped, or as having specific learning disabilities, who *because of those impairments*, need special education and related services. (*Federal Register*, 1977)

The definitions of these disabilities, as defined by P.L. 94–142, are included in Chapter 1, Figure 1–1, page 6. According to P.L. 94–142, if a student does not have a disability, that student should not be considered for enrollment in special education, regardless of his or her educational functioning level in school. The purpose of evaluation should not be to find ways to classify students to provide specially designed instruction but to ensure that, if the student does have a disability, it does not prevent that student's access to or participation in an appropriate educational program.

Adequately fulfilling both the identification and classification function and the program-planning function of evaluation usually necessitates the use of different kinds of evaluation procedures. For example, identifying and classifying a student with a disability usually requires the use of procedures that can reliably differentiate between a typical student and one with a disability. Making such a distinction requires that the student's performance be compared to other individuals rather than to an absolute standard. For this purpose standardized, norm-referenced measures are often employed.

The identification and classification function of evaluation enables schools to fulfill the administrative requirements of P.L. 94–142 for determining and reporting the numbers of students identified and/or served in each disability area. Based on this count, schools receive funding to support the special education programs of these students.

Educational Program Planning.   The second purpose of evaluation is to determine the extent and nature of the special education that the student may require. This is the educational program-planning function of evaluation. It implies that once evaluation is completed, there will be sufficient information not only to determine whether a disability exists but to determine the student's specific instructional needs. This information will, to some degree, establish the extent of the adverse educational effect(s) and thus determine whether the student requires special education. In fact, eligibility cannot appropriately be determined without fulfilling this function of evaluation. If the student is eligible for special education, the instructional needs identified during the evaluation process should provide the basis for IEP development. If the student is not eligible, this function of evaluation will designate the specific skills that need to be addressed in the regular education program. Unfortunately, this aspect of evaluation often has been neglected in favor of the identification and classification function of evaluation. Thus, it is not unusual to find abundant (though not necessarily informative) data directed at identifying the student's disability with little or no information on the specific instruction a student may require.

Program planning requires information relevant for practical classroom application and thus should emphasize how the student's performance compares to an absolute standard rather than to other individuals. Although traditional evaluation practices tend to emphasize the use of standardized and norm-referenced achievement tests, these measures may have little usefulness for the purpose of determining the specific educational needs of a student with a disability and for the development of the IEP. The failure of current evaluation practices to fulfill the program-planning function of evaluation has led many to promote the reconceptualization of the evaluation process to include more curriculum-oriented evaluation procedures.

Criteria for Selecting Evaluation Procedures.   In addition to clarifying the purposes of evaluation, the definition of evaluation provides criteria for selecting evaluation procedures by requiring that evaluation procedures be individually designed and administered. This means that no students can be determined to have a disability and to need special education based solely on systemwide tests, screening measures, standard classroom evaluation, grades, or group-administered tests. Although these measures can be used to provide a basis for pre-referral intervention, suspicion of a disability, and referral, identification of a disability and determination of the need for specially designed instruction must be based on individualized measures.

Procedural Requirements

P.L. 94–142 also imposes specific requirements on all tests and other evaluation materials used for the stated purpose of evaluation. These are designed as protections for students in the evaluation process to ensure that evaluation procedures are selected and administered so that they do not have a racially or culturally discriminatory effect.

Discriminatory evaluation practices—particularly regarding the administration and interpretation of intelligence tests used for the purpose of classifying and placing minority students in special education programs—have been documented by several court cases. These cases have provided the basis for the evaluation protections provided by P.L. 94–142. The precedent-setting, and perhaps best known, case of this nature is *Larry P. v. Riles* (1979). This case was initiated in 1971 and concerned the disproportionate classification and placement of black students in special education classes for students with intellectual disabilities based on the results of intelligence testing. The issue of cultural and racial bias in evaluation procedures and practices has been repeatedly addressed and confirmed by other court decisions including *Mattie T. v. Holliday* (1979), *Lora v. Board of Education* (1984), *PASE v. Hannon* (1980), and *Marshall v. McDaniel* (1984). The provisions of P.L. 94–142 regarding protection in evaluation procedures are similar to those provided in these cases. The law specifically requires that tests and other evaluation materials must have the following characteristics:

1. provided and administered in the child's native language or other mode of communication, unless clearly not feasible to do so.
2. administered by trained personnel in conformance with the instructions provided by their producer.
3. validated for the specific purpose for which they are used,
4. tailored to assess specific areas of educational need and not just to obtain a single general intelligence quotient,
5. selected and administered to best ensure that tests reflect aptitude or achievement or whatever factors they are designed to measure and not the effects of impaired sensory, manual, or speaking skills, unless these are the factors which are intended to be measured.
6. no single procedure can be used as the sole criterion for determining an appropriate educational program for a child,
7. The evaluation must be made by a multidisciplinary team or group of persons, including at least one teacher or other specialist with knowledge in the area of suspected disability, and
8. The child must be assessed in all areas related to the suspected disability including, where appropriate, health, vision, hearing, social and emotional status, general intelligence, academic performance, communication status, and motor abilities.

(*Federal Register*, 1977)

Primary Language. Each of the requirements from the preceding list stems from previous injustices in evaluation practices regarding student identification and placement in special education classes. For example, the seemingly obvious requirement that a student must be evaluated in his native language or other mode of communication was originally based on findings of the court in *Diana v. State Board of Education* (1970). In this case, students whose primary language was Spanish were evaluated in English using intelligence tests developed for and normed on white, English-speaking students. Not surprisingly, these students received low scores on the tests and, on the basis of the results, were classified as having mental retardation and placed in special education programs for students with intellectual disabilities. Though it may not be likely that such gross misuse of these measures would now occur, equally damaging problems can still arise when students with limited English proficiency are administered language tests in English, and are, on the basis of test results, placed in special education programs for students with learning disabilities or communication disabilities. While the academic problems of students for whom English is a second language may be

significant and real, identifying them as having disabilities and placing them in special education programs is not an appropriate way to address these problems.

Trained and Qualified Evaluators. Because of the importance of the decision to be made based on evaluation results, P.L. 94–142 requires that only those individuals who are trained and qualified to administer and use specific tests and evaluative materials be involved in the administration and interpretation of evaluation procedures. This does not mean, however, that only psychologists can perform evaluation functions. The individual qualified to administer a test or other procedure depends on the procedure to be used. For example, the administration of intelligence tests requires very specific training in administration, scoring, and interpretation. Psychologists are usually trained in these procedures. If an evaluator has not been specifically trained, that individual should not administer that measure. Other tests and procedures, which may also require specific training and expertise, are best administered by teachers. For example, use of curriculum-based evaluation techniques to identify the adverse educational effect of a disability for a student being considered for special education may require specific expertise in item development to ensure that the measure developed reflects the curriculum actually taught in the classroom. Just as it is unlikely that teachers would be trained to administer intelligence tests, it is unlikely that many psychologists have sufficient curriculum knowledge to develop and administer curriculum-based classroom evaluation measures.

In addition to being adequately trained and qualified, the individual administering the evaluation procedure must administer the test in the way directed by the producer to ensure that, to the extent appropriate, the results accurately reflect the test's intended purpose. This means that, if a commercially produced standardized test is used, the test manual should be studied carefully. The individual administering the test should be thoroughly familiar with the test's intended purpose; the nature of each subtest and its educational meaning; the procedures for administration, scoring, and interpretation; and the characteristics of the population on which the test was normed. Often, parents and other professionals ask what a particular score means, or how a particular subtest differs from another in what it actually measures and how it relates to the educational program in which the student is not performing. The individual administering the test is expected to be able to answer these questions. Evaluation has an interpretation as well as an administration component. Accurate interpretation is a vital aspect of evaluation and the aspect in which most parents and teachers are interested. It is the responsibility of the individual administering the procedure to ensure that the interpretation is accurate.

Validated for the Purpose Used. P.L. 94–142 requires that tests and other material be validated for the specific purpose for which they are used. *Validity* refers to the degree to which a test actually measures what it claims to measure. If a norm-referenced standardized test is selected, the special services committee must ensure that the test has been validated by the producer for the purpose for which the committee intends to use it with a specific student. If a criterion-based or curriculum-based measure is selected, the special services committee must also ensure that the procedure accurately measures the skill, performance, or behavior intended. Considering the many concerns currently related to issues of validity in evaluation procedures, the reader is encouraged to obtain a working knowledge of this concept. Although this book will not address the issue of validity in detail, a brief description will be provided here.

Briefly stated, validity can be demonstrated in three interrelated ways. These are content validity, criterion validity, and construct validity. Content validity is based on (1) a judgment of what the content of a measure should be, (2) whether the items included in the measure are appropriate to the identified content, (3) whether they adequately sample the intended content, and (4) whether the way in which the items are constructed accurately measures the content (Salvia & Ysseldyke, 1978). Many curriculum-based measures claim high content validity because they are based directly on the curriculum used in the school. A curriculum-based measure, however, does not automatically have content validity simply because it purports to measure a student's performance in relation to a specific curriculum. Users of these procedures must ensure that the measure does, in fact, measure the actual curriculum.

Criterion validity is based on the assumption that a specific score on a test or procedure is an actual indication of that student's performance on the criterion that the score supposedly measures (Salvia & Ysseldyke, 1978). For example, if a student's performance on one procedure, a curriculum-based measure, corresponds closely to performance on another procedure measuring the same skill, perhaps a standardized achievement test, the curriculum-based measure might be said to have criterion validity, assuming that the standardized norm-referenced test is valid.

Finally, construct (or predictive) validity is based on the degree to which the measurement of certain skills can accurately predict, through inference and evidence, performance in other areas which cannot be directly measured (Salvia & Ysseldyke, 1978). For example, college aptitude might be inferred by scores on the Scholastic Aptitude Test (SAT). The degree to which SAT scores predict success in college provides an indication of its validity as a predictive device.

Not only must tests be validated by their producer for the purpose for which they are used, but they must be used for the purpose for which they are validated. Many norm-referenced tests have been validated for the purposes for which their producers intended them to be used, but in actual evaluation practice, they may be selected and used to perform functions for which they have not been specifically validated. For example, in the previously mentioned case of *Larry P. v. Riles*, which considered the use of intelligence tests with black students, the court found that the practice of using intelligence tests with black students had the discriminatory effect of labeling a disproportionate number of black students in classes for students with intellectual disabilities. This purpose is somewhat different than the intended purpose of intelligence testing, which does not focus on placement at all but focuses on predicting future school performance. The use of scores on intelligence tests to determine placement is a decision-making function of individuals rather than the function of the test itself. As a result of the discriminatory effect that use of intelligence tests scores had on the decisions made by placement committees, the courts banned the use of intelligence testing for the purpose of labeling and placement of black students in special education programs in California.

Assessment of Specific Areas of Educational Need. The requirement of assessment of specific areas of educational need reinforces the program-planning and intervention purposes of evaluation. In addition to and regardless of the measures used to identify and classify a student according to a specific disability area, the evaluation must assess specific areas of educational need. Although a great deal of criticism has been directed at the use of standardized and norm-referenced tests for the purpose of assessing specific areas of educational need, most states currently require that districts administer these achievement tests to determine program eligibility. These tests are often preferred to less formal (though perhaps more useful) measures because they can numerically compare a student's actual performance with an expected performance. Increasingly however, many school systems are beginning to focus more on the use of criterion-referenced and curriculum-based measures to assess specific areas of educational need and to corroborate the results of standardized and norm-referenced achievement testing. The relative merits of standardized and norm-referenced measures as opposed to criterion and curriculum-referenced measures will be described later in this chapter.

Test Results Reflect Areas Measured. Evaluation procedures must be selected and administered to best ensure that evaluation results reflect the student's actual aptitude or achievement (or whatever is intended to be measured) in an area, rather than the effects of sensory, manual, or speaking difficulties on the student's performance. This means that ability and achievement tests that require and emphasize listening and understanding verbal directions should not be administered to students with hearing disabilities; tests that require writing should not be administered to students with motor disabilities that limit their ability to write; and tasks that require reading or visual attention to detail should not be administered to students with visual disabilities. Although these considerations may seem obvious components of an individually determined evaluation, the process may at times become so routine and the demands for timeliness so great that those responsible for planning the evaluation fail to pay close attention to student characteristics, which may bias the results obtained from specific measures (Bennett, 1983). Nonetheless, the special services committee's responsibility is to ensure that these factors are always considered in the selection, administration, and reporting of evaluation procedures.

In some instances evaluation measures that completely eliminate the possibility of bias are not available. When it is necessary to use a procedure that yields a potentially biased view of the student's ability or skill level, the procedure must be used very cautiously and should be supplemented by other measures that may reflect a more accurate view of the student's ability (such as adaptive behavior scales; parent, teacher, and student interviews; and direct observation). In addition, the potential effects of the student's disability on the results of the evaluation should always be discussed in the evaluation report.

Use of More Than One Procedure. No single procedure can be used as the sole criterion for determining that a student has a disability and requires special education. For example, a student with a language disorder cannot be determined to have a disability and to need special education based solely on the results of a test of language development. Likewise, to confirm an intellectual disability, an intelligence test plus a measure of adaptive behavior must be administered. For a student suspected of having a learning disability, an intelligence test plus achievement tests often are required.

The requirement for more than one evaluation procedure is often interpreted to mean that more than one standardized test must be administered. This interpretation may result in needless evaluation procedures such as administering achievements tests to students whose achievement is of no concern or administering two articulation tests to a student suspected of having an articulation disorder when one test may be sufficient to determine the presence of a disability. With a broader interpretation of the definition of evaluation, evaluation procedures might be viewed as including observation in the classroom, taped language samples, teacher report of adverse educational effect, and vision and hearing evaluation if not already completed. Some interpretations of this requirement, in fact, view standardized norm-referenced tests as only one procedure, regardless of how many are administered. This interpretation would imply that procedures in addition to standardized tests not only should, but must, be used.

Multidisciplinary Team. P.L. 94–142 requires that the evaluation be conducted by a multidisciplinary team or group of persons including at least one teacher or other specialist with knowledge in the area of suspected disability. This requirement is intended to minimize the effects of individual bias in the evaluation process and to use the collective knowledge and perspective of a team of individuals in evaluating educational concerns.

The intention of P.L. 94–142 is clear in its requirement that evaluation be multidisciplinary. It does not mean that procedures from different disciplines can be administered by one person. Thus, it is not appropriate for the school psychologist, for example, to administer, score, and interpret multiple evaluation procedures. Neither is it appropriate for the school to refer a student to a physician to unilaterally evaluate and determine whether the student is eligible for special education services. Neither should a speech therapist be the only member of the multidisciplinary evaluation team for a student with a speech or language disorder. The intention of P.L. 94–142 is that individuals from different disciplines be actively involved in the evaluation process. This means that a number of different individuals might serve on the multidisciplinary evaluation team.

Although one member of the evaluation team must be a teacher or other specialist with knowledge in the area of suspected disability, the other members of the team should be selected based on the information required to address the evaluation questions raised by the referral. Potential members might include classroom teachers who provide pre-referral information or curriculum-based assessment information; parents who provide developmental, background, and family information regarding their child; physicians who have diagnosed a physical disability; administrators who have observed the student; health personnel who monitor health disabilities in schools; psychologists who have administered formal evaluation measures; or social workers who have interviewed the student and family. Essentially, any individual who is qualified to provide needed information for appropriate decision-making should be considered. This does not mean that all team members must or should be present to determine eligibility and develop an IEP. It does mean that those synthesizing the results of evaluation and those making the eligibility determination should have access to and should consider the evaluative information provided by individuals from multiple disciplines, including information provided by parents.

In establishing evaluation procedures for a specific student, the special services committee should refer to these requirements to ensure that they are addressed in each case. Perhaps conscientious attention to fulfilling the requirements of the law will assist in alleviating some of the major concerns with current evaluation practices, which are discussed in the next section.

CONCERNS REGARDING CURRENT EVALUATION PRACTICE

Evaluation procedures used to identify a student as having a disability and needing special education continue to be the subject of much controversy. Of primary concern is the large number of students evaluated and subsequently classified as having mild-to-moderate learning disabilities. Despite rigid requirements, current evaluation practices may have fallen short of their intended purpose for many students identified and classified as having mild disabilities.

Inadequate Criteria for Diagnosing Mild Disabilities

Even though one primary purpose of evaluation is to provide a legitimate basis for identifying disabilities, research indicates that evaluation technology has not provided a reliable mechanism for identifying and isolating characteristics for the accurate diagnosis of mild learning disabilities (Ysseldyke, Algozzine, Shinn, et al., 1982). While physical disabilities, hearing disabilities, and visual disabilities are usually easily

diagnosed by medical evaluation and are characterized by clearly discernible medical criteria, procedures for diagnosing mild intellectual, learning, and emotional disabilities do not so easily distinguish students with disabilities from other underachieving students. There appear to be no reliable psychometric differences between students classified as having learning disabilities and those considered to be low achievers. For example, one study reflected a 96% overlap between scores for these two groups on more than 40 psychometric measures (Ysseldyke, Algozzine, Shinn, et al., 1982). The significance of the lack of clearly discernible criteria for identifying mild disabilities is apparent when one considers that the population of students with mild disabilities accounts for over 40% of the population identified and enrolled in special education programs (Reschley, 1987).

Bias in Classification and Placement Practices

Evaluation procedures, including test selection, scoring, and interpretation, and subsequent decision-making, have failed to eliminate bias in classification and placement practices. Although P.L. 94–142 specifically prohibits discrimination in evaluation procedures in theory, the most often used evaluation procedures and instruments to identify and classify students as having disabilities still perpetuate discrimination in diagnosis and placement of students in special education who are racially and culturally different (Heller et al., 1982 *Lora v. Board of Education*, 1984; Ortiz & Maldonado-Colon, 1986). Research consistently indicates that students from low-income and minority families score lower on tests of intelligence and achievement than do white middle-class students (Cohen, 1969; Williams, 1970) and that typical evaluation procedures tend to be biased against students from minority and low-income families. (L. S. Fuchs & Fuchs, 1986).

According to Salvia and Ysseldyke (1978), acculturation is the most important characteristic in evaluating a student's performance on a test. If a student's experiential background differs from that of the students on whom a test is normed, results and subsequent decisions based on those results may be invalid. Although some would contend that low-income and minority populations simply have disproportionate numbers of individuals with disabilities (implying that the tests themselves are valid), the technical characteristics of many evaluation measures currently used are considered to be inappropriate for identifying disabilities in minority groups because the population on which the tests are normed do not adequately represent minority segments of the population and because significant numbers of test items are based on white, middle-class values and experiences (Williams, 1970).

Although P.L. 94–142 requires that tests and procedures be validated for the purpose for which they are used, many often employed evaluation instruments provide no evidence that students with disabilities have been included in the development of test norms, items, and measures of reliability and validity (D. Fuchs, Fuchs, Benowitz, & Barringer, 1987). To be valid indicators of aptitude or achievement for students with specific disabilities, tests used should include students with disabilities in the group on which the measure is normed (Salvia & Ysseldyke, 1978).

Failure to Generate Basis for Differential Placement or Program Planning

Current evaluation procedures have, in many instances, failed to generate a basis for determining the need for differential placement based on a student's instructional needs. Heller et al. (1982), in a review of major issues related to referral, assessment, placement, and instruction of students in special education, found no evidence that students with mild intellectual and learning disabilities require instructional methodologies significantly different from those successful with other underachieving or slow-learning students. In addition, many evaluation procedures currently used to evaluate students with potential disabilities fail to identify strategies for remediating problems and fail to provide a basis for instructional planning because the content of these tests may have little relevance to the curriculum in which the child is actually instructed (J. R. Jenkins & Pany, 1978).

Many of the noted shortcomings of the evaluation process as currently used are associated with the indiscriminate use of psychological tests of intelligence and standardized, norm-referenced achievement tests in identifying, placing, and planning instruction for students with disabilities. These shortcomings, however, often reflect traditional practices and, though perhaps compounded by the use of inadequate measures, are perpetuated by established routine, resistance to change, and failure to develop and use appropriate alternatives. These are problems unrelated to the limitations of tests themselves. To change current practice, special services committees must be willing to change evaluation practices as well as to consider alternative procedures. It is important for these teams to periodically reconsider the nondiscriminatory provisions of P.L. 94–142 and consider alternative methods for appropriate consideration of student educational needs.

Misconceptions Regarding the Requirements of P.L. 94–142

An important distinction to be made when considering the process of evaluation is the use of the term *procedures* as opposed to the term *tests* in the definition of evaluation provided by P.L. 94–142. The law defines evaluation in terms of procedures used for the purpose of identification and placement of students with disabilities. This implies a broad definition of alternatives available to fulfill the evaluation function appropriately. In many respects, however, evaluation has become synonymous with the use of commercially produced norm-referenced tests to identify and classify a student's disability and to establish the need for special education. In fact, most states require that program eligibility be based on standardized and norm-referenced measures of achievement and intelligence testing. Such tests are one, but certainly not the only, procedure that might be used to fulfill this function. Other procedures might include structured interviews, systematic observation, and criterion and curriculum-based evaluation, when these procedures are used individually with a particular student and in keeping with the requirements of P.L. 94–142.

A second misconception regarding evaluation procedures is the belief that P.L. 94–142 requires the administration of intelligence tests as a part of the comprehensive evaluation process for all students suspected of having a disability. Although many states do require such a measure, P.L. 94–142 does not require the use of intelligence tests to determine eligibility for special education unless such tests are necessary to determine whether a student has a disability. Intelligence tests often may be administered unnecessarily as a component of a standard evaluation battery because schools have assigned significant value to the information that these measures provide. Schools have traditionally used intelligence tests to determine subaverage general intellectual functioning for mental retardation and to establish a student's ability for the purpose of measuring discrepancy between ability and performance for learning disabilities. Considering the heavy reliance on and confidence in these measures over a period of time, establishing new, albeit more educationally appropriate measures, may be difficult.

A third and final misconception regarding evaluation procedures is the common belief that the evaluation process begins after referral and that only information obtained during the evaluation period between referral and eligibility determination can provide the basis for considering whether a student has a disability and is eligible for special education and related services. This misconception often may be responsible for a committee's failure to consider valuable evaluation information at the point of eligibility and may have perpetuated the focus on the results of standardized and norm-referenced tests administered between referral and eligibility. In reality, P.L. 94–142 does not define evaluation in terms of, or confine evaluation activities to, a set period of time. To the extent that any evaluation measure can contribute valid information to the evaluation process, it should be considered. Evaluation may consist of procedures used throughout the pre-referral period and may even include information obtained during previous years as long as the information is currently accurate, relevant to the decision to be made, and meets the requirements of P.L. 94–142. The essential factor in designing and selecting evaluation procedures to be used with any student is the ability and cognizance of the group of individuals who make the decisions regarding the selection of evaluation procedures. Members of the special services committee must be fully informed regarding their responsibility in administering the legal requirements of P.L. 94–142 and those of the state and be responsible for the appropriate selection and use of evaluation procedures. The remainder of this chapter will provide a discussion of various evaluation procedures and will provide a systematic method of selecting appropriate evaluation procedures for students suspected of having a disability and requiring special education.

EVALUATION PLANNING

Evaluation procedures should be designed to specifically address the stated and agreed on purpose of the referral. The multidisciplinary evaluation is not intended to assess a student in all possible disability areas or to assess educational performance in and provide program planning information for all possible areas. Evaluation is intended to provide specific and detailed information related to a possible disability and specific details of performance in areas of specific educational concern. Thus, if the referral does not reflect a concern in academic areas, and the special services committee agrees, there is no reason to evaluate a student's academic performance. If there is no concern regarding intellectual functioning, then intelligence testing is irrelevant to the purpose of referral.

A Written Plan for Evaluation

Some evaluators may tend to select evaluation procedures routinely, without considering the purpose of the evaluation, the technical adequacy of the

procedures for the purpose, or even the basic test information contained in the user manual (Bennett, 1983). Considering the potential liability for using inappropriate evaluation procedures, special services committee members and others responsible for planning and administering evaluation measures should ensure that the evaluation planned for a student is carefully considered and designed appropriately for both its intended purpose and for the student being evaluated. If the special services committee considers the referral to be appropriate, a written plan for evaluation should be developed.

Development by the Committee. The development of a written evaluation plan by the special services committee can ensure that consideration is given to designing an evaluation that specifically addresses the purpose of the referral. The evaluation plan documents what assessment will be conducted based on the questions raised by the referral. Figure 5–1 provides a sample format for such a plan. The plan should be completed at the time the referral is accepted (or shortly thereafter). The referring individual should, if possible, be present to contribute any information relative to special considerations for evaluation. For example, the student may work better at a particular time of the day or may require other special considerations in evaluation procedures.

It may be acceptable for the special services committee to pass the responsibility for evaluation planning to the multidisciplinary evaluation team, once appointed. The responsibility for appropriate decision making, however, lies with the local education agency, which in most instances assigns this responsibility to the special services committee in each school. Thus, the special services committee has ultimate responsibility for ensuring that evaluation procedures are appropriate for addressing the educational concern for a particular student.

Document the Purpose of Referral. To develop the evaluation plan, the special services committee should first document the purpose of the referral, which has been confirmed with the referring individual, usually the classroom teacher, and determined to be appropriate. Depending on the purpose of the referral, and the verification and intervention information it provides, the committee can develop specific procedures to be used selectively with an individual student.

Document Procedures for Identification of a Disability. It should be remembered that evaluation, according to P.L. 94–142, has a twofold purpose (1) to identify the student's potential disability and (2) to

FIGURE 5–1
Evaluation Plan

Student's Name _____

School _____

Date of Plan _____

Purpose of Referral

_____

_____

_____

_____

Evaluation Procedures	Purpose	Person Responsible

Signatures of Those Completing Plan

_____   _____

_____   _____

Attach a copy of parent permission for assessment when received.
Attach all assessment reports to this form.

Date Evaluation Procedures Completed _____

identify areas of specific educational need. Thus, the evaluation plan might first document evaluation procedures for determining whether a disability exists. For example, the referral might indicate that an emotional disturbance is suspected and that the area of educational concern is inappropriate behavior characterized by an inability to maintain satisfactory interpersonal relationships with peers and teachers and a general and pervasive mood of unhappiness. The special services committee might first establish an evaluation procedure for determining whether the student has a disability, in this case, an emotional disturbance. If state criteria require a diagnosis by a child psychologist or a psychiatrist, this procedure would be included on the evaluation plan and the appropriate clinician included as a member of the multidisciplinary assessment team. If state-established criteria do not dictate what evaluation procedure must be used to diagnose an emotional disturbance, the special services committee should determine what evaluation procedures can best establish the existence of an emotional disturbance based on the regulations and definitions of P.L. 94–142 and include them on the evaluation plan.

Procedures for Determining Adverse Effect. The committee should next establish evaluation procedures for documenting the possible adverse educational effect of the disability. The committee might agree to use objective and well-formulated criterion-referenced or curriculum-based evaluation measures generated by the classroom teacher during the pre-referral process. These measures may consist of observational data, anecdotal records, and academic performance data gathered over a period of 6 to 8 months and may even include data collected in previous years to document the existence of the concern over an extended period of time. The committee also may determine that a standardized, norm-referenced measure of achievement, a behavior rating scale, or a social work evaluation is necessary to confirm the adverse effect of the suspected disability on educational performance. These procedures should be documented, and the name of the individual responsible for collecting or interpreting the information should be included as a member of the multidisciplinary evaluation team. All procedures used to determine that a student has a disability and requires special education must be sufficiently valid for the purpose for which they are used. Many procedures that alone may not be considered by the committee to be valid for the purpose of identification and placement may be used to support information gained from other procedures that are considered valid for this purpose.

Other Information to Assist in Eligibility Determination. The committee may document on the plan all evaluation procedures that will be used and considered at the time of eligibility determination. For example, if vision and hearing screenings have not been performed, these procedures should be included in evaluation planning. In addition to procedures to be scheduled, the evaluation plan might include some procedures that already have been completed. For example, if the referring individual conducted well-defined, curriculum-based evaluation before submitting the referral, this information should clearly be documented as an evaluation procedure to assist in making an eligibility determination. Including aspects of the pre-referral interventions that are relevant to answering referral concerns can provide valuable data for the interpretation of data collected by other measures. The teacher or the individual who collected the data should be included as a member of the multidisciplinary evaluation team.

Identification of Student Characteristics. Cultural and environmental factors must be considered in the selection of appropriate evaluation procedures. If the student is of low socioeconomic status, and/or is a member of a minority ethnic or racial group known to be at risk of discrimination in evaluation and educational decision making, or if the student has other characteristics that may bias evaluation results or subsequent decision making (such as short attention, motor problems, or poor vision), these characteristics should be noted on the evaluation plan. The special services committee should identify how these student characteristics might bias the evaluation results and should attempt to control such bias through the selection of appropriate evaluation procedures. For example, the items and normative data for an existing norm-referenced adaptive behavior scale might be considered inadequate for measuring adaptive behavior for a particular student. The special services committee might instead select a criterion-referenced measure for which items are considered to measure the skills of the student fairly. To test the intelligence of a student with poor reading ability, the special services committee might choose an intelligence test that does not require reading. When completed, the evaluation plan should include all evaluation procedures that the special services committee plans to consider in determining the student's eligibility for special education.

In addition to providing a systematic process for determining what evaluation procedures are considered appropriate for a specific student, the evaluation plan can provide written documentation of all evaluation procedures that the committee plans to consider in determining program eligibility. P.L. 94–142 requires that in interpreting evaluation data and in making placement decisions, the eligibility committee draw on information from a variety of sources including aptitude and achievement tests, teacher recommendations, physical condition, social or cultural background, and adaptive behavior. Information obtained from these sources may be considered an evaluation procedure if such consideration provides information relative to making a program eligibility decision. Including these procedures on the evaluation plan provides an indication of the variety of sources of information used to make eligibility decisions.

The use of a written evaluation plan may help the special services committee to systematically consider evaluation results in determining program eligibility. Current research indicates that placement decisions often appear unrelated to data presented during eligibility meetings (Ysseldyke, Algozzine, Richey, et al., 1982). In some instances this may be because decisions are actually based on relevant, but undocumented data, rather than on the results of norm-referenced standardized tests, which may often be the only evaluation data presented at eligibility meetings. Specifying the information (both norm-referenced and criterion or curriculum-based) that will be considered in determining eligibility can provide direction to the information discussed at eligibility meetings and can ensure that only information relevant to the eligibility decision is presented.

The evaluation plan should be signed by the recorder, and the names of those present should be listed. The date of the plan can serve as a uniform indication of the time evaluation began and can also provide a basis on which to establish the anniversary date of the 3-year re-evaluation required by P.L. 94–142.

DETERMINING THE APPROPRIATE EVALUATION PROCEDURE

Considering that few evaluation procedures used alone provide a fully accurate, valid, and relevant set of results, special services committees often must choose the elements that are of most importance in a particular evaluation situation. One way to briefly compare evaluation measures is to first consider what elements are most important in a test to obtain the evaluation data needed. Elements that should be considered in the selection of evaluation procedures include the content, norms, standardization, and validity of the evaluation measure selected.

Content

The special services committee might first consider the importance of test content in the decision to be made. Commercially produced norm-referenced tests usually sample a broad range of skills that are considered to be "typical" of the curriculum taught in most schools. Test items based on the sampled skills are administered to a large group of students to determine typical student performance. Thus, if the committee wishes to determine how a student performs relative to others on a broad range of reading skills, a norm-referenced achievement test might be selected. If, however, the special services committee requires information about the student's mastery of specific reading skills, the content of the test must fully represent the area measured with multiple test items for each skill measured. For example, if the committee wants to determine whether a student has mastered the reading skills covered in the third-grade curriculum in a particular school, the content of the measure selected in this instance would have to reflect the curriculum of the third grade in that particular school and should do so in specific detail.

If it is not essential that the content of the measure be tied to the curriculum of the local school, but careful evaluation of skills is nonetheless required, the special services committee might select a well-constructed, commercially produced criterion-referenced test designed to measure skill attainment in one area. While it would be advantageous to use evaluation measures that both compare students with one another and provide an appropriate basis for program planning, committee members should consider that many tests that purport to provide a widespread reference group for comparing students, as well as sufficient content for the purpose of instructional planning, may suffer in overall effectiveness (Salvia & Ysseldyke, 1978).

Norms

If it is important to know where a student ranks in relation to other students, the availability of test norms is essential. The norm group is a reference group chosen to provide a basis for comparison of student performance and can be selected based on the information needed by the school. For example, national norms have significance for all school systems wishing to compare the performance of their students to others in the country. The norms of the test are established and standardized to reflect patterns of performance for students nationwide. National norms, however, indicate only patterns of performance and do not purport to provide specific instructional information for individual students.

Because the items on norm-referenced tests usually provide only a sample of skills in the area measured, in-depth analysis of specific skill components is not usually possible. The necessity of norms in the evaluation procedure depends on the decision to be made based on the measure. When the purpose of evaluation is to identify a disability or to illustrate the degree to which a student differs from the "typical" student in a particular area, norms are needed.

There are other types of norms besides national norms. State, district, school, and even class norms can be developed. In addition, norms can be developed based on specific populations such as on individuals who cannot hear, or individuals in particular professions. Norms based on specific groups or geographic locations can be more accurate in comparing performances among members of that group or population. The groups on which such norms are based, however, can accurately represent only the population from which they are drawn. Thus, they can be interpreted only to define a student's performance relative to that narrowly defined group.

Standardization

Standardization refers to consistency in administering, scoring, and interpreting an evaluation measure. In a commercially produced standardized test, the producer ensures that instructions, materials, and time allowances for the test are consistent and specific so that the test can always be presented in the same way to all students. By doing so, all students will take the test under the same, and thus, comparable, conditions. A test that has been developed in this way and administered to a well-defined group can be considered standardized. Standardization is always important when the performance of a student is to be compared to that of other students. Standardization is also important in measuring student progress over a given time period (for example, from 1 year to another), because to do so accurately, the conditions under which the evaluations occur must be comparable. Both commercially produced and locally developed tests can be standardized. Commercially produced measures, however, usually have been rigorously normed and standardized, whereas locally developed measures usually lack the same level of technical adequacy.

Validity and Reliability

Validity is the extent to which a test or procedure measures what it is intended to measure. Generally, producers of evaluation instructions attempt to establish the validity of their instruments in at least one of the three areas of validity (content, criterion,

and/or construct validity). Special services committees and evaluators are responsible for ensuring that the measures used to classify and determine needed special education are both valid and reliable. Curriculum-based measures can, if properly constructed, have high criterion and content validity. For example, Deno, Mirkin, and Chiang (1982) found that curriculum-based reading measures—such as cloze procedures, saying the meanings of words underlined in the text, reading aloud from isolated word lists, and reading aloud from text passages—were highly correlated with performance on specific standardized tests of reading. This means that if both accurately measure what they intend to measure (validity) and both consistently differentiate between groups of students (reliability), the preferred measure may be the curriculum-based measure, because it is based directly on the curriculum of the classroom. Program planning relevant to the classroom curriculum is thus available. Curriculum-based evaluation procedures, if used for the purpose of identification and program planning, must also be validated for the purpose for which they are used.

Reliability is the degree to which a test provides consistent measurement. For example, if a student were to receive the same or a comparable score on repeated measures of the same test, that test would be considered to be reliable. If the scores varied significantly and unpredictably among administrations, however, the test might be considered unreliable. It is important for evaluation measures to be reliable in the information they provide. Otherwise, if scores varied significantly every time the test was administered, there would be no point in evaluating student performance.

Although standardized norm-referenced tests are often rigorously constructed to meet validity and reliability standards, it cannot always be assumed that scores resulting from tests are reliable for the purpose of program planning and evaluation (Deno, 1985). For example, scores measuring the same skill area can vary significantly among measures, and both scores can conceivably vary significantly from a student's appropriate program placement (Eaton & Lovitt, 1972). Conversely, it cannot always be assumed that locally developed, curriculum-based measures cannot be reliable in differentiating between students. In a series of studies regarding the validity and reliability of curriculum-based assessment measures, Deno et al. (1982) found that specific curriculum-based measures could consistently discriminate between students who were in special education classes and those who were not. Although this is not the same as discriminating between who needs special education and who does not, curriculum-based assessment techniques hold promise for establishing an identification system closely tied to the curriculum of the school.

STANDARDIZED AND NORM-REFERENCED MEASURES

One of the most controversial issues in evaluation is the debate over the use of norm-referenced versus criterion and curriculum-based evaluation techniques in identification and program planning for students with disabilities. In part, this controversy stems from the realization that despite their widespread acceptance and use, standardized and norm-referenced tests alone may not always be sufficiently valid and reliable for performing the required evaluation functions of P.L. 94–142, primarily, accurate identification of specific disabilities and determination of specific areas of educational need. This controversy emphasizes the need for special services committees and evaluators to accurately and systematically identify what information the evaluation is expected to yield and to selectively choose measures that will fulfill that function. Depending on the information required, both standardized and norm-referenced and criterion-referenced measures may be required, though each has specific purposes for which it is best suited.

Definition and Purpose of Standardized and Norm-Referenced Tests

Standardized and norm-referenced tests are probably the most widely accepted measures of achievement and ability in use in schools today. In many states these measures must be used to document that a student has a disability and needs special education. Although both commercially produced and locally produced tests can be standardized and even norm referenced, schools typically think of and refer to standardized and norm-referenced tests as those commercially produced. In this book standardized and norm-referenced tests refer to commercially produced tests.

The primary function of norm-referenced tests is to *differentiate between students* by showing how a particular student performs on a given measure relative to other typical students of the same age and grade. For example, the hearing acuity of a student who has a hearing disability would be expected to differ significantly from the typical individual. Likewise, a student who has an intellectual disability would be expected to differ significantly on parameters of intelligence from the typical student. Because the process of identifying disabilities (as well as

giftedness) is based on accurate identification of significant differences, tests that purport to measure these differences in a population must attempt to accurately define what is typical. By carefully selecting a broad range of test items that are considered to be representative of the entire area measured, and by including a large and representative sample of the population in test development, test makers hope to create valid and reliable measures of performance by which to determine typical performance in specific areas.

Because standardized norm-referenced tests are designed to compare a student's performance with that of other students, they are probably best suited for providing information related to the identification and classification function of P.L. 94–142. They may also provide a general indication of areas of student need. Many of these tests, however, are of questionable value for the purpose of identifying specific instructional needs and for program planning (Floden, Porter, Schmidt, & Freeman, 1980; J. R. Jenkins & Pany, 1978). Because norm-referenced tests usually are concerned with ensuring that the test provides a broad sample of items from the area to be measured (rather than a thorough measurement of each component skill within the area), a norm-referenced test may not provide enough detail for identifying specific needs. In addition, most commercially produced, norm-referenced tests are not based on any particular curriculum and thus are not likely to be useful for the purpose of program planning within an existing school curriculum.

Types of Standardized Tests

Standardized and norm-referenced measures used for the purpose of identification and educational decision making commonly include four types of tests. These include intelligence tests, achievement tests, tests of adaptive behavior, and language tests. Each will be briefly discussed here, followed by a discussion of the types of scores provided by each measure.

Intelligence Tests.   Tests of intelligence require specialized training and can only be administered by psychologists and/or other professionals who are certified or licensed to do so. These tests are designed to provide global estimates of a student's intellectual ability and by doing so, predict that student's potential to profit from instruction in a specific area. Intelligence tests often are included as part of the multidisciplinary evaluation when a student is suspected of having an intellectual disability or a learning disability. Two intelligence tests widely used by schools are the Stanford Binet Intelligence Scale and the Weschler Intelligence Scale for Children—Revised (Weschler Scales also are available for preschool children and for adults). Because potential bias in the measurement of intelligence for minority groups is of widespread concern, professionals have attempted to develop tests that are less susceptible to the effects of bias. Examples of tests that are specifically designed to minimize bias include the System of Multicultural Pluralistic Assessment (SOMPA) and the Kaufman Assessment Battery for Children (K-ABC). The development of intelligence tests requires extensive and systematic data collection, which can be time-consuming and expensive. Therefore, they usually are developed by professional test makers (Salvia & Ysseldyke, 1978).

Achievement Tests.   Standardized and norm-referenced achievement tests assess the extent to which a student has attained skills in various areas compared to other students of the same age or grade. They also can provide a very general indication of the degree to which a suspected disability adversely affects educational performance. Achievement tests may be either group administered or individually administered. However, when used to determine whether a student requires special education, achievement tests must be individually administered. Individually administered tests may assess skill attainment in only one area or in several areas. Examples of frequently used tests that measure skill attainment in one area include the Woodstock Reading Mastery Tests and Key Math Diagnostic Arithmetic Test (also criterion referenced). The Peabody Individual Achievement Test (PIAT) and the Wide-Range Achievement Test (WRAT) are examples of achievement tests that measure a variety of skills in one test.

Although most commercially produced achievement tests are norm-referenced, some frequently used measures are criterion referenced (i.e., they compare student performance to an absolute standard rather than to performance of other students). Examples of such tests are the Brigance Inventory of Basic Skills and the Key Math Diagnostic Achievement Test. A list of often employed commercially produced achievement tests is included in Appendix A.

Tests of Adaptive Behavior.   Definitions of adaptive behavior vary. Thus, tests of adaptive behavior also vary with the area of behavior being measured. Most standardized and norm-referenced tests of adaptive behavior measure the extent to which an individual meets the standards of personal independence and social responsibility expected for his age and cultural group (Grossman, 1983).

A measure of adaptive behavior must be obtained whenever a student is suspected of having an intellectual disability. Many states also require that adaptive behavior be evaluated when a student is suspected of having an emotional disturbance. Most standardized and norm-referenced measures of adaptive behavior consist of a behavior-rating scale that is based on observable operationally defined behaviors. The measures are usually designed to be completed by or administered in a structured interview with a person who is very familiar with the student (usually the parents). Examples of widely used measures of adaptive behavior include the AAMD Adaptive Behavior Scale (American Association on Mental Deficiency), The Vineland Adaptive Behavior Scale, and the Scales of Independent Behavior. Adaptive behavior scales can be criterion referenced as well as norm referenced. An example of a criterion-referenced adaptive behavior scale is the Pyramid Scales, which is a set of 20 criterion-referenced measures tied to curriculum objectives and materials for program planning.

Language Tests.   Language is typically defined as consisting of vocabulary, grammar, and phonation (Salvia & Ysseldyke, 1978). For students suspected of having a disorder of speech or a disability in the development of language, tests are usually conducted by speech therapists. However, several tests that measure the potential effect of language on educational performance may be administered by teachers. Such tests include those that measure listening comprehension (e.g., The Test for Auditory Comprehension of Language); oral expression (e.g., The Test of Language Development [TOLD]; or written expression (e.g., the Test of Written Language [TOWL]).

Scores Provided by Standardized And Norm-Referenced Tests

Results of standardized and norm-referenced tests are presented in several ways. Raw scores, seldom used alone for comparison purposes, are translated into percentiles, grade equivalents, age equivalents, and stanines for reporting purposes. These are often the scores considered and reported by special services committees when making decisions regarding the diagnosis and placement of students in special education, and thus, they warrant a brief discussion in this section.

Percentile Ranking.   A percentile ranking tells what percentage of students in the norm group obtained the same or lower score on the same measure as a particular student. For example, if a score of 25 correct answers on a test for fourth graders has a percentile rank of 52, it means that 52% of the pupils in the norm group scored 25 or lower on the test. Since the norm group is designed to be representative of all fourth graders, it may be said that a fourth-grade student scoring 25 on the test performed at the same level or above 52% of typical fourth graders in the nation.

Stanines.   A stanine is a score on a nine-unit scale from 1 to 9, where a score of 5 describes average performance. The highest stanine is 9, the lowest is 1. Except for 1 and 9, stanines divide the distribution of scores into equal parts, with 5 being average. Thus, stanine 8 is as far above average as stanine 2 is below average. Most students score in stanines 4, 5, and 6. Very few will score a stanine of 1 or 9. Because stanines are a relatively simple way to present and understand how a student performs in relation to a group, teachers and others reporting evaluation results may use stanines to describe performance on standardized tests at parent conferences. These and any derived score, however, should always be reported, noting the caveats regarding the score's degree of relevance to the school's curriculum, the student's similarity or dissimilarity to the group on which the measure was normed, and the comparative nature of the scores rather than their value as an absolute measure of performance.

Grade Equivalents.   A grade equivalent reflects the grade level in years and months for which a given score is the average or the middle score in the norm group. For example, a score of 25 with a grade equivalent of 4.6 means that, in the norm group, 25 is the average score of students in the sixth month of the fourth grade. This would indicate that the student performs at the same level as most students in the sixth month of the fourth grade on the content of the test used. If the fourth grader scores the same on the measure as a typical fifth grader, it does not mean that the fourth grader can do all fifth-grade work. It means only that on the items sampled by the measure, the fourth grader answered as many correct as the typical fifth grader. Without knowing the degree to which the test items measure the specific skills in the curriculum at that grade level in a particular school, it is difficult to determine the real value of a grade equivalent for a given student. If a student in the fourth grade obtains a grade equivalent of 2.0, it means that the student performed on the test in a similar way to that of second graders who took the test. It does not mean that the student has only learned second-grade material or that the second-grade instructional materials should be used with the student. Although grade equivalents are widely used and sound simple and useful in theory, they can (as can other norm-referenced scores) be easily misunderstood. Many publishers therefore advise against using these scores to determine or report functioning levels and suggest instead that percentile ranks and stanines be used as a more accurate and meaningful measure of a student's performance on a particular measure.

Advantages and Disadvantages Of Standardized Tests

Standardized and norm-referenced tests have several advantages that have resulted in their extensive use:

1. They are readily available and relatively easy to administer and score, producing a quantitive measure of a student's performance. Considering the large numbers of students referred for special education, this characteristic may be an important factor in the almost exclusive continued reliance on these measures during the evaluation process.
2. The testing situation is held as constant (standardized) as possible, thereby enabling comparison among students' performances.
3. Because of their widespread use and availability, standardized and norm-referenced tests provide a common base for communicating about the behavior of individual students, classes, or entire programs.
4. Standardized and norm-referenced tests provide a widespread indication of performance expectations based on the typical performance of a large number of students on a specific measure. This is an advantage for screening and program evaluation as well as for identifying and classifying disabilities.
5. Procedures for administration, scoring, and interpretation are already standardized, and validity and reliability information is already collected and provided. Many standardized tests have already been demonstrated to be technically adequate to perform the function intended by their producer.

Conversely, the disadvantages of standardized and norm-referenced tests might be summarized as follows:

1. Because standardized and norm-referenced tests usually contain only a representative sample of all the skills included in the area to be measured, and because test content is not usually specific to the curriculum used in the classroom, their validity for instructional planning is questionable.
2. Standardized norm-referenced tests do not adequately discriminate between those students who actually have mild learning disabilities and those students who learn slowly or underachieve in school.

3. To the extent that test norms and content do not adequately represent the characteristics and culture of specific populations, standardized and norm-referenced tests may produce test results that are biased against students of minority groups, those of low socioeconomic status, or students with existing disabilities.
4. Scheduling, administering, scoring, and reporting results of standardized and norm-referenced tests may be time-consuming, delaying program planning and intervention for extended periods.

It should be remembered that the advantages and disadvantages of any measure are relative to and dependent on (1) whether the intended purpose of the test is the same as the purpose of the evaluation for a given student, (2) whether the information provided by the test is the information required by the committee to make a decision regarding the student, and (3) whether the characteristics of the test are appropriate to the student. Although one measure may be appropriate in addressing a particular concern for one student, it may not be appropriate in addressing the same concern for another student. Committee members are encouraged to systematically consider such factors as (1) whether test administration procedures require the student to read, listen to, or watch directions being demonstrated; (2) whether students are expected to respond verbally, in writing, or motorically; (3) whether response formats provide choices (thus increasing the possibility that the student can guess the right answer but also providing a mechanism by which a student could point to the correct answer rather than having to write or speak); (4) whether the characteristics of the student are adequately represented in the group on which the test was normed. If, for example, a test is normed on a predominantly white, English-speaking population, the likelihood that the test norms would be appropriate for a Hispanic student with limited English proficiency would be questionable.

CRITERION-REFERENCED EVALUATION PROCEDURES

When determining the nature and extent of instructional needs and in planning an appropriate educational program, the special services committee should be concerned with knowing what skills a student does or does not have, rather than where that student performs compared to other students. When the purpose of evaluation is identification of instructional needs and program planning, criterion-referenced measures are often considered more useful than standardized norm-referenced measures.

Criterion-referenced evaluation might be defined as evaluating a student's performance in terms of a predetermined set of objectives and criteria rather than in terms of that student's performance relative to a norm group. This type of evaluation is distinguished from norm-referenced evaluation by the type of information provided by the test. For example, a score of 80% on a criterion-referenced test may indicate that a student answered correctly 80% of the test items, each correlated with an objective. Thus, the student may need instruction on the remaining 20%. A percentile score at the 80th% on a norm-referenced test indicates that a student has performed as well as or better than 80% of students at that age or grade level and that 20% of the students answered more items correctly. Thus, criterion-referenced measures compare performance against a list of learning objectives, while norm-referenced tests compare performance on selected content to a group of peers. The decision to use either a criterion-referenced measure or a norm-referenced measure should be based on what is to be measured. Figure 5–2 illustrates a criterion-referenced test that a local school system might develop.

Numerous commercially produced measures are considered criterion referenced and are used widely in schools. Examples include the Key Math Diagnostic Arithmetic Test and the Brigance Diagnostic Inventories. These tests also provide learning objectives correlated with each of the skill-analysis areas from the inventories that can be used for the development of IEPs. To the extent that these measures and accompanying objectives actually reflect the curriculum of the school, they may be an easily accessible and useful criterion-referenced measure.

Test and textbook publishers increasingly provide criterion-referenced tests to accompany basal reading programs and other textbooks. These criterion-referenced tests are developed at varying levels of specificity. Because they are based on the textbooks actually used in the school, they might be expected to better measure the school curriculum than most standardized and norm-referenced tests. The value of a commercially produced criterion-referenced test can only be determined by establishing the degree to which the objectives and content of such tests are sufficiently specific and whether they precisely match the objectives and content actually taught in the school.

Curriculum-Based Evaluations

Criterion-referenced measures that are based on a specific school curriculum are usually referred to as curriculum-based measures. Because they are based on a specific school curriculum, they have the advantage of determining how a student performs in

FIGURE 5–2
Sample Criterion-Referenced Test

OBJECTIVES

Linear Measurement

_____ 1. Identifies one foot.
_____ 2. Identifies one yard.
_____ 3. Identifies one inch.
_____ 4. Measures a 6-inch line drawn on paper, with 12-inch ruler.
_____ 5. Measures a 4-inch line drawn on paper.
_____ 6. Identifies one meter.
_____ 7. Identifies one centimeter with accuracy.
_____ 8. Measures a 6-centimeter line drawn on paper.
_____ 9. Completes:
      _____ a. one foot = _____ inches.
      _____ b. one yard = _____ inches.
      _____ c. one yard = _____ feet.
_____ 10. Orders correctly from shortest to longest: 1 foot, 1 yard, 8 inches, and 24 inches.
_____ 11. Completes numerical problem in addition and subtraction of the above measures. No conversion required.
_____ 12. Completes word problems in addition and subtraction involving the above measures. No conversion.
_____ 13. Completes numerical problems in addition and subtraction of the above measures, conversion needed.
_____ 14. Completes word problems in addition and subtraction involving the above measures. Conversion needed.
_____ 15. Reads the following words from test paper:
      _____ a. foot   _____ e. centimeter
      _____ b. inch   _____ f. feet
      _____ c. yard   _____ g. inches
      _____ d. meter   _____ h. measure
_____ 16. Measures these inches to the nearest inch:
      _____ a. chalktray
      _____ b. new piece of chalk
      _____ c. unsharpened pencil
      _____ d. length of the windowsill
_____ 17. Shows length of a figure.
_____ 18. Shows width of a figure.
_____ 19. Measures the length and width of the following objects:
      _____ a. reading or spelling book
      _____ b. top of the teacher's desk
      _____ c. classroom door
      _____ d. windowpane
_____ 20. Reads *length and width* from test paper.
_____ 21. Identifies 1/2 inch.
_____ 22. Measures lines of the following lengths:
      _____ a. 1 1/2 inches   _____ c. 6 1/2 inches   _____ e. 2 1/2 inches
      _____ b. 3 1/2 inches   _____ d. 4 1/2 inches   _____ f. 7 1/2 inches

Linear Measurement

1. How long is a ruler?
2. How long is a yardstick?
3. Show me one inch on a ruler.
4. Measure this line. How long is it? _____ inches.

5. Measure this line. How long is it? _____ inches.

(Figure 5–2 continued)

6. What is this? Look at the teacher.
7. What is this? Look at the teacher.
8. Measure this line in centimeters. How long is it? _____ centimeters

9. Fill in the blanks:
   a. one foot = _____ inches
   b. one yard = _____ inches
   c. one yard = _____ feet
10. Put these in order from shortest to longest.
    1 foot   _____
    1 yard   _____
    8 inches   _____
    24 inches   _____
11. Answer these problems.

    a.   20 inches   b.   40 feet   c.   9 yards
        +12 inches   +15 feet   +3 yards

_____

12. a. Nancy bought 7 yards of string. She used 2 yards to tie up some papers and 1 yard to mend her kite. How much string does she have left?
       _____ yards
    b. Tom needs 10 inches of tape to fix a tear in his paper. He only has 4 inches of tape. How many more inches does he need?
       _____ inches
    c. A farmer has a fence between two fields. It is now 25 feet long. If he added 14 feet of fence, how long would the whole fence be?
       _____ feet
13. Answer these problems.

    a.   1 yard   b.   1 foot   c.   2 yards
        -1 foot   -7 inches   -3 inches

_____

14. a. Jerry has 1 yard of rope. He cut off 1 foot to give to Jane. How much rope does he have left?
       _____ feet
    b. Marie needs 2 yards of ribbon to trim a dress. She has 3 feet. How many more feet of ribbon does she need to buy?
       _____ feet
    c. Mrs. Pender has 21 inches of string. She needs 1 yard. How many more inches of string does she need?
       _____ inches.
15. Read the following words.
    a. foot   e. centimeter
    b. inch   f. feet
    c. yard   g. inches
    d. meter   h. measure

16. Measure these objects to the nearest inch.
    a. the chalktray   _____ inches
    b. a new piece of chalk   _____ inches
    c. an unsharpened pencil   _____ inches
    d. the length of the windowsill _____ inches
17. Define length.
18. Define width.

(Figure 5–2 continued)

19. Measure the length and width of the following things.

	length	width
a. a reading or spelling book	_____ in.	_____ in.
a. the top of the teacher's desk	_____ in.	_____ in.
a. the classroom door	_____ in.	_____ in.
a. a windowpane	_____ in.	_____ in.

20. Read these words.
    length width
21. Show me 1/2 inch on a ruler.
22. Measure the following lines and write the length in the blank.
    (to the nearest 1/2 inch)
    a. _____ in.
    b. _____ in.
    c. _____ in.

    d. _____ in.
    e. _____ in.
    f. _____ in.

relation to the curriculum taught in his school. This section provides examples of curriculum-based procedures that might be used to identify specific areas of student need and to plan instructional programs.

Most curriculum-based measures are not designed to identify and classify student disabilities. Their usefulness lies in the identification of specific instructional needs and in program planning. However, even though many curriculum-based procedures are valid for the purpose of program planning, many states still require that determination of areas of instructional need and IEP development be based on standardized and norm-referenced procedures. When this is the case, curriculum-based evaluation measures should be used to provide additional information to that provided by the required norm-referenced procedures.

Furthermore, when used to determine a student's special education needs, curriculum-based measures, like any other measures, must be validated for the purpose for which they are used.

Types of Curriculum-Based Evaluations
Regardless of whether a student is determined eligible for special education, curriculum-based evaluation can provide program planning information for the individual responsible for instruction. Curriculum-based evaluation can include a variety of procedures. Two procedures, systematic observation and the informal reading inventory, are discussed in this section.

Systematic Observation. Teachers often use informal observation techniques to assess student performance (Salmon-Cox, 1981). For example, by looking at the student's written work, it may be difficult to determine why a student consistently forms letters incorrectly. By observing the student perform the task, the teacher may observe the incorrect procedure used by the student to form the letter and may provide appropriate remediation. Likewise, observation of a student's oral reading behavior may provide information regarding types of errors made in word recognition, word-attack techniques, phrasing abilities, and punctuation, thus alerting the teacher to needs for different instructional strategies.

The difference between the type of classroom observation that occurs most frequently in classrooms and that used for evaluation of educational performance and program planning for students with disabilities is the degree of specificity required. Observations used to determine specific areas of student need and to plan appropriate programs must reflect accurate and objective data.

Analysis of student behavior is one area in which direct observation can provide significant and relevant information regarding a student's performance. Because social behavior is spontaneous and highly individual, the use of traditional paper–pencil evaluation methods is, in most cases inappropriate. Through observation, behaviors may be systematically observed and recorded as they occur rather than in a summative manner, as is the case with many existing behavior-rating scales, which are typically completed by teachers or parents based on the student's previous behavior.

Observations of student behaviors usually occur over a period of days or even weeks and can be recorded using a variety of methods. Observation-recording methods include anecdotal recording, recording of specific events, recording the length of a specific behavior, recording behaviors during time intervals, or recording samples of behavior at regular intervals.

Anecdotal observation provides a continuous indication of all student behaviors during a specific time period. The purpose is to obtain a complete description of behaviors exhibited in specified settings. For example, if a referral indicates that a student "constantly disrupts the class," an anecdotal record of the behaviors of the entire group during that period might be conducted to determine exactly how unidentified events, group behaviors, or teacher behaviors may influence the student's behavior during that time. Although anecdotal recording is time-consuming, it has the advantage of documenting a wide range of student behaviors. Most anecdotal observation formats include recording all events in the classroom, the responding behavior of the student to each event, and events that immediately follow the student's behavior. Because this method is time-consuming and cannot easily be accomplished simultaneously with teaching, anecdotal recording is seldom conducted by classroom teachers. It is an appropriate technique for other classroom observers such as psychologists, counselors, teacher aides, administrators, resource counsultants, and educational prescriptionists.

Specific events also can be observed and recorded to define student behaviors and subsequent instructional needs. *Event recording* can most easily be used to document behaviors that have a definite beginning and end and do not occur at a high rate. For example, the teacher might record the number of student fighting episodes in a week, the number of times late or absent from school, number of times out of seat, or the number of homework assignments submitted. Event recording can occur simultaneously with teaching and can be facilitated by hand-tally digital counters, wrist golf counters, or simply by tallying behaviors on the board or on masking tape attached to the wrist. Figure 4–8 in Chapter 4 (page 104) illustrates an example of how event recording can provide systematic information on student behavior.

Another type of recording, *duration recording*, is appropriate when it is important to know how long a student engages in a particular behavior. Examples of behaviors that are appropriate for duration recording include the length of tantrum behavior, crying, or

the amount of time required for a student to complete a task. Duration recording can be done by the classroom teachers during instruction with a stopwatch, watch, or other timing device. The teacher or other observer records the time at which the behavior begins and ends and then calculates the duration of the behavior for that time period. The duration of behaviors can be examined for a specific period of the day (such as when the teacher wishes to record the length of tantrum behaviors when school begins) or for the entire day (such as how long it takes the student to complete written assignments).

Interval recording is a combination of event and duration recording and provides information on a student's behavior across time intervals (usually measured in seconds). For example, the teacher may wish to determine whether a student's off-task behavior is more pronounced during some portions of the mathematics period than others. To obtain an objective estimate of when the majority of off-task behavior occurs, an observer might divide the class period into 30-second intervals, observe the student during each of the intervals, and record whether the student is on-task during each interval. The teacher, over a period of days, can examine behavior during each of the intervals comprising the class period to determine if a pattern exists. This method requires that the observer watch the student during the entire interval to determine whether the behavior occurred or did not occur. Interval recording therefore is more suited for use by observers other than the classroom teacher.

A final type of observational recording is *time sampling*. This method is convenient and practical for use by teachers because it requires that the occurrence or nonoccurrence of the behavior be recorded only at the end of a given time interval (usually minutes) rather than during the time interval. For example, if the student is off-task at the end of a 5-minute interval, the teacher records the behavior as off-task for that interval, regardless of whether the student was on task at other times during the interval. This means that the teacher must observe the student only at the end of an established period of time (e.g., every 5 minutes). This method of recording provides a sample of student behavior at given points during the class period.

Information generated from observations can provide specific and relevant information for individualized program planning. From this information the IEP committee can develop an accurate, current level of performance and can develop intervention strategies (goals and objectives) to increase or decrease a specific student behavior. For example, the results of systematic observation may indicate that a student has difficulty staying on-task for more than 10 minutes at a time, regardless of the task involved. This information should be taken into consideration when establishing time lines for skill development on the IEP and also when developing effective strategies for teaching and providing practice for the skills to be developed.

Results of observation, in conjunction with formal evaluation results, may provide a basis for placement decisions. If the student has been observed to be so disruptive in a regular classroom that the education of other students is significantly impaired, then the regular classroom may be an inappropriate placement for the student. Observation is the only method of evaluation that can document and verify the disruptive behavior of a student in the classroom.

One major advantage of direct and systematic observation is that evaluation occurs in the natural environment, rather than in a formal evaluation setting. Thus, potential problems related to the effect of an unfamiliar environment or test examiner on student behavior may be alleviated. Additionally, systematic observation can be continuous, with the observer obtaining information at various times of the day and in various situations. By doing so, the special services committee is provided with specific information concerning when and under what conditions observed behaviors occur.

Once teachers and other observers have been trained in appropriate data-gathering techniques, observation measures may take very little time compared to traditional evaluation procedures. The teacher usually can observe the student, both in a group and individually during the course of the school day. It is not necessary to set aside time to administer test items individually unless the specific behaviors to be observed require special equipment or special administration procedures. In situations where teacher time is at a premium, observation provides a time-saving evaluation method.

One of the major disadvantages of classroom observation is the possibility of subjective rather than objective interpretation of observation results. Caution must be used in the interpretation of observation data to ensure that bias does not occur. It should be remembered that observation results document only the occurrence or nonoccurrence of specific behaviors, not the reason why they occur. The teacher may suggest reasons for the observed behavior but should not document opinion as fact unless there is substantial proof that the reasons are valid. To guard against observer bias, an independent observer should check the reliability of a teacher's observations of a student's behavior if the behaviors observed are open to subjectivity. Another disadvantage of informal observation techniques is that they usually are not formally validated for the purpose of identification and classification of handicapped students. Thus, used sin-

gularly, they may be considered inappropriate for such determination. Observation should, however, be considered in the interpretation of more formal, validated test results.

Informal Reading Inventories.   Informal reading inventories are another example of curriculum-based evaluation measures. The informal reading inventory is perhaps one of the most useful techniques for identifying areas of specific student need and for program planning in the area of reading. It provides a relatively easy and accurate way of determining a student's oral reading errors and independent, instructional, and frustration levels, based on the curriculum of the student's school. Informal inventories can be used in regular education programs, remedial reading classes, content area classes, and special education programs.

Reading inventories differ depending on the skills to be measured, but they typically include (1) a sight word test; (2) oral reading paragraphs based on the basal reading series (or other textbook used in the program); and (3) an analysis of the student's use of word-recognition techniques (phonetic analysis, structural analysis, context clue usage, and dictionary usage). To determine specific levels of student performance, test items are drawn from the reading curriculum. For example, a sight word test might be developed by randomly selecting vocabulary words from each word list found at the end of each basal reader. These words, organized into lists according to difficulty, are administered to the student, beginning with lists that can be read independently and progressing until the student reaches a level at which word identification becomes difficult, and the frustration level is reached. Figure 5–3 illustrates a sight word test that a local school system might develop.

Oral reading paragraphs are also selected from the basal text used in the school. Representative paragraphs may be selected from the middle of each text in the basal reading series to represent each level of the series. Or the teacher might develop original paragraphs, being careful to ensure that vocabulary is representative of that text or earlier texts in the series. Several literal and interpretive comprehension questions usually are developed in addition to evaluating the student's knowledge of the vocabulary used in the paragraph. As with the sight word lists, the student reads the paragraphs aloud, beginning with paragraphs estimated by the teacher to be easily read (independent level), and progressing to more difficult paragraphs, until reaching the point at which many oral reading errors are made and comprehension on the literal and interpretive questions is poor.

One of the primary purposes of the informal reading inventory is to provide indicators of various

FIGURE 5–3
Sample Informal Inventory

Basic Reading Word Lists
Directions for Administration

1. Estimate the reading level of the student and begin with the word list which is one level below the estimated reading level.

2. The teacher should give a copy of the word list to the student to read from and should retain a copy on which to indicate student responses.

3. As the student reads each word the teacher indicates incorrect responses by writing the student response beside the word read incorrectly. For example, if the word to be read is *on,* and the student says *no,* the teacher would write *no* beside the word *on.*

4. Proceed through each consecutive list until the student misses 50% of the words on any one list. This constitutes the student's frustration level in word recognition.

5. The student's instructional level for word recognition is indicated by the list on which the student can read 75% of the words.

6. The student's independent word reading level is indicated by the list on which the student is able to read 95% of the words presented.

7. Levels in basic reading vocabulary must be compared with reading comprehension ability. If the student's comprehension level is lower than the vocabulary level, instruct the student on the level of comprehension.

Pre-Primer Word List

and	fun	is	out	water
bed	funny	ladder	red	was
box	guess	lunch	sleep	work
come	help	milk	then	yard
did	ice cream	playhouse	train	you

Primer Word List

all	day	hello	night	thank
baby	friend	horse	paint	they
black	girl	kick	rain	will
candy	good	like	right	what
children	happy	music	school	yes

First Reader Word List

always	egg	just	of	under
basket	fly	keep	put	very
before	give	long	read	window
city	hill	more	seen	woman
dress	it	new	talk	yourself

levels of reading performance, usually referred to as independent, instructional, and frustration levels. These levels relate closely with the basal, instructional, and ceiling levels of many standardized tests, except that they are based on vocabulary and content from the basal reader used in the student's reading program rather than on word lists and paragraphs from a norm-referenced test. Specific criteria for determining the independent, instructional, and frustration levels may vary. According to one system (Betts, 1957), the independent level should be established at the point where the student can easily read 99% of the vocabulary with comprehension at 95%; the instructional level at the point where the student can read vocabulary at approximately 90% with 75% comprehension; and the frustration level at the point where the student reads less than 90% of the vocabulary and is less than 50% accurate in comprehension.

The primary advantage of the informal reading inventory is that it can provide specific curriculum-related information regarding the strategies used by a particular student to read. Based on this information a specific program of reading instruction can be developed. Because informal inventories usually present test items within a continuum of skills, a determination can be made not only where instruction should begin but also the order in which subsequent skills should be taught. This procedure saves time in program planning by enabling the IEP committee to establish a sequential program based on the results of the informal inventory.

Informal reading inventories can be used in content areas such as science and social studies to provide an indication of the student's ability to read the textbook. Inventories for these areas are constructed similarly to those developed for the area of reading except that inventory items are developed based on the science or social studies text used in the school. For example, a sight word test might be developed by randomly selecting specialized words from the glossary of the text. Oral reading paragraphs might be selected by choosing or constructing representative paragraphs from the beginning, middle, and end of the textbook.

The major limitation of the informal reading inventory is the time involved in development and administration. Because the inventory involves in-depth evaluation of student skills, a substantial amount of time can be involved in both the development and the administration of the instrument. It should be recognized, however, that this type of evaluation saves time once program planning begins by indicating specific skills in the order in which they should be taught, and by including a wide range of skills that assist the IEP committee in long-range planning for the student.

Another disadvantage of the informal inventory is that there are often no measures of validity associated with the measure. P.L. 94–142 requires that evaluation procedures used to determine whether a student has a disability as well as the nature and extent of special education must be validated for the specific purpose for which they are used. Informal inventories, however, like other informal means of evaluation, can be constructed so that they exhibit both content and criterion validity. For example, reading aloud from the basal text has been demonstrated to have high content validity. Deno et al. (1982) have demonstrated that a student's performance on measures such as reading aloud for 1 minute from passages from the basal reader and/or reading aloud for 1 minute from a list of vocabulary words selected randomly from the basal reader correlated highly with results of standardized tests. In addition, research is emerging that indicates that curriculum-based measures as simple as measuring the number of words read correctly and incorrectly from a basal text may reliably and validly discriminate growth in reading proficiency throughout the elementary school years (Deno, 1985).

Advantages and Disadvantages of Curriculum-Based Evaluation

Curriculum-based measures are considered by many to be superior to most standardized norm-referenced measures for the purpose of individual program planning. The advantages of these measures include the following:

1. Curriculum-based measures are directly related to the curriculum being taught in a particular school, and thus they provide a direct link between evaluation and instructional planning.
2. Because curriculum-based measures are based on existing curriculum objectives, they are often sequential. This helps the committee not only to identify where instruction should begin but also helps to plan the IEP or the instructional program in keeping with the sequence of the curriculum being taught.
3. Curriculum-based measures may be more cost effective than traditional evaluation procedures in regard to the time and personnel involved in scheduling, administration, scoring, and reporting results.
4. Curriculum-based measures may be more acceptable to teachers and other instructional personnel because results may be viewed as more instructionally relevant than those provided by standardized norm-referenced tests.

5. Curriculum-based measures can be effectively administered by teachers, thus giving teachers a role in the evaluation process. Rather than being consumers of test data produced by others, teachers are involved in and provide continuity in the evaluation process, program planning, and in subsequent IEP development.

6. Curriculum-based measures are easily understood and interpreted to parents and other professionals because the results relate specifically to the curriculum.

7. Curriculum-based evaluation measures provide an instructionally relevant basis for the evaluation of goals and objectives on IEPs, a requirement of P.L. 94–142 that is perhaps most often overlooked.

Curriculum-based evaluation does have some disadvantages, including the following:

1. Curriculum-based procedures, unless rigorously constructed, may not meet the requirements of P.L. 94–142 in regard to being sufficiently valid and reliable for identifying areas of specific instructional need and program planning for students with disabilities.

2. Curriculum-based evaluation procedures are more refined for some areas than for others. For example, curriculum-based evaluation measures for the area of reading have been studied extensively, while the area of language has received relatively little attention.

3. Development of curriculum-based evaluation measures and adequate training of teachers in their use, can be initially time-consuming. If adequate training is not provided, data collection may be inefficient, scoring and testing procedures may be inappropriately implemented, results may be inappropriately analyzed, and procedures may become cumbersome.

REPORTING EVALUATION RESULTS

The Written Report

After all evaluation information has been gathered, it must be synthesized into meaningful written form to share with parents and those who will determine program eligibility. It is not appropriate to present evaluation results as a series of unrelated findings. To accomplish synthesis, the multidisciplinary team as a group, or specific members of the team, must be responsible for compiling, analyzing, and summarizing the evaluation information obtained by each evaluator.

Meeting of Committee Members.   One way of doing this is for members of the multidisciplinary evaluation team to meet together for the purpose of synthesizing the data. This method is preferred because it enables each evaluator to interpret his own evaluation results within the context of information presented by other team members. Team meetings are multidisciplinary in the truest sense in that the results can be discussed, analyzed, and compiled from various perspectives with the final report representing the consensus reached by all involved.

The difficulty with such a procedure, however, is that scheduling time for all team members to meet to synthesize results can be overwhelming and can result in further extending an already very long process. In addition, team meetings for the purpose of synthesis can be very time-consuming. One of the purposes of such a meeting is to compose an accurate and informative, yet concise and well-organized report. This means that essential details of hashing through irrelevant data, reconciling contradictory data, and organizing the report is a necessary function of a synthesis meeting. These activities seldom are dispensed with quickly.

Reports by Individual Evaluators.   Another way of synthesizing data is for each team member contributing evaluation information to write a brief written report of findings and submit these to a case manager, psychologist, or other evaluation personnel for synthesis and drafting a written report. If this option is used, each evaluator must ensure that his report clearly summarizes significant findings. A draft of the written report should be approved by all evaluators before finalizing the report. A standard format for individual evaluation reports should also be developed to provide continuity in the synthesis process. Figure 5–4 is a sample format for reporting individual evaluation results.

Development by Subcommittee.   A variation of the preceding options is for several representatives, or a subcommittee of the multidisciplinary team, to synthesize the written evaluation findings of each evaluator into one report. This option has the advantage of shared responsibility in that more than one individual participates in synthesizing evaluation information and developing the final report.

Regardless of the method used to synthesize evaluation results, the final report should be designed to provide sufficient information for determining (1) whether the student has a disability, and if so, (2) the student's specific area of instructional need. It is not necessary to report the details of every measure used if the information provided has no

FIGURE 5–4
Individual Evaluator Report of Evaluation Results

Evaluator's Report of Evaluation Results

Student's Name_____   Age_____

Birth Date_____   Date of Report_____

School_____   Grade_____

Evaluator_____   Position_____

1. Purpose of Assessment (How does this assessment relate to the purpose of referral?)

2. Evaluation Procedure (List tests or describe procedures used.)

3. Evaluation Results (Report results that indicate student strengths, significant weaknesses, and/or disability regarding questions raised by referral.)

4. Possible Instructional Needs and Strategies Based on Results

5. Description of Potential Bias on Results of This Evaluation Procedure (Report any potential biasing effects of race, culture, existing language, sensory, motor, or speaking disability, or other significant factors.)

_____   _____

Signature of Evaluator   Date

relevance to these questions. The team, committee, or individual synthesizing the evaluation data might use the following procedures:

1. Review the purpose of the referral and summarize it in writing on the final report. All evaluation data should be reviewed and reported in relation to how it addresses questions raised by the referral.
2. Review any potentially biasing elements in evaluation procedures and specify their probable effect on the results of the evaluation.
3. Briefly review results that indicate that no disability exists or that there is no significant adverse effect on educational performance. Do not provide an in-depth discussion of a student's relative weaknesses for areas in which performance is within the range of average. Do identify the student's strengths.
4. Review and summarize data indicating that a disability exists. Specify the disability and the criteria on which the diagnosis was made.
5. Review and summarize data indicating significant adverse effects on educational performance. Specify what criteria were used to determine significance.
6. Briefly address issues raised in the referral.
7. Summarize findings.

A draft of the final report should be developed and shared with all committee members before the eligibility meeting. A completed report for Joe S., based on the referral illustrated in Figure 4–7 (page 99) is included in Figure 5–5. It should be noted that specific placement decisions are not the responsibility of the multidisciplinary evaluation team. The decision to provide special education is made at the point of eligibility, and the specific placement of a student is determined after the IEP is developed and is based on the IEP. Thus evaluation reports should not dictate placement decisions.

Reporting Evaluation Results to Parents

P.L. 94–142 requires that, before a district proposes or refuses to initiate or change the identification or placement of a student, written notice must be given to parents within a reasonable time (*Federal Register*, 1977). The notice must include the following:

1. A full explanation of all the procedural safeguards available to the parents.
2. A description of the action proposed or refused by the school, an explanation of why the school proposes or refuses to take the action, and a description of any options the school considered and the reasons why those options were rejected.

3. A description of each evaluation procedure, test, record, or report the school used as a basis for the proposal or refusal, and
4. A description of any other factors which are relevant to the school's proposal or refusal.
                                        (*Federal Register*, 1977)

P.L. 94–142 is very clear in its requirement that the school must ensure that parents not only receive written notice but that they fully understand the content of the notice. Thus the notice must be as follows:

1. Written in language understandable to the general public, and
2. Provided in the native language of the parent or other mode of communication used by the parent unless clearly not feasible to do so.
                                        (*Federal Register*, 1977)

Further, if the native language or other mode of communication of the parent is a nonwritten language, such as sign language, the school, district, or state must ensure that:

1. The notice is translated orally or by other means to the parent in his or her native language or other mode of communication,
2. The parent understands the content of the notice, and
3. There is written evidence that the notice has been translated orally or by other means and that the parent understands the content of the notice.
                                        (*Federal Register*, 1977)

Presentation of Evaluation Results at IEP Meeting.   In some states, program eligibility is determined immediately following the completion of evaluation by the special services committee without the involvement of parents and before notice of evaluation results is provided. In these states, parents are not a part of the eligibility decision but receive notice regarding the results of evaluation at the same time that they receive notice of the committee's decision to propose provision of special education services or the decision not to propose the provision of special education services. If the committee's decision is that the student is eligible for special education and that enrollment in special education will be proposed, the required notice may be sent to parents at the same time as an invitation to participate in IEP development (as in Figure 5–6, pp. 145–146). This means that, in some instances, parents may not meet with or have personal contact with school representatives until after the student has been determined by the school to have a disability requiring specially designed instruction. This also means that, when the

FIGURE 5–5
Sample Evaluation Report (Based on Referral of Joe S.)

Evaluation Report

Student: Joe S.   Date of Evaluation: 2/1/91
Birthdate: 10/1/80   Date of Report: 2/15/91
Age: 11-4   School: Adams Middle School
                                              Grade: 5

Procedures Administered:

Wechsler Intelligence Scale for Children-Revised (WISC-R)
Peabody Individual Achievement Test
Key Math
Woodcock Reading Mastery Test
System of Multicultural Pluralistic Assessment
Adaptive Behavior Inventory for Children
Informal Reading Inventory
Informal Math Inventory
Classroom Observation

1. Reason for Referral

Joe was referred by his teacher, Mrs. Snow, because of concerns about academic
performance in reading, mathematics and social emotional development. According to reading
and mathematics inventories administered by Mrs. Snow, Joe has a limited reading
vocabulary, with few effective word-attack strategies with which to decode new words. He
has difficulty with both literal and interpretive comprehension. According to systemwide tests
and curriculum-based reading evaluation, his reading is estimated to be approximately 3 years
below that of the typical fifth-grade student. In mathematics Joe has difficulty with abstract
concepts such as regrouping, place value, and zeros. He also has difficulty telling time by
the minute and counting money. Joe is cooperative but quiet in groups and does not make
friends easily. His behavior is immature for his age.

Since September, Mrs. Snow has attempted several interventions with Joe with the assistance
of the teacher assistance team within the school. Strategies used included extended work
time, individual assistance from the teacher and a peer helper, reading from taped samples,
modified materials, a behavior management program for off-task behavior, and cooperative
grouping. Although some improvement has been noted, interventions have not resulted in
signficant improvement in Joe's performance. Based on observations in the classroom,
previous school records, and interventions attempted, Mrs. Snow referred Joe for evaluation
for a suspected intellectual disability and possible instructional assistance from a resource
program in special education.

Joe had a vision and hearing evaluation in June 1990. His hearing is within normal limits.
However, he does require glasses, which he owns but seldom wears.

A parent conference was held at Joe's home with his father and mother on December 2,
1990. Because Joe's father speaks Spanish, a Spanish-speaking interpreter was present
but not needed. Joe's mother and father speak both Spanish and English. Mrs. S. speaks
English fluently. Since Joe's dominant language had not been formally established, the Test
of Language Dominance was used, which indicated that Joe does best in English. Joe has
ten family members; mother, father, grandmother, uncle, two older brothers, and three
younger sisters. Mr. S. is a migrant farmer and moves frequently. During the interview,
Joe's mother reported that Joe walked and talked somewhat later than his brothers and
sisters but that he goes about the neighborhood independently and has chores for which he
is responsible at home. She reports that Joe has always done poorly in school, although he
has only recently begun to dislike attending. She believes that the work expected of Joe is
too difficult for him.

(Figure 5–5 continued)

2. Evaluation Procedures Used

A. Wechsler Intelligence Scale for Children--Revised

Scaled Scores

Full Scale IQ = 69
Verbal IQ = 69
Performance IQ = 68

Information = 5	Picture Completion = 7
Similarities = 7	Picture Arrangement = 4
Arithmetic = 4	Block Design = 4
Vocabulary = 8	Object Assembly = 4
Comprehension = 1	Coding = 6

B. Adaptive Behavior Inventory for Children

Family	50 Percentile
Community	3 Percentile
Peer Relations	3 Percentile
Nonacademic School Roles	10 Percentile
Earner/Consumer	3 Percentile
Self-Maintenance	30 Percentile

C. System of Multicultural Pluralistic Assessment-Sociocultural Scales

Family Size	33 Percentile
Family Structure	21 Percentile
Socioeconomic Status	1 Percentile
Urban Acculturation	10 Percentile

D. Reading Inventory (From Thompson Reading Series used in school)

Sight Vocabulary
Read 24 of 25 words from list from first basal reader (independent reading level)
Read 20 of 25 words from list from second basal reader (instructional level)
Read 10 of 25 words from list from third basal reader (frustration level)
Word Analysis
Limited functional use of word-recognition strategies. Phonetic analysis: sounds out initial consonants. Structural analysis: limited use of root words, prefixes, suffixes, syllables. Context clues: attempts to guess unknown words in passage by context.
Comprehension
Reads independently in first basal reader and answers 95% of literal and interpretive questions.
Comprehends better when listening than when reading.
Instructional level, second basal. Answers 75% of literal and interpretive comprehension questions.
Frustration level, third basal. Answers less than 50% literal and interpretive questions.

E. Mathematics Inventory

Adds, subtracts, and has memorized some multiplication facts.
Has difficulty with regrouping, computing with zero's,and choosing math operations in word problems.
Can tell time to the hour and half hour and can name and count coins and dollars inconsistently. Has difficulty making change.

F. Peabody Individual Achievement Test

Math	2.7 grade equivalent
Reading Recognition	1.6
Reading Comprehension	2.7
Spelling	1.7
General Information	4.0

(Figure 5–5 continued)

G. Key Math

Total Score   2.1 grade equivalent

H. Woodcock Reading Mastery Tests

Letter Identification   3.0 grade equivalent
Word Identification   1.8
Word Attack   2.0
Word Comprehension   4.3

3. Description of Evaluation Results

During testing, Joe was reported to be initially shy with all examiners. However, he engaged in tasks readily and eventually became relaxed. When asked about his glasses, Joe said that he didn't like to wear them because other students teased him. However, he willingly wore the glasses during evaluations. Joe worked slowly on all tasks. It was difficult to tell whether he was making his best effort. He was usually unaware of errors and made no effort to correct his work.

Intellectual Performance and Adaptive Behavior
Joe is functioning in the mildly retarded range of intelligence on the Wechsler, with comparable verbal and performance abilities. All areas of intellectual performance were well below age expectancy; Joe's poorest performance involved verbal comprehension, while he did his best in defining words. Performance was consistent between subtests; however with tasks, performance was erratic; easier problems were failed, then more difficult ones were solved.

On the Adaptive Behavior Inventory for Children, Joe falls in the "at-risk" range in three areas: community involvement, peer relations, and his role as an earner and consumer. These scores probably reflect some effects of the sociocultural circumstances mentioned earlier. Nevertheless, taking language, culture, and socioeconomic status into consideration, Joe still performs substantially below that which might be expected.

On the System of Multicultural Pluralistic Assessment, Joe's family size and structure are slightly below the norm; socioeconomic and urban acculturation status are quite low.

Achievement
On the Peabody Individual Achievement Test, Joe performed from 2 1/2 to 3 1/2 years below current grade placement, depending on the subject. On diagnostic tests, he was 3 years below grade placement on the Key Math, and 1 to 3 1/2 years behind in reading on the Woodcock Reading Mastery Test. Informal inventories in reading and mathematics indicate that Joe's instructional level in reading and mathematics is approximately 3 years below that of other fifth graders in his school. These results are consistent with observations of Joe's classroom teachers and with Joe's prior school performance.

Behavioral Observations
Joe was observed in three settings by the school psychologist: group reading in the classroom, mathematics seat work, and on the playground. The teacher's referral concerns were clearly apparent. He showed little effort during seat work and did not wear his glasses. He was off-task frequently and appeared frustrated at times, even though he received assistance from both the teacher and a peer helper during seatwork and reading. He appears to participate more during group activities, although he remains shy and somewhat reluctant. Unless encouraged, he will not join a group on the playground.

4. Areas of Educational Strength and Significant Weakness

Joe's listening comprehension is relatively good, and with peer assistance he is able to participate in many group activities. He enjoys listening to taped material and reading along. Joe is good at tasks requiring memorization, and therefore he can compute mathematics

(Figure 5–5 continued)

problems when given specific procedural directions for solving the equation. He enjoys art and appears to be mechanically inclined.

Joe has particular difficulty in reading. This difficulty affects all areas of learning. His existing reading vocabulary is limited, and learning new vocabulary is difficult because he has few strategies for decoding words. Reading comprehension is difficult and is probably diminished even more because Joe must struggle to read words in a passage rather than to understand the meaning of the material. In mathematics, abstract concepts are of primary difficulty.

Joe's behavior, although not disruptive, interferes with his ability to approach and complete tasks. He often daydreams and is reluctant to interact with other students. He consequently has few friends.

It is likely that cultural and socioeconomic factors contribute to Joe's educational difficulties. However, they are not considered to be the primary reason for Joe's lack of achievement. Joe's pattern of early development, school achievement, and social emotional development is typical of students with mild intellectual disabilities.

5. **Suggested Strategies for Addressing Educational Weaknesses**

   A. Joe works successfully with reading material for which the vocabulary and concepts are controlled. His teacher has found high interest and limited vocabulary materials useful. Magazines and books with pictures from which content can be interpreted are recommended for independent reading.

   B. Joe requires strategies for expanding his reading vocabulary. Although prior attempts to develop phonetic analysis skills have been minimally successful, other strategies in addition to phonetic analysis should be attempted (structural analysis, context clues).

   C. Functional math skills should be emphasized while continuing instruction in basic mathematical procedures. Joe needs to tell time and count money accurately.

   D. Informal counseling may be helpful in addressing Joe's sensitivity to teasing, his reluctance to interact with other students, and his lack of interest in school. It is unclear whether he simply lacks the necessary social skills or whether other factors are interfering with his social adjustment. Joe needs to develop social skills necessary to make and maintain friendships, to contribute cooperatively in games and work, and to be a responsible consumer and earner in life outside school.

   E. A coordinated effort between parents and school is needed to encourage Joe to wear his glasses, without which he has a significant visual disability.

Multidisciplinary Evaluation Team Members.

Signature	Position	Date
Mrs. Snow	classroom teacher	2/15/91
Mr. LaJoie	counselor	2-15-91
Mr. Ryan	psychologist	2/15/91
Mr. Thomas	special Ed. teacher	2-15-91
Mrs. Bells	school nurse	2-15-91

FIGURE 5–6
Sample Letter to Parents Informing Them of Evaluation Results and IEP Involvement (Based on Referral and Evaluation Report of Joe S.)

Dear Mr. and Mrs. S.:

This letter will provide written notice of Joe's evaluation results and a summary of our meeting on February 17 to determine Joe's eligibility for special education.

As you are aware, Joe was evaluated last week to determine whether he might have a disability that may cause difficulty in achieving success in school. As we discussed, evaluation helps us identify whether Joe might require specially designed instruction that is not normally provided as part of the regular education program in which he is currently enrolled. We now want to (1) review the evaluation procedures used, (2) provide a written summary of the evaluation results, and (3) review recommendations made for Joe's educational program.

As you might remember, we discussed and provided a copy of your legal rights regarding Joe's educational program when you gave your permission for evaluation and when we met on February 17. Another copy of these rights is enclosed.

In Joe's evaluation, the following procedures were used:

1. Wechsler Intelligence Scale for Children--Revised (WISC-R)
2. Peabody Individual Achievement Test
3. Key Math
4. Woodcock Reading Mastery Tests
5. System of Multicultural Pluralistic Assessment
6. Adaptive Behavior Inventory for Children
7. Informal Reading Inventory
8. Informal Mathematics Inventory
9. Classroom Observation

At our meeting we discussed a written evaluation report providing the specific results of each of these procedures, and it is available to you on request. To summarize the results of the evaluation, Joe performs below average in intellectual ability as measured on the Wechsler Intelligence Scale for Children. His scores on this test indicate that he has a mild intellectual disability. He was weakest on tasks involving verbal comprehension and best in his ability to define words. At times Joe failed to complete easy items but then succeeded on more difficult ones.

When evaluating a student's intellectual ability, we also evaluate the amount of personal independence and responsibility the student demonstrates in school, at home, and in the community. The Adaptive Behavior Inventory for Children, in which you participated, indicates that Joe does have difficulty in developing relationships and friendships with other children and in the responsibilities he assumes in the community.

To ensure that Joe's difficulty at school was not due primarily to his frequent movement, differences in culture and language, and family income and educational level, we administered the System of Multicultural Pluralistic Assessment. This measure indicates that Joe's background does differ considerably from that of typical students. Although these factors probably do contribute to Joe's educational difficulties, they are not considered to be the primary cause. As noted earlier, Joe appears to have a mild intellectual disability, which is the primary cause of school difficulty.

On tests of achievement (Peabody Individual Achievement Test, Woodcock Reading Mastery Tests, Key Math, Informal Reading Inventory, and Informal Math Inventory), Joe consistently performed from 2 to 3 years below other students in the fifth grade in reading and mathematics. In reading, Joe has difficulty because he does not have the strategies to learn to read new words and because he has difficulty understanding what he reads. He does understand more when he listens to others read. In mathematics, Joe can add, subtract, and knows some multiplication facts. He often can work more difficult problems that are presented on paper if he is given a reminder on how to do them, but he has difficulty with regrouping, use of zeros, place value, and selecting the right math operation for word problems. He can tell time by the hour and half hour

(Figure 5–6 continued)

easily, but has difficulty telling time by the minute. He also can count coins to one dollar and sometimes higher, but he has difficulty making change.

At our meeting on February 17, the special services committee analyzed the results of the evaluation carefully and determined that Joe does have a disability. Because of his lowered functioning on the intellectual and adaptive behavior measures and his significant difficulties in reading and mathematics, the committee agreed that Joe qualifies for special education services. His specific disability, qualifying him for special education, is mild mental retardation.

The committee agreed that Joe has strengths on which to build including his ability to cooperate and to gain information from listening. The proposed action, based on the evaluation results, is to meet with you to plan a program designed specifically to address Joe's educational needs. At the meeting, we will develop an individualized educational program (IEP), which is a written plan of the content Joe will be taught throughout the school year and the special services he will receive. The IEP will serve as a guide to those of us responsible for his program at school and to you in helping Joe make the maximum amount of progress this year. We agreed that school representatives would develop preliminary goals and objectives in the areas of reading, mathematics, and vocational education to use as a planning document at the meeting. These will be sent to committee members before the IEP meeting.

The meeting to plan the IEP is tentatively scheduled for Tuesday, March 1, at 3:15 P.M. I will call you next week to confirm the meeting. If this is not a convenient time for you, please notify Ms. Jones, the school secretary (481-9082). Since we consider your participation very important, we can reschedule the meeting time or arrange another meeting place if more convenient for you. If we do not hear from you by February 25, we will assume that you can attend the meeting on March 1 and will look forward to seeing you at 3:15 P.M. in Joe's present classroom. The persons attending the meeting will be Mr. Thomas (the special education resource teacher), Mrs. Snow (Joe's teacher), Ms. Wrens (the principal), Mr. Ryan (the school psychologist), and myself. We would also like Joe to attend if you agree. If you would like to bring someone else to the meeting, please feel free to do so. I would appreciate your letting me know in advance if you are bringing someone. If you have any questions or concerns about the meeting, please contact me at 864-4092.

Let me assure you of our commitment to provide the best possible program for Joe. With your help, I am confident that we can do this. On behalf of all of us, we look forward to meeting with you.

Sincerely,

Steven LaJoie

Steven LaJoie
Counselor

IEP meeting occurs, an opportunity must be provided for interpretation of evaluation results, explanation of the content of the written notice, explanation of the IEP development process, and placement implications and decisions, all in the same meeting. What may often happen is that unless parents themselves request interpretation of evaluation results, or an explanation of the meaning of the written notice, the meeting may proceed with IEP development and placement. Technically, this may be acceptable. Such a procedure, however, though time-efficient for the school, often fails to establish a basis for a working partnership between parents and the school and raises serious issues regarding the degree to which parents are actually "fully informed" of the action proposed by the school.

Meeting to Discuss Evaluation Results. When at all possible, evaluation results should be reported to parents personally as well as in writing. There are several reasons for this preference. First, most parents who understand why the evaluation was conducted in the first place experience a great deal of anxiety regarding the outcome of the evaluation. Considering the magnitude of the decision to be made regarding their child, parents should be afforded an opportunity before the IEP meeting to discuss the results of evaluation with one or several members of the multidisciplinary team, the case manager, or another member of the special services committee qualified to interpret the results of evaluation. Second, provision of adequate notice is one of the least well-implemented safeguards of P.L. 94–142 in regard to ensuring that parents fully understand the implications of evaluation for the purpose of identification and placement in educational programs for the students with disabilities. A personal meeting with parents, in addition to written notice, provides an opportunity for (1) discussion, (2) emphasizing the important aspects of evaluation results, (3) ensuring that parents do, in fact, understand the content of the notice and most important, (4) establishing a personal and positive basis for future communication and cooperation between the parents and the school.

There are several ways to ensure that evaluation results are reported and interpreted to parents personally, before a student is formally classified as having a disability and a proposal made to place the student in a special education program. First, evaluation results can be shared with the parents by a member (or members) of the multidisciplinary evaluation team who compiled the final evaluation report. In such a meeting, the written multidisciplinary team report, if finalized, can provide the framework for the information provided to parents. Team members can either meet with the parents at school or go to the parents' home or other location to discuss the results. Because a meeting such as this is not required by P.L. 94–142, the participants in such a meeting can, if not governed by state or district regulation, be determined by the particular school, and can vary, depending on the situation and the available resources of the school. If this method is employed, a meeting most likely would occur before the IEP meeting. The purpose of this prior meeting is to discuss and explain evaluation results to parents and to ensure that the parents understand the content of the written notice that will be presented during the IEP meeting. In a meeting such as this, the special services committee has already made a decision regarding the student's eligibility for special education. Thus, in addition to discussing evaluation results, the proposal to change or refuse to change the student's identification and/or placement can be explained.

Another option is to conduct a meeting with the parents for the specific purpose of including them as committee members in the determination of program eligibility. In such a case, eligibility would not be determined before meeting with the parents, although the written report of evaluation results would be compiled. At such a meeting, all participants including the parents would consider the evaluation results and determine whether the student requires special education and related services to address the adverse educational effect of a disability. If the student is determined eligible for special education, the participants can schedule a date for IEP development or can proceed with the process if time allows. It should be noted that if the committee establishes a procedure to include the IEP meeting as part of an eligibility meeting, prior notice must be given to the parents that such a meeting will occur if the student is determined eligible for special education.

SUMMARY

Appropriate evaluation ultimately depends on professionals (1) to make appropriate decisions regarding procedures to be used, (2) to ensure that they are used appropriately, (3) to ensure that results provide an accurate reflection of findings, and ultimately (4) to make an appropriate eligibility determination. Though it stems from the evaluation process, eligibility determination presents its own issues. Even with appropriate evaluation procedures, wrong eligibility decisions can be made. The next chapter deals specifically with issues of eligibility determination by the special services committee.

EVALUATION

1. Review an evaluation report for a student with a disability. Develop a method and strategies for meeting the notice requirements of P.L. 94–142 regarding reporting evaluation results to parents.
2. You are the chairperson of a team responsible for planning a multidisciplinary evaluation for a student with a suspected learning disability. The student's parents speak Spanish and some English and the student speaks both English

and Spanish. Design an evaluation plan for evaluating this student, noting the potential disadvantages of traditional evaluation procedures.

3. Develop a recommendation for a standard procedure for considering the requirements for nondiscriminatory evaluation before student evaluation.

4. Assume that you are the director of special education in a local school district and have been asked to conduct a 1-hour inservice meeting on the teacher's role as a member of the multidisciplinary evaluation team. Outline your presentation, including a rationale for teacher participation, methods of informal evaluation that teachers should use, and the advantages and disadvantages of each method.

CHAPTER 6　　Eligibility Determination

OBJECTIVES

1. Identify and discuss three criteria established by P.L. 94–142 for determining that a student is eligible to receive special education services.

2. Discuss variation in eligibility criteria from state to state.

3. Identify participants in the eligibility decision-making process, and discuss the variety of sources that may be used to generate information for eligibility determination.

4. Provide guidelines for clear documentation of eligibility decisions by the special services committee.

Since the enactment of P.L. 94–142 in 1975, states have incorporated its requirements into an ongoing process of identifying and educating students with disabilities. Much evidence, however, suggests that the existing criteria and procedures established by states for determining program eligibility for students with mild learning disabilities have not clearly differentiated between those students who have disabilities and those who do not (Ysseldyke, Algozzine, Shinn, & McGue, 1982), and are not related to identifiable differences in educational needs that require special class placements (Heller, Holtzman, & Messick, 1982).

Eligibility decisions often appear to be based on reasons other than the fact that a student has a confirmed disability that requires placement outside the regular program. For example, a diagnosis of "disabled" may be one of the few ways to provide a student with individualized help. Because special education services traditionally have been available only to those students identified as having a disability, the placement committee may confirm eligibility to provide individualized instruction.

Another reason for classifying students as having a disability may be to provide assistance to the classroom teacher by removing the students from the classroom. Considering that a classroom teacher may be responsible for 25 to 30 students with varying abilities, the eligibility committee (and teachers) may consider it appropriate to remove students from the classroom when other options for providing help are available in the school.

Finally, students may be classified as having a disability to justify the existence of a special education program. Most special education programs receive funds based on the number of identified students with disabilities served in special education programs. Under these circumstances, it is necessary to determine students eligible before providing services. Unfortunately, these restrictions often prevent the student from receiving the same service as part of the regular education program without being labeled.

Although much controversy and variability exist regarding the criteria for special education eligibility, P.L. 94–142 does establish a framework within which to consider eligibility issues. This chapter will review the requirements of P.L. 94–142 regarding eligibility determination, discuss issues associated with criteria for eligibility, and provide suggestions for the special services committee in eligibility decision making.

ELIGIBILITY CRITERIA

P.L. 94–142 establishes three criteria for special education program eligibility. These include the following:

1. The student must have a diagnosed disability (impairment, handicap).
2. The disability must have an adverse effect on educational performance.
3. The student must require specially designed instruction to meet unique needs.

Figure 6–1 illustrates the use of these criteria in eligibility determination.

Diagnosed Disability

Because P.L. 94–142 is a law for students with disabilities, the first (and from a legal perspective the most important) question to be answered is whether the student has a disability that entitles her to special consideration, over and beyond that afforded to other students, to ensure an equal opportunity to benefit from education. In many instances, a disability is apparent or easily diagnosed. Hearing, vision, orthopedic, health, and even intellectual and emotional disabilities in the moderate-to-severe range can be

FIGURE 6–1
Process for Determining Eligibility for Special Education

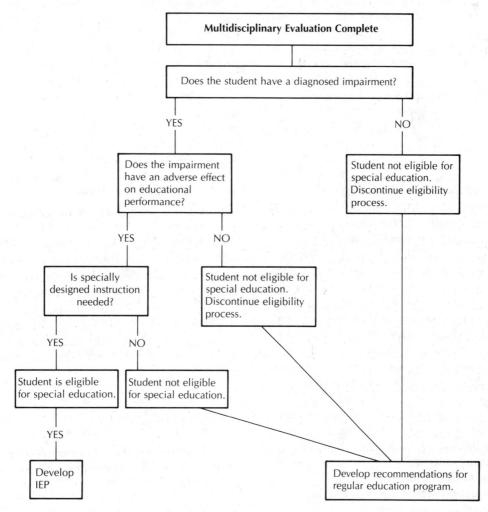

diagnosed with assurance that they represent a distinct population. However, less than 20% of students placed in special education programs are classified by rigorous physical or physiological measures (Reschly, 1988). Approximately 40% of students enrolled in special education are considered to have mild disabilities (e.g., learning disabilities, mild intellectual disabilities, or behavior disorders). For these students, it is often very difficult to differentiate the disability itself from its supposed effect, usually low academic performance and/or behavior problems in school. For example, because of the difficulty in diagnosing a learning disability, placement committees often tend to view poor performance and the student's disability synonymously. That is, low reading scores become the disability itself rather than the effect of a disability. Thus, just as the evaluation process may tend to be used simply to confirm

teacher referrals, so the eligibility decision may continue the process by confirming that a student has a disability based primarily on documentation of underachievement.

As noted earlier, eligibility decisions are often made with good intentions and in an effort to provide the student with assistance that may not otherwise be available. However, classifying an individual as having a disability to obtain these services raises serious legal and ethical issues, some of which have been tested in the courts (*Larry P. v. Riles*, 1979; *Diana v. State Board of Education*, 1970; *Lora v. Board of Education of the City of New York*, 1984). A current example is the overrepresentation of language-minority students in special education programs (Ortiz & Maldonado-Colon, 1986). Despite the clarity of P.L. 94–142 in establishing that problems arising from language differences are not, in themselves, disabling conditions, some placement committees continue to essentially disregard, fail to explore, or to misinterpret language issues when determining eligibility for those students whose behaviors do not fit the expectations of the classroom (Ortiz & Maldonado-Colon, 1986). In some instances, placement committees have fallen into the habit of treating special education programs as extensions of remedial and second-language programs without realizing the potentially serious long-term implications of labeling an individual as having a disability.

Adverse Effect on Educational Performance

Virtually every disability specified in P.L. 94–142 includes as part of its definition the phrase "adversely affects educational performance" (*Federal Register*, 1977). From an educational perspective, the disability must adversely affect educational performance in order to be considered a disability. It is entirely possible for a student to have a disability that does not adversely affect educational performance. A very common example is a student who has a speech disorder but who functions normally in school. Even some very pronounced disabilities may have little adverse effect on educational performance. Consider the student with a progressive illness who is yet able to fully participate in all aspects of the educational programs. Though somewhat controversial, it may legitimately be said that this student, while physically ill, does not have a disability that requires special education. The same might be said for a student who has a communication disorder such as stuttering, if the disorder has no adverse effect on educational performance.

Measuring the adverse effect of a disability on educational performance can be difficult for several reasons, including the following: (1) interpretation of the term *educational* varies, (2) states differ in their eligibility criteria, and (3) placement teams vary in the way eligibility decisions are made.

Interpretation of *Educational*.   The scope of the term *educational performance* is open to a wide variety of interpretations. Some systems interpret *educational* to mean *academic* and thus restrict the definition to academic performance (i.e., if the student is not failing academically and/or in physical education, then the student does not have a disability). Such a definition often excludes students with significant speech disorders who are achieving in school; students with learning disabilities who, despite discrepancies between achievement and ability, are not failing educationally; and some students with emotional disturbances who are performing adequately in school.

Whether or not the school is required to provide special education services for disorders that have a negligible effect on academic performance is a controversial issue.

If a school must generate new resources to provide services, or when existing programs are full and a mechanism must be found to reduce enrollment, a strict interpretation of *adverse effect* may be employed. For example, a student's parents may request that the school provide residential treatment for a student with an emotional disturbance who, though having difficulty socially in school, is on or near grade level academically and receives group and individual counseling through the regular program. A placement committee might, based on a strict interpretation of adverse effect on educational performance, determine that the student does not have an educational disability.

Another example of a relatively narrow interpretation of the adverse effect definition is found in the decision of the U.S. Supreme Court in *Board of Education of the Hendrick Hudson School District v. Rowley* (1982), which ruled that schools are not required to maximize a student's achievement but only to provide opportunities equal to those provided for other students. This could be interpreted to mean that if a student with a disability is already functioning adequately in school, then the school is not required to further minimize the possible adverse effect of the disability.

On the other end of the continuum is a very broad interpretation of the term *educational performance*. This definition might include social and medical as well as academic factors. Thus, a student with an articulation disorder might be classified as having a disability, while maintaining high academic achievement, because the articulation disorder adversely affects the student's self-confidence in oral reading or in social interactions. Likewise, a student with a personality disorder could be classified as having a disability based on social needs, and a student with a learning disability could be classified as having a disability because her achievement, though not near failing, is not in keeping with her ability.

Variation in State Eligibility Criteria.   The variability in states' eligibility criteria further complicates the measurement of adverse effect. The most variable criteria are those established for students with mild academic disabilities, usually included in the classification of *learning disabled*. Formulas for determining eligibility for this classification tend to vary widely. These formulas may be established on either an ability–achievement discrepancy model or an achievement-based model.

The ability–achievement discrepancy model defines adverse effect as a discrepancy that exists between measured intellectual ability and performance, usually 1.5 to 2.0 standard deviations. This model, at least for learning disabilities, tends to allow inclusion of those who are not failing and who may score within normal limits on achievement tests but who are having difficulty in school. This model, however, often excludes those who may be failing but whose assessment results do not indicate a significant discrepancy between ability and achievement. Within the discrepancy model is a wide range of other issues related to discrepancies in areas of information processing, which further complicates the definition of adverse effect. For example, in some states discrepancies do not have to be based on academic achievement. A student may demonstrate a discrepancy between intellectual ability and performance on auditory-processing tasks and thus qualify as having a disability.

States that do not adhere to a variation of an ability–achievement discrepancy formula for learning disabilities tend to define adverse effect as academic performance that is significantly below age or grade level, whether or not a significant discrepancy exists between achievement and ability. These formulas tend to be associated with "noncategorical" programs that serve students with mild learning disabilities due to academic, intellectual, and emotional disorders. A model such as this may tend to exclude students whose achievement reflects that they are surviving in the regular program, despite significant discrepancies between achievement and ability. There is also a greater likelihood that this definition of adverse effect will include poorly motivated, low socioeconomic status, and borderline-ability students.

Another issue related to the definition of adverse effect is its application to the young student. It is often difficult to measure discrepancies between ability and performance in preschool, kindergarten, and first and second grade. Thus, the application of standard formulas has often meant that young students with disabilities could not become eligible for special education until they were sufficiently far behind to demonstrate a significant adverse effect on educational performance. To improve this situation, most states have specific criteria for preschoolers and, in some instances, first and second graders. In some states, every effort is made to strictly define *adverse effect*, while in others, greater flexibility is incorporated into a category for "at-risk" students. The term *at risk* essentially means that although no adverse effect may yet exist, such effect is possible or probable if services are not provided. Figure 6–2

provides a sample of varying state eligibility criteria for establishing adverse effect for preschoolers.

Variation in Team Decision-Making Procedures. In addition to the variable interpretation of the term *educational* and the variability between and within states regarding defining *adverse effect* is the variability within school-level placement teams themselves. Although governed by state criteria for determining eligibility, committee decisions appear to violate such criteria regularly (Algozzine & Ysseldyke, 1981; Norman & Zigmond, 1980; Shepard & Smith, 1983). Yet, little evidence suggests that alternative objective criteria for determining adverse effect is established and documented during placement meetings. Research indicates that classroom referral data is frequently vague, subjective, and poorly documented (Algozzine & Ysseldyke, 1982) and that teachers appear to contribute little specific information from tests or observations on which to base eligibility decisions (Ysseldyke, Algozzine & Allen, 1981). In addition, decisions appear not to be related to data presented in meetings (Ysseldyke, Algozzine, Richey, & Graden, 1982). Considering these issues, it is unlikely that objective information on "adverse effect" is always available to or considered by the committee as the basis for eligibility decisions.

Need for Specially Designed Instruction

A final criterion of P.L. 94–142 for determining that a student is eligible for special education services is a determination that the student requires specially designed instruction. A comment in the *Federal Register* (1977) clarifies the intent of P.L. 94–142:

> The definition of "special education" is a particularly important one under these regulations since a child is not handicapped unless he or she needs special education. (*Federal Register*, 1977, p. 12478)

It is possible for a student to meet the first two criteria (presence of a disability and adverse effect) yet not need special education. For example, a student may have a confirmed physical disability that does have a limited adverse effect on performance in handwriting legibility and speed, and in physical education and athletic skills. The effect may not be significant enough, however, to prevent satisfactory completion of all work and full participation with minor modifications in the regular physical education program. In this example, the student may have a disability that does have an adverse effect, and yet the student can be well maintained in the regular program with slight modifications. Considering the

FIGURE 6–2
Examples of Eligibility Criteria for Preschool Programs

State	Age	Qualifiers
California	Birth through 4 years, 9 months	Functions 50% of chronological age (CA) level in one of the following: - Gross or fine motor - Receptive or expressive language development - Social or emotional development - Cognitive development
Colorado	Birth through 5	Exceptionalities designated for reporting purposes: - Blind - Communication disorder - Deaf - Deaf-blind - Developmentally disabled - Emotionally disturbed - Hard of hearing - Health impaired - Learning disabled - Mentally gifted - Mentally retarded - Multiple handicap - Orthopedically handicapped - Talented - Visually impaired
Louisiana	Birth through 3 years	The child must have a serious impairment as indicated by: 1. A severe physical handicap in areas such as sensory and/or motor functioning; or 2. Functioning in the low 1/3 of the normal functioning; or 3. A diagnosable condition that could result in a serious impairment if untreated; or 4. Severe inability to interact with the environment whether physical or social; or 5. Evidence that educational or developmental intervention is necessary to the future ability of the infant to benefit from the education.
Louisiana	3 years through 5 years	Children who exhibit a severe sensorial impairment, severe physical impairment, or who are suspected of being autistic, severe language disordered, or gifted or talented shall be identified categorically. Children who exhibit a suspected speech impairment (articulation, language, fluency, or voice) shall be determined eligible for services for speech impaired. If eligible, those children will be classified as nonhandicapped preschoolers.
Michigan	Birth through 5 years	A child whose primary disability cannot be differentiated through existing criteria* and who manifests an impairment in one or more areas of development equal to or greater than 1/2 of the expected CA development that cannot be resolved by medical or nutritional intervention. * Emotionally impaired, hearing impaired, severely mentally impaired, autism, educable mentally impaired, severely multiply impaired, trainable mentally impaired.

(Figure 6–2 continued)

State	Age	Qualifiers
Minnesota	Birth through 4 years	May be noncategorically classified in other than speech/language, hearing impaired or visually handicapped, or Manifest in a delay in cognitive or language development 1.5 standard deviations and supported by documented, systematic observation, or Is an identifiable syndrome known to hinder normal development.
Nebraska	Birth through 3 years	2 standard deviations if condition will require intervention.
New Jersey	Birth through 2 years 3 through 5 years	1. The child has a condition that impairs or has a high probability of impairing normal attainment of developmental milestones. Such conditions include but are not limited to hearing or vision impairment, autism, cerebral palsy, cleft palate, spina bifida, Down's syndrome, or orthopedic impairments. 2. The child has measurable developmental delays or disordered behavior showing the child to be functioning at least 25% below the CA in 2+ of the following: A. Motor B. Communication C. Cognition

North Dakota	Birth through 2 years	Performs 25% below CA norms in two or more of the following:
		- Cognitive-sensorimotor
		- Fine motor
		- Gross motor
		- Communication
		  Receptive
		  Expressive
		- Social-affective
		- Self help
		- Sensory processing
		  Auditory
		  Visual
		  Haptic
		
		Or High Risk: A child whose development is related to diagnostic disorders of known etiology that have relatively well-known expectancies for developmental outcome within specified ranges of developmental delay.

Texas	Birth through 5 years	A significant delay, beyond acceptable variations in normal development in one or more of the following areas: A. Cognitive B. Gross or fine motor C. Language or speech D. Social or emotional E. Self-help skills Or an organic defect that is very likely to result in such a delay.

(Figure 6–2 continued)

State	Age	Qualifiers
Virginia	2 years through 5 years	Age: 1.5 years SD: Delay greater than -1 Delay in months: 4.5+ Delay in %: 25%+ Age: 2 years SD: Delay greater than -1 Delay in months: 6+ Delay in %: 25%+ Age: 3 years SD: Delay greater than -1 Delay in months: 9+ Delay in %: 25%+ Age: 4 years SD: Delay greater than -1 Delay in months: 9+ Delay in %: 25%+ A child experiences a significant delay in one or more of the following areas: 1. Cognitive ability 2. Motor skills 3. Social/adaptive behavior 4. Perceptual skills 5. Communication skills
Washington	Birth through 3 years	Those children who demonstrate a 1.5 SD or 25% delay in: - Cognition - Communication - Fine motor - Gross motor - Fine and gross motor
Washington	3 years through 6 years	Those children who fall 2 SD less than X in one or more of the following: - Cognition - Communication - Fine motor - Gross motor - Fine and gross motor Those children who fall 1.5 SD less than X in two or more of the above areas or 25% delay.

current emphasis on making the regular program flexible enough to accommodate a wider range of differences, there is little to be gained by determining that this particular individual has a disability and needs special education.

This rationale clearly implies that eligibility may depend on the ability or willingness of a particular teacher to accommodate the needs of a particular child. This, unfortunately, is precisely the case at present. Although the courts have attempted to provide some guidance (by establishing that services that can "feasibly" be provided in a nonsegregated setting should be), feasible services have not been defined. Thus, some students with identical problems may receive quite different placements, based on the different characteristics of their regular classrooms (Gartner & Lipsky, 1987; Singer & Butler, 1987).

ROLE OF THE COMMITTEE IN ELIGIBILITY DETERMINATION

P.L. 94–142 establishes three committee responsibilities for eligibility determination by requiring that each local education agency ensure the following:

1. Placement decisions are made by a group of persons including persons knowledgeable about the student, the meaning of evaluation data, and the placement options.
2. Decisions draw on information from a variety of sources including aptitude and achievement tests, teacher recommendations, physical condition, social or cultural background, and adaptive behavior.
3. Information obtained from all of these sources is documented and carefully considered.

Full Committee Participation

The authority and responsibility for determining whether a student has a disability and is eligible for special education is given by law to a group of persons rather than to one individual (*Federal Register*, 1977). Although P.L. 94–142 is very clear on this point, research indicates that some committee members may tend to have an inordinate amount of influence on eligibility decisions. For example, speech therapists may decide unilaterally which students will receive speech therapy as a result of school screening. In addition, school psychologists may be viewed by both school personnel and parents as having disproportionate influence on eligibility and placement decisions, although they are not considered to be in a better position for making recommendations than other members of the committee (National

Association of State Directors of Special Education, 1985). A significant amount of evidence also indicates that the referrals of classroom teachers, in themselves, significantly influence whether a student will be determined to have a disability and to be eligible for special education services (Algozzine, Christenson, & Ysseldyke, 1982). Thus, the committee's eligibility decision may simply confirm the recommendation of specific individuals, while other committee members assume a passive role in the decision-making process.

In addressing the three criteria for eligibility discussed in the previous section, the full participation and individual expertise of all members is essential. Each member involved in determining eligibility is responsible for ensuring that data are accurately presented and interpreted and that the group makes an accurate and appropriate decision. P.L. 94–142 requires that various perspectives guide eligibility determination. To achieve this, the regulations specify that decision making must be made by individuals knowledgeable about evaluation results, about the student, and about placement options. Although these designations may appear somewhat arbitrary and overlapping, the implication is that no one perspective is sufficient for determining that a student does or does not have a disability requiring specially designed instruction. Information provided by individuals who know about test results should be considered, interpreted, and balanced by those who are knowledgeable about the student. Likewise, information provided by individuals knowledgeable about the student should be considered, interpreted, and balanced by those who know about the test results. Members of the eligibility team, then, should ideally provide a system of checks and balances to establish the accuracy of all data considered in the eligibility determination. In this way, discussion can be generated and directed toward establishing and documenting an accurate body of information on which to base an appropriate eligibility decision.

Individuals who are knowledgeable about placement options should be primarily involved in determining the need for specially designed instruction rather than in determining whether the student has a disability or whether the disability has an adverse educational effect. This individual may be an administrator, special education supervisor, curriculum specialist, or other individual who has specific knowledge about all placement options including the regular classroom and remedial programs and their suitability for different instructional needs in the context of the least restrictive environment.

Individuals knowledgeable about formal evaluation procedures may include teachers, physicians, audiologists, physical and occupational therapists, speech therapists, psychologists, educational diagnosticians, and other individuals whose primary function in the process for a particular student is assessment. These individuals can most appropriately contribute information about the first eligibility question, "Does a disability exist?" They also may contribute information regarding adverse effect by discussing the potential effects of the disability on student performance and by addressing the question of whether the disability may cause or may be related to the educational concern that prompted the referral. These individuals also can provide information on adverse effect from the perspective of standardized achievement tests, which show how a student functions in reference to the group on whom the test was normed. It should be emphasized, however, that it is not the function of these individuals to decide eligibility issues. The question "Is there a disability?" is not the same as "Is the student eligible for special education?" These individuals contribute only a portion of the information necessary to confirm program eligibility.

Individuals who are knowledgeable about the student must contribute information on which to consider program eligibility. These individuals may include the classroom teacher, parent, counselor, remedial teacher, tutor, or other individuals who work with or have knowledge of a student on a day-to-day basis and have a relationship with the student outside of the assessment situation. These individuals can contribute invaluable information for defining the adverse effect of a disability and establishing the need for specially designed instruction. They can specify the extent to which a diagnosed disability actually affects educational performance in school and away from school; interpret the meaning of test results regarding the day-to-day performance of a particular student; and can serve as an advocate in ensuring that information presented is an accurate reflection of the student. Although one might assume that classroom teachers are always involved in eligibility decisions, research indicates that classroom teachers are often not only not involved in decision making but often are not informed after decisions are made (Ammer, 1984). Because information contained in referrals tends to be somewhat vague, using the referral to represent the input of the classroom teacher at the point of eligibility is not entirely appropriate. The classroom teacher should be present not only to provide information regarding the concern but to gain information that may clarify the concern and assist in instruction.

Although P.L. 94–142 does not specifically require the involvement of parents in eligibility decisions, they are logical choices in the selection of individuals who are knowledgeable about the student. There are several good reasons for including parents

in eligibility decisions. First, parents already have very specific rights regarding the decision made. They must receive a full description of each procedure, test, record, or report used as a basis for eligibility, and a full explanation of recommendations made, with reasons why other options were rejected. They also have the right to appeal any decision made by the school. It would seem that involving parents in the eligibility decision would help to ensure that parents are fully informed about all aspects of the proposed action. Second, parents are often the only source of substantive information regarding preschool development and the actual effect that a disability may already have on a child's performance at home and in the community. Third, parents also can provide a context for the appropriate consideration of test data that may serve to avoid inappropriate identification and placement. For example, Ortiz and Maldonado-Colon (1986), in a study of eligibility and placement decisions for second-language students, noted that teacher referral and test performance in English were the most significant variables in determining placement and that substantive information on native language, which could be provided by parents, was consistently disregarded at all levels from referral to placement. Information such as home language, time and quality of exposure to English, and the type of previous instructional interventions and their outcomes may be provided by parents; such information may significantly affect the way that team members interpret test data and determine program eligibility.

Information from a Variety of Sources

P.L. 94–142 requires that eligibility be based on information from a variety of sources, including aptitude and achievement tests, teacher recommendations, physical condition, social or cultural background, and adaptive behavior. Information from aptitude and achievement tests, however, often may provide the sole basis for eligibility determination (Lambert, 1988). One reason for this may be the traditional belief that standardized tests are more valid and reliable than other data, such as curriculum-based assessment or systematic observation. Another reason may be that state-established eligibility criteria often require the use of standardized aptitude and achievement tests in confirming that a student has a disability and needs special education. In addition, eligibility determination may be viewed as completely separate from other activities in the referral process. Thus, other information, collected and available before formal assessment, may not be reviewed, synthesized, and fully considered at the point of eligibility. Although standardized aptitude and achievement tests provide one source of information on which to base eligibility decisions, used alone they provide insufficient information about the adverse effect of a disability on educational performance and little useful information for instructional planning. To reach valid conclusions regarding the functional level of students and program eligibility, the committee must systematically consider information from other sources. If the committee has access to thorough pre-referral information and well-placed and gathered assessment data, there should be sufficient information available at the point of eligibility to provide a basis for eligibility determination.

Several sources of information often may be overlooked in eligibility determinations, which may provide essential and insightful information for accurate decision making. These areas include the following:

1. Information on student characteristics that may adversely affect performance but do not constitute a disability
2. Information generated from the classroom setting
3. Information on the student's educational history
4. Information on the instructional style of the teacher
5. Information on how the student compares to other students in the same grade or class

It should be emphasized that accumulating a variety of data does not guarantee that the same data will be fully considered in the actual eligibility determination. It is the responsibility of the committee to ensure that all pertinent data are in fact available and included in the decision-making process.

Student Characteristics. Student characteristics such as physical condition, vision and hearing acuity, social/emotional functioning, distractibility, language, culture, or environment (all of which may significantly affect the measurement of student performance) must be considered at the point of eligibility determination. Considering the overrepresentation of minority, poor, and second-language students enrolled in special education programs, it appears that committees may often fail to gather and/ or consider sufficient information on student characteristics when making eligibility decisions (Ortiz & Maldonado-Colon, 1986). Because the group of individuals determining eligibility is legally bound by the nondiscriminatory assessment requirements of P.L. 94–142 to ensure that these factors have no significant adverse influence on the measurement of student skills, information gathered for eligibility determination must include data on these student characteris-

tics. The committee should ensure that this information is fully considered for students suspected of having communication, intellectual, and emotional disabilities to confirm that concerns are due to an actual disability and are not due to factors such as race, culture, language, and socioeconomic level.

Information from Classroom Setting. Information generated from the setting in which the student is not performing well is critical to the eligibility determination. If a pre-referral process is employed before referring the student to special education, valuable information directly related to the referral question should be available for consideration by the eligibility team. Consideration should be given to information provided by curriculum-based assessment, observational analyses, sociometric data, and the results of educational interventions attempted before assessment. This information can then be compared to assessment data gathered during the assessment process. Although this information should be collected and documented before referral, current research indicates that referrals often are vague and do not include all pertinent information regarding the nature of the student's educational problem (Pugach, 1985). If pertinent data were not gathered during the pre-referral, referral, or formal assessment process, the committee should obtain such data before making eligibility decisions.

Educational History. The committee should fully consider the student's educational history to determine whether poor performance has been evident for a long period of time or is recent. Previous grades, standardized achievement scores, and performance or behavior at home and in other classes can provide valuable insights into problems that a student is experiencing at school. If poor performance is a recent or isolated occurrence, the committee must question whether such performance is indeed a result of an underlying disability. Although the committee does not have to prove a relationship between poor performance and a disability, the committee should gather and consider sufficient information to reasonably assume that the two are related. The quality of the information that the committee considers may significantly affect the eligibility decision.

Instructional Style of Teacher. The instructional style of a teacher is a factor that also should be fully considered. Although this may not determine whether the student is or is not eligible for special education, it can provide an indication of whether the student's low achievement may be exacerbated by the way in which instruction has been provided. For example, a student may perform in the average range on standardized tests but may not be achieving satisfactorily in the mathematics class. If the teacher's instructional style emphasizes whole-group instruction with little individualized instruction and little supervision of homework, this factor may partially explain the difference between performance in class and performance on standardized tests.

Comparison with Other Students.   Another type of information that the committee should consider is comparison of the student's performance to that of other students in the same class or grade. It may be that as a group, students in that particular class or grade perform somewhat below average in school and below the national norm on a group-administered standardized test. It is even more likely that within a particular class, a variety of reading levels exist. Comparing the performance of the student with a possible disability to other, presumably typical, students in the school can provide a relevant framework within which to consider such issues as whether the performance of the student is, in fact, atypical; whether the instructional needs of the student differ significantly from those of other students in the classroom or grade; and whether the student should be determined eligible for special education.

For preschool students, educational performance must be considered in developmental terms. Because most identified preschool students with disabilities have a diagnosis of communication impaired (U.S. Department of Education, 1987), it is generally this area of development that is used to document an existing or potential adverse effect. In many instances, the parents must provide information regarding a student's past performance at home and with other children to determine if performance is affected or potentially may be affected in the future.

Because information gathering can be a time-consuming process, care should be taken to ensure that information already available is gathered and considered rather than regenerating the same information again at the point of eligibility. Pre-referral data, if conscientiously gathered and documented during the pre-referral process, are a readily available and excellent source of eligibility information. The committee should also ensure that data extraneous to the decision to be made do not occupy an inordinate amount of committee time and effort. Accumulation of information that is not useful to determining eligibility may not only occupy committee time but will contribute little understanding to the educational concern. For example, in an effort to ensure that more than one procedure is used to determine eligibility for students with disabilities in speech, some schools

may administer achievement tests to students referred for speech problems when there is no academic concern. This procedure may be a waste of time that could appropriately be used to establish the disorder's implications for future or present functioning in school and the disorder's social or personal effect on the student.

In summary, the committee should know what information is necessary to answer each of the eligibility questions required by P.L. 94–142 and state-established requirements and should systematically collect and fully consider information that will address those requirements. A final and very important requirement of P.L. 94–142 is the documentation of the information on which the eligibility determination is based. The next section will provide guidelines for documentation of eligibility decisions.

Clear Documentation of Decision

Ultimately, the group that determines eligibility must establish and document a clear rationale for why a student is or is not determined to have a disability that requires special education. P.L. 94–142 requires that all information on which eligibility is based be documented and carefully considered. Yet the decisions made by eligibility committees are not always apparently related to data presented at the meeting (Ysseldyke, Algozzine, Richey, et al., 1982). Furthermore, the documentation that does exist does not always justify the eligibility decision made. For example, documentation of the fact that a student has a physical disability is not sufficient to establish that the student requires special education. Likewise, documenting the fact that a student is functioning below the rest of the class is not sufficient to justify that a disability exists. It must be emphasized that eligibility is to be based on careful consideration of all relevant information, not just on the accumulation of standardized test data. Eligibility is perhaps the most important decision made regarding a student with a potential disability. This decision and the reasons for it must be clearly established and well documented.

Figure 6–3 provides a sample form for documenting eligibility decisions. Such a form provides a place in the student's record where the decision that a student does or does not have a disability is fully justified. It should be remembered that this may be the only place in the record where such information exists. It is therefore one of the most important documents to be included in the student record. In recording its decision, the committee's primary responsibility is to ensure that all requirements are met and documented in the record. If the student transfers to another school, the receiving school

FIGURE 6–3
Format for Eligibility Determination

<u>Eligibility Determination</u>

<u>ATTACH ALL REPORTS ON WHICH ELIGIBILITY DETERMINATION IS MADE</u>

1. A. Does the student have a diagnosed disability or impairment?
   Yes _____ No _____ (see attached evaluation report)

   Area of:

   _____ Speech   _____ Orthopedic   _____ Emotional
   _____ Language   _____ Other health impaired _____ Multiple
   _____ Vision   _____ Intellectual   handicap
   _____ Hearing   _____ Information processing

   Basis for determination (meets established state criteria or clear justification
   for committee application of other determining criteria)
   _____
   _____

1. B. Has it been clearly established that the data on which the diagnosis is based is
   not significantly influenced by factors other than those purportedly measured?
   Yes _____ No _____

   If no, what factors may have had significant influence on the data?
   _____
   _____
   _____
   _____

2. Does the diagnosed impairment have a significant adverse effect on educational
    performance? Yes _____ No _____

    Basis for determination (academic status, educational history, observational
    data)
    _____
    _____
    _____
    _____
    _____

3. Does this student require specially designed instruction to meet unique
    educational needs resulting from a diagnosed impairment? Yes _____ No _____

    Basis for Determination (comparison to others in same grade, class, age, etc.)
    _____
    _____
    _____

(Figure 6–3 continued)

<u>AREAS OF UNIQUE NEED</u>:

4. Based on these conclusions, the determination of this committee is:

____ The student is handicapped and eligible for special education services. (Student has a disability, it has an adverse effect on performance, and specially designed instruction is required.)

____ The student is not handicapped and therefore is not entitled to special education and related services.

5. Committee action:
Schedule IEP Meeting ____
Refer to alternate program ____
Meet with classroom teacher to recommend classroom intervention ____

The following members participated in the eligibility determination:

_____   _____
Parent   Date

_____   _____
Classroom Teacher   Date

_____   _____
Administrator   Date

_____   _____
Special Education Teacher   Date

should be able to read the eligibility documentation and understand how required criteria, both federal and state, have been met. Thus, at a minimum the committee must demonstrate that a disability does exist, that it has an adverse effect on educational performance, and that as a result the student requires special education and related services. The remainder of this section will use the three basic criteria of P.L. 94–142 to provide suggestions for committees in documenting eligibility decision.

Presence of a Disability. Assessment data usually provide the basis for establishing that a significant disability exists. These data may be medical in nature, or in the case of students with academic disabilities, more educationally or psychometrically based. An audiological assessment may establish a hearing disability, a medical report confirm a cleft palate, a psychiatrist's report confirm an emotional disorder, or a psychological evaluation confirm low or impaired intellectual functioning. As discussed earlier in this chapter, confirmation of a disability is the first step

to establishing eligibility. The committee must be able to confirm a disorder or disability that may be adversely affecting educational performance. If a disability cannot be confirmed and documented by the committee, then the student should not be determined eligible for special education. Instead, other means of addressing the educational concern should be developed.

If the committee can confirm a disability, it should be specifically named. Naming the disorder does not preclude service in a noncategorical or cross-categorical program. According to P.L. 94–142, a student must have a specific diagnosed disability to be eligible for placement in any special education program. The nature of the service delivery model (categorical, noncategorical, or cross-categorical) refers only to the way that services are provided and should not affect the specificity with which a diagnosis is made. For example, a student with a diagnosed intellectual disability ultimately may be served in the same noncategorical resource room as a student with a diagnosed learning disability. The special education programs may be similar while the specific identified disabilities may differ.

The committee should, unless clearly inappropriate to do so, document and apply the criteria established by the state and approved by the U.S. Department of Education. This is especially important for disorders that are not currently well defined such as learning disabilities and behavior disorders. Although eligibility criteria in these areas may be vague, specifically adhering to and documenting state-established criteria for confirming a disorder can demonstrate that the committee applied a set of approved criteria when diagnosing a disability rather than making an arbitrary eligibility decision.

Because P.L. 94–142 entrusts appropriate eligibility determination to the judgment of a group of individuals rather than to the outcome of a standard formula or group of tests, it is clear that informed professional judgment must guide and ensure the appropriateness of eligibility decisions. In the event that state-established criteria are clearly not applicable or appropriate for establishing the presence of a disability, or when the considered opinion of the group differs from test data, the group may find it necessary to deviate from criteria established by the state. The committee must, however, provide a clear and justifiable basis for variation. For example, some states require a specific discrepancy between measured intellectual ability on a psychological evaluation and measured achievement on standardized tests to confirm the presence of a learning disability. If all data except discrepancy data on the psychological evaluation indicate that a significant learning disability exists, then the committee must clearly document the supporting evidence and the basis for discounting the psychological evaluation. To ensure that the reasons for questioning the psychological evaluation are appropriate, a school psychologist should be involved in any meeting where the validity or interpretations of the psychological evaluation are questioned or discounted. Before moving to consideration of the adverse effect of the disability, the committee should reach consensus that a disability does or does not exist, document the sources of information that support the decision, and provide clear documentation and justification for the determination for the record.

Establish Adverse Effect. Documentation of adverse effect can be derived from both standardized and informal evaluation measures. Documentation may be most appropriately contributed by the teachers who are familiar with the student's educational performance and should be derivable in part from referral materials submitted before assessment. If an effective pre-referral process is employed before re-

ferring the student to special education, there should be sufficient data to document the adverse educational effect of the disorder. Whatever the adverse effect of the disorder may be, it is the responsibility of the eligibility committee to provide specific documentation for the record. Documentation such as "failing social studies" does not provide sufficient information to necessarily assume that a failing grade in social studies is the effect of a disorder. A better statement would be "limited vocabulary and comprehension skills affect student's ability to read and understand content area texts."

The eligibility report should clearly reflect that the adverse effect described is considered to be associated with a specific disability and not primarily attributable to other factors such as environmental disadvantage, cultural differences, or economic disadvantages. Sufficient justification for this conclusion should be provided in cases where such explanation may clearly be necessary. For example, detailed documentation of the reasons why the committee attributes language difficulties to a hearing disability is not as critical as documenting reasons why the committee attributes language problems of a second-language student to a learning disability rather than to the fact that the student's primary language is one other than English.

If, as might be the case with preschool students with disabilities, the adverse effect is not clearly apparent or is more a potential problem than an existing effect, the committee must document the potential effect of the disability and how specially designed instruction may be used to prevent or minimize such effects. Some states have eligibility provisions for children "at risk" who demonstrate characteristics likely to result later in disability and in significant adverse effect if specially designed instruction is not provided.

Establish Need for Special Education. Finally, the committee must consider and document whether the student, as a result of a disability and its adverse effect, requires specially designed instruction to meet her unique needs. This can be one of the most difficult decisions to be made and documented during eligibility determination because little information is available about what modifications are, or should be, typically or routinely made for any student enrolled in the regular program (Pugach, 1985).

Although the process of defining instructional needs can be difficult, it is impossible to establish that a student has unique needs without first identifying what those needs might be. Thus, the first step in determining whether a student requires specially designed instruction is to establish and document the student's instructional needs. Reaching a consensus on what a student's instructional needs actually are provides a basis for determining whether they in fact differ from those of other students and whether they require specially designed instruction. Identification of student needs can also provide the basis for later IEP development or for the development of remedial programs for students who do not qualify for special education. Figure 6–4 provides a list of student needs that might typically be generated by the eligibility committee in determining whether a student requires specially designed instruction. For each need identified, the committee should be able to document the sources of information used to establish the need.

After the committee has identified the student's instructional needs, a determination can be made regarding whether the identified needs differ from those of other students. One often cited criticism of special education programs is that little evidence indicates that students with mild disabilities can be characterized by different instructional needs or by different instructional strategies from those in compensatory education programs (Heller, Holtzman, & Messick, 1982). Documentation of needs forces the committee to seriously consider whether a student's needs, though stemming from a disability, are sufficiently different from those of other students to warrant specially designed instruction and possible placement in a separate program.

Sometimes it is apparent that a student has unique instructional needs. For example, a student with a physical disability may require instruction in the use of adaptive equipment, a student who cannot hear may require a system of total communication, and a blind student will require mobility training and emphasis on oral explanation. However, it is not always so apparent that a student with a learning disability, mild intellectual disability, or an emotional disorder will require specially designed instruction. Although a student with a mild intellectual disability may require concrete examples and repetition to benefit educationally, this modification might be considered one that could be provided routinely in the regular program, with or without the use of supplemental aids and materials. Thus, the committee will have to reach a consensus regarding what instructional modifications might reasonably be expected to be provided to any student in a classroom and whether a particular individual's needs might be reasonably accommodated within that structure.

It is entirely possible to confirm a disability and an adverse educational effect and still not determine that a student requires specially designed instruction. For example, even if a student has a hearing disability and reads below grade level, that student may not necessarily require instruction different from that available to other students. That student might instead benefit from small-group or individual reading provided routinely in the regular classroom to other students or from enrollment in a reading improvement program. Depending on the nature of the identified need, the committee may determine that instructional modifications normally provided through the regular program are suitable interventions for a student with a disability. Obviously, if the regular program is set up to accommodate individual differences, it is more likely that a student with mild-to-moderate educational difficulties could be maintained in the classroom using the same basic modifications that the teacher would use for other students.

It should be emphasized that the issue that the committee must address during eligibility determination is not whether the student should be enrolled in special education classes but whether, to benefit from education, she requires instruction that is not normally expected to be available to other students as part of the regular program. If the committee confirms that a disability does exist and has an adverse effect on educational performance and that as a result the student requires specially designed instruction, the committee must determine that student is eligible for special education. Where the student will receive the specially designed instruction is to be determined after the IEP is developed.

Providing Feedback to Others

If after documentation and consideration of all information necessary, the committee determines that a student is not eligible for special education, the results of the assessment and eligibility process should be shared with those who must assume responsibility for the student's instruction. Even though a student may be determined to be ineligible for special education, it is unlikely that the referral would have been submitted if the student were not experiencing difficulty in the regular classroom. Unfortunately, results of assessment and eligibility are often not shared with classroom teachers and others who may benefit from the information generated by the assessment and eligibility process (Ammer, 1984).

To extend the benefit of the multidisciplinary process beyond the determination of program eligibility, the committee might meet with the classroom teacher to discuss possible strategies for accommodating the student in the regular program. If a pre-referral intervention plan is used in the school, the committee could assist in the development of a similar written plan for the classroom teacher and

FIGURE 6–4
Index of Student Needs

Student Needs:
 1. Specification of auditory proficiency
 2. Ongoing monitoring of audiological status
 3. Sound amplification
 4. Training in tolerating and using amplification
 5. Visual presentations and modifications to supplement hearing status
 6. Speech and language training related to hearing status
 7. Lip-reading instruction
 8. Lip-reading input
 9. Manual-signing instruction
10. Manual-signing input
11. Total communication instruction
12. Total communication input
13. Specification of visual proficiency
14. Ongoing monitoring of visual status
15. Training in tolerating visual assistance aids
16. Magnification for printed materials
17. Illumination modifications
18. Paper or print color contrast
19. Enlarged print texts and materials
20. Raised print texts and materials
21. Tactile materials for information acquisition
22. Tape recorders for information acquisition because of visual acuity constraints
23. Talking books
24. An Optacon for reading
25. Instruction in using stylus and slate for note taking
26. Instruction in braille
27. Braille input
28. Instruction in orientation and mobility
29. Specification of physical proficiency
30. Assistance in ambulation
31. Ambulatory devices and training in use (i.e., crutches, braces, rollators, prosthetics)
32. Use and operation of wheelchair (manual or electric)
33. Support for sitting and/or alternative physical positions for classroom learning
34. Normalization of muscle tone
35. Lifting, carrying, and/or transferring assistance
36. Modified work surfaces (i.e., lap boards and tilted desks)
37. Use of graphomotor alternatives and/or adaptations (i.e., alternative graphics, hand styluses, head or mouth wands)
38. Eating assistance or physical adaptations because of motoric characteristics
39. Dressing assistance or physical adaptations because of motoric characteristics
40. Toileting assistance or physical adaptations because of motoric characteristics
41. The development and construction of a manual communication board and means of indicating needs
42. Use of a communication board or alternative communication mode (direct selection, scanning, or encoding devices)
43. Adaptations in physical education curricula because of motoric characteristics
44. Specification of emotional status
45. Ongoing clinical intervention for emotional integrity
46. Acquisition of inhibition of self-stimulation
47. Instruction in appropriate interpersonal social skills and acceptable social mores
48. Instruction in appropriate usage of materials

(Figure 6–4 continued)

49. Training in daily self-help skills (i.e., eating, dressing, and toileting) because of nonphysiologic characteristics
50. Development of alternative (nonoral) mode of communication because of nonphysiologic characteristics
51. Use of an alternative or nonoral communication mode because of nonphysiologic characteristics
52. Facilitation of personality development
53. Instruction in rudimentary survival skills (breathing, swallowing, primitive reflexes)
54. Instruction in rudimentary social skills (social smile, eye contact, response to touch)
55. Acquisition of a means of responding to visual and auditory input (indication of environmental awareness)
56. Acquisition of physical and/or verbal self-control (rumination, self-mutiliation, crying)
57. Instruction in sensorimotor skills
58. Instruction in preacademic skills
59. Instruction in life-experience programming
60. Instruction in use of leisure time
61. Specification of learning proficiency
62. Facilitation of arithmetic proficiency
63. Facilitation of reading proficiency
64. Facilitation of written expression proficiency
65. Facilitation of spelling proficiency
66. Facilitation of receptive language proficiency
67. Facilitation of expressive language proficiency
68. Facilitation of gross motor proficiency
69. Facilitation of fine motor proficiency
70. Facilitation of perceptual integration proficiency
71. Instruction in task strategies, organization, and completion
72. Instruction in functional academics and consumer skills
73. Instruction in experience in prevocational and career-related skills
74. Instruction in community living
75. Modifications in methods of instructional presentation and skill acquisition to accommodate preferred learning style
76. Specification of speech and language proficiency
77. Development of corrective breathing, swallowing, and eating patterns
78. Instruction in compensatory techniques for oral anomalies and organic disorders
79. Acquisition of prespeech skills
80. Facilitation of articulation proficiency
81. Facilitation of fluency
82. Remediation of voice disorders
83. Ongoing monitoring of effects of medication
84. Ongoing monitoring of existence of pain
85. Ongoing monitoring of the effects of fatigue

From *Procedural Guide for Special Education* (DS Manual 2500.13), by Department of Defense Dependents Schools, 1988, Alexandria, VA: Author. Reprinted by permission.

could recommend supplemental aids and materials that would be useful in maintaining the student in the regular program. In addition, the need statements generated by the eligibility determination should be shared with those responsible for teaching the student.

If the committee determines that the student's instructional needs are such that specially designed instruction is necessary, the student will be determined eligible for special education and an IEP developed. The IEP will define the specially designed instructional program the student requires to benefit from her educational program.

SUMMARY

This chapter has reviewed current issues related to eligibility determination and has emphasized the need to ensure that this procedure is conducted systematically and fairly for all students. Three criteria were presented and discussed to guide the collection of information and the decision-making process during eligibility determination. These criteria include (1) the student must have a diagnosed disability (2) the disability must have an adverse effect on the student's educational performance and, as a result (3) the student must require specially designed instruction. The need for full participation by all committee members was emphasized as well as the need to collect sufficient and appropriate information on which to base the eligibility decision.

The first six chapters of this book have focused primarily on the process by which a student is determined to have a disability and to need special education. They provide a context within which to understand the process of IEP development and implementation, which will provide the focus for the remainder on this book. The next six chapters will focus specifically on the development of the IEP for students who have been determined eligible for special education.

EVALUATION

1. You are the special education coordinator in a large, conservative school district and have been asked to speak to a parent organization to explain why some students qualify for special education in other states but do not qualify in your school district. Outline the reasons why criteria might differ between states and school districts.
2. Regular classroom teachers have asked you, the special education teacher in the school, to explain why students who are performing significantly below their classmates academically are not necessarily entitled to participate in your resource room program. Clarify the purpose of special education, and discuss criteria associated with eligibility determination.
3. You are a member of the committee deciding whether a fifth-grade student is eligible for special education services. The multidisciplinary evaluation indicates that the student has a significant discrepancy between measured ability and performance in reading and mathematics. The student is passing all subjects with grades of C. Provide a rationale for determining this student ineligible for special education.

PART 2

Mechanics of IEP Development

CHAPTER 7

Development of the IEP by Committee Members

OBJECTIVES

1. Define the purposes of the IEP from a legal, administrative, parental, and instructional perspective, and discuss current issues regarding these perspectives.

2. Identify pertinent information that, while not required, may make the IEP more functional.

3. Discuss four methods of IEP development.

4. Identify and discuss three types of IEP meetings.

5. Suggest factors that should be considered in planning the IEP conference, and identify planning strategies.

6. Identify and discuss seven general components of the IEP meeting.

7. Provide strategies for enhancing the participation of parents and students in IEP planning and development.

If it is determined that a student has a disability and also requires specially designed instruction, P.L. 94–142 requires that the specially designed instruction be reflected in an IEP. This document provides the central focus for program planning and placement for students with disabilities. This chapter provides a context for and serves as an introduction to the remainder of the book, which focuses on the development and implementation of each component of the IEP. Discussion will focus on the current issues related to the IEP requirement, suggestions for helpful information that might be included in the IEP format, suggested methods for developing the IEP, preparing for and conducting the IEP conference, and suggestions for maximizing parent and student involvement.

PURPOSES OF THE IEP REQUIREMENT

The IEP is clearly the most visible representation of the requirements of P.L. 94–142 regarding appropriate education for students with disabilities. As such, it serves various purposes representing legal, parental, administrative, and instructional perspectives. Each of these will be discussed briefly.

Legal Purpose

The IEP provides the legal mechanism for ensuring accountability in program planning and service delivery for students with disabilities. By requiring that a committee develop, review, and maintain a written description of the student's program, P.L. 94–142 establishes the IEP as an unprecedented and tangible statement of a student's educational program. In addition, the courts have repeatedly relied on the IEP requirements as the cornerstone for defining appropriate education (*Board of Education of the Hendrick Hudson School District v. Rowley*, 1982).

Although schools have for the most part established procedures for implementing the procedural requirements of IEP development, there remain several legal concerns regarding the appropriate implementation of the process. For example, schools still appear to routinely violate one of the most obvious and important principles related to IEP development, that of parent participation in IEP development. Despite the legal requirement of P.L. 94–142, the IEPs in many school systems continue to be developed primarily by school personnel before meeting with parents (White & Calhoun, 1987; U.S. Department of Education, 1987).

A second issue of legal concern is the practice in some schools of placing students in special education programs before the comprehensive evaluation is completed and before a determination that the student is, in fact, eligible for special education (Pugach, 1985). Again, P.L. 94–142 is very clear regarding the requirement that students cannot be placed in special education programs until eligibility has been determined and an IEP developed. In some states, a short diagnostic placement may be permissible if necessary to obtain evaluation information for identifying a student's specific areas of educational need. For example, it may be necessary to observe the interaction of a preschool student within a group to obtain accurate evaluation information before determining program eligibility. In such a case, the student might participate in the preschool program for a short period of time as part of the evaluation process. Where permissible, this procedure should be used only when evaluation information cannot be obtained by other means and only for a specified period of time.

Administrative Purpose

School administrators generally view the IEP as a management tool to document, in a general way, the student's special education program. When used for this purpose, the IEP documents that the school has fulfilled the procedural requirements of P.L. 94–142. Because most compliance-monitoring activities focus on the procedural elements of the IEP, maintaining IEP documents is useful in establishing procedural compliance or noncompliance regarding issues arising in school systems, such as due process hearings.

The IEP can also provide a useful mechanism for program monitoring and evaluation and school-wide program planning. The IEP can provide quantitative information on the types of curricula included in the special education programs of students with disabilities, the amount of time spent in separate and regular classes, and information regarding the types of IEPs that require separate placement. In addition the IEP can provide a mechanism for program supervision and evaluation.

Parent-Involvement Purpose

The IEP requirement was intended to provide several potential benefits to parents, including an opportunity to participate in the development of their child's special education program; to obtain a written definition of the specially designed educational program provided to their child; and to have at their disposal a mechanism for ensuring that the services specified in the IEP are, in fact, provided. Without question, many parents have taken full advantage of the intended benefits of the IEP. Despite the requirements of P.L. 94–142, however, the expectation that all parents of students with disabilities should and would be equal participants along with school personnel in developing, reviewing, and revising the student's IEP has not materialized (Singer & Butler, 1987; K. K. Turnbull & Hughes, 1987; U.S. Department of Education, 1987; Vaughn et al., 1988).

Studies reporting on the degree of parent involvement in IEP conferences indicate that in some districts less than 50% of parents attended their child's last IEP meeting, while in other districts attendance as high as 95% was reported (Singer & Butler, 1987). High levels of participation are particularly apparent in affluent districts and in districts where special effort is expended to encourage attendance such as scheduling the meeting outside of normal school hours (Singer & Butler, 1987). Other studies report that parents often attend the IEP meeting but play a relatively passive role during the conference (Vaughn, et al., 1988). Several reasons may account for the lack of parental participation in IEP conferences.

Parental Choice.   Although the provisions of P.L. 94–142 regarding parent involvement were intended as rights afforded to parents, these rights have in some instances taken on the tone of imperatives (A. P. Turnbull & Turnbull, 1982). Parents often are expected to assume an active and participatory role in educational decision making, advocacy, teaching, case management, and program evaluation (Allen & Hudd, 1987). Although some parents are inclined and able to participate to a great extent in their child's educational program, others may not be so inclined or able to choose an active role. This means that parents have the right to choose not to participate in the development of the IEP. Parents may wish to leave educational planning to educators while maintaining the right to review and monitor the educational program developed.

Family Characteristics.   Although parents may choose not to be involved in the IEP conference, family factors other than choice often appear to restrict the active participation of parents in IEP conferences as well as in other aspects of the educational process. Of significant concern is the continuing lack of participation by parents who traditionally have found it difficult to access the educational system, specifically parents who have low incomes, are less well-educated, who may have language and cultural differences, and who may have different attitudes toward the school problems of their children. Because the children from these families are often the very students overrepresented in special education classes for students with learning disabilities, mild intellectual disabilities and emotional disturbances, these parents may be most in need of the protections of P.L. 94–142.

Professional Attitudes.   Other parents may not participate in IEP development, because they are not encouraged to do so by professionals. Whether parents choose to be uninvolved or whether the attitudes of educators perpetuate minimal involvement is a controversial issue. Although parents clearly have preferences and make choices regarding the degree to which they prefer to be involved in the IEP development process, it appears that the attitudes of educators may, in some cases, perpetuate the passive role of parents. For example, at the time of enactment of P.L. 94–142, research indicated that parent participation in conferences tended to be primarily passive (Goldstein, Strickland, Turnbull, & Curry, 1980) and that professionals considered that role to be appropriate (Yoshida, Fenton, Kaufman, & Maxwell, 1978). Ten years later, evidence indicates that professional views may not have changed substantially. For example, in a study of 145 special education teachers in six states, P. J. Gerber, Banbury, Miller, and Griffin (1986) found that 71% of the teachers believed that parents should be given the option to waive the requirement of parent participation and place decision making solely in the hands of professionals. Further, 31% indicated that parents do not make a significant contribution to the IEP process. This information, coupled with the fact that IEPs appear in some cases to be completed even before the meeting with the parents (U.S. Department of Education, 1977; White & Calhoun, 1987), indicates that professional attitudes toward parent participation may be as much an obstacle to the achievement of this goal as family characteristics.

Research during the early years of P.L. 94–142 implementation indicated that student participation in the IEP conference was virtually nonexistent (Marver & David, 1979). As with parent participation, student participation is still low (Vaughn et al., 1988), although students at the secondary level are far more likely to participate in the conference than elementary and junior high level students.

Instructional Purpose

The IEP has provided a common focal point for those involved in the process of providing services to students with disabilities. Because the IEP must reflect both specially designed instruction and the related services necessary for the student to benefit from special education, it has provided a mechanism for interdisciplinary communication and cooperative planning to ensure that all services provided are coordinated and result in a cohesive and unified program for the student. Although much progress still must be made in the area of coordinated planning and service delivery, the IEP provides an opportunity to realize this ideal.

Although many special education teachers consider the IEP to be a potentially valuable document for long-term planning and accountability, many issues have been identified as problematic. These issues are related to (1) the relevance of the IEP for instructional planning, (2) the time involved to develop the IEP, (3) the view of the IEP conference as merely a formality, and (4) the lack of involvement of classroom teachers in the process of IEP development.

Relevance of the IEP for Instructional Planning.

Many teachers consider that the use of the IEP solely for the purpose of management, rather than instruction, does not warrant the amount of time required for its development (Dudley-Marling, 1985; Morgan & Rhode, 1983). They indicate that IEPs, as currently written, are too general to be useful for planning day-to-day instruction. Thus, they are often maintained in locked file cabinets and are referred to infrequently (Dudley-Marling, 1985).

In addition, many IEPs are based on the results of norm-referenced tests administered during the multidisciplinary evaluation. Because these tests are not usually closely related to the student's specific curriculum, they may not be useful for the specific purpose of program planning (L. S. Fuchs & Fuchs, 1986). Although currently receiving more attention, curriculum-based evaluation techniques are, as yet, minimally employed in the development of IEPs. Thus, it appears that the IEP has, at least in some cases, failed to become a working document despite the amount of time expended in its preparation.

Time Involved in the Development of IEPs.

Special education teachers indicate that the IEP requirement, like other procedural requirements of P.L. 94–142, creates excessive demands on time. In a study conducted during the first year of IEP implementation, Price and Goodman (1980) found that for a student being referred for the first time, development of the IEP involved approximately $6\frac{1}{2}$ hours, with the gathering of assessment data and actual IEP development accounting for the major proportion of time expended. Though this study was conducted during the first year of IEP implementation and involved newly referred students, the process still involves a substantial commitment on the part of teachers to develop individualized programs for students with disabilities (Ryan & Rucker, 1986).

IEP Developments as a Procedural Formality.

Educators may, in many cases, view the IEP as a routine requirement and a paperwork exercise rather than a useful vehicle for parent–school collaboration and meaningful educational planning (Dudley-Marling, 1985; Morgan & Rhode, 1983; Singer & Butler, 1987; White & Calhoun, 1987). Many would argue that too much emphasis has been placed on fulfilling the procedural requirements of P.L. 94–142 and too little emphasis on the qualitative aspects of the process.

Lack of Participation by Classroom Teachers.

The role of the regular educator beyond the referral process is still very limited in the area of IEP development (Ammer, 1984; Dudley-Marling, 1985; White & Calhoun, 1987). Many classroom teachers have no role in the development of IEPs, while others are reported as passive participants in IEP conferences. In many instances, classroom teachers view IEP development as solely the responsibility of the special education teacher (White & Calhoun, 1987).

In summary, it appears that while most schools have developed and assimilated a routine process for addressing the procedural requirements of P.L. 94–142, both procedural and programmatic issues remain that raise questions about the ability of the process as it currently functions to ensure the appropriate education of students with disabilities. The remainder of this chapter will focus on general procedures and suggestions for developing the IEP, preparing for and conducting the conference, and suggestions for enhancing the participation of parents and students.

CONTENT OF THE IEP

This section will review the required content of the IEP and discuss additional information that might be included to make the IEP a more useful document. To illustrate the variety of approaches to IEP development, Appendix C (p. 384) provides sample IEP formats required by various states. The reader is encouraged to compare the information included in these samples.

Required Content of the IEP

P.L. 94–142 requires that the IEP include certain minimum information:

1. The student's current levels of educational performance,
2. Annual goals and short-term instructional objectives,
3. The specific special education and related services to be provided and the extent of participation in regular education programs,
4. Projected dates for initiation and the anticipated duration of services, and
5. Appropriate evaluation procedures, criteria, and schedules for measuring attainment of objectives on at least an annual basis.

(*Federal Register*, 1977)

Inclusion of Other Pertinent Data
States and school districts have developed a variety of IEP formats for addressing the requirements of P.L. 94–142. IEP forms therefore will differ among states and sometimes even among school districts. Although P.L. 94–142 establishes the minimum acceptable standard for the content of the IEP, the special services committee may wish to exceed the requirements of the law to include additional pertinent information to make the IEP a more comprehensive document. Furthermore, many state agencies may require information in addition to that required by P.L. 94–142. Examples of information that may be helpful addi-

tions to the IEP include procedural checklists, student schedules, names of committee members, relevant evaluation information, health information, special materials, specification of persons responsible for teaching the objectives, and an indication of the student's specific area of disability. Each of these will be discussed briefly.

Procedural Checklist. The IEP committee may find that a procedural checklist can contribute to systematic planning and monitoring. Such a checklist might include the date of the multidisciplinary evaluation report, the date of eligibility determination, date(s) of IEP meetings to develop and review IEPs, the date of approval by the committee, the date on which the IEP is implemented and services began, and the date of annual review and 3-year re-evaluation. Such a checklist can provide essential information in one location rather than having it located throughout the student's special education record. In the event that a student transfers from or to another school, information necessary to begin special education services is readily available in one document.

Student Schedule. Including the student's schedule on the IEP helps to give a clear and concise picture of what instruction constitutes the student's educational day. Class scheduling is very important for many students with disabilities, who may achieve best when the more academic subjects, such as reading and math, occur in the morning and activities such as art, music, and physical education occur in the afternoon. The schedule may serve as a quick reference of where a student is at a given time, what subjects he is taking, and who the instructor is without having to refer to yet another file of information. Many districts require that, at the secondary level, a copy of the student's schedule of classes be attached to the IEP to document not only the amount of time but also the nature of involvement in regular education programs.

Listing of Committee Members. Each member of the IEP committee should review and approve the IEP before implementation. To document member participation and consensus, space should be provided for committee members to add their signatures to the IEP. Space might be designated for required members of the IEP committee including (1) parents, (2) teachers, (3) agency representative, (4) the student, if appropriate, and (5) someone qualified to interpret evaluation results if the student is being considered for special education for the first time. By signing the IEP, the committee certifies that all members understand the plan and agree that it established an appropriate program for that student. Although obtaining formal approval by having committee members sign the IEP is not a requirement of P.L. 94–142, it may be legally required by state regulations and is a highly recommended procedure. Signatures are also an acceptable method for documenting the presence of required participants at the IEP meeting.

Evaluation Information.   IEP regulations require that the student's current level of performance be specified on the IEP. In addition to this required information, it may be useful to include or attach a summary of all evaluation data used in the eligibility decision. Attaching or including a summary of evaluation results provides an indication of the relationship between these results and the content of the IEP. Although IEPs are supposed to be generated from student needs as identified through evaluation, some research indicates that, in actual practice, little relationship often exists between assessment data and goals and objectives on IEPs (Fiedler & Knight, 1986). One way to facilitate and ensure that evaluation data are translated into goals and objectives on the IEP is for each evaluator to summarize the findings of each evaluation in a statement at the end of the evaluator's report that can be interpreted for the formulation of educational goals. For instance, if an evaluation is conducted in reading, a major deficit in phonetic word-attack skills may be identified. This finding might be included in the summary of the evaluation and attached to or included on the IEP, along with the evaluation procedure used and the date of the evaluation. Inclusion of evaluation information may also provide a more complete picture of the student's educational strengths and weaknesses rather than focusing primarily on weaknesses, as is often the tendency.

Health Information.   Health problems may significantly affect achievement in school and therefore should be recorded on the IEP and considered in the formulation of the student's educational plan. If a student requires medication and the school must assist in its administration and/or monitoring, this information should be readily available. The student with a chronic heart disease may require a schedule adapted to accommodate potential low vitality at specific periods during the day. Students with vision and hearing impairments may require special consideration in selecting teaching methods and materials. Health problems, whether mild or severe, may not be the student's primary disability, but unless they are recognized and considered in the educational planning for that student, the resulting IEP may be inappropriate.

Special Materials and Resources.   For many students with disabilities, educational goals and objectives will be the same as for their typical peers. Special materials, however, may be necessary to enable the student to achieve in the regular education program. This may be true for the student with a visual disability who requires magnification equipment, Talking Books, braille, or large-print material, or the student with a hearing disability who requires the use of amplification equipment. A student with a learning disability who has fine-motor problems may require a word processor or a typewriter to complete written assignments, or a student with an intellectual disability may require material that provides a large amount of repetition and review. A student may require assistance from an educational aide to manage behavior or to provide other services which, though provided in the regular classroom, cannot be provided adequately by the classroom teacher alone. Although special materials and equipment often are included in the goals and objectives of the IEP, the specification of these resources can help ensure that the services are actually provided.

Agent Responsible for Objectives.   A weakness often identified in schools is the failure to identify clearly the responsibilities of each faculty member. This is especially true between regular and special education teachers. Many times a student's educational needs are quite clear, but the responsibility for addressing those needs is not always clearly established. Thus, the classroom teacher may assume that the special education teacher is responsible, while the special education teacher assumes that the classroom teacher is responsible. Unless responsibility is clarified, the instructional needs of a student may not receive appropriate consideration, even though the needs themselves are clearly identified on the IEP. To address this issue, space might be provided on the IEP for indicating the person or persons responsible for teaching each objective or providing each service. Another strategy might be for each goal and/or short-term objective to be initialed by the individual(s) responsible for instruction.

Another reason for including the responsible agent is the current focus on the integration of services into one unified and cohesive program for the student. This means that when possible, the classroom teacher, special education teacher, or instructional aide may provide services that traditionally have been provided by other specialists. For example, many occupational therapy activities can be integrated into the ongoing activities of the classroom with consultation rather than direct therapy from the occupational therapist. The IEP goals and objectives themselves do not always specify exactly how the service will be provided. Listing the agent(s) responsible provides information on the service delivery model to be used.

Total Service Plan and Individual Implementation Plan.   Some state agencies have recommended the use of both a total service plan and a more specific individual implementation plan. The total service plan is developed by the entire IEP committee and includes all required components of the IEP. The individual implementation plan is developed by the person or persons responsible for implementing the program, as determined by the total services plan. It is designed to define the more specific steps and strategies necessary for the student to accomplish the annual goals and short-term objectives identified in the total service plan. Figure 7–1 provides an example of planning forms used for the development of both the total service plan and the individual implementation plan. Despite its potential benefits, this practice is not widely used in schools, perhaps because demands on the time of school personnel result in adherence to only the minimal requirements of P.L. 94–142 rather than to the development of day-to-day instructional plans. Development of two plans may be viewed as time-consuming and, in some instances, repetitive of information already included in the total service plan. The use of instructional plans, however, does provide more continuity between the IEP and the actual instructional program that a student receives.

Designation of the Specific Disability.   Because IEPs for students with varying disabilities can often be very similar and because the titles of service-delivery programs often do not correspond to the same titles as disability areas, an indication of the student's disability category should be indicated on the IEP. This is especially helpful if the student moves to another school where programs may be called by different names. For example, the term *resource program* is often used to refer to different services in different schools. Including the student's disability category can also provide preliminary information on which to consider eligibility for students moving into a school district.

METHODS OF IEP DEVELOPMENT

A major decision for the special services committee is the determination of the method to be used to develop the IEP. Several alternatives exist, and the committee members should decide which style best meets the individual preferences of the parents. The IEP, however, cannot be completed before the IEP committee convenes with all required members present.

Contrary to practice in many schools, it is not appropriate or legal for school representatives to present a completed IEP to parents for their signature (*Federal Register,* 1977; U.S. Department of Education, 1987). Although it is permissible and expected that committee members will formulate recommendations based on assessment results, their knowledge of the student, and program options, these "recommendations," when typed on official IEP forms with multiple copies, may be interpreted by some as an indication that the IEP has already been developed and finalized. Although all participants should prepare for the meeting in advance and should bring recommendations and preliminary suggestions for goals and objectives, an IEP should not be completed until all participants have had an opportunity for mutual planning and decision making. There are a number of acceptable methods for IEP development, each with its advantages and disadvantages. These will be discussed in the following sections.

Total Committee Development

In some cases, the entire committee, including the parents and the student, will meet together as a body and develop the entire plan. The advantage of this approach is that each committee member participates from the very beginning in developing annual goals and intermediate objectives and has the opportunity to lend individual expertise to the formulation of each part of the plan. The parent participating on a committee of this nature is afforded maximum information exchange and knowledge concerning the student's school program.

The disadvantage of this total committee approach is that, because all committee members must participate in developing and approving every aspect of the IEP, the time required for development could become very lengthy. In light of the magnitude of this task and the number of IEPs to be developed within a given time line, an endeavor of this nature could first and most importantly severely limit the group's productivity. Second, since all members have obligations outside the committee, lengthy meetings might be difficult to schedule so that all members, including the parents, would be in attendance. Third, committee members may have a difficult time reaching consensus on every item of the IEP. Questions may arise as to alternative or best methods of wording an objective or, which goals should receive the greatest priority within a given subject area. While such discussion should occur before the plan is approved, it may, at this point, contribute to poor teamwork and inefficient use of time.

FIGURE 7–1
Sample Total Service Plan and Individual Implementation Plan

Individual Education Program: Total Service Plan

Child's Name _____   Summary of Present
School   _____   Levels of Performance
Date of Program Entry _____

Prioritized Long-term Goals: _____
_____   _____
_____   _____
_____   _____

Short-term Objectives	Specific Educational and/or Support Services	Person(s) Responsible	Percent of Time	Beginning and Ending Date	Review Date

Percent of Time in Regular Classroom   Committee Members Present

                                                  _____
                                                  _____
                                                  _____
                                                  _____

                                                  Dates of Meeting _____
_____   _____
Placement Recommendation

_____
Committee Recommendations for Specific Procedures/Techniques, Materials, Etc. (include information about learning style)

_____

Objective Evaluation Criteria for Each Annual Goal Statement

(Figure 7–1 continued)

Individual Education Program: Individual Implementation Plan

(Complete one of these for each goal statement specified on Total Service Plan)

Child's Name ————————————————————   Goal Statement: ——————————————————

School ————————————————————

Date of Program Entry ————————————————   Short-term Instructional Objectives

Projected Ending Date ————————————————   ——————————————————————————

Person(s) Completing Form ——————————————   ——————————————————————————

Behavioral Objectives	Task Analysis of Objectives	Strategies and/or Techniques	Materials and/or Resources	Date Started	Date Ended	Comments

Preliminary IEP Development Before Meeting

Another alternative would be for the entire committee, excluding the parents, to develop preliminary goals and objectives and criteria for evaluation of those goals and objectives. Using this procedure, the IEP committee might write the IEP in *draft* form, so that necessary changes can be made as the document is developed at the meeting. The IEP meeting would then be held to discuss the recommendations and develop the IEP with the parents. The advantage of this approach is that it provides school personnel the opportunity to engage in preliminary planning and consider instructional needs and programming options before meeting with parents. Such a procedure also saves time for parents who, to attend the meeting, may have to make arrangements to leave job or family and thus may not be available for frequent and time-consuming meetings. Furthermore, parents may be uncomfortable discussing and writing every objective. This approach provides a framework for the parent to consider in amending, approving, or rejecting the IEP.

The disadvantages of this method are, again, the time and scheduling constraints of committee members participating in the development of the IEP. School personnel may have difficulty in arranging convenient times for meeting, planning, and coordinating recommendations for the IEP before the IEP meeting occurs. Thus, this procedure usually results in the special education teacher or case manager taking full responsibility for the development of the preliminary IEP and coordinating with other members on its content before the meeting (White & Calhoun, 1987). A significant disadvantage of this approach is that it tends to create the impression that the IEP has been finalized before meeting with parents. Parents may feel as if they are being asked to "rubberstamp" the document, thus resulting in antagonism between school and parents. The parents may feel they have been denied their right to participate actively, yet the school personnel may view this method of IEP development as the most efficient use of time and resources. In using this method, school personnel must take time to assure parents that the services proposed are only recommendations for review and discussion with the parents.

Individual or Small-Group Assignments

An infrequently used but nonetheless acceptable method for IEP development is for the IEP committee members to divide into teams according to areas of expertise to develop the IEP. The parents may, in this case, serve on a single or on multiple teams to provide necessary information and assist in the formulation of goals and objectives (as opposed to the plan being developed before the total committee meeting, when the parent may not participate until the scheduled meeting). The committee may be divided so that the prospective teacher in each subject area and the special education teacher work together in developing the IEP for that subject area. For example, in developing the IEP for math, the team might consist of the prospective math teacher, the previous math teacher, the special education teacher, and the student. Other committee members who are not in a teaching position should be available and willing to assist with the development of goals and objectives in the various subject areas. When each segment of the IEP is completed, the plan must receive total committee consideraton. At this point, any necessary questions or changes should be discussed and a decision made to change or approve the plan. If the framework for the IEP has been completed before the meeting with the parents, the plan should be discussed in its entirety and the opportunity given to the parent to change, approve, or reject the IEP.

The advantages of dividing the responsibility for writing the IEP are numerous. It allows those members responsible for the implementation of the plan to have the primary opportunity for its development. Furthermore, a substantial amount of time is saved in meetings because fewer members are involved in determining the content and framework of the IEP. Finally, each small team is comprised of members who have teaching expertise in the specified area of development, thus the plan will more likely be applicable to classroom implementation. This is especially true for teachers at the secondary level or at departmentalized elementary and junior high schools, where specific aspects of curriculum are divided among various faculty members. Dividing a task into segments may make the task more approachable and manageable. The same holds true for IEP development. What may seem to be an impossible task in its entirety is more easily approached by working on one aspect at a time.

The division of responsibility for IEP development also presents disadvantages. One very significant disadvantage is that division of responsibility may result in not one annual plan for a student but rather as many separate plans as there are teams. The possibility exists that very little coordination will occur among teams, and thus each will be isolated from the others. In using an approach that divides responsibility, it is essential that the entire team meet to discuss the total plan once each individual segment has been developed. Again, if the parent is not included until after the framework is generally developed, that parent has had little opportunity to participate fully as a committee member in planning the student's program.

Provision of Preliminary Goals and Objectives to Committee Members Before Meeting

A final and suggested method of IEP development is a variation of the methods discussed previously. In using this strategy, the case manager provides preliminary goals and objectives to the parents and other committee members for consideration before the IEP meeting. This method depends on the involvement of the parents in a meeting before the IEP meeting, preferably a meeting to discuss and interpret evaluation results and to determine eligibility. The eligibility meeting would conclude with a synthesis of evaluation results and agreement among committee members, including the parents, on the areas in which specially designed instruction will be required. At this time also, the parents and school representatives could agree on a date for the IEP meeting and establish the preferred method for IEP development. If the parent prefers that the school engage in preliminary planning, it could be agreed that the case manager, or other school representative, would gather and synthesize preliminary goals, objectives, and evaluation criteria in the designated areas and send them to the parents and other committee members in sufficient time to be considered, reviewed, and revised before the IEP meeting. This draft, reviewed and revised by all members, may then serve as the basis for discussion at the IEP meeting. Such preliminary planning would include only generation of possible goals, objectives, and evaluation criteria. The specific special education and related services to be provided, time in the regular education program, and date of initiation of services would be determined at the IEP meeting, based on the goals and objectives agreed on by the committee at the meeting.

The advantages of this approach are many. First and perhaps most important, it provides maximum opportunity for parents to consider the implications of evaluation, eligibility, and program planning before attending a decision-making meeting. Second, such a strategy also provides a tangible vehicle by which the parent can prepare for and participate in the meeting. Rather than being confronted with a completed document at the IEP meeting or being placed in a position to approve a document as it is being developed, the parents have an opportunity to consider and discuss among themselves a preliminary planning document and to formulate questions and suggestions over a period of days rather than during the course of an hour. A third advantage of this procedure is that, even though there are two meetings, one for eligibility and interpretation of evaluation results and one to develop the IEP, the time spent in each is kept to a minimum. The primary disadvantage of this approach is that it places heavy responsibility for coordination and preliminary program planning on the case manager. More often than not, however, the case manager is responsible for compiling, synthesizing, and preparing the IEP regardless of the development strategy used (White & Calhoun, 1987).

If the strategy employed for IEP development is to develop the IEP before meeting with the parents, the committee may also decide whether the entire committee will meet with the parent or whether the committee will be represented only by those participants required by law. Again, there are advantages and disadvantages to both methods. When the total committee meets, all members may interact, and the parent can meet and talk with all members involved in the education of the student (Witt, Miller, McIntyre, & Smith, 1984). Firsthand information is available as to why particular objectives were chosen in each subject area. At the same time, though, a large committee may overwhelm the parent (Yoshida et al., 1978). Participation in curriculum planning will be a new experience for many parents and students, and they may feel uneasy when they find themselves substantially outnumbered by school personnel. Choosing representatives from the school team to meet with parents may greatly reduce parents' and students' anxiety. In many cases, the committee members chosen to meet with the parents should include an individual who is already acquainted with the family and can conduct the conference in an efficient, nonthreatening manner.

As noted earlier, care must be taken to ensure that preliminary IEPs, developed in draft form before the actual IEP meeting, in no way appear to be completed documents presented for parental signature. Various methods can be used to ensure that this does not occur. As in the last strategy discussed, developing only suggested goals and objectives rather than a complete draft of the IEP can avoid the perception that the IEP is a completed document. In addition, the draft goals and objectives can be written on a form other than the IEP form or on a photocopy of an IEP form. If goals and objectives are generated by computer, they might be maintained on computer paper until they are agreed on by the committee at the IEP meeting and then printed on the IEP form after the committee reaches consensus on the appropriate content of the IEP. Some districts even require that any preliminary draft be written in pencil and transferred to type only after the IEP meeting.

Again, the point must be recognized that different parents have different preferences in terms of degree of decision making with which they are comfortable. It can be difficult for educators to anticipate whether parents prefer to be involved from the very beginning in terms of specifying every goal and objective or whether they would prefer that educators initially develop a draft IEP, which parents then review and revise at the conference. If educators are in doubt about the appropriate strategy, the best way to resolve the issue is simply to ask parents and students about their preferences. Reviewing options and asking them in advance will best ensure that parents approve the strategy.

Regardless of the procedure employed, the development of the IEP represents a substantial investment of time and resources. To maximize the ultimate benefit of the resources expended, the process of IEP development must ensure that the resulting document will be a useful educational tool to guide professionals and parents in the provision of educational services.

PLANNING THE IEP CONFERENCE

The organization of the IEP conference not only can contribute to the efficient use of participant time but can also enhance the quality of member participation and provide a systematic means for clarifying the role of each committee member. However, significant variability can exist in the way that IEP conferences are conducted. This section will discuss factors to be considered in planning the conference, guidelines for preparing the meeting, and a format for conducting the conference.

Factors to Be Considered in Planning the Conference

Among those factors that should be considered in deciding how to conduct the IEP conference are the level of previous contact between the school and parents, whether the purpose of the conference is initial placement versus continuing placement in the special education program, the amount of time available for the conference, and the number of persons attending.

Level of Previous Contact Between Committee Members.   The way that the IEP conference is planned and conducted may differ, depending on the amount of information that has been provided to committee members, especially parents, before the meeting. For example, if school representatives have had ongoing and positive contact with parents during the pre-referral and referral period and have met to explain evaluation results and to determine program eligibility, the meeting to develop the IEP will likely be less time-consuming and more effective than if parents

and school representatives are meeting for the first time to discuss all aspects of evaluation, eligibility, and IEP development. The same holds true for familiarity between other committee members. If members are familiar with one another and work cooperatively on a regular basis, it is likely that the meeting will proceed more efficiently than if the IEP meeting is the first occasion for collaboration between members. In planning for the conference, the individual responsible should consider the procedural and programmatic issues that have already been addressed with the parents and plan the agenda based on those that remain to be addressed. The more information that must be included in the meeting, the longer the meeting will be.

Type of IEP Meeting.   Although the majority of this text focuses on the procedures leading up to and including initial IEP development for a student with a disability, IEP meetings also may serve several other sanctioned purposes. These include the following:

1. IEP meetings for the required annual review of the IEP
2. Intermittent reviews of the IEP as necessary or desired by the parents or school
3. IEP meetings for students transferring into the school

Depending on the type of meeting to be conducted, the focus of the agenda may vary considerably. The initial IEP meeting is the first time that the program of specially designed instruction that a student will receive is defined. As such, it may often take an extended period of time to determine the exact IEP content and educational placement appropriate to address the student's needs. In addition, if other procedural requirements have not been completed, such as providing notice of evaluation results, these results must be fully addressed at the IEP meeting. This activity can consume a large portion of conference time, especially if parents have received no prior information regarding the results and meaning of evaluation information, the eligibility determination and its meaning, and the various options considered and rejected by the school. For the reasons stated previously in this chapter, it is strongly recommended that this information be conveyed to parents in a separate meeting before the IEP meeting. However, if this information is to be provided at the IEP meeting itself, an extended conference time should be established with a specific time designated for the interpretation of evaluation results.

The annual review is a second type of IEP conference. The purpose of the annual review of the IEP is to review the student's progress toward goals and objectives included in an already established IEP. Because the student has already been determined to be eligible and is receiving special education and related services, issues of comprehensive evaluation for the purpose of identification and program eligibility are not usually the focus of annual review meetings. Instead, the meeting might focus on the degree to which the student has achieved the anticipated progress and on the need to revise the content of the existing IEP. At annual review meetings, discussion of evaluation results usually consists of reporting on the student's progress in meeting the goals and objectives of the previous IEP and applying this information as the basis for identifying strengths and weaknesses that should be addressed in the subsequent IEP, if the committee decides that continuation of specially designed instruction is required. Further, at this point parents are already familiar with the framework of the special education program and may require less explanation to ensure that they fully understand actions proposed or rejected by the school.

IEP meetings for transferring students with IEPs are a third type of IEP conference. Transfer IEPs are one of the most difficult issues for special services committees. This is primarily because eligibility criteria for special education and IEP formats may vary dramatically among states. Special services committees therefore must address issues such as whether a student who transfers into the school with an existing and current IEP is entitled to continued special education services, even if not eligible according to the criteria of the receiving state. Equally problematic is to what extent an incoming IEP should be reviewed and revised prior to being implemented in the receiving school. Rather than defining and developing an initial special education program or reviewing progress toward established goals and objectives, the activity of the committee in considering transfer IEPs often focuses on determining whether the IEP clearly defines the program that the student should receive, whether the IEP can be implemented as it is written, what additional information is required, and how the identified needs of the student will be addressed in the new school. As is true with other areas that are not clearly defined by existing laws and regulations, meetings of this nature are facilitated by the development of standard procedures that establish system policy and provide consistency in addressing these issues. Figure 7–2 provides an example of a procedural guide that one school district might develop for considering transfer IEPs.

Finally, meetings conducted to review aspects of the IEP before the required annual review are often referred to as interim reviews. These meetings may serve a variety of purposes, including a mechanism for early follow-up on a newly developed IEP; revision of an aspect of the IEP that has been inappropriate, ineffective, or perhaps accomplished; scheduled coordination with parents and other service providers; change of schedule; or requests to modify the IEP. The specific issue involved provides the agenda for meetings of this nature.

Amount of Time Available for the Meeting. Because parents and other participants often must adjust their work schedule or other commitments to attend the meeting, the time available for the meeting should be discussed and adhered to as much as possible. For example, if parents can meet for only 1 hour, the case manager must determine how the committee will accomplish its purpose in the allotted amount of time. School personnel and other service providers also have time constraints that limit the amount of time available for meetings. In addition, it should be noted that there is a reasonable limit to the amount of time that should be devoted to any one meeting. Three- or four-hour meetings to develop an IEP are often ultimately unproductive and result in negative perceptions on the part of committee members. If necessary, a second meeting can be scheduled to finalize the IEP. IEP implementation cannot be delayed, however, because of the need for more than one IEP meeting. Scheduling a second conference at a time when all participants can attend can be difficult and, considering the commitments of parents and others, can meet with resistance. If a second meeting must be held, information from those who cannot attend a second meeting must be contributed at the first meeting, or that person's contribution should be contained in a written report to which the committee can refer if necessary.

Number of Individuals Participating. The number of individuals participating in the meeting will also have an effect on the nature of the IEP conference. Increased numbers of professional service providers often indicate that multiple services may be required. Each of these services must be negotiated and integrated with the student's educational program. Meetings with large groups tend to be more formal and often, by necessity, more structured than meetings where minimal services are required and only a few individuals participate in the development of the IEP. As discussed earlier, large groups are not necessarily a disadvantage if adequate time is available to ensure that all committee members are able to contribute to the meeting (Witt et al., 1984). However, if time is limited, the extent of participation by committee members may be extremely limited. In such situations, the case manager should ensure that parents are afforded an opportunity to participate.

FIGURE 7–2
Example of Procedures for Consideration of Transfer IEPs

PROCEDURES FOR CONSIDERATION OF TRANSFER IEPs

When an incoming student arrives with a current IEP, the student must receive services immediately. As soon as possible (within 10 working days), a meeting is to be scheduled and held to review the incoming IEP. The following criteria for consideration of incoming IEPs should be used.

Review Beginning and Ending Dates of IEP
(Is the IEP current?)

YES	NO
Enroll the student in special education and implement IEP. Proceed to next step.	Do not enroll in special education. Enroll in regular classroom and proceed to next step.

Review Incoming Eligibility Information
(Does student meet established eligibility criteria?)

YES	NO
1. Maintain in special education and proceed to next step	1. If information is insufficient, initiate referral for evaluation and eligibility determination. 2. If IEP has expired but existing information indicates student is eligible, schedule eligibility meeting. 3. If student has a current IEP but existing evaluation information indicates that the student is not eligible, notify parents, maintain in special education until annual review or until formal meeting to discontinue services. Proceed to next step.

Review of Goals and Objectives
(Are IEP goals and objectives on the incoming IEP clear and of acceptable quality?)

YES	NO
If the IEP is current, the committee accepts eligibility determination, and goals and objectives are clear and of acceptable quality, a new IEP is written in receiving school format and is valid for 1 year.	1. If IEP is current and student is eligible, but goals and objectives are not clear or acceptable, a new IEP must be written. 2. If the IEP has expired, but the student is determined to be eligible for special education, a new IEP must be developed with the student's parents, based on new or existing evaluation.

Planning the Conference

The vast majority of the work for a successful IEP meeting often occurs before the meeting, during the preconference period. Adequate preparation for the conference can ensure that the conference itself will proceed smoothly, efficiently, and positively. Preconference preparation encompasses a variety of important tasks: (1) appointing a case manager if one has not already been appointed, (2) planning an agenda, (3) notifying committee members, (4) notifying parents of the IEP meeting, and (5) organizing relevant information in preparation for the conference.

Appointing a Case Manager.   Although the appointment of a case manager or coordinator for the IEP conference is not required by P.L. 94–142, local agencies have found them to be helpful, if not essential, in coordinating the IEP process. Vesting the responsibility for coordination with one person can help ensure sufficient preparation for the conference. Examples of responsibilities assumed by case managers may include coordinating the multidisciplinary evaluation, collecting and synthesizing information in advance of the IEP meeting, communicating with parents, and serving as the chairperson for the IEP meeting.

Planning an Agenda.   If the case manager serves as chairperson for the IEP conference, that individual will, in all likelihood, assume responsibility for planning the conference agenda. Planning an agenda involves arranging the logistics of the meeting. It may be time-consuming and frustrating to arrange a time convenient for all who must participate. Establishing a standard time during which all school participants are available for such meetings often helps to ensure that school representatives and those who work closely with the school will be available. If parents cannot meet during the time typically set aside for IEP meetings, the case manager may be responsible for arranging another time more convenient for the parents. Typically, IEP meetings are conducted immediately after school or during conference times established during school hours. In addition, some schools have regularly scheduled early morning or evening hours available for conferences with parents who work or cannot attend conferences held during school hours.

An important aspect of planning the agenda is to allow sufficient time for the IEP meeting. Meetings in which school representatives will meet with parents for the first time, or when evaluation results must be synthesized and interpreted and eligibility determined, will require more time than meetings in which only the IEP will be discussed or in which

extensive preliminary planning between the parents and the school has already occurred. Figure 7–3 provides a guide for planning which topics will constitute the agenda for the IEP meeting.

In addition to ensuring that important issues are not overlooked, planning an agenda in advance and sharing it with all committee members, including parents and students, before the meeting can help participants plan for the meeting and anticipate how their contributions can be incorporated into the decision-making process. The case manager should solicit comments on the agenda and invite all committee members to offer input and suggestions before the meeting. Once established, the agenda should be distributed to committee members in advance of the meeting and adhered to as closely as possible at the meeting. A sample agenda is illustrated in Figure 7–4.

Notification of Committee Members.   Another logistical aspect of preconference planning for which the case manager is usually responsible is ensuring that all legally required and necessary participants attend the meeting (White & Calhoun, 1987). This means that teachers, evaluation team members, related services providers, and others whose input into IEP development is necessary must be contacted. Committee members should be notified in writing of the meeting whenever possible. A sample invitation to the IEP meeting is illustrated in Figure 7–5, p. 188.

Because it is often difficult to coordinate the schedules of team members such as itinerant personnel, related services providers, and others outside the school, and because some parents may prefer smaller meetings, school districts may choose to accept a written report in lieu of attendance at the meeting for those participants not required by law. Such a report might include suggested goals and objectives, suggested nature and schedule of services, and even suggested times for service. This report would provide a basis for consideration by the full committee in determining the nature and extent of services for a given area. For example, if an occupational therapist has evaluated a student but cannot attend the IEP meeting, that therapist might be asked to submit a written report documenting concerns, identifying functional needs, proposing goals and objectives for remediation, and proposing recommended service levels.

Providing Notice to Parents.   After the logistical arrangements have been made for the IEP meeting, notice should be provided to the parents. As is true whenever the school proposes to change or refuses to change a student's evaluation, identification, or placement, notice must be provided to parents a

FIGURE 7–3
Guidelines for Planning the Agenda for the IEP Meeting

A. <u>**TYPE OF MEETING**</u>

1. Initial review meeting____
2. Annual review meeting____
3. Transfer IEP meeting____
4. Interim review meeting____

B. <u>**AGENDA ITEMS**</u>
   In previous contact with parents which
   of the following were accomplished?

	Yes	No	Date	Include on Agenda
1. Evaluation results explained and synthesized?	____	____	____	____
2. Eligibility determination made and explained?	____	____	____	____
3. Areas of IEP development established and agreed on?	____	____	____	____
4. Preliminary goals and objectives developed before IEP meeting?	____	____	____	____
5. Notice of evaluation results provided?	____	____	____	____
6. Due process rights explained in detail and questions answered?	____	____	____	____
7. Process of IEP development and placement previously explained?	____	____	____	____
8. Prior planning meetings with parents regarding content of the IEP?	____	____	____	____
9. Has a draft of IEP goals and objectives been developed and shared with committee members?	____	____	____	____

C. **Anticipated Extent of Curriculum Development**   **Services Anticipated**

1. Is the IEP likely to require multiple special education services? _____
2. Are related services likely to be required? _____
3. Is the IEP likely to require services unavailable in the school? _____

D. **Number of Participants and Information To Be Contributed**
1. How many potential service providers will be present at the meeting? _____
2. What information will each participant contribute?
    Member   Information To Be Contributed

_____

_____

_____

_____

_____

3. What format will be followed for information sharing? For example:
   a. Will each evaluator present and discuss individual evaluation information? _____
   b. Will evaluators submit reports indicating program recommendations _____
   c. Will one individual synthesize and report information? _____
4. Will parents be accompanied by counsel or another representative? _____
5. Will the student participate? _____

E. <u>**Time To Be Allotted for the Meeting**</u>
1. Do parents have specific time constraints? What are they? _____
2. Do other committee members have specific time constraints? _____
_____
3. Considering items A-D, how much time will be necessary for the meeting? _____
4. Can the meeting be accomplished in the time available to committee members? _____
5. Must additional meetings be scheduled? _____ Can they be scheduled in advance? _____

FIGURE 7–4
Agenda for IEP Meeting

Agenda for Meeting

<u>STUDENT:</u> Joe S.
<u>DATE OF MEETING:</u> March 1, 1991
<u>PLACE:</u> Conference Room, Adams Middle School, 17019 Lee Road
<u>TIME:</u> 9:00 AM–11:00 AM
<u>COMMITTEE MEMBERS:</u>   Mr. and Mrs. S., Parents
                            Joe S., Student
                            Mrs. Snow, Classroom Teacher
                            Mr. Thomas, Special Education Teacher
                            Ms. Wrens, Principal
                            Mr. LaJoie, School Counselor
                            Mr. Ryan, School Psychologist

<u>PURPOSE: To develop an IEP and determine the least restrictive educational placement.</u>
<u>STATUS:</u> A meeting to discuss evaluation results and to determine eligibility was
conducted on February 17, 1991. Areas in need of specially designed instruction were
established. They include reading, mathematics, and vocational education. Related
services includes counseling. Preliminary goals and objectives were distributed by
school personnel and distributed to committee members on February 22, 1991. The purpose
of this meeting is to develop the final IEP for Joe and to determine the appropriate
placement.

<u>Time</u>	<u>Activity</u>	<u>Committee Members Responsible</u>
9:00 AM – 9:05 AM	Introduction of committee members	Ms. Wrens
9:05 AM – 9:15 AM	Review of due process entitlements	Mr. Thomas, Mr. and Mrs. S.
9:15 AM – 9:30 AM	Review of decisions made and IEP development and placement process	Mr. LaJoie
9:30 AM – 10:15 AM	Discussion of draft goals and objectives Revision of draft goals and objectives Finalize IEP	Mr. and Mrs. S. Joe, Mrs. Snow, Mr. Thomas Mr. LaJoie Ms. Wrens
10:15 AM – 10:45 AM	Determine placement	All members
10:45 AM – 11:00 AM	Summary, determine necessary follow-up Clarification of answered questions.	All members

Summary of Meeting (to be completed during meeting) _____

_____

_____

_____

_____

FIGURE 7–5
Invitation to the IEP Meeting

Dear _____ :

A meeting has been scheduled to discuss the educational program for _____
(student's name), on _____ (date) at _____ (time) at _____
(location).

The purpose of the meeting is as follows:
(Check those applicable)

_____ Discuss results of initial comprehensive evaluation
_____ Determine initial eligibility or ineligibility for special education
_____ Develop an initial IEP
_____ Conduct an annual review of the IEP
_____ Conduct an interim review of the IEP
_____ Conduct a 3-year re-evaluation conference
_____ Other (specify) _____

Those invited to attend the conference include:

Name	Position	Purpose of Attendance

If you know of others who should be involved in this meeting, please contact the school
office before the meeting date to ensure that these individuals are included.

Please return the bottom portion of this invitation or call the school office to
indicate whether you will be able to attend the meeting. We look forward to seeing you
at the meeting unless we hear otherwise from you.

Sincerely,

Principal or Case Manager

PLEASE RETURN ONE COPY OF THIS FORM TO _____ , NO LATER THAN _____

Yes, I will be present for the meeting _____ .
No, I cannot be present for the meeting _____ . A better time for me would be
_____ (date).

Signature _____
Date _____

reasonable time before such changes occur. Depending on the requirements of each state and individual school district, the provision of notice can vary significantly. If only one meeting, the IEP meeting, will be conducted with parents, and evaluation results, eligibility, and the IEP all will be discussed at that meeting, the school is permitted to provide one notice of that meeting and to include in the notice the intent to review evaluation results, determine student eligibility for special education, and develop an IEP if necessary. If prior written notice of evaluation results and eligibility has already been provided (and preferably, discussed in a meeting with parents), notice of the IEP meeting may focus only on the proposal to develop an IEP and determine appropriate placement. Figure 7–6 illustrates a sample notice to parents informing them of the IEP meeting. As with all notices, notification of the IEP meeting must be provided in language understandable to the general public and in the parent's native language or other mode of communication. In addition, to ensure that one or both parents are present at the meeting or are afforded the opportunity to participate, P.L. 94–142 requires the following:

1. Notice must be provided early enough to ensure that parents will have an opportunity to attend.
2. The meeting must be scheduled at a mutually agreed on time and place.
3. The notice must include the purpose, time, and location of the meeting and who will attend.

Parents should also be informed at this time that their child may attend the meeting and that other individuals may be invited by the parent to attend.

Organizing Relevant Information and Delineating Responsibilities. Before the IEP conference, relevant information on issues to be discussed should be planned and organized. Again, the case manager usually is responsible for planning the meeting and ensuring that all participants know what information they are expected to contribute. As noted earlier, the exact nature of the information to be presented at the meeting will vary, based in part on the amount of information already presented to the parents and committee members. If evaluation results have not been previously synthesized and interpreted to parents and eligibility determination has not been previously discussed, the case manager should ensure that responsibility for this task is assigned. Those responsible for this requirement must ensure that this information is prepared in such a way that it is interpreted to parents clearly and succinctly at the IEP conference. Since classroom teachers are usually the curriculum "experts" on the committee, they should be notified of the information they will be expected to contribute (such as ensuring that results of evaluation accurately reflect the student's current level of educational performance and that evaluation results are translated into relevant, curriculum-based goals and objectives). Parents and students should also be encouraged to list questions and issues they would like to address during the meeting. A helpful strategy to ensure such organization on the part of parents and students would be to include this suggestion in the preconference communication, as illustrated in Figure 7–6. Advance planning and organization can contribute to comprehensive coverage of information at the conference as well as to the efficient use of conference time.

CONDUCTING THE IEP CONFERENCE

Introductions

The initial portion of the conference is very important in terms of creating open communication among participants. Committee members, especially parents and students, should be greeted when they arrive at the conference and introduced to the other participants in the meeting. In addition, waiting until the parents arrive to be seated and begin the meeting lends a less formal tone to the meeting than if the parents are brought into a room with all school representatives already seated. If large meetings are necessary because of the complexity of a particular student's needs, or because the parents prefer the involvement of several individuals, introductions and role clarifications take on even greater significance. In such instances, parents and students may have difficulty keeping all the names and roles straight, even if initial introductions are made. The use of nametags or the provision of a list of participants and roles can help parents, students, and other committee members remember with whom they are communicating. Meetings should begin on time, or as soon as the parents arrive, and should end on time. Parents should not be kept waiting for the meeting to start or be expected to remain beyond the time scheduled for the conference.

Review of the Agenda and Explanation of Procedures to Be Followed

Specifying an organized, efficient procedure for conducting the meeting is essential. The case manager should review and establish with all committee members the procedure to be followed at the meeting and

FIGURE 7–6
Sample Letter for Preconference Communication with Parents, Notice of IEP Meeting

Dear Mr. and Mrs. S.:

As we discussed in our meeting on February 17, we have determined that Joe has an intellectual disability which adversely affects his performance in reading and mathematics. He is therefore eligible to receive special educational services.

As you know, we will meet again on March 1, 1991, to develop an Individualized Educational Program (IEP) for Joe. I have enclosed a tentative agenda for that meeting. As agreed, we have developed preliminary goals and objectives in reading, mathematics, vocational education, and counseling to use as a planning document for developing Joe's IEP.

A copy of the draft IEP is enclosed for your review. Please feel free to make changes, suggestions, or additions directly on the form. Additional planning forms are also included so that you may list additional goals and objectives that you want to address in the meeting. As you review the plan, you may want to consider the following questions:

1.   Do you think that the goals and objectives are the ones that require the most attention in school?
2.   Are there other goals and objectives that you would like to have included on the IEP?
3.   Do you think that these goals and objectives are reasonable for Joe?
4.   How can we improve these goals and objectives to reflect Joe's educational needs?
5.   Are the goals and objectives specific enough so that you can tell exactly how Joe's educational program will be modified?

At the IEP meeting on March 1, we will review the draft plan and make all necessary changes.

After the IEP is finalized, the committee will determine whether we can implement the IEP in Joe's regular classroom or whether another setting, such as a resource room (part-time special education classroom), would be more appropriate. The placement decision will be based on the goals and objectives that we develop and on any other services that Joe may require. When at all possible, we provide special education programs as part of the regular education program. Other possibilities include having a special education teacher in the regular classroom, placing your son in a resource room for 1 or more hours per day or in a special education classroom for most of the school day, or any other appropriate arrangements.

At our meeting on February 17, we reviewed your legal rights as a parent of a student with a disability. I have enclosed another copy of these rights for your records. Please feel free to contact me before the meeting so that I may clarify any of these rights that seem unclear.

The enclosed agenda lists the persons invited to Joe's IEP meeting. We would like Joe to attend as well. Students often benefit from participating in planning their educational programs and assuming responsibility for accomplishing these goals and objectives. I would be most happy to talk with you before the meeting to discuss how Joe might participate in the meeting. And, if you would like someone else to participate in the meeting, such as a friend or representative, please feel free to invite them. Please let us know in advance who will attend the meeting with you so we can add their names to the agenda.

Please contact me if you have any questions regarding the enclosed planning document or other issues. I look forward to meeting with you on March 1.

Sincerely,

Steven La Joie

Steven La Joie
Counselor

what decisions are expected to be reached. It is especially important to review how the IEP will be developed and to use the goals and objectives agreed on as the basis for the placement decision. The parents as well as other committee members should be aware that placement depends on the goals and objectives established for a student.

Review of Procedural Rights

During the initial part of the IEP meeting, the case manager should establish whether the parents have already received written notice of their due process rights and should determine whether their rights have been appropriately explained and interpreted. Depending on what information the parent has already received, the case manager can provide the parents with a copy of their due process rights, explain them in detail, and/or simply confirm that the parents do have a copy and fully understand them. If the parents were involved in a previous meeting to discuss evaluation results and the eligibility decision, their rights regarding due process were most likely explained at that time. If they have already received an explanation of their rights and have received them in writing, the case manager need not explain them again but should provide a very brief review and confirm that the parents have no questions. If parents do not recall receiving a copy of their rights, or if they have not been explained, time should be taken to ensure that the parents fully understand. An easily implemented stategy for the case manager is to keep a copy of parents' rights in a reference notebook, used to maintain all standard information that may be needed in the course of an IEP conference. The case manager might review the parents' rights by referring to this copy with the parents while at the same time explaining the meaning of each entitlement. The copy may be retained by the parents if they do not already have one. Figure 7–7 provides an example of a written explanation of parent rights. The action taken in regard to informing parents of their rights can then be documented for the record on a form such as that illustrated in Figure 7–8.

Review of Evaluation Information and/or Current Levels of Performance

Before beginning the development of the curriculum portion of the IEP, the committee should review evaluation information. The degree to which this information must be discussed at the IEP meeting depends on the amount of evaluation information shared with the parents in previous meetings. If a previous meeting was held with parents to interpret evaluation results, determine program eligibility, and establish current levels of performance, the committee need only review the current levels of performance established as a basis for IEP development. If, however, the IEP meeting is the first meeting held with parents, the evaluation results, eligibility determination, and current levels of performance must be discussed in detail to ensure that the parents and other committee members understand the basis on which the IEP is being developed.

Development of the Curriculum Portion of the IEP

The primary activity of the IEP conference is to develop the IEP. During this portion of the conference, the committee will define the specially designed instruction to be provided to the student. Depending on the method used to develop the IEP, the format of this portion of the conference will vary. If the IEP is developed completely during the meeting by all committee members, the format should be structured to include each step of IEP development including (1) identification and agreement of the areas in which specially designed instruction is required, (2) development of and agreement on goals and objectives and evaluation criteria and schedules in each of the designated areas, and (3) identification of and agreement on necessary related services. On the other hand, if areas of IEP development were agreed on with the parents and other committee members before the meeting, and preliminary goals, objectives, evaluation criteria, and related services have been developed and distributed to committee members before the conference, the format may focus solely on reviewing, revising, and agreeing on the information included in the draft material. This process obviously saves time in the meeting but requires more work before the conference.

Determining Placement

After the curriculum portion of the IEP is developed and agreed on, the committee should determine how the specially designed instruction will be provided to the student. At this point, the committee should review all appropriate service-delivery options such as provision of consulting services in the regular program, a resource room for a specific period of time, a self-contained program, or even a placement other than the public school if necessary. The placement decision must be (1) justifiable, (2) based on the goals and objectives established by the committee, and (3) in the environment that is least restrictive and most appropriate to address the student's needs.

FIGURE 7–7
Parent and Child Rights in P.L. 94–142

As a parent of a child who has been identified as having special needs, the following rights are provided through federal legislation (P.L. 94–142):

1. A free appropriate public education with necessary related services to meet your child's needs (i.e., speech therapy, physical therapy, counseling, and transportation) must be provided by your local school system.
2. Your child should be educated in classes with children who do not have special needs if such classes are appropriate to the needs of your child. This means, for example, that your child may not be removed from regular class placement and put in a special class attended only by children with special needs unless you and the school personnel believe that the special class would be the best placement.
3. Your child may not receive an initial evaluation in order to be placed in a special education program unless you are previously informed and voluntarily give your consent.
4. You may withdraw your decision to give consent at any time.
5. You are entitled to receive an explanation of all evaluation results and an explanation of any action proposed or rejected by the school system in regard to evaluation results.
6. You have the right to request an independent evaluation (conducted by someone outside of the school) and have the results considered in discussions regarding the school placement of your child.
7. You may look at all educational records and request explanations of information contained in those records. You may also request that information be changed if you do not agree with it.
8. The privacy of your child's school records must be maintained. You may request copies of your child's school records. Furthermore, you may obtain information from the principal of your child's school concerning the particular individuals who are allowed to see your child's records.
9. You have the right to request an objective hearing (due process hearing) at any time when you disagree with the proposed procedures for evaluation and/or placement of your child. At the hearing you may have counsel, present evidence, cross-examine witnesses, and obtain written findings of the proceedings. If you are deaf or normally communicate in a language other than English, the hearing must be conducted so that all communication is completely understandable to you.

Many committee members may not be familiar with all service-delivery options. It is therefore often helpful to provide a list of the options possible as a basis for discussion. Figure 1–7 (see page 22) illustrates various placement options in the context of the least restrictive environment. This diagram may be useful as a basis for determining placement during the committee meeting.

Summary and Closing

The summary and closing portion of the meeting should be devoted to briefly recapping all decisions made and ensuring that all committee members understand and agree to the decisions made. Any questions remaining should be discussed and resolved before adjourning the meeting. Responsibility for necessary follow-up activities such as scheduling should be established and documented, and methods of future communication with parents and between services providers should be established. The meeting should close with thanks to all committee members.

In planning and conducting the IEP meeting, the case manager or other committee chairperson must remember that the IEP conference is the focal point in synthesizing many legal requirements into a meaningful educational plan for students with disabilities. The opportunities available for enhancing quality education through communication and shared decision making among school personnel, parents, and students should be used meaningfully.

ENHANCING PARTICIPATION OF PARENTS AND STUDENTS IN THE IEP CONFERENCE

A fundamental premise of P.L. 94–142 is the participation of parents and students in educational decision making. The rationale for this participation is based on several assumptions: (1) When parents speak for their child, they will represent the interest of their child. (2) Students often can identify their own needs and translate these needs into educational interventions. (3) The appropriateness of the student's IEP will be enhanced by parent and student participation in decision making. (4) Parent and student participation will contribute to increased accountability on the part of educators.

FIGURE 7–8
Documentation for Parental Participation in the IEP Committee

Name of Child _____ Date of Staffing _____

Name of Parent _____

"Each local educational agency shall take steps to insure that one or both of the parents of the handicapped child are present at each meeting or are afforded the opportunity to participate, including scheduling the meeting at a mutually agreed upon time and place."

Please check the appropriate space to indicate the actions taken to satisfy the above requirements:

_____ 1. The parent(s) attended the meeting.

      These steps were taken to insure that the parents understood the proceedings of the meeting:

      _____

      _____

      _____

_____ 2. The meeting was conducted on _____ at _____, using an:
                             date   time

          _____ individual telephone call

          _____ conference telephone call

_____ 3. A mutually agreed upon meeting time and place was not possible as verified by this evidence:

      _____ a. detailed records of phone calls

Date	Time	Who called	Result

      _____ b. correspondence sent and responses received (see attached copies)

      _____ c. detailed records of visits made to the parent's home or place of employment and results of those visits

Date	Time	Who visited	Result

From "Educational Plan Workshop Packet" by the Jefferson County School Board, Monticello, Florida. Reprinted by permission.

The nature of parent participation in educational decision-making may take many forms, including the provision of consent for evaluation, input at the IEP conference, opportunity to review records, initiation of due process proceedings, membership on advisory boards, and notification and consent before release of any personally identifiable information on the student. Although this section focuses on the participation of parents in the IEP conference, this is only one of many forms of parent involvement as specified by P.L. 94–142. This section also addresses student involvement, a topic that has to date received only negligible attention in the educational literature.

Strategies for Enhancing Parent Involvement

Methods of Scheduling the Meeting. Some schools comply minimally with the requirement of encouraging full parent participation in the IEP conference. For example, a letter may be sent three times, after which, if the parent does not respond, the meeting is conducted without them (White & Calhoun, 1987).

Other schools report making special efforts such as initial and follow-up telephone calls, home visits, and evening meetings to encourage parent participation (Singer & Butler, 1987; White & Calhoun, 1987). Not surprisingly, these efforts to assure parents that their participation is desired and necessary often result in high levels of parent participation. P.L. 94–142 also requires that such efforts be made. Personal telephone calls to parents to establish a date and time for the meeting, to follow-up and confirm the meeting, and to discuss the agenda and procedures to be followed during the meeting are helpful in ensuring that parents will attend the meeting. Scheduling evening conferences may enable parents who work to attend. In some instances transportation can be arranged for parents who do not have transportation, or conferences can be conducted at the parents' home at a time convenient to them.

Preconference Training.

If parents know what to expect at the IEP conference, they may be encouraged to participate actively. Some evidence shows that informal conferences or training before the conference can increase the number of parent contributions at the actual meeting (Brinckerhoff & Vincent, 1986). Although local agencies are not required to provide training to parents and students to prepare them for meaningful participation in the IEP conference, such training frequently is needed. Many educators themselves lack the confidence and sometimes the competence necessary to make informed decisions in IEP conferences, despite their extensive preservice and inservice training. Thus, it is not surprising that parents and students are often not prepared to assume an active role in interpreting evaluation information, specifying goals and objectives, and deciding on an appropriate placement and related services. Training on these topics may contribute substantially to meaningful participation. Figure 7–9 lists competencies that parents may need to enhance their active decision making in the IEP conference. In addition, many states and school systems have developed training and information materials for use by parents.

Provision of Information to Parents Before the Meeting.

Providing information before the meeting is a strategy that can assist parents to participate more fully in the actual IEP meeting. If a drafted IEP is sent home or explained to parents before the meeting, the parents and the student will have an opportunity to review the information and formulate questions before the IEP meeting. Copies of draft IEPs, a list of potential questions that the parent may want to ask before or during the conference, a list of information that the parent may wish to share, or even a copy of the state's or school district's regula-

tions regarding special education programs may be helpful to parents in preparing for the IEP conference. The notice illustrated in Figure 7–6 provides information that parents can use to prepare for the meeting.

Designating a Parent and Student Sponsor.

Although it is not legally required, many parents and students might benefit from having another participant at the IEP meeting designated in advance to serve as a sponsor for them (Goldstein & Turnbull, 1982; Strickland, 1983). The sponsor might ensure the following: (1) The parents are introduced to all participants. (2) They are involved in the conference (i.e., questions are directed to them). (3) Educational jargon is clarified. (4) Parents' contributions are considered and reinforced by the committee. (5) Decisions are summarized at the end of the conference. A comparison of conferences in which a parent-sponsor role was assumed by counselors with conferences that did not have a parent sponsor indicated that the sponsor's presence resulted in significantly more parent comments during the conference (Goldstein & Turnbull, 1982).

If such a strategy is implemented, the designation of which committee member will serve in this capacity should be made before the conference. However, some parents may prefer to bring their own sponsor to the meeting—someone who is not an employee of the educational agency. This issue can be discussed with parents when they are notified of the IEP conference.

Assigning Parent Responsibilities in IEP Implementation.

It is important that goals and objectives viewed as important by the parents and student be incorporated into the IEP (Witt et al., 1984). In addition, it is entirely appropriate to ask parents if they would be willing to assume responsibility for teaching or reinforcing some objectives at home. Parents may agree to assume full responsibility for particular objectives, or responsibility may be shared between teachers and parents. If parents do assume responsibility for teaching, they may need some assistance with analyzing the tasks into subskills or with selection of appropriate teaching methods. Providing parents with the opportunity to participate in planning the educational program will likely result in parents assuming greater responsibility for implementing the developed plan.

Parent Reference Book.

Although the school is responsible for ensuring that an appropriate educational program is provided for a student with a disability, parents must ultimately be the best advocates for their children. One way to assist parents in

FIGURE 7–9
Parental Competencies Associated with Involvement in the IEP

1. To state federal and state legislative requirements pertaining to the following six principles: zero reject, nondiscriminatory evaluation, individualized educational programs, least restrictive environments, due process, and parental participation.

2. To explain the purpose of the IEP committees, required components, time lines, and rationale for annual review.

3. To state the purpose, nature, and method of providing parental notices and obtaining parental consent for the preplacement evaluation and placement into a special education program.

4. To ensure that specific concerns are addressed and questions answered when discussing evaluation results with professionals.

5. To communicate with professionals in a manner characterized by respect, self-confidence, persistence in getting answers to questions, and nondefensiveness.

6. To discuss and negotiate the following aspects of IEP development with professionals: (a) levels of performance, (b) annual goals, (c) short-term objectives, (d) evaluation procedures, (e) special education placement and related services, (f) extent of time in the regular class, and (g) method of reviewing the IEP on at least an annual basis.

7. To engage in active decision-making strategies in IEP meetings, such as initiating questions and asking for clarification on unclear issues.

8. To state special concerns related to the child and to ensure that these concerns are carefully considered by the IEP committee.

9. To state the particular follow-up responsibilities from the IEP committee meeting that are manageable for the family in consideration of the other responsibilities of family members.

10. To negotiate preferred strategies for parent-teacher communication throughout the school year.

11. To recognize available due process alternatives if agreement cannot be reached within the committee on the approval of the IEP.

12. To be aware of the procedure and to use parent advocates as support if necessary in fulfilling roles and responsibilities associated with IEP development and implementation.

13. To participate in monitoring procedures related to IEP development and implementation.

From Turnbull, A.P., B. Strickland & S. Goldstein. Training professionals and parents in developing and implementing the IEP. *Education and Training of the Mentally Retarded,* 1978, *13,* 414–26.

this role is to help them to identify, gather, and maintain information about their child that will be consistently useful to them during the course of their child's education. A parents' reference book might provide this type of tool for parents.

The IEP committee might compile a notebook with several sections. For example, sections might be delineated as legal and procedural references; student-specific information; names of local, statewide, and national parent support groups; and names of school and community contacts. Reference books for parents of older students may include a list of colleges and universities with programs for students with disabilities. Other items to include in a reference book for parents include the names, addresses, and phone numbers of individuals and agencies in the school and community who may provide information or services to families.

Assisting parents to establish and maintain a reference book can benefit the school as well as the parents. The book might contain copies of written material provided by the school that the parents can refer to, as necessary. This eliminates the need to provide multiple copies of records, policies, and due process rights at meetings. Such a procedure facili-

tates communication between the parents and the school by providing a reference point for discussion about the student's IEP, parent rights, or evaluations. For example, despite the requirement of P.L. 94–142, and schools' efforts to ensure that parents understand their due process rights, research indicates that many parents do not fully understand their entitlements even after attending committee meetings in which efforts were made to explain their rights (Barton, 1984; U.S. Department of Education, 1987; Vaughn et al., 1988). In part this may be due to the fact that during IEP meetings parents are typically required to consider and make decisions on a number of issues in a short period of time. Although most parents are unlikely to review and fully assimilate due process information at the IEP meeting (unless that information is particularly important at the time of the meeting), they may find the information useful at a later date.

Visiting the School Program. Before the IEP meeting and/or before agreeing to placement, school representatives should suggest to parents that they observe in the programs in which their child may be placed. The school should make every effort to ensure that parents have this opportunity and that they are provided information related to the program. Schools may develop and provide to parents a list of classroom elements by which to review the program or formulate questions. Figure 7–10 provides a list of classroom elements that may assist the parent in observing a program in which their child may be placed. Parents should also be encouraged to monitor their child's program after placement by observing in the classroom periodically. Although parents may lack formal strategies for monitoring the educational program, they almost certainly will use the information available to them as a basis for program evaluation (Strickland, 1983). If parents have only written progress reports and no encouragement to obtain other information, then the program will be evaluated based on that criterion. Schools should make every effort to provide parents with the skills and opportunities for obtaining accurate and relevant program information.

Student Participation in the IEP Conference

Practically no literature is available on student involvement in the IEP conference. However, in many ways the IEP represents a formal agreement between the parties involved that all will work toward the accomplishment of the goals as stated on the IEP. Because the student is the focus of that agreement and will obviously play an important part in its accomplishment, his involvement is vital. There are many potential benefits of student participation, including the following:

1. Students can contribute firsthand information regarding areas that present the greatest and least amount of difficulty. They can also evaluate methods of intervention in terms of their effectiveness in providing helpful strategies for learning.
2. Student presence at the IEP meeting can personalize the meeting for committee members, who may not know the student. Committee members can ask the student directly about his interests, skills, and so on, rather than relying solely on reports of others.
3. Including the student in the IEP conference indicates to the student that parents and teachers are receptive to the student's input and consider what students have to say as important.
4. Participation in IEP development and/or in the IEP conference promotes the notion that the student is expected to behave maturely and responsibly. Involvement in decision making can encourage shared responsibility for the results of the decision.

5. Student participation in the IEP process may foster self-advocacy by providing an opportunity for the student to speak for himself regarding interests, academics, and the educational program.
6. By participating in the IEP conference and listening to the ideas communicated by individuals within the group, the student may communicate more effectively with parents and with groups in general.

The decision to involve the student in the IEP conference is often left to the parent, or the student, if appropriate. At a minimum, the school must inform parents in the notice of the IEP meeting that parents may invite their child to participate. However, the school should exceed these minimal requirements to actively encourage student participation whenever feasible and to inform parents and students about appropriate methods of participation. The school should discuss the possibility of student participation with the parents before a decision is made to determine whether the student's attendance will be helpful in developing the IEP and whether participation will benefit the student. Criteria that might be considered to determine when students should participate in the IEP conference include (1) the age of the student, (2) the type and level of disability, (3) the student's ability to participate.

Age of the Student.   Active student participation in the IEP conference depends to some degree on the student's age. Attendance and participation of students in kindergarten and early elementary years seldom is considered necessary, or even appropriate. However, as age increases, the frequency of student participation should increase so that by high school, student participation in program planning not only should be expected but should be considered essential. As emphasis on transition planning for postschool employment increases, the need for students with disabilities to develop appropriate decision-making skills has received increased attention. By the time many students with disabilities reach graduation, they should be able to assume primary responsibility for decision making, with parents and other conference participants providing coordination of services, support, and assistance in determining future training and employment goals.

Decision making is a skill acquired over time and through repeated opportunities for participation in decision-making activities. Thus, parents and schools should begin early to encourage student participation at appropriate levels. Although young students with disabilities participate infrequently in the IEP conference, it should be noted that they can

FIGURE 7–10
Checklist of Classroom Elements That Parents May Wish To Consider Before Placement

Special Education Classroom

	Yes	No	Uncertain
1. Is the classroom located in the same building as and in proximity to classrooms for students without disabilities?	___	___	_____
2. Is the classroom accessible?	___	___	_____
3. Is the equipment consistent with that of the needs of the students and with that provided in the rest of the school?	___	___	_____
4. Is there adequate opportunity for interaction with students without disabilities? When? At what times? For what activities?_____	___	___	_____
5. Can parents visit whenever they like? Are there specific procedures to follow regarding visits for classroom observations?	___	___	_____
6. Are there opportunities available for learning in other settings within the school and community? Is the library accessible and used? Are there field trips and work and social experiences in the community?	___	___	_____
7. Are there opportunities available for developing job training and employment skills? Vocational education? Home economics? Shop? Are these experiences with typical students in the school or segregated?_____	___	___	_____
8. Are physical education and other recreational and therapeutic activities available?	___	___	_____
Are they provided with students without disabilities?	___	___	_____

Regular Classroom

	Yes	No	Uncertain
1. Does the teacher grade students based on the same standards established for other students, or are individual considerations made? For example, does the teacher have a policy that students with disabilities can attain no higher than a grade of "C" if they are on a modified program?_____	___	___	_____
2. Do students work in small groups and individually as well as in one large group for all curriculum areas? Does the teacher individualize instruction for the students in the classroom?	___	___	_____
3. Are there opportunities for individualized and small-group instruction? Are there a teacher's aide, peer helpers, volunteers?	___	___	_____
4. Does the classroom contain all necessary equipment, or is it set up to accommodate necessary equipment?	___	___	_____
5. Are there written discipline policies? What is the teacher's philosophy about discipline? How is it handled in the classroom?_____	___	___	_____
6. Are specialized services integrated into the classroom or other settings?	___	___	_____

Classroom Observations

	Yes	No	Uncertain
1. Does the teacher praise the students often?	___	___	_____
2. Does the teacher provide clear, but gentle guidance when individually instructing students?	___	___	_____
3. Is the time in the program used intensively and in challenging ways? Is there minimum inactive time?	___	___	_____
4. Are teaching materials appropriate? Are they interesting and varied?	___	___	_____
5. Does the classroom have a pleasant environment and age-appropriate or age-free decor?	___	___	_____
6. Do interactions between the teacher and students appear to be positive and age appropriate?	___	___	_____
7. Do teaching strategies focus on skills that my child needs?	___	___	_____

nonetheless contribute valuable information for IEP planning. Research indicates that even by the age of 6, some students may have a general understanding of their limitations and by age 8 may understand many of the implications of their disability (Minde, Hackett, Killon, & Silver, 1972). Questions that students ask at school and at home regarding their disability, as well as the reaction and curiosity of peers, often can provide the basis for IEP conference planning. For example, a goal for a young student with a physical disability might be the development of a positive self-image and open communication between the student and his peers. As a means of promoting the goal, the teacher or parent, as members of the IEP committee, may ask the student to help think of ways to let other students know about disabilities.

Type and Level of Disability. Students with mild disabilities can often participate directly in the IEP conference. Participation may focus on identification of interests, strengths, weaknesses, and strategies that may assist in the development of an effective educational plan. The student also may provide evaluative information on the effectiveness of the existing program. Even students with mild disabilities, however, cannot be expected to generate program-planning information without some assistance. The IEP committee should develop strategies to enhance the student's ability to participate effectively in the meeting. One way to do this is for the parents or a teacher or both to meet with the student before the IEP conference to discuss and perhaps prepare the information to be shared with or by the student at the meeting.

The type and level of the student's disabilty should be considered in determining *how* not *whether* the student will participate in the IEP conference. Students with severe intellectual disabilities and communication disabilities can contribute valuable information for IEP planning. It is the responsibility of the IEP committee to establish a means of student participation that will minimize the effects of the student's disability on the ability to participate. Students with alternative methods of communication might participate through a parent or teacher familiar with the student's communication style. In addition, professionals and parents can observe students in various activities to determine their preferences, interests, and needs. For example, if a student with a significant intellectual disability is observed to feel comfortable in quiet, structured environments, this information should provide the basis for locating community employment options with these characteristics.

Responsibilities of IEP Committee in Planning Student Participation

The ability of the student to participate positively and importantly depends heavily on the information he is asked to provide, how the student is expected to participate, and the degree to which the student understands what is expected. Figure 7–11 provides guidelines for planning student involvement in the IEP conference.

Defining the Information That the Student Will Contribute. The information that the student is asked to contribute should be based on the student's age, area of educational difficulty, type of disability, and personality characteristics. Contributions could include explaining personal strengths and weaknesses, identifying perceived needs and interests on which goals and objectives can be formulated, stating preferences for special education placement and related services, and generally providing insights into the instructional strategies that have been educationally successful in the past as well as those most likely to promote future success. The IEP committee should make certain that the student is able and willing to provide the requested information before the IEP meeting. An informal discussion with the student before the IEP conference may provide an opportunity for the student to think and talk briefly about the information that will be provided during the conference.

Method of Student Participation. The manner in which the student is expected to participate should also be determined before the IEP conference. Few students should be expected to participate in the same manner as professionals. Some students can participate actively throughout the meeting, while others may appropriately participate for a short period of time. IEP committee members should consider various nonthreatening ways for students to participate. Options might include attendance at only a portion of the meeting (this is often a necessary requirement for younger students); selection of a student sponsor to attend the meeting with the student; attendance as an observer with the prerogative to contribute information as preferred; preparation and presentation of written information such as a list of interests, likes, and dislikes, or effective learning strategies; development of goals that parents and professionals can help accomplish at home and at school; and meeting with only one or two members of the IEP committee. Methods of indirect participation might include observation of the student in various settings to determine interests and skills, videotapes at a worksite or in the community, or an

FIGURE 7–11
Suggestions for Including Students in IEP Meetings

1. The way in which the student is to be involved should be determined on a case by case basis. Older students with mild disabilities may be able to participate more fully than younger students and students with limited ability. The parents, IEP committee members, and the student should determine in advance the role that the student will be expected to play.

2. Parents and/or teachers should review the agenda and draft goals and objectives with the student before the meeting to familiarize the student with what will be discussed and how the student might participate.

3. If the student does not feel comfortable attending the meeting, information related to the educational program can be discussed before the meeting and incorporated into the IEP at the meeting. A conference might be conducted with the student before the IEP meeting to determine to what extent he feels comfortable participating in IEP development.

4. The physical setting should be arranged so that the student sits with the rest of the committee as a full and participating member. A warm atmosphere should be established, and IEP committee members should view the student as a full and responsible member of the committee.

5. Ask questions of the student that cannot be answered with a yes or no response. Instead of asking, "Do you like math?" ask, "What do you like or dislike about math?" Instead of asking, "Do you think this will help you?" ask "How do you think we can help you?"

6. Plan time for the student to speak, and do not interrupt while the student is talking. This communicates that what the student is saying is important. Encourage the student to ask questions for clarification.

7. Use brief remarks. Do not confuse the student with long complicated questions or comments. If necessary, assist the student to clarify, interpret, and summarize what has been said after the student has presented his ideas.

8. The meeting should be nonthreatening and should emphasize the positive growth of the student and the willingness and commitment of the IEP committee in assisting the student to achieve the goals and objectives established.

9. Students should be informed of their legal protections offered them through their parents' representation of their interests. Although not required by P.L. 94-142, including students in the decision-making process should also carry the responsibility of providing them with full information.

10. Students should be asked to "officially" sign the IEP. This practice reinforces the notion that their participation and endorsement is important rather than perfunctory. In addition, signing the IEP represents a commitment by the student to make a good faith effort toward achieving the goals and objectives included on the IEP.

interview with a group of students on topics of common interest (such as career interests).

Define Expectations. Finally, the IEP committee must ensure that the student knows what to expect before the IEP conference. One option is to provide training to groups of students at the same time. Although practically no literature is available on training students for IEP involvement, such training is necessary for shared decision making. A variety of sponsors for student training could be considered, including the local education agency, parent organizations, mental health centers, and advocacy groups comprised of adults with disabilities. Training strategies, involving simulations of conferences with student participation, values-clarification exercises, and assertiveness training, are likely to be highly relevant. Students with disabilities who have previously participated in conferences could share their experiences with students who have not yet had the experience.

Planning an agenda in advance and sharing it with students before the meeting can also assist them to anticipate the manner in which their contributions can be incorporated into the decision-making process. The agenda should be flexible enough to be modified according to the student's preferences and method of participation.

In summary, student participation in the IEP process can enhance the quality and relevance of the educational program and provide the student an opportunity for self-direction and self-assertion. When given an appropriate opportunity to share their perspective in a supportive and individual manner, most students with disabilities can contribute information for or participate in the planning of educational programs. Educators and parents alike need to remind themselves that students can contribute valuable information about themselves, which can significantly enhance the quality of the program and the student's commitment to its success.

SUMMARY

This chapter has attempted to provide a general context within which to develop and implement the components of the IEP. Suggestions for IEP formats, methods of IEP development, and suggestions for conference planning were presented, along with a rationale and suggestions for participation of parents and students in the process. Beyond the planning aspects of the IEP process, it should be remembered that for an IEP to be effective, it must be appropriately developed and implemented. The IEP committee is responsible for ensuring that the IEP's content is technically accurate and that once developed, the IEP can be appropriately implemented. The remainder of Part 2 will provide suggestions for accomplishing the technical development of the IEP.

EVALUATION

1. You have been asked to present information about the IEP to members of the school board. Outline your presentation, noting the purposes of the IEP from a legal, administrative, parental, and instructional perspective. What are the identified advantages and disadvantages of the IEP?
2. Develop a format for writing IEPs, which not only meets all requirements but also is functional for planning an appropriate curriculum for a student with a disability in your school.
3. You are the director of special education in a large school system. One school has asked that you provide inservice training on methods of IEP development. Outline the requirements for development of the IEP and provide three alternative IEP development methods, noting the advantages and disadvantages of each.
4. Discuss three factors to be considered in planning the IEP conference and three activities that should be conducted during the preconference planning period.
5. Provide a rationale for conducting the IEP conference separately from a meeting with parents to discuss eligibility and/or evaluation results. How might two meetings affect the IEP conference? What are the advantages and disadvantages of such a procedure?
6. At a group parent meeting sponsored by the local education agency, you have been asked by the director of special education to give a 15-minute presentation on the rationale and importance of parent involvement in the IEP conference. Outline your presentation.

CHAPTER 8

Determining Levels Of Performance

OBJECTIVES

1. Establish that levels of performance for program planning are an expected outcome of the evaluation process.

2. Identify and discuss three ways of stating performance levels, depending on the information to be conveyed by the statement.

3. Discuss five guidelines for developing levels of performance statements.

4. Identify and discuss advantages of curriculum-based evaluation information as the basis for levels of performance statements.

The first step in translating student evaluation information into practical programming for the student with a disability is the determination of current levels of educational performance. Indicating present levels of performance is one of the legal requirements for IEP development, and establishes the basis for formulating annual goals and short-term instructional objectives and the evaluation criteria by which the objectives will be measured.

Levels of performance are an important issue throughout the pre-referral, referral, evaluation, and IEP development process. For example, low levels of performance are the source of concern that prompts initial prereferral and referral activities. Performance levels are also crucial elements considered in the evaluation process to determine the presence of a disability. (Identification of disabilities is, in fact, based on discrepancies between a student's actual and expected performance in the areas of intelligence, health, communication, and emotional status.) At the point of eligibility determination, the "adverse effect" of a disability is again often determined by comparing the student's performance level to some expected level of performance. Thus, identifying levels of performance actually begins long before the point of IEP development and is in fact the focus of virtually every activity, from referral to placement in a program of specially designed instruction.

Despite many opportunities to clearly articulate levels of performance in clear educational terms before the IEP is developed, IEP committee members may not always have sufficient performance level information on which to base development of an appropriate IEP. This may be because the type of performance data typically generated during the evaluation process may be suited primarily for identifying and classifying the student's disability rather than for program planning (J. R. Jenkins & Pany, 1978). Levels of performance for the purpose of identification and classification of disabilities are typically represented by scores, grade equivalents,

and percentile rankings from commercially produced norm-referenced tests, rather than by specific statements of which curriculum-related skills the student actually has or has not achieved. As a result, many teachers conduct additional evaluation after eligibility has been determined to obtain specific information for determining levels of performance and developing goals and objectives for the IEP (White & Calhoun, 1987). This chapter will discuss the importance of evaluation information in developing appropriate levels of performance statements for IEP development and will provide guidelines for ensuring that levels of performance statements included on the IEP provide clear and useful information for instruction.

EVALUATION RESULTS AS A BASIS FOR DETERMINING LEVELS OF PERFORMANCE

Appropriate Evaluation

Because the establishment of useful levels of performance hinges on the availability of accurate and educationally useful evaluation information, evaluation must be planned in advance to generate the kinds of information that will be required for the purpose of program planning. By anticipating the program-planning function of evaluation, as well as the identification and classification function, the special services committee can ensure that evaluation procedures include appropriate curriculum-related measures, as well as those traditional measures necessary to obtain norm-referenced information.

Eligibility determination, program planning, and placement are not three separate and unrelated decisions but are three inextricable aspects of the same process, all directed at providing an appropriate educational program to a student with a disability. Decisions made throughout the identification and program-planning process should have their basis and justification in a common and appropriate body of evaluation information. A student cannot be determined eligible for special education without having been determined to require specially designed instruction. This determination cannot be appropriately made without identifying student needs on which such a determination might be based. Further, it is difficult to determine student needs without some general indication of levels of performance in particular areas. Thus, if eligibility has been appropriately determined, areas in which specially designed instruction is thought to be necessary (based on levels of performance) will have been identified before IEP development. The function of the IEP committee then becomes one of further translating general performance levels into specific curriculum-related statements on which annual goals and objectives can be based.

To make information on levels of performance readily accessible, evaluation reports should provide adequate information on levels of performance and data for individual program planning. Figure 8–1 illustrates a report of the multidisciplinary team in which levels of performance are clearly indicated.

Designation of Areas in Which Specially Designed Instruction Will Be Provided

Making a specific determination of which areas will require specially designed instruction is a committee function and should be completed before IEP development begins. Evaluation results should be thoroughly reviewed and used as a basis for determining which general areas will be provided with specially designed instruction. Based on the results of evaluation, the team, preferably including the parents, should agree on the general areas that will require specially designed instruction. Areas of specially designed instruction will depend to some extent on characteristics of the student's disability and the educational area(s) affected.

Characteristics of the Student's Disability. A student's need for specially designed instruction could be indicated by several factors. First, academic achievement may be significantly below that of other students of the same age or grade. For example, students with intellectual or learning disabilities may have poor reading skills and thus may be failing in all academic areas that have reading requirements. Second, evaluation may indicate a need for alternative instructional equipment or materials to minimize the adverse effects of the disability. For example, a student with a visual disability may require magnification equipment while a student with a hearing disability may require auditory training equipment for use in the classroom. Alternative response strategies such

as verbal rather than written responses or use of a typewriter or word processor for a student who has a physical or visual disability may be required. Third, an emotional disturbance may be so extreme as to require specially designed management strategies or psychological counseling. If the student is encountering difficulty with social relationships in the school setting because behaviors are considered annoying by others, social adjustment might be designated as an area of IEP development. The insights of parents and of students themselves can be especially helpful in making decisions as to which areas may require specially designed instruction. Because behavioral determinations to a large extent often involve value judgments, parental and student opinion should be solicited and heeded.

Educational Area Affected. A student may require specially designed instruction in some areas but not in others. A student with a specific learning disability, for example, might require specially designed instruction in reading and language but not in vocational education or other areas. A student with a physical disability may require specially designed instruction only in physical education. It is inappropriate to assume that, because a student requires specially designed instruction in one area, all areas should be included. Similarly, it is also inappropriate to conclude that because a student does not require specially designed instruction in an academic area, the student is not eligible for specially designed instruction in nonacademic areas. Academics are only one component of the educational program, which when interpreted in a broader sense, includes all aspects of a student's schooling. As specifically designated by P.L. 94–142, schooling includes physical education and vocational education. Figure 8–2, p. 207, provides a format for generating and documenting areas in which specially designed instruction is required. After the specific skill areas on which the IEP will be based are identified and agreed on, levels of performance can be generated for these areas.

Developing Statements Of Levels of Performance

Levels of performance statements must be developed for each of the areas in which it is determined that instruction must be specially designed to meet the needs of the student with a disability. After broad subject areas have been identified, the committee should identify the specific skills to be addressed in each area. The specific skill areas established will be determined by and vary according to the identified needs of each student. In a typical breakdown, the area of mathematics might be further broken down

FIGURE 8-1
Example of Evaluation Report with Clear Indication of Levels of Performance

PREVOCATIONAL ASSESSMENT REPORT

Student: Michael Ashton   Birthdate: June 5, 1974
Age: 16   Test Date: 25 Sept. 90

Reason For Referral

To determine prevocational aptitudes, independent living skills, and
needs to assist in the development of appropriate vocational goals and
curriculum planning.

Test Administered

The Street Survival Skills Questionnaire (SSSQ). The Street Survival
Skills Questionnaire is an inventory that evaluates and measures
functional knowledge and skills that are important for independent
living in a community. Evaluation data obtained from SSSQ can help to
provide a curriculum blueprint to direct a student from current
baseline of skills to higher levels of functioning more consistent with
community demands. The inventory consists of nine tests, each of which
measures abilities in different skill areas.

Behavioral Observations

Michael arrived promptly for each testing session and appeared
motivated to perform at his optimal level throughout most of the
evaluation. Although he was somewhat withdrawn at the outset of the
meeting, we established rapport by familiarizing Michael with the
surroundings, introducing him to students, and talking with him about
himself, schoolwork, and the school activities he prefers. During the
testing, Michael seemed to be particularly concerned about the
whereabouts of his father and had to be often reassured that he would
pick him up once we were finished with the session.

Throughout the morning session, Michael worked diligently and
persevered through tasks that appeared most difficult for him. He was
able to follow oral directions reasonably well, and his ability to
focus on tasks was good. Michael worked slowly, yet easily mastered 3-
step work tasks (with frequent repetitions) quite successfully. Verbal
encouragement and praise were used to reinforce positive and
cooperative behaviors exhibited during the session.

At the beginning of the afternoon session, Michael became upset on
the departure of his father. He was reluctant to work with the same
enthusiasm that he had exhibited during the morning. His attention to
task was limited, and he appeared to lose patience easily. As a
result, testing in the afternoon was very minimal. It is felt, however,
that this assessment is representative of his skills and abilities.

Assessment Results

Michael completed eight of the nine subtests. Scaled scores were not
reported because of the nature of the normative group. Generally,
individuals scoring 80% or better are generally considered to possess
functional living skills consistent with the kinds of community demands
needed for independent living. The results were as follows:

(Figure 8–1 continued)

Component Scale	Percentage Score
Basic Concepts	58
Functional Signs	54
Domestics	37
Health & Safety	37
Public Services	45
Time	25
Monetary	16
Measurement	25
Total	56

Levels of Performance

Basic Concepts

Strengths	Needs
1. Visually matches colors 2. Understands basic comparative concepts 3. Understands basic directional concepts	1. Knowledge of basic positional concepts 2. Basic comparative concepts

Functional Signs

Strengths	Needs
1. Understands some symbolic signs	1. Knowledge of signs with symbolic information 2. Read signs with one four-letter word 3. Read signs with sentences

Domestics

Strengths	Needs
1. Can describe basic food preparation and storage	1. Knowledge of cleaning products 2. Knowledge of body parts for measurement and proper fit of clothing 3. Operation of dials for washing and drying clothes

Health and Safety

Strengths	Needs
1. Bathes and dresses self on request	1. Distinguish between safe and unsafe conditions 2. Select the correct materials to administer first aid 3. Review of basic personal hygiene/health practices

Public Services

Strengths	Needs
1. Identifies basic community public services (telephone, post office, library, bank)	1. Use of telephone and telephone book 2. Use of checking account 3. Review of post office, addressing, stamping, and mailing letters

(Figure 8–1 continued)

Time

Strengths	Needs
1. Reads numerals 1-10	1. Tell time to the hour, half hour, and minute 2. Read digital time 3. Read calendar time 4. Time activities

Money

Strengths	Needs
1. Identifies nickle, dime, and quarter	1. Identify coins and currency 2. Formulate equivalence of coin and currency 3. Make change

Measurement

Strengths	Needs
1. Identifies basic measurement instruments (thermometer, cup, ruler)	1. Read a thermometer 2. Make liquid measures 3. Use a ruler in measurement of length

Summary

The SSSQ suggests that Michael's living skills are not consistent with those needed for independent living. Vocational planning should include a curriculum that is functional and multifaceted. Skill training should have utility in more than one area of instruction. Continuous and direct measurement of performance during training, such as charting and graphing work behaviors, may help to enhance learning of tasks and provide reinforcement for Michael.

Stephen Nelson

Steven Nelson

Vocational Evaluator

FIGURE 8–2
Format for Documenting Levels of Performance

1. Student Name: <u>Janice</u>
    Age: <u>9</u>   Grade: <u>4</u>
    Date: <u>October 15, 1990</u>

2. **Areas of Educational Concern**
    <u>   Reading   </u>
    <u>   </u>
    <u>   </u>

3. <u>   </u>

Evaluation Measure	Summary of Results in Areas of Concern	Area for IEP? Yes	No
Reading from basal readers (Four trials in three basals)	Recognizes fewer than 50% of words in selected passages from grade-level reader. Has difficulty answering questions related to comprehension when she reads but can answer some questions when teacher or another student reads the passage. Reading style is hesitant with little inflection. Uses finger to point to words. Can read most basic sight vocabulary for first-grade reader but confuses words such as when, where, went, in, on etc.	X	
Systemwide Achievement Test	10th percentile in vocabulary 15th percentile in comprehension		
Peabody Individual Achievement Test	Reading Recognition 1.5 Reading Comprehension 2.5 Spelling 2.0 Mathematics 3.5		

4. **Signatures of Committee Members**
<u>Olive Hanley</u>   Date: <u>10 15/90</u>
<u>Sara E. Wright</u>   Date: <u>10-15-90</u>
<u>Thomas Oldenburg</u>   Date: <u>10/15/90</u>
<u>Adrian L Copeland</u>   Date: <u>10-15-90</u>

into skills of addition, subtraction, money concepts, and telling time; reading into vocabulary development, comprehension, and word-attack skills; motor development into fine and gross motor coordination; communication into language and articulation; adaptive behavior into social competence and self-help; and vocational education into career awareness and vocational training.

For each specific skill identified, statements of current performance levels must be included on the IEP. Performance statements can be illustrated in numerous ways, including norm-referenced scores, criterion-referenced skill statements, curriculum-based statements, observational statements, and even anecdotal information. The type of information included will depend on the specific skill area to be addressed on the IEP and on the type of information that best describes student functioning in terms of that skill area. The next section of this chapter will provide criteria for determining the type of information to be included in developing statements of current performance levels.

CRITERIA FOR SELECTING PERFORMANCE STATEMENTS

The information used to document current levels of performance depends on what the committee determines to be important and of value in developing the educational program for the student in a specific area. Committee members must keep in mind that levels of performance must serve two purposes. First, they should provide a basis for projecting the goals and objectives that will be developed for a student. Second, they should also provide a benchmark for establishing the criteria for determining when the goals and objectives have been achieved.

In selecting information to be used to document performance levels, committee members must consider and define the purpose for which levels of performance statements will be used and must fully understand what kinds of data will provide the necessary information. For example, if the committee agrees that for the area of reading it is most important to indicate the specific reading skills that a student does and does not have, but then selects only a grade equivalent to indicate the reading performance level, the performance statement falls short of the intended purpose of the committee. In determining what information the performance statements should provide, the committee should consider which of the following purposes the statements are intended to serve:

1. Provide an indication of the student's level of performance in a particular area relative to a large sample of other students.
2. Provide an indication of the student's specific skills and weaknesses.
3. Provide an indication of the student's level of skill attainment in a particular curriculum.

Comparison with a Large Sample of Students

In some instances, it may be helpful to include norm-referenced performance statements on the IEP. Many parents want information related to how their child performs compared to other students as well as information on specific skill attainment. Including this information may make explanations to parents easier by providing a context within which to explain student strengths and weaknesses. Including norm-referenced statements may also be helpful in situations where students move frequently from school to school. Because norm-referenced scores are widely accepted and often used by schools as a basis for estimating initial placement in graded instructional programs, scores on standardized achievement tests, if considered accurate, can be helpful indicators for estimating placement in instructional materials such as basal reading programs. Examples of performance statements that provide comparison information include the following:

1. Woodcock Reading Mastery Test, Grade Score = 3.0 (Date administered, May 5, 1988). Jonathan performed similar to the typical third-grade student in the norm group.
2. Susan performed as well as or better than 20% (score at the 20th percentile) of other students taking the statewide competency test in mathematics. (Administered May 1989.)
3. On the AAHPR Youth Fitness Test, Kate performed at the 50th percentile for sex and age group on sit-ups and standing broad jump; 25th percentile for pull-ups and soft-ball throw for distance, and 15th percentile for 600-yard dash run–walk. (Administered October 1988.)

If the committee considers it important to include information that indicates how a student performs relative to others, results of standardized and norm-referenced achievement tests might be included. This type of evaluation information, however, is generally designed to identify and classify and thus may appear to be more useful than it actually is for the purpose of instructional planning. Although grade-equivalent scores may indicate the level at which a particular student performs relative to other students who took the test, little information is usually provided about the specific skills represented by the score or about the group to which the student is being compared. Likewise, test scores indicate performance on a wide range of test items. If the sample of items included on the test is not similar to the curriculum in which the student must perform in school, these scores are meaningless for the purpose of program planning. Although test scores may be useful in providing a mechanism for general and widely recognized comparison of students, developers of the IEP must be aware of the limitations of these measures for obtaining information for instructional planning. Although test scores will likely continue to be used as one indicator of levels of performance, they should be used with other information that provides specific information about the student's performance relative to the curriculum in which she will be instructed.

Identification of Specific Skill Attainment

The committee may also determine that it is important to include statements on the IEP that reflect the specific skills that a student does or does not have. These statements provide specific information to parents and professionals about skill development in particular areas, such as reading or math. For example, rather than telling that a student performed similarly to other third graders on a mathematics test, performance statements might indicate that a student can add and subtract with regrouping and can tell time but that division, multiplication, and changing money are areas of weakness. Examples of performance statements based on criterion-referenced tests might include the following:

1. Jonathan can read orally from a third-grade reading passage without experiencing difficulty in pronouncing more than one word in 20. (Brigance Diagnostic Inventory of Basic Skills, administered May 5, 1988.)
2. Given three problems for each operation, Susan can add, subtract, multiply and divide using whole numbers with 90% accuracy. (Brigance Diagnostic Inventory of Basic Skills, administered May 5, 1988.)
3. Kate can throw and catch small objects, follow a sequence of directions to perform physical skills, and kick balls of various sizes using either foot. (Inventory of Body Awareness and Balance Survey, administered October 1988.)

Information for developing performance statements that reflect specific skills can be obtained from criterion-referenced tests administered during the evaluation process. Schools frequently use measures

such as the Key Math Diagnostic Inventory and the Brigance Diagnostic Inventories to obtain levels of performance and to generate goals and objectives for the IEP (White & Calhoun, 1987). However, unless the skills measured by the test reflect the curriculum taught in the school, these measures still may not be sufficient for instructional planning.

Skill Attainment Relative To a Specific Curriculum

If the committee determines that it is necessary to include performance statements that indicate how the student performs in the curriculum of the school, then curriculum-based measures must be used, because they are the only source of this information. Performance statements based on curriculum-based evaluation have the distinct advantage of providing specific information about a student's actual performance because they are derived from the school's specific curriculum. These measures can include not only tests but also observational measures. Examples include the following:

1. Jonathan applies structural analysis to read regular and irregular plurals of nouns and contractions; identifies the plural form of nouns by attending to the *s* and *es* plural markers; identifies the root word in its plural form; changes a singular noun to its plural form. (Skill 3.2 in Sweetwater Union Curriculum, administered October 1989.)
2. Susan multiplies by three digits with regrouping; divides by two digits with or without remainders; adds and subtracts decimals to thousandths; tells time using minutes; makes change from $20. (Scope and Sequence Sequential Learning Objectives, Martin School District, administered January 1990.)
3. Kate catches a small ball thrown from 20 feet with two hands; throws a small ball 50 feet; floats in water; swims 20 feet using arms and legs. (Bridge School District Physical Skills Curriculum, administered March 1990.)

Curriculum-based measures are not always available or even valid for documenting levels of performance for all areas. In some instances, the committee may have to decide whether to give up a measure of technical validity in favor of a measure that provides information more useful for instructional planning.

A suggested procedure in developing level of performance statements for the IEP is to include a variety of performance indicators. In so doing levels of performance can be viewed from various perspectives. For example, Figure 8–3 provides three per-

FIGURE 8–3
Examples of Levels of Performance Statements

INDIVIDUALIZED EDUCATION PROGRAM

Student Name: _Kay_   School: _Lincoln_
Age: _9_   Grade: _4_

Levels of Performance

1. Comprehensive Test of Basic Skills (4/89). Compared to other fourth graders who took the test, Kay performed as follows: Vocabulary 15th percentile; Comprehension 25th percentile; Spelling 25th percentile. The CTBS Interpretive Profile indicates that Kay is strong in letter identification and identifying initial-consonant sounds and blends. The average performance on these sections of the test in the fourth grade in Kay's school was at the 45th percentile. This measure may underestimate Kay's actual performance in that she is a slow worker and does not follow directions well.

2. Kay likes to look at pictures in magazines and books. She does not like to read with a group or alone. She attends for only short periods of time and has difficulty remaining on task for periods exceeding 3 to 4 minutes. Although Kay will work alone with an adult or peer to completion of a task, she rarely completes a task on her own without frequent prompting.

3. Informal Reading Inventory (10/89)
   a. Is able to recognize the words found on the Dolch Basic Sight List.
   b. Can recognize and apply consonants, consonant blends, vowels to word attack.
   c. Is able to recognize a base or root word and differentiate between syllables.
   d. Can answer literal or factual questions posed from pictures and from readers when passage is read to her.
   e. Does not understand and apply all rules of phonetic analysis in reading.
   f. Does not use context clues to determine meaning of unknown words in passage.
   g. Does not answer literal, interpretive, or evaluative comprehension questions from passages that she must read.

Annual Goals

_____

_____

_____

Short-Term Instructional Objectives

_____

_____

_____

spectives on levels of performance. The first is a norm-referenced perspective indicating where the student performs relative to others who took a system-wide achievement test. Though the score has little value for specific program planning, it provides a useful indicator of the student's performance on the systemwide test relative to the performance of others in the school. The second statement provides observational information about the student's study habits, which cannot be obtained from tests but which is useful for providing insight that should be considered in program planning. The third statement of performance is derived from the reading curriculum of the class and indicates the skills that the student has and has not achieved within the curriculum of the regular program. These statements together provide useful information for the development of goals and objectives and for developing appropriate evaluative criteria for measuring progress.

GUIDELINES FOR WRITING STATEMENTS OF PERFORMANCE LEVELS

After designating the curricular areas in which specially designed instruction will be developed and also determining what information should be included as indicators of levels of performance, attention should focus on the actual writing of levels of performance statements. Sometimes, because of time constraints, established routine, and unavailability of relevant information, levels of performance may be stated inapproprately. For example, reading levels may be reported from norm-referenced tests that are outdated and no longer accurate because more recent scores are unavailable. Or level of performance statements may be omitted in some areas such as vocational education because norm-referenced information is not gathered. Because level of performance statements provide the basis on which the rest of the IEP is based, accurate and complete information relative to these levels must be provided. To ensure that the time spent in developing the IEP is worthwhile, those developing the IEP should ensure the levels of performance have the following characteristics:

1. Relevant and directly related to other components of the IEP
2. Stated in terms of strengths as well as weaknesses
3. Accurate in describing the adverse effect of the disability on educational performance
4. Current at the time of IEP development
5. Written in clear concise language

Relevant and Directly Related To Other IEP Components

There should be a direct relationship between the present levels of educational performance and the other components of the IEP. Thus, if reading comprehension is designated as an area in need of specially designed instruction, the level of performance should reflect current performance in the area of reading comprehension, and reading comprehension should be the focus of the goals and objectives subsequently developed. Although continuity between levels of performance and other components of the IEP should go without saying, overemphasis on such indicators as grade equivalents and percentile rankings from commercially produced measures have, in some cases, resulted in these scores being used as indicators of performance in any and every area designated for IEP development, regardless of their appropriateness.

Stated in Terms of Strengths As Well as Weaknesses

The level of performance statements should indicate not only what the student cannot do but what skills the student does have regarding the designated area of IEP development. In this way the IEP reflects both what the student has attained as well as specific problems. Including statements related to student strengths can assist those teaching the student to capitalize on these characteristics of the student. For example, a student may have very poor skills in mathematics but may be persistent and task oriented in completing assignments. This information provides insight into instructional strategies that might be successful in working with the student. In addition, providing specific information on the skills a student has already attained in specific areas can prevent reteaching of the same skills once the IEP is implemented. For example, if the level of performance on an IEP indicates that the student cannot tell time, it might be assumed that the student had no skills in this area. If the student can tell the hour, count by fives, or has other component skills, these should be indicated as strengths on the IEP.

It is also necessary to state the specific weaknesses that provide the basis and justification for the annual goals and short-term objectives in a particular area. If specific weaknesses are not identified in the level of performance statement, it may be unclear to those implementing the IEP exactly what need is being addressed by the goals and objectives. For example, if a student is physically aggressive toward other students, and the IEP states only strengths as levels of performance, there may be no apparent basis for an annual goal that is clearly directed toward modifying aggressive behavior. All performance statements should reflect an appropriate and accurate balance of the student's strengths and weaknesses.

Accurately Describe the Disability's Adverse Effects

The level of performance should accurately describe the disability's effect on student performance in any area of education that is affected, including academic areas such as reading, math, and language and nonacademic areas such as mobility, social emotional development, and fine and gross motor skills. Test scores that provide information on student performance might be included where appropriate. The scores, however, should be able to be interpreted by all who use the IEP, including parents and should provide usable information related to the area in which specially designed instruction will be provided.

It should be noted that labels such as "mentally retarded" or "deaf" and scores such as intelligence quotients are not functional indicators of educational performance and should not be used as such. Although the type and severity of the student's disability are important to know in developing specialized educational programs, level of performance statements are intended to provide information related to the student's functional instructional needs and should therefore be stated in terms of the student's functional skills.

Based on Information Current at the Time of IEP Development

Perhaps one of the most often observed violations of the requirements for IEP development is the use of outdated information to document current levels of performance. Although it is logical that the statement of current performance level should be based on current information, it is not unusual practice to use behavior statements from previous IEPs or previous reports as a basis for current levels of performance. For example, IEP committee members might use information from a previous but still current IEP to develop a new IEP for a student transferring into the school. In an effort to save time, the committee might fail to consider that the student's level of performance may well have changed since the date that the incoming IEP was developed. Statements of current performance developed in this way, without confirmation of present accuracy, are unlikely to provide appropriate information on which to base instruction. Behavioral concerns present at the time of

referral or reflected in previous reports are especially prone to being perpetuated in statements of current levels of performance, even though they may have long since disappeared and are no longer relevant.

Failure to ensure that levels of performance are current can occur as a result of overreliance on standardized test scores. Many educators believe, and indeed some systems require, that current levels of performance must be defined in terms of grade equivalents, percentile rankings, or other norm-referenced measures. This presents a potential dilemma because it is inappropriate and impractical (not to mention unnecessary) to administer standardized and norm-referenced tests every year to ensure that performance levels are current. Thus, scores generated at the time of eligibility determination and not updated until the required 3-year re-evaluation, may be used inappropriately to indicate levels of performance on current IEPs.

Generally, for information to be considered current, it should be generated during the current referral and/or evaluation process. Performance statements that are based on the student's performance and progress within the curriculum of the school or class are most likely to ensure that the information contained on the IEP is current.

Stability of Information Over Time.   What is current also depends on the stability of the information over time. For example, it may be helpful to indicate levels of physical development as part of performance levels for students with severe disabilities, even if little change is anticipated. Thus, a report indicating limited use of limbs and poor prognosis for future use may, if still accurate, be used as a source of information (in conjunction with observational data) even if it is several years old. Generally, the only data likely to be stable over time are data related to relatively permanent disabilities such as blindness, deafness, and permanent motor disabilities. Use of this information in conjunction with, or to support, current levels of educational performance should be considered in terms of its utility in providing useful information for program planning in designated areas. Information that is likely to change over time must be current when the IEP is developed. This usually includes such information as achievement levels, statements of specific skills attained, and observational data.

Regulated Definitions of the Term Current.   Some states and districts quantify the term current by requiring that information used to generate levels of performance be not more than 6 months olds. Although a standard definition of the term current does set some parameters for ensuring the appropriateness of information, some information ceases to be current very rapidly. For example, if a preschool student is not toilet trained during the summer when an initial evaluation is completed but is trained when school starts in the fall, it is inappropriate to develop or maintain an IEP based on toilet-training skills, even though the information on which it is based is only 2 months old.

To provide an indication of the recency of the information on which performance levels are based, it is suggested that each performance statement be accompanied by the date or month when the information is obtained. This information is especially helpful for students who frequently transfer between schools. A receiving school may decide that a statement based on a reading inventory administered 3 months previous to the student's transfer is sufficient information on which to implement an existing IEP. If the statement, however, is dated 9 months previous to the date of transfer, the school may decide to administer additional evaluation to update the current level of performance before implementing the IEP. In addition, dated performance levels can provide a reference for locating appropriate evaluation reports in the student's record if additional information is needed by those implementing the IEP.

For annual or interim reviews, levels of performance should be updated based on curriculum-based measures developed to measure attainments of the objectives included on the IEP. Based on these measures, levels of performance should be revised on the IEP at least annually. It is not usually necessary or appropriate to administer norm-referenced tests to document progress toward goals and objectives on the IEP.

Use of Concise and Clear Language

Use of concise and clear language is another important criterion to consider when developing statements of current performance. The committee should consider specifying all performance levels in observable and measurable language, similar to that used for instructional objectives. The use of observable and measurable language can increase the possibility that all committee members will have the same understanding of each performance statement. For example, if the performance level in math includes the statement, "knows addition," many different interpretations could be drawn. On the other hand, if the statement were written as, "adds two two-digit numbers with regrouping in the ten's column," the skill level of the student is concisely and clearly pinpointed. In developing this and all aspects of the IEP,

the committee should remember that the document represents the specially designed instruction that a student receives, and the levels of performance provide the basis and rationale on which the rest of the plan is based. As such, these statements should be clearly and logically written so that others, including teachers, parents, and possibly other schools, can interpret and implement the plan.

Using proper measures, it is relatively easy to identify specific skills in areas such as reading, math, self-help, and mobility. In the content areas such as social studies and science, however, committee members may find it more difficult to specify current levels of performance in terms of specific skill statements. Difficulty arises because skills identified within these areas are closely associated with other basic areas, especially reading. Thus, failing grades in social studies are often directly related to a deficit in reading. In addition, skills specific for these areas do not necessarily occur in the same structured sequence as the more basic areas of reading and math. If content areas such as science and social studies are to be included on IEPs as areas in which specially designed instruction is necessary, the student's reading level should be indicated if the committee considers that a low reading level may be the primary cause of failure in any subject area in which progress depends on the ability to read the textbook or reference material.

The curriculum checklists included in Appendix E (p. 465) can be especially helpful in specifying performance levels. As teachers use such checklists to evaluate students and chart their continuing progress, the current level of achievement can be readily pinpointed. The current achievement or performance level could then be translated from the checklist to the IEP.

CURRICULUM-BASED INDICATORS OF PERFORMANCE LEVELS

Using student performance information generated from the existing curriculum or classroom environment can effectively resolve many problems related to the development of level of performance statements. Curriculum-based evaluation measures differ from most commercially produced norm-referenced and criterion-referenced tests because they are measures of the student's performance in the curriculum of her own school. Informal reading and mathematics inventories, systematic observation, and even weekly tests and projects are curriculum-based measures. Those that provide a valid indication of the student's performance in a given area can be used to generate level of performance statements. Like criterion-referenced tests, curriculum-based measures compare a student's performance to objective criteria (the student either does or does not tell time to the hour) rather than to the performance of other students. Unlike commercially produced criterion-referenced tests, however, the skills measured are drawn directly from the student's curriculum. The advantage of determining performance levels from measures of the school curriculum are discussed in the following sections.

Relevance to the Curriculum

One of the major advantages of curriculum-based performance statements is that they are relevant to the instruction that the student will actually receive. For this factor alone they are preferred to statements generated by other means, because they are based on the same body of information that provides the basis for classroom instruction. This relevance eliminates the disparity often found between the statement of the student's current level of performance and the information that provides the basis for classroom instruction. Performance statements that are relevant to the curriculum of the classroom greatly facilitate the integration of the IEP curriculum into the student's ongoing instructional program.

Stating performance levels in terms of the established curriculum means that evaluation, documentation of skill levels, and planning and delivering instruction are all related. Performance statements come from evaluation measures that reflect the classroom curriculum and are translated into goals and objectives related to the curriculum and are implemented within the classroom curriculum.

Facilitation of Identification of Annual Goals and Objectives

Curriculum-based performance statements provide precise information related to skill levels within the broader context of the scope and sequence of the school curriculum. Because there is an established sequence in which information is presented within the school curriculum, projecting annual goals and short-term objectives from statements of current performance is greatly facilitated. In addition, the usually difficult task of developing goals and objectives in the content areas is easier because the curriculum specifies the knowledge that the student is expected to master and provides the sequence in which skills in these areas are to be presented.

Timeliness and Currency of Information

One of the greatest advantages of stating levels of performance in terms of the curriculum of the school or class is that skill levels can be continually monitored, revised, and updated using ongoing classroom methods rather than traditional standardized assessment or other commercially prepared materials. It is not necessary to continually subject students to the stress of formal and unnecessary evaluation procedures to obtain current information related to student performance. An additional advantage of curriculum-based statements related to timeliness is that the often long waiting periods to obtain updated performance information are essentially eliminated because this information is generated within the classroom as part of the ongoing educational program.

Using the curriculum as the basis for generating IEPs will be discussed further in the next two chapters.

SUMMARY   This chapter has discussed the identification of current levels of educational performance, which is the first step in developing the IEP. The importance of basing these statements on accurate and meaningful evaluation results was emphasized, and criteria and guidelines for developing appropriate statements were presented. The value of using the curriculum as the basis for determining instructional levels was discussed. Using the curriculum as the basis for generating IEPs will be further discussed in the next two chapters, Specifying Annual Goals and Short-Term Instructional Objectives and Evaluation of Goals and Objectives.

EVALUATION   1. Assume you are a teacher serving on an IEP committee. A parent points to an IEP form and asks you what the level of performance means and why it is included on the IEP. Outline your response.

2. You are responsible for conducting a 45-minute inservice training program for the faculty at the junior high school where you teach, on the topic of "Guidelines for Stating Levels of Performance on the IEP." Outline the major points you would cover in your presentation.

3. Review evaluation information available for a student in special education in your school. Based on this information, develop level of performance statements to serve each of these three functions: (1) comparison with other students, (2) skill attainment according to a specific criterion, and (3) skill attainment specific to the school's curriculum.

CHAPTER 9

Specifying Annual Goals and Short-Term Instructional Objectives

OBJECTIVES

1. Identify five criteria to be considered in the formulation of annual goals.

2. Identify and discuss three criteria for ensuring the specificity of short-term instructional objectives.

3. Discuss five methods for specifying criteria for attainment of objectives.

4. Illustrate three methods of sequencing short-term instructional objectives by the process of task analysis.

5. Identify eight curriculum areas in which IEPs might be developed for a student with a disability.

6. Discuss advantages and disadvantages of computer-generated goals and objectives for the IEP.

7. Discuss the use of curriculum guides and curriculum-based checklists as resources for developing goals and objectives for the IEP.

Based on the student's current level of educational performance, the formulation of annual goals and objectives constitutes the basic curriculum that specialized instruction should deliver to a student with a disability. Both annual goals and short-term objectives must reflect the careful planning of the IEP committee to provide a systematic guide for instructing the student.

Although the IEP clearly is intended to describe the specially designed instruction that will be provided to address a student's unique needs, some controversy exists regarding the amount of detail that should be involved in developing the IEP. From an administrative perspective, most states view the IEP as a management document that sets the general direction to be taken in working with a student rather than a document intended to address the specific objectives that are traditionally found in daily, weekly, or monthly lesson plans. Many teachers, however, report that an IEP, constructed in this general way, has little value for specific instructional planning (Dudley-Marling, 1985; Singer & Butler, 1987). Many consider that, to be educationally useful, the IEP should be more relevant to the actual instructional program and used as a guide for day-to-day programming.

The determination of how specific the IEP should be to enhance its value as a tool for specific instructional planning is a critical question. IEP committee members must determine at what point the lack of specificity eliminates the IEPs usefulness for later planning and instructional guidance. The committee must also determine how much specificity is feasible, considering the time available for IEP development. This chapter discusses the development of annual goals and short-term objectives in the context of specific program planning and focuses on the inclusion of more detailed curricular goals and objectives than may be legally required. This detail is provided to facilitate the translation of IEP goals and objectives into the components of the instruc-

tional plan. Even if the IEP is not developed to be a specific instructional plan, the IEP committee should ensure that annual goals and short-term objectives nonetheless meet the following criteria:

1. Relate directly to the current levels of educational performance
2. Relate directly to the special education instructional plan
3. Serve as the basis for developing a detailed instructional plan
4. Set the general direction for working with the student.

DEVELOPING ANNUAL GOALS

An annual goal represents the achievement anticipated for the student over a period of 1 year in the program of specially designed instruction. The formulation of annual goals is an educated guess or estimate of where a particular student will be at the end of 1 year if a prescribed sequence of instruction is followed. In making this estimate, the committee should consider the following criteria for choosing annual goals:

1. The student's past achievement
2. The student's present levels of performance
3. The student's preferences
4. The practicality of the chosen goals
5. The student's priority needs
6. The amount of time to be devoted to instruction related to the goal

Past Achievement

The student's past achievement represents a pattern of progress or lack of progress identified with previous schooling. By examining previous placements, instructional methods, achievement records, rate of previous achievement, and student behavior patterns, the IEP committee members can gain information that may be unavailable through test administration or formal diagnosis. Periods indicating stronger or weaker progress should be noted and examined. The rate of progress during such periods could be attributed to specific characteristics such as the learning environment, family problems, illness, or adjustment difficulties. In addition, if a student's school records indicate that past achievement has been slow and that the student tends to fall behind more each year, it would be unreasonable to project annual goals based on achievement rates expected of typical students. When such characteristics are identified, they should be considered in the development of the student's IEP.

Current Performance Levels

As described in Chapter 8, the student's current levels of performance indicate educational strengths and weaknesses and serve as a basis for educational programming. It is essential, therefore, that the committee accurately determine the student's levels of performance so that long-term goals, based on progress from the levels of performance, will be realistic. If current levels of performance are based on the student's progress within the specific curriculum of the student's school or class, these performance levels can provide a systematic starting point for the development of annual goals that are both relevant to the student's needs and easily translated into classroom instruction.

Student Preferences

Students with a disability have preferences based on their interests and goals, similar to students without a disability. Increasingly, however, researchers have documented that the preferences of students with a disability are often ignored in programming decisions (Houghton, Bronicki, & Guess, 1987; Shevin & Klein, 1984). When instruction is based on student preferences, student performance is enhanced (Dattilo & Rusch, 1985; Peck, 1985). Thus, an important aspect of determining appropriate annual goals is to identify the curriculum in which the student is most interested in investing time and energy. An important consideration is the student's career interest.

Practicality

The practicality of annual goals chosen for a student is also an important consideration. Because many students with a disability have fallen behind their

non-handicapped peers academically and may continue to do so throughout their school career, care must be taken to ensure that goals chosen are practical and relevant to the social and vocational needs of the student. For example, it might be considered to be a misuse of valuable time to spend an entire school year tutoring a secondary student in social studies when the student has no vocational skills and will soon leave school.

Priority Needs

After selecting annual goals that indicate the most essential needs of the student, the committee should prioritize these goals for each area included in the IEP. Although prioritization of goals is not a requirement of P.L. 94–142, this practice can assist the IEP committee to select and focus on a reasonable amount of instruction for 1 year. For instance, 10 goals may be identified for a high school student in the area of vocational training. Obviously, all 10 goals cannot be addressed immediately and concurrently. The committee responsible for the development of the IEP should sequence the goals from simple to complex and ensure that prerequisite skills are taught before more complex ones. Furthermore, the committee must decide which goals reflect the most immediate needs of the student and then record them on the IEP in the order in which they are to be taught.

Because priorities may differ depending on individual perspectives, all participants involved in IEP implementation should contribute to prioritizing annual goals. These participants should include the student's parents, the classroom teacher, the special education teacher, and/or the referring teacher if the student has not previously received special education. The student should also participate whenever appropriate, but especially at the secondary level. Because the school and the home serve different functions for the student, the parent's and the school's perceptions of the student's needs may differ. Although the school may be interested in teaching a student how to tell time, the parents may be concerned about the student's inability to tie his shoes. The active participation of parents, therefore, is necessary to ensure that skills of everyday living and home life are incorporated into the educational plan.

Time Allocated to Goals

The time to be devoted to attaining the annual goals will have a substantial influence on goal selection. More instructional time will usually lead to greater progress toward a specified goal. The committee may either define annual goals in terms of instructional time available or allot instructional time according to the priority of specific annual goals. Regardless of the method chosen, the committee must estimate how much instruction can occur within a given amount of time and must determine annual goals accordingly.

Because many goals take more than 1 year to accomplish, the IEP should not be seen as a plan to provide a student with all necessary skills in 1 year. Instead, it serves as an ongoing plan of instruction. Hence, annual goals may be viewed in a sense as the short-range goals leading to much broader ultimate educational goals that will enable students to achieve their maximum potential on leaving school. Developing the annual goals for a student, then, is a step in the process of long-range planning. Although no hard and fast rule can be made, a general guideline is that three or four annual goals should be developed for each specific need area. Because they will broadly encompass the more specific short-term instructional objectives, these annual goals will be more general and less specific. They should also, however, be detailed enough to be understood by another parent or professional and explicit enough that other possible skills will not be mistaken for the desired skill.

DOMAINS FOR SELECTION OF ANNUAL GOALS

In considering areas for IEP development, it should be remembered that the IEP is intended to focus on offsetting or reducing the problems that result from the student's disability and that adversely affect educational performance. Annual goals may be developed for addressing problems in three general areas: the cognitive domain, the affective domain, and the psychomotor domain.

Cognitive Domain

The theory of the cognitive domain, based on Bloom's taxonomy (Bloom, Engelhart, Furst, Hill, & Krathwohl, 1956), is concerned with intellectual responses of the learner and accounts for most of the curricula related to academic areas of learning. For students who are behind academically, the IEP may comprise primarily annual goals in the cognitive domain. Goals in this area may deal with the recall or recognition of facts and the development of intellectual abilities and skills. Most goals developed for IEPs in the areas of reading, math, language, and the content areas are in the cognitive domain. Examples include the following:

1. John will apply rules of capitalization and punctuation in written class assignment and in writing personal and business letters.
2. John will count money and make change up to $50.00.
3. John will compute the total cost of buying, owning, operating, and maintaining a car.
4. John will demonstrate skills necessary to plan and prepare a balanced meal.

Affective Domain

Goals that specify learning in the affective domain describe changes in interest, attitudes, and values. They also deal with the development of appreciations and adequate adjustment. Most goals dealing with adaptive behavior, social development, and emotional development are of the affective domain. Within this area, it is sometimes quite difficult to specify clear goals because of the unobservable nature of human emotions, which are the focus of the affective domain. We may tend to interpret the meaning of particular behaviors vaguely and often incorrectly. For example, we sometimes typify the behaviors of a student as being indicative of a "poor self-concept." This is an often heard phrase that may be used to collectively describe any number of behaviors that may or may not be behaviors we wish to change. Another example of a vague phrase used to describe student behavior is reflected in the statement "Tony picks on other students." From the information provided by this phrase, it is not clear what exactly Tony does that constitutes "picking on" other students. He may be either verbally or physically abusive, or both.

To establish clear goals for changing a student's social behavior, the behavior to be changed must be clearly defined before the way that the behavior will change is specified. Goals and objectives must be developed based on specific behaviors and then translated into specific acceptable behaviors. This procedure requires that the teacher and others involved in developing goals assume that certain observable behaviors relate to and reflect unobservable feelings and emotions.

For the student identified as having a poor self-concept and in need of an IEP in the area of social adjustment, a variety of goals might be developed, depending on what specific behaviors are assumed to indicate a positive self-concept. Goals might include the following:

1. Jake will participate in group activities without hitting other students.
2. Jake will seek out positive interaction with another student.

3. Jake will make positive statements about himself and other students.
4. Jake will demonstrate appropriate verbal conduct during conflicts.

By translating feelings into observable events, teaching of the objective is made manageable. Such specificity will enable the development of a systematic program of instruction rather than depending on haphazard means of controlling behaviors that are not clearly delineated.

Psychomotor Domain

The psychomotor domain represents the motor skill area of development, which includes fine and gross motor coordination, muscle control, reaction time, and other physical activities. Goals in this domain may be most apparent for children with physical disabilities but may also be applicable to students with mild motor coordination problems. A goal developed in this area may require that the student actually demonstrate the physical activity specified in the goal. The following are some examples of goals in the psychomotor area:

1. Linda will feed herself independently.
2. Linda will dress herself without assistance.
3. Linda will stand supported in an adapted chair.

P.L. 94–142 specifically requires that physical education be provided to students with disabilities and that it be specially designed when necessary. In developing goals in this domain, attention should be given to adapting methods and approaches normally used so that a variety of ways of reaching the same goal can be achieved. Some suggested adaptations include substituting walking, wheeling, or rolling for running; allowing some students four, five, or six strikes in softball or kickball; and permitting an additional bounce of the ball in wheelchair tennis. The provision of well-planned physical education to students with disabilities allows the attainment of specific physical and motor goals and objectives based on individual interest, needs, abilities, and disabilities of each student. An example of IEP goals and objectives for the area of adapted physical education is included in Figure 9–1.

Physical and occupational therapists may also develop goals primarily in the psychomotor domain to improve, develop, or restore functions impaired or lost through illness, injury, or deprivation (*Federal Register*, 1977). Examples of goals and objectives that might be included in an IEP for these areas are included in Figures 9–2 and 9–3.

Once annual goals are specified, the IEP committee will have established the student's current levels of performance, which represent the instructional starting points toward those goals, and the attainment or termination of instruction anticipated by the end of the school year. The task still remains to provide the intermediate steps, or objectives, for attaining the specified goals.

CRITERIA FOR SPECIFYING SHORT-TERM INSTRUCTIONAL OBJECTIVES

IEP objectives are measurable intermediate steps between a student's present levels of educational performance and the annual goals that are established for that student. The objectives should be based on a logical breakdown of the major components of the annual goals and should serve as milestones for indicating progress toward meeting the goals. IEP objectives, like objectives in an instructional plan, are used to describe what a student is expected to accomplish in a particular area within some specified period of time and to determine the extent to which the student is progressing toward those accomplishments. The major difference between IEP objectives and those included in a instructional plan is the amount of detail. While IEP objectives provide an indication of progress toward meeting annual goals and may, for example, be projected on a quarterly or semester basis, objectives in instructional plans deal with specific outcomes to be accomplished daily, weekly, or monthly.

To move the student from one level of performance to another, the IEP must include short-term instructional objectives that sequentially identify skills lying between the current levels of performance and the annual goals. The short-term instructional objectives should specify the instructional sequence for achieving the annual goal. Measures therefore must be taken to ensure that short-term objectives are both specific and sequential. This is often accomplished by the process of task analysis, in which general skills are analyzed and broken into their component sequential parts for instruction. The process of task analysis is discussed later in this chapter.

P.L. 94–142 requires that short-term objectives be stated in instructional terms. This means that IEP objectives require the same degree of specificity as behavioral objectives. Objectives stated behaviorally include the following elements:

1. A statement of the expected behavior

FIGURE 9–1
Sample IEP Goals and Objectives for Adapted Physical Education

INDIVIDUALIZED EDUCATION PROGRAM

Student: James Morrison   **School**: Brundage Jr. High
Age: 13   **Program Entry Date**: 9-5-90
Birth Date: 6-5-77   **Annual Review Date**: 9-4-91

ANNUAL GOAL
To improve upper limb coordination and dexterity to enable participation in group physical education activities.

LEVEL OF PERFORMANCE
James can catch a beachball with arms extended at elbow when tossed from a distance of 5 feet. He throws underhanded with little coordination or accuracy. Kicks at ball with little power or coordination.

SHORT-TERM OBJECTIVES	EVALUATION CRITERIA
Catching	
1. James will catch a large ball with arms flexed rather than extended at elbow from a distance of 5 feet.	9 of 10 trials on 5 consecutive days
2. James will catch a large ball with hands rather than arms.	9 of 10 trials on 5 consecutive days
3. James will catch an 8" ball with two hands, using an intermediate skill-catching pattern.	9 of 10 trials on 5 consecutive days
4. James will catch a tossed softball-size ball with two hands in a mature catching pattern.	Latchaw Motor Ability Test 80%
5. James will catch a bounced softball-size ball with two hands in a mature catching pattern.	Latchaw Motor Ability Test 80%
Throwing	
1. James will throw an 8" ball overhanded a distance of 5 feet with two hands.	9 of 10 trials for 5 consecutive days
2. James will throw an 8" ball overhanded a distance of 5 feet with accurate placement with two hands.	9 of 10 trials for 5 consecutive days
3. James will throw an 8" ball overhanded a distance of 5 feet with accurate placement and stepping forward with one foot, using two hands.	9 of 10 trials for 5 consecutive days
4. James will throw a softball one-handed, overhanded, a distance of 5, then 10, then 15 feet with accurate placement.	Latchaw Motor Ability Test 80%
Kicking	
1. James will kick a stationary ball a distance of 15-20 feet in a desired direction using a mature kicking pattern.	Latchaw Motor Ability Test 80%
2. James will kick a moving ball a distance of 15-20 feet in a desired direction using a mature kicking pattern.	

FIGURE 9–2
Sample IEP Goals and Objectives for Occupational Therapy

INDIVIDUALIZED EDUCATION PROGRAM

Student: Mandy Cole
Age: 4 **Birth Date**: 4-16-87
School: Estes Road Elementary

Program Entry Date: 9-10-91
Annual Review Date: 9-10-92
Three-Year Re-evaluation Date: 8-94

ANNUAL GOAL
Mandy will feed herself with a spoon independently.

LEVEL OF PERFORMANCE
Grimaces, gags, and spits out food during feeding at home. Lower frequency of these behaviors during feeding at school. Requires frequent physical guidance and cueing to feed self. Social interactions at meal times are positive unless new food is introduced. Mandy has an abnormal gag reflex and oral hypersensitivity. Removes food from spoon independently with prompting.

INSTRUCTIONAL OBJECTIVES	EVALUATION CRITERIA
1. Mandy will grasp spoon when physically guided by holding spoon in her hand.	90% of opportunities during mealtime at school/at home for 5 days
2. Mandy will grasp spoon independently with teacher assisting in appropriate positioning of grasp on spoon.	90% of opportunities during mealtime at school/at home for 5 days
3. Mandy will scoop food with spoon when physically guided and with verbal prompt of "scoop."	80% of opportunities during mealtime at school/at home for 5 days
4. Mandy will scoop food when signaled by tapping bowl with spoon.	80% of opportunities during mealtime at school/at home for 5 days
5. Mandy will carry spoon to mouth with physical guidance, bringing elbow toward shoulder and guiding spoon to mouth, if necessary.	80% of opportunities during mealtime at school/at home for 5 days
6. Mandy will carry spoon to mouth with physical touching at elbow.	80% of opportunities during mealtime at school/at home for 5 days
7. Mandy will remove food from spoon independently.	90% of opportunities during mealtime at school/at home for 5 days
8. Mandy will return spoon to bowl when teacher physically guides hand back to bowl.	80% of opportunities during mealtime at school/at home for 5 days
9. Mandy will return spoon to bowl with physical cue and verbal prompt.	80% of opportunities during mealtime at school/at home for 5 days

FIGURE 9–3
Example of Functional Objectives in the Area of Physical Therapy

INDIVIDUALIZED EDUCATION PROGRAM

Student: Eric Wilson
School: Githens Elementary
Birthdate: September 9, 1982

Parents: Mr. and Mrs. Wilson
Date of Meeting: March 3, 1990
Annual Review Date: March 1, 1991

AREA:
Physical Therapy

ANNUAL GOAL
To be independently mobile in a school environment.

CURRENT LEVEL OF PERFORMANCE
Eric is beginning to use a joystick control with his left hand to operate an electric wheelchair as his primary form of mobility in school. Currently, he can maneuver into the school building and down hallways without assistance. He has difficulty maneuvering through doorways and around desks and furniture. Eric is not yet able to move himself from the wheelchair to toilet independently and to participate in floor activities within the classroom.

SHORT-TERM OBJECTIVES	EVALUATION CRITERIA
1. Eric will navigate through doorways and over carpet to his desk, tables, and to other points within the classroom and school.	9 of 10 trials on 5 consecutive days
2. Eric will position his wheelchair at desks and tables.	9 of 10 trials on 5 consecutive days
3. Eric will move his wheelchair up to the bus ramp and lock the chair to be lifted into the bus.	10 of 10 trials in morning and afternoon on entering and leaving the bus
4. Eric will complete a standing pivot transfer from his wheelchair to toilet independently.	Completion of toileting with no adult assistance in all toileting activities
5. Eric will independently transfer from his wheelchair to the floor during floor activities in the classroom.	9 of 10 trials on 5 consecutive days

2. A statement of the condition under which the behavior will occur
3. A statement of the criteria for attainment.

The IEP formulation process is a timely opportunity for educators to become familiar with the use of behavioral objectives as an essential aspect of educational planning. This section will provide a brief overview of the process of writing an instructional objective.

The Expected Behavior

The most obvious characteristic of a behavioral objective is that the expected behavior is stated in observable and measurable terms. For example, a poorly written objective for a student in the vocational skill area of tool use may be stated ambiguously, "Will know how to use tools." Or a better written objective may be stated in terms of specific behaviors:

1. Given a hammer, nails, and a board, John will hammer 20 nails straight into the board.
2. Given a saw and three boards with lines drawn at the midpoint, John will saw the boards in half.

There are distinct advantages to the latter examples. Using specific, observable terms helps the teacher clarify exactly what will be expected of the student to demonstrate mastery of a task. This procedure also serves to clarify for the teacher how the skill will be taught. It is difficult, if not impossible, to determine appropriate teaching strategies for achieving an unspecified behavior. If objectives are not clearly specified, the teacher may inadvertently teach or evaluate content other than that intended. If instructional outcomes are specific, the teacher can systematically identify instructional procedures and plan lessons designed to meet a specific desired outcome.

Specifying expected behaviors is not difficult. The teacher must simply consider what the student will be expected to *do* to demonstrate that the objectives have been achieved. To do this, terminology must be specific, observable, and open to few interpretations. If the terminology of the objective is vague, there is little likelihood that those implementing the IEP will be able to measure the attainment of objectives. The terms listed following are examples of terminology that is open to many interpretations and thus is inappropriate for use in the specification of short-term instructional objectives:

to understand	to know
to realize	to learn
to gain knowledge	to master
to like	to be concerned
to appreciate	

Terminology open to fewer interpretations and, thus, preferable in developing short-term instructional objectives includes the following:

to indicate	to compare
to contrast	to repeat
to design	to classify
to count	to solve
to group	to explain

In choosing terminology, the teacher must remember, as discussed later in this chapter, that different skills incorporate various levels of difficulty.

Specifying the Condition under Which Behavior Should Occur

Behavioral objectives should also state the conditions under which specified behaviors should occur. "Conditions" typically include the materials, instructions, time limits, and prompts that make up the task required of the student. In many instances, the conditions may be assumed. For example, for any student required to write a paragraph, the conditions would include giving the student paper and pencil. For the sake of brevity and to reduce redundancy in the IEP, conditions that can be assumed without being stated do not have to be included in the objective. Committee members, however, must exercise caution in establishing whether conditions can or cannot be assumed. When conditions differ from those normally expected for any student, the committee is advised to include the conditions in the statement of the objective.

Quite often, special conditions for certain behaviors are warranted. For example, a student might be expected to add numbers with the use of a number line or might be expected to achieve a specified grade on a test when time lines are extended or specific prompts provided. Other examples may include physically disabled students who will use typewriters to complete assignments or blind students who will use tape recorders to study. The objective for a student with a physical disability that affects mobility may be that he travel between classes unassisted for 10 consecutive days. If the student requires a walker, however, the objective should be stated to include this equipment. For example, "Christa will travel from class to class alone with the use of a walker for 10 consecutive days."

If special conditions are required to attain the objective, they must be stated as part of the IEP, and preferably as part of the objective, so that others involved in the student's educational program will be aware of the conditions under which the student can attain the desired performance. If special conditions are not included as part of the objective itself, these conditions should be specified in another appropriate part of the IEP. For example, in some IEP formats, the conditions under which the objective will be demonstrated are included in a separate section designated for specifying the criteria for achievement of objectives.

Criteria for Attainment

Finally, when developing short-term instructional objectives, the teacher must establish the acceptable criteria for determining mastery of the short-term objectives. Development of specific criteria will tell the teacher and others involved in the instructional process when the objective has been achieved. That is, how well the student has to perform the skill before all concerned agree that he has "learned" that skill. If criteria for the attainment of objectives are not established, mastery may be mistakenly assumed or may even remain unmeasured.

It cannot be assumed that because a skill is taught it is necessarily mastered by the student. For example, it is quite possible for a student to get three out of four math problems correct without mastering the process involved. It is also possible to read a word correctly without mastery. By assuming that a student has mastered a concept when, in fact, he has not, the teacher may find that subsequent achievement becomes increasingly difficult for the student. To ensure that mastery of a task has occurred, standards must be established by which the student's knowledge of the skill can be evaluated. Failure to delineate specific attainment criteria for objectives on the IEP, and subsequent failure to adequately evaluate progress toward the stated goals and objectives, may become a troublesome issue during the annual review process, when objective criteria must be employed to determine whether short-term objectives are being achieved.

Criteria for attainment of objectives may be delineated in several ways. The committee must select the method appropriate and best suited to the type of objective specified. Examples of options include establishing requirements for time limits, percentage or ratio of items correct, minimum number of appropriate responses, specific statements of criteria, and combination of criteria.

Time Limits. Establishing time limits for the completion of tasks is one method of delineating criteria for the achievement of objectives. For example, a time limit might require that a student be able to run 100 yards within 14 seconds in a physical education class, or a time limit might be established that requires a student to complete all assigned work by the end of the school day. Time limits are often appropriate criteria for the area of physical education

and in other objectives in which the skill or behavior is measured on a duration basis (e.g., in-seat behavior; socializing)

Percentage or Ratio of Items Correct. The objective might require that the student answer a percentage of given items correctly. For example, correctly answering 80 of 100 or 80% of basic addition facts might be established as the attainment criterion for an objective in the area of mathematics. Or the student might be required to reproduce a specific speech sound in 10 of 10 words containing that sound. Percentage requirements are perhaps the most used indicators of attainment criteria. Because their use has become almost routine, these indicators are often used inappropriately. Committee members must ensure that percentage criteria, when used, are appropriate to the objective being measured.

Minimum Number of Appropriate Responses. In some instances the possible number of correct responses is not established or is not relevant to the objective. In such cases percentages or ratios of correct responses are not useful or appropriate indicators of achievement. When there is no established number of possible opportunities for correct responses, the objective might instead require only that the appropriate behavior be demonstrated a specific number of times during a specified time period. For example, the objective for a student might require that the student initiate positive conversation with a peer a minimum of three times a day. With such a criterion the number of possible opportunities is not so important as the number of occurrences of the appropriate behavior sometime during the day.

Specific Statements of Criteria. In some instances, the emphasis of the objective may be on the student's ability to perform a behavior in a certain way rather than with a specific amount of accuracy. For example, to require that a student write his name with 100% accuracy is not as appropriate as establishing the specific criteria on which accuracy will be judged. More appropriate criteria might require that the student write his name with all letters in proper sequence and of proportionate size. This method of stating criteria might also be applied to other skill areas for objectives that focus on the quality with which a skill is performed. Examples might include skills such as kicking a ball or bowling.

Combination of Criteria. Types of criteria may be, and often are, combined in an objective. For example, an objective might require that the student be able to compute the sums of 100 addition facts with 100% accuracy within 2 minutes. Repeated trials might also be included as part of the criteria for objectives to ensure that skill attainment is measured on more than one occasion. Thus, an objective that requires a student to accurately reproduce the *sh* sound in five consecutive words might also require that the criteria be met on five trials spread over a 2-week period.

In stating the criteria for mastery, the committee must consider the appropriateness of the criteria in relation to the student and to the stated objective. Many objectives are not designed to be completed within specified time periods, and many are not designed to require 100% performance. For example, a student who has an intellectual deficit may not be able to complete a curriculum goal that requires the completion of 100 addition problems in 2 minutes with 90% accuracy. The committee must determine whether such criteria are appropriate or essential to the student's instructional program. If the goal of completing addition facts is considered to be appropriate, the committee might decide to modify the criterion for this particular student to 80% accuracy with a 10-minute time limit. Criteria are also determined by the nature of the skill. For example, attainment criteria for a spelling objective may be lower than criteria for an objective for street crossing. The committee must seek the best opinion of the teacher to determine the level of mastery necessary for each skill to be useful to the student's future achievement.

SEQUENCING OBJECTIVES BY TASK ANALYSIS

Task analysis, the process by which tasks are broken down into sequential components, involves isolating, describing, and sequencing all the necessary subtasks, which, when mastered, will enable the student to perform the terminal behavior or annual goal. The concept of task hierarchies has a very useful application in making the development of short-term instructional objectives systematic, sequential, and inclusive.

Most skills can be broken down into component parts, which develop in a sequential fashion. For instance, in mathematics, one typically does not begin instruction in division until the component skills of subtraction and multiplication are mastered. In the area of reading, it is difficult to comprehend written words that are not first a part of a student's sight vocabulary. In teaching dressing skills, putting on shoes occurs before learning to tie them. Even content-area skills are often task analyzed according to the sequence in which they are introduced in the curriculum. For example, one does not usually learn the capitals of states in social studies until after the names of the states are learned.

Although all skill development follows some broad sequence, many skill areas are not bound to one strict developmental order. For example, given the assignment of developing a task analysis to teach a student how to balance a checkbook, 10 teachers would probably develop 10 different sequences, each appropriate and yet indicative of individual teaching preference. As long as each objective or subskill follows the preceding skill in a logical, sequential order, the task analysis may be considered to represent an appropriate teaching sequence.

Many teachers have difficulty breaking skills down into very small components. For students with significant learning problems, it is often necessary to categorize skills in minute detail to ensure the attainment of established goals. Although tedious at the outset, this process becomes less difficult with continued use and encourages the educator to look closely at the smaller skill components included within a particular subject area. Figure 9–4 illustrates task hierarchies in the area of self-feeding skills that are appropriate for many young and severely disabled students. In addition, sample IEPs found in Appendix D (p. 411) illustrate how the process of task analysis may be applied to the development of a systematic instructional strategy.

Task analysis can provide a checkpoint to ensure that established goals are both manageable and realistic. Established annual goals may seem attainable before all the prerequisite component subskills are identified. Once all subskills are determined, however, the committee may realize that too much or too little progress has been projected for the student. Because revision of the IEP goals is much easier during the planning stage than after the plan has been implemented, the IEP must be made as relevant and practical as possible before attempting to implement it in the classroom. A practical, systematic, and sequential IEP stands a far greater chance of being successfully implemented by those involved in the student's instructional program than one that has been haphazardly constructed.

Annual goals and short-term instructional objectives can be isolated, described, and sequenced by the following steps:

1. Working in reverse from the established annual goal or terminal behavior
2. Working forward from the present level of performance to the annual goal
3. Establishing the annual goal by working forward from the present level of performance

FIGURE 9–4
Task Hierarchy for Feeding

Student Name _____
Date _____
Evaluator _____

KEY: M = Mastered at time of observation
       PM = Partially mastered
       NI = Skill was not introduced

Skill	Level of Performance		
	M	PM	NI
1. Jaw remains open with no noticeable movement in response to utensil.			
2. Jaw opens in response to utensil and closes with manual assistance.			
3. Opens and closes jaw smoothly over utensil.			
4. Initiates jaw thrust or bite reflex on contact with utensil.			
5. Lips close over spoon.			
6. Lips close over spoon and purse together to actively remove food from spoon.			
7. Tongue moves upward and forward in an attempt to swallow.			
8. Tongue elevates to the roof of the mouth and moves food back to swallow.			
9. Lips approximate closure during swallow.			
10. Lips close tightly to prevent food loss during swallow.			
11. Swallows food without excess loss.			
12. Moves jaw vertically to chew.			
13. Bites off solid piece of food and chews functionally.			
14. Tongue able to control position of bolus.			
15. Places lips over rim of glass.			
16. Sips liquids from glass.			
17. Sips liquids from glass and swallows repeatedly.			
18. Sips liquids from glass and swallows repeatedly with no excess loss.			
19. Swallows food with no hypersensitivity (coughing, gagging).			

Reverse Analysis

Short-term objectives may be identified by working in reverse from the annual goal and answering the question, What skill must be taught immediately before the skill indicated by the annual goal? For example, an annual goal, as illustrated in Figure 9–5, might require that a student be able to subtract a two-digit number from a two-digit number with regrouping in five consecutive trials. The skill that immediately precedes the annual goal might be that the student be able to subtract a one-digit number from a two-digit number with regrouping. Preceding that skill, the student should be able to subtract a two-digit number from a two-digit number without regrouping, and before that, be able to subtract a one-digit number from a two-digit number without regrouping. Skills should be listed in descending order until the identification of subskills reaches the current level of performance of the student, in this case, addition and subtraction of two one-digit numbers.

Forward Analysis

Another method of systematic identification of short-term objectives is to begin with the student's current levels of performance and proceed forward, identifying each subsequent skill until reaching the annual goal. The last short-term objective, or subskill, should be the same as the annual goal. For example, the performance level of a student in telling time may be that he recognizes the numbers 1 to 12. The annual goal may be that the student will tell time by 5-minute intervals. The skill immediately following the level of performance may be to tell the function of the large and small hands on a clock. The next subsequent skills may be pointing to o'clock, "past" and "before" sides of the clock, half-past an hour, and so forth, until the annual goal is reached. Again, the sequence of skills may differ according to the curriculum of the school or class, or according to who is developing the plan. Figure 9–6 illustrates the process of forward analysis by using the mathematics sequence identified in Figure 9–5 as a basis for comparison.

Determining Annual Goals By Forward Analysis

Committee members may begin the process of goals formation with the identification of short-term instructional objectives rather than annual goals. Using this process, skills are identified by moving forward from the student's present level of performance until the committee or subcommittee believes that enough skills have been identified to constitute an appropriate year's plan in a particular skill area. The last skill identified would then become the annual goal. One

distinct advantage of this procedure is that formulation of annual goals is based on systematic identification and development of skill areas and is established only after the committee has determined how far along the skill sequence the student can be expected to advance during one school year. This process is illustrated by Figure 9–7.

Regardless of the procedure chosen, in the resulting instructional plan, each objective should be presented logically and systematically, and each should be necessary for the attainment of the annual goal.

Sequencing According to Skill Complexity

A critical aspect of task analysis is determining which skills are more and less complex. This is necessary to ensure that, when task analyzed, skills are appropriately sequenced in their order of difficulty. Objectives too, may range from simple to complex. Consider, for example, the following statements:

1. The student will state the three nutrients needed for plant growth.
2. Using classroom plants as an example, the student will describe in writing the relationship between plant life and the nutrients of water, sun, and soil.

The first statement may require the student to name, write, or point to the nutrients needed for plant life. In the second objective, however, the student, required to describe a relationship between plants and nutrients, must understand that relationship, thus requiring a higher level skill than simply recalling information.

Bloom et al. (1956) have formulated six levels of classification: knowledge, comprehension, application, analysis, synthesis, and evaluation. The terminology used to reflect each of these levels is described in Figure 9–8, p. 232.

Knowledge. Objectives at the knowledge level may require that the student remember specified instruction such as word meanings, dates, events, and places. The vast majority of information presented in schools requires learning at this level. According to Bloom (1984), over 95% of test questions posed on both teacher-made and standardized tests are largely tests of remembered information. Although information at this level is essential, educators must remember that most students, given the opportunity, can learn higher mental processes if these processes are included in the teaching-learning process.

Comprehension. The level of comprehension indicates that students understand what is communi-

FIGURE 9–5
Task Sequencing—Reverse Analysis

Annual Goal: Subtract two-digit number from two-digit number with borrowing.

Step

1. Subtract one-digit number from two-digit number with borrowing.

2. Subtract two-digit number from two-digit number without borrowing.

3. Subtract one-digit number from two-digit number remembering to bring down the one in the ten's column: 11 – 1 to 19 – 9.

4. Subtract combinations of tens: 10 – 10 to 90 – 96.

5. Subtract one-digit number from two-digit number without borrowing; combinations of 11 through 18 (11 – 2 to 18 – 9).

6. Add two-digit numbers; carrying from one's and ten's column.

7. Add two-digit numbers; carrying from ten's column.

8. Add three two-digit numbes with carrying from one's column.

9. Add a two-digit number to a two-digit number with carrying from one's column.

10. Add a one-digit number to a two-digit number; sums 10 through 1 without carrying.

11. Add three two-digit numbers without carrying.

12. Add a two-digit number to a two-digit number without carrying.

13. Add a one-digit number to a two-digit number without carrying.

14. Add tens from 10 + 10 to 90 + 10.

15. Add three one-digit numbers to sums 10 through 19.

16. Add two one-digit numbers to sums 11 through 19.

17. Add three one-digit numbers to sums 0 + 0 + 0 to 9 + 0 + 0.

Current Level
of Performance: Add and Subtract two one-digit numbers.

From *Data-Based Program Modification: A Manual* **(p. 81) by Stanley L. Deno and Phyllis K. Mirkin, 1977, Minneapolis, MN: Leadership Training Institute/Special Education. Courtesy of the Council for Exceptional Children.**

cated to them. Objectives at this level may require such skills as translating given information into one's own words orally or in writing, or defining listed terms. Comprehension is most often associated with objectives that require reading but may be expanded to include any cognitive skill.

Application.   Application of a skill requires the student to comprehend material presented and use that information for the solution of novel problems. Most of what is learned is intended for application to

problem situations in daily life, thus some skill at this level is essential. Objectives at the application level should require the student to apply concepts and principles to new situations. In the area of math, a student might be required to solve a word problem using basic computation skills. Generalization of skills also occurs at the application level.

Analysis.   The analysis level deals with the student's ability to break information down into its constituent parts and evaluate the relevance of each. The student

FIGURE 9–6
Task Sequencing—Forward Analysis

Annual Goal: Subtract two-digit number from two-digit number with borrowing.

Step

17. Subtract one-digit number from two-digit number with borrowing.

16. Subtract two-digit number from two-digit number without borrowing.

15. Subtract one-digit number from two-digit number remembering to bring down the one in the ten's column: 11 – 1 to 19 – 9.

14. Subtract combinations of tens: 10 – 1 to 90 – 96.

13. Subtract one-digit number from two-digit number without borrowing; combinations of 11 through 18 (11 – 2 to 18 – 9).

12. Add two-digit numbers; carrying from one's and ten's column.

11. Add two-digit numbers; carrying from ten's column.

10. Add three two-digit numbers with carrying from one's column.

9. Add a two-digit number to a two-digit number with carrying from one's column.

8. Add a one-digit number to a two-digit number; sums 10 through 1 without carrying.

7. Add three two-digit numbers without carrying.

6. Add a two-digit number to a two-digit number without carrying.

5. Add a one-digit number to a two-digit number without carrying.

4. Add tens from 10 + 10 to 90 + 10.

3. Add three one-digit numbers to sums 10 through 19.

2. Add two one-digit numbers to sums 11 through 19.

1. Add three one-digit numbers to sums 0 + 0 + 0 to 9 + 0 + 0.

Current Level
of Performance: Add and Subtract two one-digit numbers.

From *Data-Based Program Modification: A Manual* (p. 81) by Stanley L. Deno and Phyllis K. Mirkin, 1977, Minneapolis, MN: Leadership Training Institute/Special Education. Courtesy of the Council for Exceptional Children.

should be able to distinguish between facts and inferences. The student may be asked to diagram, outline, or point out distinguishing features of such information. An example may be found in the area of reading comprehension when a student is asked to identify the main idea of a paragraph, or in history when the student is required to outline the most influential battles of the Revolutionary War. The student may also demonstrate analytic ability by selecting the "best" answers to objective questions.

Synthesis. Synthesizing information requires that the student be able to combine segments of information with other bits of information to form a conclusion that was not necessarily present before. Providing for creative behavior by the student, synthesis combines the knowledge, comprehension, application, and analysis levels and requires the student to come to conclusions not prespecified by the teacher, while at the same time presenting a logical rationale for such conclusions. Evaluation proce-

FIGURE 9–7
Task Sequencing—Forward Analysis to Determine Annual Goals

Subtract one-digit number from two-digit number with borrowing.

Subtract two-digit number from two-digit number without borrowing.

Subtract one-digit number from two-digit number remembering to bring down the one in the ten's column: 11 – 19 – 9.

Subtract combinations of tens: .10 – 10 to 90 – 96.

Subtract one-digit number from two-digit number without borrowing; combinations of 11 through 18 (11 – 2 to 18 – 9).

Add two-digit numbers; carrying from one's and ten's column.

Add two-digit numbers; carrying from one's and ten's column.

Add two-digit numbers; carrying from ten's column.

Annual
Goal: 10.   Add three two-digit numbers with carrying from one's column.

9.   Add a two-digit number to a two-digit number with carrying from one's column.

8.   Add a one-digit number to a two-digit number; sums 10 through 1 without carrying.

7.   Add three two-digit numbers without carrying.

6.   Add a two-digit number to a two-digit number without carrying.

5.   Add a one-digit number to a two-digit number without carrying.

4.   Add tens from 10 + 10 to 90 + 10.

3.   Add three one-digit numbers to sums 10 through 19.

2.   Add two one-digit numbers to sums 11 through 19.

1.   Add three one-digit numbers to sums 0 + 0 + 0 to 9 + 0 + 0.

Current Level
of Performance: Add and Subtract two one-digit numbers.

From *Data-Based Program Modification: A Manual* (p. 81) by Stanley L. Deno and Phyllis K. Mirkin, 1977, Minneapolis, MN: Leadership Training Institute/Special Education. Courtesy of the Council for Exceptional Children.

dures at this level may include asking the student to give a well-organized speech, to write a position paper, or possibly to write a musical composition.

Evaluation of Information. When students are required to make judgments about information, the ability to evaluate information is being appraised. For example, a teacher may ask students to evaluate their own compositions, using such criteria as neatness, grammar, and content. In doing so, students must compare their work with specific criteria, discriminate between positive and negative features of the work, describe those features, draw a conclusion concerning the quality of the work, and justify that conclusion. The teacher may then re-evaluate the students' work by using the same criteria and procedure to determine if, in fact, the students are skilled in appraising their own work. Students may also be asked to evaluate different alternatives to a situation in terms of the consequences that each might pro-

FIGURE 9–8
Model for Differentiating Indicators of Behavior on Basis of Time and Mental Process

BEHAVIORAL OBJECTIVES

Mental Process / Time Interval

MORE SIMPLE ⟶ ⟶ ⟶ ⟶ MORE COMPLEX

COGNITIVE PROCESSES

Time Interval	1.0 KNOWLEDGE	2.0 COMPREHENSION	3.0 APPLICATION	4.0 ANALYSIS	5.0 SYNTHESIS	6.0 EVALUATION
3rd Level Immediate 1–4 day periods	Count Define Draw Identify Indicate List Name Point Quote Read Recall Recite Recognize Record Repeat State Tabulate Trace Write	Associate Compare Compute Contrast Describe Differentiate Discuss Distinguish Estimate Extrapolate Interpret Interpolate Predict Translate				
2nd Level Intermediate 5 days to 2, 3, 4, 5, 6 weeks		Classify Compare Contrast	Apply Calculate Classify Complete Demonstrate Employ Examine Illustrate Practice Relate Solve Use Utilize	Order Group Relate Transform		
1st Level Long-Range 6 weeks to 1 semester or 1 year or more				Analyze Detect Explain Infer Separate Summarize Construct	Arrange Combine Construct Create Design Develop Formulate Generalize Integrate Organize Plan Prepare Prescribe Produce Propose Specify	Appraise Assess Critique Determine Evaluate Grade Judge Measure Rank Rate Recommend Select Test

This model incorporates the principles of complexity in the cognitive process with time intervals typically associated with school operations.

From S. Leles and R. Bernabei, *Writing and Using Behavioral Objectives* (Northport, AL: Lern Associates, 1969), p. 72.

duce. It must be remembered that the teacher is evaluating the student's ability to evaluate information and not the amount of information a student can recall (knowledge). When requiring a student to evaluate information, the teacher may either allow the student to develop the necessary criteria for evaluation or may specify what criteria are to be used.

In summary, some skills such as counting, naming, and pointing are quite simple, while other skills such as judging, explaining, and analyzing are much more difficult. When writing and sequencing instructional objectives for a student with a disability, one must consider the difficulty or level of the task relative to the student's skill level.

CURRICULAR AREAS FOR IEP DEVELOPMENT

Other than the basic requirements established by law and regulation, there is no one required way in which to write an IEP. Thus, the instructional focus of the goals and objectives developed are to be guided by the student's established needs, as defined by the IEP committee, rather than by preconceived notions of how the IEP should be written. For example, contrary to the opinion of many, programs labeled as "tutorial" are not illegal. Although many IEPs tend to reflect specialized instruction in the acquisition of basic reading and mathematics skills, others may appropriately provide for reteaching and tutoring of classroom material for the purpose of maintaining success in the regular education program. Others may appropriately focus on the development of social skills necessary to function within the educational environment. Still others may focus on functional living skills. Particularly at the secondary level, the committee must consider and make choices regarding the focus of instruction. It may be decided that development of vocational skills, rather than instruction in basic reading or achieving an average grade in biology should receive primary emphasis for a student who will soon be leaving school. Conversely, a student may desire and realistically expect to graduate from high school with a diploma. In such a case, a tutorial program established to meet this goal may be the priority established for a particular student. Each of these IEPs may be written from a different curricular perspective. Nonetheless, all may be appropriate. This section will briefly discuss various curricular areas in which IEPs may be developed. Sample IEPs are included in Appendix D (p. 411).

Vocational Education

Some studies indicate that goals and objectives specifically addressing vocational education are often omitted from IEPs and that when they are included, they often lack present level of performance statements or indicators that vocational assessment has occurred (Cobb & Phelps, 1983; Office of Civil Rights, 1980). Because preparation for future employment is often one of the IEP's primary ultimate purposes, IEP committees should carefully and fully address this area. The extent to which vocational goals and objectives are specified on the IEP may differ from student to student. Vocational goals and objectives for many students may focus on adaptation of existing vocational education courses. When a student can participate in the regular vocational education program, only that aspect of the program that must be modified need be included in the IEP. For example, the student may require repeated demonstration of specific skills within the regular vocational curriculum or may require specially adapted equipment such as an adapted keyboard for computer programming courses. It is not necessary to rewrite all of the curriculum goals and objectives of the regular curriculum onto the IEP.

When the student's needs require separate provision of vocational education, the IEP should reflect the specific goals and objectives that will make up the student's curriculum. For example, a student with a moderate-to-severe intellectual disability may be enrolled in a program to develop skills for supported employment. These vocationally related skills may not be part of the regular vocational education program, and thus the goals and objectives on the IEP would constitute the curriculum to be followed with the student. An example of this type of IEP is included in Appendix D (p. 448). Finally, vocational goals and objectives might include job-related skills such as punctuality, completion of job applications, or other specific work behaviors. An example of work behaviors often included in vocational education programs is included in Figure 9–9.

Motor Development

Motor development is an obvious component of the IEP for students with physical disabilities. It is typically included as a program component for students with disabilities whose participation in the physical educational program is adversely affected. Physical and occupational therapy programs often consist of motor goals and objectives, as does adaptive physical education. Goals and objectives developed in this area may include such areas as fine and gross motor

FIGURE 9–9
Checklist of Work Behaviors for Vocational Education

Skills	Mastered	Developing	Not Introduced
Develops Functional Career Awareness			
1. Adheres to school and class rules			
2. Recognizes self as a co-worker in the classroom			
3. Match various jobs with developing interests and skills			
4. Works independently			
5. Completes work on time			
6. Works steadily at task for an established period of time			
7. Takes pride in class work			
8. Applies functional academic skills such as telling time, counting money, making change			
9. Maintains personal hygeine for employment			
Job-Seeking Skills			
1. Reads and selects a possible job from help-wanted ads			
2. Writes a job-application letter			
3. Fills out a simple job application			
4. Identifies transportation options for getting to work			
5. Uses public transportation to get to job site			
6. Demonstrates appropriate interview techniques			
7. Maintains appropriate appearance and dress			
On-the-Job Skills			
1. Works without excessive supervision			
2. Arrives to work on time			
3. Resumes work after break			
4. Attends work regularly			
5. Can maintain a time card			
6. Seeks assistance from supervisor when necessary			
7. Works steadily at a task for established period			
8. Works at task to completion			
9. Works without interfering with co-workers			
10. Exhibits courteous behavior toward co-workers			
11. Is courteous in verbal interactions with supervision			
12. Follows verbal/written directions			
13. Observes rules			
14. Maintains own work area			
15. Works accurately at job assignment			
16. Works at job assignment with adequate speed			
17. Accepts constructive criticism			

development, body control such as balance and posture, or may consist of adaptation of specific motor activities to accommodate the student with a disability in a program of physical education. Figure 9–10 provides an example of a skills hierarchy in the motor area.

Functional Living Skills

For some students, especially those with significant intellectual and physical disabilities, the emphasis of the IEP will be on the development of functional life skills necessary for independent living. Goals and objectives in this area may include skills in several areas including personal care, safety, housekeeping, dressing, telling time, counting money, and social interactions, to name only a few. The primary purpose of goals in this area is to develop the student's ability to perform basic functional activities independently. Depending on the student's age, various functional areas may be contained in the IEP. For example, emphasis for one student may be to learn to bathe, dress, and feed oneself. For another student, emphasis might be placed on telling time, using public transportation, and housekeeping. Current research indicates that these skills are best taught in natural settings (Brown et al., 1986). Thus, the IEP committee should consider developing goals and objectives that can be demonstrated in the community. Figure 9–11 provides an example of a skills sequence in this area.

Communication

Goals and objectives developed for the area of communication may include those directed at remediating or improving specific disorders of articulation and/or language or may focus on the development of appropriate and functional general communication skills within the classroom. The area of speech and language therapy has, in recent years, moved from a clinical orientation to one that focuses on the classroom as the normal language-learning environment (Goetz, Schuler, & Sailor, 1979; McCormick, 1985). Thus, goals and objectives developed for language and communication often focus on demonstration of skills within the classroom environment rather than only in the clinical setting. Figure 9–12, p. 238, provides a skills sequence in the area of communication.

Social Skills

Although in most states, behavior problems, in themselves, are not sufficient to determine that a student has a disability and requires special education, some students with disabilities may have difficulty with social and associated behaviors that adversely influence the ability to function adequately in a social environment. When this is the case, the IEP should include goals and objectives addressing the area of social skills. Goals and objectives in this area may focus on remediating inappropriate classroom behaviors or developing appropriate social skills for everyday living. Counseling and therapeutic goals and objectives would also be included in this area. Figure 9–13, p. 239, illustrates a list of social behaviors often identified on IEPs.

Learning Strategy-Training Skills

Many students with disabilities lack organizational strategies and study skills that can be applied across academic learning situations. For example, a student who is tutored in science may do well. The same student, however, may fail social studies because of the inability to apply the same learning strategies in that area. Methods used to train students in the acquisition and application of learning strategies that are applicable across areas of the curriculum are generally referred to as cognitive training strategies. IEPs may include procedures such as memorization and other self-instructional strategies and study skills. These strategies may also be applied to the area of behavior self-management. Figure 9–14, p. 240, provides examples of strategy-training skills that might be included in IEPs for specific students.

Leisure Skills

For students with moderate-to-severe disabilities, it is often necessary to develop functional and age-appropriate leisure skills. This skill area, however, is often neglected, both in programming and in the IEP. Leisure skills might include training in group and individual sports such as swimming and bowling or may include actually teaching a student how to engage in basic leisure activities such as watching television, listening to music, or interacting with a group. Figure 9–15, p. 241, illustrates a skills list that might be developed for swimming.

Academic Skills

Most IEPs consist of goals and objectives in traditional academic areas, especially reading, mathematics, and language. There are numerous skills sequences, checklists, and task analyses available for each of these areas. When at all possible, however, goals and objectives should be drawn from the curriculum in which the student is actually enrolled rather than from skills sequences derived from other sources.

FIGURE 9–10
Task Hierarchy in Motor Development

Student Name_____

Date_____

Person Completing Checklist _____

KEY: M   =   Mastered at time of observation
　　　 PM =   Partially mastered
　　　 NP =   Skill was not performed

Skills	Levels of Performance			Goals
	M	PM	NP	
1. Sits supported				
2. Sits without support on floor				
3. Pushes up on hands and knees				
4. Changes from sitting to prone				
5. Changes from prone to sitting				
6. Crawls on belly, using arms				
7. Pulls self to standing				
8. Stands holding onto rail				
9. Makes stepping movements				
10. Lowers self from rail				
11. Pivots in sitting				
12. Crawls on hands and knees				
13. Walks with one or both hands held				
14. Stands alone				
15. Stands alone and takes steps				
16. Walks alone				
17. Stoops to pick up objects				
18. Crawls up steps				
19. Stands on one foot				
20. Walks up stairs with help				
21. Runs				
22. Pushes and pulls large objects				
23. Jumps in place				
24. Walks up and down stairs				
25. Jumps from chair				
26. Walks on tiptoe				
27. Hops on one foot				

FIGURE 9–11
Checklist for Functional Living Skills

Personal Health Care	Date Introduced	Date Mastered
Bathing		
1. Distinguishes between hot and cold water		
2. Prepares water for bathing at suitable temperature		
3. Washes, rinses, and dries body after bathing		
4. Washes when necessary without reminders		
5. Cleans bath after use		
Hair Care		
1. Brushes and combs hair, including parting		
2. Brushes and combs hair at regular intervals as necessary		
3. Washes hair following instructions		
4. Washes hair adequately without supervision		
5. Dries hair		
6. Uses hair dryer		
7. Washes and dries hair without reminders		
Dressing		
1. Dresses independently including shoelaces, buckles, tie, buttons, zippers, and hooks.		
2. Puts on clothes right-side out.		
3. Dresses appropriately for the occasion		
4. Dresses appropriately for the weather		
5. Selects own clothes from closet, choosing clothes that coordinate		
6. Changes underwear daily		
7. Chooses appropriate clothes, dresses independently, changes clothes as necessary		
Clothes Care		
1. Hangs clothes in closet		
2. Folds clothes to put in drawers		
3. Does simple sewing repair (hems, seams, buttons)		
4. Launders and dry cleans clothes regularly		
5. Assumes responsibility for maintenance of own wardrobe		
Meal Preparation		
1. Assembles items and makes a bowl of cereal		
2. Makes sandwiches with a simple filling		
3. Prepares uncooked snacks without supervision		
4. Prepares food from a can involving heating up only		
5. Prepares food by frying		
6. Prepares food by boiling		
7. Uses oven to heat up food		
8. Follows a recipe card or instructions to make a meal		
9. Follows instructions on a packet to prepare food		
10. Prepares a simple meal without supervision or instruction		

FIGURE 9–12
Sample Skills Sequence in Area of Functional Communication

Student Name _____
Date _____
Evaluator _____

KEY: M = Mastered at time of observation
      PM = Partially mastered
      NI = Skill was not introduced

Skills	Levels of Performance		
	M	PM	NI
Understanding of Language			
1. Identifies nonlanguage sounds (fire alarm, phone, horns)			
2. Follows two part instructions			
3. Delivers simple messages verbally			
4. Locates a specific person and delivers message			
5. Delivers a complex message			
6. Comprehends a sequence of events			
Using Language			
1. Uses mainly gestures to make wants known			
2. Uses single words or short sentences that are understood by familiar individuals but not strangers			
3. Uses appropriate language but is not clearly understood by strangers			
4. Secures peer and adult attention appropriately			
5. Answers questions promptly and appropriately			
6. Asks relevant questions and listens to reply			
7. Describes people, objects, and places in detail			
8. Describes emotions and comments on own actions			
9. Holds conversation with adults and peers			
10. Is clearly understood, uses appropriate language, and requests, gives, receives, and remembers information			
Language in the Community			
1. Can give on request:			
a. first name			
b. full name			
c. name and address			
d. telephone number			
e. age and date of birth			
2. Can make an appointment			
3. Can make enquiries from community service individuals (policemen, shopkeepers)			
4. Restates rules or directions when asked			
5. Explains, justifies own behavior			

FIGURE 9–13
Checklist of Behavior

INDEPENDENT WORK
1. Begins work within an appropriate time without excessive teacher direction
2. Stays on task without excessive teacher supervision
3. Seeks assistance appropriately
4. Completes tasks within allotted period of time
5. Completes task to criterion
6. Transitions from task to task as specified by class routine

CLASSROOM INTERACTIONS
1. Responds in a friendly manner when approached by adults
2. Responds in a friendly manner when approached by peers
3. Initiates positive social contact with others in the class
4. Participates in group activities in a friendly manner
5. Volunteers comments while in a group
6. Demonstrates truthful behaviors
7. Demonstrates ability to wait for turn
8. Responds to teacher correction with appropriate response

SCHOOL ROUTINES
1. Attends school regularly
2. Goes to and from school appropriately
3. Reports to class on time
4. Brings required materials to school
5. Changes classes independently
6. Uses equipment and materials appropriately
7. Uses appropriate cue for teacher recognition
8. Follows directions

RECOGNITION OF AUTHORITY
1. Acknowledges and accepts authority at home, school, and community
2. Participates with classroom authority in development of goals and rewards
3. Complies with requests of authority figure

PERSONAL BEHAVIORS
1. Practices acceptable personal hygiene
2. Expresses feelings when asked
3. Initiates expression of feelings
4. Identifies appropriate methods of dealing with feelings
5. Demonstrates appropriate outlets for feelings
6. Identifies appropriate alternatives to specific inappropriate behaviors
7. Identifies consequences for inappropriate behaviors
8. Responds appropriately to consequences of inappropriate behaviors
9. Identifies frequent sources of frustration
10. Develops a plan for alternative strategies for dealing with frustration

FIGURE 9–14
Examples of Strategy-Training Skills

Strategies	Date Introduced	Date Mastered
1. With assistance from teacher, analyzes inefficient strategies for approaching reading task		
2. Analyzes appropriateness of specific alternative strategies for reading tasks		
3. Verbally describes the advantages of using the new strategy in place of previous practice		
4. Verbally rehearses steps involved in the new strategy		
5. Practices new strategy in controlled reading materials, and with several examples		
6. Practices new strategy using classroom reading materials and multiple examples to promote generalization of the learning strategy		
7. Performs reading tasks to criterion with corrective feedback from special education teacher		
8. Performs reading task to specific criterion without prompts or cues from the special education teacher		
9. Generalizes acquired strategy to regular classroom when using regular class materials		
10. Cues others, including teachers, for reinforcement of learning strategies acquired and applied		
12. Applies learning strategies to regular classroom tasks with varying formats and instructions to approximate real learning situations		
13. Applies learning strategy in alternative settings with alternative teachers, including peers		

Adapted from "Instructional Practices for Promoting Skill Acquisition and Generalization in Severely Learning Disabled Adolescents." by D. D. Deshler, G. Alley, M. M. Warner, & J. B. Schumaker, 1988, *Learning Disability Quarterly, 4,* pp. 415–421.

FIGURE 9–15
Skills Sequence for Leisure Education

SWIMMING

Student Name _____

Date _____

Evaluator _____

KEY: M = Mastered at time of observation
 PM = Partially mastered
 NO = Skill was not observed

Skills	Levels of Performance		
	M	PM	NO
1. Lies on back and kicks with arm bands and supported by an adult			
2. Lies on front and kicks with arm bands and supported by an adult			
3. With arm bands, treads water holding one hand of an adult			
4. With arm bands, treads water independently			
5. With arm bands, treads water and paddles with arms			
6. Treads water with one chamber of arm band deflated			
7. Dog paddles to side of pool with arm bands completely deflated			
8. Swims a width of pool (8 m) on front			
9. Swims a width of pool on back			
10. Treads water for 30 seconds			
11. Jumps into deep water			
12. Swims one length of pool (20 m) on front			
13. Swims one length of pool on back			
14. Treads water for 1 minute			
15. Does a standing dive			
16. Dives in, treads water for 1 minute, and swims to side			
17. Swims four lengths of pool on front			
18. Swims four lengths of pool on back			

Goals and objectives in academic areas may be written to replace the instruction provided in the regular education curriculum. Or they may focus on maintaining the student in the regular education curriculum, focusing on reteaching or tutoring the student on the same skills as those taught in the regular classroom. Figure 9–16 illustrates a reading sequence based on the regular curriculum of a public school.

All of the areas discussed in this section may overlap. For example, reading skills not only may be considered an academic skill but may also be taught as a functional skill for a student with a moderate-to-severe disability, or the goal may require that the student apply a learning-strategy approach to attain reading goals.

COMPUTER-GENERATED GOALS AND OBJECTIVES

One of the most notable advances in special education has been the development and widespread availability of computer technology. Computers are used for a number of purposes in the classroom including tutoring, drill and practice, student motivation, and word processing to bypass or compensate for specific student impairments such as the inability to write. Computer programs are also available and used for management purposes to store and organize records and other information on students, to develop and generate reports, and to generate goals and objectives for IEPs, as well as for most other management functions. This section will focus on the use of computers to generate goals and objectives for the IEP.

Advantages of Computer-Generated Goals and Objectives

Research indicates that computer-generated goals and objectives may have many advantages over noncomputerized programs. First, computerized goals and objectives are usually less time-consuming to generate (M. W. Jenkins, 1987; Ryan & Rucker, 1986). Rather than being written by hand and/or typed each time an IEP is developed, reviewed, or revised, computer-generated goals and objectives can be printed automatically, based on assessment results or selected by the committee directly from the computer bank and printed within a short period of time. Considering that teachers must still spend a great deal of time engaged in noninstructional tasks such as referral, conferring with other teachers and parents, assessment, and lesson planning, time saved in IEP development can allow more time for direct instruction with students.

Second, computer-generated IEPs may be less costly than noncomputerized systems. Ryan and Rucker (1986) noted that even with the cost of computer hardware and software or of using a commercial vendor service, computer-assisted IEPs were less costly than noncomputerized IEPs when considering participants' salaries and fringe benefits, and costs associated with developing the IEP such as printed forms, paper, postage, copying, and other related costs.

Third, computer-generated goals and objectives have been reported to be of higher technical quality than those produced without the assistance of a computerized objective bank. Jenkins (1987) noted that this may be because manually writing goals and objectives can be tedious and time-consuming. To save time, teachers may write less comprehensive and less precise documents.

Finally, computer-generated goals and objectives may result in more positive attitudes on the part of teachers using this system (M.W. Jenkins, 1987; Ryan & Rucker, 1986). The time saved in IEP development is most certainly a significant factor in improved teacher perceptions of the IEP process. Of even greater importance, however, is the finding that teachers who use computerized IEPs may also tend to view the process of IEP development as more valuable for planning instruction in the classroom (Ryan & Rucker, 1986). Considering that much research indicates that teachers question the value of the IEP for planning instruction (Dudley-Marling, 1985; Sabatino, 1981; Singer & Butler, 1987), it appears that computer-generated goals and objectives may be instrumental in improving teacher attitudes toward the process.

Potential Disadvantages of Computer-Generated Goals and Objectives

Although there are many obvious advantages to computerized goals and objectives, the IEP committee should also be aware of potential disadvantages and misuses of this procedure. One of the primary concerns regarding the generation of educational programs by computer is that the individualization and personal consideration guaranteed by P.L. 94–142 will be lost in the mechanization of the process of IEP development (Hummel & Degnan, 1986). If computerized goals and objectives are used as the IEP itself rather than as a source for generating possible goals and objectives, individual considerations such as the relevance, practicality, and priority of the goals for a particular student may be overlooked.

FIGURE 9–16
Reading Sequence from Public School Curriculum

<u>Kindergarten</u>
1. Recognizes auditory likenesses and differences of letter sounds in words, repetitive jingles, and rhymes
2. Recognizes likenesses and differences in basic geometric shapes, patterns, and colors, lower case and upper case letters, and names
3. Recognizes directionality
4. Recognizes own name in print
5. Follows simple directions
6. Interprets pictures and stories
7. Selects books

<u>First Grade</u>
1. Demonstrates understanding of letter-sound relationship of alphabet letters with consonant sounds and blends, long and short vowels, and consonant digraphs
2. Applies structural analysis to read word endings, compound words, possessive forms of singular nouns, and simple contractions
3. Recognizes selected sight words and word opposites; uses context clues
4. Interprets poems and stories using art media
5. Follows simple oral and written directions; comprehends details; relates sequence of events through pictures
6. Predicts outcomes; makes inferences from a picture or story; distinguishes fact from fantasy
7. Alphabetizes a list of words by using the first letter
8. Identifies common school and safety signs
9. Reads for enjoyment

<u>Second Grade</u>
1. Demonstrates understanding of letter-sound relationship of consonant blends/clusters, short and long vowels, vowel digraphs, and dipthongs
2. Applies structural analysis to read root words, plurals of nouns, singular, possessive, contractions, and compound words
3. Recognizes sight words, antonyms, homonyms, synonyms; uses context clues
4. Reads aloud with fluency and expression
5. Identifies main idea, details, and sequence of events
6. Alphabetizes a list of words to the second letter
7. Interprets poetry and story selections
8. Identifies clues to correctly answer multiple-choice test items
9. Reads for enjoyment

<u>Third Grade</u>
1. Applies consonant and vowel generalization
2. Applies structural analysis to read regular and irregular plurals of nouns and contractions
3. Recognizes multiple meaning words, homographs, homonyms, antonyms, synonyms; uses context clues
4. Understands main ideas, details, sequence, and oral and written directions with multiple commands
5. Makes inferences, interprets influences, mood, and conclusions
6. Uses classification, alphabetical order to the third letter, dictionary skills, glossaries, maps, charts, and guide words
7. Reads aloud with fluency and expression
8. Interprets consumer information from books, signs, and food packages
9. Proofs answers before handing in test
10. Reads for enjoyment

A second potential disadvantage of computerized IEPs is that school systems, in an effort to save time in the process of IEP development, may adopt a system that fails to match the needs of the school system (Hummel & Degnan, 1986). For example, the adopted system may have an already complete bank of goals and objectives that do not reflect the school's curriculum. There is little advantage to having a computerized system that generates goals and objectives that have no relationship to what is taught. Although goals and objectives may be well written and presented professionally, the resulting IEP may well be useless for instructional purposes and may not even reflect the program the student actually receives.

Commerically Versus Locally Developed Computerized Systems

Computer programs for the production of goals and objectives may be either commercially produced or developed by the local school system or state.

Commerically Produced Systems. Commercially produced systems vary in the amount of structure they impose on the IEP development process used by the school. For example, some commercially produced systems have established objective banks, which cannot be modified, while other systems have partially developed banks, which allow the school system to add to or otherwise modify the existing program. In addition, some systems are keyed to existing assessment instruments. For example, the Talley Goals and Objectives Writer is based on the Brigance Diagnostic Inventory and the Enright Inventory. Similarly, the PIAT Error Analysis Report is based on the Peabody Individual Achievement Test. If these assessment instruments are used to assess the student's needs and also closely reflect the student's curriculum, these computerized goals and objectives programs may be especially useful in the development of IEPs. Commerically produced systems, however, can be expensive and may require significant investments in both hardware and software to maintain the program.

Before purchase of a computerized IEP-development system, it is imperative that the school system carefully consider its specific philosophy, needs, and resources related to IEP development. Philosophy and needs can then be matched to the characteristics of potential commercially produced systems before purchase. For example, if the school system believes that the IEP should be a guide for planning day-to-day instruction, the program selected must be able to reflect the school curriculum and, in most cases, should be amenable to modification of goals and objectives contained in the program.

Locally Produced Systems. To match the specific curriculum of the school to the process of IEP development, many school systems have developed their own programs for generating goals and objectives. Again, these systems range from the simple to the complex. A program may consist only of a catalog of curriculum goals and objectives from which the IEP committee chooses those appropriate for a specific student or may be more systematically based on curriculum-based assessment measures from which specific goals and objectives within the curriculum are identified. Although locally produced systems can be significantly less costly than commercially produced systems, the time involved in developing a workable system may be great. School systems considering development of a computerized program for generation of goals and objectives must also go through the process of clarifying how the IEP is intended to be used, what functions such a program would be expected to serve, and the cost versus the benefit of developing a locally specific program.

RESOURCES FOR DEVELOPING CURRICULUM-BASED ANNUAL GOALS AND OBJECTIVES

Writing relevant and appropriate IEPs requires the use of relevant and appropriate resources. To ensure the relevance of goals and objectives and to avoid haphazardness in the process of IEP development, school systems should establish a procedure for ensuring systematic specification of goals and objectives based on the curriculum in which the student is enrolled. Resources that may assist in this effort might include goals and objectives from existing curriculum guides and curriculum-based checklists.

Existing Curriculum Guides

One way to provide the needed support system for the systematic specification of goals and objectives is through the use of existing curriculum guides, the purpose of which is to provide a basis or framework for instruction. Many curriculum guides contain skills within particular subject areas, which are sequentially arranged in levels of increasing complexity or in the order in which the skill is typically presented to students. Typically, all children follow the same developmental process in learning. While a fifth-grade student may not be at fifth-grade level in a particular skill sequence, his specific level of performance could still be found within the broad skill sequence identified in the curriculum guide. Figure

9–16 illustrates a skills sequence taken from the curriculum of a regular education program.

Existing curriculum guides are usually organized so that a multitude of objectives are listed for each subject area for each grade level. In selecting objectives for a student with a disability, the IEP committee may choose those objectives that can be adapted to meet the student's needs. For example, a goal that focuses on the analysis of the Constitution may require students to evaluate the value of the Constitution as a basis for governance in a modern society. The goal for a student with a mild intellectual disability might be to tell what the Constitution is and its purpose. Or, the student who is blind may be required to meet the same criteria as his classmates without disabilities, except that instead of reading from the text, he may use Talking Books or tapes, and instead of a written examination, he may be required to take an oral examination or to participate in a debate. In this way the goals and objectives for the student with a disability are, as much as possible, based on the goals established for other students in the school.

Many existing curriculum guides have potential weaknesses that make them difficult to use as a basis for instructional planning. First, objectives may not always be sufficiently specific in stating what the student is to learn and how the student is expected to demonstrate what has been learned. Second, curriculum guides may be geared primarily to the average student and provide little flexibility for curricular planning for other populations within the school. Third, instruction in the classroom may not always be based on the existing school curriculum.

If IEPs are to be based on objectives drawn from the curriculum, it is necessary that the curriculum of the school actually reflect the instruction being provided in the classroom. The process of curriculum development in every school system provides for the periodic review and revision of goals and objectives found in existing curriculum guides. During the curriculum review process, a curriculum committee might consider how the format of the curriculum guide might be made more useful as a tool for addressing the diverse needs of all students in the school, including both advanced and underachieving students. Such a process would greatly enhance the usability of the curriculum as a tool in the development of the IEP for students with disabilities. For example, rather than offering only one way in which the student might demonstrate understanding of the objective, curriculum guides might be revised to provide a list of several criteria by which students with different characteristics may demonstrate understanding of stated objectives. In addition, objectives for specific subject areas might be broadened to include a greater variety of objectives at various skill levels. For example, the science teacher might have a list of objectives from which to choose in the area of ecology, rather than only one objective stating the need for clean air. If none of the listed objectives meets the needs of the student, the teacher may then develop a list that does meet those needs.

To make curriculum guides useful for the purpose of curriculum-based IEP development, general educators from all subject areas should collaborate with special educators. By combining the broad curriculum knowledge of the subject area teacher and the knowledge of the special educator concerning the characteristics of the student with a disability, it is possible to develop a curriculum guide that will serve as a common reference to all teachers. A suggested procedure for developing such guides might include the following steps:

1. Committees might consist of teachers assigned by subject areas and grade levels, including a special educator on each committee to develop a broad sequence of skills related to the specific subject area.
2. Once consensus is reached on the continuum of skills, the subcommittee may divide by grade levels, such as K to 2, 3 to 5, 6 to 8, and 9 to 12, with each level assuming responsibility for a designated portion of the continuum of skills as well as development of specific objectives for each skill. Objectives can be identified by the process of task analysis to ensure sequence and comprehensiveness.
3. When the subcommittee has completed the identification of objectives, appropriate evaluation procedures might be developed to assess student mastery of stated objectives. Although some form of paper—pencil test is often used to evaluate performance, other methods are possible. A variety of procedures might be provided for use with students with varying characteristics.
4. Finally, the larger group should reconvene to refine and approve the work of all subcommittees and ensure that the guide reflects the scope and sequence of each subject area.

The Development and Use of Curriculum-Based Checklists

Another resource in curriculum-based planning is the use or development of curriculum checklists. Sample curriculum checklists developed in the area of mathematics, vocational education, health, social studies, and social competence are included in Appendix E. These checklists, focusing on relevant, functional skills associated with everyday living demands, would be appropriate for consideration with students achieving significantly below grade level.

Curriculum-based checklists comprise broad skill areas broken down into specific component subskills, by a systematic procedure of task analysis. The procedure for developing curriculum checklists is the same as for curriculum guides, with the exception that materials and activities are not included. Several advantages accrue to the development and use of curriculum checklists, not only in the writing of IEPs but also in the provision of systematic instruction to all students. The advantages of these checklists include the following:

1. Curriculum-based checklists provide a task hierarchy of specific skills and provide the basis for teaching higher order skills. Once the lists are developed, the teacher will not have to recreate the task hierarchy every time consideration is given to the sequence in which a skill is taught. Valuable time can be saved in the writing of IEPs through the use of specific checklists in which skills are arranged systematically according to the order in which they should be taught.

2. Curriculum-based checklists provide a basis for classroom evaluation. Often, it is difficult to pinpoint where a student is having difficulty in the acquisition of a skill and to provide a program for the development of that skill. Curriculum-based check-lists provide the basis for the construction of curriculum-based tests based on a systematic task hierarchy that, when administered to the student, will provide the teacher with an indication of which skills have not been mastered as well as those that have. The teacher may then plan an effective intervention strategy based on the skill sequence indicated by the curriculum checklists.

3. Curriculum-based checklists can be shared with parents to delineate the sequential instructional steps that will be taken between the student's current level of educational performance and the goals and objectives documented on the IEP. The checklists can provide a specific and ongoing point of reference between the school and home for monitoring and reporting student progress.

4. Finally, curriculum checklists focus only on those skills necessary for the accomplishment of targeted skills. The checklist may serve as a plan for teachers and can help ensure that the classroom activities designed to teach a specific skill are necessary for the attainment of that skill. A curriculum checklist assists the teacher in effective planning by providing direction for the teaching of necessary skills. The teacher is therefore aware of what skill is to be taught, how many subskills remain to be taught before the target skill is achieved, and how mastery of each subskill will be demonstrated.

SUMMARY

This chapter has discussed the process of developing the annual goals and objectives for the IEP. Criteria for the selection of goals were presented, along with guidelines for developing short-term instructional objectives. The process of task analysis was discussed as a method for breaking down annual goals into sequential component parts for the purpose of instruction. Just as levels of performance indicate where to begin instruction, annual goals and short-term objectives tell the teacher what is to be taught. The next chapter will provide guidelines for the next required step in IEP development, evaluation of the student's progress toward achieving the goals and objectives stated on the IEP.

EVALUATION

1. The IEP committee in your school is attempting to develop a rough draft of an IEP for David, a fourth-grade boy with a mild intellectual disability. You are meeting with the committee to ensure that the goals and objectives developed are relevant and individually determined. What criteria might you suggest that the team apply in developing goals and objectives for David's IEP?

2. Name three elements of an instructional objective. Why is each important?

3. In monitoring IEPs in your school district, you have noticed that the criteria for attainment of objectives are almost always noted as "teacher observation" or "100% accuracy," regardless of the skill to be taught. Prepare an outline of your meeting with special services committee members to discuss the problems with these criteria, and suggest alternative methods for indicating criteria for achievement of objectives.

4. Using a method of task analysis, develop goals and objectives for instructing a student with a mild intellectual disability in the skill of counting money, beginning with counting money to $1.00 and moving to the skill of making change for $5.00.
5. Develop a sample task analysis of goals and objectives for a student in your school in one of the following areas: vocational education, functional living skills, communication, social skills, strategy training, or academic skills.
6. Your school district is considering the purchase of a computer program for generating IEP goals and objectives. You have been asked to provide the school board with a brief overview of the advantages and disadvantages of such a move. Outline your presentation.

CHAPTER 10

Evaluation of Goals And Objectives

OBJECTIVES

1. Identify the legal requirements related to evaluating goals and objectives of the IEP.

2. Examine the influence of objectives, time requirements, and student characteristics as determinants for choosing appropriate evaluation procedures.

3. Identify and compare five methods of documenting student progress toward goals and objectives specified on the IEP.

4. Discuss four potential outcomes of revision of IEPs.

5. Discuss three modified grading procedures that may be used with students with disabilities.

P.L. 94–142 provides for the periodic review and evaluation of the IEP by requiring that the document include the following:

> Appropriate objective criteria and evaluation procedures and schedules for determining on at least an annual basis whether the short term instructional objectives are being achieved. (*Federal Register*, 1977)

The educational rationale underlying this requirement is that to be effective, instruction requires systematic monitoring and evaluation of progress toward objectives. Evaluation of student progress provides the classroom teacher with information regarding the effectiveness of teaching strategies and with information on which to modify and plan future instruction. Evaluation should be an ongoing procedure so that both the student and the teacher know at all times where the student is in terms of the stated objectives and goals.

REQUIREMENTS RELATED TO EVALUATION OF GOALS AND OBJECTIVES

Of the legal requirements related to the development of the IEP, three pertain specifically to the evaluation of goals and objectives included in the document. They include the following:

1. Determination of objective criteria for evaluation
2. Determination of appropriate evaluation procedures
3. Determination of evaluation schedules

Each of these requirements will be discussed in this chapter.

Determining Objective Criteria

Writing instructional objectives requires that the specific criterion for completing the behavior or task be included in the objective. By including such criteria, the measurement of the objective is outlined. If instructional objectives have been appropriately stated, then the criteria are already established for evaluation. For example, an objective in reading for a student may be, "Given a set of stimulus cards, the student will be able to sound out in isolation the consonant blends of *spl, spr, sma,* and *sna* accurately in five consecutive trials." The determination has been made that the task must be completed accurately in five consecutive trials. When the student completes the task as stated, the criterion has been met.

As noted in Chapter 9, it is essential to carefully consider the selection of accuracy requirements. Arbitrary selection of criteria may result in inappropriate and unrealistic expectations concerning student progress. The objective that requires a student to run the 50-yard dash with 100% accuracy is inappropriate. Since running the 50-yard dash is not reflected in terms of accuracy percentiles, it is impossible to reflect mastery in such terms. A more appropriate criterion would be to require the student to run the 50-yard dash in less than 30 seconds. This can be measured in terms of the task and thus provides appropriate criteria for evaluation.

The purpose of stating criteria is to provide a basis for knowing when a specified objective has been met. Unless criteria are specified, evaluation becomes open to the subjectivity of the evaluator. If criteria are not stated, it will be difficult, if not impossible, to tell when the objective has been achieved. For example, if a student is expected to recite the multiplication tables of 2, 3 and 4, consideration should be given to how many errors the student will be allowed, how much time will be allotted for the student to complete the task, and how many chances will be allotted to complete the task correctly. Each of these questions must be answered initially when the objective is formulated. Such early determination guides both the student and the teacher through the instructional and evaluation process toward the mastery of specified objectives and goals.

Determining Evaluation Procedures

The choice of particular evaluation procedures depends on the nature of objectives, time requirements to complete the procedure, and the characteristics of the student.

Nature of Objectives.   The type or domain of objectives selected for the IEP quite often requires the use of specific procedures in evaluation. An objective in the cognitive domain may focus on the recall or recognition of knowledge and the development of intellectual abilities and skills. Procedures for evaluation in this area may include both achievement tests and informal measurement. For example, an objective in the cognitive domain may require that the student recall the names of the four basic food groups with no mistakes. The teacher may determine mastery of the objective by having the student write, say, or point to the names of the food groups. The teacher must be certain, however, that the procedure selected for evaluation measures the intent of the objective, which is, in this case, the recall of the four basic food groups. If the objective requires that the student be able to *apply* knowledge of the four basic food groups, the method of evaluation would be different and might include a trip to the grocery store, where the student would select foods from the four basic food groups to plan a meal.

The affective domain includes objectives related to interests, attitudes, values, appreciations, and adjustment. Also included in this domain is the area of social behavior, which is often a major focus of IEP development for some students. Goals for social behavior usually cannot be adequately evaluated by formal norm-referenced tests or by paper—pencil tests administered by the teacher. Thus, various methods of observation are often used to evaluate objectives in this area. Because the internal feelings of individuals cannot be observed, it is usually necessary to identify outward behaviors that can be assumed to indicate the affective domain. To evaluate an objective in this area, the desired outcome must be stated in terms of the student's observable behavior. For example, if the IEP committee wishes to measure change in the withdrawn behavior of a particular student, the desired outcome for the IEP objective might be stated in terms of observable

behaviors such as (1) an increase in the number of a student's verbal responses, (2) an increase in participation in group or free-time activities, or (3) establishing and maintaining eye contact for a specified period of time. Several alternative methods of observing student progress (e.g., role playing and simulation of predetermined situations) provide the teacher with effective means of evaluating otherwise unobservable growth.

In the psychomotor domain, the motor skill area of development, objectives may be evaluated by having the student demonstrate the physical activity specified in the objective. Procedures for evaluating objectives in the psychomotor domain include tests that focus on reaction time, speed, balancing, and other coordination tests and may also include measures of strength and endurance.

In addition to the type or domain of the objective being measured, the level of the skill specified in the objective will also be a determining factor in the selection of measurement procedures. Skills may range from simple to complex, with varying types of evaluation procedures used to measure various points on the continuum. For instance, one objective in the area of language may focus on the improvement of spelling skills at the knowledge level, while another objective focuses on organization of written language at the synthesis level. An evaluation procedure for both objectives may require that a student write a theme about personal hobbies. For the spelling objective, the evaluation procedure would include attention to spelling errors in the paper. However, to measure the student's ability to write a well-organized paper at the synthesis level, the evaluation procedure would focus on the organizational factors within the theme. Thus, before selecting an evaluation procedure, the IEP committee must determine the level of the skills or behaviors to be evaluated.

An instructional objective that states the special conditions by which a student will demonstrate knowledge of a skill also provides measures by which the student should be evaluated. An objective may state, "Given a map of the United States with only the outline of each state illustrated, the student will fill in the names of 45 of 50 states correctly." To evaluate progress toward this objective, the procedure should comply with the condition stated in the objective, which requires that the student be given a map of the United States to complete the task. If the conditions stated in the objective are not implemented, the actual desired skill will not be evaluated, and the student instead may be evaluated on her ability to perform a task that was not taught. In the case of a student learning to fill in a map of the United States, if the teacher required the student to list all the states on a blank sheet of paper, it is possible that the student would be unable to do so. The map provides visual clues for recalling the names of states, whereas simply listing the states provides no clues. Conditions for completing a task should be clearly stated in the objective so that the evaluation procedure selected will be appropriate.

Depending on the skill being taught, the acceptable criteria for attainment of an objective may be stated in various ways. As discussed in Chapter 9, criteria may specify a timed procedure, a percentage of time, percentages of items to get correct, the minimal number of items to get correct, or a combination of these. Evaluation procedures should be selected based on consideration of the type of criteria specified in the objective. An objective may indicate the following, "Given a work sheet, the student will solve 100 basic addition facts within 5 minutes with 80% accuracy." The evaluation procedure for this objective should include both the time and percentage requirements to indicate whether or not the student has met the stated objective. Such an objective may be designed to teach immediate recall with a high degree of accuracy. If the evaluation procedure is not timed, the student may achieve 80% but may take 20 minutes to complete the task by counting fingers. If the percentage requirement is not considered, the student may complete all items but correctly answer only 20%. In either situation, the intent of the objective is not being met.

The established criterion for attaining an objective may be found to be inappropriate for a particular student. For example, the student may not complete 100 basic addition facts in five minutes with 80% accuracy. It may be decided that the attainment of the objective at that criterion level does not warrant the expenditure of an inordinate amount of additional instructional time on that skill. At this point criteria can and should be adjusted in light of the student's needs and abilities and the relevance of the objective for future school and life success. (Because this constitutes a change in the IEP, parents must be notified before implementing the change. For *minor* IEP changes, most school systems notify the parent by telephone, and if parents agree to the change, send them a copy of the revised IEP.)

Time Requirements.   The time required for evaluation of goals and objectives will vary, depending on the type of evaluation procedure selected. It may be difficult for the regular classroom teacher with large numbers of students to evaluate individual progress continuously. High teacher–pupil ratios can seriously limit the amount of time available to consider the progress of individual students on a day-to-day basis. In such cases, evaluation should be scheduled to occur as often as is manageable but at least weekly.

Evaluation procedures vary in amount of time necessary to use them. In general, the more removed the procedure is from the ongoing methods used to evaluate student progress in the classroom, the more time will be required. In some instances, an evaluation procedure may be time-consuming yet provide the most appropriate means of measuring achievement toward the stated goal. For example, a procedure that requires that a student actually use public transportation to achieve a goal that requires the student to be able to get to various locations in the community may be time-consuming but far more appropriate than simulating the experience within the school. On the other hand, requiring that the student be scheduled for a formal achievement test in reading every year as a procedure for determining whether reading achievement has increased is both time-consuming and, in most cases, inappropriate. The committtee must consider whether the benefit of a particular evaluation procedure is both appropriate and worth the amount of time required.

Many educators voice the concern that frequent and direct measurement of a student's progress may take an inordinate amount of time (Wesson, King, & Deno, 1984). However, the requirement to evaluate progress toward stated goals and objectives does not necessarily demand that instructional time be decreased. If teachers are properly trained and efficient in planning instruction so that progress lends itself to ongoing measurement, evaluation may be incorporated into the ongoing instructional process. Evaluation information may be obtained by use of curriculum-based measures such as student observation, work samples, and regularly scheduled classroom tests. Instructional strategies used during the day-to-day classroom instructional routine often can be modified to document day-to-day student progress.

Teacher observation is a continuous source of evaluation information and may be applied to all aspects of curriculum, ranging from academic skill areas to the area of social adjustment. Observation can vary in its degree of specificity, but according to P.L. 94–142, it must be objectively derived if used to evaluate student progress toward achievement of goals and objectives (*Federal Register*, 1977). For example, while listening to a reading group, the teacher may make a mental note that the student seems to be beginning to apply word-attack skills to reading. A more objective method of observation used in the same situation may incorporate the use of a reading checklist on which the teacher notes that the student has begun to apply knowledge of specific initial-consonant sounds in reading. The use of checklists enables the teacher to document progress made in the instructional setting without reducing instructional time.

Samples of assignments completed by the student provide documentation of progress toward the objectives specified in the IEP. *Dated work samples* that are representative of the student's performance should be chosen periodically, beginning when the IEP is implemented and ending when the IEP is evaluated. This strategy allows the teacher to determine not only how much progress was made but also at what rate the student progressed. Comparison of work samples may indicate that the student learned to multiply quickly but that division was much more difficult and progress was slow.

Regularly scheduled tests are a type of work sample that provide confirmation related to classroom progress. They also provide a means of determining progress toward attainment of objectives. Samples of tests may be numerically fewer but more individually comprehensive than work samples. For instance, a test may include all spelling words presented to the student in a 2-week period, whereas a work sample may represent spelling words given daily. Tests should be evaluated in terms of the student's ability to remember previous information acquired while, at the same time, applying new skills. For example, after having mastered addition with regrouping, the student should still encounter test items dealing with this skill, even while working on subtraction with regrouping. Including previously acquired skills in ongoing work can help ensure that such information is not forgotten as new skills are acquired.

More comprehensive evaluation procedures would likely be chosen at standard grading periods, such as every 9 weeks, rather than daily or weekly. At this point, time should be set aside to administer curriculum-based tests such as informal inventories or formal observation to document progress made during that grading period. Some school systems or individual schools might choose to administer standardized tests at the midpoint of the IEP or at the end of the year to formally document the student's progress in terms of the standardized level of performance. Such a procedure, however, is likely to yield limited correlation between the standardized test questions and the objectives on the student's IEP and thus is not likely to provide valid information related to progress toward goals and objectives stated on the IEP (unless goals and objectives are norm referenced).

Various schedules and methods of documenting evaluation data exist, each of which varies in time required. Regardless of the evaluation-documentation method, frequent and systematic evaluation enables the teacher to make daily decisions concerning appropriate instructional strategies for achieving the objectives specified in the IEP.

Student Characteristics.   To ensure the appropriateness of evaluation procedures, the student's learning characteristics must be considered. The choice of evaluation procedures will depend on such characteristics as the student's type of disability, cultural background, reinforcement schedule, and the approach to tests.

Many students with disabilities will be able to acquire content equivalent to their peers without disabilities but at a different level or with instructional modifications. For example, a student with a mild-to-moderate intellectual disability may be able to participate in a history unit and, as an evaluation measure, may be asked to locate a state on a map and name the major state products. Other students having participated in the same unit, but perhaps with more extensive study and understanding of the information, may be asked to verbally compare the natural resources of their state with those of similar geographical locations. Likewise, in the same history unit, another student with limited speaking ability may be asked to write a report comparing the natural resources and major products of three states that differ significantly from one another regarding these factors.

The nature of the student's disability may be a determining factor in how the student will be evaluated. P.L. 94–142 requires that evaluation not penalize the student on the basis of the disability except when the degree or nature of the disability is the focus of such evaluation. When evaluating progress toward a stated objective on the IEP, the teacher should choose a procedure by which the student can operate at optimal potential. A written history examination that must be completed within a specified time period would be inappropriate for a student with a learning disability whose poor eye–hand coordination results in laborious and extremely slow handwriting. Nor would an oral examination be appropriate for a student with a significant disorder in expressive language.

The student's cultural background must also be considered in choosing evaluation procedures so that methods selected do not penalize the student for lacking skills not stressed in the student's cultural environment. For example, some students come from cultures where high levels of verbal response are not encouraged or required. Requiring this mode of response when evaluating student progress may not provide an accurate picture of what the student actually knows.

Many students with disabilities require reinforcement on a frequent basis. Test situations quite often do not provide frequent enough support to ensure that the student is continually performing at maximum potential. If the student requires continuous reinforcement, or shorter duration of testing sessions because of a short attention span, the evaluation procedure should reflect that need. This may be achieved by scheduling evaluation sessions in short time periods so that a small amount of information may be evaluated and reported to the student. Evaluation measures requiring that the student attend for long periods of time with no immediate feedback would be inappropriate for the student who requires continuous reinforcement.

As a result of repeated failure, many students with disabilities feel anxious when placed in a testing situation. Evaluation should be structured to minimize the threat to the student. To establish success from the outset, tests should begin with information the student already knows. For some students, evaluation procedures may have to be presented informally to lessen anxiety about the situation.

In all likelihood, if the student feels comfortable with a particular evaluation procedure, progress will be more accurately reflected in the results. Many students feel most comfortable with procedures with which they are familiar. Prior successful experience with one or more evaluation procedures affords the student familiarity with, and therefore confidence about, the method of evaluation. Introducing students to novel evaluation situations, however, is desirable and quite often necessary. This can be done by informing students of the procedure in terms of people involved, information included, time involved, and the nature of student involvement. It may be helpful to simulate the situation with students before the actual evaluation occurs so that they know what to expect.

Determining Evaluation Schedules

Ongoing Curriculum-Based Evaluation. To be of maximum benefit, evaluation should occur continuously rather than annually and should be directly related to the curriculum in which the student is engaged. Continuous evaluation should occur daily, if possible. This is not to say that the teacher must give a test or even record progress every day. Rather, by observing the student daily while he works on a specified task or participates in group activities, the teacher can monitor student progress informally. Then, when the student completes the skill being taught, more structured methods of evaluation should be used. By evaluating instruction and student progress as each skill is taught, the teacher can ensure student mastery at each step. With this type of evaluation, the teacher maintains current, accurate information concerning the student's progress and gains insight into the effectiveness of various materials and methods. Based on the continuous information obtained, the decision may be made to change a student to another reading group based on rapid progress in the acquisition of reading skills; or it may be decided that the student needs an additional week on the multiplication tables of 4 and 5. Continuous evaluation provides justification for the teacher's decision to change the instructional methods or instructional materials when necessary and to revise the IEP if the student is not achieving in terms of the curriculum designed for the student.

Periodic Home–School Communication. Parent–teacher communication can be greatly enhanced if both the parent and the teacher know where the student is achieving in terms of the IEP. The IEP document may be the parents' only link with the student's instructional program (other than report cards), and thus, it should provide a basis for reporting progress information. Questions may arise concerning the student's progress in terms of stated objectives. In the event that the parents ask about skills the student is achieving at a given time, it is to the teacher's advantage to be able to answer in specific statements. Statements such as, "Joe is doing well, but I can't tell you exactly where he is until after the 6-week test," are not nearly as satisfying to the teacher or parent as a more specific statement such as, "Joe has completed the objectives for this month in math, which include learning basic division facts. He is now working on dividing three-digit numbers by a one-digit divisor with no remainder." This type of communication also enables parents to know what skills they might work on at home with their child, if they so choose.

Parents should also be informed when objectives are not being met. Although the IEP is not a legally binding document, parents may believe, unless they hear otherwise, that the plan is going smoothly and that the goals stated on the IEP will be achieved by the end of the year. Keeping parents adequately informed either by letter, phone call, or conference creates confidence and provides a basis for future cooperation and educational planning between the school and the home. Because parents may differ in their preferences for information from and contact by the school, schedules and methods for communicating with parents might be established at the IEP meeting.

Annual Schedules of Evaluation. At a minimum, progress toward goals and objectives included on the IEP must be evaluated annually. The obvious disadvantage of this procedure is that it provides no mechanism for monitoring student progress or lack of progress throughout the year and provides no method for determining whether the instructional methods employed daily are appropriate for a particular student. Because there is no mechanism established for linking the goals and objectives to a functional and ongoing evaluation system, IEPs may be filed away until the annual review, at which time the arbitrary judgment of the committee or inappropriate methods of evaluation such as standardized achievement testing may provide the only basis for determining whether the goals and objectives have been achieved. If an annual evaluation schedule is the only schedule to be included on the IEP, the committee should discuss when and how interim progress will be evaluated and reported to parents and should ensure that the annual evaluation methods are appropriate for accurately measuring the student's progress toward the goals developed by the committee.

METHODS OF DOCUMENTATION

Alternatives for documenting progress toward the short-term objectives and annual goals specified in the IEP include the following methods: (1) the IEP form, (2) skills checklists, (3) graphing, (4) anecdotal records, and (5) work samples.

The IEP Form
The method of dating completed objectives on the IEP as they are achieved can provide a relatively simple means of indicating student progress. A space may be provided beside each objective so that the teacher can mark the date the student meets the criteria indicated in the objective. Figure 10–1 provides an example of this type of documentation. Using the IEP form to document student progress simplifies record-keeping procedures by including all such information on one form. Such a procedure also contributes to systematic monitoring procedures.

Documentation of student progress on the IEP form provides complete information concerning achievement in terms of the stated objectives. By specifying objectives in instructional terms, the basis for evaluation is clearly indicated on the IEP form. The teacher has already documented the condition under which evaluation will occur, the task to be performed, and the acceptable criteria for completion of the task. The teacher, the parent, the student, or those responsible for monitoring the IEP can readily observe not only how much progress was made toward short-term instructional objectives but also the conditions and the criteria under which such progress has been made.

Indicating when the dated objectives are achieved on the IEP form also provides a basis for IEP revision. If an objective that was projected to take 1 month to complete is not completed in 2 months, revision of the IEP should be considered. This information can also contribute to planning more realistic IEPs in the future.

Because short-term objectives on the IEP usually are not written daily, initial progress may be difficult to document. Some short-term objectives include several skills and may take weeks or months to achieve. A short-term instructional objective may require a student to identify in oral reading passages all initial-consonant sounds with 90% accuracy over a 3-week period. In this case, documentation would occur only when the student was able to perform the entire task at the stated criterion level. The IEP would contain no indication of documented progress when the student could identify one consonant sound or when the task was performed with only two errors. Being able to recognize and document even small gains is important for students, teachers, and parents. Consequently, documenting progress on the IEP form may not provide the frequent reinforcement often necessary to ensure maximum motivation and achievement for the student.

Skills Checklists
Skills checklists, such as the samples found in Appendix E, provide an alternative method of documenting student progress. Checklists are arranged by skill areas and are presented in a sequential order according to task hierarchies within the student's curriculum. Teachers who use a checklist as the basis for planning instruction may also use them to indicate which of the component skills the student has mastered and which have not been mastered. Skills not mastered are incorporated into the instructional plan or as objectives on the IEP. Figure 10–2 illustrates the procedure of documentation by skills checklists.

Skills checklists have the advantage of locating objectives within the context of a continuum of related skills, thus enabling the teacher to indicate where along that continuum the student is achieving. Because skills checklists can be developed to represent each small component task required to master a skill, it is possible to document even small student gains. Thus, even though the objective may be to identify all initial consonant sounds with 100% accuracy, the teacher may document mastery of three consonant sounds to indicate progress toward the broader short-term objective.

Skills checklists are most useful when developed based on the curriculum of the school, grade, or class in which the student is enrolled. They may also be

FIGURE 10–1
Documentation by Dating IEP Objectives

Individual Education Plan (IEP)

Student's Name: __Linda Lawler__

Subject Area: __Physical Education__

Teacher: __Ms. Tennison__

Level of Performance: __Has coordination of basic fine motor skills; can walk, skip, run, jump, and hop to even and uneven dance rhythms; and has been introduced to games of low organization, team games, and elementary gymnastics.__

Annual Goals: 1. __The student will demonstrate good body mechanics, movement, and form in a wide variety of running, throwing, catching, and hitting activities.__

2. __The student will participate in individual and team sports by acquiring the fundamental skills and by knowing the basic rules of those sports.__

	September	October	November

Objectives	1. Review of Movement Combinations: The student will be able to: gallop, skip, slide, land and stop, dodge, stretch and bend, swing and sway, turn and twist, throw overhand, throw underhand, catch, push and pull, lift, and carry. (Accuracy will be measured by the student demonstrating that she can perform the movement.) 2. The student will be able to move into the following formations upon command:
	9-15 circle 95%
	9-15 shuttle
	9-15 zig zag
	9-17 square
	9-17 corner
	3. The student will be able to perform the following track and field events:
	9-25 run a 50-yd. dash in 10 seconds
	9-27 run a 100-yd. dash in 20 seconds
	9-25 throw a ball 20 yds. 90%
	9-25 dribble a ball with control 90%
		Unit of Study: Soccer
		1. The student will be able to participate in a game of soccer by demonstrating the ability to perform the following skills: 85%
		a. Kicking
		   9-30 (1) Instep kick
		   10-15 (2) Punting
		   10-15 (3) Volley kick
		b. Dribbling
		c. Trapping
		   10-5 (1) foot trap
		   10-5 (2) shin trap
		   10-10 (3) inside of leg trap
		   10-15 (4) chest trap
		d. Heading 10-25
		e. Throwing the ball 10-10
		f. Tackling 10-10
		2. The student will play soccer according to the basic rules and regulations. 90%
		10-26
			Unit of Study: Volleyball
			1. The student will be able to participate in a game of volleyball by demonstrating the ability to perform the following skills: 85%
			a. Two-hand overhand hit 11-15
			b. Two-hand underhand hit 11-20 (bumping)
			c. Serving
			   10-20 (1) Underhand serve
			   10-27 (2) Overhand serve
			2. The student will play volleyball according to the basic rules. 90%
			10-27

Evaluation	Observation The AAHPER Youth Fitness Test The Oregon Motor Fitness Test	Observation Soccer Skills Test Teacher-Made Test on Soccer Rules	Observation Volleyball Skills Test Teacher-Made Test on Volleyball Rules

FIGURE 10–2
Documentation of Student Progress by Checklists

Arithmetic—Intermediate

I. Basic Concepts, Facts, and Procedures

A. Counts, Reads, and Writes Numbers

Entered Program

✓ 1. Counts objects from 0 to 50 by 2's, 5's, and 10's.
✓ 2. Reads and writes number symbols 0–50.
✓ 3. Recognizes and understands the ordinal positions 6th, 7th, 8th, 9th, and 10th and knows the relations to the numbers 6, 7, 8, 9, 10.
✓ 4. Counts objects from 0–100 by 1's.
✓ 5. Reads and writes number symbols 0–70.
9-27 6. Reads and writes number names: zero, one, two, three, four, and five.
10-20 7. Writes the missing numerals in an incomplete sequence using numerals 0–50.
9-20 8. Counts objects from 0–100 by 2's.
____ 9. Reads and writes number symbols 0–100.
____ 10. Reads and writes number names zero–ten.
10-15 11. Counts objects 0–100 by 1's, 2's, 5's, and 10's.
____ 12. Reads and writes number symbols 0–100.
____ 13. Reads and writes number names zero–fifteen.
____ 14. Knows the meaning of ordinals: first, twentieth.
11-5 15. Distinguishes between even and odd numbers.
11-1 16. Writes the missing numerals in an incomplete sequence using numerals 0–100.
____ 18. Reads, writes, and spells cardinal and ordinal number names through twenty.

B. Facts and Processes

____ 1. Using one-to-one relation, matches smaller set to larger ones telling how many objects of larger set are not matched.
____ 2. Adds to smaller set to make it match larger set.
____ 3. Solves addition equations with sums through 20 or less with no carrying using real objects and sets.
____ 4. Solves word problems involving addition problems with sums through 20 or less with no carrying.
____ 5. Determines if the number of objects in a set is greater than, less than, or equal to the number of objects in another set.
____ 6. Uses symbols less than (<) and greater than (>) with numberals 0–25.
____ 7. Arranges objects into sets of 10 when the total number of objects is a multiple of 10.
____ 8. Joins two given subsets into one set and tells how many objects there are.
____ 9. Uses symbols less than (<) and greater than (>) with numerals 0–50.

obtained, however, from commerical sources, although commercially produced checklists do not usually reflect the specific curriculum in which the student is actually enrolled. Thus, they may not be entirely applicable to the objectives chosen for a particular student and may not provide an appropriate basis for documenting student progress. For example, an objective based on the student's curriculum may require the following: "The student will correctly use present, past, and future tenses of verbs in classroom conversations structured to elicit these responses in five consecutive trials." A commercially developed skills checklist may emphasize learning the rules of grammar with the use of a work book, while the teacher's method for achieving the objective may be to structure specific classroom conversational situations, with the student responding verbally. Checklists developed by the teacher or school are more likely to be appropriate for documenting student progress. Such development, however, requires teacher time and effort, which may be unavailable.

Because of their comprehensiveness, checklists are quite often bulky, especially if the teacher uses detailed checklists for each skill area to be developed. Therefore, if skills checklists are made available to everyone involved in writing, implementing, and evaluating the IEP, duplication will require extra expenditure by the school system.

Graphing

Graphing provides a visual representation of student progress and may take many forms. Progress toward a goal may be charted daily or weekly by the teacher or by the student. Based on a specified objective, the student's performance is charted in terms of progress toward that objective. For example, a short-term objective may require a student, given a set of stimulus cards, to read 20 new sight words in a 20-day period with 100% accuracy. The graph developed to illustrate student progress would begin at zero. As new words are learned, the student's progress would be indicated on the graph. Figure 10–3 illustrates how graphs may be used to document student progress in acquiring new vocabulary words.

The use of graphing procedures has the advantage of providing a continuous visual indication of progress made by the student toward specified objectives. Each small gain made by the student is recorded on the graph to indicate such progress. The degree to which the student has accomplished the objective is readily apparent on the graph. Thus, the student and the teacher can tell how far the student has come since instruction was initiated and how much remains to be accomplished in terms of the short-term instructional objective. This type of visual representation illustrates each successive achievement of the student and, therefore, can provide a strong stimulus for motivating the student toward further achievement.

Graphs are sensitive to even small changes in achievement and may indicate such changes even when they are not apparent to the teacher or the student. Increased student achievement becomes apparent when illustrated on a graph, providing reinforcement for progress that may have otherwise gone unnoticed. On the other hand, decreased performance by the student also becomes readily apparent by graphing and alerts the student and the teacher to determine what may be interfering with the student's progress.

In addition to illustrating how much achievement is made, graphs also indicate the rate at achievement. The student may make greater progress during certain times; for example, she may learn more words during 1 week than another. By averaging daily or weekly achievement, the teacher establishes an average instructional achievement rate, which provides a basis for appropriate educational programming.

The construction and maintenance of graphs can be time-consuming if the teacher is attempting to keep daily graphs on many students. Graphs can be simply constructed, however, enabling most students to maintain their own graphs. Even at the secondary level, graphs can be developed to look sophisticated and yet be simple enough to be maintained by the students themselves.

Anecdotal Records

The teacher may use anecdotal records to document student progress. This procedure requires the teacher to record comments concerning student progress in narrative form daily or weekly. Such records should be kept in a notebook to maintain continuity among entries. Figure 10–4 provides an example of an anecdotal record maintained to document student progress.

The major advantage of keeping an anecdotal record is that it allows the teacher to document information that might not always be apparent by other means of documentation. Such information may include student absence or illness, interruption of the usual class schedule, or changes in the instructional methods or materials. Any or all of these circumstances may affect student performance. By recording both student data and instructional procedures, the teacher can gain insight concerning circumstances that improve or reduce student performance. For example, the seating arrangement within the classroom may be changed because the student is engaging in frequent conversation with another student. This may be noted in the anecdotal record maintained on the student. If performance increases, the teacher has documentation indicating the possible reason for such increase. Knowledge of circumstances that increase or decrease achievement for a particular student is of substantial educational value. Information contained in anecdotal records may be passed on to future teachers to be considered in planning appropriate instructional strategies for the student.

The primary disadvantage of anecdotal records is that they may contain subjective impressions made by the teacher, thus failing the requirement for objectivity established by P.L. 94–142. Observations made in one situation may not be true in another and may be interpreted differently by different people. Consider the student who is very shy and seldom participates in class discussions. One teacher may interpret this behavior as acceptable and, thus, not view it as creating a barrier to achievement. Another teacher may interpret the same behavior as inappropriate and likely to impede the student's achievement. Caution must be exercised to consider the possible bias inherent in anecdotal records. Anecdotal records should not be used as the only method for documenting student progress. Other more objective

FIGURE 10–3
Graphing Student Progress Toward Objectives

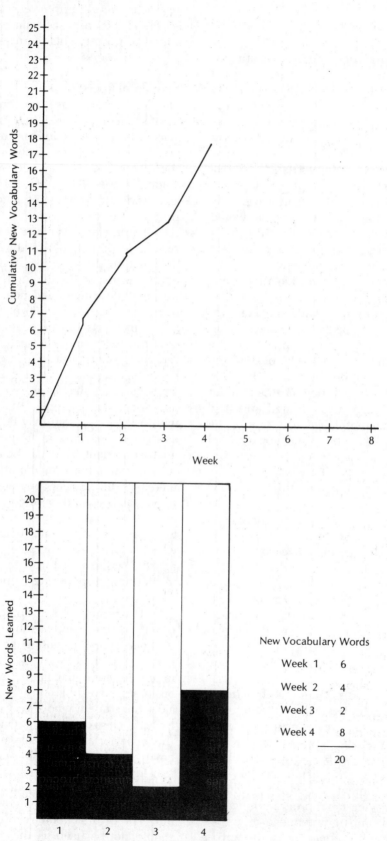

FIGURE 10–4
Anecdotal Record

Sept. 4, —Introduced subtraction with regrouping in ten's column in math group of six.

Sept. 5, —Joyce did not complete the math assignment on time today. She seemed to be struggling through the work. Five of ten answers were incorrect.

Sept. 6, —Joyce turned in math assignment very early; accuracy level was 60%. Paper returned for her to correct.

Sept. 7, —Still working on math paper from yesterday. Tried to help her for a few minutes during the 50-minute period. Not enough time. Perhaps a peer tutor tomorrow.

Sept. 8, —Cindy worked with Joyce today. Seems to be making progress. Cindy solved the first few problems, then helped Joyce with the next six. Joyce did the last two alone. Made one mistake. Cindy helped her correct it.

measures must be used to substantiate subjective information provided by such records.

The process involved in maintaining anecdotal records can be time-consuming. Such a procedure may be feasible only when the teacher has some free time at the beginning or at the end of the school day to devote to this method of documentation.

Work Samples

Another method for documenting student progress is by maintaining student work samples to compare at different points in the instructional process. For some areas, such as handwriting and written language, work samples are better evaluative devices than other methods because they provide an actual example of the student's work rather than a report describing the type and amount of progress made. Although it is certainly possible to quantify why a student's handwriting has improved by indicating that the consistency of letter size has improved and spacing between words is appropriate and consistent, samples that illustrate these points by comparing "before" and "after" samples are far more valuable for the student and for the parents than a narrative progress report. The same is true for the area of written language. A student may well use more complex sentences and descriptive vocabulary. However, comparing samples of written language at the point of IEP implementation, at midyear, and at the end of the year can provide a more dramatic and comprehensive indication of the student's progress.

Work samples, when used appropriately, are excellent methods for motivating students and reporting progress to parents. Teachers often make the mistake of collecting too many work samples that may or may not indicate the student's performance level. Often these samples are given to parents in a folder at the point of parent-student conferences. Too

many samples in different areas provide little basis for comparison and little time to sort through to gain useful information regarding the student's progress. Teachers should maintain from one to three representative samples of a student's work when the IEP is implemented and the same number of representative samples as instruction progresses, perhaps every month or 6 weeks. At interim reviews or the annual review, selected samples can be compared and reviewed with parents. The teacher should ensure that work samples are dated so that it is clear what period in the instructional process is represented.

REVISING IEPs, BASED ON EVALUATION OF GOALS AND OBJECTIVES

It should be emphasized that an IEP cannot be revised without the knowledge and participation of the student's parents. P.L. 94–142 is not clear on whether a review meeting must be convened every time a minor change in the IEP is anticipated. Most school systems, however, differentiate between a minor and a major revision of the IEP. For a minor revision such as an anticipated change in evaluation procedures or criteria, schools typically notify and consult with parents by phone, and if parents agree to the revision, send them a copy of the revised portion of the IEP. For major modifications such as an anticipated change in time in program or a change in placement, review meetings are convened.

Systematic evaluation of objectives can result in the decision to revise the IEP at any point that the student's instructional needs or learning rate differ from the original projection made by the IEP committee. If evaluation of objectives is conducted continuously and is closely related to the student's curriculum, the need for revision will be recognized before a significant gap results between anticipated and actual achievement. Evaluation can point out the need for redefining objectives and annual goals, time lines, amount of service provided, and teaching strategies contained in the original IEP.

Redefinition of Objectives and Goals

If evaluation indicates that the objectives are clearly unrealistic, they should be redefined in terms more appropriate to the student's needs. Such redefinition may include changing the specific behavior expected of the student, the conditions under which the behavior is to occur, or the minimum criteria expected for attainment. Annual goals may or may not change with short-term objectives. The committee should review annual goals to determine whether they continue to be appropriate or whether they should be modified to reflect the revised objectives.

Modification of Time Lines

If, after evaluation, the originally specified objectives are still considered to be appropriate, the decision may be made to extend the original time lines rather than change the content of the objectives. In such a case, a greater amount of time would be allotted to the teaching of the originally specified objectives. Annual goals would be adjusted in scope according to the amount of time reallocated to the short-term instructional objectives.

Modification of the Amount Of Service Provided

Lack of student progress may indicate the need for revision in the amount of special education specified at the original IEP committee meeting. For example, it may be determined that to attain specified objectives more instructional time is required with the resource teacher, who comes to the classroom to work with the student individually. Attention should be directed toward obtaining the additional services determined necessary for the student to benefit from special education.

In addition to providing a basis for spontaneous IEP revision, evaluation of goals and objectives can contribute to identifying the student's learning rate, which will be helpful in planning next year's IEP for the student. Documenting student progress throughout the year provides an indication of how much material the student learned in a specified amount of time. Such information should provide the basis for future appropriate planning.

Modification of Teaching Strategies

Before the decision is made to revise the IEP, the teacher should closely examine the strategy being used to teach the objectives. Alternative instructional strategies should be employed before the decision to revise goals and objectives is made. Perhaps the student who does not attend well in class and is consequently progressing slowly in math and reading might benefit from the use of a peer tutor, a contract, high-interest materials, or an individual project. Thus, the problem may be a "teaching deficiency" rather than a "student deficiency." If various teaching strategies fail to improve student performance and IEP revision is indicated, the IEP committee, including the student's parents and the student if appropriate, should participate in and approve such revision.

EVALUATION FOR THE PURPOSE OF GRADING

It is often appropriate to evaluate goals and objectives on the IEP at the same intervals as those established by the school for grading and reporting progress to parents. The issue of grading in schools involves all students but is compounded when applied to students with disabilities. While grades are in some cases reinforcing, they are in many cases devastating to students who do not meet the established "criteria" for "passing." Although some states and school districts have developed uniform procedures for grading students with disabilities, research indicates that in practice, student evaluation and grading remain somewhat idiosyncratic and teacher dependent (Zigmond et al., 1985). The criteria for achievement of objectives on the IEP can provide continuity for grading a student with a disability. This section will discuss guidelines for developing uniform criteria for modifying grading procedures in schools.

Modification of the Regular Grading Criteria

Modification of the grading of a student with a disability is as individual as the goals and objectives contained in the IEP and is based on the student's demonstrated need for modification. Thus, it is inappropriate for a school to establish a separate grading system for all students who are enrolled in special education. Many students with disabilities do not require modified grading, while others require criteria entirely different from that of nondisabled students. The concept of least restriction applies to a student's right to be included in the regular grading system if appropriate, as well as to the student's right to access to the regular classroom.

Modified grading systems should maintain as many characteristics of the regular grading system as possible. For example, the same report card format, color, and cover should be used for all students, regardless of whether the actual grading system is modified. In addition, and to the extent possible, the same grading indicators should be used whenever possible to ensure continuity between the regular and special education programs. For example, if a student with a moderate disability is likely to receive modified grades in some subjects but not in others, or in some years but not others, incompatible grading indicators may interfere with documenting the accumulation of units for graduation and may interfere with communication between parents and the school regarding the relative value of the different grades. In addition, P.L. 94–142 guarantees confidentiality in the disclosure of information that may unnecessarily identify a student as having a disability. Maintaining similar grading procedures for all students can serve to protect the student's right to confidentiality.

Standard grades can be accompanied by other, more subtle, indicators when it is necessary to document that the student has received a modified grade. Accompanying indicators might include an asterisk beside the grade with an explanation provided elsewhere on the grade card or record that the grade is based on the functional level of the student rather than on current grade placement. Or, the decision might be made to provide a written progress report to accompany the report card. This report would refer directly to the student's progress relative to the goals and objectives stated on the IEP. An example of a progress report of this type is illustrated in Figure 10–5. Another option to be used alone or in combination with other indicators is the use of modified course titles. For example, a modified course in biology might be entitled Biology for Everyday Living and be designated as a functional rather than an academic course.

Grading procedures may be modified to fit the needs of the individual student. Some students will require only minor modification, whereas others will require different grading criteria altogether. Three examples of different levels of modification are provided in the remainder of this section.

Minor Modification of the Regular Grading Criteria.

For some students only minor modifications in grading are appropriate or necessary. In such cases, the standard grading format is accessible and should serve as the basis for modifications made to address the individual needs of the student. Students should receive the same report card as nondisabled students and the same grading scale should be used. Minor modifications might include modification of time limits for completion of tests, administering tests orally rather than in writing, modifying the format of written test items from narrative to short answer (such as true–false or completion), and modification of the degree that specific course requirements count toward the final grade. Minor modifications are those modifications that provide alternative methods of enabling the student to achieve the same criteria as other students. Figure 10–6 provides an example of an IEP that defines minor grading modifications.

Major Modification of the Regular Grading Criteria.

Many students can participate in the regular program but cannot, regardless of minor modifications, meet the standard requirements established for grading. They do not, however, require a completely different curriculum. These students often do not fit neatly into either the regular or an alternative program. To ensure a measure of success, grading for these students may require the modification of the basic standards established for grading. For example, instead of a grade of 70% being required for passing, the standard may be lowered to 60% or even 50%. Course requirements may be altered to focus on those that are most important, with less crucial requirements omitted. Classroom teachers often may resent modifications such as these; they understandably may consider it inappropriate to significantly modify course requirements to maintain a student in the regular program. An often voiced concern is that making special exceptions for some students is unfair to others and creates an inaccurate picture of the student when progress is reported. Nonetheless, it is not always necessary to grade students competitively based on the class average. It is possible to grade students individually to reflect motivation, interest, and effort as well as on assignments and class work. When major modifications are made and implemented in the regular education curriculum, procedures noted earlier, such as providing an additional report that interprets the student's grade, or indicating with an asterisk that the course requirements have been modified, or even renaming the course to reflect a modified curriculum, are appropriate and should be included. A grading system that significantly modifies the standard grading criteria for a classroom is included in Figure 10–7, p. 264.

Alternative Grading Systems.

In some instances, the standard grading format used for most programs will be inappropriate for use with specific students with disabilities. This may be a result of the type of

FIGURE 10–5
IEP Progress Report

Name: _____ Date Form Initiated: _____ Teacher: _____ Grade: _____

Birth Date: _____ Chronological Age: _____ IEP Implementation Date: _____

1. Skill Mastered
2. Satisfactory Skill Improvement
3. Skill Improvement—Slow
4. No Observable Progress
5. Objective Not Initiated
6. _____

Objective	Qtr.	Qtr.	Qtr.	Qtr.	Comments: (Qtr. ___)
					Comments: (Qtr. ___)
					Comments: (Qtr. ___)
					Comments: (Qtr. ___)

FIGURE 10–6
Example of Minor Modifications to Regular Grading Procedure

INDIVIDUALIZED EDUCATION PROGRAM:
MINOR MODIFICATIONS TO GRADING PROCEDURES

Rationale
The IEP committee has identified relative strengths in verbal expression, short-term memory, problem-solving skills, social/interpersonal skills, listening skills, mathematical calculation, and artistic ability. Relative weaknesses include reading comprehension and written language skills. The grading format of the regular science class is as follows:

Grading Scale	Course Requirements	Percent of Grade
A = 90%-100%	Research Paper	30%
B = 80%-89%	Test (Essay, Objective)	50%
C = 70%-79%	Homework	10%
D = 60%-69%	Classroom/Lab Work	10%
F = 0%-59%		100%

The committee determined that the present system is based on reading and writing proficiency and therefore may not afford John the opportunity for success. The committee redesigned course requirements to accentuate John's verbal ability and reduce demands relative to reading and writing tasks. Criteria for letter grades were not changed. The weight of course requirements was altered slightly, as follows:

Modifications

Grading Scale	Course Requirements	Percent of Grade
A = 90%-100%	Oral Research Presentation	20%
B = 80%-89%	Tests (Objective Format)	40%
C = 70%-79%	Homework	20%
D = 60%-69%	Classroom/Lab Work	20%
F = 0%-59%		100%

Criteria for mastery is a C average for the semester. This grading plan will be monitored by the Special Education teacher and adjusted accordingly by the IEP committee.

The following objectives were added to John's IEP:

1. Following library research of animal habitats, John will prepare a 10-minute oral presentation of his findings. Diagrams, clay models, and a written outline of the speech will accompany his presentation. Criterion for mastery is 70% of possible 100 given for the presentation.

2. John will demonstrate mastery of unit concepts by successful completion of four objective tests. Questions will consist of true-false, multiple choice, matching, fill-in-the-blank, and short answer questions. Memorization of key vocabulary words will be measured through matching tasks rather than through dictation. Criterion for mastery of each test is 70%.

Committee Members
Science Teacher_____   Student_____

Special Education Teacher _____   Other_____

Parents_____   _____

FIGURE 10–7
Sample of Major Modifications to the Regular Grading Procedure

INDIVIDUALIZED EDUCATION PROGRAM: MAJOR MODIFICATIONS TO GRADING PROCEDURES

Rationale

Janice has been identified as having a serious emotional disturbance, which adversely affects her educational performance. She is frequently late for class and arrives without books, materials, or her homework assignments. During class Janice finds it difficult to concentrate on assignments. She seldom completes homework assignments. Although she is capable of completing grade-level work, she is failing in Algebra, English, and American History. The IEP committee has determined that grading criteria should be modified to accommodate the adverse affects of Janice's disability.

Modifications

1. A grade will be given each day that will determine the class grade for each week.
2. Up to 20 points can be earned each day for a total of 100 points per week.
3. Weekly grades will be averaged as a test grade.
4. The six elements of the procedure are as follows:

Requirements	Possible Points
a. Arrives to class on time, is seated and ready to begin when class starts	1
b. Brings books, pencil, paper, and other materials required for class	1
c. Homework assignments are completed from the previous day and meet criterion established	4
d. Works steadily on assignments in class:	5
1. 5 points if teacher does not have to give more than one reminder to continue working	
2. After one reminder, student will lose 1 point for each time reminded until end of work period	
e. Class assignments complete	5
f. Class assignments mostly correct	4

a. 90%–100% = 4 points   Total possible daily points   20
b. 80%–89% = 3 points
c. 70%–79% = 2 points
d. 60%–69% = 1 point
e. below 60% = 0 points

Grading scale is as follows: 90%–100% = A, 80%–89% = B, 70%–79% = C, 60%–69% = D, below 60% = F. Criterion for mastery is a C average for the semester. This grading plan will be monitored by the Special Education teacher and adjusted accordingly by the IEP committee.

The following objective was added to Janice's IEP:

1. Janice will maintain a minimum grade of C in Algebra, English, and American History by arriving to class on time with all materials, beginning work on time, continuing work to task completion, and by completing to criteria all homework and class assignments.

IEP Committee Members

Parent_____	Agency Representative_____
Special Education Teacher_____	Other _____
Student_____	_____
Classroom Teachers_____	_____
_____	_____
_____	_____

program in which the student is enrolled or because the student's needs vary significantly from those of most other students. For programs such as speech therapy and occupational and physical therapy, using a standard grading format may be entirely irrelevant and inappropriate for providing information on student progress. Thus, an alternative reporting procedure would be used, based on progress toward the goals and objectives identified in the IEP. For programs such as these, which are not a part of the curriculum on which promotion and graduation are based, there is little need for or pressure to produce standard grades. When a student's educational needs vary significantly from the standard curriculum of the school, modification of existing grading procedures may be inappropriate for reporting student progress. The IEP committee should explore a reporting format that better communicates student progress for parents and the school. Although the system might retain the same report card cover and color to maintain confidentiality, the report itself may deviate totally from the standard reporting format. Reporting may be based on attainment of IEP objectives as defined by the criteria for achievement, or on objectives related to a specific competency-based curriculum. Figure 10–8 provides an example of an alternative grading system designed for an individual student enrolled in a community education program.

Regardless of the level and type of modification made, the IEP committee should define the modification on the IEP before implementation. In addition, the rationale for the modification should be clearly established either on the IEP or in the minutes of the meeting. As noted earlier, it is inappropriate to modify the grading system simply because the student is enrolled in special education. Providing a clearly stated justification on which the committee's decision is based can assist teachers and parents to understand the reasons for and the parameters of the modifications made. The parents must be fully informed of the modified or alternative plan and must have the opportunity to contribute to the determination that the proposal is in the best interest of their child.

MONITORING IEPs, BASED ON EVALUATION OF GOALS AND OBJECTIVES

Evaluation of goals and objectives constitutes a means of monitoring the IEP. Documenting student progress is directly related to the monitoring process because such documentation serves as a major source of information in making decisions about potential program changes. If the student is not making the projected gains, effort should be made to identify and eliminate the barriers to student progress.

Systematic evaluation can also provide data on the appropriateness of the IEP developed by the committee and competencies of teachers related to implementation of the IEP. If the teacher feels the student is not making progress commensurate with that projected, the teacher should consider the quality of procedures used to develop the IEP. Perhaps the responsibilities of the committee members were not well defined during planning, or the placement decision for the student was inappropriate. Such procedural weaknesses in developing IEPs are quite often reflected in low attainment of students.

Monitoring student progress provides an opportunity to document whether anticipated gains are being made. This documentation can be used as a basis for modifying the IEP based on discrepant findings and also as a guide in developing the student's IEP for the next academic year. Perhaps the most important outcome of monitoring student progress is pinpointing the factors that are impeding progress, in the case of delayed gains, and enhancing progress, in the case of unanticipated acceleration. Again, the purpose of compiling this documentation is to eliminate barriers and build on success.

Interviewing Students

In addition to evaluating student progress toward achievement of stated goals and objectives, the IEP committee might also choose to interview students and teachers to obtain additional insight into student progress. The IEP committee can gain useful insight on student performance and interfering problems from talking directly with the student. An interview might include the following questions:

1. What lessons did you cover yesterday in class?
   a. How much do you believe you learned?
   b. Did you ever feel "lost" during class?
   c. Did you understand what the teacher expected of you?
   d. Did you need extra help to complete your assignments?
   e. Were you provided with extra help? By whom?
   f. If you were going to assign yourself a grade for the work you did yesterday, what grade would you assign?
2. What are your best subjects in school? Why do you think you do your best in these subjects?
3. What are your weakest subjects? What seems to cause the problems in these subjects?
4. If you could change anything about your school day, what would it be?

FIGURE 10–8
Sample Alternative Grading Procedure

INDIVIDUAL EDUCATION PROGRAM:
ALTERNATIVE MODIFICATION TO GRADING PROCEDURE

Rationale

The IEP committee has determined that a life-skills curriculum, including participation in community-based instruction, most suits Jerry's educational needs. Further, the committee decided that the instructional goals required for a standard high school diploma do not adequately address Jerry's educational needs. The committee determined that a standard grading format was incompatible with the curricular goals of Jerry's program; thus, an alternative format was designed.

Description of Grading Procedure

The reporting system will include a listing of the short-term objectives, which consist of competency-based performance objectives, the criteria for mastery, and a space for coded notation of student performance. The notation system consists of four codes (A, P, M, R) to document achievement, progression toward, maintenance of, or regression from a specific objective.

Example: Objective   Grading Period

Using a grocery list containing at least 10 familiar generic   1 2 3 4
items, Jerry will, within 20 minutes, scan the aisles and
locate the items independently, and put all items in the
grocery cart as they are located.

                            Criterion
At least 8 of 10 items in 5 trials in 2 stores

Progress summaries will be prepared at the same reporting intervals as the general education program (each 9 weeks). A standard report card jacket will be used to send the progress report to the parents.

Grading System:
A = Achieved Skill
P = Progressing, showing improvement
M = Maintaining, retaining skills without regression
R = Regressing, declining in skill level

The following documentation of the alternative grading system was added to Jerry's IEP:
As a result of Jerry's participation in a non-diploma program consisting of a life-skills curriculum, the standard grading format cannot communicate Jerry's individual performance objectives. Therefore, an alternative system for reporting progress was developed. The alternative system evaluates student progress toward attainment of specific instructional objectives. Each objective will be evaluated on an ongoing basis. A summary of student performance will be communicated to the parents every 9 weeks. A notation system of A-achieving, P-progressing, M-maintaining, and R-regressing, will record student progress. The grading system will be monitored by the IEP committee following each 9-week grading period. Modifications will be made as necessary.

IEP Committee Members

Parents_____   Agency Representative_____
Teacher_____   Other _____
Student_____   _____

5. What does your teacher do that helps you the most?
6. What does your teacher do that sometimes confuses you?
7. What causes you to get in trouble at school?
8. Who are your closest friends? Why did you choose them for friends?
9. What makes you happy when you are with your classmates?
10. What makes you angry when you are with your classmates?
11. What can your teachers and friends do to help you improve your school work?

Student responses should be recorded. An analysis of these responses can pinpoint problems that might be interfering with the student's progress. For example, if a student states in response to question 6 that her teacher makes assignments in books she cannot read, leaves her out of group work, and excessively scolds her in front of the class, she is providing insight into possible sources of the problem. The IEP committee should then document these findings through classroom observation and teacher interviews.

Students with various types of disabilities frequently can identify sources of problems they are having that teachers may have never considered. For example, a student with a visual disability may be able to identify that purple ditto sheets are more difficult to read than any other type of printed material to the point of being barely legible, yet the student may feel hesitant in expressing this to the teacher in an unsolicited fashion. A monitoring strat-

egy that encourages students to speak out can identify many such problems that can be relatively simple to overcome.

Interviewing Teachers and Parents

Teachers and parents likewise can be valuable sources of information regarding assessing student progress and analyzing the source of problems. Sometimes formal evaluation of the progress of students on the IEP objectives may indicate only marginal gains, yet the perceptions of the teacher and parents may be very different. Teachers and parents may believe that substantial gains have been made in areas not precisely covered on the IEP that may be as important or more important than, for instance, the science objectives. These gains could be related to improved peer relationships, self-concept, attitudes toward school, or work habits. Interviews need to cover the full spectrum of the student's school day and adjustment, rather than considering the IEP the singular basis for determining progress. Individual students should be the focus of interviews with questions pertaining to their strengths, weaknesses, areas of improvement, areas of needed concentration, and any special problems. Information from an interview of this nature may suggest that the IEP committee needs to reconvene to consider a change in placement, revision of the IEP, or solutions to documented problems. The important point is that program review and modification, based on data gathered during the monitoring process, are to enhance the progress of the student.

SUMMARY

This chapter has discussed the requirements related to the evaluation of the goals and objectives included on the IEP and provided strategies for ongoing evaluation of student progress. The discussion of IEPs has thus far focused on determining the starting point for specially designed instruction (levels of performance), identifying the curriculum that will be taught (goals and objectives), and determining objective criteria for evaluating progress toward attainment of objectives (evaluation of goals and objectives). If a student requires additional services to enable her to benefit from special education, related services must be identified and included on the IEP. The next chapter will provide guidelines for inclusion of related services on the IEP.

EVALUATION

1. This is your first year as special education coordinator in a local school system. You have found that no provision has been made for evaluating IEPs in the system. You decide to have an inservice meeting to acquaint all teachers with the legal requirements pertaining to the evaluation of the IEP and to give them suggestions to consider in evaluation. Outline your suggestions for determining objective evaluation criteria and appropriate evaluation procedures.

2. Discuss the importance of considering the nature of the objective, time requirements, and student characteristics when determining procedures for evaluating progress toward goals and objectives on the IEP.

3. The teachers in your secondary school are looking for ways to document the progress of students other than the usual weekly testing procedures. Suggest four alternative methods of documenting progress, and state the advantages and disadvantages of each.

4. Conduct a survey in your school to determine how grading procedures for students with disabilities are modified and documented. Develop suggestions for alternative grading systems based on the needs of the student.

5. Discuss the use of interviews with parents, students, and teachers as a mechanism for monitoring student progress on IEP goals and objectives.

CHAPTER 11

Documentation and Provision Of Related Services

OBJECTIVES

1. Define related services regarding their relationshiop to special education services.
2. Identify and discuss issues related to the provision of related services.
3. Discuss three criteria for determining when related services are necessary.
4. Provide examples of related services often provided by schools.
5. Discuss four service-delivery models for providing related services.

Often, the provision of a free appropriate public education requires more than just the adaptation of the educational program that will be provided to the student with a disability. P.L. 94–142 therefore provides not only for the provision of specially designed instruction to address the unique instructional needs of students with disabilities but also requires the provision of any related services that are necessary for the student to benefit from the special education provided. P.L. 94–142 has defined related services as follows:

> ... transportation and such developmental, corrective, and other appropriate supportive services as are required to assist a handicapped child to benefit from special education, and includes speech pathology and audiology, psychological services, physical and occupational therapy, recreation, early identification and assessment of disabilities in children, counseling services, and medical services for diagnostic or evaluation purposes. The term also includes school health services, social work services in schools, and parent counseling and training. (*Federal Register*, 1977)

Figure 11–1 provides a description of related services that may be necessary to enable some students with disabilities to benefit from their special education programs. This list is not exhaustive and could include such services as art, music, and dance therapy, if they are necessary to assist the student to benefit from special education. This chapter will discuss issues surrounding the provision of related services, criteria for the IEP committee in determining the need for related services, guidelines for determining the type and extent of services required, and service-delivery and payment options.

ISSUES CONCERNING THE PROVISION OF RELATED SERVICES

Determining whether a student requires related services can be difficult because specific legal criteria for making such a determination are lacking. Primary issues regarding the provision of these services include (1) the level and scope of services that must be provided to enable a student to benefit from the educational program provided, (2) the lack of definitive explanation regarding what services are and are not included as related services, and (3) which students with disabilities are and are not entitled to receive related services. Each of these issues will be discussed briefly.

Level and Scope of Services to Be Provided

Although the term *appropriate* is a central theme throughout P.L. 94–142, the legislation itself provides little insight into its meaning regarding the level and scope of services that might be considered sufficiently appropriate for a given student. Thus, criteria used to determine which students should receive what services are inconsistent among states and school systems.

The Supreme Court has provided some preliminary clarification on the definition of the term *appropriate* in its interpretation in *Board of Education of the Hendrick Hudson Central School District v. Rowley* (1982). In this case, the court determined that the provision of an interpreter as a related service for a student who cannot hear was not required to provide an appropriate educational program, because the student was "benefiting" from the existing program, as was evidenced by average or above-

FIGURE 11–1
Related Services in Special Education

Audiology	(a) Identification of children with hearing loss;
	(b) Determination of the range, nature, degree of hearing loss, including referral for medical or other professional attention for the habilitation of hearing;
	(c) Provision of habilitative activities, such as language habilitation, auditory training, speech reading (lip reading), hearing evaluation, and speech conservation;
	(d) Creation and administration of programs for prevention of hearing loss;
	(e) Counseling and guidance of pupils, parents, and teachers regarding hearing loss; and
	(f) Determination of the child's need for group and individual amplification, selecting and fitting an appropriate aid, and evaluating the effectiveness of amplification.
Counseling Services	Services provided by qualified social workers, psychologists, guidance counselors, or other qualified personnel.
Early Identification	Implementation of a formal plan for identifying a disability as early as possible in a child's life.
Medical Services	Services provided by a licensed physician to determine a child's medically related handicapping condition which results in the child's need for special education and related services.
Occupational Therapy	(a) Improving, developing, or restoring functions impaired or lost through illness, injury, or deprivation;
	(b) Improving ability to perform tasks for independent functioning when functions are impaired or lost; and
	(c) Preventing, through early intervention, initial or further impairment or loss of function.
Parent Counseling and Training	Assisting parents in understanding the special needs of their child and providing parents with information about child development.
Physical Therapy	Services provided by a qualified physical therapist.
Psychological Services	(a) Administering psychological and educational tests, and other assessment procedures;
	(b) Interpreting assessment results;
	(c) Obtaining, integrating, and interpreting information about child behavior and conditions relating to learning.
	(d) Consulting with other staff members in planning school programs to meet the special needs of children as indicated by psychological tests, interviews, and behavioral evaluations; and
	(e) Planning and managing a program of psychological services, including psychological counseling for children and parents.
Recreation	(a) Assessment of leisure function;
	(b) Therapeutic recreation services;
	(c) Recreation programs in schools and community agencies; and
	(d) Leisure education.
School Health Services	Services provided by a qualified school nurse or other qualified person.
Social Work Services	(a) Preparing a social or developmental history on a handicapped child;
	(b) Group and individual counseling with the child and family;
	(c) Working with those problems in a child's living situation (home, school, and community) that affect the child's adjustment in school; and
	(d) Mobilizing school and community resources to enable the child to receive maximum benefit from his or her educational program.
Speech Pathology	(a) Identification of children with speech or language disorders;
	(b) Diagnosis and appraisal of specific speech or language disorders;
	(c) Referral for medical or other professional attention necessary for the habilitation of speech or language disorders;
	(d) Provisions of speech and language services for the habilitation or prevention of communicative disorders; and
	(e) Counseling and guidance of parents, children, and teachers regarding speech and language disorders.
Transportation	(a) Travel to and from school and between schools;
	(b) Travel in and around school buildings; and
	(c) Specialized equipment (such as special or adapted buses, lifts, and ramps), if required to provide special transportation for a handicapped child.

From the *Federal Register*, August 23, 1977, *42* (163).

average progress in the classroom, and because the school had demonstrated that access to comparable educational opportunity had been provided to the student. With this decision, the Supreme Court confirmed that the intent of P.L. 94–142 is not to guarantee *optimal* services to a student with a disability but to provide *reasonable* opportunity for that student to participate in and benefit from the educational program provided by the school. The generalizability of this decision, however, is limited. The student in this case was enrolled in the regular classroom and was progressing in an average manner. It is difficult to know how the decision would apply to a student enrolled in a special education program and performing well below average, as is true of many students with disabilities (Turnbull, 1986).

Services Included and Not Included As Related Services

P.L. 94–142 defines related services as any service necessary for a student to benefit from special education, except those that must be provided by a physician. The exclusion of services provided by a physician is the element of the definition that has provided the basis for controversy in determining which services are and are not included as related services.

In some instances, the services that can be provided by someone other than a physician differ among states, depending on state licensure requirements. For example, in some states, only licensed psychiatrists or psychologists can provide psychotherapy. In other states, social workers, counselors, and other professionals can be trained and licensed to provide this service. In states where a psychiatrist must provide psychotherapy, the school is not required to provide psychotherapy. In states where other professionals may provide the service, psychotherapy may be considered a related service, if it is necessary for the student to benefit from special education. Thus, related services might be more appropriately defined by who provides the service rather than by the type of service itself (Vitello, 1986).

The courts have also provided additional clarification on services that must be provided by a physician. In *Irving Independent School District v. Tatro* (1984), the Supreme Court required that the school provide a student who had spina bifida with clean intermittent catheterization (CIC) as a related service to enable that student to attend the educational program available in the public school. The decision affirmed that CIC is a related service that can be performed by a lay person, rather than a medical procedure, which can only be performed by

a physician. As such, it is a procedure that must be provided to a student if that procedure is necessary to enable the student to come to school, participate in, and benefit from the educational program.

In similar decisions, schools have been required to provide such related services as an air-conditioned room for a student who could not regulate his own body temperature (*Espino v. Besteiro*, 1981), and maintenace of a tracheostomy tube (*Hawaii Department of Education v. Katherine D.*, 1983) to ensure access to special education services. These decisions clarify the intention of P.L. 94–142 that related services may be any service required to enable a student with a disability to attend school and participate in the educational program, provided that service does not have to be provided by a physician.

Who is Entitled to Receive Services

The provision of related services, by law, is inextricably tied to the provision of special education. As the definition indicates, related services are those services necessary for a student to benefit from special education. This means that only those students whose disability adversely affects educational performance and who require specially designed instruction are entitled to receive related services (*Federal Register*, 1977). Even if the IEP committee can agree that the student meets these criteria, agreement must still be reached on whether the service is necessary for the student to benefit from special education.

Differences in the way school systems define the terms *adverse effect* and *specially designed instruction* determine who will receive special education and thus who will receive related services. A study of the implementation of P.L. 94–142 (Education Turnkey Systems, 1981) found extreme variations in the way states defined and delivered related services, with the most indicative determinant being the level of state funds appropriated for special education. Thus, the wealthier the school system, the broader the criteria and the greater the level of related services provided.

The wealth of the school system may prove to be a determining issue in the provision of related services to increasing numbers of students who rely on daily specialized nursing procedures (Palfrey, DiPrete, Walker, Shannon, & Maroney, 1987). As technology increases the options for community-based living, these students are increasingly being presented to the public schools for enrollment. Because support services for students with medical dependency can be very expensive, the courts, in some instances, have begun to address the parameters of appropriate services in terms of expense. *Irving Independent School District v. Tatro* (1984) addressed this issue by indicating that the specific exclusion of medical services from the definition of related services was to protect schools from assuming responsibility for costly medical care. It might be expected then, that future definition of related services may focus on inordinate cost as a factor for limiting the responsibility of schools to provide some related services, even though cost has been specifically excluded as an issue in the past.

Finally, issues have arisen regarding the provision of related services to students with chronic and physical disabilities when the student does not receive special education. In some instances, students do have confirmed and legitimate disabilities but do not appear to require specially designed instruction in the traditional sense. Students with physical and health impairments are most frequently in this situation. Without proper support services, the disability could seriously limit participation in school programs. For example, a student with severe asthma may not require specially designed instruction in the sense that the academic program must be modified on an ongoing basis. The student, however, may require that the school have established emergency procedures in the event of an asthma attack. Because this student may not receive special education, a dilemma arises as to whether the student is entitled to receive services under P.L. 94–142 or whether such an accommodation would depend on the availability of existing resources in the regular program.

IEP COMMITTEE CONSIDERATION OF APPROPRIATE RELATED SERVICES

The decision to provide necessary related services is the responsibility of the IEP committee, based on the evaluation results and recommendations of the multidisciplinary evaluation team, including qualified related services providers. If the committee determines that the student does require related services, the committee must determine the type of service, the extent of services to be provided, and the service-delivery model to be employed. Often, recommendations regarding the student's needs are made by professionals other than those employed by the school. For example, a parent may obtain an independent evaluation that indicates that a particular student requires occupational therapy provided directly to the student twice a week. Although it is helpful to be aware of the recommendations of other profes-

sionals, and P.L. 94–142 requires that the school consider any independent evaluation in its determination of the services that will actually be provided to the student, this is a group decision and is based not on whether the service is one that may benefit the student but on whether the service is necessary for the student to benefit from the educational program provided.

Attendance at the IEP Meeting

Although certainly appropriate and preferable at times, attendance at the IEP meeting is not required of related services providers. The obvious advantage of having related services personnel at the IEP meeting is to facilitate the development of an integrated method of service delivery. Meeting together enables cooperative planning toward common goals for the student with less opportunity for misinterpretation and loss of information. Related services providers are available to explain, in detail, the nature of the proposed service and answer any questions from parents or other committee members. When many related services are involved, however, full representation may make the size of the IEP meeting unmanageable, create scheduling problems, and perhaps be somewhat threatening to parents. For example, in making specially designed instruction available to a student with a hearing disability, provision of one or all of the following related services may be necessary: audiological evaluation; auditory training; counseling of students, parents, and teachers; individual and group amplification; psychological services, and speech therapy.

Written Recommendations

Securing written recommendations before the meeting provides an alternative to the presence of service providers at the meeting. The obvious advantage of this procedure is that it reduces the number of people at the committee meeting and avoids scheduling problems, which may often cause lengthy delays in meetings. In addition, the committee can use the written proposal as a basis for discussion and determination of appropriate services. The disadvantage of this procedure is that the related services provider is not present to discuss the recommendations and suggestions with committee members who are developing the IEP or to determine how related services can best be provided to enhance the special education program designed for the student. If a question arises that cannot be answered by the committee members present, another meeting may have to be conducted to discuss the proposed service with the service provider.

Determining Related Services
After the IEP Meeting

Obtaining input from service providers after the IEP meeting and reconvening the committee to finalize the arrangements for related services is a procedure that, while not alone sufficient, has some distinct advantages. Because related services are often essential to the successful education of a student with disabilities, it may be advantageous to determine what special education is necessary and where it will be provided before determining what related services are required. Once the educational program has been determined, the service providers may be better able to determine the nature and extent of necessary related services. The obvious disadvantage of this procedure is that two meetings would be necessary. In addition, for some students, related services may make up the primary element of the special education program. Thus, omitting related services providers from the initial IEP meeting may result in inadequate program planning.

CRITERIA FOR DETERMINING WHETHER
RELATED SERVICES ARE NECESSARY

Despite vague criteria, the IEP committee must often determine when a related service is necessary for a student to benefit from special education. Based on the information provided at the IEP meeting, the committee might apply the following criteria as a starting point:

1. Is the student receiving specially designed instruction (special education)?
2. Is the related service necessary for the student to benefit from special education?
3. Could the related service in question be provided by someone other than a licensed physician?

Receiving Specially Designed Instruction

If the student is receiving no specially designed instruction, there can be no related service, because by definition, related services are designed to support the specially designed instruction that a student receives. As noted earlier, this distinction is clear in some instances, but difficult to interpret in others. For example, it is relatively clear that if a student is difficult to manage in school, but no serious emotional

disturbance has been confirmed, that student is not entitled to special education in most states and therefore is not entitled to counseling or other related services. Although counseling may be provided as part of the regular program, the student would not be entitled to services under P.L. 94–142. Less clear is the case noted earlier, when a student has a legitimate disability but may not be enrolled in a special education program. To ensure that students receive the services to which they are entitled, the IEP committee should keep in mind the following three aspects of the definition of special education, on which the provision of related services depends.

Not Necessarily in Separate Program. First, it must be emphasized that special education means specially designed instruction not necessarily placement in a special education classroom. Regardless of where it takes place, instruction might be considered to be specially designed if the adaptations necessary to accommodate a student are (1) significantly different from adaptations routinely or normally expected or made for other students in that setting and (2) if the adaptations are necessary to offset or reduce the adverse effect of the disability on educational performance. The first criterion has little to do with the difficulty of the adaptation or whether it is possible to provide the adaptation in the regular classroom. Regardless of the complexity of the adaptation, it may be considered specially designed if it is different from that normally provided to other students. For example, a student with a hearing disability may require preferential seating and a written outline or notes. These may be adaptations that are not provided to all students as a matter of course but are certainly specially designed instruction that can be provided in the classroom. Another student may require adaptations that cannot be provided in the regular classroom. For example, a student with a congenital heart disorder may require a rest period during the day. In both instances the adaptation may be considered specially designed.

The second (and determining) criterion emphasizes that, in the case of a student with a disability, the specially designed or adapted instruction must be necessary to offset or reduce the adverse effect of the disability on educational performance. Thus, for specially designed instruction to qualify as special education, the special adaptations made in a classroom for a student with a disability must be necessary. In the example of a student with a hearing disability, preferential seating and written outlines and notes are considered specially designed instruction because they are not, as a matter of routine, provided to all students and because without these specially designed adaptations, the student could not participate equally in the class. Thus, these adaptations may be considered special education because they are necessary to offset or reduce the effect of the disability on the student's educational performance. This student would be eligible for related services if needed.

Includes All Areas of the Educational Program.   The second point to be made about the definition of special education is that it includes all areas of the educational program not just the academic portion. As such, any student with a diagnosed disability who requires specially designed instruction only in physical education, for instance, should not be considered ineligible for special education. Physical education and vocational education are both as much a part of the educational program as reading, math, and language and should be considered as such in determining a student's eligibility for special education.

Thus, if a student with a confirmed disability requires special consideration in seating, adaptive physical education, and adaptations in vocational training, these necessary adaptations may be considered specially designed instruction. Necessary related services such as physical therapy would then be provided to support the specially designed instruction provided to the student.

Related Services May Be Considered Special Education.   The third and final point to be made regarding the definition of special education and related services is that a related service can be considered special education under standards established by individual states. Those services that consist of specially designed instruction to meet the unique needs of a student with a disability, and that are provided at no cost to the parent, may in some cases meet the criteria for both related services and special education (*Federal Register,* 1977). Speech therapy is an example of a service that may be defined as special education, or as a related service, or as both. If a student has a speech disability and displays no other disability, then the provision of speech therapy may be considered special education rather than a related service. Likewise, if a student has a physical disability that has an adverse effect on ability to move about or participate in physical education or other aspects of the educational program, physical therapy may be viewed as the special education provided, rather than a related service. In such a case the physical therapist would, in fact, be providing the specially designed instruction.

If the IEP committee determines that a student does not have a disability, or that there is a disability but there is no adverse effect on educational performance, the student would not be eligible for special education and thus not entitled to related services. Likewise, if the IEP committee decides that the student is eligible for special education but that no additional services are necessary for the student to benefit, the student would not be entitled to related services.

It should be pointed out that the school is not responsible for the provision of related services not related to, or necessary for, the student to benefit from the educational program. For example, a student may have a serious emotional disturbance but be progressing adequately at school in a specially designed program of instruction. The student may not, however, be managing well at home or in the community. In such a case the student may require and receive psychotherapy from a source other than the school. The school, however, would not be responsible for paying for this or other services necessary to address the problems that the student is having at home.

Necessary to Benefit from Special Education

The second criterion that the IEP committee should consider in determining whether a student requires related services is whether it is necessary for the student to benefit from special education. Both *Board of Education of the Hendrick Hudson Central School District v. Rowley* (1982) and *Irving Independent School District v. Tatro* (1984) recognize that to be provided, a related service must be necessary for the student to benefit from the educational program. These cases, however, deal with situations that, regarding this criterion, seem clear-cut compared to most cases in the schools. In the *Rowley* case, the student was enrolled in a regular classroom and clearly was realizing benefit without an interpreter. In the *Tatro* case, the student clearly would be unable to benefit or even attend school without related services.

For many students, it may be difficult to establish that a related service is, in fact, necessary for the student to benefit from the program provided. For example, is language therapy necessary for a student with a learning disability that affects the area of reading and expressive language? Or is occupational therapy necessary for a preschool student with a poor pencil grip or inability to dress independently? As noted earlier, the degree to which related services are determined to be necessary often appears to depend on the level of services available in the school system (Education Turnkey Systems, 1981). For example, school districts with ample speech and language services may provide speech and language as a related service to a greater extent than a system whose resources are limited. Related services may also vary, depending on the composition of IEP committees and the political strength within the school system of the professional group delivering the services (Singer & Butler, 1987).

Nonmedical Services, Excluding Those For Diagnosis and Evaluation

Although the list of possible related services is not exhaustive, services are limited to those that are not medical, except for medical services necessary to evaluate or diagnose a disability. This means that if a licensed physician must provide a particular service, it is considered a medical service rather than a related service and is therefore not an entitlement of P.L. 94–142. As noted earlier, state laws differ regarding who can provide certain services. The IEP committee is advised to determine what licensing standards exist in their state to distinguish between medical and related services. As reflected by *Irving Independent School District v. Tatro* (1984), students who may require specialized health services are increasingly found in public schools. Thus, there is an increasing need to ensure adequate availability and training of health personnel.

TYPES OF RELATED SERVICES MOST OFTEN PROVIDED

Obviously, not all students with disabilities require related services to benefit from their special educational program. For example, a student with a mild learning disability may need only minor adjustments in provision of the educational program. When the IEP does not indicate that related services are necessary for a student to benefit from special education, the student is not entitled to receive those services at school expense.

Schools appear to be providing the majority of speech therapy, occupational therapy, physical therapy, and counseling services that students with disabilities receive (Palfrey, Singer, Raphael, & Walker, 1987; U.S. Department of Education, 1987). Although the list of possible related services is not exhaustive, some related services tend to be provided more often than others, and appear to represent the majority of expenditures for related services. These services include transportation, speech therapy, occupational and physical therapy, student counseling, medical diagnosis of various disabilities, and school nursing services (Singer & Butler, 1987). Because these services represent those most often provided, each will be discussed briefly below.

Transportation

Not all students with disabilities require special transportation. When the IEP committee determines, however, that transportation by usual or conventional means is inappropriate because of the nature and/or severity of the student's disability, special transportation may be warranted. The specific transportation requirements should be included on the IEP. For example, if the committee determines that the student must be transported with a seat harness and an aide to manage behavior, these requirements should be included and agreed upon by all committee members including the parents.

In determining the need for special transportation, the IEP committee should ensure that the determination is based on the nature and severity of the student's disability and not on the basis of administrative convenience. It is inappropriate to deny a student access to the same transportation system used by other students if the student can reasonably and safely be transported by those means. Transportation of the student to and from school represents a part of the educational program, and as such, its determination should be based both on the principle of least restriction and on appropriateness.

Special transportation may be required in several instances. First, the nature and severity of the disability may be such that transportation by conventional means is dangerous and inappropriate. For example, it is inappropriate for a student who uses a wheelchair to ride a conventional school bus unless that bus has a lift and wheelchair accommodation inside. For such a student, a modified van or bus appropriately equipped might be used. Second, special transportation might be provided for students who are too young to ride the school bus unattended. Many school systems provide special vans, buses, or even taxicabs for preschool students with disabilities, or provide aides to attend these students on the school bus. Third, special transportation might be provided if a student's behavior or intellectual functioning makes transportation by usual means inappropriate. Again, in these instances, special buses or even taxicabs may be used with aides often employed to accompany students to school and home.

As illustrated in Figure 11–1, transportation includes not only transportation to and from school but also any necessary transportation in and around school buildings and to and from any service provided as part of the student's educational program. In addition, if a student would normally walk to school, but the nature of the disability makes walking dangerous or inappropriate, the school is responsible for providing appropriate transportation for the student. The school system is also responsible for transportation of students placed by the school system in schools other than the one they would normally attend. For example, if a student is placed in a private day school, transportation must be provided on the same basis as if the student attended the local school. Likewise, if a student is placed in a residential school, the local school system is responsible for all transportation costs to and from the facility, transportation on holidays, and other transportation as decided on a case by case basis.

Finally, if should be emphasized that parents cannot be held responsible for transporting their child to and from school. In some instances, schools may make arrangements with willing parents to provide transportation for which the parents are reimbursed. Parents, however, are not obligated to provide this service. Even when agreements are made with parents to transport students, schools are advised to arrange appropriate backup transportation for the student.

Speech Therapy

Speech and language therapy is one of the therapeutic support services most often provided to students with disabilities (U.S. Department of Education, 1988). Most schools have their own speech and language programs, many of which are well developed, enabling comparatively ample services to students. Speech therapy might be provided as a related service when a student has a disability that interferes with the student's receptive and expressive language abilities or when the student has a related articulation, fluency, or voice-quality disability, which may affect the student's ability to benefit from the educational program.

Occupational Therapy

Occupational therapy programs in the public schools have evolved from a medically oriented model of providing a multitude of services to a wide variety of persons with physical and mental disabilities to a program designed specifically for students whose disability adversely affects educational performance in school. Occupational therapy focuses on improving, developing, or restoring functions impaired or lost through illness, injury, or deprivation (*Federal Register*, 1977). Specific programs might include training in gross and fine motor skills, organizing and using materials appropriately, improving coordination skills, and learning to dress or to feed oneself.

Occupational therapy is provided to enhance students' abilities to adapt to and function in educational programs. . . . The primary goal of occupational therapy in carrying out the mandates of the law is to offer students the predetermined services that will improve their ability to adapt, thus enhancing their potential for learning. Occupational therapy services must, therefore, have a direct impact on the students' abilities to learn and benefit from their educational programs. (American Occupational Therapy Association, 1981)

Like other related services, occupational therapy programs in schools are available only to those students who have a diagnosed disability that also adversely affects educational performance. Similar to other related services such as speech therapy, this exclusionary criterion is often controversial in schools because many students who might benefit but do not meet the criterion are excluded. Examples of conditions that may not be considered disabling from an educational perspective might include clumsiness, scoliosis, traumatic injury to nerves or muscles of the hand, mild cerebral palsy, an amputee who is independent in the use of his prosthesis, or any child who has reached maximum benefit from therapy (American Occupational Therapy Association, 1987).

Physical Therapy

When the unique physical needs of a student with a disability interfere with his educational performance, physical therapy may be provided as a related service. As more students with physical disabilities have enrolled in public schools, the demand for physical therapy has increased significantly. Like occupational therapy, physical therapy in schools has evolved from a clinical emphasis to an emphasis on the development of functional skills to enable a student with a disability to participate in and benefit from the educational program. In theory, physical therapy focuses on motor development and functional activities such as positioning, handling, sitting, lifting and transferring, and ambulation, while occupational therapy tends to focus on functional activities such as dressing, hygiene, self-feeding, and methods of nonverbal communication. In educational practice, however, these programs are often provided as one service focusing on the integration of services to the student with a disability. Thus, the delineation on an IEP that a student receives "OT/PT" is not unusual. However, unlike occupational therapy in most states, physical therapy can be provided only on referral from a physician.

Because of the increased demand for therapeutic services for students with disabilities, a major issue in providing physical and occupational therapy to students is the availability of therapists. Even more problematic is the scarcity of therapists trained in pediatric therapy and familiar with therapeutic programs in public schools.

Counseling

The related services provisions of P.L. 94–142 provide for counseling in a variety of contexts. One of the most often provided counseling services (and one of the most controversial) is the provision of direct therapeutic counseling services to students with disabilities (Osbourne, 1984). A large number of students may well receive counseling services from resources already available in the school, such as counselors, social workers, or school psychologists. In addition, as noted earlier, some states provide psychotherapy licensure for counselors and social workers. In these states, psychotherapy may be considered a related service. Other areas of counseling delineated as related services by P.L. 94–142, such as counseling of parents regarding their child's special needs and counseling of teachers regarding various disorders and their accommodation in the classroom, appear to occur at a minimal level.

Medical Services for Evaluation And Diagnosis

As noted earlier, P.L. 94–142 includes the provision of medical services for evaluation and diagnosis. Ongoing treatment or other medical services, however, are specifically excluded. Because the responsibility of the public school does not extend to the medical treatment a student may receive, ongoing communication between medical and school personnel would seem imperative to ensure continuity between the medical treatment program and the school's educational program. Yet research indicates that direct and coordinated collaboration between physicians and school personnel is minimal (Palfrey, Singer, Walker, & Butler, 1986). Because medical personnel are seldom paid by the school system for student consultations, there are few incentives or rewards for physicians to participate in educational planning. In addition, communication barriers continue to exist in terms of the information that professionals in each field want from one another (Palfrey, Singer, Walker, et al., 1986).

The school can enhance communication between the student's medical and educational program by improving school personnel's presentation of information to and request of information from medical professionals. When referrals are made or information requested, the reason for the referral should be clearly stated in terms of functional statements that provide a basis for the school's concern. In some instances referrals may request information such as "a neurological examination" as part of an evaluation for a student with a learning disability without any indication of what question such an evaluation is supposed to answer. In other instances, referrals to medical facilities for evaluation may request medical professionals to make eligibility determinations by asking if the student "qualifies for special education." In making referrals for medical evaluation and diagnosis, it is appropriate to provide functional information about the student that provides a basis for referral. The referral should request medical information in functional statements. For example, referral questions might include questions such as "Does the student have a health disability? What is it and what are the potential adverse effects on educational performance? Could the diagnosed health disability cause or be related to the school-related observations included in the referral? Are there classroom considerations that must be considered in programming for this student?"

School Health Services

As the area of school health services is increasingly redefined to include services that at one time were considered to be medical procedures, the provision of services is becoming increasingly controversial. The distinction between medical and health services remains problematic despite preliminary clarification on specific issues such as those addressed in *Irving Independent School District v. Tatro* (1984). P.L. 94–142 defines medical and health services only in terms of who provides the service, without adequate definition of the criteria to be used in distinguishing between related and medical services. Even though the role of school health personnel is changing dramatically, states have yet to establish substantive guidelines for nursing procedures in schools. Examples of services that have been the focus of controversy include catheterization, suctioning, care of tracheostomies, and various forms of counseling, including psychotherapy. In the absence of clear federal guidelines, policy regarding health-related services is being developed in the courts and through due process hearings.

The need for some related services is not as clear-cut as it is for others. For example, it is often simpler to agree that a student with a physical disability needs physical therapy than it is to agree that the parents need counseling to understand the special needs of their child. When the necessity of a related service is disputed among committee members, every effort should be made to negotiate a settlement agreeable to all members. When this is not possible, the issue may be settled by mediation or due process procedures.

DELINEATION OF RELATED SERVICES ON THE IEP

Because related services are considered to be a part of the specially designed instruction provided to a student with a disability, the goals and objectives for these services should be included as part of the student's IEP. Goals and objectives should be developed following the same general guidelines included in Chapter 9. Three additional points, however, should be emphasized regarding delineation of related services on the IEP. The IEP committee should ensure that the related services to be provided are (1) clearly identified and defined, (2) incorporated into one IEP for the student, and (3) are designed to support the goals and objectives of the educational program.

Clear Definition

Unless the related service determined to be necessary is clearly specified on the IEP, it may be difficult for individuals unfamiliar with the student's program to determine specifically what services are to be provided. Often, the goals and objectives of special education services and related services are similar, with the primary difference being the service provider, the method of intervention, or the level of service. For example, a preschool student with a disability may have IEP goals and objectives focusing on dressing and feeding. Depending on the needs of the student and the way that the program is provided, goals and objectives in these areas might be provided by either the teacher or an occupational therapist. However, whether the student actually receives services from an occupational therapist depends on how the IEP committee determines that these needs must be addressed. Similarly, an adaptive physical education program may have goals similar to those of a related services program of physical therapy. Because a teacher of adaptive physical education is not usually licensed as a physical therapist, that individual is not qualified to provide the related service of physical therapy. Clearly identifying which elements of the IEP are related services can also greatly enhance the continuity of services among schools and from year to year for a specific student.

Incorporation in the Existing IEP

As noted earlier, the program of related services that a student receives is part of the specially designed instructional program provided to a student. The goals and objectives developed for related services must therefore be incorporated into the same IEP as the goals and objectives developed for rest of the student's program. Thus, speech therapy should not have a separate IEP if the student also receives specially designed instruction in other aspects of the educational program. Detailed intervention plans that may not normally be a part of the IEP may be developed and maintained by the service provider. In addition, and again because they are one plan, related services components and educational components of the IEP should be reviewed together at the annual review.

Designed to Support the Educational Program's Goals and Objectives

Related services provided in public schools are designed specifically to assist the student in achieving the educational goals established and to enable the student to participate to the maximum extent appropriate in the least restrictive educational setting. As such, related services goals and objectives should clearly focus on the student's educational needs and should be stated so that they reflect that relationship. For example, goals and objectives established for speech therapy should indicate how achievement of those goals and objectives will help the student benefit from the special education program.

The provision of an appropriate educational program depends not only on the identification of necessary related services but also on the appropriate provision of services necessary to make the program appropriate. The IEP committee may recommend, for example, that a student with a hearing disability be placed in the regular classroom and that the classroom teacher receive counseling and guidance, which is part of the related service of audiology. Unless the classroom teacher actually receives the consultation necessary, the regular classroom may be an inappropriate placement. When decisions regarding related services are made, the IEP committee must ensure that the necessary services are available and procedures for provision of those services are established. The representative of the public agency, a required member of the IEP committee, is responsible for committing the resources of the school system to the provision of necessary services to students.

EXTENT OF RELATED SERVICES

In addition to a statement of the specific services to be provided, the IEP should also include a statement of the amount of related services to be provided to the student.

Amount of Time

The specification of time to be committed to each of the services should be stated so that the exact commitment of resources on the part of the school is clearly defined. In addition to indicating the amount of time committed, some other indication of the parameters of the services may also be necessary for clarity. For example, it may not be appropriate to indicate that a student with an emotional disorder will receive 3 hours of counseling a week. A clearer indication of the number of times weekly and the time involved for each session should be indicated on the IEP. It is important to recognize that some related services may be provided only periodically, rather than daily or weekly. Identification and documentation of these types of related services can often be overlooked but are apparent in dealing with progressive or fluctuating disabilities. For example, one aspect of audiology is the selection and fitting of an appropriate hearing aid. If the hearing loss increases in severity and the effectiveness of amplification is not monitored periodically, the student may not receive the full benefit of the educational program.

SERVICE-DELIVERY MODELS

Similar to special education, the specification of related services on the IEP is a commitment by the public agency to provide the services, either directly or through contract or agreement with other services providers. The IEP should list all related services needed by a student with a disability, regardless of the availability of the service in the school system.

Services Provided Within the School

Related services, like special education services, must be provided in the least restrictive environment. Traditionally, related services have been provided in separate, usually clinical settings, with limited coordination between the therapy and the student's educational program. In recent years increased emphasis has been placed on the need to develop and implement programs for students that integrate all services into one unified program. As a result, a broader range of service-delivery models has evolved. Depending on the needs of the student, and the type of related service to be provided, the IEP committee should agree at the IEP meeting on how services will be provided. Options might include direct therapy, monitoring, or a consultation program.

Direct Service. Direct service is provided when specific therapeutic techniques are provided "directly" to the student by the related services professional. Therapy might be provided individually or in small groups. This individual or small-group therapy may be provided in a location separate from the regular classroom or within the classroom. When services are incorporated into the student's ongoing program, the model might be considered to be an integrated service-delivery model. The integrated services model is similar to team teaching in that the professionals involved with a student work together in the same environment on the same broad goals for a particular student within the existing curricular framework. Professionals plan cooperatively to design activities in which the goals of the related services program can be addressed through the ongoing curriculum. Services are provided in the student's classroom when at all possible. An excerpt from a sample IEP developed around the notion of an integrated service-delivery model in included in Figure 11–2.

Indirect Service. Often, it is not necessary for a therapist to provide direct services to a student. For example, an occupational therapist may train and supervise another professional or paraprofessional to implement a therapeutic program. In this monitoring model, the therapist would evaluate the student, design the program for another individual to implement, and periodically monitor the program to determine whether adjustments are necessary. Teaching assistants, regular or special education teachers, and physical education teachers may be taught to implement the goals of the related services program when appropriate. Monitoring is appropriate when the program to be implemented does not require in-depth expertise to ensure appropriate implementation. The individual delivering services, however, must be able to implement the program correctly. Examples of programs that are often conducted through a monitoring service delivery model include feeding, dressing, and adaptive physical education programs.

When related services are designed and monitored by a related services professional but actually provided by another professional, an aide, or the student's parents, the responsibilities of each individual should be indicated on the student's IEP to avoid

FIGURE 11-2
Related Services Integrated with Other Program Goals

Date January 15, 1990

(1) Student

Name: Sue James
School: Winston High School
Grade: 11
Current Placement: Community-based education
Date of Birth: 1-3-72   Age: 18

(2) Committee

Name:	Position:
Lawrence King	Principal
Robert James	Father
Kathryn Jones	Teacher
Sue James	Student

IEP From 1-20-90 To 6-20-90

Initial: *[signatures]*

(3) Present Level of Educational Functioning	(4) Annual Goal Statements	(5) Instructional Objectives	(6) Objective Criteria and Evaluation
Sue enjoys eating out. She waits her turn in line at the supermarket and at fast food restaurants. She tends to become impatient quickly.	Sue will use appropriate social, communication, and eating skills when dining in a restaurant.	When entering a restaurant, Sue will wait in line to be seated. When leaving the restaurant, Sue will wait in line to pay the check (Teacher).	4 of 5 dining experiences in community education. 4 of 5 dining experiences with family.
Sue speaks clearly when prompted, using primarily two- to three-word phrases. She imitates short sentences.		When ordering from a menu, Sue will speak clearly and in complete sentences (Speech Therapist, Teacher). Sue will engage in conversation in a low voice while dining (Teacher, Speech Therapist).	
Sue has poor trunk control as a result of cerebral palsy. She can hold and move an eating utensil and a glass to her mouth to eat but eats very slowly.		When seated at the table, Sue will eat and drink independently and will complete the meal within 45 minutes (Occupational Therapist, Teacher).	

miscommunication of responsibility. For example, when appropriate the speech therapist might be assigned responsibility for designing a language intervention program with parents and classroom teachers, training an aide to implement it, and observing, reviewing and revising the program with the aide and the classroom teacher twice monthly.

Consultation.   Developing a specialized and regularly provided program of related services for a student with a disability is not always necessary; the student's needs may be addressed by the related services provider consulting informally with the classroom teacher on an as-needed basis. Consultation differs from direct service and monitoring in that an ongoing program of services is not provided to the student. Thus, this model is appropriate for students who require no regular intervention. This model is cost-effective and is recognized as a viable and unobtrusive service-delivery model for students whose needs are minimal and can be incorporated by the teacher into the ongoing activities of the class. For example, the teacher of a student who no longer requires physical therapy may receive periodic follow-up and consultation services from a physical therapist. A psychologist might consult with the classroom teacher periodically to adapt established classroom routines to accommodate the needs of an emotionally disturbed student. Consultation might also be used to adjust the height of a chair or table to facilitate learning. Demonstration of individual and group activities in the classroom is also a form of consultation.

As noted earlier, the process of working out the mechanics of service delivery is a major aspect of the effective delivery of services. Attention to these details in the formative stages of IEP development will help to alleviate implementation problems at a later date.

Cooperative Agreements Between School Systems

School districts (especially rural ones) often form special education cooperative agreements, through which they combine resources for providing related services to students with low-incidence needs. Physical therapy and occupational therapy are examples of related services often provided through such agreements. Cooperative agreements enable school systems to provide services locally, which they might otherwise have to obtain through private contract or by hiring full-time personnel. In cooperative agreements, related services providers often travel between schools to provide the necessary services to students.

In some instances, students who require specific related services are required to attend schools where those services are located. This arrangement

may reduce or eliminate the travel time necessary for the service provider to travel between schools and thus allow more time for direct services to students. However, significant problems arise if the student must travel a long distance to the school where related services are provided or must be placed in a more restrictive setting than necessary (a special school, for example) to obtain needed related services. P.L. 94–142 requires that a student with a disability be educated as close to home as possible and, when possible, in the school which he would normally attend unless the IEP requires some other arrangement. In planning the provision of related services for individual students, the IEP committee must consider the distance the student must travel to attend school where services are provided and the extent to which the placement provides educational services in the least restrictive environment.

Interagency Service Agreements

It is sometimes difficult for the public school to provide, or arrange to share, related services that are not readily available within the school. In such cases, a student may receive necessary related services from public agencies other than the public school. These agencies may include local health or human resources departments, community agencies, or medical service agencies. For example, a student may receive physical therapy through a local health department or hospital, or a student with an emotional disability may receive counseling through the local mental health agency. A local department of vocational rehabilitation may provide mobility training for a student who is blind. When related services are provided by multiple agencies, special effort must be made to ensure communication between agencies and continuity between the educational and the related services programs. Because related services are a required part of the student's educational program, the public school is responsible for transportation to and from the related service if the service is not provided at school or if it must be provided after school hours.

Contracts with Private Service Providers

In some instances, private contracts can be less expensive on a per-pupil basis than employing full-time personnel to provide related services. When services within the school system or other public agencies are unavailable or inappropriate, the IEP committee may choose to contract with private organizations or professionals for the provision of services. Such services may include, for example, the selection and fitting of an appropriate hearing aid for a student with a hearing disability, the evaluation and diagnosis by a physician of a medical disability, or occupational and/or physical therapy for a student who has lost limbs through an accident. One issue that may arise with the provision of services by private contract is that private service providers may make program recommendations that are inconsistent with or beyond the school's obligation to provide. For example, a private occupational therapist may recommend that a student receive occupational therapy three times a week on a one-to-one basis. This recommendation may, in the opinion of the school, represent an optimal rather than a reasonable level of services. However, the school's decision that a lesser amount of services is appropriate may tend to alienate parents and the private therapist, who may question the school's authority to determine who should receive therapy and how much is appropriate. (Singer & Butler, 1987).

The public school is responsible only for providing services that are documented on the IEP, and the provider of the services is also determined by the IEP committee. In most cases, the school system is not required to maintain services provided privately before the IEP was developed, unless the IEP committee decides that such services are necessary and should continue for the student to benefit from special education. For example, if a student's parents have obtained speech therapy provided by a private source before the IEP is developed, the school is not obligated to provide the same service, extent of service, or service provider, unless agreed on by the IEP committee. The parents, however, may choose to maintain these services at their own expense.

RESPONSIBILITY FOR PAYMENT

One of the most controversial issues in the provision of special education and related services is the determination of who is responsible for paying for the services provided. P.L. 94–142 requires that special education and related services be provided at public expense, under public supervision and direction, and without charge (*Federal Register*, 1977). This means that services agreed on by the IEP committee must be provided at no cost to the parent. P.L. 94–142 also establishes that state educational agencies are ultimately responsible for ensuring that services are provided according to the criteria established. Thus, school systems have often assumed full financial responsiblity for their provision. P.L. 94–142, however, also establishes that each state may use whatever state, local, federal, and private sources of support are available to ensure the provision of appropriate services.

When related services are provided through agreements between public agencies other than the public schools, costs in some cases may be covered by the other agency, if provision of that service is an established function of that agency. For example, vision, hearing, and health screening are often responsibilities of local health departments. Departments of human resources often are responsible for providing psychological counseling and other mental health services. Thus, school systems should not have to pay for these services. However, because P.L. 94–142 requires that educational agencies must assume ultimate responsibility for ensuring that services are provided, some public health, mental health, and health insurance organizations have withdrawn their financial support, allowing school resources to supplant their own. (Singer & Butler, 1987).

When related services must be obtained from a private agency or professional, three payment options are generally possible. First, if parents, against the advice of the IEP committee, choose to obtain private services, they must bear the cost of the service unless an agreement is reached or a due process hearing decision requires such payment by the school system. Second, when the IEP committee agrees that provision of a service by a private agency is necessary for the student to benefit from special education, then the school system often assumes the full cost of the related service, including transportation. A third source of payment is some instances is an insurance provider. P.L. 94–142 states that nothing relieves an insurer or similar third party from an otherwise valid obligation to provide or to pay for services provided to a student with a disability (*Federal Register*, 1977). Many insurance policies provide coverage for medically related services, some of which are related services required by P.L. 94–142. Such benefits often include physical therapy, occupational therapy, and speech therapy as a result of accidental injury. While insurance proceeds may be used to pay for related services, the public agency cannot require parents to use insurance coverage to pay for these services. Since parents have paid an insurance premium for such coverage, they will have incurred financial cost. Under these circumstances, using parents' insurance coverage to pay for related services should be voluntary.

COORDINATION OF RELATED SERVICES

Planning and coordination of services is vitally important to ensure that the student with a disability receives the appropriate type(s) and extent of related service that the school system is required to provide. Once the necessary related services are identified, the extent of service determined, and the provider documented, the task of coordination must be addressed. Since the concept of related services is based on the premise that they are necessary for the student to benefit from special education, these services should be coordinated in such a way that they enhance the student's educational program. Arranging periodic meetings, allowing service personnel to observe the student in the educational setting (and vice versa), and distributing copies of the IEP to related services professionals involved with the student are strategies that can serve to enhance the coordination of services.

Coordination with agencies other than the pub-lic school should include the same considerations as those necessary within the school system. Interagency coordination, however, can be difficult to plan, implement, and monitor, because procedures outside the public school system are different and under the control of an agency other than the public school. In such cases, the identification of related services often becomes time-consuming and the services often difficult to arrange. It is essential to the delivery of appropriate education, however, that these components be identified and provided. The availability of related services, in many cases, will determine the overall effectiveness of the special education provided to the student.

SUMMARY

The inclusion of related services as a component of the IEP ensures that the student will receive the services necessary to benefit from the special education program provided. This chapter has discussed issues regarding the level and scope of services to be provided, those services included as related services, and students who are entitled to receive them. Three criteria for determining when related services are required were reviewed. These criteria included (1) the student must be receiving special education, (2) the related service must be necessary for the student to benefit from special education, and (3) the service must be able to be provided by someone other than a physician. Each of these criteria was discussed in detail. Related services most often used in public schools were defined, and methods of service delivery discussed. The determination and documentation of related services on the IEP completes the delineation of services to be provided to the student. The next and final step in IEP development is the determination by the IEP committee of how the services identified will be provided. The next chapter will discuss the placement decision.

EVALUATION

1. Discuss three current issues regarding the provision of related services. Consider additional issues that may be evident in your school.
2. You are the director of special education in a small school district. A parent has made a request that the school system provide or pay for psychotherapy as a related service for her son, who has an identified learning disability. What criteria should the IEP committee apply to determine whether this student requires psychotherapy as a related service?
3. You are the school principal. You have five students who require direct physical therapy twice a week. Your options are to either hire a part-time therapist for the school year or to contract the services privately. What are the advantages and disadvantages of both?
4. What is the difference between direct and indirect provision of related services? What models might be considered indirect service? Provide examples of student characteristics that might be considered appropriate for each model.

CHAPTER 12

Committee Agreement Concerning IEP Appropriateness and Placement Decision

OBJECTIVES

1. Identify current issues related to placement of students in special education programs.

2. Discuss five criteria for determining student placement.

3. Provide and discuss examples of the continuum of services required by P.L. 94–142 for special education placement.

4. Discuss criteria for the provision of an extended school year for some students with disabilities.

5. Define and discuss the "regular education initiative" regarding the preference for least restrictive placement.

6. Identify placement information that must be included on the IEP.

7. Discuss documentation of dissenting opinions regarding the appropriateness of the IEP.

The final step in the development of the IEP occurs when the committee agrees that the program defined by the IEP is appropriate and makes a placement decision based on the IEP. This process allows all committee members involved in the education of the student to reach a consensus concerning the curriculum planned for the coming year. The decision to implement the plan should be a committee decision and should be based on the support of all committee members. The IEP committee should follow a systematic process in completing these final steps. This chapter discusses issues related to placement, reviews the criteria established by P.L. 94–142 in considering placement, and discusses the requirements for documentation of the decision on the IEP. In addition, options related to placement and IEP approval are discussed.

CURRENT ISSUES RELATED TO PLACEMENT

Variability in Placement among States

Placement in the least restrictive environment is one of the cornerstones on which P.L. 94–142 is based. The regulations governing placement require that:

> Each public agency ensure that special classes, separate schooling, or other removal of handicapped children from the regular educational environment occurs only when the nature or severity of the handicap is such that education in the regular class with the use of supplementary aids and services cannot be achieved satisfactorily. (*Federal Register*, 1977)

States vary widely in the number of students with disabilities placed in separate classrooms and facilities (Office of Special Education and Rehabilitative Services, 1985; Singer et al., 1986). According to a report by the U.S. Department of Education (1988), over 70% of students with mild-to-moderate disabil-

ities spend at least a portion of the school day with students who do not have disabilities. This report indicates that 44% of students counted are served in resource rooms and 26% are served in regular classes. Further, 94% of all students with disabilities are reported to be served in regular school buildings, with only 6% being educated outside the regular school building. According to the same report, however, placement statistics among states vary considerably, depending on policies and procedures established by individual states and school districts. For example, according to data reported, the rate of placement in segregated day and residential facilities in the District of Columbia is 25 times the rate in Oregon. State by state variation in segregated placement is illustrated in Figure 12–1.

Even though statistics indicate that most students with disabilities receive at least a portion of their education in regular schools and classes, these statistics cannot define the quality and nature of the educational programs actually provided to students with disabilities. For example, these indicators do not tell us whether students are appropriately placed and actively participating in the regular classes they attend or whether necessary support services are available and provided in those settings. Nor do they provide information regarding the degree to which individual needs are, in fact, addressed in the placement selected. The special services committee in each school is responsible for ensuring that the program in which a student is enrolled actually addresses the student's needs, as identified in the IEP.

The Regular Education Initiative

A renewed emphasis on the legal preference for maintaining students with disabilities in the regular classroom with appropriate support services, rather than creating separate programs (typically referred to as the "regular education initiative"), has generated

FIGURE 12–1
Placement Rate for Students with Disabilities in Separate Schools and Residential Facilities

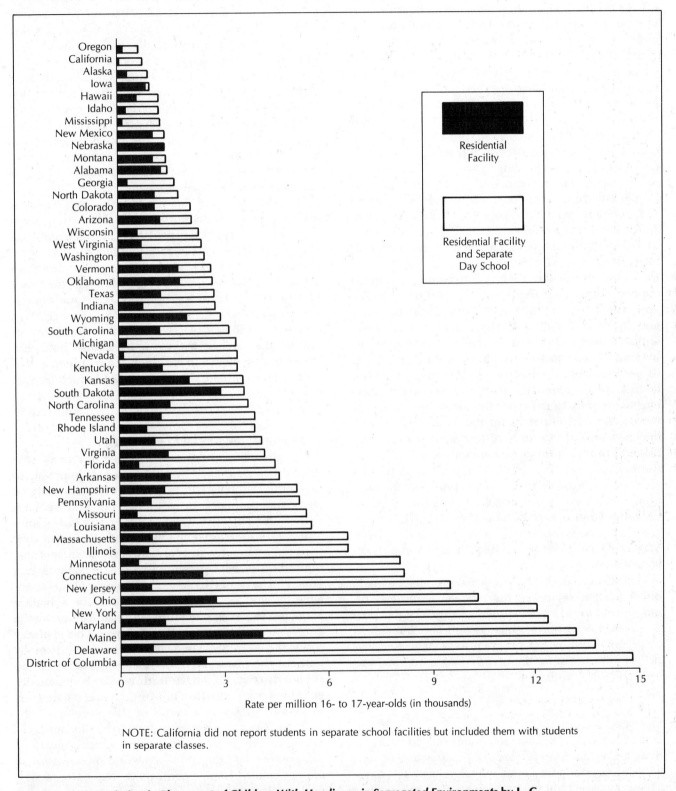

Rate per million 16- to 17-year-olds (in thousands)

NOTE: California did not report students in separate school facilities but included them with students in separate classes.

Source: *State Variation in Placement of Children With Handicaps in Segregated Environments* by L. C. Danielson and G. T. Bellamy, 1988, Washington, DC: Office of Special Education Programs. U.S. Department of Education.

much recent support (Gartner & Lipsky, 1987; Heller et al., 1982; S. Stainback & Stainback, 1984; Wang & Reynolds, 1985; Will, 1986). The preference for maintaining students with disabilities in the regular education program is based on several factors. These include (1) students with disabilities have a legal right to be educated with students who do not have disabilities (*Federal Register*, 1977); (2) data to document the instructional and social efficacy of special classes are unavailable (Carlberg & Kavale, 1980; Madden & Slavin, 1983); and (3) existing special education labels for students and programs are not necessary for addressing students' educational needs, interests, and capabilities and may instead perpetuate the view of special education as separate and unequal (Lipsky & Gartner, 1987; S. Stainback & Stainback; 1987; Will, 1986).

Although most would agree that students with disabilities should receive their education in an appropriately integrated setting, there remains a great deal of controversy regarding the readiness and/or appropriateness of the regular education program for addressing the educational needs of students with disabilities. Critics of the movement toward integration of students with disabilities into the regular classroom cite as evidence of this position (1) lack of an adequate data base for determining effective instructional strategies for maintaining students with disabilities in regular programs, (2) lack of readiness on the part of the regular education teachers to appropriately accommodate students with disabilities, and (3) unrealistic expectations that all students with disabilities can be appropriately managed and taught in the regular education program (Braaten, Kauffman, Braaten, Polsgrove, & Nelson, 1988; D. Fuchs & Fuchs, 1988; Hallahan, Keller, McKinney, Lloyd, & Bryan, 1988; Schumaker & Deshler, 1988).

Although all placement decisions must be made on an individual basis, the renewed emphasis on attempting to maintain students in the regular program when appropriate has created new interest in the regular education program as a viable service-delivery option for students with mild, moderate, and even severe disabilities.

Extended School Year

One of the most controversial issues related to placement is the provision of special education and related services beyond the usual school year of 180 days. This concept is known as the *extended school year* and may apply to the student whose disability is such that extended periods of time, such as summer vacations, without specialized instruction may result in regression over and beyond that normally experienced by other students. The primary concern related to such regression is that students with severe disabilities may be more susceptible to regression and may have a substantially more difficult time recouping lost skills once instruction is resumed. In *Armstrong v. Kline* (1979), *Battle v. Commonwealth* (1980), and *Birmingham and Lamphere School Districts v. Superintendent of Public Instruction for the State of Michigan* (1982), the courts have established that state policy governing the usual length of the school year cannot be used to prevent the provision of extended school services to students with disabilities when such services are necessary. Such a policy, it is contended, significantly inhibits consideration of the student's educational needs and may, in some instances, preclude the provision of an appropriate education. The courts have essentially supported the consideration of extended school years for those students with severe and profound intellectual disabilities and for those with severe emotional disturbances who are susceptible to significant regression and extreme difficulty in recoupment of skills. States and local school districts must establish policy for determining the extent to which other students with disabilities might be eligible for extended school-year services.

Private and Residential Placement

Although only a small percentage of students with disabilities are placed by public schools in private or residential schools and facilities, this issue is one of significant concern to both parents and schools. Criteria for objectively determining at what point a student's educational needs cannot be addressed by the public school system are often vague and confusing to both school personnel and especially to parents. The issue of what services the school is responsible for and under what conditions the school is expected to pay is currently being addressed by the courts in several states. For example, when parents place their children in private schools unilaterally without the involvement or recommendation of the school district, they have traditionally been considered to be responsible for tuition and related expenses incurred as a result of the placement. The Supreme Court, however, in *Burlington School Committee of the Town of Burlington, Massachusetts v. Department of Education of the Commonwealth of Massachusetts* (1985), confirmed that parents who unilaterally place their children in private schools pending the resolution of a placement dispute may be entitled to reimbursement, if the program is eventually approved.

A final issue related to placement is the responsibility of the public school in providing and paying for residential placement for students with severe disabilities. Despite the mandate for placement in the least restrictive environment, some parents, as is evidenced by the large number of due process hearings and litigation related to this issue, prefer that their children be placed in more restrictive settings, such as residential facilities. In addition, school systems are not always able to provide for the educational and related services needs of students with severe and multiple disabilities. At issue in these instances is whether requests for residential placement are based on educational need rather than family problems or medical needs. In most instances, the courts have held that the school is responsible only for the cost of residential placement when such placement is necessary for the student to be provided an appropriate special education program. Thus, if the IEP is reasonably calculated to enable the student to receive educational benefit and the student is benefiting educationally from the special education provided locally, in most instances the school system would not be responsible for the cost of residential placement, even if the student is experiencing problems at home and in other environments.

CRITERIA FOR DETERMINING PLACEMENT

The issues discussed briefly in this chapter are but a few that school districts and parents must consider in making placement decisions for students with disabilities. Despite numerous unresolved issues related to the provision of special education and related services, P.L. 94–142 is clear in establishing the basic criteria on which placement decisions are to be based. Public agencies are required to ensure the following:

1. Each student's educational placement is based on his or her IEP.
2. To the maximum extent appropriate, students with disabilities are educated with students who do not have disabilities.
3. A full continuum of alternative service-delivery models is made available to the extent necessary to implement the IEP.
4. The student is placed in the school he or she would attend if not disabled, unless the IEP requires otherwise, in which case the placement must be as close to the student's home as possible.
5. Each student's placement is determined at least annually.

Placement Based on the IEP

Research indicates that in some instances placement decisions may be somewhat arbitrary and based more on standard administrative procedure than on a specific relationship with the goals and objectives of the IEP, evaluation data, or consideration of the least restrictive environment (U.S. Department of Education, 1988; Algozzine & Ysseldyke, 1983; Ysseldyke, Algozzine, Richey, et al., 1982). Factors such as teacher referral, types and numbers of established programs, availability of space, and pupil characteristics may tend to influence placement decisions. It is the responsibility of the IEP committee to ensure that the placement decision is determined individually and is based on the provisions of the IEP, rather than on other factors.

It should be noted that not all goals and objectives of the IEP will require the same placement. Some goals may potentially be addressed by specially designing the instruction provided in the regular classroom, while other goals and objectives may require the student to leave the regular classroom for special instruction. For example, if a student with a physical disability requires the use of a word processor or typewriter to complete written assignments, this might be viewed as specially designed instruction. It is unlikely, however, that the student would have to leave his classroom to go to the resource room to benefit from this specialized program. The committee should ensure that the necessary equipment is available in the classroom.

The IEP defines the specially designed instruction to be provided to the student and should also provide the basis for determining how much and what type of instructional intervention is necessary to appropriately address the goals and objectives included in the plan. To ensure that the instructional portion of the IEP accurately reflects the intentions of the committee, the IEP committee should review each component of the IEP, before determining where the specially designed instruction will take place. At this point, the IEP should include these required elements: (1) levels of performance, (2) annual goals and short-term instructional objectives, (3) schedules and procedures for evaluation, and (4) related services. To ensure that the process of reaching agreement on the appropriateness of the IEP occurs systematically, criteria, including those that follow, should be specified.

1. The IEP's compliance with the legal requirements of P.L. 94–142
2. The relevance of goals, short-term instructional objectives, evaluation procedures, and related services

3. The manageability of the total plan
4. The clarity with which the plan has been written

A checklist outlining such criteria, as illustrated in Figure 12–2, can assist committee members in careful documentation of appropriateness. Before specifying the particular placement decision, all committee members should agree that the goals and objectives included on the IEP have been reasonably calculated to enable the student to receive educational benefit.

Full Continuum of Service-Delivery Models

When the committee has ensured that the curriculum has been appropriately defined on the IEP, alternative service-delivery models for providing the specified curriculum should be considered. Alternative placements can be viewed as ranging from less restrictive to more restrictive environments. For example, for some students, the service-delivery model continuum might range from the regular classroom, as least restrictive, to a full-time special class, to homebound instruction, and ultimately to the hospital, as most restrictive (see Figure 1–7, Chapter 1, p. 22). For some students, however, homebound instruction might be considered the most restrictive instructional setting, as the student is segregated not only from students who do not have disabilities but also from other students with disabilities.

When determining the setting in which special education services will be provided, the committee must choose alternatives that will be most conducive to the progress of the student, while at the same time placing the student as close to nondisabled students as possible. A brief discussion of placement options follows.

Regular Classroom. The regular classroom is the preferred placement for all students whose identified educational needs can be addressed appropriately in that setting. This preference includes using supplemental aids and materials whenever necessary to maintain the student in that environment. Modifying the regular education program to accommodate the specialized instructional needs of the student can enable the student to remain a part of the curriculum and activity of the rest of the school, rather than being removed to a separate program, which can sometimes result in stigmatization and isolation of the student (Will, 1986). Although the benefits of maintaining the student in the regular education program are well documented and provide the basis for the legal requirement of least restrictive placement, it should be pointed out that the regular classroom, while it enables maximum integration

with students who do not have disabilities, also is the setting with the largest student–teacher ratio and therefore usually provides less specialized and less one-to-one support to the student than any other available alternative. The student who is placed in the regular classroom, therefore, should be able to benefit from adaptations and supplementary aids and services that can feasibly occur in this environment. For example, (1) preferential seating, (2) use of braille materials accompanied by clear verbal directions, (3) modification of instruction to accommodate motor and communication difficulties, and (4) strategies such as cooperative grouping, peer tutoring, and small-group instruction can all be provided as part of the regular education program. When the needs of the student cannot be addressed in a large-group setting, even with individualized assistance within that setting, other alternatives should be considered.

Consultation. When the student's identified special education needs do not require ongoing direct services or when indirect services are required in addition to direct services from a special education teacher, a consultation model might appropriately be used to provide the necessary support. Consultation models are specifically designed to provide support services to teachers and other classroom personnel to assist them in working effectively with students in the classroom. Consultation may be provided by an individual (such as consulting teacher, or a resource teacher) or in a collaborative fashion by a team of individuals including special education teachers, regular classroom teachers, and administrators (Idol, Paolucci-Whitcomb, & Nevin, 1986). Consultation models have been increasingly recognized as a viable method of assisting classroom teachers and parents who work directly with the student (Idol & West, 1987; West & Idol, 1987). Consultation might include providing information and assistance to the classroom teacher and/or aide, demonstration teaching, provision of materials, adaptation of curriculum and equipment, observation, and assistance in monitoring student progress.

Although both classroom teachers and special education teachers view this service as desirable and necessary, many school systems tend to combine consultative services with the ongoing instructional and case management responsibilities of resource teachers and other direct service providers (Idol & West, 1987). Few states have developed special consultation roles and responsibilities to ensure the effective implementation of the model. In addition, research indicates that special education teachers do not automatically have the skills necessary to provide effective consultation services (Idol & West,

FIGURE 12–2
Checklist for Documenting Appropriateness of the IEP

Student Name _____

Date of Committee Meeting _____

Committee Chairperson _____

	Yes	No	Comments
Legal Requirements			
1. Does plan include all information required by law?			
a. level of performance			
b. annual goals			
c. short-term instructional objectives			
d. schedules of evaluation			
e. procedures for evaluation			
f. related services			
g. specific special education			
h. extent of participation in the regular classroom			
i. projected dates for initiation and duration of services			
Relevance			
1. Are goals, objectives, evaluation procedures, placement, and services:			
a. appropriate to the disability of the student?			
b. determined in consideration of identified strengths and weaknesses?			
c. appropriate to the student's level of performance?			
2. Are the specified evaluation procedures correlated with the goals and objectives?			
3. Do the minimum acceptable criteria stated in objectives seem realistic for the student?			
Manageability			
1. Is the anticipated progress proportional to the amount of instructional time available?			
2. Are the procedures scheduled for evaluation reasonable considering the time and methods involved?			
3. Has the method for provision of related services been determined?			
Clarity			
1. Is the terminology used in the plan understandable to all other committee members?			
2. Is the student's level of performance specified in terms of specific skill statements?			
3. Do short-term instructional objectives clearly state:			
a. the specific behavior to be required of the student?			
b. the condition under which the behavior is to occur?			
c. the minimum acceptable criteria for attaining the objectives?			
4. Do annual goals indicate what the student will be able to do when the IEP is terminated?			
5. Do evaluation procedures specify the type of evaluation to be used and, where appropriate, specific tests?			
6. Does the schedule of evaluation clearly indicate how often evaluation will occur?			
7. Is the special education to be provided stated in specific terms?			
8. Are related services clearly specified in terms of extent or amount of services to be provided?			

1987). Thus, for consultation to be effective, training must be provided to those who will serve in this capacity. When a consultation model of service delivery is determined to be appropriate to address the student's educational needs, the IEP committee should be particularly careful to designate responsibility for the achievement of the goals and objectives included on the IEP. In many instances, both the classroom teacher and the consulting teacher can appropriately be designated as responsible.

Integrated Special Education Services. If the regular classroom is considered appropriate to meet the student's needs, but in the IEP committee's opinion, the student or teacher requires more support than is generally available in this setting alone or with consultation support, an in-class service delivery might be employed. As used here, *integrated services* means any special education or related service provided directly to the student in the regular classroom by a special education teacher, related services professional, or an aide. For example, rather than requiring that the student leave the classroom for assistance in reading, speech therapy, or occupational therapy, the specialist might come to the student's classroom to provide necessary services, either to individual students or a small group.

A more integrated method of providing services in the classroom occurs when the goals of the special education program are one and the same with those of the regular-education program and all staff teach together to attain the common goals. One way that this is often accomplished with speech and language therapy is for the therapist to work with the teacher on specific program goals within the context of a large or small group within the classroom. The goals of the individual student are incorporated into the activities of the classroom. In this way, services are provided in the setting where language naturally occurs rather than in an isolated clinical situation. While there are times when a separate setting will be necessary, direct services, when appropriate, should be provided in the regular classroom.

Resource Program. The majority of students with mild-to-moderate disabilities receive a portion of their education in a resource room (U.S. Department of Education, 1988). A resource room is a separate special education instructional setting that provides an opportunity for the student to receive specially designed instruction, for various amounts of time, in an environment removed from the activity of the regular classroom, while still receiving the majority of her instruction in the regular program. There are a number of variations on the resource program model. For example, the student may receive instruction either individually, or in small groups in which the special education teacher schedules students with similar needs from different classrooms during the same time period. The resource program schedule may also vary among students and schools, but generally it is organized into time segments ranging from 1 to 3 hours a day, depending on the student's needs. In addition, some resource programs are specifically designed to serve students categorically, while others provide services to students on a multicategorical or noncategorical basis. For example, one resource program in a school may be established to serve only students who have diagnosed learning disabilities, while another may serve only students diagnosed as having emotional disturbances. In another school, however, resource programs may be organized to serve students with varying disabilities but may be organized according to age or grade level. Finally, the instructional approach used may vary from program to program. For example, one secondary resource program for students with learning disabilities may focus on teaching students basic skills such as reading, while another focuses primarily on tutoring in the content areas, and still another focuses on teaching vocationally related skills.

A resource room model is appropriate for students who require very specific instruction for a period of time to enable them to participate in the regular curriculum. For example, a student with a specific reading disability may receive reading instruction in a resource room, or a student with a hearing disability may receive auditory training in a resource room. In both instances, the majority of the instructional program is provided in the regular program. The resource room program has the advantage of being the least restrictive of the pull-out type programs, not only because it removes the student from the regular program for only a portion of the school day, but also because it is similar to pull-out programs within the regular program, such as programs for advanced study, reading improvement, and compensatory education.

Self-Contained or Modified Self-Contained Program. An instructional setting that provides for more specialized education than that of the resource room is the self-contained or modified self-contained program. Students whose primary educational needs cannot be met in the regular classroom or in a resource program may receive most of their education in a special class setting for most of the day, while still participating, where appropriate, in activities of the regular classroom. Depending on the nature of the student's disability, participation in regular class activities may include art, physical education, music, or any other subject area appropriate to the identified needs of the student.

The self-contained program can provide, in a small group setting, an alternative curriculum to that of the regular classroom. Students whose disabilities have a significant adverse effect on their ability to benefit from the regular-education program typically receive the majority of their education in special class settings. These students, however, may differ dramatically regarding their educational needs. For example, students with serious emotional disturbances are often placed in self-contained programs to implement and maintain effective behavior management programs and to provide a therapeutic learning environment. These students may, however, receive the same academic curriculum as students who do not have disabilities. Self-contained programs may also provide an entirely different curriculum from that provided in the regular program. If, for example, a student with a moderate-to-severe intellectual disability requires a curriculum that emphasizes areas of functional living, these skills might be addressed in a self-contained or modified self-contained program, with a substantial amount of the educational program provided in a community setting.

Special School. Special schools include segregated special day schools, private schools, or training facilities that segregate students with disabilities from students who do not have disabilities. Although special schools are recognized as a potential placement option, P.L. 94–142 specifically states that separate schooling can occur only if the nature or severity of the student's disability is such that education in a regular school cannot be achieved satisfactorily. As noted earlier in this chapter, a great deal of variability exists between states in the degree to which separate facilities are used to provide educational services to students with disabilities (U.S. Department of Education, 1988). This variability might indicate that some states have been more successful than others in building a capacity to accommodate a wider range of students within the regular school building.

The continued maintenance of separate schools and facilities, however, apparently continues to receive significant support. For example, many states and school districts continue to support intermediate units, which cluster students with disabilities in separate settings, as a preferred service-delivery model (Gartner & Lipsky, 1987). Despite the requirements of P.L. 94–142 for placement in the least restrictive environment, proponents of separate schools and facilities justify the maintenance of separate programs by citing such factors as cost benefits

of locating services in one location, ability to concentrate curriculum on the similar needs of a population of students, and increased availability and continuity of services. In addition, some parents and parent advocacy groups continue to support special schools for low-incidence disabilities (Gartner & Lipsky, 1987; Singer & Butler, 1987). For these groups, preference for separate schools may represent a backlash against the perceived poor quality of services for low-incidence disabilities in public schools (Gartner & Lipsky, 1987).

The use of separate facilities will no doubt continue to be a controversial issue in the provision of services to students with disabilities. Nonetheless, every service provided in special facilities or separate schools has been provided in regular facilities and integrated schools. That is not to say that every regular facility and integrated school in the country is ready to provide an appropriate education to every student; the state of the art is not so far advanced throughout the United States. But what has been done in some regular facilities and integrated schools can be done in all of them, and as all schools begin to respond to students' needs and to meet them in regular and integrated settings and programs, there will be less reason to support special facilities and separate schools. Although many school systems will continue to house special education programs in separate schools or buildings, or contract with other agencies to provide services in facilities apart from nondisabled students, placing students in separate facilities for administrative reasons rather than because the student requires separate placement is a violation of the least restrictive environment provisions of P.L. 94–142.

Homebound Instruction. Students who might be included in a program of homebound instruction are those who, because of accident, chronic illness, or acute health problems, are not able to attend school for extended periods of time. Homebound instruction for a student with a disability is usually distinguished from homebound services provided to students with temporary disabilities. For example, a student injured in an automobile accident who may be at home or in a hospital for a short period of time or a pregnant teenager who may be absent from school for a designated period are usually not considered to be eligible for special education because of the temporary nature of the disability.

Various methods are available for providing hospital or homebound instruction. Many hospitals have educational facilities and teachers as a part of their programs. These programs can greatly facilitate coordination with the student's school. Other methods for providing special education services to students with disabilities at home or in the hospital include visiting teachers, coordinated volunteer programs, telecommunications systems using the telephone for home instruction, and SPECIALNET, a computer-based communication system available to many school systems that uses mechanisms such as electronic mail and electronic bulletin boards to communicate information to students (Latham & Burnham, 1985).

It must be emphasized that home instruction is considered by some to be the most restrictive educational setting because it segregates students from other students both with and without disabilities. Home instruction is not an acceptable service-delivery model for students who, except for the lack of appropriate services, could be served in a school-based program. Thus, establishing home instruction as the service-delivery model for a student with a severe emotional disturbance or for a student with multiple physical disabilities is inappropriate in most instances. When the service that is considered to be both appropriate and least restrictive is not available in the school district, the district must develop and/or locate the service privately or from another source.

Residential Schools. Some IEP committees and some parents have the opinion that, for a specific student, an appropriate education is feasible only in residential schools. Although every service provided in residential facilities can also be provided in community-based and integrated programs, sometimes students are placed in residential facilities. In those cases, the student's local educational agency is required to pay for the cost of the education in that facility, if it places the student there. Such placements occur most frequently in three instances. In the first instance, the necessary services may simply not be available locally to address the identified needs of the student. For example, in rural areas special education programs for students who can neither see nor hear may not be available locally or within driving distance of the parents' home. These disabilities, though significant, do not require that a student be placed in a residential setting to receive an appropriate education. Lack of local services, however, may require that the student reside at a school that does offer the necessary program if that program is not within commuting distance. In such an instance, the school is required to pay for the full cost of the placement including transportation, nonmedical care, and room and board.

In the second instance, the nature of the student's needs may provide the basis for residential placement. For example, if a student with a serious emotional disturbance requires a consistently structured management program on a 24-hour basis to

benefit from education, the school might be required to provide a residential setting, regardless of the existence of a day program. If the local educational agency cannot provide an appropriate educational program for a student with a disability, the school may agree to place the student in a residential school that provides the required educational services. However, residential placements made for this reason can be especially controversial for several reasons. First, it is often difficult to differentiate educational problems from other problems that may actually provide the basis for the need (such as a medical or family problem). In addition, it is often parents who request that the school district assume responsibility for placement in private schools and residential facilities, even though the school may consider the student to be appropriately served in the public school program.

A third instance when the school might provide education in a residential facility is when the placement has been made by another agency but the school agrees to pay the educational portion of the cost of the placement. Cooperative agreements between service agencies may result in the sharing of costs of residential placements. The progress of students enrolled in residential facilities should be continuously monitored so that when appropriate, the student may be moved progressively closer to a typical educational setting with students who do not have disabilities.

The current trend in residential placement is away from institutional settings and toward community living alternatives. Community-based residential facilities, such as group homes, and community-based residential treatment centers that serve fewer students are emerging alternative placements for students who may require a 24-hour care or treatment program but who can benefit from education in the regular school during the day.

Noneducational Services. Although P.L. 94–142 is very clear in establishing that all school-aged individuals, regardless of the nature or severity of their disabilities, are entitled to receive appropriate educational programs, it is sometimes very difficult to distinguish between the educational and noneducational service needs of students. In such instances, educational services might be very similar to or actually be incorporated into services providing medical care and supervision. Such might be the case for students whose disabilities are so severe that they have profound adverse effects not only on their ability to participate in educational programs but on their ability to participate in any functional activity. In such cases (such as for a nonresponsive student with profound intellectual and physical disabilities), educational services might be defined by such activities as ensuring that a student's limbs and body are routinely exercised; that attempts are made to encourage, develop, and elicit a system of communication; or that the student learn to chew and swallow food.

Interagency Agreements. In most cases, the local educational agency serving the student can provide appropriate educational programs for students with disabilities. However, some students with low-incidence and/or severe disabilities may not be provided for within every local education agency. If the school system cannot provide an appropriate educational placement with its own resources, interagency agreements, typically referred to as special education cooperative arrangements, or co-ops, might be developed with other school systems and with other state agencies providing services to students with disabilities.

Small school systems may be unable to maintain the full range of special education services required by P.L. 94–142. Services for students with low-incidence disabilities may not be feasible to provide locally because the cost of maintaining personnel likely would be out of proportion to the number of students being served. In these cases, two or more school systems may establish agreements to cooperatively share personnel and programs for the provision of specific services. Examples of services that often are shared between school systems include physical and occupational therapy programs, programs for students with visual and hearing disabilities, and programs for students with multiple disabilities. Advantages of shared services include the availability within the participating public school systems of a full continuum of services, shared costs of services that, if purchased privately might be excessively expensive, and the ability to provide services to students in the local school during the school day, rather than transporting the student to the services after school.

Despite obvious advantages, cooperative agreements do have some disadvantages. Cooperative programs often require that either the service provider travel between schools or the student be transported to where the necessary services can be provided. The time spent by the service provider in transit may substantially reduce the amount of time available for direct services to students, while transporting the student to the service might create a hardship for the student and substantially reduce participation in the rest of the educational program. An alternative might be for the student to attend a school where special educational services are centralized. This arrangement, however, may require that the student travel a long distance to and from a school other than the

one that she would attend if there were no disability. P.L. 94–142 requires that the student's educational placement be as close to the student's home as possible (*Federal Register*, 1977). It might therefore be inferred that expensive travel time, beyond that normally established as acceptable for all students, would be considered an inappropriate method for providing appropriate educational services to a student with a disability.

When cooperative agreements between school systems are arranged, all school systems involved share the cost of providing the program or service. Costs may either be shared equally or may be prorated, based on the number of students receiving the service from each school system. For example, each school system might pay for its own transportation costs, while sharing the program start-up costs and salary expenses. Another option in cooperative agreements is sharing the contribution of resources rather than sharing the cost of each program. For instance, one school system may hire an occupational therapist, while another system hires a physical therapist. Many states have formalized these service agreements by establishing administrative support units to administer shared programs. School systems within these agencies may identify mutual needs and pool resources. The administrative unit then may hire, direct, and supervise the staff under the direction of the participating school systems. Thus, while still assuming the cost of services, the participating school systems can share the expenses.

Agreements with Other State Agencies. In some instances, public agencies other than the public school may provide special education services. For example, departments of mental health or human resources may maintain residential facilities for students who have emotional disabilities. Interagency agreements often are developed to provide residential placement in a state facility operated by another state agency.

Problems can arise when education, health, and social services agencies attempt to share the responsibility for providing similar services to students with disabilities. In addition to possible duplication of services and potential difficulty with coordination, ensuring that the terms of the interagency agreement are upheld often may become problematic. For example, the school district may determine that a student requires residential placement and thus refer that student to a residential facility operated by another agency within the state. If the agency is unable to provide services for the student, the school district must find other means of providing the required service. Reasons for lack of follow-through in providing agreed on services may vary. Programs and services operated by other agencies may already be overextended, causing the agency to refuse to accept further referrals or to establish excessively long waiting periods. (Although not permissible for educational agencies, other agencies can, and often do have excessively long waiting periods for services.) In other instances, agencies may disagree regarding the appropriateness of the recommended placement. Just as states differ in their eligibility criteria, agencies within the same state may differ in their definition of various disabilities. A final reason for failure to honor interagency agreements is the contention by some public agencies that P.L. 94–142 does not apply to or regulate agencies other than the public school. In situations such as these, despite the existence of interagency agreements, public schools may be left to assume full responsibility for ensuring that the necessary services are provided.

Interagency agreements may be developed on a student by student basis or may be developed at the program level. If agreements are completed for each student receiving services in a shared program or by another agency, the IEP committee should participate in the development of, or review, the agreement to ensure that provisions are included for addressing all requirements for the maintenance and reviewing the IEP as well as monitoring the program provided to the student. If the interagency agreement focuses primarily on elements of a shared program, the IEP committee should clarify responsibility for these procedures within the parameters of the agreement.

Although interagency agreements have the advantage of maximizing services while minimizing expenses, their development and maintenance require a great deal of coordination between all agencies involved in the provision of services. It is recommended that any agreements be in writing. Although such a procedure does not always ensure that services will be provided as agreed, it does provide a basis for coordination and does reinforce the commitment of the agencies involved to fulfill the terms of the agreement. To further promote coordination of services, these interagency agreements should be clearly and simply written, specific in designation of responsibilities shared between the agencies, flexible, and realistic.

Placement in the Least Restrictive Environment

In addition to requiring that placement decisions be based on the IEP and that a continuum of alternative placements be available to address the needs of each student, P.L. 94–142 established placement criteria, which require that students with disabilities be educated to the maximum extent appropriate with students who do not have disabilities and that removal from the regular education program occurs only when the nature of the disability is so severe that an appropriate education cannot be provided in that setting (*Federal Register*, 1977).

Compliance Standards.   In developing standards to ensure compliance with this legal requirement, the U.S. Department of Education (1986) established that "decisions as to the type of placement that is appropriate must not be based on any of the following factors used alone or in combination: 1) category of handicapping condition, 2) configuration of the service delivery system, 3) availability of educational or related services, 4) availability of space, and 5) curriculum content or methods of curriculum delivery" (U.S. Department of Education, 1986). This requirement essentially confirms that placement decisions are to be based on the student's needs as identified in the IEP, rather than solely on the existing administrative structure of the special education program. For example, students cannot be excluded from an otherwise appropriate program because of lack of space. Nor could a student diagnosed as having a hearing disability be placed in a separate program simply because that program has been designated by the school district as the program for all students with hearing disabilities. Eliminating this often used criterion presents a challenge to public schools to design educational placements based on the student's functional needs and the degree to which the regular-education programs can be modified to appropriately accommodate those needs.

The legal preference for mainstreaming and the arrangement of alternative services according to their proximity to nondisabled students should not be misinterpreted to mean that the least restrictive environment for all students is the regular classroom. The regular classroom may, in some instances, be a more restrictive environment than a self-contained program if the student's needs cannot be met in that setting. Furthermore, the inappropriate placement of a student in the regular classroom, under the guise of least restriction, may compound the adverse effect of the student's disability on educational performance by adding undue failure to the factors with which the student must already contend. To avoid this situation, services must be chosen on the basis of the individual strengths and weaknesses and the identified needs of each student. The placement chosen should be the educational setting in which the student can participate, realize educational benefit, and have maximum association with peers who do not have a disability.

Severity of the Disability. Although the preceding list of elements that cannot be used as a sole basis for determining placement in the least restrictive environment seems extensive, P.L. 94–142 has established that the severity of a disability can and should be used as a criterion for determining the least restrictive educational setting for a student with a disability. The nature of specially designed instruction and the setting in which it can most appropriately be provided depends, in part, on the nature and severity of the disability and the degree to which an alternative curriculum may be required.

Despite the obvious importance of severity in determining educational placement, few functional definitions can be generally applied for drawing parameters between the mild, moderate, or severe nature of a disability. For example, whether a learning disability should be described as mild, moderate, or severe is not always apparent. Because of the lack of criteria for specifically defining levels of severity, educators often address this issue by referring to severity in terms of ranges such as mild to moderate, moderate to severe, or severe to profound, which provide more general indicators of severity.

In addition to vague and inconsistent definitions of severity, differences between the severity of the disability itself and the severity of its educational adverse effect further compounds this issue. For example, what may appear to be a severe physical disability may not present a severe educational problem at all and may well be accommodated in a regular classroom with support from physical and occupational therapy. Conversely, a student whose behavior is completely unmanageable in the regular program may be considered to have a severe disability at school yet not have a clinical diagnosis of severe emotional disturbance and, by some eligibility criteria, may not even qualify for special education services.

One programmatic and functional way that educators have addressed this issue is to determine severity by the type of curriculum necessary for the student to realize educational benefit from the program provided. When addressing the issue of severity in this strictly educational way, students who require a functional life-skills curriculum in an alternative educational program would be considered to have a more severe disability than a student who could participate in the regular education program with support from a resource program for the majority of the school day. Many schools have established criteria for determining severity based on the type of curriculum required. For example, students who are enrolled in a special education program for 20% or less of the school day may be considered to have a mild disability, those enrolled for 21% to 50% may be considered to have a mild-to-moderate disability, those enrolled for more than 50% of the school day may be considered to have a moderate-to-severe disability, and those enrolled full-time in an alternative program may be considered to have a severe to profound disability.

DOCUMENTATION OF PLACEMENT INFORMATION ON THE IEP

After the IEP committee has determined how the IEP will be implemented, specific details regarding the type and amount of service must be documented on the IEP. In regard to defining and documenting the placement decision on the IEP, P.L. 94–142 requires that the IEP committee include the following:

1. the specific special education to be provided to the student,
2. the extent to which the student will be able to participate in regular education programs, and
3. the projected dates for initiation and duration of the services.

(Federal Register, 1977)

This statement is necessary to provide an accurate record of the student's special education needs as well as to document participation in the least restrictive setting. The statement essentially represents the placement decision made by the IEP committee.

Specific Special Education To Be Provided to the Student

The definition of special education is twofold. First and foremost, it is defined as instruction. This instruction must be (1) specially designed to meet the unique needs of a student with a disability and (2) provided at no cost to the parent (*Federal Register,* 1977). The instructional component of the definition is defined in the goals and objectives developed by the IEP committee and included in the IEP. Thus, the committee, in developing and documenting the curriculum portion of the IEP, partially addresses this IEP requirement.

The second aspect of the requirement has to do with the location in which specially designed instruction can take place, including (but not limited to) classroom instruction, instruction in physical education, home instruction, and instruction in hospitals and institutions (*Federal Register,* 1977). To fulfill this component, the IEP committee should document the service-delivery model selected to provide services to the student. For example, a student may have fine-motor difficulties that in the past may have been addressed by an occupational therapist in therapy sessions apart from the classroom. Current educational preference is that, if the therapy consists of skills that can be incorporated into the educational portion of the student's program, then the special education teacher, paraprofessional, or even the classroom teacher may actually be responsible for implementing and maintaining the therapy program under the therapist's direction. The same may be true for students who have physical disabilities, speech and language disabilities, and emotional disabilities, if the need for therapy can be addressed through a consultation program. In such cases, the individual responsible may be the classroom teacher or special education teacher, with direction and consultation from the therapist. In designating the specific special education to be provided, the location of the service provided may be essential to the appropriateness of the program. If the IEP form requires that the service provider be indicated, it is usually best to include the position of the service provider rather than the name of the individual providing the service. The IEP is not designed to ensure that a particular individual will provide services but that a particular service will be provided by a qualified service provider. In addition, if the service provider changes, the need for an IEP meeting to revise the name on the IEP is avoided.

Determining the Extent of Participation In the Regular Classroom

Because there is a legal preference for placement in the regular classroom whenever appropriate, the IEP must document the extent to which the student with a disability participates in the regular program (*Federal Register*, 1977). This information may reflect a percentage of instructional time or the number of hours spent in the regular classroom daily or weekly. In most instances, the extent of participation in the regular program may be determined by simply subtracting the amount of time spent in special education from the amount of time in a school day or week. However, when students receive their special education in the regular classroom or within a consultation model, variation often occurs in the way regular classroom participation is indicated on the IEP.

The documentation of time spent in the regular classroom and special education programs is relatively easy to determine and has the advantage of providing immediate information to IEP committee members and school administrators regarding the amount of time spent in each setting. The purpose of

the requirement, similar to all other requirements, is to help ensure the appropriateness of the education provided to students. Although it is relatively simple to document the legal requirement of the amount of time a student spends in regular education programs, it is quite difficult to ensure that the student will actively participate in the activities of the program. Unfortunately, many students are assigned to regular classrooms all day and seldom participate in class activities. Although the IEP committee cannot guarantee the extent to which a student will be socially and instructionally integrated, the committee's determination of the appropriate environment for meeting the objectives designed for the student should constitute a setting in which maximum participation is achieved. After placement, if the student is unable to participate because of the inappropriateness of the setting, another placement should be considered.

Specifying Projected Dates for the Initiation and Duration of Services

In documenting the provision of special education and related services, the IEP committee must record the projected dates of initiation and duration of special education and related services (*Federal Register*, 1977). In most instances, special education services are indicated as being of 1-year duration, because the IEP is considered an annual plan. This does not mean, however, that services must end after 1 year or that services cannot end before 1 year has elapsed. Some services may be required for less than 1 year. For example, a student making a transition from a special education resource room to receive special education in the regular program may receive direct services from a special education teacher for a short transition period. Likewise, physical and occupational therapy are not always provided for the entire duration of the IEP. Other services, for example community education, may be provided year after year, being reviewed and continued with each subsequent IEP.

There are various methods for indicating the dates for initiation and duration of services on the IEP. One frequently used method is to base the specified duration of services on a calendar year. For example, services documented as beginning on September 5, 1990, would be documented as ending on September 5, 1991. The advantage of this method is that projecting the duration of services and the annual review date is simplified, because it is always 1 year from the date when services began. In addition, such a method enables the plan to be in effect at the beginning of the school year without the need to develop a new plan immediately on the opening of the school year. Finally, this method enables the school system to stagger the dates when annual reviews must be conducted for all students receiving special services.

One disadvantage of this method is that it may imply that services are to be extended through the summer. To avoid misinterpretation, IEP formats using this method should state on the IEP form that, unless otherwise specified, services are provided on a school-year basis only. Another disadvantage of this method is that the IEP that spans a calendar year may not be reviewed at the end of the school year, when the program actually ends, or at the beginning of the school year, when a new one would actually begin. Thus, the plan, though not expired, may not appropriately reflect changes in the student's program or changes in the student's needs that may have occurred during the summer.

A second frequently used method of specifying the duration of services is to terminate all IEPs at the end of each school year, regardless of the date of initiation of services. The advantage of this method is that the duration of services is very clear in specifying that services end when the school year ends. A second advantage is that the IEP can be revised at the end of the current program, based on the anticipated program for the following year. For example, if a student is moving from elementary to junior high school, reviewing the IEP at the close of the school year would enable the IEP to be reviewed and revised, based on the program that the student would require for the coming year. Or the review meeting could be conducted before the beginning of the new school year, with revisions based on current student information after the summer months. The major disadvantage of such a method is that the number of IEPs to be reviewed during the same time period could be overwhelming and extremely time-consuming at a point in the year when time is especially limited.

Regardless of the method used to document the duration of special education and related services, it is useful to indicate similar beginning and ending dates for all services. This enables all services to be reviewed at the same time rather than in separate review meetings. Such a procedure is consistent with the philosophy that the IEP is one document rather than several separate service documents. If all services cannot be initiated at the same time, the ending dates may still be selected to ensure consistency with other services listed on the IEP. For instance, if a student receives specially designed instruction in reading beginning in September, and physical therapy services begin perhaps a month later in October and are expected to last for the entire school year, review dates for both services should be established for the same time.

All services must be reviewed at least annually but may be continued in the subsequent IEP. When the parents or school representatives believe that a change or modification in services is necessary during the school year, a review meeting should be scheduled.

Provisions for Extended School Year

As discuss earlier, the issue of providing special education and related services beyond the established school year to some students with disabilities has been controversial. Although there appears to be little question that extended services must be provided to those students for whom they are required, establishing criteria for eligibility and procedures for implementation of extended school-year programs remains problematic (Alper & Noie, 1987).

Relatively few students with disabilities require extended school-year services. Thus, it is usually assumed, unless otherwise indicated on the IEP, that special education and related services will be provided during the school year only. By documenting the need for an extended school year on the IEP, the school district acknowledges that the student's program will not end with the close of the regular school year. The need for extension of services beyond the school year should be determined by the IEP committee at the time that the IEP is developed, at the annual review, or at an interim review meeting convened for the purpose of considering the need for an extended school year. Such meetings should be scheduled early enough to allow for planning on the part of the parent, the administrative unit, and if necessary, the agency providing the educational and related services.

Few states have established uniform and specific procedures for considering on a case by case basis those students who may require an extended school year to benefit from the special education and related services they receive (Alper & Noie, 1987). Thus, these decisions often are made at the local level, according to locally established criteria. Individual school districts continue to struggle with concerns such as hiring of staff for summer programs, use of school facilities, and acquisition of required related services that are required as part of the student's educational program. To ensure continuity in the way that the provision of an extended school year is determined on a case by case basis, school districts should establish systemwide procedures for providing extended school years. Figure 12–3 provides an example of extended school-year procedures developed for use in one school district.

As noted earlier, the purpose of the extended school year is to prevent regression or loss of skills

FIGURE 12–3
Extended Instructional Year for Handicapped Students

1. <u>GUIDELINES</u>

   The following are guidelines used in developing the mandatory procedure to determine the need for an extended instructional year.

   a. <u>Purpose</u>

   The primary purpose of the extended instructional year is to prevent serious regression of previously learned skills. An extended instructional year should be provided when significant regression of those learned skills occurs as a result of a break or interruption in educational programming and the regression would be compounded by limited capacity to recoup lost skills.

   b. <u>Student Eligibility</u>

   Students eligible are those handicapped students whose multidisciplinary assessment data and IEP clearly identify areas of instructional programming where a significant regression/recoupment cycle requires an extension of the instructional year program. Such areas must be identified by the IEP committee on the basis of data taken during the school year or by the fact that history has demonstrated that there is a great likelihood of significant regression and lengthy recoupment following an extended break in services. Regression is viewed as significant only when the time required to regain the skills to an approximate level of previous accomplishment exceeds an unacceptable recoupment time. An unacceptable recoupment period is one in which the time spent relearning a previously acquired skill significantly detracts from teaching a new skill.

   Research indicates that significant regression generally occurs within the handicapped population in the areas of motoric development, adaptive behavior, and functional skills.

   c. <u>Assessment Considerations</u>

   (1) Each student should be evaluated on IEP goals and objectives to measure retention/attainment level at least at the following times:

   (a) The beginning of any given school year.
   (b) Pre/post any extended vacation (or absence) period within the school year.
   (c) The end of any given school year.

   (2) Assessment data can be formal and/or informal and should include parent and teacher interviews, anecdotal reports, and records checks.

   (3) Formal and/or informal educational assessment data, past history records, parent interviews, teacher reports, and/or medical evaluations must be described in the minutes of IEP meetings when the need for an extended instructional year is being considered.

(Figure 12–3 continued)

2. STUDENT NEEDS TO BE CONSIDERED

Any student meeting eligibility for special education and related services is subject to consideration for an extended instructional year. The following areas are to be evaluated in determining the need for an extended instructional year:

a. Motoric Development

A student exhibiting severe delays in motoric development and requiring extensive physical and/or occupational therapy in relation to his/her special education may be eligible if an extended break in programming would result in tightening of muscles necessary for self-feeding, weight bearing, head control, positioning, etc. At least one of the following conditions must be met to determine if a student is eligible based upon significant regression/recoupment:

(1)   The need to inhibit the development of scoliosis.

(2)   The need to inhibit the deterioration of range of motion.

(3)   The need to continue the development of head control, midline control, or trunk stability without which the student would regress to a less developed stage.

(4)   The need to continue initial progress toward ambulation, without which the student would regress to a prior developmental stage.

(5)   The need to inhibit the deterioration of oral muscular competence required for proper feeding skills.

(6)   The need to continue the adjustment to special prosthetic devices when interruption in programming would render the devices inadequate.

For any of the above, a representative of the appropriate medical treatment facility *must* confirm the condition.

b. Adaptive Behavior

A student exhibiting severe problems in adaptive behavior and/or categorized as seriously emotionally disturbed may be eligible for an extended instructional year program if an interruption in program increases the likelihood that the student will revert to inappropriate behaviors and show evidence of significant social/emotional regressions. One of the following conditions must be considered to determine if a student is eligible based upon significant regression/recoupment:

(1)   Self-abusive behavior, such as head banging, biting, hitting, picking, etc., and those behaviors associated with possible deficits in the competence of the sensory motor integration system.

(Figure 12–3 continued)

(2)   Physically aggressive behaviors, which pose potential harm or threat, directed at other individuals.

(3)   Severe withdrawal which may further isolate the student from his/her environment.

(4)   A severely limited attention span in a student who has developed from the point of nonattending and who may regress to a point of virtually no attention span.

c. Functional Skill Development

A student may be eligible for an extended instructional year program when he/she is at a critical learning stage in the acquisition of a functional skill. One of the following conditions must be considered to determine if a student is eligible based upon significant regression/recoupment:

(1)   Demonstration of a breakthrough in the understanding of a communication system by a nonverbal student.

(2)   Extreme difficulty attaining goals related to self-sufficiency in skills such as eating, toileting, dressing, etc., and independence from caretakers.

3.   INDIVIDUALIZED EDUCATION PROGRAM (IEP)

A supplement to the student's current IEP must be written at the meeting, indicating an extended instructional year program, and is to include the following:

- goals
- short-term instructional objectives
- present level of performance
- criteria for achievement of objectives
- amount of time per day/week
- beginning/ending dates
- hours of instruction
- location(s)
- service provider(s)
- transportation

The supplement would be attached to the student's current IEP.

4.   PROCEDURE TO IMPLEMENT THE PROGRAM

a. Schools having students requiring an extended instructional year will submit requests in writing to the District Superintendent's Office, Attn: Special Education Specialist. Requests must include the following information:

(Figure 12–3 continued)

(1)   A copy of the IEP containing the specific goals and objectives for an extended instructional year program.

(2)   A copy of the minutes identifying the problems the student will experience without such a program and justifying an extended instructional year.

(3)   The specific hours of instruction.

(4)   The beginning and ending dates the instruction is to be provided.

(5)   Location of services to be provided.

(6)   The transportation requirement. (A special transportation request must be included, as appropriate, for any student requiring an extended instructional year program [Attachment B]).

(7)   If possible, the name of a local special education teacher available to provide the required services.

(8)   The total number of man-hours required.

b. The District Superintendent's office will:

(1)   Review the requests for completeness and compliance with the outlined procedures.

(2)   Summarize the request on Attachment A (one for *each* school and *each* program, i.e., preschool, learning impaired: moderate to severe.)

(3)   Forward one copy of each to the Finance, Personnel, and Logistics Office. A copy of each student's transportation requirement, Attachment B, must be included.

(Figure 12–3 continued)

Attachment A

Request for an Extended Instructional Year

STUDENT: _____, _____ AGE:___
               (Last Name)   (First Name)

SCHOOL: _____

HOME ADDRESS: _____

                  _____

HOME TELEPHONE: _____

<u>ENCLOSURES/REQUIREMENTS:</u>

1. A copy of the student's current IEP with the appropriate attachment.

2. A copy of the minutes identifying the problems the student will experience without such a program and justifying an extended instructional year.

3. Hours of daily instruction: 8:30 to 12:00/Other: _____

4. Beginning/Ending dates: June 29 to August 7, 1990
                 Other: _____

5. Location: Educational Services: _____

            Related Services: _____

6. Transportation requirement: enclosed

7. Special Education teacher available: _____

8. Total number of man-hours: _____
   (1 teacher: 20 hours per week for 6 weeks = 120 total)

                          _____
                          Principal

(Figure 12–3 continued)

Attachment B

Request for Special Transportation, Extended School Year

Name of Student: _____   Date of Birth: _____

Residence: _____   Enrollment Code:_____

Sponsor: _____

Address: _____

Home Telephone: _____   Work Telephone: _____

Place of Pickup/Dropoff (If Not Residence): _____

_____

School: _____   Grade: _____

Requested Time of Arrival (If Not 8:30 A.M.): _____

Requested Time of Departure (If Not 12:00 noon):_____

Frequency of Service (If Not Daily): _____

Special Requirement: _____

_____

_____

Requested Period of Service (If Not June 29–August 7):_____

_____

Figure 12–3 is from *Procedures for an Extended School Year for Handicapped Students for 87–88* by Department of Defense Dependents Schools—Germany Region.

that cannot be recouped in a reasonable length of time once instruction resumes. Thus, the primary elements in determining the need for extended school year tend to include (1) the likelihood of significant regression and (2) the rate of probable recoupment of skills. In the vast majority of states, it is the IEP committee's responsibility to determine in which areas a student is likely to regress, whether such regression is likely to be unusual in relation to that experienced by other students, and whether it is likely that lost skills will be recouped in a reasonable amount of time (Alper & Noie, 1987). Wide discrepancies exist among states regarding the type of data collected to demonstrate regression and skill recoupment. Because the courts have established the precedent for requiring extended school-year services only to students with severe disabilities of mental retardation and emotional disturbances, some states and school districts tend to restrict eligibility to these areas rather than extending the option for such programming to other students.

To determine regression, some school districts require that regression actually be demonstrated before providing an extended school year. For example, one procedure for documenting regression includes summarizing daily and weekly progress data at three points each year, for example in September at the beginning of the year, in January at midyear, and in June at the end of the school term (W. C. Stainback, Stainback, & Hatcher, 1983). If the student progresses from September to January and from January to June but regresses significantly from June to September, a regression problem might be suspected. To determine how long it would take to recoup the lost skills, the same daily record-keeping system would continue through the following school year, documenting the point when the student had recouped those skills lost during the summer months.

An option to requiring that the student actually demonstrate regression before receiving an extended school year might be to make a decision based on the best opinion of professionals and on existing information that delineates those student, family, and educational characteristics that might tend to be associated with significant regression and slow recoupment of educational skills. For example, the IEP committee might consider the student's domestic environment, the degree of parental involvement in the student's education during breaks in the school year, medical information, IEP objectives, training sites, and alternatives to summer programming (Alper & Noie, 1987).

Although most school systems have summer school programs for students with disabilities, it should be carefully noted that the concept of ex-

tended school year goes far beyond the permissive and somewhat standard concept usually associated with summer school. Although an extended school-year requirement for a given student may in some cases be addressed through an existing summer school program, the provision of an extended school year is a required element of the student's IEP and as such is based on the provision of the specific services defined in the IEP. The provision of an extended school year and the determination of services to be provided must be determined on a case by case basis. Thus, the extended school-year services provided to one student may not be the same as those provided to another.

REACHING CONSENSUS THAT THE IEP IS APPROPRIATE

After the IEP components have been reviewed and a placement decision made, most school districts require that committee members indicate approval of the completed plan by signing the document. A place for signatures is usually provided on the IEP so that committee endorsement of the plan is readily apparent. Final approval of the IEP indicates that the plan meets all legal requirements and that the committee considers the plan to constitute an appropriate educational program for the student. Figure 12–4 provides a completed IEP for Joe S., based on referral and evaluation information provided earlier in the text.

Since initial placement in special education requires the written consent of parents, many school districts incorporate this requirement into the process of agreeing that the IEP is appropriate. For example, parents might be asked to sign the IEP, indicating approval of the educational plan and consent for the proposed placement. Such a procedure can satisfy the consent requirements of P.L. 94–142 if the IEP includes a statement in which the parents agree that they (1) have been fully informed of all information relevant to the placement, (2) understand and agree to the placement, (3) agree that the consent document describes the placement and lists all records that will be released and to whom, and (4) understand that their consent is voluntary and may be revoked at any time (*Federal Register*, 1977).

Approval of the IEP and consent for placement are not one and the same procedure. P.L. 94–142 requires that parents provide written consent before initial placement in a special education program can occur. P.L. 94–142 does not require, however, that parents provide written approval of the IEP's entire content before services can begin. Thus, parents can conceivably not approve of the entire IEP yet still consent to placement in the special education program. This distinction is important when differences of opinion develop among committee members regarding the services to be provided to the student. For example, if the committee disagrees regarding the necessity of speech therapy, with the consent of the parents, other services included can be initiated, with negotiations continuing regarding the disputed services.

Although the parents' signatures are not a binding agreement that the IEP and the subsequent placement will not later be challenged, the signature of the agency representative on the IEP provides the parents with a confirmed and binding record of the services the school has agreed to provide.

Documentation of Dissenting Opinions

Because P.L. 94–142 requires no written indication that the entire IEP committee has approved the IEP, neither does it provide a mechanism for documenting dissenting opinions of those members who do not agree with the document's content. The need to document dissenting opinions is an outgrowth of individual states' and school districts' requirement that committee members must sign the IEP. Disagreements regarding the appropriateness of the IEP may develop regarding the appropriateness of the program goals and instructional objectives, the proposed method of service delivery, the amount of services to be provided, or the nature of services to be (or not to be) provided. For example, a classroom teacher may disagree with the IEP provision that a student's needs in reading can be appropriately addressed in the regular education program. Or a special education teacher may disagree with an eligibility determination that a student is eligible for special education services. A related services provider may feel that a student must receive direct occupational therapy, though other committee members agree that consultation services are sufficient.

The committee may not reach consensus regarding the necessary elements of appropriate education for a specific student. Many school systems therefore have developed methods for enabling dissenting committee members to document the reasons for their disagreement. In some school districts, records of dissenting opinions are maintained in the student's special education record with no additional requirement for follow-up. In other school districts, an administrator or administrative panel might hear the dissenting opinion and make a determination regarding the disposition of the complaint.

Regardless of whether or not they sign the IEP, parents may disagree with or request a change in the IEP or placement at any time they consider such a change to be necessary. As IEP committee members, parents may use any procedures established by the school system and available to other committee members for documenting a dissenting opinion. They may also use the more formal and legally sanctioned due process procedures established by P.L. 94–142. There are instances, however, when parents, while disagreeing with elements of the IEP, do not wish to initiate formal complaint procedures. For example, the parents may disagree that the educational needs of their child with a learning disability can best be addressed in a multicategorical program that also serves students with other disabilities. However, they may not consider such a program to constitute an inappropriate educational program for the student. In such a case, documentation of the reasons for the disagreement can provide an opportunity to indicate that consent for placement is provided, but with reservations.

The IEP must be in effect before the student is placed in a special education program. When specific aspects of the IEP are being negotiated, the parents and school can agree to initiate the agreed on components of the IEP. Once the entire IEP has been developed and deemed appropriate by both school personnel and parents, the special education and related services agreed on should begin immediately. The only exception to this policy is when the IEP is developed during the summer or vacation period, or when a short delay is necessary to work out such details as transportation. If a delay is necessary, it should be specified in the minutes of the IEP meeting and agreed to by the parents. For students already receiving special education and related services, the IEP must be in effect at the beginning of each school year. This does not mean that all IEPs must be reviewed and revised at the beginning of the year but that an IEP that has been reviewed within 1 year of its development is in effect when the school year begins.

REVIEWING THE IEP

Once the IEP is approved, the committee should determine the procedure for its review and revision. P.L. 94–142 requires school systems to arrange meetings to review each student's IEP periodically and to revise it if necessary. A meeting must be held for this purpose at least annually. The timing of such a meeting might be on the anniversary date of the last IEP meeting, but this is left to the discretion of the

FIGURE 12–4
Sample IEP (based on psychoeducational report presented in Chapter 5)

INDIVIDUAL EDUCATION PROGRAM

Date ___3-1-91___

(1) Student

Name: Joe S.
School: Adams
Grade: 5
Current Placement: Regular Class/Resource Room

Date of Birth: 10-1-80   Age: 11-5

(2) Committee

	Initial
Mrs. Wrens	Principal	
Mrs. Snow	Regular Teacher	
Mr. LaJoie	Counselor	
Mr. Thomas	Resource Teacher	
Mr. Ryan	School Psychologist	
Mrs. S.	Parent	
Joe S.	Student	

EP from ___3-15-91___ to ___3-15-92___

(3) Present Level of Educational Functioning	(4) Annual Goal Statements	(5) Instructional Objectives	(6) Objective Criteria and Evaluation
MATH **Strengths** 1. Can successfully compute addition and subtraction problems to two places with regrouping and zeros. 2. Knows 100 basic multiplication facts. **Weaknesses** 1. Frequently makes computational errors on problems with which he has had experience. 2. Does not complete seatwork. Key Math total score of 2.1 Grade Equivalent.	Joe will apply knowledge of regrouping in addition and renaming in subtraction to four-digit numbers.	1. When presented with 20 additional problems of 3-digit numbers requiring two renamings the student will compute the answer at a rate of one problem per minute and an accuracy of 90%.	Teacher made tests (weekly)
		2. When presented with 20 subtraction problems of 3-digit numbers requiring two renamings the student will compute the answer at a rate of one problem per minute with 90% accuracy.	Teacher made tests (weekly)
		3. When presented with 20 addition problems of 4-digit numbers requiring three renamings the student will compute the answer at a rate of one problem per minute and an accuracy of 90%.	Teacher made tests (weekly)
		4. When presented with 20 subtraction problems of 4-digit numbers requiring three renamings the student will compute the answer at a rate of one problem per minute with 90% accuracy.	

(Figure 12—4 continued)

INDIVIDUAL EDUCATION PROGRAM

Date __3-1-91__

(1) Student

Name: Joe S.
School: Adams
Grade: 5
Current Placement: Regular Class/Resource Room

Date of Birth: 10-1-80   Age: 11-5

(2) Committee

	Initial
Mrs. Wrens — Principal	
Mrs. Snow — Regular Teacher	
Mr. LaJoie — Counselor	
Mr. Thomas — Resource Teacher	
Mr. Ryan — School Psychologist	
Mrs. S. — Parent	
Joe S. — Student	

IEP from __3-15-91__ to __3-15-92__

(3) Present Level of Educational Functioning	(4) Annual Goal Statements	(5) Instructional Objectives	(6) Objective Criteria and Evaluation
MATH	Joe will multiply 2- & 3-digit numbers requiring regrouping.	1. Will multiply 2, 3 & 4 digits by 1 digit without regrouping in 20 problems with 90% accuracy. 2. Will multiply 2 & 3 digits by 1 digit with regrouping in 20 problems with 90% accuracy. 3. Will multiply 2 & 3 digits by 2 digits with no regrouping in 20 problems with 90% accuracy. 4. Will multiply 2 & 3 digits by 2 digits with regrouping in 20 problems with 90% accuracy.	Key Math (after 7 mos.) Teacher made tests (weekly)
	Joe will use linear, volumnar, weight, temperature, & money measurements.	1. Will write dictated money values up to $200.00 with 90% accuracy in 9 of 10 trials. 2. Will accurately identify various weights in lbs. & ounces using a scale in 9 of 10 trials. 3. Will read a thermometer in 9 of 10 trials. 4. Will measure items to the nearest foot, yard and inch in 9 of 10 trials.	Teacher observation (daily) Key Math (after 8 mos.)

(Figure 12-4 continued)

INDIVIDUAL EDUCATION PROGRAM

Date ___3-1-91___

(1) Student	(2) Committee

Name: Joe S.
School: Adams
Grade: 5
Current Placement: Regular Class/Resource Room

Date of Birth: 10-1-80   Age: 11-5

	Initial
Mrs. Wrens	Principal
Mrs. Snow	Regular Teacher
Mr. LaJoie	Counselor
Mr. Thomas	Resource Teacher
Mr. Ryan	School Psychologist
Mrs. S.	Parent
Joe S.	Student

IEP from ___3-15-91___ to ___3-15-92___

(3) Present Level of Educational Functioning	(4) Annual Goal Statements	(5) Instructional Objectives	(6) Objective Criteria and Evaluation
READING **Strengths** 1. Comprehends reading material at 2nd grade level. 2. Can identify main idea of a paragraph at 2nd grade level. **Weaknesses** 1. Poor word attack skills and word identification. (See grade equivalents next page.) 2. Has difficulty identifying words written cursively.	Joe will successfully identify long and short vowels.	1. When requested by the examiner, the student will correctly sound out the long and short sounds of five vowels (a, e, i, o, u) in 9 of 10 trials. 2. When presented with 3-letter words having the pattern "consonant, vowel, consonant," the student will correctly pronounce the vowel with its short sound. He will be able to perform this task for all 5 of the vowels in 9 of 10 trials. 3. When presented with one-syllable words having the pattern "consonant and final e" or "consonant, double vowel, consonant," the student will pronounce the vowel(s) with a long sound. He will be able to perform this task for all vowel sounds in 9 of 10 trials.	Brigance Diagnostic Inventory of Basic Skill (after 2 mos.)

(Figure 12–4 continued)

INDIVIDUAL EDUCATION PROGRAM

Date ___3-1-91___

(1) Student

Name: Joe S.
School: Adams
Grade: 5
Current Placement: Regular Class/Resource Room
Date of Birth: 10-1-80   Age: 11-5

(2) Committee

		Initial
Mrs. Wrens	Principal	*J.A.W.*
Mrs. Snow	Regular Teacher	*A.S.*
Mr. LaJoie	Counselor	*L.J.*
Mr. Thomas	Resource Teacher	*M.T.*
Mr. Ryan	School Psychologist	*N.R.A.*
Mrs. S.	Parent	*J.S.*
Joe S.	Student	*Joe S.*

IEP from ___3-15-91___ to ___3-15-92___

(3) Present Level of Educational Functioning	(4) Annual Goal Statements	(5) Instructional Objectives	(6) Objective Criteria and Evaluation
READING Woodcock Reading Mastery Tests Grade Equivalent Letter identification 3.0 Word identification 1.8 Word Attack 2.0 Word comprehension 4.3	The student's oral reading rate for reading material at his comfortable reading level will increase from 30 words per minute to 36 words per minute. Student will improve his reading fluency.	1. When presented with a list of 250 basic sight vocabulary words listed in order of difficulty and/or commonly taught, the student will correctly pronounce 200 of them by the end of the year. 2. When presented with a list of 37 direction words listed in order of difficulty and/or commonly taught, the student will correctly pronounce 24 of them. 3. When presented with a list of 40 words and phrases frequently seen on signs listed in order of difficulty the student will correctly pronounce 30 of them.	Brigance Diagnostic Inventory of Basic Skill (after 4 and 9 mos.) Teacher observation (daily) Brigance Diagnostic Inventory of Basic Skill (after 4 and 9 mos.) Teacher observation (daily) Brigance Diagnostic Inventory of Basic Skill (after 4 and 9 mos.) Teacher observation (daily)

(Figure 12—4 continued)

INDIVIDUAL EDUCATION PROGRAM

Date ___3-1-91___

(1) Student

Name: Joe S.
School: Adams
Grade: 5
Current Placement: Regular Class/Resource Room
Date of Birth: 10-1-80   Age: 11-5

(2) Committee

		Initial
Mrs. Wrens	Principal	
Mrs. Snow	Regular Teacher	
Mr. LaJoie	Counselor	
Mr. Thomas	Resource Teacher	
Mr. Ryan	School Psychologist	
Mrs. S.	Parent	
Joe S.	Student	

IEP from ___3-15-91___ to ___3-15-92___

(3) Present Level of Educational Functioning	(4) Annual Goal Statements	(5) Instructional Objectives	(6) Objective Criteria and Evaluation
		4. When presented with a second grade reading passage student will read it orally without experiencing difficulty in pronouncing more than one word in 20 (95% accuracy). (He is presently reading at a 1.8 instructional level.)	Brigance Diagnostic Inventory of Basic Skill (after 4 and 9 mos.) Teacher observation (daily)
	Student will apply context clue to decode difficult words.	When presented with sentences which contain difficult words, the student will use context clues to decode the difficult words. This task will be performed at the 2–3 grade level.	Brigance Diagnostic Inventory of Basic Skill (after 4 and 9 mos.)

(Figure 12–4 continued)

INDIVIDUAL EDUCATION PROGRAM

Date ___3-1-91___

(1) Student

Name: Joe S.
School: Adams
Grade: 5
Current Placement: Regular Class/Resource Room
Date of Birth: 10-1-80   Age: 11-5

(2) Committee

		Initial
Principal	Mrs. Wrens	*yatz*
Regular Teacher	Mrs. Snow	*a.g.*
Counselor	Mr. LaJoie	*8.19.*
Resource Teacher	Mr. Thomas	*MT*
School Psychologist	Mr. Ryan	*N.R.R.*
Parent	Mrs. S.	*J.S.*
Student	Joe S.	*g-s.*

IEP from ___3-15-91___ to ___3-15-92___

(3) Present Level of Educational Functioning	(4) Annual Goal Statements	(5) Instructional Objectives	(6) Objective Criteria and Evaluation
SOCIAL EMOTIONAL			
Strengths	Joe will speak about himself in a positive manner.	1. In a one-to-one situation with the teacher Joe will talk about his personal strengths for five min. a day.	Teacher observation (daily) for 15 days.
1. Joe cooperates in group activities.		2. In a one-to-one situation with the teacher Joe will state 5 strengths he possesses for 3 days in a row.	Anecdotal records (daily) 3 consecutive days
2. Attentive and cooperative in class.			
Weaknesses	Joe will participate with peers in small groups on the playground and in class.	3. After a small group activity (3–4 students), Joe will tell the teacher 3 things he did well in the group.	Anecdotal records (daily) 5 consecutive days
1. Reluctant participant on playground.		4. After a small group activity Joe will tell the teacher 6 things he did well in the group.	Anecdotal records (daily) 5 consecutive days
2. Makes derogatory comments about himself frequently during the school day.		5. In a small group activity Joe will ask a peer for help instead of asking an adult:	Teacher observation. Data collected 30 min. a day, 3 days a week
3. Has few friends, is ignored by peers.		a) With verbal reminders from an adult in 80% of opportunities.	
		b) With nonverbal reminders in 80% of opportunities.	
		c) With no signals in 80% of opportunities.	
		6. In a small group activity Joe will offer assistance to a peer:	Teacher observation. Data collected 30 min. a day, 3 days a week
		a) With verbal reminders from an adult in 80% of opportunities.	
		b) With nonverbal reminders in 80% of opportunities.	
		c) With no signals in 80% of opportunities.	

(Figure 12—4 continued)

INDIVIDUAL EDUCATION PROGRAM

Date ___3-1-91___

(1) Student	(2) Committee

Name: Joe S. Adams
School: Adams
Grade: 5
Current Placement: Regular Class/Resource Room
Date of Birth: 10-1-80   Age: 11-5

	Initial
Principal	Mrs. Wrens	*V.a.W.*
Regular Teacher	Mrs. Snow	*a.s.*
Counselor	Mr. LaJoie	*L.J.*
Resource Teacher	Mr. Thomas	*M.T.*
School Psychologist	Mr. Ryan	*N.R.R.*
Parent	Mrs. S.	*J.S.*
Student	Joe S.	*Joe S.*

IEP from ___3-15-91___ to ___3-15-92___

(3) Present Level of Educational Functioning	(4) Annual Goal Statements	(5) Instructional Objectives	(6) Objective Criteria and Evaluation
SOCIAL EMOTIONAL	Joe will increase on-task behavior to 75% of class time.	1. Using a behavior chart, Joe will chart weekly progress in two academic areas of his choice.	Chart, weekly
		2. Given 30-minute intervals 4 times a day, Joe will evaluate and plot success of goals he has set for himself and discuss his feeling concerning his progress with the group.	Daily teacher conference and chart
		3. Joe will independently complete 80% of his assignments.	Daily charting
		4. Joe will remain on task during entire group activity in 5 of 6 daily activities.	Teacher observation (daily) and anecdotal records (weekly)
		5. When given a difficult or frustrating assignment, Joe will raise his hand and ask for assistance.	Teacher observation (daily) and anecdotal records (weekly) and charting (daily)

(Figure 12–4 continued)

INDIVIDUAL EDUCATION PROGRAM

Date ___3-1-91___

(1) Student

Name: Joe S.
School: Adams
Grade: 5
Current Placement: Regular Class/Resource Room
Date of Birth: 10-1-80   Age: 11-5

(2) Committee

		Initial
Mrs. Wrens	Principal	
Mrs. Snow	Regular Teacher	
Mr. LaJoie	Counselor	
Mr. Thomas	Resource Teacher	
Mr. Ryan	School Psychologist	
Mrs. S.	Parent	
Joe S.	Student	

IEP from ___3-15-91___ to ___3-15-92___

(3) Present Level of Educational Functioning	(4) Annual Goal Statements	(5) Instructional Objectives	(6) Objective Criteria and Evaluation
HANDWRITING	Joe will identify and write letters and words in proper cursive handwriting.	1. Writes name in cursive	
Strengths		Traces first and last name accurately in 9 of 10 trials.	
1. Attentive and cooperative during one-to-one instruction.	Joe will write neatly in cursive.	Copies first and last name accurately in 9 of 10 trials.	Completion of Cursive Writing and alphabet practice cards.
2. Prints all letters.		Writes first and last name from verbal cue accurately in 9 of 10 trials.	
3. Holds pencil appropriately.		2. Writes alphabet in cursive	
Weaknesses		Traces upper case letters accurately in 9 of 10 trials.	
1. Does not use cursive writing.		Copies upper case letters accurately in 9 of 10 trials.	
2. Has difficulty naming words in cursive.		Writes upper case letters from verbal cue accurately.	
3. Does not wear his glasses.		Traces lower case letters.	
4. Has poor letter formation and word spacing.		Copies lower case letters.	
		Writes lower case letters from verbal cue.	Teacher observation.
		3. Writes words in cursive	
		Traces words.	
		Copies words.	
		Writes words from verbal cue.	
		4. Writes legibly	
		Forms manuscript letters correctly.	Informal tests.
		Forms cursive letters correctly.	
		Forms words of correct size.	
		Spaces between words.	

(Figure 12–4 continued)

INDIVIDUAL EDUCATION PROGRAM

(7) Educational Services to be Provided

Services Required	Date Initiated	Duration of Service	Individual Responsible for the Service
Regular Reading–Adapted	3-15-91	3-15-92	Reading Improvement Specialist and Special Education Teacher
Resource Room	3-15-91	3-15-92	Special Education Teacher
Counselor Consultant	3-15-91	3-15-92	Counselor
Monitoring diet and general health	3-15-91	3-15-92	School Health Nurse

Extent of time in the regular education program: 60% increasing to 80%

Justification of the educational placement:

It is felt that the structure of the resource room can best meet the goals stated for Joe; especially coordinated with the regular classroom.

It is also felt that Joe could profit enormously from talking with a counselor. He needs someone with whom to talk and with whom he can share his feelings.

(8) I have had the opportunity to participate in the development of the Individual Education Program.

I agree with the Individual Education Program (✓)

I disagree with the Individual Education Program ( )

Mrs. J.

Parent's Signature

school system. Some school systems will prefer to review and revise all IEPs in the spring and/or summer so that prospective teachers for the following year may be included in the meeting.

Frequently, and especially in the initial stages of IEP implementation, review must be conducted more often than once a year. Even though careful consideration may have been exercised in the original determination of goals and objectives, circumstances such as accidents, permanent injury, or simply the miscalculation of a student's ability to achieve specified tasks may negate the appropriateness of originally specified goals and objectives. If the student is not achieving goals and objectives as projected in the IEP, and major revision is considered necessary, an IEP review meeting must be conducted to determine what changes must be made in the IEP to make the document appropriate to address the needs of the student.

P.L. 94–142 requires that parents be involved throughout the entire process of IEP development, including participation in the revision of the IEP. When revisions are necessary, the parents must be notified of the proposed change and be invited to

attend the IEP meeting. If the parents are unable to attend the meeting, their participation may be obtained by conference telephone call, written comments, or by other methods of parental involvement.

Although P.L. 94–142 is clear that the program delineated in the IEP should not be changed without conducting an IEP meeting with the parents, the law is unclear regarding what changes might be made in the IEP without conducting a formal review meeting. Changes in the goals, short-term instructional objectives, and evaluation criteria that constitute the special eduation program that the student will receive; changes in the amount or schedule of services to be provided; and changes in the type or extent of related services to be provided all might be considered program changes that require an IEP review meeting. When minor changes such as clarification of services, corrections, or changes in service providers occur, the modification might be discussed with the parent by phone and a copy of the modified IEP sent to the parent. In the absence of clear federal guidelines, it is necessary for state and local educational agencies to develop procedural guidelines in this area.

SUMMARY

Agreement by the IEP committee that the IEP is appropriate and that the student will receive special education in the least restrictive environment is the final step in IEP development. This chapter has reviewed current placement issues, including the variability in service delivery among states, the regular education initiative, private and residential placement, and the need for extended school years for some students. Various service-delivery options were defined, and criteria for determining placement were presented. Requirements for documenting placement information on the IEP were reviewed, and procedures for reaching consensus and reviewing the IEP were discussed. Once the IEP is completed, the task still remains to ensure its appropriate implementation. The final section of this book focuses on the implementation of the IEP.

EVALUATION

1. You have been asked by a local parents group to speak on the topic of "How Special Education Placement Decisions Are Made." Outline the points you will cover, including local criteria as well as the criteria established by P.L. 94–142.
2. You are making a presentation entitled, "The Regular Education Initiative: Implications for Placement of Students With Disabilities" to a group of parents and faculty from your school. How do you explain the concept of "the regular education initiative" in terms of the continuum of services required by P.L. 94–142?
3. You are the principal of your school. A parent comes to you to request that the school system provide an extended school year to her 5-year-old son, who has a profound hearing disability. What criteria will you use to determine whether an extended school year will be provided?

PART 3

Implementation Of the IEP

CHAPTER 13

Coordination Between Service Providers

OBJECTIVES

1. Discuss two ways in which the IEP can serve as a means of coordination among service providers.

2. Discuss the need for increased involvement of classroom teachers, related services providers, and medical representatives in coordinating services for students with disabilities.

3. Identify four strategies for increasing coordination and communication with parents.

4. Discuss four levels of team planning and coordination.

5. Identify strategies for coordination with non–public school placements.

6. Identify strategies for coordinating transition into public school, transition between services, and transition from school to work.

The effective coordination of the IEP among service providers is essential for enhancing the successful education of students with disabilities. Yet coordination can pose a major barrier unless systematic efforts are made to ensure it. This chapter will discuss various strategies for facilitating coordination among service providers, beginning with initial IEP development and continuing through program implementation and review of the student's program.

ISSUES RELATED TO COORDINATION OF SERVICES

Despite the requirements of P.L. 94–142, achieving effective coordination among service providers has continued to be problematic in many aspects of special education service delivery. For example, there is little evidence of dedication and coordination of resources during the pre-referral and referral process to maintain students in the regular education program (Christenson, Ysseldyke, Wang, & Algozzine, 1983). In addition, the multidisciplinary team evaluation process is often described as a process of separate assessments, completed by each required discipline, rather than a coordinated effort to produce a comprehensive and synthesized overview of the student. Finally, the IEP planning process continues to be characterized as one in which the IEP committee meets to approve an IEP already developed by a special education teacher rather than a process based on the coordinated effort of a team of individuals including the parents (White & Calhoun, 1987).

Coordination at the implementation phase of the IEP also appears to be limited in that there is often little collaboration between regular and special education teachers in planning, implementing, and ensuring continuity between the regular education

program and the specially designed instruction provided to the student (Ammer, 1984; Skrtic, 1987). Further, the IEP document is often viewed as being of little value for instructional planning and service delivery and may seldom be referred to in making instructional decisions (Dudley-Marling, 1985). If the IEP is not used to make instructional decisions, it can hardly be viewed as a useful means of coordination of services among providers.

THE IEP DOCUMENT AS A METHOD FOR FACILITATING COORDINATION

A very basic issue related to IEP coordination is ensuring that the program, as defined and approved by the IEP committee, is actually implemented. Unfortunately, the fact that an IEP is developed and approved by the IEP committee does not always constitute assurance that the program will occur as planned (Strickland, 1983). Although the IEP itself may be considered to be appropriately written, either its implementation may not be achieved, or it may not occur as envisioned by the IEP committee. In some cases, required services may not be provided at all, even though they are included on the IEP. In other cases, providers may fail to provide the services in the manner stated on the IEP. The failure of school systems to implement the program documented on the IEP has been a primary basis of frustration for many parents and in some cases has resulted in due process hearings (Strickland, 1983).

Although, as it is presently used, the IEP may not always be a useful document for instructional planning, its potential value for facilitating coordination should not be underestimated. The specificity with which the IEP is developed can significantly enhance its value for facilitating coordination among service providers. If IEP goals, objectives, evaluation schedules, and criteria as well as service providers are thoroughly discussed by those responsible for their implementation and clearly delineated before IEP implementation, the probability that the program will be appropriately implemented will be significantly increased.

Clarifying Roles of Service Providers

When more than one individual is responsible for implementing the IEP, each individual's role must be clearly defined. Therefore, designating the individual who will be responsible for the specific elements of the student's IEP is a helpful first step in coordinating services. Although not a specific requirement of the IEP, such a designation is included in many IEP formats developed by school districts to ensure that responsibilities are clearly defined. If more than one individual is responsible for particular aspects of a goal, both individuals should be designated by their position, such as speech therapist, special education teacher, or regular classroom teacher. Such a procedure enables committee members to identify and resolve potential implementation and coordination issues before they become problems. For example, one goal for a student may be to speak using complete sentences. Both a speech therapist and the classroom teacher may be responsible for the goal. The classroom teacher, however, may focus on promoting generalization of the spontaneous use of complete sentences in classroom activities, while the speech and language therapist may provide consultation services to the teacher and/or may provide direct therapy and strategy training to the student. If the individual responsible for each of these aspects of language development is not clearly articulated on the IEP, coordination between the therapeutic component of the goal and the generalization of the skill in the classroom may not occur systematically.

Another advantage of designating the service provider on the IEP is that it provides a written indication to parents of the professional(s) responsible for each goal included on the IEP. Although responsibility for providing services may be discussed at the IEP meeting, parents do not usually interact daily with school personnel and are not always familiar with the school's service-delivery models. Thus, after the IEP meeting, parents may not be likely to remember which professionals are responsible for which goals and objectives.

Accessibility of the IEP

The practice of distributing copies of the IEP to the student's parents and teachers has become generally accepted since the implementation of P.L. 94–142 and constitutes sound educational practice. Nonetheless, what happens to the IEP after it is distributed to committee members is of some concern. Some research indicates that IEPs are rarely referred to and are often stored in locked file cabinets rather than kept easily accessible for reference by those responsible for implementation (Dudley-Marling, 1985; Pugach, 1982). If implementers must leave their classrooms or offices to walk to the school's main office and engage in appropriate confidentiality procedures to obtain and review the IEP for instructional purposes, it is not surprising that some educators seldom consult the IEP during the implementation period.

Likewise, related services providers who are expected to provide services to support the goals and objectives identified in the IEP may find it similarly inconvenient to use the IEP in developing daily or weekly individual treatment or instructional plans. Although confidentiality procedures apply to the IEP, these requirements should not prevent the distribution of copies to those individuals who are responsible for the implementation of the program. On the contrary, one might question the appropriateness of the program provided to a student with a disability if individuals responsible for programming, for example, the classroom teacher, have not received a copy of the IEP on which to base the student's instructional program.

It is also important for parents to receive a copy of the IEP. Although P.L. 94–142 requires only that parents be provided a copy on request, many parents may not be aware of this option and thus may not make a request. A sound policy for local educational agencies would be to ensure that all parents are provided with a copy of the approved IEP once it is completed. Keeping a copy of the IEP, parents know what educational services are being provided to their child and have an opportunity to monitor progress toward the goals and objectives on the IEP as implementation occurs. In addition, many parents assume responsibility for reinforcing or even teaching some IEP objectives and can help their child work toward objectives being taught at school. Both home and school programs should be coordinated to ensure that the goals and objectives on the IEP provide the focus for these efforts.

Another consideration regarding distribution of copies of the IEP is to provide a copy to the student when appropriate. When students are familiar with and understand the content and purpose of the IEP, they can be helpful in adding a measure of coordination to the services provided by various professionals. For example, in one instance, a student at the high school level had participated in her IEP conference and had received a copy of the IEP, which she kept in the front of her notebook. One of the stipulations of the IEP was that she would be allowed additional time on classroom tests and assignments because she wrote at a very slow speed and became extremely anxious under pressure. This student, in effect, monitored the implementation of her own IEP. When teachers gave tests and assignments and did not allow her the agreed-on additional time, she took out her IEP and diplomatically reminded the teacher that agreement had been reached that this type of specially designed instruction would be available to her. This example demonstrates the potential for students learning to be their own case managers to promote the coordination of their educational programs while in school. An exciting consideration is that once this skill is learned during school years, students may continue to demonstrate it in coordinating the special services they will need as adults.

Although the distribution of multiple copies of the IEP can have many benefits, making multiple copies can be time-consuming and expensive. Recognizing the need to distribute copies of the IEP to committee members, many school systems have begun to use pressure-sensitive or carbon-paper formats to obtain multiple copies of the document.

COORDINATION AMONG SERVICE PROVIDERS

To foster coordination of services during IEP implementation, service providers should be in close contact with one another, either informally or in regularly scheduled team meetings of all individuals providing services to a particular student. Despite the seemingly obvious need for active participation of these individuals, research continues to indicate that responsibility for program development is still primarily the responsibility of the special education teacher. It is usually the special education teacher who develops the specific instructional programs after overall IEP development (White & Calhoun, 1987). Often, classroom teachers who provide instructional services to the student after IEP development are not substantively included in initial IEP development or in ongoing activities designed to facilitate coordination of the student's program (Ammer, 1984; Dudley-Marling, 1985).

Classroom Teachers

A major consideration in facilitating coordination among providers is to involve the classroom teacher of the student in ongoing program monitoring and coordination activities. Although a substantial number of students with disabilities are placed into

regular classes for at least a portion of the day, the active participation of the classroom teacher in the program planning remains at a low level (Ammer, 1984; Goldstein et al., 1980; Pugach, 1985). The lack of meaningful teacher involvement in the development of the student's educational program is viewed as a major obstacle to effective IEP implementation (Dudley-Marling, 1985).

To facilitate the participation of classroom teachers in program planning, many schools attempt to schedule meetings during commonly established planning times to make it possible for teachers to attend. In other school systems, substitute teachers are made available so that teachers may attend IEP meetings for their students. If periodic meetings are not conducted or if the classroom teacher is unable to attend, other opportunities should be made available for involvement with the other service providers. It should be remembered that of all the service providers, the classroom teacher is probably the individual who knows the curriculum best and is therefore the most appropriate individual to consider IEP implementation in the context of its appropriateness in the classroom.

The classroom teacher's involvement is particularly important when the student will participate for all or a portion of the day in the regular program. Although individuals other than the classroom teacher may be able to identify goals and objectives for a particular student with a disability, it is unlikely that these individuals will be thoroughly familiar with the curriculum, routines, and schedules of the regular program. With the involvement of the regular teacher, goals and objectives can be developed that complement the regular classroom structure, thereby increasing the probability that the IEP will be effectively implemented. An important system of checks and balances occurs when persons responsible for implementation actually participate in the planning process.

Related Services Providers

Despite the requirement of P.L. 94–142 that related services are those services necessary to enable the student to benefit from the educational program provided to a student, these services traditionally have been developed and provided separately from the student's educational program. For example, a speech therapist might conduct a speech and language evaluation, develop a therapeutic program, and provide speech and language therapy in a separate setting, with little initial or ongoing coordination with the classroom teacher or the special education teacher. As mentioned previously, however, in recent years increased emphasis has been placed on integrating related services into the ongoing educational program rather than providing them in traditional "pull-out" settings removed from the regular program (Rainforth & York, 1987). This process requires cooperative planning and coordination between teachers and related services providers both during the initial stages of program development and throughout the year. Depending on the type of service provided and whether the service provider is based in the school, attendance at team meetings may or may not be possible. Privately contracted and itinerant service providers may be unable to attend team meetings regularly. It is nonetheless important that these individuals be involved in the planning and decision making process.

One strategy for ensuring involvement of related services providers in the student's educational program may include developing a coordinated written instructional plan and schedule, based on the IEP, to guide coordination among service providers and instruction on a daily, weekly, and monthly basis. Another strategy might be use of a service log to provide progress information to other service providers on a routine basis. Each service provider might provide a written update of service providers on a routine basis. Each service provider might provide a written update of service activities each time the student is seen. The service log might be maintained in a specific location in the school, or it may remain with the student, with the parents having an opportunity to review the services provided each week. Each service provider would read new updates before providing services and making an entry at the completion of each session.

Physicians and Other Medical Representatives

As student's with complex disabilities increasingly enroll in public school programs, the need for improved communication and coordination with members of the medical profession has become increasingly vital. Although P.L. 94–142 implies the need for coordination between physicians and schools in planning and providing special education and related services to students with disabilities, few physicians attend school planning conferences, and communication between these agencies has been characterized as minimal (Palfrey, Sarro, Singer, & Wenger, 1987; Palfrey, Singer, Walker, et al., 1986). This is not surprising, considering that many physicians and educators lack information and training related to the contribution that the one discipline may make to another. In addition, because physi-

cians usually are not paid to collaborate with professionals in school-related activities, physicians may assign this type of interaction low priority, except when such collaboration is an established part of an educational or treatment program (such as in therapeutic settings).

Although physician participation in team planning of educational programs has traditionally been minimal, improved partnerships with medical services providers can greatly enhance the educational program provided to students with disabilities. For example, physicians may have established close, long-term relationships with the student's family and thus may provide necessary communication links between the school and the family. In addition, physicians can offer evaluation and diagnosis of medically related disabilities, as well as perspectives on issues that might affect the student's educational program such as nutrition, allergies, and chronic illness. When a student takes or is being considered for medication, the physician can be an invaluable resource for educating school personnel and parents regarding the medication's therapeutic value and potential side effects.

Methods that might enhance communication between the school and physicians might include published call hours within school systems and pediatric practices to establish common conference times, training programs in which each discipline could learn more about the other, and flexibility in scheduling planning and coordination conferences.

COORDINATION AND COMMUNICATION WITH PARENTS

Parents often are the primary coordinators of services between the school and other service agencies (Allen & Hudd, 1987). It is usually parents who provide information to other service providers, such as physicians, on how their children are performing in school, and it is usually they who are initially responsible for informing a new school about their child's disability and the previous educational program provided. In addition they are often called on to provide continuity and support for the IEP through activities conducted at home. Examples of ways that parents might be asked to be involved in implementation of the IEP include ensuring that homework is completed satisfactorily, managing behavior in a way consistent with that used at school, facilitating language development and use of correct speech, and implementing specific programs for motor development or maintenance.

To enable parents to participate effectively in IEP implementation, effective communication and coordination strategies are essential. Although teachers and parents may meet periodically for required conferences, such meetings do not, however, seem to necessarily enhance coordination and communication. Studies reviewing the amount and nature of communication between parents and school personnel during IEP conferences indicate that parents may not fully understand decisions made during formal IEP conferences, that verbal participation of parents is limited, and that parent responsibilities regarding the IEP are only minimally discussed (K. K. Turnbull & Hughes, 1987; Vaughn et al., 1988).

School personnel, too, may consider the formal conference to be a relatively ineffective mechanism for communication and coordination between parents and the school program. Although perhaps achieving the purpose of IEP development, such conferences may not promote sufficient familiarity between parents and school personnel to ensure a coordinated effort toward the successful implementation of the student's program.

In one study of interaction between parents of preschool students and their teachers, a major obstacle identified by school personnel in establishing linkages with parents was difficulty in communicating with parents. Results of the study indicated that more time is usually spent with parents in formal and structured conferences, or in indirect communication such as note writing, than in direct personal contacts. Teachers, however, felt that the direct, less formal type of communication was more effective in promoting satisfaction with parent involvement (Fuqua, Hegland, & Karas, 1985). Some suggestions for enhancing communication and interaction with parents follow.

Parent Group Meetings

A casual group meeting of school representatives and several parents may provide a nonthreatening mechanism for coordination and communication between parents and service providers. Open-house meetings provide an informal way to meet and talk about student programs. Meetings may also be more structured to provide an opportunity for parents to ask questions about the IEP document itself.

Volunteer Programs

Many parents volunteer as room parents and class sponsors because they recognize that this is an effective method for keeping abreast of what is going on at school and for communicating informally with their child's teacher(s). Interestingly, it is often teachers rather than parents who may need training regarding the use of volunteers in the classroom. In some instances, teachers may find it difficult to determine what types of activities can appropriately be delegated to volunteers. Parents, however, often have excellent individual skills that can be used in a variety of ways. Simply asking parents how they would like to be involved can present a number of options, ranging from involvement in actual teaching or tutoring activities to providing supportive services such as gathering of teaching resources outside the classroom.

Observing in the Classroom

The relationship between the written IEP and actual classroom practice is often difficult for parents to determine. If parents are expected to understand the process by which special education and related services are provided to their child, and also support that program at home, they should be encouraged to observe in the classroom when they desire to. Although teachers and other service providers may feel somewhat uncomfortable when being observed by parents, such an opportunity can provide a valuable and positive experience for both parents and teachers. Rather than speculating about the services being provided to their child, parents can observe firsthand the kinds of activities, materials, and methods used. In addition to adding a measure of accountability for teachers and therapists, observation by parents can enable a different level of communication and can provide a basis for suggesting activities for use at home.

Home Visits

Just as observation in the classroom can greatly enhance the parents' understanding of the educational program provided to their child, home visits can provide the same valuable insight for the teacher or therapist. Such visits can enable the teacher to develop appropriate teaching strategies at school and to suggest realistic goals for implementation at home. For example, observing established after-school routines can enable the teacher to suggest effective and workable homework routines that fit the family's established patterns. In a home with several young children, the teacher may observe that parents do not have the time or opportunity to work individually with one child. Depending on the ages of other children in the family, however, the teacher may assist the parents in developing a homework routine in which an older sibling assists with homework, or in which all children participate at the same time.

THE ROLE OF THE TEAM IN PROMOTING COORDINATION OF SERVICES

Service providers tend to interact with one another in a variety of ways, depending on the nature of the task to be completed and the communication and coordination skills of the team members themselves. Coordination in the implementation of special education programs can generally be defined in terms of levels of interaction among team members, with isolated and individually determined programming and service delivery being the lowest level of coordination and fully integrated and unified programming representing the highest, and perhaps most desirable, level of team interaction. Levels of coordination are often conceptualized as multidisciplinary, interdisciplinary, and transdisciplinary, with multidisciplinary coordination requiring minimal interaction among team members and transdisciplinary coordination representing maximum coordination.

It should be noted that not every student with a disability requires the same amount of service coordination. For example, a speech therapy program for one student might be easily coordinated among individuals responsible for providing services to that student, while for a student with a severe physical disability, coordinating and integrating multiple therapies into an appropriate program might require frequent collaborative planning between all service providers. The IEP committee must consider the coordination needs of each student's program to ensure that a sufficient level of coordination is maintained while not overcommitting resources to achieve levels of coordination beyond those necessary. Four levels of coordination are discussed below.

Isolated Programming and Service Delivery

Even though there is general consensus of opinion that coordination of service delivery is often essential for students with disabilities, coordination may not always occur in actual practice. Even when professionals agree that coordination is necessary to effectively implement a student's program, service providers may continue to deal with students autonomously. Despite the fact that isolated programming might be appropriate for some students (depending on the nature of the service provided), lack of coordination probably occurs more often than it should. Because of limited time, and perhaps because of lack

of experience with team approaches, some professionals seldom interact with other service providers except in a perfunctory manner. When professionals interact minimally with one another, there can be little communication or coordination. Thus, in such cases, there is no team approach to programming for the student.

Multidisciplinary Participation in Evaluation And Planning Activities

P.L. 94–142 requires professional interaction and coordination through the multidisciplinary evaluation team. This method of coordination is characterized by the inclusion of individuals from a variety of disciplines in diagnostic or planning activities. At this level of coordination, service delivery may continue to remain isolated and independent, affected little by contributions from other team members (Bailey, 1984; Campbell, 1987). In many instances, the focus of the multidisciplinary team may center more on the number of individuals involved in the administration of tests, rather than emphasizing joint or coordinated evaluation, synthesis and program development. Although this level of coordination may achieve the minimal legal requirements for nondiscriminatory evaluation, it is ineffective for ongoing program coordination (Bailey, 1984; Campbell, 1987).

When the focus of coordination continues to be on the number and type of team members required for meetings to plan and review the student's program, there may be little emphasis on ongoing collaboration or coordination related to implementing the student's program. As a result, the multidisciplinary team may experience particular difficulties in coordinating services to the same client (Bailey, 1984). For example, the classroom teacher who is responsible for a particular student with a disability in the classroom may focus primarily on including the student in class instruction, based on the established curriculum of the school. Even though the teacher may participate in the IEP meeting, he may not be aware of the specific types of instruction provided by other service providers. At the same time, the special education teacher may see the same student for a portion of the day in the resource room, during which he provides specialized methods and materials for teaching the student isolated reading skills in accordance with the short-term objectives on the IEP. This individual may know little about the reading curriculum of the regular classroom or the reading skills currently being addressed in that program. In addition, a speech therapist may also see the student in the speech therapy room, focusing entirely on encouraging the same student to describe various objects to develop expressive language skills. The therapist may know little about the structures of the regular program to which expressive language skills must eventually be generalized and may have little, if any, interaction with the special education resource teacher. In such a situation, the student may have difficulty synthesizing these instructional efforts into a meaningful educational experience.

Coordination in Program Planning and Delivery

Beyond multidisciplinary evaluation and a committee's writing of the IEP, it is the school's responsibility to ensure that the actual provision of the student's educational program is coordinated to represent a unified program with common goals rather than several separate programs. To accomplish this, the concept of team coordination must extend beyond the multidisciplinary evaluation process, to actual coordination and interaction among disciplines in the planning and delivery of a comprehensive program of services. A team functioning in this way might be referred to as functioning at an interdisciplinary level.

The interdisciplinary team differs from the multidisciplinary team in that the goals of the team, in this case the goals and objectives on the IEP, can only be accomplished by an interactive effort and contributions from the disciplines involved (Fordyce, 1981). Although members of an interdisciplinary team may still conduct assessments individually, and may still provide direct services via pull-out programs, emphasis is placed on systematic sharing of evaluation results to ensure a well-documented and comprehensive educational plan. Coordination among team members after implementation generally occurs through regularly scheduled team meetings. Interdisciplinary team planning enables professionals to be more aware of each person's contribution to the whole education of the student.

Integrated Service Delivery

A final level of team functioning is characterized by full integration of services and is often referred to as transdisciplinary coordination. Although not a frequently achieved level of coordinated service delivery, transdisciplinary coordination often is considered the optimal organization level for effective delivery of coordinated services to students with disabilities. This model is characterized by three distinctive team functions:

1. team members perform the various services together,

2. the expertise of individual team members is used to train other team members, and
3. roles and responsibilities are shared by more than one team member.

(Lyon & Lyon, 1980)

Coordination at this level enables professionals to become familiar with, and share, roles traditionally maintained by separate and distinct disciplines. In this way, the primary service provider or other team members can become proficient in, and in many instances teach, most skills in the student's ongoing curriculum (Rainforth & York, 1987).

Integrating related services (e.g., speech therapy) into the student's educational program to promote functional skill development and meaningful performance is one example of coordination at the level of transdisciplinary coordination. Another example includes designing instruction to enable clustering of skills from various disciplines to facilitate the development of functional concepts.

Despite the obvious appeal of an integrated service-delivery model, many professionals have not been adequately trained to assume team roles such as those required for this level of coordination. In addition, few school programs are logistically organized to facilitate the maintenance of such a program. Service-delivery models in both regular and special education should be reviewed and modified to facilitate and support transdisciplinary coordination in planning and delivery of services. In addition, training opportunities, provided in conjunction with employment, should be provided to enable teachers, related services providers, and school support personnel to acquire skills necessary to implement this model.

COORDINATION WITH NON–PUBLIC SCHOOL PLACEMENTS

P.L. 94–142 addresses the coordination of services between agencies at three levels. First, in accordance with the child-find requirement of P.L. 94–142, the public school must coordinate with all public and private schools and institutions to ensure the location, evaluation, and identification of students with disabilities within the jurisdiction of that public school.

Second, in an attempt to provide special education and related services to students who are not placed by the public school but who are enrolled by their parents in private or parochial schools, public schools may coordinate with those facilities to provide equipment, dual enrollment, educational radio and television, and the provision of mobile educational services and equipment (*Federal Register*, 1977). In addition, public school personnel in some instances may provide direct services to students enrolled in non–public schools.

Third, P.L. 94–142 firmly establishes that when the public school places a student in a non–public school facility to receive special education and related services, that agency is responsible for ensuring the appropriateness of the program provided (*Federal Register*, 1977). The requirements of P.L. 94–142 address the issue of coordination of services with private schools in three ways, as follows:

1. A representative of the private school facility must attend the meeting conducted to develop the student's IEP, or, if unable to attend, the representative's participation must be ensured by methods such as individual or conference telephone calls.
2. Both the parents and a representative of the public school must be involved in, and agree to, any decision related to the student's IEP and before implementation of any change in the student's program.
3. The compliance of the private school program must be monitored by the public agency by methods such as written reports, on-site visits, and parent questionnaires.

Although these requirements do facilitate coordinated planning and review of the student's IEP between the public school and the private facility, they do not address issues related to ongoing communication between the agencies. This is particularly critical with students for whom private services or placement is temporary. Examples include students who are placed in correctional institutions, students with emotional disturbances who are placed for short-term treatment in residential treatment facilities, and students with chronic health disorders who are enrolled both in hospital programs and public school programs. Because these students come from and will return to the public school, it is vital that continuity and communication be maintained between the public school and alternative educational settings.

Even if a private school implements a student's IEP, responsibility for compliance remains with the public school. Schools should therefore develop mechanisms to ensure ongoing coordination of services. Suggested strategies for facilitating such coordination include establishing liaison personnel to coordinate student services between the private school and the public school, developing procedures for routine contact with the private school or facility,

and ensuring appropriate information exchange between the agencies.

Appointment of Liaison Personnel

Few school systems delegate staff specifically to establish and maintain linkages with private schools and other facilities that provide special education to students with disabilities. For example, in a study of correctional institutions, Lewis, Schwartz, and Ianacone (1988), found that the majority of representatives polled from correctional institutions (71%) and public schools (79%) indicated that services are never coordinated by a person whose primary responsibility is to facilitate coordination between agencies. Nonetheless, the majority of representatives surveyed agreed that such a role was needed in their states. In a large school system, establishing a position to coordinate services can enhance the planning and development of services before they are initiated, ensure the maintenance of services for their duration, and facilitate return to and continuity with the public school program when the services are completed. In small school systems where the incidence of non–publicly provided services is low, liaison responsibilities might be assumed by existing professional staff such as social workers and counselors.

Establishing Routine Contact with Non–Public Service Providers

Even though P.L. 94–142 requires that the public school monitors private programs in which it places students with disabilities, the tendency may exist to provide minimal (if any) supervision after private services are implemented. Although placement in a private facility usually is based on the understanding that the services the student requires are present and available, private facilities, like public schools, sometimes have difficulty maintaining staff and services at levels commensurate with those required by a student's IEP. When this occurs, the level of services provided to students may be reduced for extended periods of time. If the public school does not maintain routine contact with the service provider, the disparity between the requirements of the IEP and the level of services actually provided may go unnoticed. As noted earlier, the public school is ultimately responsible for ensuring that services are provided in accordance with the IEP. Schools should establish strategies for routine contact with service providers, including monthly scheduled meetings, site visits, telephone conferences, and/or periodic reports documenting that services are provided in accordance with the IEP.

Exchange of Information

When students receive special education and related services from agencies other than the public school, information related to the student's progress may not always be exchanged freely and in a timely manner between service providers. Confidentiality requirements may differ between the agencies, required information exchanges may be overlooked, or parents may request that information not be shared. Needless to say, access to necessary and appropriate information is critical if communication is to occur between the agency providing the service and the agency responsible for ensuring the appropriateness of the program provided. This is particularly critical when the student moves from one service provider to the next. A lack of information may delay the provision of an appropriate program and perhaps even may prevent the successful integration of the students into the program provided. To avoid unnecessary delay and difficulties in exchange of student information, school systems might develop specific procedures and agreements for information transfer with agencies providing services to students with disabilities.

COORDINATION OF TRANSITION FROM ONE PROGRAM TO ANOTHER

Facilitating transition from one program to another has in recent years become a major focus of special education programs at virtually every level. P.L. 99–457, The Education of the Handicapped Amendments Act of 1986, addresses transition both for preschool students with disabilities and for secondary students preparing to leave school for employment in the community. Coordination of transition is also a necessary consideration for students moving from or to private schools and facilities. Finally, transition from elementary to junior high and from junior high school to high school is also a coordination issue that schools must address. This section will provide suggestions to facilitate coordination of transition services.

Transition to Preschool

For a prospective preschool student with a disability preparing to enter a special education program sponsored by the public school, an individualized family services plan (required by P.L. 99–457 for infants and toddlers with disabilities) may already exist. This plan outlines the steps to be taken supporting the transition of the preschooler to services provided by the public school. In addition, the provision of a case manager to coordinate services between agencies is a required component of this plan.

Schools currently attempt to coordinate services for preschool students in several ways. Most schools conduct kindergarten screening activities to identify students with disabilities. In addition, child-find activities may include referrals from medical facilities, local health departments, day-care centers, and parents. Child-find activities, however, are not always sufficiently timely for service coordination far enough in advance to ensure that an appropriate public school program is available.

With the implementation of required services to 3- to 5-year-old students, public schools must develop strategies for coordinating with agencies currently providing services to this population. The fact that public schools not already providing services to the 3- to 5-year-old population must begin to provide these services by 1991 provides a strong incentive to begin necessary coordination activities. Strategies for coordinating transition of preschoolers with disabilities to public school programs might include improved child-find activities, the establishment of transition groups, the development of individual or group transition plans, and cooperative agreements with other agencies. Each of these coordination strategies will be discussed briefly.

Improvement of Child-Find Activities.   By improving coordination of child-find activities with day-care centers, local parent groups, health departments, and clinics, public schools can obtain information for more accurately projecting the number of preschool students who may need services in sufficient time to ensure availability of adequate programs. This type of information enables the school to plan systematically for the types of services that may be required for coming years and when those services should be available. Collaborative efforts may include developing a central child-find program for all agencies. Many states have initiated efforts to develop computerized programs between agencies for storing and organizing information on students located through child-find efforts. These cooperative child-find efforts may greatly reduce the replication of child-find information between agencies.

Transition Groups.   For many parents of young preschool students, transition from home or community services to a public school program can be a difficult experience. The difficulty can be compounded when knowledge of the new program is limited and when no relationship has been established with the public school to assist with transition. Transition groups sponsored by the public school for incoming preschool students can provide an opportunity for parents and school representatives to meet with one another regularly before the student actually enrolls in the school. Such an arrangement has many benefits, including the potential for parents and school personnel to establish a positive basis for future coordination and the opportunity for both the school and parents to gain information and resolve issues informally before school begins. Transition groups can provide special services committees with valuable information regarding the needs of students and families who will be enrolled in their programs, enhancing planning for coordinated programming.

Transition Plans. In some instances, a written transition plan is developed to ensure that transition occurs smoothly. Although such a plan could be developed for any student, it is especially appropriate for students who need multiple services or for whom transition may be particularly difficult or cumbersome. For example, if a student has a rare medical disability that requires special health procedures at school as well as coordination with medical services providers, a written transition plan may serve to organize all essential elements that must be considered and arranged before enrollment in school. Figure 13–1 illustrates a transition plan for a student preparing to enter a public school program from a community day-care center.

Cooperative Arrangements with Other Agencies.
Before entering public school for the first time, many preschool students with disabilities will be enrolled in programs other than those sponsored by the public school. These programs might include private preschools, day-care centers, play groups, or home intervention programs. One way to facilitate transition from these programs to the public school is by establishing cooperative agreements between agencies that enable service providers in the public school to visit and perhaps to work with the student in the preschool environment before the student's enrollment in the public school program. In this way, future service providers can observe and even participate in the program provided to the student, thus gaining valuable knowledge on which to plan the student's future program. Another option might be for the preschool student to spend a portion of the week in the public school program before the beginning of the school year in which enrollment would actually begin. For example, the student might participate once or twice a week during the spring before school enrollment. Arrangements such as this not only provide professionals with information about the student but also can provide the preschool student with an orientation to the new program.

Development and Coordination of Transition Services for Secondary Students

In recent years, increased attention has been focused at the secondary level to strengthen and coordinate special education programs for students with disabilities currently in school or who recently left school to assist them in the transition to post secondary education, vocational training, competitive employment, continuing education, or adult services. Although public school administrators tend to agree that the public school should assume responsibility for transition activities (Benz & Halpern, 1987), research indicates that cooperation and coordination between schools and adult agencies has, to date, been virtually nonexistent (Hasazi, Gordon, & Roe, 1985; Wehman, Kregel, & Barcus, 1985). Coordination of services to address this goal requires that public schools coordinate services with community adult agencies. Hardman and McDonnell (1987) suggest several strategies for facilitating coordination between service providers at the secondary level. These include transition teams, written transition plans, cooperative tracking systems, and transition-planning guides.

Transition Teams. One strategy for increasing coordination at this level includes the development of a transition team for students preparing to leave high school. These teams should include representatives from the school (e.g., special education teachers and vocational education teachers) and also representatives from adult agencies (e.g., vocational rehabilitation and developmental disabilities agencies). The student should be an active member of his transition team. Even if the student cannot participate fully in all decisions regarding his future, it is inappropriate for professionals alone to decide what the student will do and where he will go, without information from the student. The student's case manager, often a special education teacher, typically assumes responsibility for organizing and coordinating the transition team for a particular student.

The transition team's purpose is to coordinate planning for the student in preparation for leaving school to facilitate meaningful employment and independent living after graduation. Transition teams should be established early in the student's high school years to allow time to identify and access throughout high school those community services necessary to support the student when leaving school.

Written Transition Plans. At the secondary level, the written transition plan provides a mechanism for systematically identifying those activities that must occur to facilitate the student's entry into adult

FIGURE 13–1
Preschool Transition Plan

Child's Name: _____

Age: _____ Birth Date: _____

Date of Plan: _____

Sending Program: _____

Receiving Program: _____

Planning Committee Members:

1. _____   3. _____

(Coordinator)

2. _____   4. _____

Responsibilities

Transition Event	Date of Completion	Sending Staff	Receiving Staff	Parents
1. Conduct comprehensive evaluation.	4-91	Will conduct functional assessment in preschool routines.	Will conduct multidisciplinary assessment and share results with parents and sending agency.	Will provide copies of all records and will participate in evaluation process.
2. Conduct eligibility conference.	4-91	Will attend eligibility conference of receiving school system to assist in eligibility decisions.	Will schedule and conduct eligibility conference with all participants.	Will be a member of the interdisciplinary team determining eligibility.
3. Parent observation in possible placement sites.	5-91	Will accompany parent on observations to placement sites.	Will schedule observations in possible placement sites.	Will review possible placement sites and assess.
4. Conduct IEP meeting.	5-91	Will attend and share progress reports, program goals, and other evaluation information.	Will provide tentative program planning information to all participants prior to IEP meeting.	Will participate in IEP development and contribute goals.
5. Identify related services.	5-91	Provide information on current therapy program.	Establish need for type and method of continuing therapy.	Participate in establishing need for therapy.
6. Conduct placement meeting.	5-91	Will attend placement meeting to assist in placement decision.	Will schedule placement meeting with all participants.	Will participate in placement decision.
7. Receiving staff observes child in current program.	5-91	Will arrange one day for receiving staff to observe and work with child in current environment.	Will observe child to obtain information for successful transition to receiving program.	Will attend observations.
8. Child participates in receiving program.	6-91	Will share program information and strategies with receiving school program.	Will arrange one week for child to participate in receiving program prior to enrollment.	Will observe child in receiving program and make suggestions for integration.

(Figure 13–1 continued)

Responsibilities

Transition Event	Date of Completion	Sending Staff	Receiving Staff	Parents
9. Identify skills needed for successful integration.	6-91	Will incorporate agreed on objectives into existing program for remainder of program.	Will continue agreed on strategies for skill development in receiving program.	Will participate in identification of necessary skills and will reinforce skills at home.
10. Identify equipment needed for successful integration.	6-91	Identify current equipment needs and share equipment with receiving school if needed.	Ensure availability of necessary program equipment.	Ensure availability of needed personal equipment.
11. Arrange transportation to and from school.	6-91	Share information regarding current transportation.	Ensure availability of appropriate transportation and share information with parents.	Provide information regarding current transportation methods.
12. Enroll in school.	9-91		Implement IEP in receiving program.	Participate in classroom program.
13. Follow-up	9-91	Sending program will provide follow-up contact during first month of enrollment.	Evaluate effectiveness of program. Contact sending program if necessary.	Evaluate effectiveness of program. Contact sending program if necessary.

living—whether postsecondary education or sheltered employment. The transition plan should be written by parents, teachers, adult agency representatives, and the student. The document should provide for the gradual assumption of case management responsibilities by adult services agencies so that as the student approaches graduation, a community program is already in place. The transition plan may be incorporated into the students IEP.

Figure 13–2 provides an example of a transition plan for a student preparing to leave high school. In this example, service goals are identified, based on such factors as student and family values, student capabilities, student and family preferences, and availability of services. Levels at which action should appropriately occur are identified, along with specific corresponding activities that will be completed to attain the goal. To ensure coordination of activities, the person and agency responsible are noted.

Cooperative Tracking System.   Another strategy for facilitating coordination in postschool transition activities is to develop with adult service agencies a cooperative information system for tracking students as they move from school to postsecondary activities. Very few districts use systematic procedures to obtain follow-up information from former students (Benz & Halpern, 1987), possibly because schools assume that after the student leaves school their responsibility has ended or because resources for extended follow-up activities are limited or nonexistent. In many instances, however, valuable information can be obtained on the effectiveness of the high school program by developing cooperative agreements between adult agencies and the public schools. Such a mechanism can provide for periodic monitoring of the employment status of former students and can make available specific and longitudinal student information on which to base program evaluation and revision.

Transition-Planning Guides.   In addition to written plans for individual students, school systems, together with adult service agencies, might develop a general transition-planning guide that describes for parents and service providers the process of transition from school to community living and employment. Such a guide might include (1) a sequential list of transition activities, the year in high school when these activities would typically begin, and which agency is responsible; (2) a list and description of services provided by adult service agencies; (3) employment and service options within the local community; and (4) procedures for accessing services in the community. Such a guide may assist parents in becoming familiar with the kinds of decisions they may have to make as well as time lines for making

those decisions. It may also be used to provide training both to parents and professionals regarding the service delivery developed between the school and community agencies. A helpful resource in compiling a local guide to transition needs is *Disabililty and the Family: A Guide for Adulthood* (H. R. Turnbull, Turnbull, Bronicki, Summers, & Roeder-Gordon, 1988).

Transition between Levels within School

Transition issues occur not only when a student enters or leaves school but also when a student moves from one level to another within school. For example, the programs of students moving from a middle school or junior high to a high school require coordination between sending and receiving schools to ensure that the program is appropriate to address the student's needs as identified in the IEP. Strategies for promoting coordination between school programs include joint IEP review meetings, joint program-planning meetings, and systematic exchange of records and information.

Joint IEP Meetings.   Many schools require that at least one representative of the receiving school participate in the annual review meeting for a student with a disability who is transferring to another school within the school district the following school year. This procedure has several advantages for the student, parent, and school personnel. It can assist the receiving school in planning for the efficient use of resources for the coming year by early determination of incoming students' needs. With adequate planning, such a meeting can provide an opportunity for receiving teachers and other service providers to meet the student and his parents, thus providing a point of contact for both parents and the school. Joint planning and development of the student's new IEP can also provide continuity between the programs provided to the student.

Joint Program-Planning Meetings.   To ensure that coordination occurs at the program level as well as on an individual basis, special services committees representing sending and receiving schools should meet at least yearly to systematically discuss the nature of the student population served by each school and any apparent trends or programmatic issues that may require long-term program planning. For example, if a blind student enters the third grade at an elementary school, the special services committee at the middle school should be aware that special provisions likely will be necessary when the student enters the fifth grade and changes schools. One way of accomplishing this type of transition

FIGURE 13–2
Individualized Transition Plan
(instructions on page 341)

INDIVIDUALIZED TRANSITION PLAN

Student _____

Date of
ITP Meeting _____

Expected Year
of Completion _____

Parent/Guardian's
Signature & Date _____

ITP Coordinator _____

VOCATIONAL/ EDUCATIONAL SERVICES		Annual Action Plan to Access Service Goal			
Vocational/ Educational Service Goal	Sequence of Action	Action Step	Person Responsible (S, F, A)	Time Frame	Date Accomplished
___ Independent Employment	**Awareness** 1. Values Clarification 2. Service Options Inquiry 3. Assessment(s) 4. Career Awareness				
___ Military					
___ Community College	**Exploration** 5. Community Support Service Options 6. Transportation Options 7. Assessment(s) 8. Skill Training				
___ University					
___ Supported Employment	**Integration** 9. Assessment of Values and Service Options 10. Site Visits 11. Program Application 12. Transportation 13. Assessment(s) 14. Skill Training				
___ Sheltered Employment					
___ Prevocational Training					
___ Day Treatment	**Access/Mastery** 15. Support Services 16. Transportation 17. Assessment(s) 18. Skill Training 19. Employment/Advanced Placement				
___ Other					

(Figure 13–2 continued)

INDIVIDUALIZED TRANSITION PLAN

Student _____

Date of
ITP Meeting _____

Expected Year
of Completion _____

Parent/Guardian's
Signature & Date _____

ITP Coordinator _____

FINANCIAL SUPPORT SERVICES

Annual Action Plan to Access Service Goal

Financial Support Service Goals	Sequence of Action	Action Step	Person Responsible (S, F, A)	Time Frame	Date Accomplished
____ Social Security	**Awareness** 1. Values Clarification 2. Service Options Inquiry 3. Assessment(s) of Need				
____ Supplemental Security Income	**Exploration** 4. Options Exploration 5. Assessment(s) of Need				
____ Social Security Disability Income	**Integration** 6. Assessment of Values, Options, and Needs 7. Service Application				
____ Food Stamps	**Access** 8. Service(s) Secured 9. Transportation				
____ General Assistance	_____				
____ Medicaid	_____ _____ _____				

(Figure 13–2 continued)

INDIVIDUALIZED TRANSITION PLAN

Student _____

Date of
ITP Meeting _____

Expected Year
of Completion _____

Parent/Guardian's
Signature & Date _____

ITP Coordinator _____

HEALTH SERVICES

Annual Action Plan to Access Service Goal

Health Service Needs/Goals	Sequence of Action	Action Step	Person Responsible (S, F, A)	Time Frame	Date Accomplished
___ Major Health	**Awareness** 1. Service Options Inquiry 2. Assessment(s) of Need				
___ Orthopedic					
___ Speech	**Exploration** 3. Options Exploration 4. Assessment(s) of Need				
___ Hearing					
___ Vision	**Integration** 5. Assessment of Options 6. Service Application 7. Transportation 8. Assessment(s) of Need				
___ Neurological					
___ Physical Therapy	**Access** 9. Service(s) Secured 10. Transportation 11. Assessment(s) of Need				
___ Occupational Therapy	_____				
___ Counseling	_____				

337

(Figure 13–2 continued)

INDIVIDUALIZED TRANSITION PLAN

Student _____

Date of
ITP Meeting _____

Expected Year
of Completion _____

Parent/Guardian's
Signature & Date _____

ITP Coordinator _____

CITIZENSHIP AND GUARDIANSHIP			Annual Action Plan to Access Service Goal			
Citizenship and Guardianship Service Goals	Sequence of Action	Action Step		Person Responsible (S, F, A)	Time Frame	Date Accomplished
___ Self as Guardian	**Awareness** 1. Values Clarification 2. Options Inquiry 3. Assessment(s) 4. Civic/Consumer Awareness					
___ Public Guardianship of Person						
___ Public Guardianship of Property	**Exploration** 5. Options Exploration 6. Support Service Options 7. Transportation Options 8. Assessment(s) 9. Skill Training					
___ Private Guardianship of Person	**Integration** 10. Assessment of Values and Options 11. Service Application 12. Transportation 13. Assessment(s) 14. Skill Training					
___ Private Guardianship of Property						
___ Self-Advocate	**Access/Mastery** 15. Service(s) Secured 16. Support Services 17. Transportation 18. Skill Training					
___ Public Advocate						
___ Private Advocate						

(Figure 13–2 continued)

INDIVIDUALIZED TRANSITION PLAN

Student _____

Date of
ITP Meeting _____

Expected Year
of Completion _____

Parent/Guardian's
Signature & Date _____

ITP Coordinator _____

HOME AND FAMILY

Annual Action Plan to Access Service Goal

Home and Family Goals	Sequence of Action	Action Step	Person Responsible (S, F, A)	Time Frame	Date Accomplished
___ Independent Living	**Awareness** 1. Values Clarification 2. Service Options Inquiry 3. Assessment(s) 4. Skill Training				
___ Independent Living with Support					
___ Family Home	**Exploration** 5. Community Support Service Options 6. Transportation Options 7. Assessment(s) 8. Skill Training				
Supervised:					
___ Apartment	**Integration** 9. Assessment of Values and Service Options 10. Site Visits 11. Service Application 12. Assessment(s) 13. Skill Training				
___ Boarding					
___ Congregate					
___ Group	**Access/Mastery** 14. Residential Tryout 15. Support Services 16. Maintenance of Family Relations 17. Transportation 18. Assessment(s) 19. Skill Training				
___ Foster					

(Figure 13–2 continued)

INDIVIDUALIZED TRANSITION PLAN

Student _____

Date of ITP Meeting _____

Expected Year of Completion _____

Parent/Guardian's Signature & Date _____

ITP Coordinator _____

RECREATION AND LEISURE

Annual Action Plan to Access Service Goal

Recreation and Leisure Service Goals	Sequence of Action	Action Step	Person Responsible (S, F, A)	Time Frame	Date Accomplished
___ Hobby	**Awareness** 1. Values Clarification 2. Service Options Inquiry 3. Assessment(s) 4. Recreation/Leisure Awareness				
___ Art/Music/ Dance Enrichment					
___ City and County Recreation/ Fitness (General)	**Exploration** 5. Community Support Service Options 6. Transportation Options 7. Assessment(s)/Tryouts 8. Skill Training				
___ City and County Recreation/ Fitness (Handicapped)	**Integration** 9. Assessment of Values and Service Options 10. Site Visits 11. Program Application 12. Transportation 13. Assessment(s) 14. Skill Training				
___ Private Recreation/ Fitness (General)					
___ Private Recreation/ Fitness (Handicapped)	**Access/Mastery** 15. Support Services 16. Transportation 17. Assessment(s) 18. Skill Training 19. Placement				
___ Social/Service Club					

(Figure 13–2 continued)

INSTRUCTIONS FOR COMPLETING THE IEP/ITP

I. The ITP

A. Service Goal   A list of postsecondary goal options is provided. Check one goal option or prioritize goal options based on (a) student and family values; (b) student and family preferences; (c) student capabilities; and (d) service availability.

B. Annual Action Plan to Access Service Goal   The columns under this heading indicate the steps that the school, family, and adult service providers agree to take during the current year to plan for and access the postsecondary service goals selected in the first column of the form.

1. Sequence of Action   The sequence provides options for action to assist in planning. Each year options should be selected from the sequence and should proceed from lower to higher numbered activities. Blank lines at the bottom of the sequence allow for options to be added by the ITP/IEP team. When a line appears within the list of options, options above the line can be carried out by members of the ITP team, while options below the line must be incorporated into the IEP for completion. Circle the numbers of the items, which the ITP/IEP team agrees to address during the current year.

2. Action Step   This column provides space to write specific descriptions of the action steps, which will be taken during the current year toward attainment of the service goal. The action steps are drawn from the sequence in the second column. Action steps should be written in specific and measurable terms. Record the corresponding number chosen from the sequence, and then write a description of the action to be taken.

3. Person Responsible   The name of the person responsible for coordinating each action step is recorded in the fourth column. Record the last name of the person responsible, followed by S (school), F (family), or A (adult service provider), as appropriate.

4. Time Frame   The projected time frame for accomplishing each action step is recorded in this column. The time frame should be a realistic appraisal of the actual time needed to accomplish the individual step during the current year. Record the time frame as beginning date (month) and ending date (month).

5. Date Accomplished   In this column, record the month that the action step is actually completed.

II. The IEP   The annual IEP goals and objectives developed for each transition area should contribute to the achievement of the postsecondary service goal(s) selected in the ITP, as indicated in the annual ITP action steps.

From Hawaii Transition Project, COMTEP, Department of Special Education, University of Hawaii—Manoa.

planning might be for professionals of the same service area to meet together. Occupational therapists might meet with occupational therapists, special education teachers with special education teachers, and speech therapists with speech therapists. Although many schools have informal mechanisms for conveying this information to one another, systematic and long-range program planning may be lacking in many systems. If schools meet to systematically share and discuss demographic data available for the purpose of long-term program planning, program resources can be planned for the comprehensive programs developed.

Exchange of Records.   Sharing information between schools, even within the same district, can sometimes be problematic if procedures for doing so do not exist. To coordinate transitions for students moving from one level to another within a school district, the sending school might be required to send to the receiving school early in the spring written notification of the names and special needs of students with disabilities who will be transferring. At this time, a copy of the students' current IEPs might be sent so that these may be reviewed and questions formulated before a meeting between the schools. Students' special education records should be transferred to the chairperson of the special services committee at the close of the school year including a list containing the names of the records. The chairperson of the special services committee of the receiving school should ensure that all records on the list are included in the records received and should formally accept the records. Service providers should review the records of incoming students before the close of school to become familiar with the names and special needs of each student to be enrolled in the program for the coming year.

ADMINISTRATIVE AND SUPERVISORY RESPONSIBILITY

Effective coordination of both IEP development and implementation requires that clear administrative and supervisory responsibility be identified within the local educational agency. Often, the superintendent appoints one individual as the agency administrator for IEPs. When this is the case, a job description delineating specific duties associated with IEP coordination should be developed. In many instances, the director of special education, curriculum, or special services also serves as the IEP administrator. In local educational agencies with an especially high student enrollment, an individual may be singularly assigned to administer the IEP process.

The procedures for supervision of IEP implementation at individual schools within the agency should be specified by the administrator, working with the principal and special services committee. Alternatives include assigning supervisory responsibility to the IEP administrator, the principal, chairperson of the special services committee, or a combination of these individuals. Guidelines for supervisors should be specified by the administrator and should cover specific duties, time lines, and methods of reporting to the IEP administrator. The active support and involvement of administrators is essential for the effective coordination of services. To achieve this goal, teachers and other service providers require time to plan and meet with one another as well as inservice training in planning and coordination strategies. Administrators can be responsive by recognizing and supporting these needs.

SUMMARY

Coordination between IEP service providers is critical to the successful implementation of the educational plan and thus has provided the focus for this chapter. The importance of the IEP for facilitating coordination was discussed, and strategies for enhancing communication among service providers and parents were presented. Alternative levels of team coordination were discussed, including multidisciplinary, interdisciplinary, and transdisciplinary coordination. Strategies for coordinating service delivery with non–public schools were presented as well as strategies for transition from one program to another.

EVALUATION

1. Conduct a survey in your school to determine whether classroom teachers have copies or ready access to IEPs for students with disabilities in their classes and whether the IEP indicates which professionals are responsible for each goal and/

or objective stated on the IEP. How well is the program provided in the regular classroom coordinated with that of the special education program?

2. In a meeting of the school special services committee, you have been asked to discuss the topic of increasing communication with parents. Discuss at least four strategies other than formal conferences that may involve parents in substantive and interesting ways.

3. You have observed that multidisciplinary evaluation teams in your district coordinate and collaborate very little, even in the development of the written evaluation report. You decide to set up an inservice meeting to discuss strategies for increased collaboration. Outline the levels of coordination that typify multidisciplinary team planning, and outline the characteristics of the level(s) you prefer for your district.

4. Describe three strategies for communicating and coordinating with non–public school facilities.

5. Identify and describe three types of transition issues, and discuss strategies for facilitating transitions between services.

CHAPTER 14

Systemwide Program Monitoring, Evaluation, and Inservice Training

OBJECTIVES

1. Define and state the purpose of monitoring.
2. Identify and discuss three strategies for monitoring the mechanics of IEP development.
3. Discuss two strategies for monitoring the competencies of educators.
4. Identify the requirements of P.L. 94–142 regarding the state's responsibility for developing and carrying out a personnel development program.
5. Identify strategies for inservice training.
6. Describe three levels of program evaluation.

To monitor a program basically refers to investigating or checking on its operations and quality. Monitoring includes (1) collecting data regarding the development and implementation of the program and (2) analyzing that data to make judgments related to the strengths of the program and areas of needed remediation. The process is evaluative in nature and should ultimately lead to program improvement. Thus, the purpose of monitoring is to enhance efficiency in procedural operations of development and to ensure that IEP development and implementation result in the provision of an appropriate education for students.

CONDUCTING PROGRAM-MONITORING ACTIVITIES

P.L. 94–142 requires each state educational agency to develop monitoring procedures to ensure that school systems comply with the requirements of the law. These monitoring activities must include on-site visits to schools, comparison of a sample of written IEPs with the program actually provided to the student, audit of federal fund expenditures, and compilation of data and reports (*Federal Register*, 1977). The standards by which programs are to be monitored are included in "Standards and Guidelines for Compliance With Federal Requirements for the Education of the Handicapped" available from the U.S. Department of Education, Office of Special Education Programs (1986).

The focus of this section is on monitoring to be conducted by the local agency, which would be in addition to the monitoring activities conducted by the state agency. Although many of the monitoring strategies included in this section would also be appropriate for state agency use in its monitoring processes, local agency monitoring is emphasized. The rationale for this emphasis is that, compared to state and federal personnel, local officials and educators are in the best position to assess and improve the quality of their own programs.

Systematic local monitoring has the potential to substantially strengthen the procedures and process of IEP development and implementation through systematic identification of strengths and weaknesses, and subsequent inservice training. At a recent inservice training session, a classroom teacher who had been involved in developing several IEPs commented that she hoped effort would be directed toward increasing the skills of teachers to promote meaningful rather than paper compliance with IEP regulations. She stated that, because of the rush to meet the deadlines for having approved IEPs on file, the IEPs in her system tended to be developed haphazardly and were generally irrelevant to the needs of students with disabilities. She stated that she hoped her system would not continue to "crank out" IEPs without taking systematic steps to improve the quality of the product. This teacher was basically asking for the development of monitoring procedures to pinpoint the factors contributing to the haphazard approach so that inservice training could be directed toward improving the IEP process. By monitoring IEP development and implementation and immediately initiating procedures to correct problems, a strong foundation can be established for IEP effectiveness.

LOCAL RESPONSIBILITY FOR MONITORING

The local educational agency's monitoring activities should surpass those initiated by the state agency to ensure that IEPs are being developed and implemented systematically. To develop local procedures for monitoring, the local school administration might establish an advisory committee with membership representing the special interests of all persons who have rights and responsibilities associated with the IEP. Representatives of the following groups should be considered for advisory committee membership: principals, classroom teachers, special education teachers, school psychologists, counselors, related services representatives, and parents. The chairpersons of special services committees could be particularly important persons to include on such a committee because they are likely to coordinate a substantial portion of the IEP process in their individual schools.

The purpose of having a broadly based advisory committee is to examine many different perspectives on issues and questions related to the IEP. Such a committee can address multiple issues related to the IEP rather than being restricted only to monitoring. To enhance the coordination of all facets of the IEP process, the advisory group could be the focal point for all systemwide planning related to the IEP.

Monitoring the Mechanics Of IEP Development

Before monitoring procedures can be established, the advisory committee needs to consider the legal requirements related to IEP development and implementation. By law, these are the required components:

1. Participants at IEP committee meetings
2. Documentation of attempts to involve parents when they do not attend the IEP meetings
3. Content of the IEP
4. Time lines
5. Provision of needed special education and related services
6. Committee meetings to review the IEP
7. Private school regulations

The required components should be monitored to ensure their compliance with P.L. 94–142. If state law or local educational agency policies specify further required components, the monitoring procedures should be extended to include these components. The advisory committee might also be encouraged to identify additional qualitative issues associated with IEP development and implementation. Examples of such issues might include problems such as a low percentage of parental involvement in IEP meetings or objectives generally not being stated behaviorally on the IEP. By identifying known problems in advance of implementing monitoring procedures the committee can ensure that monitoring procedures, when implemented, are sensitive to these problems and that documentation results in identifying the precise nature and extent of the problem.

After the areas that require monitoring have been identified by the advisory committee, the next decision involves choosing an appropriate strategy to collect the desired data. Strategies to consider in monitoring IEP development and implementation include the following:

1. Reviewing completed IEPs
2. Interviewing participants after IEP committee meetings
3. Observing at IEP conferences

Reviewing Completed IEPs.   A representative sample of IEPs might be reviewed at each individual school in the local educational agency. The sample should include IEPs on students at different grade levels and should represent the full spectrum of disabilities and special education placement alternatives. Ultimate responsibility for conducting this review should be assigned to the advisory committee or to the chairperson of the special services team in each school. Outside consultants from regional staff development centers, the state educational agency, colleges and universities, professional organizations, and parent organizations may also be invited to participate in the review process. To ensure that reviews of completed IEPs are consistent and systematic, the advisory committee might develop a questionnaire to be completed on each IEP reviewed. The use of a questionnaire ensures the systematic documentation of information resulting from the review. Clear documentation or record keeping is an essential element of effective monitoring procedures. Such a questionnaire is illustrated in Figure 14–1. It is important to note that this questionnaire assesses whether or not basic legal requirements were met. It does not address the issue of quality or the appropriateness of the IEP. It is possible for an IEP to comply with all legal requirements and still not be appropriate in light of the student's strengths and weakness.

Interviewing Participants after IEP Committee Meetings.   To monitor the dynamics of IEP committee meetings and the perceptions, roles, and responsibilities of each individual, participants of a representative sample of conferences could be interviewed by a designee of the advisory committee to elicit their responses and insights. The educators at a committee meeting may believe that the parents of a student were extremely satisfied with the conference's progress and may have considered parental involvement to be significant. An interview with the parents, however, may reveal that the parents' perspective is quite different. They may have felt intimidated and excluded. Interpersonal dynamics are an extremely important variable in successful IEP development.

FIGURE 14–1
Completed IEPs Questionnaire

Yes   No

—— —— 1. The IEP was completed within the specified time line.

  a. Date of referral ————

  b. Date student was determined to be handicapped ————

  c. Date of approved IEP ————

—— —— 2. The IEP committee included all required participants.

  a. Name of teacher attending ————————————————————————

  b. Name of individual responsible for providing or supervising special education attending ————

  ——

  c. Name of evaluator attending ————————————————————————

  d. Name of parent attending ————————————————————————

  e. Other persons attending ————————————————————————

  ——

  ——

—— —— 3. The IEP included all required components.

  Check if included:

  a. Present levels of performance ——

  b. Annual goals ——

  c. Short-term objectives ——

  d. Special education and related services ——

  e. Extent of participation in regular education program ——

  f. Projected date of initiated and anticipated duration of services ——

  g. Objective criteria and evaluation procedures ——

—— —— 4. Services specified on the IEP are being delivered.

  a. Services specified ————————————————————————

  ——

  ——

  b. Services delivered ————————————————————————

  ——

  ——

—— —— 5. All follow-up information that parents requested in the IEP conference has been provided to them.

  a. Information requested ————————————————————————

  ——

  ——

  b. Information provided ————————————————————————

  ——

  ——

—— —— 6. Evaluation of instructional objectives is being conducted on a periodic basis.

  a. Type of evaluation specified ————————————————————————

  ——

(Figure 14–1 continued)

b. Type of evaluation completed _____
_____
_____

c. Frequency of evaluation _____
_____

___ ___ 7. If necessary, the IEP has been revised to specify more appropriately the student's instructional program.

a. Reason for revision _____

b. Nature of revision _____

c. Date of reapproved IEP _____

___ ___ 8. An IEP committee meeting for the purpose of periodic review has been scheduled.

Date of meeting _____

9. Specify obstacles that may have prevented the appropriate development and implementation of the student's IEP. _____
_____

A questionnaire such as the one in Figure 14–2 can be used as a guide in structuring the interview and as a method of documenting information. Because interviews require a significant amount of time for both the individual conducting the interview and the participant from the IEP committee meeting, an alternative monitoring strategy would be to ask participants to provide a written response to the questionnaire as the primary method of collecting information. An interview would be necessary, of course, for parents who cannot read or who are blind.

In reviewing the responses of the participants, consistent negative reaction to various portions of the conference should be interpreted as warning signals of problems. If participants believe that the conference was not helpful or that the goals set were inappropriate, a communication problem among participants is likely. Documentation of participants' concerns should lead to recommendations of needed changes.

Observing at IEP Conferences. Observation of IEP conferences can also be used as a strategy for monitoring interpersonal dynamics. The observer, however, should not be a participant at the conference. In addition, permission to observe should be obtained before the IEP conference occurs. If any participant is uncomfortable with the observation, it should not be done, as it may inhibit the effective functioning of the committee and thus negatively affect the quality of the programming developed for the student. This strategy is recommended in instances when interviews and questionnaires have documented the fact that participants view committee meetings negatively. An objective observer could provide specific recommendations for improvement.

Analyzing Monitoring Data. After the initial data related to the mechanics of IEP development and implementation have been collected, the advisory committee or special services committee in each school should analyze them very carefully. As problem areas are identified, the committee members should determine their sources. For example, low parental involvement in IEP meetings may be attributed to any combination of the following factors: lack of information on the part of the parent of what an IEP is, inconvenient scheduling, transportation problems, difficulty locating baby sitters, feelings of intimidation on the part of the parent, lack of previous contact between the home and school, fear on the part of the parent of being told that their child has a disability, or strained relations between the teacher and parents. The type of intervention planned to increase parental involvement must be tailored to the exact source of the problem.

After problems are initially identified, it is frequently necessary to develop additional strategies to pinpoint problem sources. When parents do not attend the IEP conference, telephone or personal interviews might be scheduled with parents to find out their reasons for not attending and to secure recommendations from them pertaining to actions the school could take to involve them positively in the future. Because the purpose of monitoring is program improvement, it is insufficient to stop at the

FIGURE 14–2
IEP Conference Questionnaire

1. Has the IEP committee meeting been helpful in planning the student's educational program?

   very little   1   2   3   4   5   very much

2. Can the goals set for the child be accomplished during the current school year?

   definitely not   1   2   3   4   5   definitely yes

3. Did you have all your questions concerning the student answered at the committee meeting?

   definitely not   1   2   3   4   5   definitely yes

4. Are you satisfied with the placement decision?

   definitely not   1   2   3   4   5   definitely yes

5. Can the school system offer the resources to implement the IEP effectively?

   definitely not   1   2   3   4   5   definitely yes

6. As a result of the IEP meeting, do you have a better understanding of the student?

   definitely not   1   2   3   4   5   definitely yes

7. Do you have a definite responsibility in achieving the goals of the IEP?

   definitely not   1   2   3   4   5   definitely yes

8. Do you feel that your time at the meeting was well spent?

   definitely not   1   2   3   4   5   definitely yes

9. In thinking back on the conversation at the meeting, what were the topics most frequently discussed? What were the topics most infrequently discussed? Please list in priority order

Most Frequently Discussed: Least Frequently Discussed:
1. _____   1. _____
2. _____   2. _____
3. _____   3. _____

10. Which participant talked the most? _____

11. Which participant talked the least? _____

12. Approximately how many placement conferences have you attended in the past? _____

13. How much influence do you think you had in defining the student's curriculum? _____

point of mere problem identification. Analysis of data should lead to answering the question, "What can be done to enhance the success of IEP development and implementation?"

A further outgrowth of data analysis should be the identification of strengths and successes in IEP development and implementation. Such data need to be shared with all individuals who have assumed IEP responsibility. There is a tendency to point out problems, yet rarely to highlight the successes. Educators and parents need recognition and reinforcement for a job well done. The systematic improvement of mechanics associated with the IEP process can be fostered by building on strengths and ensuring that the participants are commended for their success.

Monitoring Competencies of Educators

To a large extent, the effective development and implementation of IEPs depends on the competencies of educators. IEPs require a more systematic approach to evaluation, curriculum development, and individualized instruction than has generally been practiced in regular education programs in the past.

FIGURE 14–3
Competency Analysis Guide

	Needs Improvement	Satisfactory	Excellent

A. INDIVIDUALIZED EDUCATION PROGRAMS

1. To be able to identify federal and state legislative requirements associated with the IEP.
2. To be able to develop an IEP for a student with a disability.

Assessment

   a. To be able to administer formal and informal diagnostic tests to determine level of functioning.

   b. To be able to demonstrate ways to modify paper-pencil evaluation techniques for various student needs.

   c. To be able to develop a system to collect and record data by which to evaluate student progress toward goal attainment.

Long-Range Goals

   d. To be able to determine long-range goals for students within the range of student ability.

Short-Term Objectives

   e. To be able to formulate behaviorally stated objectives for each learner based on diagnostic information collected.

   f. To be able to analyze a task for the skills required to learn that task (task analysis).

   g. To identify appropriately related services based on the needs of students.

   h. To be able to demonstrate skills for obtaining information from and giving information to parents, students, and other professionals.

   i. To be able to serve as a supportive counselor for parents in implementing a planned program for the student's intellectual and social development.

3. To be able to demonstrate appropriate instructional strategies in the classroom with students with disabilities.

   a. To be able to identify techniques for individualizing instruction to meet the specific learning needs of each student.

   b. To be able to design a variety of alternative learning strategies for students with disabilities who are unable to learn from commonly used strategies.

   c. To be able to modify activities within a wide range of difficulty so that students of varying abilities can participate at their own level, pace, and style.

   d. To be able to break tasks into component steps and teach in sequence.

   e. To be able to identify methods of teaching social and vocational skills to students with disabilities.

4. To be able to use effectively commercial and teacher-made instructional materials.

   a. To be able to identify characteristics of materials that bear consideration in selecting materials appropriate for specific learning situations (format, process, grade level, etc.).

   b. To be able to evaluate commercial materials in terms of efficiency in obtaining stated goals.

   c. To be able to identify potential sources of information concerning instructional materials and other resources.

   d. To be able to utilize diagnostic information on the selection and use of media and materials appropriate to the needs of the student.

   e. To be able to adapt instructional materials in accordance with the exceptionalities of the individual student.

5. To be able to develop individualized programming for students with disabilities using a variety of resources including peer tutors, community volunteers, and self-instructional materials.

6. To be able to apply behavior management skills in improving the academic performance and the general classroom behavior of students with disabilities.

(Figure 14–3 continued)

	Needs Improvement	Satisfactory	Excellent

B. ZERO REJECT

1. To be able to identify federal and state legislative requirements associated with the principle of zero reject.

2. To be able to develop and implement a child-find program.

3. To be able to collaborate effectively with personnel from other educational agencies regarding contracted services for students with disabilities.

C. NONDISCRIMINATORY EVALUATION

1. To be able to identify federal and state legislative requirements associated with the principle of nondiscriminatory evaluation.

2. To be able to describe educationally relevant characteristics of handicapping conditions.

3. To be able to assess the educational usefulness of standardized tests (IQ, achievement) in regard to evaluation of students with disabilities.

4. To be able to assess the educational usefulness of criterion-referenced tests in regard to evaluation of students with disabilities.

5. To be able to identify state and local criteria for special education services/placement.

6. To be able to describe the functioning of a special services committee in regard to referral and evaluation.

D. LEAST RESTRICTION

1. To be able to identify federal and state legislative requirements associated with the principle of mainstreaming.

2. To be able to define what mainstreaming is and what it is not.

3. To be able to state the rationale for mainstreaming in regard to the following issues: efficacy studies of the academic progress of students with mild disabilities in special vs. regular classes, labeling, minority status, and legislation.

4. To be able to identify the interactive roles and responsibilities of various groups of educators (regular teacher, resource teacher, school psychologists, counselors, and administrators) in promoting the approach of shared responsibility in order to successfully implement least restrictive policies.

5. To be able to assess the ancillary services (speech therapy, physical therapy, etc.) required to meet the educational needs of students with disabilities.

6. To be able to assess educational placements in identifying the least restrictive appropriate placement for a student with a disability.

E. DUE PROCESS AND PARENT PARTICIPATION

1. To be able to identify federal and state legislative requirements associated with the principles of due process and parent participation.

2. To be able to specify a plan of preventing due process hearings by obtaining necessary parental consent and involvement.

3. To be able to state roles and responsibilities of participants in a due process hearing.

4. To be able to communicate effectively with parents regarding evaluation results and placement recommendations.

5. To be able to conduct parent conferences related to reviewing the student's records and discussing proposed amendments.

6. To be able to demonstrate in professional and personal interactions the protection of personally identifiable information.

Monitoring procedures need to be implemented to identify those competencies that educators need to strengthen or develop. Before establishing such monitoring procedures, it is first necessary to specify the behavioral competencies associated with effective IEP development and implementation: Figure 14–3 is a rating scale that includes behaviorally stated competencies associated with the IEP, in addition to competencies related to implementing the legislative principles of zero reject, nondiscriminatory evaluation, least restriction, due process, and parent participation. This list is not exhaustive and certainly could be expanded by the advisory committee. Using such a competency list as a guide, an advisory committee should identify the particular competencies or the various roles and responsibilities of the participants involved in the IEP process. For example, counselors have different responsibilities regarding IEP development and implementation than do classroom teachers. These different responsibilities should be reflected in stated competencies for each group. A separate listing of competencies could be made by the advisory committee for the various positions of educators, according to particular job expectations and assignments in the school system.

After competencies have been identified, the committee should decide on the strategy for investigating whether or not educators actually possess the competencies. Two strategies that might be considered by the committee include (1) self-ratings and (2) supervisor ratings.

Self-Ratings. The self-rating strategy involves asking all educators who have responsibility associated with the IEP to complete a rating form, such as the one depicted in Figure 14–3, indicating whether they meet the criteria of "needs improvement," "satisfactory," or "excellent" for each competency. Another column of "not applicable to job duties" could be added to the rating form if the advisory committee chooses not to develop separate competency lists for the various positions of educators.

Before using the self-rating procedure, an atmosphere needs to be created within individual schools and the school system that the assessment of professional strengths and weaknesses is a constructive rather than a punitive process. Educators need to be assured that they will not be penalized by acknowledging their areas of needed improvement. One method of building this type of professional trust and respect is for members of the advisory committee to state openly that successful IEP development and implementation require (1) new or refined skills on the part of all individuals and (2) the identification of personal areas of needed improvement. Advisory committee members can provide a model for other

educators and contribute to lowering the threat often posed by the act of monitoring competencies. It is also important to stress from the outset that identification of needs will lead to designing inservice training that is both relevant and practical. Specifying areas of competencies should be viewed as a means to an end rather than an end in itself.

Each self-rating could be reviewed with the principal or other immediate supervisor. The advisory committee should compile all data into a report summarizing the number of persons who responded at each criterion level to the competencies. Such a summary report has utility in identifying the strengths and weaknesses of the faculty as a total group. The committee should make recommendations on strategies for responding to the needs of educators through inservice training.

Supervisor Ratings. Supervisor ratings can be completed using the same format as self-ratings. The major difference in the two strategies is in the person who completes the form. The caution indicated in the previous section relative to the threat of monitoring is often heightened in supervisor ratings. The advisory committee needs to introduce this monitoring procedure very carefully to reduce the atmosphere of threat as much as possible. In most cases, it is impossible to eliminate totally the threat of supervisor ratings.

Before completing the rating scale, the supervisor should gather firsthand information from observation and interviews. Teacher skills in individualizing instruction could be pinpointed by actually observing the teachers in the classroom working with students with disabilities. School psychologists and counselors might be observed in IEP committee meetings or teacher conferences as a method of identifying the competencies they demonstrate in their job performance. Sometimes there is a distinction between the knowledge possessed by the educator and the application of the knowledge related to educational problems. For this reason, observation can be a valuable tool for documenting the level at which competencies are demonstrated.

Interviews can be another valuable strategy for gathering firsthand information of an individual's competencies. Such knowledge areas as legislative principles and state and local criteria for special education placement can be assessed through interview procedures. Since both observations and interviews require a substantial amount of time on the part of the individuals who implement these monitoring strategies, the competencies of a representative sample of educators could be assessed, rather than the competencies of all faculty members. The assessment of competencies is a prerequisite to the planning of systematic inservice training, as discussed in the next section.

PROVIDING INSERVICE TRAINING

The IEP requires new or refined skills on the part of a substantial number of educators. In recognition of this need, P.L. 94–142 requires that each state develop and implement a comprehensive system of personnel development for regular and special education teachers, related services providers, and others involved with the education of students with disabilities. This training system, along with assurance that the established procedures will result in personnel qualified to carry out the purposes of the act, must be specified in the state's annual program plan, which is submitted to the Commissioner of Education in the U.S. Department of Education for approval.

Requirements of P.L. 94–142

P.L. 94–142 defines inservice training as any training other than that received by an individual in a full-time program that leads to a degree (*Federal Register*, 1977). Each annual program plan developed by the state agency must include the following components:

1. A description of the inservice training needs of personnel responsible for providing appropriate educational programs to students with disabilities, based on an annual needs assessment; a description of the process used to determine the needs must also be included
2. An identification of the areas in which training is needed
3. An identification of the groups requiring training
4. A description of the content and nature of training related to each area identified
5. Specification of the method of delivering training in terms of geographical scope and staff-training resources
6. An identification of the funding sources and time frame of training
7. Specification of evaluation procedures to ensure that program objectives are met

Furthermore, the state agency must ensure that ongoing inservice training programs are accessible to all personnel involved in providing educational services to students with disabilities. These programs must provide incentives for teacher participation such as release time, payment, and an option for academic and renewal credit. In addition, the programs must involve local staff and must incorporate

innovative practices that have been demonstrated to be effective (*Federal Register*, 1977).

The state education agency is responsible for the development of the comprehensive system of personnel development plan. This responsibility, however, is not to be executed in isolation. The state agency must instead ensure that all interested public and private institutions of higher education and other agencies and organizations (including representatives of parent advocacy groups) located in the state have an opportunity to participate in the development, review, and annual revision of the personnel development plan. The state agency may enter into contracts with higher education institutions and other agencies and organizations to implement innovative inservice training programs, develop or modify instructional materials, and disseminate the relevant findings of educational research and demonstration projects.

Developing Inservice Training At the Local Level

Successful inservice training programs reported in the literature consistently emphasize the importance of local control and management. Two elements of local control include conducting school building-based programs and having educators participate in planning and executing inservice training programs. Regarding school building-based programs, the Commission on Education for the Profession of Teaching of the American Association for Teacher Education has recommended that school systems become the primary focus for inservice training efforts to enhance the responsiveness of training to school and community needs (Agne & Ducharme, 1977). Furthermore, the Rand Change Agent Study (Berman & McLaughlin, 1975) indicated that effective staff development activities should be related to school-site program-building efforts to foster professional learning.

A second feature of local control is the degree to which educators participate in the design and delivery of inservice training. Documentation exists to support the value of eliciting the strong input of educators in the planning and implementation process (Berman & McLaughlin, 1975; Lawrence, Baker, Elzie, & Hansen, 1974; Reilly & Dembo, 1975). Skrtic, Knowlton, and Clark (1979) suggest that because all participants in inservice training activities possess various combinations of strengths and needs, it is appropriate for each individual on different occasions to assume the role of planner, teacher, and learner. Thus, the focus of this section is on the delivery of inservice training at the levels of the school system or individual school building that involve teachers in leadership roles.

The development of effective inservice training requires the development of a systematic process. Too many educators can recall specific instances that meet Flanders's description of inservice training:

> [It is a] giant spectator sport for teachers, costing at least 20 million dollars annually. As spectators, teachers gather to hear speeches, usually choosing seats in the rear of the room. They plan a passive role in which their ideas and questions are not adequately considered. They react as one does to any performing art and are more impressed or disappointed by the quality of the performance than with how much they learned. (Flanders, 1963, p. 26)

To enhance the probability that relevant training will be provided and that participants' time will be well spent, it is imperative that a systematic planning process be followed. Just as it is important to specify the required level of performance, goals and objectives, special services, and evaluation criteria when developing the IEP, similar components must be planned relative to the development of inservice training. Such a planning process includes the stages of assessing needs, specifying goals and objectives, identifying training strategies, locating resources, and conducting evaluation. If the school or school system has identified an advisory committee to oversee monitoring activities within the school, this group can also be designated as responsible for coordinating the entire planning and implementation process associated with inservice training.

Assessing Needs. The National Education Association (NEA) has taken the position that training "be established largely on the basis of teacher needs as identified by teachers" (Edelfelt, 1977, p. 14). Because the IEP involves a multidisciplinary team, the importance of involving teachers in identifying needs can be broadened to recognizing the importance of identifying the needs of all educators involved in the development and implementation of the IEP, including administrators, school psychologists, counselors, therapists, and other related services personnel.

One needs-assessment strategy is the analysis of data compiled through the previously discussed monitoring procedures established by the local school or district. Because the purpose of monitoring is to pinpoint areas of needed improvement, monitoring methods used in schools should document the individual needs of educators. The monitoring procedure discussed in this chapter that has the strongest applicability to assessing needs for inservice training is the competency analysis guide included in Figure 14–3. Educators must first know what they should be able to do before determining whether they, in fact, do possess the requisite knowledge and skills. Even if the competency analysis guide is not used for program monitoring, it can be used to assess inservice training needs. For example, educators could be asked to complete such a form by ranking a specified number of competencies they believe most represent their needs and which, consequently, should become the objectives addressed in training sessions.

Having educators complete a needs-assessment form and then ensuring that these data are used in the planning process can boost educators' morale and can motivate them. If educators perceive the system as responsive to their training needs, participation in inservice training will likely be significantly enhanced. Use of a needs-assessment form can also help to assure participants that their questions and needs will be adequately considered. Relevance is a key concern of educators, especially in light of the fact that inservice training is only one of many responsibilities. The competency analysis guide is a time-efficient procedure for involving participants in the needs-assessment phase of the planning process.

If the competency data have already been collected as a part of monitoring procedures by the special services committee through observing IEP conferences with teachers, the needs assessment for inservice training essentially has been completed with no extra effort. It is imperative that the special education supervisor or the special services committee chairperson reach a consensus with teachers and other educators observed and interviewed regarding identified needs. If a discrepancy of opinion exists, it should be clarified before planning inservice training to ensure that training sessions reflect the participants' felt needs.

Goals and Objectives. The goals and objectives for the inservice training related to the IEP can be specified after examining the needs-assessment data. Because the needs-assessment data should pinpoint the participants' current level of performance, the purpose of stating goals and objectives is to move the participants systematically forward to higher levels of skill development.

The goals and objectives must clearly specify the content outcomes of the training sessions. These outcomes should be stated in advance and understood by all participants. An analysis of the needs-assessment data might reveal a high level of response consistency. For example, the majority of participants might indicate a preference for training on the development and use of curriculum-based assessment measures or pre-referral intervention strategies. If this is the case, the skill could be translated into a general goal statement and the specific competencies could be translated into behaviorally stated objectives, depending on the analysis of needs-assessment data and the amount of time allocated to training sessions. If a one-day session will be provided on the topic of curriculum-based assessment measures, the goals and objectives might be as follows:

GOAL:
Develop a curriculum-based assessment measure in one area using the existing school curriculum.

OBJECTIVES:
1. Participants will define curriculum-based assessment and identify four advantages for classroom application.
2. Participants will identify one skill area for development of curriculum-based assessment measure, list skills required, and sequence the skills list.
3. Participants will write one objective for each skill on the list.
4. Participants will develop two appropriate test items for each listed objective.
5. Participants will plan materials and methods necessary for administering the measure.

Even in cases in which a high level of consistency is indicated on the needs assessment relative to areas of need, participants will vary in their current skill levels relative to those areas. The trainer must be prepared to provide multiple levels of training to meet the varied instructional needs of each participant. This can be accomplished by adapting the degree to which each participant must address all of the stated objectives or by providing information at varying levels of difficulty. When the majority of participants want training on developing and using curriculum-based assessment measures or pre-referral intervention strategies, the trainer might assist participants in selecting models of varying complexity for development of measures or may assist participants in selecting curriculum areas that lend themselves to development of curriculum-based measures.

When the information gathered through the needs assessment indicates a wide variety of needs that do not cluster around any consistent themes, the planning group must consider alternatives to providing training to participants based on their particular preferences. For example, school psychologists might be interested in obtaining more information on curriculum-based assessment, while classroom teachers might be more interested in pre-referral classroom intervention strategies. If this is the case, goals and objectives might be based on individual needs and then categorized according to various themes and disciplines. The inservice program could then offer choices of content based on the identified goals and objectives.

Individual Training Plans.   Another method for specifying goals and objectives is to work with individuals in developing an individual training plan, similar to the IEP, representing the participant's proposed inservice program. The data from the needs assessment could document the current level of performance. The individual could specify goals and objectives based on her specific perceived needs, responsibilities, and career plans. Thus, an opportunity would be provided to learn competencies associated with the IEP process in the meaningful and personal context of developing an IEP for oneself. If this method is followed, the group responsible for designing inservice training would be responsible for devising strategies applicable to individual plans and for providing opportunities for addressing the stated goals of the individual. It would violate every principle of the IEP to develop individual training plans, only to finally combine all participants together in sessions irrelevant to their identified needs. If inservice tailored to the identified goals and objectives of each participant is provided for in the inservice model of the school system, participants are likely to welcome the opportunity to work with trainers who provide a model for the processes they teach.

STRATEGIES FOR INSERVICE TRAINING

After specifying the goals and objectives for training, the advisory committee should decide on the strategies to be used in delivering the content. The issue of strategies involves asking the question of how the goals and objectives will be met. Godhu, Crosby, and Massey (1977) have suggested the following basic principles in considering effective inservice strategies:

1. Opportunity should be provided for active participation on the part of the learner.
2. The agenda should allow for physical movement and exploration.
3. Individualization of pace and level of knowledge should occur.

Strategies for delivering inservice training on the IEP that might be considered include small-group problem solving, simulation, media, "show-and-tell," and self-instructional packages. The inservice committee must decide on the particular strategy in light of factors such as goals and objectives, time allocated to training sessions, resource leaders, and any stated preferences of participants. Each strategy will be briefly examined regarding its application and appropriateness.

Small-Group Problem Solving

Small-group problem solving involves the application of concepts or instructional strategies to hypothetical or real educational situations. This training strategy allows for a high level of participant interaction and can be tailored to the unique concerns of educators working together in the same building. Many IEP competencies are suited for small-group problem solving, including those related to developing a system to collect and record data by which to evaluate student progress, stating goals and objectives, developing a task analysis for a variety of skills, developing daily lesson plans, designing a variety of pre-referral intervention strategies for students with disabilities, and developing effective strategies for involving parents in IEP committees. When using this technique in training, small groups could be instructed to solve a problem or to develop a product. An example of product development could be actual forms of data collection of student progress or a series of task-analyzed skills, which could, in turn, be used as a reference for teachers in formulating goals and objectives.

Simulation

Simulation can be an effective learning strategy because it allows participants to actually enact or experience various tasks associated with the IEP. An example of such a task is an IEP committee meeting in which the special education supervisor, teacher, parent, and student work together to develop an IEP. Participants can be encouraged to take different roles from the ones they actually assume in their job capacities to gain a clearer idea of the roles and responsibilities of each team member. When simulation is used, time should be provided in the training session to reflect on the reactions and insights of the participants after the simulation has been completed. A high level of active participation and individualization can be provided through simulated activities. The simulations can be based on data on a student in the school as long as personally identifiable information is changed so that the student's identity is absolutely protected. Another method is to assign roles and some background information on a hypothetical student. Figure 14–4 includes short descriptions of three roles and a rough draft of an IEP that could be used in a simulated activity of a committee meeting to develop an IEP. Videotapes of simulated conferences could be made in inservice sessions, which could be used as examples in later training sessions or in parent groups in discussing parental involvement associated with the IEP committee.

Media

Films, filmstrips, slide-audiotape packages, and videotapes can be used as possible training strategies in preparing educators in competencies associated with the IEP. Another alternative is for school systems to work with state departments of education and regional staff development centers in developing slide-audiotape packages on topics such as the federal and state legal requirements for developing IEPs, task analysis, and techniques for individualizing instruction. These media packages have a higher motivational appeal than lectures for many participants and are relatively inexpensive to produce, particularly in light of the number of times they can be used, and are available through commercial companies and professional organizations.

Show-and-Tell

The show-and-tell strategy for inservice training is particularly applicable to teaching competencies associated with the effective use of commercially produced and teacher-made instructional materials. This strategy could involve teachers demonstrating instructional materials that have been effective in meeting the needs of students with disabilities. In the process of sharing materials, teachers could also provide information on the general characteristics of materials that are appropriate for different types of students and on techniques of adapting materials. The conclusion of the inservice session could provide an opportunity for participants to actually construct materials based on the principles that had been identified. Developing products, such as instructional materials, can be an extremely beneficial outcome of inservice training.

Since the successful implementation of IEPs in a school system requires a multitude of specially designed instructional materials, consideration can also be given to training volunteers to make materials. Volunteers can be a valuable resource in individualized instruction if they receive the prerequisite training and direction.

RESOURCES

The identification of resources is the fourth major step in the planning process and can only be completed after the specification of needs, goals and objectives, and training strategies. Accessibility of resources from one school to another can be extremely variable. Both human and financial resources must be considered. Human resources for delivering training could include the following alternatives:

1. Special services faculty, such as special education consultants, resource teachers, classroom teachers and school psychologists, from within the school system or geographical area

2. Central administrators, including directors of special education and directors of curriculum
3. Regional staff development specialists
4. State department consultants
5. College and university faculty members
6. Private consultants
7. Adults with disabilities

The use of adults with disabilities as trainers is a valuable, yet often overlooked, resource. P.L. 94–142 requires that school systems take positive action in hiring individuals with disabilities in programs assisted financially by the law. One method of employment is hiring individuals with disabilities as consultants in planning and/or providing inservice training. For example, an adult who is blind and has successfully been through the educational system has probably discovered alternative learning strategies and adaptations of instructional activities that have likely never occurred to sighted persons. In addition to offering practical and functional curriculum suggestions, persons with disabilities may positively influence the inservice participants' attitudes because the disabled person is functioning as a trainer, with emphasis on her abilities rather than disabilities.

Trainers who can provide certification credit or college or university credit toward a graduate degree often bring an additional incentive to participants. This alternative should be considered when resources are being identified. Additionally, consideration should be given to the nature of desired follow-up. If follow-up on individual problems of IEP development or implementation is desirable, choosing a trainer within the school system might be given priority. Geographical distance between the trainer and participants can contribute to a gap between the content of the inservice training and actual implementation of the content into educational practice.

Financial resources frequently dictate the nature of inservice training. It is imperative that school systems carefully attend to the problem of identifying sufficient funds to deliver the training that will enable them to meet the legislative requirements. Financial resources for IEP training could directly or indirectly originate from the following:

1. Local inservice funds
2. Regional staff development centers
3. The state's personnel development program
4. State or federal staff development grants

FIGURE 14–4
IEP Committee Meeting Simulation

Teacher Perspective

You are the teacher of Tim, a 5-year-old boy who has a mild intellectual disability. He had a psychological assessment from a developmental clinic last spring and received an IQ of 58 on the Stanford-Binet Intelligence Test. On the Vineland Social Maturity Scale, Tim's adaptive skills were at the 4-year, 1-month level.

Tim has an extremely high activity level and tends to have a hard time getting along with other children. Tim is one of six children and both of his parents work. Although Tim's teacher last year had several contacts with Tim's parents, this is your first contact.

You have the following areas to discuss:

1. Parents' rights (you have asked the Special Education Coordinator to explain this).

2. The individualized education plan (sample provided).

3. The placement decision.

Special Education Coordinator Perspective

You have been asked to be a participant in the IEP conference with Tim, his teacher, and parent. You assisted his teacher in the spring in securing the psychological evaluation. You have helped the teacher draw together the necessary materials for the conference. The teacher has asked you to explain the parent's rights.

Parent Perspective

You are the parent of Tim, a 5-year-old who was evaluated with your permission last spring. You have been asked to attend an IEP meeting, but you are not sure what the IEP means. You are wondering if Tim has been a problem in his class. Last spring you were told that he was not developing at a normal rate. You are concerned about his slow development.

(Figure 14—4 continued)

Name of Student Marten, Tim   Subject Area Self-help Skills

Annual Goals (1) Can go through lunch line then eat lunch independently. (2) Dresses independently including tying shoes. (3) Chooses appropriate clothing to weather/occasion (independently). (4) Can bathe and brush teeth independent of adult reminders and adult supervision.

Objectives	Special Materials	Person(s) Responsible	Evaluation	Date Achieved
(1) Tim can walk through lunch line, get milk, tray of food, silverware, napkin, and then give lunch ticket to cashier with no teacher supervision.	Articles mentioned	Teacher	(1) Tim can complete task in 8 of 10 trials with no teacher supervision or intervention.	
(2) Tim can correctly locate top of milk carton marked "open," push flaps back, then makes opening to form spout.	Milk carton	Teacher	(2) Tim can complete task independently without tearing the spout in 8 of 10 trials.	
(3) Tim can cross one shoe lace over the other at top of shoe (independently).	Shoe	Teacher Parent	(3) Tim independently completes task in 8 of 10 trials.	
(4) Given a zippered jacket/coat, Tim can correctly zip or unzip jacket/coat.	Jacket/coat with zipper	Teacher Parent	(4) Tim completes task independently in 9 of 10 trials.	
(5) After removing coat, Tim can hang it on a hanger in the closet with no reminders, supervision or help.	Coat hanger	"	(5) Tim completes task independently with shoulder seams of jacket at the top of hanger in 8 of 10 trials.	
(6) Given various clothes (or pictures of) and a description of the weather for the day by an adult, Tim can choose clothing appropriate to the weather.	Pictures of articles of clothing	"	(6) Selects heavy, warm, clothes for winter days, rainwear, umbrella for rainy days, light clothing for summer days, remembers jacket on cool days, etc., in 9 of 10 trials.	

358

(Figure 14—4 continued)

Objectives	Special Materials	Person(s) Responsible	Evaluation	Date Achieved
(7) Given a choice between "school clothes" or "dress clothes" (or pictures of), Tim will choose clothes appropriate to the situation or occasion.	Pictures of clothing	Parent Teacher	(7) Selects clothing appropriate to the situation in 9 of 10 trials.	
(8) Tim can wash face/hands adequately without adult supervision.	None	"	(8) Adult judgement-total area washed, rinsed, dried completely in 10 of 10 trials.	
(9) Tim washes hands before eating without adult supervision/reminders.	None	"	(9) Must do task in 9 of 10 trials without being reminded.	
(10) Tim washes hands/face in morning and/or before going to bed without being reminded.	None	Parent	(10) Must do task in 8 of 10 trials without being reminded.	
(11) Tim brushes his teeth adequately with no supervision.	None	Parent Teacher	(11) Adult judgement-must brush all teeth, front and back in 9 of 10 trials.	
(12) Tim brushes teeth after eating with reminders 20% of the time.	None	"	(12) Must do task in 8 of 10 trials without reminders.	

(Figure 14-4 continued)

Name of Student Marten, Tim

Subject Area Interpersonal Relationships

Annual Goals (1) During free time on the playground, Tim will seek out other students to play with or with whom he can talk. (2) Tim will relate to others in a manner appropriate to home, school, neighborhood.

Objectives	Special Materials	Person(s) Responsible	Evaluation	Date Achieved
(1) Surrounded by other kids participating in an activity, Tim will watch what they are doing.	None	Parent Counselor Teacher	(1) Given the situation, Tim will respond in the desired manner in 9 of 10 trials.	
(2) Surrounded by other kids participating in an activity, Tim will walk toward the group to watch.	None	"	(2) Given the situation, Tim will respond in the desired manner in 8 of 10 trials.	
(3) Tim will initiate some activity or appropriate conversation with another child (other than classmate).	None	" Speech Therapist	"	
(4) When approached by another child other than a classmate, to join in a conversation or an activity, Tim will make a relevant, appropriate response and will participate in an acceptable, appropriate manner.	None	"	"	

(Figure 14—4 continued)

Name of Student Marten, Tim

Subject Area Fine Motor Skills

Annual Goals (1) Tim can print legibly his full name and telephone number independently. (2) Tim can reproduce numerals 1–10. (3) Tim can use scissors to cut along a straight line and/or cut out a simple picture following general lines. (4) Tim can fold a paper evenly and neatly into thirds.

Objectives	Special Materials	Person(s) Responsible	Evaluation	Date Achieved
(1) Following a model, Tim can write his first name legibly.	None	Teacher	(1) Does task accurately in 8 of 10 trials.	
(2) Following a dot pattern, Tim can trace the numerals 1 and 2.	Worksheet Dot pattern	"	"	
(3) Following a dot pattern, Tim can trace his last name legibly.	"	"	"	
(4) Tim can use scissors to cut a straight 5" line.	Scissors	"	"	
(5) Tim can fold a piece of paper (8-1/2 x 11) in half, having edges even.	None	"	"	
(6) Given a picture or design to color with areas measuring approximate square inches, Tim can color the entire area while remaining inside the lines.	Worksheets	"	"	

5. Institutes or conferences sponsored by colleges and universities
6. Institutes or conferences sponsored by professional organizations

The chairperson of the inservice committee should work with the system administrators having overall responsibility for special education in locating and securing funding.

EVALUATION OF TRAINING

Evaluation is essential to quality control of training as data are reviewed, analyzed, and used as guides in future planning and delivery. Evaluation can be conceptualized at three levels, including documen-tation, satisfaction, and impact. Documentation data are usually quantitative and provide, for example, information on increases in the number of partici-pants in a training program, number of inservice training sessions provided, or number of IEP meet-ings conducted. Satisfaction data provide qualitative information related to the perceptions of individuals participating in a program. For example, teachers may be asked to rate their satisfaction with an inservice program. Impact data are also qualitative and indicate whether a program or intervention has had the desired impact. For example, a school system may evaluate the systemwide reading program to evaluate its impact or evaluate a systemwide disci-pline program to determine if the desired effect was achieved. Figure 14–5 gives examples of evaluation questions at each of these levels. All three levels are important to include when evaluating inservice training.

FIGURE 14–5
Levels of Evaluation—Inservice Training

Documentation: *Quantity*

How many teachers received training?

How many instructional hours were provided?

How many reference books were purchased?

Satisfaction: *Reactions, feelings, perceptions*

Do teachers believe their needs were met?

Do teachers believe the format of training was appropriate?

Was the time of training convenient?

Was the leader perceived to be organized and effective?

Impact: *What difference did training make?*

To what extent did teachers increase their competencies related to the instruction of students with disabilities?

To what extent did teachers become more willing to include students with disabilities in their classrooms?

FIGURE 14—6
Project Objectives With Evaluation Components

Objectives:
1. After participating in a 4-hour workshop on the special learning characteristics of students with disabilities, classroom teachers will identify four learning characteristics associated with each disability area with 100% accuracy.
2. After participating in a 6-hour workshop on methods and materials for working with students with disabilities, classroom teachers will develop five daily lesson plans for a student with a disability. These lesson plans will be evaluated by the special services committee on the following criteria and meet an accuracy standard of 90%: objective, task analysis, curriculum adaptation, and documentation of student progress.
3. Every classroom teacher will serve as a member of an IEP committee and participate in the development of an IEP for a handicapped student in a minimum of three subject areas. The IEP must be judged to be appropriate by the total committee.

Evaluation Focus	Source of Data	Instrument Used	Date Instrument Administered	Data Analysis
1. To what extent were teachers able to identify characteristics associated with area of disability?	56 classroom teachers, grades K-12, in seven schools; 8 teachers from each school	Teacher questionnaire	At end of the 4-hour workshop held in September. Workshops will be conducted on September 10 for grades K-6 and on September 12 for grades 7-12	Percentage analysis
2. How accurate are lesson plans developed by teachers? Focus will be on: objectives task analysis curriculum adaptation documentation of progress	5 daily lesson plans developed by classroom teachers for students with disabilities in their classes	Rating scale	Week following participation in 6-hour workshop on methods and materials for working with students with disabilities. Dates of workshop: October 2 October 5	Percentage analysis
3. Have teachers served on an IEP committee? Have teachers participated in the development of an IEP in at least three subject areas?	Lists of IEP committee members and subject areas in which participated Week following participation in 6-hour workshop on methods and materials	Comprehensive log	September-June	Frequency count
Has IEP been judged to be appropriate by committee?	IEPs developed on selected students and signed by committee members			

When goals and instructional objectives are specified from the outset by the inservice committee, evaluation should involve assessing the outcomes of instruction (or whether the stated criteria were achieved). This type of evaluation is at the level of impact, as outlined in Figure 14–5. A planning guide, providing a model for conducting impact evaluation of inservice training, is depicted in Figure 14–6. In this guide, an evaluation method is pinpointed for three inservice training objectives. A guide such as this can be helpful in ensuring that evaluation is systematic. Modification of training content, strategies, and resources should be made in accordance with evaluation data.

The competency analysis guide identified in Figure 14–3 can be used as a means of assessing needs and documenting progress. When evaluation data indicate that teachers have mastered competencies, the checklist should be filled in to reflect the teacher's additional refinement of skill.

Planning and delivering systematic inservice training requires substantial time and effort but is essential to ensure the effective development and implementation of IEPs. Local and state education agencies who invest their time in providing relevant and functional training will reap high dividends.

SUMMARY

This chapter has reviewed the requirements of P.L. 94–142 regarding the ongoing monitoring of special education programs and requirements for ensuring that personnel are adequately prepared for the roles they are expected to fulfill. Strategies for ongoing monitoring within the school system were suggested, including (1) reviewing completed IEPs, (2) interviewing participants after IEP committee meetings, and (3) observing at IEP meetings. The need for ongoing and individualized inservice training was also discussed. A process of needs assessment, developing goals and objectives, and developing individual training plans was presented, noting the similarities between planning for inservice training and planning the IEP for a student with a disability. Several strategies for inservice training were suggested.

EVALUATION

1. Interview one elementary and one secondary teacher regarding problems they have encountered in implementing IEPs. Select a strategy they could use to minimize or eliminate each problem they identify.
2. What are the requirements of P.L. 94–142 regarding the state's responsibility for developing and carrying out a personnel development program?
3. Develop a needs-assessment procedure related to IEPs to implement with a small sample of educators in a local school. After collecting needs-assessment data, write objectives for a 6-hour inservice workshop based on the identified needs.
4. Based on the objectives identified in number 3 for inservice training, specify the strategies, resources, and evaluation to be used as the basis for delivering the 6-hour workshop.
5. Name and describe three types of program evaluation information.

APPENDIX A   Summaries of Achievement Tests

LISTENING COMPREHENSION

Test and Publisher	Grade Ranges	Components Evaluated	Norm or Criterion Referenced	Scores Obtained	Comments
Assessment of Children's Language Comprehension. Palo Alto, CA: Consulting Psychologists Press, Inc., 1972.	3-7	Receptive vocabulary of 50 common words combined into 2, 3, and 4 element phrases. Child points to appropriate picture in response to word or phrase spoken by examiner.	Criterion	Percentiles	Normative, reliability, and validity data incomplete
Clinical Evaluation of Language Functions. (Diagnostic battery) Columbus, OH: Charles E. Merrill Publishing Company, 1980, 82.	K-12	Six language processing subtests, i.e., word and sentence structure, concepts, oral directions, spoken paragraphs	Norm	Grade/age levels	Elementary and advanced level screening tests also available; norms available as of 3/82
Diagnostic Reading Scale (Spache). Monterey, CA: CTB/McGraw Hill, 1972.	1-12	Auditory comprehension (passages available as part of reading test to be read aloud by examiner)	Norm	Grade level	Standardization sample not described in manual
Durrell Analysis of Reading Difficulty. New York, NY: Harcourt, Brace, Jovanovich, Inc., 1955.	1-6	Listening comprehension subtest (examiner reads paragraph and asks specific comprehension questions)	Norm	Grade level	Tests auditory memory for details
Durrell Listening-Reading Series. New York, NY: Harcourt, Brace, Jovanovich, Inc., 1970.	1-9	Listening comprehension (vocabulary, sentences, paragraphs)	Norm	Grade/age levels, percentiles, stanines	Group test, extensive reliability and validity data, large standardization sample
Peabody Picture Vocabulary Test-Revised. Circle Pines, MN: American Guidance Service, 1981.	2½-Adult	Single word receptive vocabulary *only*	Norm	Age level, standard scores, percentiles, stanines	Adequate standardization
Stanford Achievement Test. New York, NY: Harcourt, Brace, Jovanovich, Inc., 1973. (Listening Comprehensive subtest)	1.5-6.9	Dictated passages	Norm	Grade/age levels, percentiles, standard scores	Group test, standardization excellent
Test for Auditory Comprehension of Language. Hingham, MA: Teaching Resources, 1973.	3-7	Auditory comprehension of vocabulary and structure (syntax and grammar)	Norm	Age level, percentiles	High test-retest reliability

From *Learning Disabilities: A Diagnostic Handbook* by The Maryland Learning Disabilities Project, 1986. Baltimore, MD: Maryland State Department of Education.

Oral Expression

Test and Publisher	Age Ranges	Components Evaluated	Norm or Criterion Referenced	Scores Obtained	Comments
Carrow Elicited Language Inventory. Learning Concepts, 1974.	3-0 to 7-11	Oral grammar	Norm	Percentiles, stanines	Limited standardization sample, not useful with children who have severe articulation problems or who suffer severe echolalia
Clinical Evaluation of Language Functions. (Diagnostic battery) Columbus, OH: Charles E. Merrill Publishing Company, 1980, 82.	Grades K-12	Five language production subtests, i.e., words, sentences, associations	Norm	Grade/age levels	Elementary and advanced level screening tests also available; norms available as of 3/82
Illinois Test of Psycholinguistic Abilities. Urbana, IL: University of Illinois Press, 1968.	2-4 to 10-3	Verbal expression, grammatic closure, auditory association	Norm	Psycholinguistic age, mean scaled score, median scaled score	Inadequate norms, poor reliability, questionable validity
Meeting Street School Screening Test. East Providence, RI: The Easter Seal Society for Crippled Children & Adults of Rhode Island, Inc.	5-0 to 7-5	Language subtest surveys listening, memory sequencing, and language formulation	Norm	Scaled scores	Standardization sample not described in manual
Preschool Language Scale, Revised. Columbus, OH: Charles E. Merrill Publishing Co., 1979.	1-5 to 7	Auditory comprehension, verbal ability, and language	Norm	Auditory comprehension age and quotient; language age and quotient	No reliability, validity date reported
Structured Photographic Language Test. Sandwich, IL: Janelle Publications, 1974.	4-0 to 8-11	Expressive grammatical structures	Norm	Grammatical performance is compared to age guidelines	Adequate norms
Test of Adolescent Language. Austin, TX: Pro-Ed, 1980.	11-0 to 18-5	Speaking/vocabulary, speaking/grammar	Norm	Scaled scores, quotients	Standardization adequate
Test of Language Development-Primary Edition. Austin TX: Pro-Ed, 1971	4-0 to 8-11	Oral vocabulary, grammatic understanding, sentence imitation, grammatic completion	Norm	Language age, scaled score, language quotient	Standardization adequate
Test of Language Development-Intermediate. Austin, TX: Pro-Ed, 1982.	8-6 to 12-11	Sentence combining, word ordering	Norm	Percentiles, scaled score, language quotient	Reliability and validity adequate
Woodcock Language Proficiency Battery. Hingham, MA: Teaching Resources, 1980.	3-0 to 80 +	Picture vocabulary, antonyms-synonyms, analogies	Norm	Oral language cluster score, standard score, percentile rank	Composed of selected subtests from the Woodcock-Johnson Psycho-Educational Battery; standardization adequate

Basic Reading Skills

Test and Publisher	Grade Ranges	Components Evaluated	Norm or Criterion Referenced	Scores Obtained	Comments
Peabody Individual Achievement Test. Circle Pines, MN: American Guidance Service, Inc., 1973.	K-12	Word recogntion	Norm	Grade/age levels, percentiles, standard scores	Designed as a screening instrument standardization excellent
Stanford Achievement Test. New York, NY: Harcourt, Brace, Jovanovich, Inc., 1973.	1.5-6.9	Word study skills subtest (phonics)	Norm	Grade/age levels, percentiles, standard scores	Group test: standardization excellent; five levels
Stanford Diagnostic Reading Test. New York, NY: Psychological Corp., 1976.	1.6-13	Word recognition, phonics, structural analysis	Norm	Grade level, percentile ranks, stanines, scaled scores, standard scores	Multiple choice test, standardization excellent
Wide Range Achievement Test. Wilmington, DE: Jastak Associates, Inc., 1978.	K-12	Word recognition, letter identification	Norm	Grade level, percentiles, standard scores	Limited behavior sampling: inadequate standardization: no reliability and validity data
Woodcock-Johnson Psycho-Educational Battery. Part 2 Achievement. Hingham, MA: Teaching Resources, 1977.	K-12	Letter/word identification, word attack	Norm	Grade/age levels, percentiles, functional levels, standard scores	Adequate standardization
Woodcock Reading Mastery Tests. Circle Pines, MN: American Guidance Service, Inc., 1973.	K-12	Letter identification, word identification, word attack	Norm	Grade/age levels, percentiles, standard scores (mean 50, SD 10)	Adequate standardization
Botel Reading Inventory. Chicago, IL: Follett Publishing Co., 1970.	1-12	Word recognition phonics	Norm	Grade level	Normative data not described in manual
Brigance Diagnostic Inventory of Basic Skills. North Billerica, MA: Curriculum Associates, 1976, 77.	K-6	Oral reading, word recognition, word analysis, spelling	Criterion	Grade level	Informal measure, useful in planning instruction
Brigance Diagnostic Inventory of Early Development. North Billerica, MA: Curriculum Associates, 1978.	Preschool-2 (Birth to 7 years)	Visual and auditory discrimination, letter names and sounds, word recognition, oral reading	Criterion	Age level	Format of record book may be confusing; informal measure: useful in planning instruction
Brigance Diagnostic Inventory of Essential Skills. North Billerica, MA: Curriculum Associates, 1981.	4-11	Word recognition, word analysis, oral reading, functional skills	Criterion	Grade level	Informal measure, useful in planning instruction
California Phonics Survey. Palo Alto, CA: Consulting Psychologists Press, 1963.	7-12	Phonics	Norm	Scaled scores	Normative sample inadequately described in manual
Classroom Reading Inventory (Silveroli) Dubuque, IA: Wm. C. Brown Company Publishers, 1976.	2-8	Word recognition	Criterion	Independent instructional frustration levels	Informal measure
Criterion Test of Basic Skills. Novato, CA: Academic Therapy Publications, 1976.	1-6	Letter recognition, phonics, sight vocabulary	Criterion	Mastery, instructional frustration levels	Useful in planning instruction

Basic Reading Skills

Test and Publisher	Grade Ranges	Components Evaluated	Norm or Criterion Referenced	Scores Obtained	Comments
Diagnostic Reading Scales (Spache). Monterey, CA: CTB/McGraw Hill, 1972.	1-8	Word recognition, phonics	Norm	Grade level	Standardization sample not described in manual
Durrell Analysis of Reading Difficulty. New York, NY: Harcourt, Brace, Jovanovich, Inc., 1955.	1-6	Word analysis skills, word recognition	Norm	Grade level	Normative population, reliability, validity studies are not reported
Gates-McKillop Reading Diagnostic Tests. New York, NY: Teachers College Press, 1962.	1-6	Word analysis, word recognition, sound blending	Norm	Grade level	No description of norming sample and no reliability and validity studies reported
Macmillan Reading Readiness Test. Riverside, NJ: Macmillan Publishing Company, 1970.	K-1	Visual discrimination, auditory discrimination, word recognition	Norm	Percentiles	Normative date limited, screening test
Metropolitan Readiness Test. New York, NY: Harcourt, Brace Jovanovich, Inc., 1976.	K-1	Level I-auditory memory, rhyming, letter recognition, visual matching Level II-beginning consonants sound/letter correspondence, visual matching	Norm	Percentiles, stanines, performance ratings, standard scores	Multiple choice format; group administered; screening; adequately normed
Mann-Suiter Developmental Word-Recognition Inventory. Boston: Allyn & Bacon, Inc., 1979.	Reading levels Preprimer-eighth	Word recognition-timed and untimed	Criterion	Frustration, instructional, and independent levels	Informal measure

Reading Comprehension

Test and Publisher	Grade Ranges	Components Evaluated	Norm or Criterion Referenced	Scores Obtained	Comments
Brigance Diagnostic Inventory of Basic Skills. North Billerica, MA: Curriculum Associates, 1976.	K-6	Vocabulary, oral paragraph reading, comprehension	Criterion	Grade level	Useful in planning instruction
Brigance Diagnostic Inventory of Essential Skills. North Billerica, MA: Curriculum Associates, 1981.	4-11	Oral and silent comprehension	Criterion	Grade level	Useful in planning instruction
California Achievement Test. Monterey, CA: CTB/McGraw Hill, 1977, 78. (Vocabulary and Comprehension subtest)	1.5-12	Word meaning, sentence and passage comprehension	Norm	Grade level, percentiles, stanines, scaled socres, NCE	Reliability is adequate; validity data not described in manual; useful at screening-level; multiple choice format; group test
Classroom Reading Inventory. (Silveroli) Dubuque, IA: Wm. C. Brown Company, 1976.	2-8	Oral paragraph reading and comprehension	Criterion	Independent instructional and frustration levels	Informal measure
Diagnostic Reading Scales (Spache). Monterey, CA: CTB/McGraw Hill, 1972.	1-8	Oral and silent reading comprehension	Norm	Grade level	Standardization sample not described in manual
Durrell Analysis of Reading Difficulty. New York, NY: Harcourt, Brace, Jovanovich, Inc., 1955.	1-6	Oral and silent reading comprehension	Norm	Grade level	Normative population reliability and validity data not reported in manual
Durrell Listening-Reading Difficulty. New York, NY: Harcourt, Brace, Jovanovich, Inc., 1970.	1-9	Vocabulary, sentence paragraph comprehension	Norm	Grade/age levels, percentiles, stanines	Group test; extensive reliability and validity data; large standardization sample
Ekwall Reading Inventory. Boston: Allyn and Bacon, Inc., 1970.	1-8	Oral paragraph reading and comprehension	Criterion	Independent, instructional and frustration levels	Informal measure
Gates-MacGinitie Reading Tests. Los Angeles, CA: Western Psychological Services, 1972.	1-12	Vocabulary and comprehension	Norm	Grade level, percentiles, stanines, standard scores (mean 50, SD 10)	Group screening test; multiple choice; well normed
Gilmore Oral Reading Test. New York, NY: Harcourt, Brace, Jovanovich, Inc., 1968.	1-8	Accuracy, comprehension, rate of oral reading	Norm	Grade level, percentiles, stanines	Standardization sample inadequately described in manual
Gray Oral Reading Test. Indianapolis, IN: Bobbs-Merrill, 1963.	1-12	Oral reading and reading speed	Norm	Grade level	Norms reliability and validity are limited (reading rate significantly affects grade score)
Iowa Test of Basic Skills. Boston, MA: Houghton Mifflin, 1978. (Vocabulary and Reading subtests)	1-9	Word meaning and passage comprehension	Norm	Grade/age levels, percentiles, stanines, standard scores	Standardization is adequate; useful at screening; group test; multiple choice format.
Mann-Suiter Developmental Paragraph Reading Inventory. Boston, MA: Allyn & Bacon, Inc., 1979.	Reading levels Preprimer 3-8	Silent and oral comprehension	Criterion	Frustration, independent, and instructional levels	Informal measure

Reading Comprehension

Test and Publisher	Grade Ranges	Components Evaluated	Norm or Criterion Referenced	Scores Obtained	Comments
Metropolitan Achievement Test. New York, NY: Harcourt, Brace, Jovanovich, Inc., 1978. (Reading subtest)	K-9	Passage comprehension at lower levels; students select sentences to describe pictures	Norm	Percentiles, stanines, grade level, standard scores	Normative sample is adequate; reliability and validity are adequate; multiple choice screening test
Peabody Individual Achievement Test. Circle Pines, MN: American Guidance Service, 1970.	K-12	Child reads passage and chooses a picture (given four) that goes with it	Norm	Grade/age levels, percentile rank at age and grade, standard scores	Standardization excellent; designed as a screening instrument
Stanford Achievement Reading Test. New York, NY: Harcourt, Brace, Jovanovich, Inc., 1973.	1.5-9.5	Vocabulary and passage comprehension at first two levels; passage comprehension at upper levels	Norm	Grade/age levels, percentiles, standard scores	Group test; standardization excellent, six levels, upward extension available for grades 9-12
Stanford Diagnostic Reading Test. New York, NY: Harcourt, Brace, Jovanovich, Inc., 1978.	1-12	Reading comprehension and rate of comprehension	Norm	Percentiles, stanines, grade level, scaled scores	Standardization is excellent
Woodcock-Johnson Psycho-Educational Battery. (Tests of Achievement) Hingham, MA: Teaching Resources, 1977.	1-12	Passage comprehension using cloze procedure	Norm	Age/grade levels, percentiles, functioning levels, standard scores	Adequate standardization
Woodcock Reading Mastery Tests. Circle Pines, MN: American Guidance Service, 1973.	K-12	Word meaning, passage comprehension using cloze procedure	Norm	Grade/age levels, percentiles, standard scores (mean 50, SD 10)	Adequate standardization

Written Expression

Test and Publisher	Grade Ranges	Components Evaluated	Norm or Criterion Referenced	Scores Obtained	Comments
Brigance Diagnostic Inventories. North Billerica, MA: Curriculum Associates, 1980.	Preschool-12	Handwriting, mechanical skills of capitalization, punctuation, spelling, and some functional writing skills	Criterion	Grade levels	Useful in planning instruction
California Achievement Tests. Monterey, CA: CTB/McGraw Hill, 1977, 78. (Language and Spelling subtests)	1.5-12	Language arts skills of capitalization, punctuation and grammar, usage and structure; in the spelling subtest the student is required to choose from four responses the correct spelling of a word to fill in the blank in a sentence.	Norm	Percentiles, stanines, grade level, NCE	Reliability is adequate; validity data not described in manual; useful at screening multiple choice format; group test
Iowa Test of Basic Skills. Boston, MA: Houghton Mifflin, 1978. (Language subtest)	1-9	Language is assessed in four areas: spelling, identification, capitalization, punctuation and usage.	Norm	Age level, percentiles, stanines, standard scores, grade level	Standardization is adequate; useful at screening; group test; multiple choice format
Larsen-Hammill Test of Written Spelling. Austin, TX: Pro-Ed, 1976.	1-8	Written spelling of predictable and unpredictable words	Norm	Grade/age levels; spelling quotient similar to standard score	Standardization adequate
Metropolitan Achievement Test. New York, NY: Harcourt, Brace, Jovanovich, Inc.; 1978. (Language and Spelling subtests)	K-9	Language subtest assesses knowledge of rules of punctuation, capitalization and usage. Spelling assessed through written dictation.	Norm	Percentiles, stanines, grade level, standard scores.	Standardization, reliability and validity are adequate; useful at screening; multiple choice format; group test
Peabody Individual Achievement Test. Circle Pines, MN: American Guidance Service, 1970. (Spelling subtest)	K-12	Spelling at recognition level	Norm	Grade/age levels, percentile rank at age and grade, standard scores	Excellent standardization. The area of spelling is tested by a multiple choice format with no writing involved. Designed as a screening test.
Picture Story Language Test. New York, NY: Grune & Stratton, 1965.	1-12	Written sample is evaluated in five areas: total sentences, words per sentence, syntax and an abstract-concrete score.	Norm	Mean age scores, percentiles, stanines	Validity information is excellent
Slingerland Screening Tests for Identifying Children with Specific Language Disability. Cambridge, MA: Educators Publishing Service, 1962-74. (Subtests 1,2,5,6 and 7)	1-6	Subtests 1 and 2: Copying from near and far points. Subtest 5: Writing from memory with a visual stimulus. Subtest 6: Writing from memory with an auditory stimulus. Subtest 7: Writing sounds from an auditory stimulus.	Criterion	Error analysis	Useful in planning instruction

Written Expression

Test and Publisher	Grade Ranges	Components Evaluated	Norm or Criterion Referenced	Scores Obtained	Comments
Test of Adolescent Language. Austin, TX: Pro-Ed, 1980. (Subtests of Writing/Vocabulary and Writing/Grammar)	6-12	Writing/vocabulary subtest requires student to write vocabulary words in a meaningful sentence; Writing/grammar subtest requires student to combine sentences into a single sentence which incorporates all the important elements of the stimulus sentences.	Norm	Scaled scores, quotients	Standardization, reliability, and validity are adequate
Test of Written Language. Austin, TX: Pro-Ed, 1978.	3-8	Written sample is evaluated for vocabulary, thematic maturity, handwriting, and thought; other areas evaluated are word usage, style, (capitalization, punctuation), and spelling.	Norm	Scaled scores for each subtest; a written language quotient is obtained; grade level.	Reliability is adequate; validity data is mixed. Authors caution use of grade equivalent scores on students under 14½ years of age.
Wide-Range Achievement Test. Wilmington, DE: Guidance Associates of Delaware, 1976.	K-12	Written dictated spelling	Norm	Grade level, percentile at age, standard score	Inadequate standardization; absence of reliability and validity data
Woodcock-Johnson Psycho-Educational Battery. (Test of Achievement) Hingham, MA: Teaching Resources, 1977.	Preschool to Adult	Written language achievement; two subtests are administered. The dictation subtest requires student to only spell isolated single words. Proofing section requires student to locate either punctuation, usage, or spelling errors in a printed sample.	Norm	Grade level, percentile rank by age and grade, and a relative functioning level	Standardization, reliability, and validity are adequate

Mathematics Calculation

Test and Publisher	Grade Ranges	Components Evaluated	Norm or Criterion Referenced	Scores Obtained	Comments
Basic Skills in Arithmetic. Chicago, IL: Science Research Associates, 1973.	6-12	Computation	Norm	Percentiles	Inadequate norming sample, useful in planning instruction
Brigance Diagnostic Inventory of Basic Skills. North Billerica, MA: Curriculum Associates, 1976.	K-6	Operations including whole numbers, fractions, decimals, and fractions	Criterion	Grade level	Useful in planning instruction
Brigance Diagnostic Inventory of Essential Skills. North Billerica, MA: Curriculum Associates, 1978.	4-11	Number facts, computation of whole numbers, fractions, decimals and percents, metrics	Criterion	Grade level	Useful in planning instruction
California Achievement Tests. Monterey, CA: CTB/McGraw Hill, 1977. (Computation subtest)	1.5-12	Computational problems of increasing difficulty, multiple choice items	Norm	Percentiles, stanines, grade level, scaled scores, anticipated achievement scores	Reliability is adequate; validity data not described in manual; useful at screening level; multiple choice format
Criterion Test of Basic Skills. Novato, CA: Academic Therapy, 1976.	1-6	Computation	Criterion	Mastery, instructional and frustration levels	Useful in planning instruction
Iowa Test of Basic Skills. Boston, MA: Houghton Mifflin, 1978. (Mathematics subtest)	1-9	Mathematics computations of increasing difficulty	Norm	Grade/age levels, percentiles, stanines, standard scores	Multiple choice format; standardization is adequate; useful at screening; group test
KeyMath Diagnostic Arithmetic Test. Circle Pines, MN: American Guidance Service, 1971.	K-6	Operations including whole numbers, decimals, and fractions	Norm	Grade level, standard scores	Does not yield reliable individual subtest scores
Metropolitan Achievement Test. New York, NY: Harcourt, Brace, Jovanovich, Inc., 1978.	K-9	Computation of single digit numbers to complex multiplication and division	Norm	Percentiles, stanines, grade level, standard scores	Multiple choice format; normative sample is adequate; reliability and validity are adequate; useful at screening; group test
Stanford Achievement Tests. New York, NY: Harcourt, Brace, Jovanovich, Inc., 1973.	1.5-9.5	Operations including whole numbers, fractions, and decimals	Norm	Grade/age levels, percentiles, standard scores	Lower and upper extension available; group test; standardization excellent
Stanford Diagnostic Mathematics Test. New York, NY: Harcourt, Brace, Jovanovich, Inc., 1976.	1-12	Operations including whole numbers, decimals, and fractions	Norm	Grade level, percentiles, stanines	Four levels, group administered; standardization excellent
Wide-Range Achievement Test (Revised) Wilmington, DE: Jastak Associates, Inc., 1978.	K-12	Counting, written computation	Norm	Grade level, percentiles, standard scores	Limited behavior sampling; inadequate standardization; no reliability and validity data
Woodcock-Johnson Psycho-Educational Battery. (Tests of Achievement) Hingham, MA: Teaching Resources, 1975.	K-12	Written computation including whole numbers, decimals, and fractions, basic algebra and trigonometry	Norm	Grade/age levels, percentiles, standard scores	Adequate standardization

Math Reasoning

Test and Publisher	Grade Ranges	Components Evaluated	Norm or Criterion Referenced	Scores Obtained	Comments
Kraner Preschool Math Inventory. Hingham, MA: Teaching Resources Corporation, 1976.	Preschool-2	Counting, sequence, measurement, spatial and directional concepts, geometry	Criterion	Age level	Group screening test available with test kit; small standardization sample; informal developmental measure
Metropolitan Achievement Test. New York, NY: Harcourt, Brace, Jovanovich, Inc., 1978. (Mathematical Concepts and Problem Solving)	K-9	Number systems, measurement, place value, sets, geometry, problem solving	Norm	Grade level, percentiles, stanines, standard scores	Adequate standardization; group test; multiple choice format
Peabody Individual Achievement Test. New York, NY: Harcourt, Brace, Jovanovich, Inc., 1976.	K-12	Mental arithmetic (with visual and auditory stimulus)	Norm	Grade/age levels, percentile rank at age and grade, standard scores	Individually administered multiple choice format, designed as a screening test
Stanford Achievement Tests. New York, NY: Harcourt, Brace, Jovanovich, Inc., 1973.	1.5-9.5	Math concepts and applications	Norm	Grade/age levels, percentiles, standard scores	Lower and upper extensions available; group test; standardization excellent; six levels
Stanford Diagnostic Mathematics Tests. New York: NY: Harcourt, Brace, Jovanovich, Inc., 1976.	1-12	Numeration, number systems, applications	Norm	Scaled scores, grade level, percentiles, stanines	Four levels; group administered; standardization excellent
Woodcock-Johnson Psycho-Educational Battery. (Tests of Achievement) Hingham, MA: Teaching Resources, 1977.	1-12	Applied problems (visual and auditory stimulus) including time, measurement, money, fractions	Norm	Grade/age levels, percentiles, functioning levels, standard scores	Adequate standardization
Brigance Diagnostic Inventory of Early Development. North Billerica, MA: Curriculum Associates, 1978.	Preschool-2 (Birth to 7 years)	Number concepts, time, and money	Criterion	Age level	Informal developmental measure, useful in planning instruction
Brigance Diagnostic Inventory of Basic Skills. North Billerica, MA: Curriculum Associates, 1976.	K-6	Measurement, geometry, functional skills, math vocabulary	Criterion	Grade level	Informal measure, useful in planning instruction
Brigance Diagnostic Inventory of Essential Skills. North Billerica, MA: Curriculum Associates, 1978.	4-11	Measurement, metrics, functional skills	Criterion	Grade level	Informal measure, useful in planning instruction
California Achievement Tests. Monterey, CA: CTB/McGraw Hill, 1977, 78. (Mathematics Concepts and Problems)	1.5-12	Measurement, sequences, money, time, geometry, place value	Norm	Grade level, percentiles, stanines, scaled scores	Reliability is adequate; validity data not described in manual; useful at screening; multiple choice format; group test
Iowa Test of Basic Skills. Boston, MA: Houghton Mifflin, 1978. (Mathematical Concepts)	1-9	Number concepts, time, money, measurement, fractions	Norm	Grade/age levels, percentiles, stanines, standard scores	Adequate standardization; group test; useful at screening; multiple choice format
KeyMath Diagnostic Arithmetic Test. Circle Pines, MN: American Guidance Service, 1971.	K-6	Money, missing elements, word problems, measurement, time numeration, geometry, symbols, fractions	Norm	Grade level, standard scores	Does not yield reliable individual subtest scores

APPENDIX B   Checklists of Concerns: Preschool and School

PRESCHOOL

I. Self-Help Skills

Using Utensils

1. does not use utensils for eating _____
2. uses spoon _____
3. uses fork _____
4. uses knife, fork, and spoon _____

Eating Habits

1. is not able to handle foods alone _____
2. is untidy in handling food _____
3. is tidy under supervision _____
4. usually eats in acceptable manner _____
5. eats acceptably in all situations _____

Dressing

1. cannot manage any clothing _____
2. can manage most clothing except zipping and buttoning _____
3. dresses self except for tying shoes _____
4. dresses self completely _____

Washing Face and Hands

1. cannot wash face and hands _____
2. can wash face and hands with assistance _____
3. can wash face and hands without assistance _____

Toilet Training

1. does not make needs known _____
2. expresses needs but has occasional accidents _____
3. expresses needs — avoids accidents _____
4. uses toilet without assistance _____

Avoids Dangers

1. does not recognize common dangers _____
2. recognizes dangers, but must be watched _____
3. avoids dangers _____

II. Communication Skills

Nature of Communication

1. communicates by gesture only _____
2. communicates by sound and gesture _____
3. uses single words or short phrases _____
4. uses complete sentences _____

Intelligibility of Speech

1. no understandable speech _____
2. speech understood only when combined with gestures _____
3. speech understood by immediate family _____
4. speech understood by listener in known situation _____
5. speech understood by almost everyone _____

Name

1. does not respond to name _____
2. sometimes responds to name _____
3. frequently responds to name _____
4. can give first _____ first and last names _____ full name _____
5. can identify name when sees written _____
6. can write first name _____ first and last name _____

Stories, Records, Television

1. does not listen to stories _____
2. listens, but loses interest before end _____
3. listens and answers simple questions about _____
4. can retell or explain story _____

Response to Verbal Directions

1. does not respond to verbal directions _____
2. responds to short directions _____
3. responds to series of directions _____
4. responds to directions after a time lapse _____

Experiences

1. does not relate own experiences _____
2. indicates that experience took place _____
3. tells highlights _____
4. relates experience with detail _____

III. Physical Development Skills

Walking

1. is not ambulatory _____
2. is ambulatory with braces _____ crutches _____ or wheel chair _____
3. walks, but is clumsy _____
4. walks, well coordinated _____
5. walks and runs _____
6. climbs _____

Grasp

1. cannot grasp objects _____
2. grasps objects clumsily _____
3. can grasp large objects _____
4. can grasp small objects (pencil, crayon) _____

Catching

1. cannot catch ball _____
2. traps ball against chest with two hands _____
3. catches ball with both hands _____
4. catches ball with one hand _____

Scissors

1. cannot cut with scissors _____
2. can cut with scissors with assistance _____
3. cuts a straight line with scissors _____
4. cuts design with scissors _____

Drawings

1. cannot trace straight line or circle _____
2. copies straight line and circle _____
3. draws straight line or circle _____
4. copies square _____
5. copies triangle _____
6. draws square _____ triangle _____ unaided
7. colors within lines _____

IV. Preacademic Skills

Age

1. does not know _____
2. shows with fingers _____
3. tells _____

Home Address

1. does not know _____
2. tells house number _____ street _____ town _____ state _____
3. tells telephone number _____

Body Parts

1. head   shows _____ names _____
2. eyes   shows _____ names _____
3. ears   shows _____ names _____
4. nose   shows _____ names _____
5. mouth   shows _____ names _____
6. hair   shows _____ names _____

Matching

1. can match common objects _____ or pictures of common objects _____
2. can match objects by size _____ shape _____ color _____ use (utility) _____
   directionality _____
3. can find one object in a series that is different by size _____ shape _____ color _____
   directionality _____
4. can work simple puzzles _____
5. can work complex puzzles (more than 12 pieces) _____

Colors

1. can match objects by color _____
2. can point to a color that is named _____
3. can identify a color when asked red _____ yellow _____ blue _____ green _____
   others: _____

Alphabet

1. does not know letters _____
2. recognizes a few of the letters _____
3. sings the alphabet song _____
4. identifies a few letters (can name them) _____
5. can name all the letters in sequence _____
6. can name letters out of sequence _____

Names of the Days of the Week, Months, and Seasons

1. does not know the names of the days of the week _____ the months _____ the seasons _____
2. knows a few of the names of the days _____ the months _____ the seasons _____
3. knows all the names of the days _____ the months _____ the seasons _____
4. can name the days _____ months _____ seasons _____ in order

Morning/Night, Yesterday/Today/Tomorrow

1. does not know morning _____ night _____ yesterday _____ today _____
   tomorrow _____
2. knows sometimes morning _____ night _____ yesterday _____ today _____
   tomorrow _____

Money

1. does not recognize money _____
2. recognizes penny _____ nickel _____ dime _____ quarter _____ dollar _____
   more _____
3. attaches value to money _____
4. makes change for amounts less than a dollar _____ more than a dollar _____

Writing

1. scribbles _____
2. copies recognizable straight line _____ circle _____ square _____
   triangle _____ other forms:
3. draws recognizable straight line _____ circle _____ square _____
   triangle _____ other forms: _____
4. can trace _____ copy _____ write spontaneously _____ letters of the alphabet
5. can trace _____ copy _____ write spontaneously _____ words
6. can write letters _____ words _____ when dictated

Numbers

1. does not say numbers _____
2. can count to 3 _____ 5 _____ 10 _____ 20 _____ other: _____
3. can recognize numbers in sequence _____
4. can recognize numbers presented randomly _____
5. attaches quantity to numbers _____
6. has the concept of more _____ less _____ same as _____
7. can sequence objects by size _____
8. can identify objects which are first _____ last _____ in the middle _____
   next to last _____ in a series _____

V. Behavior

Please check the following behaviors as to whether they occur frequently, infrequently, or seldom.

	frequently	infrequently	seldom
1. refusal to do as asked	_____	_____	_____
2. unresponsive	_____	_____	_____
3. short attention span	_____	_____	_____
4. easily upset	_____	_____	_____
5. cannot wait or take turns	_____	_____	_____
6. demands immediate rewards or help	_____	_____	_____
7. leaves group or class	_____	_____	_____
8. does not work with a group	_____	_____	_____
9. cannot work alone	_____	_____	_____
10. easily confused	_____	_____	_____
11. displays immature behavior	_____	_____	_____
12. forgetful	_____	_____	_____
13. shows signs of anxiety (crying)	_____	_____	_____

14. easily distracted   _____ _____ _____

15. difficulty changing activities   _____ _____ _____

16. easily tired   _____ _____ _____

17. overly active   _____ _____ _____

size of the class the child is in _____

number of adults working in the class _____

special services which the child receives _____

_____

_____

SCHOOL

I. Scholastic Information: Check problem areas.

A. READING   Present level: _____

                                 Book: _____

                                 Publisher: _____

*Listening Comprehension
   and Speech*

_____ comprehension of orally presented material

_____ expressive language

_____ speech (intelligibility)

_____ other: _____

Visual Perception

_____ matching letters

_____ copying letters

_____ identifying letters

Phonic Abilities

_____ sounds of consonants

_____ sounds of vowels

_____ sounding out words

_____ other: _____

Word Analysis Abilities

_____ using phonic skills

_____ using structural analysis (syllables, root words, etc.)

_____ using context clues

_____ sight vocabulary

Reading Comprehension

_____ gets main idea

_____ singles out details

_____ sequences events

_____ draws inferences

_____ follows written directions

_____ recall of material

_____ other: _____

Does Child Have Difficulty With:

_____ listening comprehension/speech

_____ visual perception of word elements

_____ phonics

_____ word analysis

_____ reading comprehension

_____ spelling

Note any significant reading behaviors (slow, reversals, loses place easily, etc.)

Spelling and Structure

_____ letter-sound relationships (phonics)

_____ irregular words (nonphonetic)

_____ oral spelling

_____ written spelling

_____ other: _____

B. ARITHMETIC   Present Level: _____

                      Book: _____

                      Publisher: _____

Number Concepts

_____ meaning of bigger (more), smaller (less), same as (number vocabulary)

_____ number recognition

_____ counting orally

_____ counting objects

_____ sequencing alternate numbers (by 2's, 5's, 100's, etc.)

_____ meaning of +, –, = signs

Computation

_____ meaning of place values (ones, tens, hundreds, etc.)

_____ simple addition facts

_____ simple subtraction facts

_____ regrouping (borrowing and carrying)

_____ multiplication tables

_____ division tables

_____ telling time

_____ fractions

_____ decimals

_____ word problems

_____ money values

_____ other: _____

II. Behavior

Please check the behaviors the child exhibits during the school day as to whether the behavior is a frequent problem, an infrequent problem, or no problem at all. Any specific descriptions or examples will be appreciated.

	Frequent Problem	Infrequent Problem	No Problem
1. refusal to do as asked			
2. short attention span			
3. lack of tolerance for tasks not enjoyed			
4. cannot wait or take turns			
5. leaves group or class (walks out, "sick")			

	Frequent Problem	Infrequent Problem	No Problem
6. does not work with group			
7. overconforms to rules			
8. seeks attention excessively			
9. cannot work alone			
10. easily confused or disoriented			
11. forgetful, needs constant reminders			
12. overly sensitive to criticism			
13. shows signs of anxiety (crying, nail biting)			
14. puts blame for behavior on external causes			
15. will not speak up			
16. shows off (clowning, bragging, teasing, etc.)			
17. speaks inappropriately (threatens, curses, etc.)			
18. antisocial tendencies (steals, lies, fights, etc.)			
19. hurries through work			
20. works too slowly			
21. easily distracted from work			
22. difficulty changing activities			
23. tires easily			
24. overly active (not sit down, etc.)			
25. relationships with other children			
26. relationships with adults			
27. other:			

When do behavior problems *occur most frequently?*

_____ morning   _____ mid-day

_____ afternoon   _____ before a class change (to playground, lunch, class, etc.)

_____ after a class change   _____ before a specific subject (Please list subject: _____)

_____ in a large group   _____ with the teacher(s)

_____ in a small group

_____ with peers

What remedial and/or behavioral techniques have been attempted with the child? (Please be as specific as possible.)

From the Clinical Center for the Study of Development and Learning, The University of North Carolina at Chapel Hill. Reprinted by permission. Adapted with permission from the *Pre-Academic School Checklist*, Clinical Center for the Study of Development and Learning, The University of North Carolina at Chapel Hill, Chapel Hill, N.C.

APPENDIX C　　Sample IEP Formats

INDIVIDUAL EDUCATION PROGRAM
Instructional/Implementation Plan

Student Name:_____　I/IP for Skill Area:_____

School:_____　Special Education Program and/or
　　　　　　　　　Date of　　　　　　　　Related Service:
Teacher:_____　I/IP:_____　_____

Long-term Program Goal (from Total Service Plan):

Student has/has not reached long-term goal:　Date:

SHORT-TERM INSTRUCTIONAL OBJECTIVES
(in sequence of estimated achievement)

Date Begun	Target Com-pletion Date	Objectives Behavior	Conditions	Mastery Criteria	Mastery Date

From *Individual Education Programs for Idaho's Exceptional Children,* Boise, Idaho. Department of Education, Special Education Section, 1977. Reprinted by permission.

Material: _____

Developer: _____

Level: _____

Sequence Steps	Short-Term Objectives				Measurement Procedures
	who (learner)	will do what (observ. behavior)	in what setting/stimulus (conditions)	at what level (standard)	

INDIVIDUALIZED EDUCATION PROGRAM
DISTRICT OF COLUMBIA
AGENCY_____

PART A Total Service Plan
CHILD STUDY TEAM

(1) Identifying Information

Name of Student_____Birthdate_____

Age_____School_____Class_____

(2) Hours/Days per week in mainstream_____

Hours/Days per week in regular and/or adaptive Physical Education_____

(3) Special Notations_____

_____

_____

_____

_____

_____

_____

(4) STUDENT'S PROFILE	(5) PRIORITIZED ANNUAL (LONG—TERM) GOALS
Academic Achievement	
Language Development	
Psychomotor Skills	

From *Manual for Development of Individualized Education Programs for Handicapped Students in the District of Columbia.* Additional information from Dr. Doris A. Woodson, Assistant Superintendent, Division of Special Education, D.C. Public Schools, 415 12th Street, N.W., Washington, D.C. Reprinted by permission.

PART A

(4)   STUDENT'S PROFILE (con't)

Social Adaptation

Self-Help Skills

Prevocational/Vocational Skills

Other

(5)   PRIORITIZED ANNUAL
         (LONG-TERM) GOALS (con't)

PART A

Name of Student_____Birthdate_____

Age_____School_____Class_____

(6) Short-Term Instructional Goals (incl. a time period)	(7) Services and Resources	(8) Person(s) Responsible for Implementation

PART A

Name of Student_____Birthdate_____

Age_____School_____Class_____

(6) Short-Term Instructional Goals (incl. a time period)	(7) Services and Resources	(8) Person(s) Responsible for Implementation

(9) Interim Review Date(s) by CST_____

Annual Review Date by CST_____

(10) Comments and Recommendations:_____

Observed Learning Style:_____

(11) Recommendations and Justification for Placement:

_____

_____

_____

_____

(12) Date of Child Study Team (CST) Meeting(s)_____

Persons Present - Name/Position   Signature(s)
        (print or type)

_____   _____

_____   _____

_____   _____

Chairman_____

INDIVIDUALIZED EDUCATION PROGRAM

DISTRICT OF COLUMBIA

AGENCY_____

PART B Individual Implementation Plan

IMPLEMENTERS

Complete this sheet for each goal statement.

(13)   Identifying Information

Name of Student_____Birthdate_____

Age_____School_____Class/Teacher(s)_____

Date of Entry into Program_____

Information from Total Service Plan

Goal   Statement:_____

_____

_____

Current performance level as related to goal statement:_____

_____

_____

Responsible Staff_____
Hours/days per week_____

_____

(14) Behavioral Objectives	(15) Date Started	Date Ended

PART B

Name of Student_____Date of Birth_____

Age_____School_____Class_____

(16) Learning Activities (Methods, Materials, Media)	(17) Method of Evaluation	(18) Interim Review Dates Performance Summary

(19) Additional Comments and Recommentations:_____

_____

_____

_____

_____

_____

_____

INDIVIDUAL EDUCATION PROGRAM

Child's Name _____

Birthdate _____   Grade _____

School _____

Date Referred to Committee _____

SUMMARY OF PRESENT LEVELS OF PERFORMANCE

_____

_____

_____

_____

_____

_____

PRIORITIZED LONG-TERM GOALS

_____

_____

_____

_____

_____

_____

_____

From *Individual Education Program (IEP) Procedures.* Des Moines, Iowa: State of Iowa Department of Public Instruction, Special Education Division, 1977. Reprinted by permission.

IEP SAMPLE

SHORT-TERM OBJECTIVES	SPECIAL EDUCATION & RELATED SERVICES	PERSON RESPONSIBLE	BEGINNING AND ENDING DATES	REVIEW DATE

IEP SAMPLE

PLACEMENT DECISIONS

PERCENT OF TIME IN REGULAR CLASSROOM

FOR THE COMMITTEE RECOMMENDATIONS FOR
SPECIFIC PROCEDURES/TECHNIQUES, MATERIALS,
INFORMATION ABOUT LEARNING STYLE, ETC.

CRITERIA FOR EVALUATION

COMMITTEE MEMBERS PRESENT

DATES OF MEETINGS

Classification _____

INDIVIDUALIZED EDUCATION PROGRAM

Child's Name _____ Birthdate _____ Age ____ School _____ Grade _____

Date of Referral _____ Date of Eligibility Determination _____ Date of Beginning Service _____

Anticipated Length of Service _____

A statement of the child's present levels of educational, psychological, and adaptive behavior functioning including strengths and weaknesses:

Instructional Levels:

Reading _____

Math _____

Spelling _____

IQ Range:

Above Average _____

Average _____

Below Average _____

(optional)

_____
_____
_____

Justification for placement in special education:

_____
_____
_____

Person(s) responsible to provide service(s):

_____
_____
_____
_____
_____
_____

A statement of Annual Goals:

Specific educational and/or support services needed to meet annual goals:

_____
_____
_____
_____
_____
_____
_____
_____
_____
_____

From Rules and Regulations for Programs for the Handicapped. Salt Lake City, Utah: Utah State Board of Education, Division of Staff Development, 1977. Reprinted by permission.

A description of the extent of the child's participation in the regular classroom, including physical education activities:

_____

_____

_____

Additional pertinent information as needed: _____

_____

_____

Participant and anticipated involvement: _____

_____

EVALUATION/PLACEMENT TEAM MEETINGS and Participant Signatures and Titles   ANNUAL REEVALUATION

Date_____   Date_____

_____

_____

_____

Parent(s): _____

RECOMMENDATIONS:

_____

_____

_____

Classification _____

INDIVIDUAL IMPLEMENTATION PLAN

Child's Name _____ Birthdate _____ Age _____ School _____

Date of Referral _____ Date of Eligibility Determination _____ Date of Beginning Service _____

Anticipated Length of Service _____

SHORT-TERM INSTRUCTIONAL OBJECTIVES	SPECIAL INSTRUCTIONAL MEDIA/MATERIALS	CRITERIA FOR MASTERY
To meet Annual Goal #1:		
To meet Annual Goal #2:		
To meet Annual Goal #3:		

INDIAN RIVER SCHOOL DISTRICT
DEPT. OF PUBLIC INSTRUCTION
(302) 436-8222

DIVISION OF MENTAL RETARDATION
DEPT. OF HEALTH & SOCIAL SERVICES
(302) 934-9231

INDIVIDUALIZED EDUCATIONAL PROGRAM
TOTAL SERVICE PLAN

Child's Name _____ Age: _____ Birth Date: _/_/_ Grade Level: _____
Parents/Guardians: _____ Address: _____ Telephone: _____
Reasons for Referral: _____ Program Location: _____

Individual Initiating Referral: _____
Present Levels of Performance: _____

Student Strengths: _____   Student Weaknesses: _____
_____   _____
_____   _____
_____   _____

.... IPRD COMMITTEE RECOMMENDATIONS ....

Date Prepared: _/_/_   Annual Review: _____
Primary Exceptionality: _____   Initial Placement: _____
Secondary Exceptionality(ies): _____   Medication (if any): _____
Major Goals (in order of priority): _   Reason: _____
_____

Specific "short-term" Objectives	Educational and/or Related Service(s) Required to meet Stated Objective(s)	Person(s) Responsible For Providing Basic Service

Parent/Guardian Approval: ___ Yes ___ No   IPRD Committee Members: _____

Implied Consent if parent/guardian unavailable to sign: Committee chairman: _____
___ Yes ___ No _____   _____   _____   _____
                   Signature   Date   Signature
Date of Verification: _/_/_ _____ _____
Due Process Hearing Requested: ___ Yes ___ No   Title of Authorized Agency Representative
Date of Request: _/_/_   Authorized Representative Resident District:
                                                 _____ _____
                                                       Signature   Title

cc: Parent/Guardian (white); Resident District (pink); Administrator, Programs for Exceptional Children
     (yellow); Pupil Personnel Services (gold); Child's Folder (green)

From "Profile Documentation Folder" by the Indian River School District, Frankford, Delaware 19945, and Delaware Hospital for the Mentally Retarded, Georgetown, Delaware. Reprinted by permission.

SAMPLE

DISTRICT INDIVIDUAL EDUCATION PLAN

Date of Next Review _____

SCHOOL: _____ /GRADE: _____

STUDENT: _____

Date of Meeting: _____

Participants in Meeting

Date of birth: _____   Representative of district/agency _____
                                   Child's teacher(s) _____
Date of   Child's parents(s) _____
Program Entry: _____   Other individuals (identify) _____
                                        Name   Agency

The IPRD planning committee has reviewed
all pertinent data and determined that
_____ placement will be
recommended.

Total % of Time: Regular _____

            Special Education _____

Hours per week of special education
for State unit funding _____

I. PRESENT LEVELS OF PERFORMANCE

	Pre	Post	LEARNING STRENGTHS/MODALITIES	WEAKNESS MODALITIES
Word Recognition				
Reading Comprehension				
Spelling				
Math				
General Information				
IRI				
Social Adaptation				
Other(s)				

II. ANNUAL GOALS	III. SHORT-TERM OBJECTIVES	CRITERIA AND EVALUATION PROCEDURES	SPECIFIC EDUCATIONAL SERVICES	Dates Begin End	SUGGESTED MATERIALS (Optional)	STAFF RESPONSIBILITIES Name Position

399

FORM A
(9)

INDIVIDUALIZED EDUCATION PROGRAM: RECOMMENDED TOTAL SERVICE PLAN

Name of Student: _____ (1) _____

District: (2) _____ School: _____

Home Language: (3) _____ Ethnic Bkgd.: _____

Date of Birth: (4) _____ Age: _____ Grade: _____

Eligibility Recommendation:(5) Yes _____ No (6) Handicap _____

The consensus of the diagnostic team is that this

child (7) needs a minimum of _____ in special education in order to receive appropriate remediation for all

recommended areas. _____ % of time

Staffing Conference Members: (8)

Name: _____ Position: _____

Name: _____ Position: _____

Name: _____ Position: _____

Name: _____ Position: _____

Name: _____ Position: _____

Date of Meeting: _____

IEP: FORM A must include the following categories: I. Achievement Levels; II. Speech/Language Skills;
III. Behavioral Data; IV. Learning Style; V. Relevant Medical–Developmental Data; VI. Relevant
Social–Family Information. Additional comments may be included.

(10) Diagnostic Data/Functional Performance Level	(11) Areas of Remediation	(12) Support Services	(13) Parental Respon.

From *Individualized Education Program (IEP) Interim Guidelines.* Copyright 1977 by the Department of Education, State of Hawaii.
Reprinted by permission.

STATE OF HAWAII
DEPARTMENT OF EDUCATION
INDIVIDUALIZED EDUCATION PROGRAM: INSTRUCTION PLANS

Name of Student: (1)
Date of Birth: (2)   Age: Grade:
District: (3)   School:(Receiving)
Means of transportation: (4)
Date of Entry to Program: (5)   Educational Arrangement: (6)
Percent of time in special education class: (7)
Projected Ending Date(SLD only):   (8)   IEP Review Date: (9)

Meeting Participants: (10)   Date of Meeting: (11)
Name:_____Position:_____
Name:_____Position:_____
Name:_____Position:_____
Name:_____Position:_____

(12)
SUMMARY OF PRESENT LEVELS OF PERFORMANCE

(13)
PRIORITIZED ANNUAL GOALS

(14)
STRATEGIES AND/OR TECHNIQUES

(15)   SHORT-TERM INSTRUCTIONAL OBJECTIVES

20,21b

(16) PERSON(S) RESPONSIBLE	(17) TEACHING TOOLS/ACTIVITIES

20,21c

DURATION OF SERVICES			EVALUATION (21)				
EST.(18) ATTAIN. DATE	(19) DATE STARTED	(20) DATE ENDED	PROGRESSING	NO PROGRESS	MASTERED	EVALUATION	COMMENTS

(22) .

<u>Statement of the extent to which child will be able to participate in regular</u>
<u>educational programs</u>.

I have reviewed the educational plan.

Name_____

Date_____

Additional Information

INDIVIDUALIZED EDUCATIONAL PLAN

Plan Covers the Period From: _____ To: _____

Meeting Date: _____

Type of Meeting (Check One):

Initial Evaluation: _____

Review: _____

Re-evaluation: _____

Date 3-Year Re-evaluation Due: _____

Student Name: _____

Parent(s) Name(s): _____

Identification No: _____

School: _____

Grade: _____

Student's Dominant Language: _____

Language of Home: _____

Prototype: _____

Liaison Name: _____

Liaison Position: _____

Birth Date: _____

Address: _____

Home Phone No: _____

Work Phone No: _____

TEAM PARTICIPANTS

Name	Role/Assessment Responsibility
	Chairperson/

Signature, If in Attendance

STUDENT PROFILE, including but not limited to the child's performance level, measurable physical constraints on such performance, and learning style:

SPECIAL EDUCATION SERVICE DELIVERY:

Type of Service	Focus on Goal Numbers	Type of Setting				Location	Personnel	Projected Date Service Begins	Frequency and Duration of Service per Day/Week	Total Hours per Week
		Class	Small Group	Individual	Regular	Special					

Total Hours of Special Education Service Delivery per Week: _____

CRITERIA FOR MOVEMENT TO NEXT LESS RESTRICTIVE PROTOTYPE, including entry skills to be met by the student and accommodations to be made in the regular or special education program:

ANNUAL/DAILY DURATION OF PROGRAM: _____ **Days per Year,** _____ **Hours per Day**

TRANSPORTATION PLAN: (Check One)

_____ **Regular Transportation**

_____ **Parent-Provided Transportation With Reimbursement**

_____ **Special Transportation as Follows:** _____

405

ADDITIONAL INFORMATION: including a description of the child's participation in regular education and physical education, recommendations regarding state-mandated testing programs, a description of the program for transition from private to public school, and other applicable information:

Need for Continuing Services: For students 2 years before graduation or age 22, the TEAM has determined that there _____ IS, _____ IS NOT a need for continuing services to be provided by a human service agency.

Discipline: The student's handicapping condition requires a modification of the rules and regulations outlined in the student handbook. _____ NO _____ YES If YES, describe modifications below.

Graduation/Diploma: For students 14 years or older, the TEAM has determined that the student _____ IS expected to graduate in _____ , _____ IS NOT expected to graduate.
(Month/Year)

If the student is expected to graduate, the criteria for graduation and the plan for meeting those criteria are noted below:

PRIORITY NUMBER	CURRENT PERFORMANCE LEVEL	GENERAL STUDENT-CENTERED GOALS	TEACHING APPROACH AND METHODOLOGY MONITORING AND EVALUATION TECHNIQUES SPECIALIZED EQUIPMENT AND MATERIALS

PLAN COVERS THE PERIOD FROM: _____ TO: _____

Goal Number	Objective Number	SPECIFIC STUDENT-CENTERED OBJECTIVES	QUARTERS DURING WHICH OBJECTIVES WILL BE ADDRESSED			
			1 From: ____ To: ____	2 From: ____ To: ____	3 From: ____ To: ____	4 From: ____ To: ____

RESPONSE TO EDUCATIONAL PLAN: Parent(s)/Guardian/Surrogate Parent/Student over age 18.

In the space below, check the option(s) of your choice, sign and date this form, and make any comments you wish. You may request an independent evaluation under the following circumstances: if you postpone a decision, if you reject the plan in full, if you reject the finding of no special needs, if you reject the plan in part.

OPTION CHOICES

_____ I accept the educational plan in full.

_____ I accept the finding of no special needs.

_____ I postpone a decision until the completion of an independent evaluation.

_____ I request an independent evaluation.

_____ I reject the educational plan in full.

_____ I reject the finding of no special needs.

_____ I reject the following portions of the educational plan with the understanding that the portions that I accept will be implemented immediately.

_____

_____

_____

Signature: _____ Date: _____
         (Parent/Guardian/Surrogate Parent/Student Over Age 18)

Comments: _____

_____

_____

_____

_____

I certify that the goals in this plan are those recommended by the TEAM and the indicated services will be provided.

Principal: _____ Special Education Administrator: _____
         (Signature/Date)   (Signature/Date)

If placement outside the local education agency is recommended, I certify that _____
is able to provide the services stated in this plan.   (Facility Name/Address)

Director of Accepting Facility: _____
                                      (Signature/Date)

409

STATE-MANDATED TESTING PROGRAMS

Student: _____ Grade: _____ School: _____

State-mandated testing in _____ will be given to all students in grade _____ in _____ .
(Basic Skills/Curriculum Assessment)   (Month/Year)

Your child, _____ , is eligible to participate in the testing program, which consists of tests in the following areas:

You should know that although testing will be appropriate for most special-needs students, modifications to the testing procedures may be made when necessary. These modifications would be similar to those that are usually made in the child's instructional program.

Under Massachusetts law, parents may excuse their child from taking all or part of the test. If you do not want your child to participate, please check the appropriate space(s), sign and date this form, and return it to _____ by _____ .
(Name)   (Date)

If you do not respond in writing on this form, testing will be administered on the scheduled date.

_____ I do not want my child to participate in the state testing program described above.

_____ I do not want my child to participate in the following areas of the state testing program described above:

_____

_____

_____

(Parent Signature)

_____

(Date)

APPENDIX D

Sample Individualized Education Programs

INDIVIDUALIZED EDUCATION PROGRAM (IEP)

STUDENT'S NAME: Laura Jordan

PARENTS' NAME: Mr. & Mrs. Jordan

SCHOOL: Matton Elementary

Date of Birth: June 10, 1980

Age: 10

GRADE: 3

School Authority Approval:

On behalf of the

Matton Elementary   School, I approve this IEP.

Alice Mays

Principal/Designee

August 25, 1990

Date

Parental Approval:

(1) My due process rights have been explained to me, and I understand them fully.

(2) I agree / ~~disagree~~ (cross out one) with this IEP.

(3) I have received a copy of this IEP.

James E. Jordan

Parent(s) / Guardian(s)

26 August 90

Date

Signatures of Participants in the IEP Meeting:

James E. Jordan
(Parent/Guardian)

Alice Mays
(Principal/Designee)

Jim Pirlli
(Regular Teacher)

Fred Wright
(Special Education Teacher)

Brenda Sottie
(Speech Therapist)

(   )

(   )

IEP Time Lines:

Program Entry Date: 26 Aug 1990

Review Date: _____

Review Date: _____

Review Date: _____

Annual Review Date: 25 Aug 1990

Time in Regular Program		
37%		

Parental agreement with major modifications

Initials	Date:
_____	_____
_____	_____

Three-Year Re-evaluation Date: May 1993

Date of Termination of special education services: _____

Parent(s) / Guardian(s) _____

(1) Yellow Copy: Permanent School File

(2) Salmon Copy: Parent's Copy

(3) Blue Copy: Special Education Teacher

(4) Pink Copy: Regular Teacher

(5) Green Copy: Distribution Copy

From Department of Defense Dependents Schools, Atlantic Region, 1986.

412

STUDENT'S NAME: Laura Jordan

Note: The timelines on this IEP do not include summer vacation or school holidays.

(1) Annual Goals and (2) Short-Term Instructional Objectives	(3) Present Level of Performance	(4) Criteria for Achievement of Objectives	(5) Service Provider	(6) Time in Program or Service	(7) Projected Dates Begins	(7) Projected Dates Ends
1. Given support from the resource room and from home, Laura will increase reading, sight words, word-attack, and comprehension skills. Laura will be able to:			Special Ed. Teacher and Regular Ed. Teacher with Educational Aide monitoring exercise cards & support activities	Resource Room 60 minutes daily (Approx. 18% of total school program)	26 Aug 1990	13 June 1991
A. Complete assigned work in the Merrill Linguistic Reading Program by guided reading of stories, silently and orally, and answering comprehension questions orally and in workbooks.	Merrill Linguistic Reader—Level B	A. 70%-100% accuracy on all reading tasks.			26 Aug 1990	13 June 1991
B. Complete exercise cards in the SRA Schoolhouse Word Attack Kit to reinforce the concepts of rhyming, sound/symbol, long and short vowel sounds, blends, and digraphs.	Currently achieving in the Violet (first) Level of the kit with help.	B. 70%-100% accuracy on assigned cards.		Included in above time.	26 Aug 1990	13 June 1991
C. Complete assigned phonics worksheets with a minimum of teacher assistance.	Partial mastery of consonant sounds and blends. Can give sound in isolation, but weak in applying.	C. 70%-100% accuracy on all worksheets.		Included in above time.	26 Aug 1990	13 June 1991
D. Read orally 20 direction words, in the order commonly taught, when presented one at a time on flash cards.	Brigance: Inv. of Basic Skills +1/37 Direction Words (3 June 1990) +1/40 Common Sight Words (3 June 1990)	D. 100% accuracy within 5 seconds on each direction word.		Included in above time.	26 Aug 1990	13 June 1991
E. Read orally 15-20 sight words, in the order commonly taught, when presented one at a time on flash cards.		E. 100% accuracy within 5 seconds on each common sight word.		Included in above time.	26 Aug 1990	13 June 1991

413

STUDENT'S NAME: Laura Jordan

(1) Annual Goals	(2) Short-Term Instructional Objectives	(3) Present Level of Performance	(4) Criteria for Achievement of Objectives	(5) Service Provider	(6) Time in Program or Service	(7) Projected Dates Begins	Ends
2. Given support from the resource room and from home, Laura will increase her computational and math skills. Laura will be able to:				Special Ed. Teacher and Regular Ed. Teacher with Educational Aide in classroom	Resource Room 60 minutes daily (Approx. 18% of total school program)	26 Aug 1990	13 June 1991
	A. Write or verbalize the answer when given addition and subtraction combination facts 1-18, one at a time, auditorily or visually.	Brigance: Inv. of Basic Skills Math Grade Placement Test 1.9 (4 June 1990)	A. 100% accuracy within 5 seconds on each fact.				
	B. Write the numbers 1-500 when given paper and requested to do so.		B. 100% mastery on number formation & order.				
	C. Complete addition and subtraction problems.		C. 70%-100% accuracy on assigned problems.				
3. Given support from the resource room and from home, Laura will increase her spelling skills. Laura will be able to:		Informal tests put present level at a beginning first-grade level. Mastery of all consonant sounds in the initial & final positions has not been achieved with 100% mastery.		Special Ed. Teacher and Regular Ed. Teacher	Resource Room 30 minutes daily (Approx. 9% of total school program)	26 Aug 1990	13 June 1991
	A. Complete a first-grade spelling book.		A. 70%-100% accuracy on spelling units.				
	B. Complete weekly word and sentence dictation tests.		B. 70%-100% accuracy on weekly word & sentence dictation tests.				
4. Given support from the resource room and from home, Laura will increase her written language skills. Laura will be able to:				Special Ed. Teacher and Regular Ed. Teacher	Resource Room 30 minutes daily (Approx. 9% of total school program)	26 Aug 1990	13 June 1991

STUDENT'S NAME: Laura Jordan

(1) Annual and Short-Term Instructional Objectives		(3) Present Level of Performance	(4) Criteria for Achievement of Objectives	(5) Service Provider	(6) Time in Program or Service	(7) Projected Dates	
(1) Annual Goals	(2) Short-Term Instructional Objectives					Begins	Ends
A. Write simple sentences of two (2) or more words when given lists of words to choose from.		Informal tests indicate that Laura is unable to write simple sentences.	A. 70%–100% on assigned sentences.	Educational Aide in classroom		26 Aug 1990	13 June 1991
B. Discriminate between asking and telling sentences.			B. 70%–100% accuracy on sentences.			26 Aug 1990	13 June 1991
C. Punctuate simple sentences using periods and question marks.			C. 70%–100% accuracy on end punctuation marks.			26 Aug 1990	13 June 1991
D. Use capital letters for people's names and for the beginning letter of the first word in sentences.			D. 70%–100% accuracy on capitalization of people's names and first letters in sentences.			26 Aug 1990	13 June 1991
PHYSICAL EDUCATION:		No modifications. Laura will complete the regular P.E. program.					
REGULAR EDUCATION:		MODIFICATIONS A. Laura will attend all large-group specialist classes without modifications (art, music, p.e.). B. Laura will be a part of social studies, science, and health classes but will not be required to do the written assignments. She will receive modified grades based on participation rather than skills mastery. C. Laura's program will be reviewed at the end of the first marking period.					

STUDENT'S NAME: Laura Jordan

(1) Annual Goals and (2) Short-Term Instructional Objectives	(3) Present Level of Performance	(4) Criteria for Achievement of Objectives	(5) Service Provider	(6) Time in Program or Service	(7) Projected Dates Begins	Ends
RELATED SERVICES: Speech and Language Therapy						
1. To improve production of the following sounds: th, sh, ch, j. Each objective applies to each sound.	Articulation Test identified the following errors (May 1988): f/th-initial t/th-initial and medial sh/j-medial and final sh/ch-initial and medial ch/sh-initial b/g-medial		Speech/Lang. Therapist OR Educational Aide	30 minutes daily in classroom (Approx. 9% of total school program)	26 Aug 1990	13 June 1991
A. To correctly identify and discriminate the target sound from all other speech sounds.		A. 90% accuracy on 20 pictures labeled by therapist.				
B. To correctly produce the sound in isolation.		B. 90% accuracy in 20 trials in 3 consecutive sessions.				
C. To correctly produce the sound in single words—initial, medial, and final positions.		C. 90% accuracy on 20 target sound words.				
D. To produce the target sound correctly in sentences when concentrating on speech.		D. 90% accuracy on 20 sound sentences.				
E. To consistently produce the target sound correctly in conversational speech.		E. 90% accuracy on spontaneous speech sample.				
2. To improve production of the following vowel sounds (long and short) a, e, i, o, and u. A. To correctly identify and discriminate a target vowel sound from all other vowel sounds.	Often uses long vowels in place of short vowels. Articulation Test: Vowels were distorted, or long vowels were used in place of short vowels.	A. 90% accuracy on 20 pictures labeled by therapist.	Speech/Lang. Therapist OR Educational Aide	Included in above time.	26 Aug 1990	13 June 1991

STUDENT'S NAME: Laura Jordan

(1) Annual Goals and (2) Short-Term Instructional Objectives	(3) Present Level of Performance	(4) Criteria for Achievement of Objectives	(5) Service Provider	(6) Time in Program or Service	(7) Projected Dates Begins	Ends
B. To correctly produce long and short vowel sounds in words in a structured context.		B. 90% accuracy on 20 pictures labeled by therapist.				
C. To correctly produce long and short vowel sounds in sentences in a structured context.		C. 90% accuracy in 10 sentences modeled by therapist, teacher, or aide.				
3. To develop receptive/expressive language skills: form/content and language organizational skills.	Peabody Picture Vocabulary Test Age Equivalent 4 years, 0 months.		Speech/Lang. Therapist OR Educational Aide OR Regular Ed. Teacher		26 Aug 1990	13 June 1991
FORM A. To correctly form and use regular/irregular noun plurals in a structured context.	Informal test of language functioning (8 Aug 1988): inconsistent use of plurals, tenses, subject/verb agreement, and comparative adjectives.	A. 90% accuracy in 20 trials using picture tasks.				
B. To correctly form and use regular past-tense verbs in a structured context.		B. Same as above.				
C. To correctly form and use proper subject/verb agreement in a structured context.		C. Same as above.				
D. To correctly use comparative/superlative adjective forms in a structured context.		D. 90% accuracy in 10 trials when using pictures and objects.				
E. To demonstrate a knowledge of antonyms (opposite word pairs).		E. 90% accuracy in 10 trials when asked to verbalize opposites.				
CONTENT F. To describe an object by assigning a label to it.		F. 100% accuracy when tested over 3 new vocabulary words per week.				

STUDENT'S NAME: Laura Jordan

(1) Annual Goals and (2) Short-Term Instructional Objectives	(3) Present Level of Performance	(4) Criteria for Achievement of Objectives	(5) Service Provider	(6) Time in Program or Service	(7) Projected Dates Begins	(7) Projected Dates Ends
G. To describe an object by naming 3 attributes about it.		G. Upon presentation of 5 common objects and 5 uncommon objects, Laura will describe 3 attributes about each object.				
LANGUAGE ORGANIZATIONAL SKILLS H. To correctly classify objects and pictures into categories.	Has difficulty following directions and retelling stories.	H. 100% accuracy when asked to categorize 20 objects or pictures.				
4. To improve memory skills (particulary sequencing). A. To correctly retell a story using picture clues. B. To correctly complete 2- to 4-step commands to complete a task.		A. 90% accuracy. B. Will complete given task 9 out of 10 times.	Speech/Lang. Therapist in classroom OR Educational Aide and Regular Ed. Teacher	Included in above time.	26 Aug 1990	13 June 1991

Individual Education Plan (IEP)

Identification Information

Name __James S.__

School __C. L. Bishop__

Grade __2nd__

Birthdate __9/2/84__

Parents' Names __H. R. and Betty S.__

Address __1029 Langley Avenue__
__Lawrence, KS 66044__

Phone: Home __841-0920__ Office __869-4098__

Continuum of Services

	Hours Per Week	Dates
Regular class	23	9/28/91 - 6/2/91
Resource teacher in regular classroom		
Resource room	5	9/29/91 - 6/2/92
Reading specialist		
Speech/language therapist		
Counselor		
Special class		
Transition class		
Others:		
Counseling	2	9/30/91 - 5/29/92

Yearly Class Schedule

Time	Subject	Teacher
9:00	Language Arts	Miller
10:45	Math	Miller
11:30	Social Studies	Miller
12:00	Lunch	
1:00	Science	Miller
2:00	Resource Reading	Houston

Testing Information

Test Name	Date Admin.	Interpretation
Stanford-Binet	9/13/88	low average range
Key Math	9/15/88	functioning on 1.8 level
Zaner-Bloser	9/22/88	scored "low for grade"
Slingerland	9/20/88	difficulty copying near & far points
Physical exam	8/15/88	mild paralysis left hand seizure prone

Disability Area __Physical Disability__

Checklist

9-2	Referral by __Mrs. Jenkins__
9-8	Parents informed of rights; permission obtained for evaluation
9-21	Evaluation compiled
9-24	Parents contacted
9-26	IEP committee meeting held
9-26	IEP completed
9-26	Parent consent notification
9-27	Placement made

Committee Members

Lou Ashley Teacher

Lois Seibler Other LEA representative

Mrs. Betty S. Parents

Date IEP initially approved ____

Health Information

Vision: __Normal__

Hearing: __Normal__

Physical: __Normal__

Other: __Medication-tegratol__

419

Individual Education Plan (IEP)

Student's Name **James S.** Subject Area **Handwriting** Teacher **Houston/Miller**

Level of Performance **recognizes all manuscript letters; exhibits proper sitting & writing position; can write 7-10 letters per minute; makes frequent erasures; handwriting is often illegible, slow, and laborious.**

Annual Goals **Print legibly all letters of alphabet (upper- and lower-case); write numerals 1-10 with no erasures; write 35 letters per minute with 4 or less erasures.**

Objectives

September
referral/evaluation, IEP development

October
1. Following a model, writes legibly letters: Aa, Cc, Dd, Ee, Gg, Oo
2. Following a model, writes legibly numbers 1-5
3. Following a model, writes legibly his first name
4. Writes legibly 10 letters per minute with 50% or less erasures

November
1. Following a model, writes legibly letters: Bb, Pp, Qq, Uu, Mm, Nn, Hh
2. Writes legibly numerals 1-5—no model
3. Writes legibly first name—no model
4. Writes legibly 13 letters per minute with 45% or less erasures

December
1. Following a model, writes legibly letters: Ll, Tt, Ff, Kk, Ii, Jj
2. Writes legibly numerals 6-10 with a model
3. Writes legibly last name with a model
4. Writes legibly 14 letters per minute with 40% or less erasures

January
1. Following a model, writes entire alphabet legibly
2. Writes legibly numerals 6-10—no model
3. Writes legibly first and last name—no model
4. Writes legibly 19 letters per minute with 35% or less erasures

Special Materials
"Beginning to Learn Fine Motor Skills" by Thurstone & Lillie

Agent
1, 4-Houston
2, 3-Miller

Evaluation
Informal assessment 80% accuracy of objectives 1-3 on 3 consecutive days

420

Individual Education Plan (IEP)

Student's Name ___James S.___

Subject Area ___Handwriting___   Teacher ___Houston/Miller___

Level of Performance ___recognizes all manuscript letters; exhibits proper___   Annual Goals ___Print legibly all letters of alphabet (upper and lower-___

___sitting & writing position; can write 7-10 letters per minute; makes___   ___case); write numerals 1-10 with no erasures; write 35 letters per___

___erasures 50%-60% of time; handwriting is often illegible___   ___minute with 10% or less erasures___

	February	March	April	May	June
Objectives	1. Following a model, writes the entire alphabet legibly 2. Writes legibly numerals 1-10 in math lesson with 4 or less erasures 3. Writes legibly first and last names on all class assignments 4. Writes legibly 23 letters per minute with 30% or less erasures	1. Writes legibly Aa, Cc, Dd, Ee, Gg, Oo, Bb, Pp from dictation 2. Writes legibly numerals 1-10 in math lessons with 2 or less erasures 3. Writes 28 words per minute with 20% or less erasures	1. Writes legibly Qq, Uu, Mm, Nn, Hh, Ll, Tt from dictation 2. Writes legibly numerals 1-10 in math lessons with 1 or less erasures 3. Writes 30 words per minute with 20% or less erasures	1. Writes entire alphabet from dictation 2. Writes legibly numerals 1-10 with no erasures 3. Writes 35 letters per minute with 10% or less erasures	
Special Materials	"Beginning to Learn Fine Motor Skills" by Thurstone & Lillie			→	
Agent	1, 4-Houston 2, 3-Miller	1, 3-Houston 2-Miller		→	
Evaluation	Informal assessment 80% accuracy of objectives 1-3 on 3 consecutive days	Informal assessment 80% accuracy of objectives 1-2 on 3 consecutive days		→	

INDIVIDUAL EDUCATION PROGRAM

Identification Information

Name _____ Wendy _____

School _____ Oak Hill _____ Grade _____ 4th _____

Birthdate _____ 3/15/77 _____ Age _____ 11 _____

Mother's Name _____ Miriam D. _____

Address _____ 1861 Alvamar Dr. _____

Phone _____ 732-9225 _____ _____ 933-7353 _____
     Home   Business

Father's Name _____ Paul D. _____

Address _____ E-5, Four Seasons Apts. _____

Phone _____ 967-0541 _____ _____ 984-1477 _____
     Home   Business

Medical Information

Vision _____ within normal limits _____

Hearing _____ within normal limits _____

Physical Condition _____ no known health problems. _____

Medication _____ none _____

IEP Committee

Name	Position
Marilyn Fleisher	Principal
Thelma Rillon	Classroom Teacher
Bruce Ballard	Sp. Ed. Teacher
for W. Quinn	Psychologist
Paul M. Diedrich	Parent

Procedural Checklist

11/26/88   Referral by _____ Dr. Lewis _____

12/5/88   Parents informed of rights

12/7/88   Permission obtained for evaluation

12/19/88   Evaluation Compiled

1/7/89   IEP development begins

1/12/89   IEP completed; ready for approval

1/13/89   Placement recommendations made

1/13/89   Parental permission for placement

1/13/89   IEP approved and signed by all
           committee members

IEP from _____ 1/14/89 _____ to _____ 1/14/90 _____

Evaluation Information

Name ___Wendy___

IEP from ___1/14/89___ to ___1/14/90___

Test Name	Date Administered	Administered by	Results and Interpretation
WISC-R	12/10/88	Gaines	Verbal - 65; Performance - 62; Combined - 63.
AAMD Adaptive Behavior Scale	12/9/88	Gaines	Intelligence test scores are in the mild range of mental retardation, indicating that problems in school are due to an intellectual deficit.
PIAT	12/12/88	Ballard	Math—2.4; Reading Recognition—2.7; Reading Comprehension—2.3; Spelling—2.6; General Information—3.0; Total Test—2.6.
KeyMath	12/14/88	Ballard	Total Test—2.7; Significant subtest scores include: Addition—2.8; Subtraction—2.4; Multiplication—2.8; Division—2.3; Word Problems—2.4; Time—2.7. Taken together, the PIAT and KeyMath indicate school performance approximately two years behind her present grade placement.
Curriculum-based measure of word-attack skills	11/15/88	Dillon	
Informal Reading Inventory	11/10/88	Dillơn	Informal reading inventory indicates that Wendy can sound out phonetically regular words with short vowels, consonant blends, and digraphs. She reads in a second-grade basal reader.

Name **Wendy**

IEP from **1/14/89** to **1/14/90**

Subject **Reading**

Present Level of Performance	Annual Goal Statements	Instructional Objectives	Evaluation Procedure
Strengths: 1. Can sound out phonically regular words with short vowels, consonant blends and digraphs. 2. Can read level 1 Dolch words with 95% accuracy. 3. Can read fluently and accurately from 2-1 basal reader. 4. Answers comprehension questions on passages from 2-1 basal reader. 5. When prompted, reads as a leisure activity. **Weaknesses:** 1. Cannot consistently sound out words with silent e or double vowel. 2. Reads level 2 Dolch words with 70% accuracy. 3. Reads orally from 2-2 basal reader at less than 75 words/min. correct and more than 5 words/min. incorrect.	1. Wendy reads phonically regular words orally. 2. Wendy reads common sight words through level 3 orally. 3. Wendy reads orally from 3-2 basal reader fluently and accurately. 4. Wendy demonstrates understanding of silent reading passages from level 3-2 basal reader.	1.1. Given lists of phonically regular words, including nonsense words, ending in silent e, she will read words orally with 95% accuracy. 1.2. Given lists of phonically regular words, including nonsense words, containing double vowel, she will read words orally with 95% accuracy. 2.1. Wendy reads orally from Dolch word list through level 2 with no more than two errors. 2.2. Wendy reads orally from Dolch word list through level 3 with no more than two errors. 3.1. Wendy reads orally passages from level 2-2 basal reader at 100 words/min. correct and less than 2 words/min. incorrect. 3.2. Wendy reads orally passages from level 3-1 basal reader at 100 words/min. correct and less than 2 words/min. incorrect. 3.3. Wendy reads orally passages from level 3-2 basal reader at 100 words/min. correct and less than 2 words/min. incorrect. 4.1. On being given passages from a level 2-2 basal reader and instructed to read silently, Wendy answers literal comprehension questions with 90% accuracy and inferential comprehension questions with 80% accuracy.	weekly teacher-made CRT weekly teacher-made CRT weekly CRT based on Dolch list weekly CRT based on Dolch list weekly teacher-made CRT weekly teacher-made CRT weekly teacher-made CRT weekly teacher-made CRT

Name **Wendy** IEP from **1/14/89** to **1/14/90** Subject **Reading (cont.)**

Present Level of Performance	Annual Goal Statements	Instructional Objectives	Evaluation Procedure
4. Answers inferential comprehension questions on passages from 2-2 basal reader at less than 60% accuracy.		4.2. On being given passages from a 3-1 level basal reader and instructed to read silently, Wendy answers literal comprehension questions with 90% accuracy and inferential comprehension questions with 80% accuracy.	weekly teacher-made CRT
		4.3. On being given passages from a 3-2 level basal reader and instructed to read silently, Wendy answers literal comprehension questions with 90% accuracy and inferential comprehension questions with 80% accuracy.	weekly teacher-made CRT
5. Rarely chooses to read as leisure activity without prompting.	5. Wendy will read one book each week as a leisure activity.	5.1. Wendy will select and read a book every two weeks for three months.	student record of books read and discussion with teacher
		5.2. Wendy will select and read a book every week for three months.	student record of books read and discussion with teacher

Name __Wendy__   IEP from __1/14/89__ to __1/14/90__   Subject __Arithmetic__

Present Level of Performance	Annual Goal Statements	Instructional Objectives	Evaluation Procedure
Strengths:			
1. Knows basic addition and subtraction facts.	1. Wendy will correctly perform subtraction of three-digit numbers requiring regrouping twice.	1.1. Wendy will subtract one-digit numbers from two-digit numbers with regrouping in 4/5 trials.	weekly teacher-made CRT
2. Solves three-digit addition problems with regrouping.		1.2. Wendy will subtract two-digit numbers from two-digit numbers with regrouping in 4/5 trials.	weekly teacher-made CRT
3. Solves two-digit subtraction problems without regrouping.		1.3. Wendy will subtract two-digit numbers from three-digit numbers with regrouping twice in 4/5 trials.	weekly teacher-made CRT
4. Tells time to nearest 15 minutes.		1.4. Wendy will subtract three-digit numbers from three-digit numbers with regrouping twice in 4/5 trials.	twice weekly teacher-made CRT
5. Identifies values of coins.	2. Wendy will correctly multiply two-digit numbers by one-digit numbers.	2.1. Wendy will give answers on basic multiplication facts in 4/5 trials.	weekly teacher-made CRT
Weaknesses:		2.2. Wendy will multiply two-digit numbers by one-digit numbers in 4/5 trials.	twice weekly teacher-made CRT
1. Does not know basic multiplication or division facts	3. Wendy will correctly divide two-digit numbers by one-digit numbers without remainder.	3.1. Wendy will give answers on basic division facts in 4/5 trials	weekly teacher-made CRT
2. Does not consistently identify the operation required in one-operation word problems.		3.2. Wendy will divide two-digit numbers by one-digit numbers without remainder in 4/5 trials	weekly teacher-made CRT
3. Makes change inconsistently.	4. Wendy correctly solves one-operation word problems.	4.1. Given a one-operation word problem requiring addition or subtraction, identifies required operation and gives correct answer in 4/5 trials.	weekly teacher-made CRT
4. Tells time to nearest five minutes inconsistently.		4.2. Given a one-operation word problem requiring addition or subtraction, identifies required operation and gives correct answer in 4/5 trials.	weekly teacher-made CRT
		4.3. Given a one-operation word problem requiring addition, subtraction, or multiplication within her computational competence, identifies the required operation and gives the correct answer in 4/5 trials.	weekly teacher-made CRT
		4.4. Given a one-operation word problem requiring addition, subtraction, or multiplication or division within her computational competence, identifies the required operation and gives the correct answer in 4/5 trials.	weekly teacher-made CRT

Name __Wendy__   IEP from ___1/14/89___ to ___1/14/90___   Subject ___Arithmetic (cont.)___

Present Level of Performance	Annual Goal Statements	Instructional Objectives	Evaluation Procedure
	5. Wendy will correctly make change from $1.	5.1. Wendy adds given number of coins total value up to $1 in 4/5 trials.	weekly teacher-made CRT
		5.2. Makes change following purchase of up to $1 in 4/5 trials.	weekly teacher-made CRT
	6. Wendy will solve one-operation word problems with addition or subtraction of time.	6.1. Tells time to nearest five minutes in 4/5 trials.	weekly teacher-made CRT
		6.2. Given a one-operation word problem requiring addition or subtraction of time identifies the required operation and gives answer in 4/5 trials.	weekly teacher-made CRT

EDUCATIONAL SERVICES TO BE PROVIDED

Services Required	Date Initiated	Date Terminated	Extent of Time	Individual Responsible for Service
resource room mild disabilities	1/14/89	1/14/90	25%	Ballard, Dillon

Extent of time in regular education program: 75%

I have had the opportunity to participate in the development of the Individual Education Program.

I agree with the Individual Education Program (✓)

I disagree with the Individual Education Program ( )

I agree with the placement of my child in the resource room for students with mild intellectual disabilities (✓)

I further understand that no records on my child will be released to unauthorized persons without my written permission. I also understand that my consent to the placement of my child in special education is voluntary and I may withdraw it at any time.

Paul M. Diedrich _1/12/89_
Parent's Signature   Date

Signatures Indicating Approval

Bruce Ballard
Thelma Dillon
Marilyn Fischer
Jon W. Jones
Paul M. Diedrich

INDIVIDUALIZED EDUCATION PROGRAM

STUDENT'S NAME: Jennifer Newsome

PARENTS' NAME: Jean and Ron Newsome

SCHOOL: Peterson Elementary

Date of Birth: 12-15-81

Age: 8

GRADE: 3

School Authority Approval:

On behalf of the _____

Peterson Elementary School, I approve this IEP.

Richard L. Keys

Principal/Designee

9-10-90

Date

Parental Approval:

(1) I acknowledge that my due process rights have been explained to me, and I understand them fully.

(2) I agree / ~~disagree~~ (cross out one) with this IEP.

(3) I have received a copy of this IEP.

Jean Newsome

Parent(s) / Guardian(s)

9-10-90

Date

Signatures of Participants in the IEP Meeting:

Ron Newsome
(Parent/Guardian)

Richard L. Keys
(Principal/Designee)

Phyllis Markus
(Regular Teacher)

Barbara A. Simon
(Special Education Teacher)

Kathleen Adams
(Counselor)

E. Ambrath
(Educational Aide)

Lamar Owens
(PE Teacher)

IEP Time Lines:

Program Entry Date: 9-16-90

Review Date: Crisis intervention

Review Date: as necessary

Review Date: _____

Annual Review Date: 9-15-91

Time in Regular Program

90%

Three-Year Re-evaluation Date: May 1993

Date of Termination of special education services: _____

Parent(s) / Guardian(s) _____

Parental agreement with major modifications

Initials	Date:

---

(1) Yellow Copy: Permanent School File

(2) Salmon Copy: Parent's Copy

(3) Blue Copy: Special Education Teacher

(4) Pink Copy: Regular Teacher

(5) Green Copy: Distribution Copy

NAME OF STUDENT Jennifer Newsome

SUBJECT AREA Social-Emotional Development

LEVEL OF PERFORMANCE Will attend well with teacher assistance. Imitates behavior of peers, dependent on adults, withdraws from situations; minimal group participation and/or contributions; demands instant need gratification, frequently says "I can't do this" when approaching tasks; completes assignments only with teacher's direction.

ANNUAL GOALS (1) Jennifer will demonstrate skills for interacting with adults and peers. (2) Jennifer will demonstrate group interaction skills. (3) Jennifer will demonstrate positive self-identity skills. (4) Jennifer will complete academic assignments within a specified amount of time.

OBJECTIVES	SPECIAL MATERIALS	PERSON(S) RESPONSIBLE	EVALUATION		DATE ACHIEVED
			METHOD	SCHEDULE	
Annual Goal: Jennifer will demonstrate skills for interacting with adults and peers.			A teacher-made checklist will be used to evaluate progress in this area.		
Instructional Objectives:					
1. Jennifer will share a task with another student without withdrawing from the task.	none	Consultation from teacher of the emotionally handicapped (EH teacher). Classroom teacher and aide will manage behavior program. Crisis intervention as necessary by EH teacher.	Anecdotal records, behavior charting, and checklist	Daily (Mastery 80% of opportunities provided)	
2. Jennifer will respond to requests made by a familiar adult.	"		"		
3. Jennifer will respond to requests made by an unfamiliar authority figure.	"		"	"	
4. Jennifer will demonstrate a "chum" relationship (where she is able to perceive and meet the needs of others and demonstrate compassion or empathy for that person) with at least one same-sex peer.	"		"	"	

430

IEP: Social-Emotional Development

OBJECTIVES	SPECIAL MATERIALS	PERSON(S) RESPONSIBLE	EVALUATION		DATE ACHIEVED
			METHOD	SCHEDULE	
5. Jennifer will participate in a group and respond to the group leader.	<u>none</u>	Classroom teacher and aide	Anecdotal records, behavior charting, and checklist	Daily	
6. Jennifer will participate in a group and act as group leader.	"	"	"	"	
<u>Annual Goal</u>: Jennifer will demonstrate group interaction skills. <u>Instructional Objectives</u>:			A teacher-made checklist will be used to evaluate progress in this area		
1. Jennifer will engage in a short-term group task without withdrawing.	<u>none</u>	Classroom teacher and aide	Anecdotal records, behavior charting, and checklist	Daily (85% of opportunities provided)	
2. Jennifer will participate in a short-term group task by seeking assistance from other group members rather than teacher.	"	"	"	"	
3. Jennifer will give assistance to other group members.	"	"	"	"	

IEP: Social-Emotional Development

OBJECTIVES	SPECIAL MATERIALS	PERSON(S) RESPONSIBLE	EVALUATION		DATE ACHIEVED
			METHOD	SCHEDULE	
Annual Goal: Jennifer will demonstrate positive self-identity skills.			A teacher-made checklist will be used to evaluate progress in this area		
Instructional Objectives:					
1. When presented with a task, Jennifer will accurately assess her capabilities and limitations.	none	Classroom teacher with consultation from EH teacher and counselor	Anecdotal records, behavior charting, and checklists	Daily (80% of opportunities provided)	
2. When presented with an athletic task she cannot perform, Jennifer will demonstrate acceptance of her limitations by not withdrawing or crying.	"	PE teacher with consultation from EH teacher and counselor	"	"	
3. When involved in a situation requiring her personal needs to be met, Jennifer will state ways that she can independently meet her needs.	"	Classroom teacher, counselor once weekly	"	"	

IEP: Social-Emotional Development

OBJECTIVES	SPECIAL MATERIALS	PERSON(S) RESPONSIBLE	EVALUATION		DATE ACHIEVED
			METHOD	SCHEDULE	
4. When asked to make decisions about her personal goals, Jennifer will state these goals and a means of achieving them.	none		Anecdotal records, behavior charting, and checklists	Daily	
Annual Goal: Jennifer will complete academic assignments within a specified amount of time.		Classroom teacher and educational aide	Contracting will be done with the student to determine the number of problems or assignments, the amount of time allowed for completion, and reinforcement for completion.		
Instructional Objectives:					
1. Jennifer will complete one assignment within the specified time with verbal cues or reminder.	none	Monitoring and consultation by EH teacher	Anecdotal records, behavior charting, and contract evaluation	Daily (80% accuracy on assignments)	
2. Jennifer will complete one assignment within the specified time without cues or reminders.	"		"	"	
3. Jennifer will complete two assignments without cues or reminder.	"		"	"	
4. Jennifer will complete three assignments without cues or reminders.	"		"	"	
5. Jennifer will complete four assignments without cues or reminders.	"		"	"	

NAME OF STUDENT Jennifer Newsome

SUBJECT AREA Language Development

LEVEL OF PERFORMANCE Describes objects by function, uses functional and descriptive words to classify objects inconsistently, identifies what happened first and last in a story, spells and writes words independently.

ANNUAL GOALS (1) Will increase vocabulary of descriptive words. (2) Will increase classification skills. (3) Will increase sequencing skills. (4) Will tell and write simple stories that involve making inferences and drawing conclusions.

OBJECTIVES	SPECIAL MATERIALS	PERSON(S) RESPONSIBLE	EVALUATION		DATE ACHIEVED
			METHOD	SCHEDULE	
Annual Goal: Jennifer will increase vocabulary of descriptive words. Instructional Objectives:			System Fore Criterion-Referenced Test (Language) will be administered monthly to assess progress.		
1. When shown an object, Jennifer will tell at least 3 things about how it looks.	various objects	Classroom teacher and aide	Teacher observation and System Fore checklist	Daily until attained	
2. When shown a picture, Jennifer will give one sentence describing the action shown in the picture.	pictures	Special education teacher in class 40 minutes daily	"	"	
3. Given 4 pictures, Jennifer will use the comparisons "-er" and "-est" to compare the pictures.	"	"	"	"	
4. When shown an object, Jennifer will tell at least one thing each about how it looks, is used, and is classified.	various objects	"	"	"	
5. When shown a picture, Jennifer will give a descriptive comment regarding the composite picture. Ex.: "What kind of face is this?"	pictures	"	"	"	

IEP: Language Development

OBJECTIVES	SPECIAL MATERIALS	PERSON(S) RESPONSIBLE	EVALUATION		DATE ACHIEVED
			METHOD	SCHEDULE	
6. Given a picture, Jennifer will interpret the pictured action by giving 2 sentences describing what is happening.	pictures	Classroom teacher or aide	Teacher observation and System Fore checklist	Daily until attained	
7. Given objects or pictures, Jennifer will describe the difference between 2 objects.	objects or pictures	Special education teacher in classroom 40 minutes daily	"	"	
8. After listening to a poem, Jennifer will correctly answer questions about the poem. Ex.: "Yours + mine" by F.G. Resser. "Is the author describing things he likes?" "Who owns the song of birds?"	poem	"	"	"	
9. Jennifer will correctly answer descriptive riddles.	none	"	"	"	
10. When playing a guessing game, Jennifer will use at least 3 complete descriptive sentences to describe an object. Ex.: "Pick an animal, but don't tell us what it is. Tell me everything you can about it so I can guess what it is."	"	"	"	"	
11. After listening to a descriptive sentence, Jennifer will select a word that is similar in meaning to the descriptor. Ex.: "A baby kitten is small. Can you think of another word that means small?"	"	"	"	"	

435

IEP: Language Development

OBJECTIVES	SPECIAL MATERIALS	PERSON(S) RESPONSIBLE	EVALUATION		DATE ACHIEVED
			METHOD	SCHEDULE	
12. Given a stimulus word, Jennifer will give at least 2 words that describe the stimulus word. Ex.: "water" ___ ___ "house" ___ ___	none	Classroom teacher or aide Special education teacher in classroom 40 minutes daily	Teacher observation and System Fore checklist	Daily until attained	
13. Given 2 objects or pictures, Jennifer will use two complete sentences to tell how they are alike. Ex.: "How are a ___ and a ___ alike?"	"		"	"	
14. After listening to an example, Jennifer will make up riddles using at least 2 complete descriptive sentences	"	"	"	"	
15. After listening to a question, Jennifer will answer the question with at least one complete sentence using descriptive language relating to sensory perception. Ex.: "What sounds do babies make?"	"	"	"	"	
16. After listening to a description of a situation, Jennifer will use at least 3 words to describe her feelings. Ex.: "How do you feel when your mother gets angry at you?"	"	"	"	"	
17. After listening to a story, Jennifer will give at least 3 adjectives describing a character in the story. Ex.: "What was the wolf in 'Little Red Riding Hood' like?"	"	"	"	"	

IEP: Language Development

OBJECTIVES	SPECIAL MATERIALS	PERSON(S) RESPONSIBLE	EVALUATION		DATE ACHIEVED
			METHOD	SCHEDULE	
Annual Goal: Jennifer will increase classification skills			System Fore Criterion-Referenced Test (Language) will be administered monthly to assess progress.		
Instructional Objectives:					
1. Given 3 pictures, Jennifer will state the relationship between the pictures. Ex.: "Which of these pictures go together? Why?"	pictures	Classroom teacher and aide	Teacher observation and System Fore checklist	Daily until attained	
2. When given a general classification, Jennifer will spontaneously name at least 8 objects in that classification. Ex.: "Tell me all the toys you can think of until I say 'stop'."	none	Special education teacher in classroom 40 minutes daily	"	"	
3. After listening to a list or looking at pictures of objects in a class, Jennifer will state their general classification. Ex.: "What do we call beds, chairs, and tables?" (furniture)	classification pictures	"	"	"	
4. Given a set of pictures or objects, Jennifer will state which ones "do not belong."	pictures objects	"	"	"	
5. Given a set of pictures, Jennifer will use relationships described by prepositions to classify the pictures. Ex.: "Find all the pictures where the ball is under something."	classification pictures	"	System Fore CRT (Language)	On attainment of objective	

437

IEP: Language Development

OBJECTIVES	SPECIAL MATERIALS	PERSON(S) RESPONSIBLE	EVALUATION METHOD	SCHEDULE	DATE ACHIEVED
Annual Goal: Jennifer will increase sequencing skills			System Fore Criterion-Referenced Test (Language) will be administered monthly to assess progress.		
Instructional Objectives:					
1. Given a set pictures, Jennifer will put them in sequential order.	sequence pictures	Classroom teacher and aide	Teacher observation and System Fore checklist	Daily until attained	
2. Given a picture, Jennifer will state logical events that may have preceded the event.	story pictures	Special education teacher in classroom 40 minutes daily	"	"	
3. Given a picture, Jennifer will state logical events that may have followed the pictured event.	"	"	"	"	
4. When asked a question, Jennifer will relate at least 3 events in correct sequential order. Ex.: "Tell me what happened before you came to school today."	none	"	"	"	
5. When shown pictures of 4 animals in a row, Jennifer will use the terms first, second, third, or fourth to identify the animals. Ex.: "The lamb is number 4. He is fourth in line."	animal pictures	"	"	"	
6. When telling experiences, Jennifer will relate 2 or more events that appear to be in order. Ex.: "Tell me what you did from the time you woke up until you came to school."	none	"	System Fore CRT (Language)	On attainment of objective	

IEP: Language Development

| OBJECTIVES | SPECIAL MATERIALS | PERSON(S) RESPONSIBLE | EVALUATION | | DATE |
			METHOD	SCHEDULE	ACHIEVED
Annual Goal: Jennifer will write simple stories that involve making inferences and drawing conclusions.			System Fore Criterion-Referenced Test (Language) will be administered monthly to assess progress.		
Instructional Objectives:					
1. When asked a question, Jennifer will comprehend the question and formulate a logical response. Ex.: "What must you do when you have lost something?"	none	Classroom teacher and aide	Teacher observation and System Fore checklist	Daily until attained	
2. Given a situation, Jennifer will create an original narrative of at least 3 complete sentences. Ex.: "Tell me a pretend story about a dog on Halloween."	none	Counselor will write stories with Jennifer once weekly	"	"	
3. When asked a question related to feelings, Jennifer will respond with at least 2 complete sentences. Ex.: "How do you feel when you're happy?"	none	"	"	"	
4. When given a picture and asked a question requiring an inference, Jennifer will make a logical response. Ex.: "Why did the girl say 'Thank you'?"	pictures	"	"	"	
5. After drawing a picture, Jennifer will respond to the question. "Tell me what your picture is about" by writing a caption of at least one complete sentence.	paper, crayons	"	"	"	

IEP: Language Development

| OBJECTIVES | SPECIAL MATERIALS | PERSON(S) RESPONSIBLE | EVALUATION | | DATE ACHIEVED |
			METHOD	SCHEDULE	
6. Given a picture, Jennifer will write at least 2 complete sentences telling about the picture.	picture paper pencil	Classroom teacher and aide	Teacher observation and System Fore checklist	Daily until attained	
7. Given a topic, Jennifer will write a story with at least 2 complete sentences.	paper pencil	Special education teacher in classroom 40 minutes daily	"	"	
8. After looking at a picture, Jennifer will tell a story about it stating what, whe, where, why, and how it happened.	pictures	"	"	"	
9. When given a picture, Jennifer will tell a story suggested by the picture and invent a logical ending.	pictures	"	"	"	
10. After looking at a picture, Jennifer will create a logical dialogue about what the characters are saying. Ex.: "What are the mother and father saying in this picture?"	pictures	"	System Fore CRT (Language)	"	

NAME OF STUDENT Jennifer Newsome

SUBJECT AREA Math

LEVEL OF PERFORMANCE Identifies numerals, rate counting, counts objects in sets, addition and subtraction facts 0-10 with concrete objects.

ANNUAL GOALS (1) Jennifer will demonstrate understanding of terminology and perform operations on sets. (2) Jennifer will add two 2-digit numbers with regrouping. (3) Jennifer will subtract two 2-digit numbers with regrouping.

OBJECTIVES	SPECIAL MATERIALS	PERSON(S) RESPONSIBLE	EVALUATION		DATE ACHIEVED
			METHOD	SCHEDULE	
Annual Goal: Jennifer will demonstrate understanding of terminology and perform operations on sets.			Teacher-made criterion-referenced test will be administered monthly to assess progress.		
Instructional Objectives:					
1. When asked what a set is, Jennifer will say that it is a group of objects.	none	Classroom teacher and aide	Teacher questions and teacher-made CRT checklist	Daily until attained	
2. When asked how many objects are in the empty set, Jennifer will say "none" or "zero."	none	"	"	"	
3. When shown a set of concrete objects, Jennifer will identify the subset. Ex.: "Here is a set of shapes. Show me the subset of circles."	counters, shapes, or small objects	"	"	"	
4. Using concrete aids, Jennifer will make sets with "one more than" or "one less than" a given set.	counters	"	"	"	
5. Given a worksheet with rows of sets, Jennifer will make the set with "one more than" the first set.	worksheet pencil	"	"	"	

441

IEP: Math

OBJECTIVES	SPECIAL MATERIALS	PERSON(S) RESPONSIBLE	EVALUATION		DATE
			METHOD	SCHEDULE	ACHIEVED
6. Given a worksheet, Jennifer will mark the set with "one less than" the first set.	worksheet pencil	Classroom teacher and aide	Teacher questions and teacher-made CRT checklist	Daily until attained	
7. Using concrete aids, Jennifer will use a 1 to 1 relation to match a smaller set to a larger set and tell how many objects in the larger set are not matched.	counters	"	"	"	
8. Using concrete aids, Jennifer will add to a smaller set to make it match a larger set.	"	"	"	"	
9. Given pictures of two sets, Jennifer will tell the difference in the sizes of the sets by saying "This set has ___ more than this set."	pictures of sets	"	"	"	
10. Given two sets, Jennifer will write the symbols >, <, or = to identify if the number of objects in a set is greater than, less than, or equal to the number of objects in another set.	worksheet pencil	"	"	"	
11. Given a set of an even number of concrete objects, Jennifer will divide the set into halves.	counters	"	"	"	
12. Given concrete objects, Jennifer will arrange them into sets of n when the total number of objects is a multiple of n.	counters	"	"	"	

IEP: Math

OBJECTIVES	SPECIAL MATERIALS	PERSON(S) RESPONSIBLE	EVALUATION METHOD	SCHEDULE	DATE ACHIEVED
13. Given equal sets of concrete objects with up to 5 members, Jennifer will tell how many objects she will have if she has n sets.	counters	Classroom teacher and aide	Teacher questions and teacher-made CRT checklist	Daily until attained	
Annual Goal: Jennifer will add two 3-digit numbers with regrouping.	"		System Fore Criterion-Referenced Test (Math) will be administered monthly to assess progress.		
Instructional Objectives:					
1. Given a worksheet, Jennifer will write additional facts with sums to 10 from memory with 90% accuracy.	worksheet pencil	Classroom teacher and aide	Teacher observation and System Fore checklist	Daily until attained	
2. Given a worksheet, Jennifer will work additional problems with sums to 10 with place holders (i.e., ☐) in all 3 positions with 90% accuracy. Ex.: 2 + ☐ = 5, ☐ + 5 = 7, 6 + 3 = ☐	"	"	"	"	
3. Given a worksheet, Jennifer will work addition problems with sums to 10 demonstrating the cummutative property with 90% accuracy. Ex.: 3 + 2 = ☐ + 3	"	"	"	"	
4. Given a worksheet, Jennifer will regroup numbers through 99 as tens plus ones with 90% accuracy. Ex.: 67 = 60 + ____	"	"	"	"	

IEP: Math

OBJECTIVES	SPECIAL MATERIALS	PERSON(S) RESPONSIBLE	EVALUATION METHOD	SCHEDULE	DATE ACHIEVED
5. Given a worksheet, Jennifer will solve vertical addition problems with 3 addends to sums of 10 with 90% accuracy.	worksheet pencil	Classroom teacher and aide	Teacher observation and System Fore checklist	Daily until attained	
6. Jennifer will represent addition facts with sums to 19 using concrete aids with 90% accuracy.	counters	"	"	"	
7. Jennifer will use a number line to solve addition problems with sums to 19 with 90% accuracy.	worksheet pencil number line	"	"	"	
8. Given a worksheet, Jennifer will complete sentences with a missing addend or sum with sums to 19 with 90% accuracy.	worksheet pencil	"	"	"	
9. Jennifer will write addition facts, sums to 19 from memory with 90% accuracy.	"	"	"	"	
10. Given a worksheet with addition problems with sums to 19, Jennifer will use 10s in regrouping addends with 90% accuracy. Ex.: 000000000 O 000 9 + 4 = 13 10 + 3 = 13	"	"	"	"	
11. Given a worksheet, Jennifer will correctly solve addition problems with 3 addends and sums to 19 with 90% accuracy.	"	"	"		

IEP: Math

OBJECTIVES	SPECIAL MATERIALS	PERSON(S) RESPONSIBLE	EVALUATION — METHOD	EVALUATION — SCHEDULE	DATE ACHIEVED
12. Given a worksheet, Jennifer will use the associative property when adding 2-digit and 1-digit numbers with 80% accuracy. Ex.: $12 + 5 =$ $(10 + 2) + 5 =$ $10 + (2 + 5) =$ $10 + 7 = 17$	worksheet pencil	Classroom teacher and aide	Teacher observation and System Fore checklist	Daily until attained	
13. Given a worksheet, Jennifer will correctly add by 10s with 90% accuracy. Ex.: 9 12 +10 +10	"	"	"	"	
14. Given a worksheet, Jennifer will add two 2-digit numbers without regrouping with 90% accuracy	"	"	"	"	
15. Given a worksheet, Jennifer will add two 2-digit numbers with regrouping with 90% accuracy.	"	"	System Fore CRT (Math)	On attainment of objective	
Annual Goal: Jennifer will subtract two 2-digit numbers with regrouping.			System Fore Criterion-Referenced Test (Math) will be administered monthly to assess progress.		
Instructional Objectives:					
1. Given a worksheet, Jennifer will use the number line to solve subtraction problems related to sums to 10 with 90% accuracy.	worksheet pencil number line	Classroom teacher and aide	Teacher observation and System Fore checklist	Daily until attained	
2. Given a worksheet, Jennifer will solve word problems with sums to 10 with 90% accuracy.	worksheet pencil	"	"	"	

IEP: Math

OBJECTIVES	SPECIAL MATERIALS	PERSON(S) RESPONSIBLE	EVALUATION		DATE ACHIEVED
			METHOD	SCHEDULE	
3. Using concrete aids, Jennifer will represent subtraction facts related to sums to 19 with 90% accuracy.	counters	Classroom teacher and aide	Teacher observation and System Fore checklist	Daily until attained	
4. Given a worksheet, Jennifer will use a number line to solve subtraction facts related to sums to 19 with 90% accuracy.	worksheet pencil number line	"	"	"	
5. Given a worksheet, Jennifer will write subtraction facts related to sums to 19 with 90% accuracy.	"	"	"	"	
6. Given a worksheet, Jennifer will solve problems involving subtraction by 10s with 90% accuracy. Ex.: 20 33 −10 −10	"	"	"	"	
7. Given a worksheet, Jennifer will subtract two 2-digit numbers with regrouping with 90% accuracy.	"	"	"	"	
8. Given a worksheet, Jennifer will subtract two 2-digit numbers with regrouping with 90% accuracy.	"	"	System Fore CRT (Math) Key Math Diagnostic Arithmetic Test will be administered at the end of the time covered by this IEP.	On attainment of objective	

446

(7) Educational Services to be Provided

Services Required	Date Initiated	Duration of Service	Individual Responsible for the Service
Crisis Intervention: Classroom (as needed)	9-16-90	6-15-91	Special Education Teacher
Counseling	9-16-90	6-15-91	School Counselor
Small group and individual	9-16-90	6-15-91	Special Education Teacher
instruction in the regular classroom			Classroom Teacher
			Educational Aide

Extent of time in the regular education program: none

Justification of the educational placement: Past documentation of Jennifer's behavior reveals that she lacks skills for participating independently and effectively in group instruction in the regular classroom. She requires a very structured, consistent educational program based on the regular curriculum low teacher-pupil ratio to provide the support needed to function in academic situations. This will be provided in the regular classroom with an educational aide and daily in-class instruction from the special education teacher. Emotional and behavioral problems will be dealt with by the special education teacher in the crisis-intervention classroom as necessary and by the counselor in weekly small-group counseling sessions.

(8) I have had the opportunity to participate in the development of the Individual Education Program

I agree with the Individual Education Program (X)

I disagree with the Individual Education Program ( )

Jean Newsome   _Ron Newsome_
_____
Parent(s) Signature

447

CONFIDENTIAL

Office of Special and Alternative Education
MONTGOMERY COUNTY PUBLIC SCHOOLS
Rockville, Maryland

INDIVIDUALIZED EDUCATION PROGRAM: TOTAL SERVICE
PART A

Last Name	First	M.I.	Date of Birth	Student ID No.	Present School	Present Grade	Present Program
Norman	Melissa	W	3-3-69	44120	Heights H.S.	12	Community Based

Home School: Heights H.S.

The IEP is a two part document (Part A and Part B) which is drafted prior to initiation of services or program placement. It establishes a teaching and/or services plan for the pupil at the beginning of each year, upon initial placement, or upon program/placement changes. It cannot reflect all activities of the pupil, nor guarantee a specified rate of progress. If more space is needed for Part A, use MCPS form 335-69-A1 — Part A Addendum.

SUMMARY OF CURRENT LEVELS OF PERFORMANCE: (Include observation(s), educational, ability and pertinent health information.)

EVALUATOR/OBSERVER	DATE	DATA SOURCES	SCORES/LEVELS OF PERFORMANCE	INDICATED STRENGTHS	INDICATED NEEDS
Masters, Sam	2-18-90	WAIS-R	V-60 P-53 FS-54	Wide range of good skills	Decreased distractibility
Nelby, Kathy	2-90 - 3-90	Adolescent & Adult Psychoeducational Profile (AAPEP)	Completes one- to two-step tasks	Self-help skills	Improved attending skills
					Improved functional life skills
					Improved functional use of money
					Improved knowledge of basic survival signs
					Improved leisure skills

PROGRAM DECISIONS

Disability code 01

Related services _____

Program School/Community-based Grade 16 DATE OF MEETING 8/25/90

Project Basic objectives in IEP Yes (No) Test accommodations needed Yes (No) (see ARD notes)

School assigned Heights High School

Start date Sept 1, 1990 Prelim. review date Oct 2, 1990 Annual review date June

Projected end date _____ Percent of time in regular classes _____

PARENTS

I authorize MCPS staff to implement Parts A and B of this program. My rights to appeal the educational services/program recommendations have been explained. I authorize MCPS to forward information for the Special Services Information System to the Maryland State Department of Education. I understand that this IEP will be maintained in a confidential file. I have been informed of Project Basic requirements.

Catleen Norman   Aug. 25, 1990
Signature(s) of Parent/Guardian   Date

MEETING PARTICIPANTS   TITLE:

Gary Forme   ARD Chair
Cathleen Norman   Parent(s)
Sara Collins   Teacher
Mark P. Seibler   Support Teacher
Scott McClary   Principal
nancy jane   Job site coordinator

The signature establishes completion of the IEP, Part A and B, and authorizes the initiation of the program.

Scott McClary   8/25/90
Signature of Principal/Program Coordinator   Date

MCPS Form 335-69-A. Revised September 1984

NOTE: This is a 5-part form. No carbon paper is required. Remove 5 copies before completing.
Original to Student's Confidential Record; copies to: Service Provider, Parent, Coordinator, and Other

From Office of Special and Alternative Education, Montgomery County Public Schools, Rockville, Maryland.

Office of Special and Alternative Education
MONTGOMERY COUNTY PUBLIC SCHOOLS
Rockville, Maryland

INDIVIDUALIZED EDUCATION PROGRAM:
INSTRUCTIONAL GOALS AND OBJECTIVES

Last Name	First	M.I.	MCPS ID. No.
Norman	Melissa	W	44120

Date of Meeting
August 25, 1990

PRIORITY ANNUAL GOALS/ SHORT TERM INSTRUCTIONAL OBJECTIVES	PERSON RESPONSIBLE (TITLE)	PROJECTED START DATE	EVALUATION CRITERIA	PROJECTED COMPLETION DATE	DATE OBJECTIVE ACHIEVED
To demonstrate improved functional life skills. 1. Will demonstrate improved functional use of money. 2. Will identify basic survival signs. 3. Will demonstrate improved leisure skills. 4. Will demonstrate improved pre/voc and vocational skills. 5. Will improve on task behavior/attending skills.	Special education teacher/staff	9-90	Task analysis Teacher checklists Formal & informal evaluations	6-91	
To demonstrate community independence. 1. Will utilize stores & services. 2. Will utilize transportation. 3. Will utilize recreational facilities. 4. Will utilize fast-food restaurants. 5. Will demonstrate appropriate social interactions.	Special education teacher/staff	9-90	Task analysis Teacher checklists Formal & informal evaluations	6-91	

NOTE: This is a multipart form—no carbon paper required. Remove copies before completing. Original to student's confidential record; copies to: service provider, parent, coordinator, and others as needed.

449

INDIVIDUALIZED EDUCATION PROGRAM   PAGE 1

FOR: MELISSA NORMAN
STUDENT NUMBER: 44120
EFFECTIVE: 1990–91 SCHOOL YEAR

Goal / Objective	PERSON (TITLE) RESPONSIBLE	PROJECTED START DATE	PROJECTED END DATE	ACTUAL END DATE	EVALUATION CRITERIA	PERCENT MASTERY
Goal Area: To demonstrate mathematics skills						
Annual Goal: Will use money	Classrm tchr	9/90	6/91		Will perform the task with 95% accuracy for 4 out of 5 trials	
Short-Term Objective: Will show recognition of coins needed for lunch money, pay phones, and vending machines						
Short-Term Objective: Will determine how many dollar bills are necessary for a purchase						
Annual Goal: Will tell time	Classrm tchr	9/90	6/91		Will use a daily schedule	
Short-Term Objective: Will relate daily activities to appropriate time segments						
Annual Goal: Will develop measuring skills	Classrm tchr	9/90	6/91		Will perform the task with 95% accuracy for 4 out of 5 trials	
Short-Term Objective: Will measure with measuring cups and spoons designated in a recipe						
Goal Area: To demonstrate home living skills						
Annual Goal: Will interact with others	Classrm tchr	9/90	6/91		Teacher observation	
Short-Term Objective: Will identify own feelings						
Short-Term Objective: Will share feelings with others						
Short-Term Objective: Will use constructive methods for dealing with feelings						

IEP FOR: MELISSA NORMAN PAGE 2	PERSON (TITLE) RESPONSIBLE	PROJECTED START DATE	PROJECTED END DATE	ACTUAL END DATE	EVALUATION CRITERIA	PERCENT MASTERY
Goal Area: To demonstrate community living skills						
Annual Goal: Will use the telephone	Classrm tchr	9/90	6/91		Will perform the task with 95% accuracy for 4 out of 5 trials	
Short-Term Objective: Will make local phone calls to friends and parents						
Goal Area: To prepare for the world of work						
Annual Goal: Will interact successfully	Classrm tchr	9/90	6/91		Teacher observation	
Short-Term Objective: Will initiate conversation when appropriate						
Short-Term Objective: Will maintain eye contact during conversations						
Short-Term Objective: Will maintain conversation topic as appropriate						
Short-Term Objective: Will show ability to cope with change in school						
Goal Area: To participate in the world of work						
Annual Goal: Will develop work skills	Classrm tchr	9/90	6/91			
Short-Term Objective: Will engage in out-of-school work programs						
Annual Goal: Will demonstrate positive work behaviors	Classrm tchr	9/90	6/91		Teacher observation & specific data collection methods (e.g., rate, freq, etc.)	
Short-Term Objective: Will greet co-workers and supervisors appropriately						

451

IEP FOR: MELISSA NORMAN PAGE 3	PERSON (TITLE) RESPONSIBLE	PROJECTED START DATE	PROJECTED END DATE	ACTUAL END DATE	EVALUATION CRITERIA	PERCENT MASTERY
Short-Term Objective: Will remain on task for increasing lengths of time						
Short-Term Objective: Will work with increasing speed and accuracy						
Short-Term Objective: Will ask for assistance if necessary						
Short-Term Objective: Will use sign-in and sign-out procedures						
Goal Area: Stores and services						
Annual Goal: To acquire the skills necessary to use a fast food restaurant and/or snack bar/shop	Classrm tchr	9/90	6/91		Will perform the task with 95% accuracy for 4 out of 5 trials	
Short-Term Objective: Will acquire skills for verbally ordering predetermined items pictured on an ordering card and paying for the items						
Annual Goal: To acquire the skills necessary to use a supermarket, drug and/or convenience store	Classrm tchr	9/90	6/91		Will perform the task with 95% accuracy for 4 out of 5 trials	
Short-Term Objective: Will acquire the skills for using pictures/labels displayed in a shopping notebook/list to locate predetermined items and will purchase the items						
Goal Area: Domestic living						
Annual Goal: To acquire the skills necessary in food preparation	Classrm tchr	9/90	6/91		Will perform the task with 95% accuracy for 4 out of 5 trials	
Short-Term Objective: Will acquire the skills to prepare an entree, using a picture recipe book						

IEP FOR: MELISSA NORMAN	PERSON (TITLE) RESPONSIBLE	PROJECTED START DATE	END DATE	ACTUAL END DATE	EVALUATION CRITERIA	PERCENT MASTERY
Short-Term Objective: Will acquire the skills to prepare a cold beverage from a powdered/liquid mix						
Short-Term Objective: Will acquire the skills to prepare a hot beverage from a powdered/liquid mix						
Short-Term Objective: Will acquire the skills to prepare a dessert item using a picture recipe book						
Short-Term Objective: Will acquire the skills to operate and use a small appliance to prepare a food item (i.e., can opener, mixer, blender, food processor, toaster oven, toaster)						
Short-Term Objective: Will acquire the skills to operate and use a microwave to cook/heat a food item						
Short-Term Objective: Will acquire the skills to operate and use a stove to cook/heat a food item						
Annual Goal: To acquire the skills necessary to maintain a household	Classrm tchr	9/90	6/91		Will perform the task with 95% accuracy for 4 out of 5 sessions	
Short-Term Objective: Will acquire the skills to put groceries/ household items away in their proper location following shopping						
Short-Term Objective: Will acquire the skills to set a table before a meal						
Short-Term Objective: Will acquire the skills to unload clean dishes from a dishwasher						
Short-Term Objective: Will acquire the skills to load dirty dishes into a dishwasher						

IEP FOR: MELISSA NORMAN   PAGE 5

	PERSON (TITLE) RESPONSIBLE	PROJECTED START DATE	PROJECTED END DATE	ACTUAL END DATE	EVALUATION CRITERIA	PERCENT MASTERY
Short-Term Objective: Will acquire the skills to sweep a floor						
Short-Term Objective: Will acquire the skills to vacuum						
Annual Goal: To acquire the skills necessary to maintain clothing and linens	Classrm tchr	9/90	6/91		Will perform the task with 95% accuracy for 4 out of 5 trials	
Short-Term Objective: Will acquire the skills to sort clothing/ linens for washing						
Short-Term Objective: Will acquire the skills to use a washing machine						
Short-Term Objective: Will acquire the skills to use a dryer						
Short-Term Objective: Will acquire the skills to fold clothing/ linens						
Goal Area: Recreation/leisure						
Annual Goal: To acquire the skills necessary to participate in community-based recreational/leisure activities	Classrm tchr	9/90	6/91		Will perform the task with 95% accuracy for 4 out of 5 trials	
Short-Term Objective: Will acquire the skills to participate in aerobic exercises						
Short-Term Objective: Will acquire the skills to use a public library						
Short-Term Objective: Will acquire the skills to use a vending machine						

IEP FOR: MELISSA NORMAN PAGE 6	PERSON (TITLE) RESPONSIBLE	PROJECTED START DATE	PROJECTED END DATE	ACTUAL END DATE	EVALUATION CRITERIA	PERCENT MASTERY
Annual Goal: To acquire the skills necessary to play/participate in table games Short-Term Objective: Will acquire the skills to play a card game	Classrm tchr	9/90	6/91		Will perform the task with 95% accuracy for 4 out of 5 trials	
Goal Area: Transportation Annual Goal: To acquire the skills necessary to use public transportation Short-Term Objective: Will acquire the skills to ride a public bus to a predetermined destination	Classrm tchr	9/90	6/91		Will perform the task with 95% accuracy for 4 out of 5 trials	
Goal Area: Community preparations Annual Goal: To acquire the skills necessary to prepare for the use of a restaurant Short-Term Objective: Will acquire the skills to select choices from photographs of actual food items and use a hand calculator to determine price/money needed	Classrm tchr	9/90	6/91		Will perform the task with 95% accuracy for 4 out of 5 trials	
Annual Goal: To acquire the skills necessary to prepare for the use of a supermarket/drug/convenience store Short-Term Objective: Will acquire the skills to select needed shopping items using photographs and labels and estimating to the nearest dollar for the prices	Classrm tchr	9/90	6/91		Will perform the task with 95% accuracy for 4 out of 5 trials	

IEP TEAM

Student __Kelly R.__

Parent(s) __Mr. and Mrs. R.__

Teacher(s) __Ms. Brown (voc. ed.), Mr. Jones__

__(sp. ed.), Mr. Turner (rd. spec.)__

Agency Representative __Mrs. Johnson__

__(principal)__

Other(s) _____

STUDENT INFORMATION

D.O.B. __6-2-72__ Age __16__ Grade __10__

Phone __555-4162__ Address __12 Holly Court - Apt. 3__

School __West View High School__

PROCEDURAL CHECKLIST - DATE

	Persons Responsible	Date Initiated	Duration
Written notice about program initiation/change	Turner/Stone	12-01-88	review IEP
	Brown	12-01-88	8-10-89
	Jones	12-03-88	
Consent for preplacement evaluation 11-20-88	Jones	12-08-88	
Consent for initial placement 10-02-81	Jones	11-11-88	
11-06-81			

SPECIAL EDUCATION AND RELATED SERVICES TO BE PROVIDED

remedial reading and math - daily
vocational education - in-class help 3 times weekly
tutorial help in social studies & science; lab assistance
special class in basic skills one hour weekly
bi-weekly consultation with 4 core subject area teachers

EXTENT OF TIME IN REGULAR EDUCATION PROGRAM __80% in regular classes & 20% in special education__

EVALUATION DATA

WISC-R (10-88) Verbal - 65, Performance - 72, Full Scale - 68
PIAT (10-88) math - 6.7, word recognition - 4.4, comprehension - 4.0, spelling - 4.8, total - 5.0
WRAT (10-88) math - 6.9, reading - 4.6, spelling - 5.0
Vineland Social Maturity Scale - 83 (10-88)
Informal inventory of vocationally related skills (9-88): low performance in application of language and
grammar to work related tasks; Application of functional skills to work related task in mechanics
and repair is good

DISABILITY AREA UNDER WHICH STUDENT QUALIFIES FOR SPECIAL EDUCATION:

Mild Intellectual Disability

PRESENT LEVELS OF PERFORMANCE	ANNUAL GOALS	SHORT-TERM INSTRUCTIONAL OBJECTIVES	EVALUATION PROCEDURES	PERSON RESPONSIBLE
No work experience using basic mechanical principles. Interest in mechanics and simple repair.	Kelly will attain pre-employment skills at an employable level including an understanding of the free enterprise system.	Job Skills: Given the requisite materials, tools, equipment, and training, Kelly will . . . Compare/contrast the American private enterprise system with other economic systems. Discuss investment opportunities, competition, automation, specialization, taxation. List the influences of labor organizations on the economy, business, and individuals. Name 5 reasons that demonstrate the value of work.	Participation in class discussions and work sample activities. Observation, oral and written quizzes. Bi-weekly check scale used for all objectives through oral and written assessment: ☐ Unfamiliar ☐ Maintaining ☐ Progressing 50-70% success ☐ Productive 70-85% success ☐ Employable 85-100% success	Vocational education and special education teachers
	work possibilities and basic principles	Explore various jobs and occupational clusters. Demonstrate a working knowledge of basic mechanical principles (e.g., levers, screws, pulleys, vacuums).		
	good work habits	List characteristics, abilities, attitudes, and habits of successful workers. Maintain appropriate personal hygiene and dress. Be on time consistently and accept consequences for tardiness. Work dependably and independently without direct, continuous supervision. Demonstrate concern/adherence to safety precautions.		
Basic reading level approximately 4th grade and weak in technical vocabulary. Strong in spelling with good dictionary skills	occupational communications.	Read and follow written instructions correctly (e.g., labels, procedural manuals, street signs). Define and correctly use technical vocabulary at a level sufficient for work experience communication.		
As determined by a work sample inventory, Kelly's manual dexterity is somewhat clumsy	Kelly will improve his manual dexterity.	Coordinate eye-hand-foot movements accurately. Coordinate the use of both hands effectively, including lifting, turning, pulling, placing, and using small hand tools and equipment. Demonstrate effective finger agility.	Monthly work sample assessment and successful completion of work sample kit activities as determined by teacher observation. All activities must be completed without mistakes.	

457

PRESENT LEVELS OF PERFORMANCE	ANNUAL GOALS	SHORT-TERM INSTRUCTIONAL OBJECTIVES	EVALUATION PROCEDURES	PERSON RESPONSIBLE
Reads with difficulty from newspapers, magazines, and textbooks written at 4th-grade level	Kelly will increase functional reading and spelling skills in preparation for competency exam. Kelly will develop functional writing skills using occupational tasks.	**Reading Lab:** Given small group instruction, Kelly will ... Spell & define survival words, words typically found on a job application, and other vocationally related words. Write simple sentences & paragraphs correctly. Accurately complete such forms/letters as applications, registration forms, thank you notes, want ad replies. Evaluate information in want ads. Communicate effectively on the telephone. Define abbreviations commonly used on application forms. Describe a resume verbally; list reasons for using a resume; write a resume for himself. List 5 elements of a successful interview; appropriately answer 10 sample interview questions. Read high interest-low level books, selected by Kelly and approved by Mr. Turner, no less than 1 bi-weekly. Read a 15-minute daily assignment from the newspaper, with an occupational emphasis, or in workbook.	80% accuracy expected on all daily assignments. 85% accuracy expected on all teacher-made weekly quizzes. Criterion-referenced tests will be used to test achievement	Reading specialist Vocational education & Special education teachers
Reads, writes, and interprets correctly numerical information, cardinal and ordinal numbers. Progressing in subtracting decimals. Uses calculator for most computation.	Kelly will increase quantitative and numerical skills. Kelly will attain basic money management skills.	**Math Lab:** In an individualized math lab, Kelly will ... Discriminate among different sizes, shapes, textures. Define and correctly use such common numbers as zip codes, phone numbers, social security numbers. Estimate distances, sizes, and weights accurately. Correctly measure perimeter, weight, time, temperature. List common financial responsibilities and describe how to accommodate each; include obligations and luxuries. Discuss principles of banking; include credit, loans, savings. Match common coins/bills with their correct names. Accurately make change using up to $100. Distinguish between gross and net pay. Write sample checks correctly; balance checkbook. Fill in and compute time cards. Prepare biweekly and monthly budgets — data furnished.	All objectives will be checked on the following scale through weekly quizzes: ☐ Unfamiliar ☐ Introduced ☐ Progressing 50-70% success ☐ Productive 70-85% success ☐ Mastery 85-100% success Criterion-referenced tests will be used to test achievement semi-annually	Remedial math teacher Special education consultation

PRESENT LEVELS OF PERFORMANCE	ANNUAL GOALS	SHORT-TERM INSTRUCTIONAL OBJECTIVES	EVALUATION PROCEDURES	PERSON RESPONSIBLE
		Social Studies/Science		
About a 4th grade reading level.	Same as those for regular class using small group instruction.	Receives tutorial aid daily and lab assistance weekly. Follow basic objectives of class using alternative texts on third-grade reading level.	Graded according to regular class criteria and schedules, using a contract system.	Classroom teacher
Below age-appropriate behaviors in memory, organizing, decision making, and listening. Attentive to written detail. Learns best through demonstration and active participation.	Kelly will improve organizational and study skills.	Basic Skills: Given small group instruction in a resource class, Kelly will . . . Organize class and homework assignments. Correctly order/sequence numbers, dates, directions, etc. Organize information to solve mathematical problems systematically. Select appropriately from decision-making alternatives. Listen carefully to discriminate sounds and their meanings and to remember oral instructions.	Maintain calendar of assignments, homework, and schedule 8 events for 2 months.	Special education teacher
Does not sustain conversations with peers and adults. Does not ask for assistance when needed.	Kelly will demonstrate appropriate social skills and occupational interests.	React appropriately to nonverbal cues, such as gestures, tones, body language. List personal strengths and correlate them with qualities sought by employers. Ask questions appropriately to gain information. Describe how to address others in a businesslike manner, including customers, fellow employees, supervisors, and management. Demonstrate acceptable work attitudes and behavior. Exercise patience and self-control under stress.	Weekly class grades should improve if the resource help is effective. A semi-annual self-appraisal and observational scale will determine progress in social skills and occupational development.	

Individual Education Program

Identification Information

Student's Name: **Shane W.**
School: **Rosewood**
Grade/Placement: **Infant Treatment Program**

Birthdate: 1-19-87
Age: 14 months
Parent's Name: Stephen and Valerie W.
Address: 320 W. 19th St.
Phone: (Home) 621-0662   (Business) 621-9792

Medical Information

Vision: **Within normal limits**

Medication: **none**

Hearing: Within normal limits (December 13, 1987)

Physical Condition: Extremely hypotonic, quadriplegic cerebral palsied. Frequent problems with upper respiratory infections and ear infections.

Schedule of Services

Monday	Tuesday	Wednesday	Thursday	Friday
		9:30–10:00 Group Time (Art or Music)		9:30–10:00 Group Time (Art or Music)
		10:00-11:30 Individual lessons in cognitive, gross motor areas		10:00-11:30 Individual lessons in cognitive, gross motor areas
		11:30-12:00 Snack (self-help) with mother		11:30-12:00 Snack (self-help) with mother

Comments

Infant Treatment Group meets only on Wednesday and Friday morning. The group helps show the parents effective ways to work with their children and helps the parent devise objectives to work on at home.

Date of Beginning Service: 3-19-1988
Projected Ending Date: 3-1989
Date IEP Initially Approved: 3-14-1988
Review Date: 6-1-1988; 9-1-1988

Committee Members
Teacher: *Susan Jeffrey, Agiola founder*
LEA Representative:
Parents: *Mr. Stephen W.*
Other: *George Griffin, Physical Therapist*

TESTING INFORMATION

Student's Name: ___Shane___

Carolina Curriculum for Handicapped Infants (a curriculum-based checklist that accompanies the curriculum used at the Infant Treatment Group).

Adaptive Performance Instrument

January 25, 1988

January 30, 1988

* fine motor—Shane is developing at an almost age-appropriate rate in this area. He has a nice superior pincer grasp. He responds positively to most tactile stimulation activities. His reaction and grasp are well directed, though it takes him a long time to reach objects placed at arms length sometimes (12 month level).

* gross motor—
  a) prone—Shane is just developing the ability to lift his head in this position. He works best over a wedge (2-3 month level).

  b) supine—Shane's preferred position. He is developing the ability to roll from this position (3 month level).

  c) upright—Shane is developing the ability to lift his head upright for longer periods of time in this position. He does not have much trunk awareness in this position (2-3 month level).

* language skills—
  a) receptive—Shane does not consistently respond to his own name yet. He is beginning to understand "up" and "bye." He is not particularly attentive to the human voice (6-7 month level).

  b) expressive—Shane vocalizes a variety of vowel and consonant sounds, but he vocalizes very frequently. He occasionally repeats sounds made by his caregiver which are already in his repertoire. (5-6 month level).

* Cognitive—Shane has an inconsistent understanding of object permanence. Shane likes games and is beginning to anticipate frequently occurring events in a game he plays with his mother.

* fine motor—well directed reach, good pincer grasp.

* gross motor—beginning to be able to hold up head in prone . . . ability to hold head steady when upright is also emerging.

* social skills—not very "people oriented"—developing a stronger attachment to his mother.

* language skills—ability to produce a variety of vowel-consonant sounds. Has differential cries his mother can understand.

* cognitive—object permanence is not well established.

Individual Education Program

Name of Student: Shane

Subject Area: Gross Motor

Present Level of Educational Functioning	Annual Goals/Criteria	Instructional Objectives/Criteria	Date Achieved
I. Shane is beginning to consistently lift his head or turn his head to the side when he is placed in prone. When over a wedge or a person's knee while in the prone position, Shane is inconsistently able to lift his head and chest up far enough to look around. He still tires quickly in this position, though.	I. In a prone position, Shane will be able to support himself on his hands with his arms extended and his head upright for ≥ 30 seconds, 4/5 times on 5 consecutive days.	1. Shane, when placed in a prone position, will consistently lift his head and free his nose, 5/5 times on 3 consecutive days.	[05/88]
		2. With a wedge, or prone over a person's knee, Shane, will lift his head to a 45° angle; supporting himself on his elbows, ≥ 30 seconds, 5/5 times on 3 consecutive days.	[08/88]
		3. Shane will lift his head to a 45° angle; supporting himself on his elbows for ≥ 30 seconds, 5/5 times on 3 consecutive days.	[11/88]
II. Shane's ability to roll from his back to his stomach is improving rapidly. He is able to perform this roll fairly consistently, though it often takes him a long time. Shane's not able to roll over completely when placed upon his stomach.	II. Shane will be able to roll smoothly from his stomach to his back, or from his stomach to his back, 5/5 times on 3 consecutive days.	1. Shane will roll from his stomach to his back or vice-versa by arching his back, 5/5 times on 3 consecutive days.	[05/88]
		2. Shane will roll from his back to his stomach and return to his back again when placed on a moderate incline, 5/5 times on 3 consecutive days.	[08/88]
		3. Shane will roll from his stomach to his back quickly and readily; leading with an arm or leg and showing trunk rotation, 5/5 times on 3 consecutive days.	[11/88]
III. Shane is able to hold his head erect when he is held upright. After several minutes of being upright, Shane's head tends to "wobble" a bit. Shane is able to hold his head steady inconsistently when the person holding him sways about. Shane can hold his trunk steady for very brief periods of time when in an upright position.	III. Shane, when placed in a sitting position will be able to sit unsupported for 1 minute, 4/5 times on 5 consecutive days.	1. Shane will be able to maintain his head erect and steady for 1 minute as adult holding him sways back and forth, 5/5 × on 3 consecutive days.	[06/88]
		2. Shane will hold his trunk steady without support while being held for ≥ 30 seconds, 5/5 times on 3 consecutive days.	[09/88]
(*Note - Shane should not work in the sitting position until he has mastered Gross-Motor goals I.3. and III.3).		3. Shane will maintain trunk steadiness and balance while adult holding him sways back and forth for 60 seconds, 5/5 times on 3 consecutive days.	[12/88]

Individual Education Program

Name of Student: __Shane__

Subject Area: Cognitive

Present Level of Educational Functioning	Annual Goals/Criteria	Instructional Objectives/Criteria	Date Achieved
I. Shane inconsistently watches people talking and/or gesturing. Shane inconsistently imitates gestures he is already known to perform if they are imitated by the caregiver. (Example: will shake a bell following the caregiver shaking the bell).	I. Shane will imitate new activities which are modeled for him by an adult, 5/5 times for the same activity on 3 consecutive days.	1. Shane will look at person talking and/or gesturing, 5/5 times on 3 consecutive days. [06/80]	[06/88]
		2. Shane will continue an activity he is performing if it is imitated by the caregiver, 3/4 times on 3 consecutive days. [07/80]	[07/88]
		3. Shane will begin an activity already in his repertoire if the same activity is begun by his caregiver, 3/4 times on 2 consecutive days.	[09/88]
		4. Shane will approximately imitate an activity when his action is visible to himself, 3/4 times on 2 consecutive days.	[11/88]
		5. Shane will imitate unfamiliar activities which are out of sight of his own body, 3/4 times on 2 consecutive days.	[01/89]
II. Shane likes to play games like patty-cake. He sometimes smiles, vocalizes, or moves about when playing games with an adult. He anticipates when his mother will tickle him in their "I'm gonna getcha" game, but he has not generalized this skill to other people or other games yet.	II. Shane, will initiate activities with adults by starting movements at least 1 time per day on 5 different days.	1. Shane will anticipate (demonstrated through vocalization or movement), frequently occurring events in games or nursery rhymes, 3/5 times on 2 consecutive days.	[05/88]
		2. Shane will repeat activities which get interesting results/reactions from others, repeats for 3 different behaviors for at least 2 different days.	[08/88]
		3. Shane will get an adult to continue an activity by starting body movements at least 2 times per day for 5 consecutive days.	[11/88]

463

Name of Student: __Shane__

Individual Education Program

Subject Area: Cognitive

Present Level of Educational Functioning	Annual Goals/Criteria	Instructional Objectives/Criteria	Date Achieved
Shane usually shakes most of the toys placed in his hands. He is currently learning to squeeze a squeeker toy.	III. Shane will demonstrate different activities with toys having obviously different properties; 5 appropriate activities with 5 different toys on 3 separate days.	1. Shane commonly performs 2 or more activities with objects, 2 or more activities on 3 separate days.	[05/88]
		2. Shane commonly performs 3 or more activities with objects, 3 or more activities on 3 separate days.	[07/88]
		3. Shane commonly performs 4 or more activities with objects, 4 or more activities on 3 separate days.	[09/88]
		4. Shane explores toys and responds to their differences, 5 successful trials on 3 separate days.	[11/88]

APPENDIX E   Curriculum Checklists

ARITHMETIC—PRIMARY

I. Basic Concepts, Facts, and Procedures

A. Counts, Reads, and Writes Numbers

_____ 1. Reads and writes symbols 0–10.

_____ 2. Can count groups of objects with sums, 0–10.

_____ 3. Writes in missing numerals in an incomplete sequence using numerals 1–10.

_____ 4. Recognizes and states numbers along the number line (0–10).

_____ 5. Recognizes and names patterns of 2, 3, 4, and 5 without counting.

_____ 6. Counts the number of objects in a set (0–10).

_____ 7. Completes dot-to-dot pictures by drawing marks that connect the numbers 0–10 in order.

_____ 8. Counts by 2's from 0–10 using number line.

_____ 9. Names the ordinal positions 1st, 2nd, 3rd, 4th, 5th and matches ordinal positions to the numbers 1, 2, 3, 4, and 5.

_____10. Rote counts from 0 to 50 by 1's.

_____11. Reads and writes symbols from 0 to 25.

_____12. Reads and writes number words to 10.

_____13. Tells age, address, and telephone number.

_____14. Writes, age, address, and telephone number.

_____15. Uses numbers in daily situations, such as counting children, finding page in book, and keeping score during ball game.

B. Facts and Processes

_____ 1. Matches groups of objects through 5.

_____ 2. Counts number of objects through 5.

_____ 3. Matches groups of objects through 10.

_____ 4. Counts number of objects through 10.

_____ 5. Matches equivalent sets having the same number.

_____ 6. Points to empty sets containing no objects.

_____ 7. Identifies by pointing to subsets within sets of objects.

_____ 8. Solves simple puzzle involving concepts of number set.

_____ 9. Demonstrates the meaning of *more* and *less* by utilizing the concept of "one more than" and "one less than" in making sets.

_____10. Recognizes and states the meaning of the symbols > and < .

_____11. Recognizes and states the meaning of the symbols =, +, and −.

_____12. Solves simple addition equations with sums through 10 or less using real objects and sets.

_____13. Solves simple word problems involving addition problems with sums through 10 or less.

_____14. Solves column addition using 3 numbers with sums to 10.

C. Geometry

———— 1. Names geometric shapes such as circle, square, triangle, star.
———— 2. Traces geometric shapes on paper and cuts them out.

II. Measurement

1. Can match the following size and amount terms:

———a. more—less	———h. tall—short
———b. big—little	———i. all—enough—some
———c. long—short	———j. none
———d. large—small	———k. fat—thin
———e. many—few	———l. young—old
———f. heavy—light	———m. far—near
———g. high—low	

———— 2. Compares objects according to the previously mentioned terms.
———— 3. Can state and demonstrate the meaning of 1/2 and 1.
———— 4. Recognizes and understands the measures of pint, 1/2 pint, and cup.
———— 5. Recognizes and understands the measures of tablespoon and teaspoon.
———— 6. States that a thermometer measures temperature.
———— 7. Can distinguish between body and weather thermometers.

III. Time

1. Can tell how time relates to each of the following:
———a. To begin school.
———b. To end school.
———c. For lunch.
———d. To get up in the morning.
———e. To go to bed at night.
2. Identifies sequences of events in time:
———a. Yesterday, today, tomorrow.
———b. Before, after.
———— 3. Can state the relationship of morning, afternoon, evening, and midnight.
———— 4. Can state that clocks and watches are used to tell time.
———— 5. Can read the numerals on the clock.
———— 6. Can tell which is the hour hand and which is the minute hand.
———— 7. States that there are 60 minutes in an hour.
———— 8. States that there are 30 minutes in a half-hour.
———— 9. Tells time by the hour.
————10. Tells time by the half-hour.
————11. States the number of days in a week.
————12. Tells the names of the days of the week.
————13. Can recognize the words for the names of the week when they are pointed to.
————14. Uses the calendar with teacher assistance to interpret the date.
————15. Verbalizes and writes birth date.
————16. Can state number of months in a year.
————17. States the names of the months of the year.
————18. Recognizes the words for the months of the year when they are pointed to.
19. Can tell which months the following holidays occur in:
———a. Christmas.
———b. Thanksgiving.
———c. Halloween.
———d. Valentine's Day.

IV. *Money*

_____ 1. Can point to the following coins: penny, nickel, dime (when they are named).

2. Can state the following monetary relationships:

_____a. 5 pennies = 1 nickel

_____b. 10 pennies = 1 dime

_____c. 2 nickels = 1 dime

_____ 3. Tells the cost of certain items around school, such as lunch, pencils, ice cream, drinks.

_____ 4. Tells the difference between buying and saving.

_____ 5. Tells the difference between saving and spending.

_____ 6. Solves addition problems involving sums to 10 related to values of penny, nickel, and/or dime.

_____ 7. States the meaning of cents sign.

_____ 8. Writes monetary value using cents sign.

ARITHMETIC—INTERMEDIATE

I. Basic Concepts, Facts and Procedures

A. Counts, Reads, and Writes Numbers

_____ 1. Counts objects from 0 to 50 by 2's, 5's, and 10's.

_____ 2. Reads and writes number symbols 0–50.

_____ 3. When presented with ranked objects, can point out the ordinal positions 6th, 7th, 8th, 9th, and 10th and tells the relationship to the numbers 6, 7, 8, 9, and 10.

_____ 4. Counts objects from 0–100 by 1's.

_____ 5. Reads and writes number symbols 0–70.

_____ 6. Reads and writes number names; zero, one, two, three, four, and five.

_____ 7. Writes the missing numerals in an incomplete sequence using numerals 0–50.

_____ 8. Counts objects from 0–100 by 2's.

_____ 9. Reads and writes number symbols 0–100.

_____10. Reads and writes number names zero–ten.

_____11. Counts objects 0–100 by 1's, 2's, 5's, and 10's.

_____12. Reads and writes number symbols 0–100.

_____13. Reads and writes number names zero–fifteen.

_____14. Can state the meaning of ordinals: first, twentieth.

_____15. Distinguishes between even and odd numbers by giving a few examples of each.

_____16. Writes the missing numerals in an incomplete sequence using numerals 0–100.

_____17. Reads, counts, and writes by 1's, 2's, 5's, and 10's to 100.

_____18. Reads, writes, and spells cardinal and ordinal number names through twenty.

B. Facts and Processes

_____ 1. Using one-to-one relation, matches smaller set to larger one telling how many objects of larger set are not matched.

_____ 2. Adds to smaller set to make it match larger set.

_____ 3. Solves addition equations with sums through 20 or less with no carrying using real objects and sets.

_____ 4. Solves word problems involving addition problems with sums through 20 or less with no carrying.

_____ 5. Writes or states if the number of objects in a set is greater than, less than, or equal to the number of objects in another set.

_____ 6. Uses symbols less than (<) and greater than (>) with numerals 0–25.

_____ 7. Arranges objects into sets of 10 when the total number of objects is a multiple of 10.

_____ 8. Joins two given subsets into one set and tells how many objects there are.

_____ 9. Uses symbols less than (<) and greater than (>) with numerals 0–50.

_____10. Arranges objects into sets of ten when the total number of objects is not a multiple of 10 with objects left over being 1, 2, 3, 4, or 5.

_____11. Shows the relationship of ten and ones that makeup the "teen family."

_____12. Arranges objects into sets of ten when total number of objects is not a multiple of 10 with objects left over being 6, 7, 8, or 9.

———13. Supplies the missing addends in addition combinations.

———14. Uses greater than and less than symbols correctly when comparing any two numbers 0–100.

———15. Masters 100 basic addition facts.

———16. States the meaning of *place value* in two-digit numbers.

———17. Uses mental solutions without the use of written computation to find solutions to written problems.

———18. Adds by "counting on" a number line.

———19. Adds any two 2-digit numbers involving no carrying.

———20. Demonstrates knowledge of place value of 3-digit number by telling which is the 100's, 10's, and 1's column.

———21. Adds any two 3-digit numbers involving no carrying.

———22. Solves word problems utilizing 2- and 3-digit numbers involving no carrying.

———23. Solves column addition of 0–8 one-digit addends—equations and word problems.

———24. Solves column addition with 2–4 two-digit addends involving no carrying.

———25. Adds two 2- and 3-digit numerals involving carrying one to tens column only—equations and word problems.

———26. Adds three–five 2-and 3-digit numerals carrying 2 or more to 10's column only—equations and word problems

———27. Adds two 3-digit numbers carrying to 100's column only—equations and word problems.

———28. Adds two–four 2- and 3-digit numbers carrying to 10's and 100's column—equations and word problems.

———29. Solves subtraction problems with minuends 1–10—equations and word problems.

———30. Solves subtraction problems with minuends 11–20—equations and word problems.

———31. Uses number line to solve subtraction problems.

———32. Shows the relationships between addition and subtraction by writing the inverse operation when an equation is given.

———33. Writes subtraction equation when shown a set of specific objects.

———34. Masters 100 basic subtraction facts.

———35. Subtracts 2- and 3-digit numbers with no borrowing—equations and word problems.

———36. Subtracts digits of unequal length with no borrowing—equations and word problems.

———37. Subtracts numbers of 2 and 3 digits borrowing from 10's column only—equations and word problems.

———38. Subtracts numbers of 3 digits borrowing from 100's column only—equations and word problems.

———39. Subtracts numbers of 3 digits borrowing from 10's and 100's column—equations and word problems.

C. Geometry

——— 1. Identifies and draws squares.

——— 2. Identifies and draws triangles.

——— 3. Identifies and draws rectangular shapes.

4. Can point out the following shapes in functional settings as well as in isolation:

———a. Circles.

———b. Squares.

———c. Triangles.

———d. Rectangles.

——— 5. Draws a line, circle, square, triangle, and rectangle when the word name is given.

——— 6. Refers to geometric forms by their geometric names.

II. Measurement

——— 1. When shown a ruler and a yardstick, can tell which is equal to a foot and which is equal to a yard.

2. States the following relative values:

———a. 1 foot = 12 inches

———b. 1 yard = 36 inches

———c. 1 yard = 3 feet

——— 3. Converts values from one measure to another.

——— 4. Uses ruler and yardstick to measure environmental objects.

——— 5. When shown containers which measure gallons, half-gallons, quarts, and cups, can state the measurements of the containers.

6. States the following relative values:

———a. 1 gallon = 4 quarts

———b. 1 half-gallon = 2 quarts

_____c. 1 quart = 2 pints

_____d. 1 quart = 4 cups

_____ 7. Converts values from one measure to another.

_____ 8. Tells the meaning of the measure of a dozen.

_____ 9. States the meaning of 1/2 as it relates to measures of pint, cup, foot, yard, quart, gallon, dozen, etc.

_____10. Uses previously mentioned measures in addition and subtraction problems related to situations in daily living.

_____11. Tells that scales are used to weigh pounds.

_____12. States that body weight is measured in pounds.

_____13. Tells that height is measured in feet and inches.

_____14. Keeps a monthly record of weight and height.

_____15. Reads a weather thermometer.

_____16. States the average room temperature.

_____17. Tells that the freezing point is 32°F.

_____18. Lists articles that form a pair.

III. Time

_____ 1. Counts by five's around the face of the clock to determine the number of minutes in an hour.

_____ 2. Tells time by five-minute intervals (3:05, 3:10, 3:15, etc.).

_____ 3. Tells what the concepts of before and after mean as they are related to the hour.

_____ 4. Interprets the written form of a time equivalent.

_____ 5. Writes a time equivalent in correct form.

_____ 6. States the number of seconds in a minute.

_____ 7. Tells the number of hours in a day.

_____ 8. States the difference between A.M. and P.M.

_____ 9. States that the beginning of the day is 12:01 A.M.

_____10. Tells the number of days in a month.

_____11. States the number of days in a year.

_____12. Can categorize months according to corresponding seasons.

_____13. Tells about changing length of day as related to season.

_____14. Identifies and writes days of week and date.

_____15. Reads and spells days of week.

_____16. Reads and spells months of year.

IV. Money

_____ 1. Recognizes the following coins and bills: quarter, half-dollar, silver dollar, one dollar bill, five dollar bill.

2. Can state the following monetary relationships:

_____a. 5 nickels = 1 quarter

_____b. 25 pennies = 1 quarter

_____c. 2 dimes and 1 nickel = 1 quarter

_____d. 2 quarters = 1 half-dollar

_____e. 4 quarters = 1 dollar

_____f. 2 half-dollars = 1 dollar

_____g. 20 nickels = 1 dollar

_____h. 10 dimes = 1 dollar

_____i. 100 pennies = 1 dollar

_____ 3. Counts coins up to $1.00.

_____ 4. Counts bills up to $5.00.

_____ 5. Makes correct change from purchase up to $1.00.

_____ 6. Tells the meaning of _decimal point_ and _dollar mark._

_____ 7. Writes monetary value with correct decimal point and dollar mark.

_____ 8. Adds and subtracts monetary values using problems of daily living.

_____ 9. Can state the approximate monetary value of personal items such as food treats, paper, pencil, crayons, books, etc.

_____10. Tells what the common postage rates are.

ARITHMETIC—JUNIOR HIGH

I. Basic Concepts, Facts, and Procedures

   A. Counts, Reads, and Writes Numbers

——— 1. Counts by rote from 0–500.
——— 2. Reads and writes number symbols 0–500.
——— 3. Tells the meaning of ordinals—first–fiftieth.
——— 4. Reads and writes number words—zero–fifty.
——— 5. Reads and writes Roman numerals I–XII.
——— 6. Uses symbols for more than and less than with numerals 0–500.
——— 7. Counts, reads, and writes from 0–1000.
——— 8. Uses symbols for more than and less than with numerals 0–1000.

   B. Facts and Processes

——— 1. Demonstrates place values of 2-,3-, and 4-digit numerals (10's, 100's, 1,000's).
——— 2. Knows all addition and subtraction facts.
——— 3. Demonstrates skill in all addition and subtraction processes.
——— 4. Solves multiplication problems using 1 through 5's table—equations and word problems.
——— 5. Masters the basic multiplication facts.
——— 6. Solves multiplication problems using 6 through 10's table—equations and word problems.
——— 7. Multiplies 2- and 3-digit mutiplicand with 1-digit multiplier involving no carrying—equations and word problems.
——— 8. Multiplies 2- and 3-digit multiplicand with 2-digit multiplier involving no carrying—equations and word problems.
——— 9. Multiplies 2- and 3-digit multiplicand with 1-digit multiplier involving carrying—equations and word problems.
———10. Multiplies 2- and 3-digit multiplicand with 2-digit multiplier involving carrying—equations and word problems.
———11. Shows or tells that zero is a place-holder in multiplication problems.
———12. Shows the short way of multiplying by 10, 100, and 1,000.
———13. Solves basic division facts with 2–5 as divisor and no remainder—equations and word problems.
———14. Solves basic division facts with 6–9 as divisor and no remainder—equations and word problems.
———15. Masters basic division facts.
———16. Divides 2- or 3-digit quotient involving no borrowing always getting zero when subtracting from dividend—equations and word problems.
———17. Divides quotient of 2 or more digits involving no borrowing and no remainder—equations and word problems.
———18. Divides quotient of 2 or more digits involving borrowing and remainder—equations and word problems.
———19. Divides problems with zero in the quotient and involving no remainder—equations and word problems.
———20. Divides problems with zero in the quotient with a remainder—equations and word problems.

   C. Fractions

——— 1. Tells what a fraction is.
——— 2. Can point to the fractional parts, 1/2, 1/3, 1/4, 3/4, when presented with diagrams of these fractional parts.
——— 3. Relates fractional parts to liquid, dry, and linear measure.

II. Measurement

——— 1. Tells what a mile is.
      2. Tells the approximate number of miles between significant points such as:
        ———a. Home to school.
        ———b. Home to friend's house.
        ———c. Community to neighboring community.
——— 3. Can point out the measurements of bushel and peck.
——— 4. Tells about the following relative values: 2 gallons = 1 peck, 4 pecks = 1 bushel, 8 gallons = 1 bushel.
——— 5. Can convert values from one measure to another.

_____ 6. Uses various measurement devices for length such as yardstick, tape measure, carpenter's ruler.

_____ 7. Can correctly measure all objects in classroom.

_____ 8. Uses various measurements in multiplication and division problems related to situations in daily living.

_____ 9. Uses thermometer to take body temperature.

_____10. States that normal body temperature is 98.6°F.

_____11. Illustrates the meaning of 1/2 and 1/4.

_____12. Tells what an ounce is.

_____13. States the number of ounces in a pound.

_____14. States that some produce items and meat are usually sold for a certain price per pound.

_____15. Utilizes liquid measurements in following cooking recipes.

_____16. Gives a simple definition of area.

_____17. Shows the meaning of square inch, square foot, square yard, etc.

_____18. Converts inches to square inches, feet to square feet, yards to square yards, etc.

III. Time

_____ 1. Tells time to the minute.

_____ 2. Constructs various time schedules for activities such as school, church, meals, radio programs, television programs, etc.

_____ 3. Sets an alarm clock for any particular hour.

_____ 4. Tells that most public transportation runs on prescribed time schedules.

_____ 5. Secures information related to public transportation time schedules.

_____ 6. Tells what daylight saving time is.

IV. Money

_____ 1. Recognizes instantly all coins.

_____ 2. Recognizes the following bills:

_____a. One-dollar bill.

_____b. Five-dollar bill.

_____c. Ten-dollar bill.

_____d. Twenty-dollar bill.

_____ 3. Counts up to $5.00 in coins.

_____ 4. Counts up to $100.00 in bills.

_____ 5. Makes correct change after purchase up to $25.00.

_____ 6. Writes amounts to $200.00 with proper decimal placements.

_____ 7. Tells the approximate value of environmental items such as food, clothing, household items, rent, car, etc.

_____ 8. Uses newspaper to compare prices on items such as food and clothing.

_____ 9. Keeps a daily record of personal purchases.

_____10. Can tell what sales taxes are.

_____11. Computes sales tax on purchases up to $25.00.

_____12. Tells why it is important to get a receipt for purchases.

_____13. Explains the value of standard work rates per hour.

_____14. Computes gross pay for a 40-hour work week at minimum wage.

_____15. Explains the purposes of state and federal income tax.

_____16. States the purposes of social security.

ARITHMETIC—SENIOR HIGH

I. Basic Concepts, Facts, and Procedures

A. Counts, Reads, and Writes Numbers

_____ 1. Demonstrates understanding of number value to 10,000.

_____ 2. Writes numbers from 0 to 10,000 upon verbal presentation of number.

_____ 3. Reads and writes number words—zero–hundred.

_____ 4. Reads numbers up to 6 digits.

B. Facts and Processes

———— 1. Uses addition, subtraction, multiplication, and division facts.
———— 2. Applies processes of addition, subtraction, multiplication, and division within limits of capability.
———— 3. Applies above processes to demands of daily living.
———— 4. Demonstrates knowledge of arithmetic processes associated with particular chosen vocation.

C. Fractions

———— 1. Explains fractional concepts: 1/2, 1/4, 1/3, 2/3, 3/4.
———— 2. Tells the relative value of fractional parts (1/2 is less than 3/4, etc.).
———— 3. Adds and subtracts mixed numbers and fractional parts with same denominator.
———— 4. Adds and subtracts fractions with different denominators.
5. Applies knowledge of fractions to demands of daily living:
————a. Can follow recipe.
————b. Can double and half recipes.
————c. Explains the concept of sale—1/2 off.

II. Measurement

———— 1. Understands and practices measurement skills as related to the demands of the pupil's desired vocation.
———— 2. Uses postal scales to determine the correct amount of postage for letters and small packages.
———— 3. Uses scales to determine the weight of various objects.
4. Practices measuring as related to household needs:
————a. Measures rooms in house and computes size of floor covering.
————b. Measures windows and computes size of curtains and length of rods.
————c. Measures door frame for screening.
———— 5. Practices measuring for basic shop work.
———— 6. Uses legend on map to estimate miles.
———— 7. Tells how to use an odometer and speedometer.

III. Time

———— 1. Shows or tells how to use a time clock.
———— 2. Explains the meaning of time and a half and double time.
———— 3. Practices the habit of being on time for work.
———— 4. Tells that there are different time zones in the United States and knows the names of them.
———— 5. Given the time in a particular zone, computes time in the three remaining zones.
———— 6. Relates time to factors such as distance, cooking, wages, etc.

IV. Money

———— 1. Counts up to $10.00 in coins.
———— 2. Makes correct change after purchase up to $50.00.
———— 3. Writes amounts to $2,000.00 with proper decimal placements.
———— 4. Tells the cost of utilities and rent.
———— 5. States the cost of various licenses.
———— 6. Tells the value and the cost of upkeep and repair.
———— 7. Explains how to evaluate sales and bargains.
———— 8. Explains basic bank functions.
————a. Can tell the importance of banking.
b. States function of checking and saving accounts.
————(1) Explains how to open an account.
————(2) Tells how to make a deposit.
————(3) Shows how to write a check.
————(4) Tells how to endorse a check.
————(5) Memorizes own bank account number.
————(6) Tells that interest is paid on savings account.

    c. Shows how to find total savings.

        _____(1) Tells how to balance account.

        _____(2) Interprets bank statement.

    d. Explains loans.

        _____(1) Tells procedure in getting loan.

        _____(2) States procedure in paying back a loan.

_____ 9. Tells function of credit unions.

_____10. Tells function and danger of finance companies.

11. Explains income tax deductions:

    _____a. Federal income tax.

    _____b. State income tax.

    _____c. Union dues.

    _____d. Employer's purchases.

    _____e. United Fund.

    _____f. Social Security.

_____12. Completes basic steps in filing federal and state income tax returns.

_____13. Tells how and when to use installment buying.

_____14. Tells how to get and keep a good credit rating.

HEALTH—PRIMARY LEVEL

I. Personal Hygiene

—————— 1. Washes hands before meals, after going to the bathroom, and at other appropriate times.
—————— 2. Washes face regularly.
—————— 3. Practices brushing teeth at appropriate times.
—————— 4. Takes a bath as needed.
—————— 5. Practices proper procedure for blowing nose, coughing, and sneezing.
—————— 6. Changes socks and underwear daily.

II. Food and Nutrition

—————— 1. Distinguishes between edible and nonedible items.
—————— 2. Tells order of meals and approximate correlating time.
—————— 3. Recognizes and names common foods.
—————— 4. Associates common foods with meal at which they are usually eaten.
—————— 5. Recognizes foods important to being healthy and nonhealthy.
        6. Develops good eating habits.
           ——————a. Eats what is on the plate.
           ——————b. Eats a variety of foods.
           ——————c. Chews properly and doesn't rush.
—————— 7. Eats food from the four basic food groups.
—————— 8. States the importance of drinking milk.

III. Preventing and Treating Illness
     (related section: HEALTH—Section V, Part 3)

—————— 1. Performs daily habits associated with sanitation.
           ——————a. Washes hands at appropriate times.
           ——————b. Covers mouth when coughing and sneezing.
           ——————c. Uses tissue or handkerchief.
           ——————d. Drinks properly from water fountain.
           ——————e. Practices sanitary ways of sharing food.
—————— 2. Keeps fingers and objects out of nose, mouth, and ears.
—————— 3. Gets a minimum of eight hours sleep at night.
—————— 4. Wears proper seasonal attire.
—————— 5. Dresses properly for cold and rainy weather.
—————— 6. Stays in bed when ill.
—————— 7. Uses good posture when sitting and standing.
—————— 8. Tells the role of the school nurse.
—————— 9. Explains how doctors, dentists, and nurses help people.
——————10. Explains the role of hospitals in treating illness.
——————11. Gets immunizations against common diseases.

IV. Basic Body Functions and Structure

—————— 1. Names the basic body parts (arms, legs, face, neck, etc.).
—————— 2. Explains the difference and functions of primary and permanent teeth.
—————— 3. Explains the role of the five senses.
—————— 4. Tells that physical growth is slow but steady.
—————— 5. Tells that the basic body frame is bone.
—————— 6. States that our bodies absorb food and that the waste is eliminated.

V. Alcohol, Tobacco, and Narcotics

     1. Alcohol.
           ——————a. Tells that alcohol is used every day for medical purposes.
           ——————b. States that beer, wine, and whiskey are forms of alcoholic beverages.

        _____c. Explains that drunkenness is a result of excessive drinking.

        _____d. Tells that drinking alcohol can be very dangerous.

_____ 2. Explains that smoking tobacco has harmful effects on the body.

    3. Narcotics.

        _____a. Tells that medicine comes in different forms (tablets, capsules, liquids, etc.).

        _____b. Recognizes poisonous symbols on labels.

        _____c. Tells about harmful effects of taking medicine incorrectly.

        _____d. Explains that doctors prescribe medicine for us.

        _____e. States that medicine should be administered by an adult.

        _____f. Tells that medicine is sold in drug stores.

HEALTH—INTERMEDIATE LEVEL

I. Personal Hygiene

_____ 1. Shampoos hair correctly and as frequently as needed.

_____ 2. Bathes correctly and as frequently as needed.

_____ 3. Practices trimming and cleaning fingernails in a proper manner.

_____ 4. Practices using his own comb and brush.

_____ 5. Wears clean clothes.

II. Food and Nutrition

_____ 1. Explains the value of eating three well-balanced meals.

_____ 2. Categorizes foods into four basic food groups.

_____ 3. Selects and eats new foods.

_____ 4. Explains the sources of basic foods.

_____ 5. Eats food from the four food groups daily.

_____ 6. Explains the importance of cleanliness.

_____ 7. Explains that some food must be kept under refrigeration.

_____ 8. Explains the importance of vitamins.

III. Preventing and Treating Illness
(related section: HEALTH—Section V, Part 3)

_____ 1. Practices basic sanitary habits.

_____ 2. Correctly demonstrates that certain clothes must be worn for various seasons and weather conditions.

_____ 3. Removes wet clothes and coats when inside.

_____ 4. Explains that personal items such as clothing, toilet articles, and glasses should not be worn or used by others.

_____ 5. Contacts an adult when ill or injured.

_____ 6. Explains the importance of rest.

_____ 7. Practices getting appropriate amount of sleep.

_____ 8. Arranges appropriate lighting when reading or doing close work.

_____ 9. States that room temperature should be approximately 68 degrees F.

_____10. Explains the relationship between appropriate room temperature and staying healthy.

_____11. States that yearly visits should be made to the dentist for examination and cleaning.

_____12. Tells the importance of regular physical examinations from the doctor.

_____13. Tells how to make a doctor's appointment and the importance of keeping it.

_____14. Explains the services offered from the local health department.

_____15. Tells what it means to have an operation.

_____16. Tells the normal body temperature.

_____17. Uses a thermometer correctly.

_____18. Explains what it means to have a fever.

_____19. Explains how to obtain emergency medical services.

IV. Basic Body Functions and Structure

———— 1. Explains basic functions of brain

2. Gives name, location, and general function of:

   ————a. Heart.

   ————b. Lungs.

   ————c. Liver.

   ————d. Kidneys.

   ————e. Stomach.

———— 3. Explains that blood circulates through vessels and carries food and oxygen through the body.

———— 4. Explains the body's dependency on oxygen.

———— 5. Tells the function and location of muscles.

———— 6. Names body parts and the location of organs on model of skeleton.

———— 7. Explains that tissues are composed of various kinds of cells.

———— 8. Explains that all human beings have the same kinds of systems, organs, tissues, and cells.

V. Alcohol, Tobacco, and Narcotics

1. Alcohol

   ————a. States that intoxication affects one's mental processes and often leads to inappropriate behavior.

   ————b. Tells that alcohol has a potential harmful effect on the body.

   ————c. Explains that experimenting with alcohol is very dangerous for children.

   ————d. States that through excessive use people become dependent on alcohol.

   ————e. States that one should never ride in the car when the driver is intoxicated.

   ————f. States that the death rate caused by drunkenness is very high.

   ————g. Will not antagonize a person who is drunk.

2. Tobacco

   ————a. Explains the warning: "The Surgeon General has determined that cigarette smoking is dangerous to your health."

   ————b. Tells that people can become addicted to cigarettes.

   ————c. States reasons why people begin the habit and why it is hard to stop.

3. Narcotics

   ————a. States that some medicines are for external use only.

   ————b. Tells how medicine can harm us if we take the wrong kind or too much.

   ————c. Lists the basic household aids that are poisonous.

   ————d. Tells and follows the proper precautions when working with compounds that give off toxic fumes.

   ————e. Explains hazards involved when people are exposed to toxic fumes.

   ————f. Names the different kinds of drugs that are commonly used.

   ————g. Explains the adverse effects of common drugs.

   ————h. Tells that people react to drugs in different ways.

   ————i. States the meaning of drug abuse.

   ————j. Tells how the government tries to regulate drug abuse.

HEALTH—JUNIOR HIGH LEVEL

I. Personal Hygiene

———— 1. Uses deodorant as needed.

———— 2. Practices keeping hair clean and combed.

———— 3. Practices regular shaving as needed.

———— 4. Practices proper hygiene during menstrual period.

———— 5. Tells why body odor begins to be a greater concern during adolescence.

———— 6. Devotes special attention to complexion care.

———— 7. Accepts responsibility for keeping clothes clean.

II. Food and Nutrition

_____ 1. Tells the amount of foods from the four food groups which should be eaten daily.

_____ 2. Plans well-balanced meals.

_____ 3. Explains sanitation as it relates to purchasing food, preparation, and storage.

_____ 4. Explains that calories indicate the amount of energy in food.

_____ 5. States that to find out the necessary number of calories, one can multiply his weight by the number of calories per pound for his age.

_____ 6. States that a girl 13–15 years old needs approximately 24 calories per pound per day.

_____ 7. States that a boy 13–15 years old needs approximately 29 calories per pound per day.

_____ 8. Evaluates his own food habits as related to good nutrition.

_____ 9. Keeps food, dishes, and the kitchen clean.

_____10. Speaks of the necessity for family financial planning for food.

_____11. Recognizes safe and unsafe diets.

_____12. Explains there are various ways to serve the same food.

III. Preventing and Treating Illness
(related section: SAFETY—Section V)

_____ 1. Explains how a good diet, rest, and exercise all contribute to staying healthy.

2. States some information about the causes, symptoms, treatment, and prognosis for the following diseases and disorders:

    _____a. Flu.

    _____b. Measles.

    _____c. Mumps.

    _____d. Heart disease.

    _____e. Cancer.

    _____f. Venereal disease.

    _____g. Sickle cell anemia.

    _____h. Diabetes.

    _____i. AIDS

_____ 3. Tells the importance of immunization.

_____ 4. States the importance of water sanitation.

_____ 5. Tells why sewage should be disposed of properly.

_____ 6. States the importance of relaxation.

_____ 7. Explains the importance of rest and restricted activity when ill.

_____ 8. Uses a thermometer and reads it appropriately.

_____ 9. Utilizes public health services.

_____10. Explains the role of specialists in treating diseases and providing particular services.

_____11. Gets routine medical and dental examinations.

_____12. Tells it is important to follow the doctor's recommendations.

_____13. Explains the method of using the emergency room at the hospital.

IV. Basic Body Functions and Structure

_____ 1. Explains role of nervous system in directing body's response.

2. Explains role of each of the following in the digestive process:

    _____a. Saliva.

    _____b. Esophagus.

    _____c. Stomach.

    _____d. Small intestine.

    _____e. Large intestine.

3. Gives name, location, and general function of:

    _____a. Pancreas.

    _____b. Gall bladder.

    _____c. Urinary bladder.

4. Tells basic functions of the respiratory system including the contribution of each of the following:

———a. Nose.

———b. Mouth.

———c. Windpipe.

———d. Larnyx.

———e. Bronchial tube.

———f. Lungs.

——— 5. Tells the basic functions of blood as it circulates through the body.

——— 6. Gives the name, location, and general function of the reproductive organs.

V. Alcohol, Tobacco, and Narcotics

1. Alcohol

———a. States that there is a difference in the content of alcoholic beverages.

———b. Tells that alcohol may affect judgment, speech, balance, vision, and coordination.

———c. Explains the nature of alcohol addiction.

———d. States that driving under the influence is against the law.

———e. Explains the potential benefit of organizations like Alcoholics Anonymous.

———f. Tells why the majority of coaches do not allow smoking by the athletes.

———g. Explains economic factors associated with alcohol.

———h. States effects of peer group pressure on drinking.

———i. Tells that alcoholism is a chronic disease.

2. Tobacco

———a. Tells that many people begin to smoke to gain recognition from peers.

———b. Tells that smoking may cause lung cancer, bronchitis, emphysema, and heart disease.

———c. Explains that tobacco is made from a leaf of a plant which contains the drug nicotine.

———d. Explains different ways people use tobacco.

———e. States that smoking can be a very expensive habit.

———f. Tells why the majority of coaches do not allow smoking by the athletes.

3. Narcotics

———a. Recognizes marijuana and explains its history, physical characteristics, effects, and laws pertaining to it.

———b. Explains the effects of hallucinogens.

———c. Gains information on LSD—its history, physical characteristics, effects, and laws pertaining to it.

d. Explains the following concepts:

———(1) Tolerance.

———(2) Addiction—psychological and physiological.

———(3) Withdrawal.

———e. Explains the physical characteristics, common effects, and dangers of barbiturates.

———f. Tells the physical characteristics, common effects, and dangers of amphetamines.

———g. States that there are laws regulating drug use and transportation.

———h. Explains the harmful effects that volatiles like gasoline, glue, lighter fluid, etc., can have on the body.

———i. States that there is still much unknown and many exaggerated claims related to narcotics.

———j. Explains the serious legal and social problems to which drug abuse leads.

HEALTH—SENIOR HIGH LEVEL

I. Personal Hygiene

——— 1. Practices the habit of being clean and well-groomed.

——— 2. Supervises younger children in keeping their bodies clean.

II. Food and Nutrition

——— 1. Develops increased ability to plan, prepare, and serve food.

——— 2. Makes a list of food the family likes and also a list of new recipes to try.

_____ 3. Explains meal planning according to income and number in family.
_____ 4. Practices making a shopping list according to family size and income.
_____ 5. Develops skill in conserving food for present and future use.
_____ 6. Tells the danger of crash diets or overeating.
_____ 7. Explains the importance of a well-balanced diet during pregnancy.
_____ 8. Explains the nutritional requirements of babies.

III. *Preventing and Treating Illness*

_____ 1. Practices simple techniques of home nursing.
_____ 2. Explains differences between proper medical treatment and nonmedical treatment.
_____ 3. Encourages family and younger children to develop habits of getting regular physical and dental examinations.
_____ 4. Explains the importance and cost of medical insurance.
_____ 5. Tells the benefits of Medicare and Medicaid.
_____ 6. Tells the common illnesses and ailments of babies and how to treat them.
_____ 7. Arranges for proper ventilation, lighting, and heating in house.
_____ 8. Tells proper procedure for getting admitted to the hospital.

IV. *Basic Body Functions and Structure*

1. Explains the general contribution of each of the following glands:
_____a. Adrenal.
_____b. Pituitary.
_____c. Thyroid.
_____ 2. States the importance of proper hormonal balance.

V. *Alcohol, Tobacco, and Narcotics*

1. Alcohol
_____a. Tells that alcohol affects the central nervous system.
_____b. Tells the dollar cost of drinking alcoholic beverages.
_____c. States that mature individuals make wise decisions concerning the use of alcohol.
_____d. Explains moderation in drinking.
_____e. Tells about arrests and punishment procedures associated with intoxication.
_____f. Tells that if one chooses to drink, it should be done in appropriate places.
_____g. Explains local laws governing the sale of liquor, beer, and wine.
_____h. Tells the usual uses of liquor revenue within the community.

2. Tobacco
_____a. Tells techniques used to break the smoking habit.
_____b. States the benefits of never acquiring the smoking habit.
_____c. Explains effects of smoking on the circulatory, respiratory, digestive, and nervous systems.
_____d. Tells why cigar and pipe smoking are generally less harmful than cigarette smoking.
_____e. Computes the cost of smoking one pack of cigarettes per day for a year.

3. Narcotics
_____a. Explains the physical characteristics, common effects, and dangers of opium and its derivatives.
_____b. Tells federal and state laws pertaining to narcotics.
_____c. Tells the costs of using drugs.
_____d. Explains the effects of various drugs on the body and on behavior.
_____e. Names state and federal facilities providing treatment for drug addicts.
_____f. Formulates personal value system in regard to the use of drugs.
_____g. Accepts responsibility of informing other persons about the dangers of drug abuse.

SOCIAL STUDIES—PRIMARY

I. Understanding One's Heritage

    1. Associates a few well-known persons and stories with holidays.

        ——a. Tells that Columbus discovered America.

        ——b. States that Indians and Pilgrims were the first to celebrate Thanksgiving in America.

        ——c. Associates Santa Claus with Christmas by being able to recognize his picture.

    2. Participates in patriotic customs.

        ——a. Pledges the flag in the correct manner: puts hand over heart, stands at attention.

        ——b. Names or sings a patriotic song.

        ——c. Recognizes the American flag.

  ——— 3. Tells the name of his race.

  ——— 4. States the name of his religion.

II. Understanding One's Rights, Responsibilities, and Privileges

  ——— 1. Begins to be aware that people vote.

  ——— 2. Tells the difference between a good rule and a bad rule.

  ——— 3. Can tell about some of the rules set down by the authority in the classroom, school, and home.

  ——— 4. Tells who makes rules in the family and at school.

  ——— 5. States that all people live by rules.

  ——— 6. States that he should treat others as he would like to be treated.

  ——— 7. Participates in making classroom rules.

  ——— 8. Assumes appointed classroom duties.

  ——— 9. Participates in making simple group choices.

  ———10. Explains why he should come to school every day.

III. Understanding One's Community

  ——— 1. States that people live together in families.

  ——— 2. Tells that families live together in homes.

  ——— 3. Gives the name of his community.

  ——— 4. Tells his address.

  ——— 5. States that all communities are not alike.

  ——— 6. Tells the occupation of his parents.

  ——— 7. Names some essential elements of a community such as homes, stores, and churches.

  ——— 8. Tells the names of some community helpers such as the doctor, grocer, etc.

  ——— 9. Tells that people get paid for the work they do.

  ———10. States that people use money to get things they need.

  ———11. Tells general climate of community.

  ———12. Explains how people go from one place to another within the community.

  ———13. Finds various areas of neighborhood and school by looking at a map of school or neighborhood.

IV. Understanding One's State

  ——— 1. Tells the name of his state.

  ——— 2. Tells that states are comprised of many different communities.

V. Understanding One's Country

  ——— 1. Gives the name of his country.

  ——— 2. Tells that the U.S. is comprised of many different states and communities.

VI. Understanding One's World

  ——— 1. Tells that the world is round.

  ——— 2. States that the world is made up of both land and water.

  ——— 3. States that there are other countries in the world.

  ——— 4. Gives the name of the planet earth.

SOCIAL STUDIES—INTERMEDIATE LEVEL

I. Understanding One's Heritage

      1. Practices respect for flag:

         _____a. Pledges the flag.

         _____b. Shows proper display.

         _____c. Show correct use of hands.

_____ 2. Sings the National Anthem and other patriotic songs.

_____ 3. Tells that the country was discovered by many explorers.

      4. Explains contribution of historical figures:

         _____a. Columbus.

         _____b. Washington.

         _____c. Lincoln.

         _____d. Martin Luther King.

      5. Tells why we observe and how we celebrate:

         _____a. Christmas.

         _____b. Thanksgiving.

         _____c. Easter.

         _____d. Valentine's Day.

         _____e. Halloween.

         _____f. Fourth of July.

_____ 6. Takes an active part in the celebration of holidays.

_____ 7. Tells that forefathers fought for the freedom of our country.

_____ 8. Explains that times and customs have changed since the founding of our country.

II. Understanding One's Rights, Responsibilities, and Privileges

_____ 1. Develops and helps to enforce classroom rules.

      2. Begins to participate in the democratic process:

         _____a. Pays attention to particular qualifications for job.

         _____b. Practices different methods of voting—secret ballot, show of hands, voice.

         _____c. Abides willingly by majority rule.

_____ 3. Explains importance of following rules.

_____ 4. Uses the proper procedure for expressing legitimate discontent with classroom rules.

      5. Demonstrates methods of showing respect to authority:

         _____a. Does not use slang or smart remarks.

         _____b. Does not "talk back."

         _____c. Uses common courtesy.

III. Understanding One's Community

_____ 1. Tells the names and functions of community workers.

_____ 2. States names of some community businesses, grocery store, drugstore, and churches within the community.

_____ 3. Tells the roles of family members as community participants.

_____ 4. Tells about some of the local institutions, occupations, and businesses and knows jobs people perform.

_____ 5. Tells location of and how to use the nearest fire alarms and police station.

      6. States the transportation facilities available to get around in the community:

         _____a. Cars.

         _____b. Taxis.

         _____c. Bicycles.

      7. Tells the services of each of the following:

         _____a. Post office.

         _____b. Hospitals.

         _____c. Fire department.

         _____d. Water department.

         _____e. Sheriff's office.

_____f. Police department.

_____g. Banks.

_____ 8. Names and lists the components of a "typical" community.

IV. *Understanding One's State*

_____ 1. Locates state on map of United States.

_____ 2. Tells that there are different geographical divisions of the state.

_____ 3. Names the state capital.

_____ 4. Locates own community and the state capital on a state map.

_____ 5. Locates on a map the northern, southern, eastern, and western parts of the state.

_____ 6. Tells the major transportation systems used in the state.

V. *Understanding One's Country*

_____ 1. Locates the U.S. on a globe or world map.

_____ 2. Tells that the U.S. is made up of 50 states.

_____ 3. Identifies northern, southern, eastern, and western parts of the country.

_____ 4. Locates state in specific section of the U.S.

_____ 5. Tells that all the states are grouped together except Alaska and Hawaii.

_____ 6. States that New York City is the largest city in the U.S.

_____ 7. Tells that different parts of the country can be characterized by different weather conditions.

_____ 8. Lists the major transportation systems that are used throughout the country.

_____ 9. Tells that the U.S. is bound on the east by the Atlantic Ocean and on the west by the Pacific Ocean.

10. Tells the major geographical features of the country:

_____a. Mountains.

_____b. Lakes.

_____c. Rivers.

_____d. Coastal areas.

_____e. Plains.

_____f. Plateaus.

_____11. Names the president of the U.S.

_____12. Says that George Washington was the first president.

_____13. States that Washington, D.C., is the national capital.

VI. *Understanding One's World*

_____ 1. States the globe is a model of the world.

_____ 2. Locates U.S. on the globe.

_____ 3. Says that there are five huge bodies of water known as oceans.

_____ 4. Tells that groups of countries are clustered together in larger units known as continents.

_____ 5. Shows on the globe that there are seven continents.

_____ 6. Tells that the U.S. is in North America.

_____ 7. Tells that Columbus found the New World while trying to prove that the earth was round.

SOCIAL STUDIES—JUNIOR HIGH LEVEL

I. *Understanding One's Heritage*

1. Is familiar with some famous inventors:

_____a. Benjamin Franklin.

_____b. Robert Fulton.

_____c. Alexander Graham Bell.

_____d. Eli Whitney.

_____e. George Washington Carver.

_____ 2. Explains the meaning of a democratic government.

3. Tells the general contributions of some of the more recent political leaders:

_____a. Franklin D. Roosevelt.

_____b. John F. Kennedy.

———c. Lyndon B. Johnson.

———d. Richard Nixon.

4. Tells the significance of a patriotic day, such as:

———a. Labor Day.

———b. Veteran's Day.

———c. Columbus Day.

———d. Independence Day.

———e. Memorial Day.

———f. Election Day.

5. Tells some of the principles upon which this country was founded:

———a. Lists and discusses many of the reasons for people coming to this country.

———b. Explains some of the many sacrifices people made to gain their rights.

———c. States that the Constitution is a document that insures certain rights to all people.

——— 6. Tells that the U.S. is a "melting pot" for people of different races.

——— 7. Tells the names of various religious denominations.

II. Understanding One's Rights, Responsibilities, and Privileges

——— 1. Gives some information about institutions, such as schools, governmental agencies, and churches.

——— 2. Gives some information about social groups, such as peers and community figures.

——— 3. Exercises self-control in classroom situations.

——— 4. Explains the impact of the civil rights movement on the process of social change.

——— 5. States that our governmental officers are elected by the people.

——— 6. Tells that it is a basic civic responsibility to vote.

——— 7. Explains the importance of securing information on the person for whom he votes.

8. Tells that certain freedoms are guaranteed to all people in the U.S.:

———a. Freedom of speech.

———b. Freedom of religion.

———c. Freedom of assembly.

———d. Freedom of protection under the law.

9. States that one must be ready to serve in the military:

———a. Explains the legal and moral responsibility associated with military service.

———b. Tells the benefit of service.

———c. Gives some locations of recruiters.

III. Understanding One's Community

——— 1. Names the mayor or city manager.

——— 2. Tells that communities have a governing board—usually called a city council.

3. Explains services that a community provides:

———a. Power.

———b. Water.

———c. Sewage.

———d. Telephone.

——— 4. Names some of the job opportunities in the community.

——— 5. Tells about community laws.

——— 6. Explains proper method of expressing concerns or complaints related to community matters.

——— 7. Tells the relationship of a community and county.

——— 8. Reads and interprets maps of the community.

IV. Understanding One's State

——— 1. Tells that states have a constitution that contains the basic laws for running the state.

2. Gives basic information on role of governor:

———a. Name of the governor.

———b. Highest ranking officer.

———c. Elected by people.

        d. Serves four-year term.

        e. Head of executive branch.

        f. Helps make laws.

        g. Has staff of people to assist him.

3. Tells basic information on role of legislature:

        a. Tells it is comprised of Senate and House of Representatives.

        b. Tells the number in each group.

        c. Tells legislators are elected from each district.

        d. States the length of term in office.

        e. Tells they are elected officials.

        f. Tells where the legislature is housed.

        g. Names the major duties.

4. Understands basic information on role of state courts:

        a. Tells that the state supreme court reviews and interprets laws pertaining to the state.

        b. States that courts in the community are part of the state court system.

        c. Tells that judges in state courts are either elected by the people or appointed by the governor.

   5. Tells the importance of voting in state elections.

   6. States that there are many different kinds of state government workers.

   7. Tells that state tax is paid to support state services.

8. Tells that various services are supplied by the state:

        a. Schools.

        b. Highways.

        c. Police force.

        d. Protection of natural resources.

   9. Gives some of the reasons why the state was founded.

V. Understanding One's Country

   1. Tells basic reasons why colonists first came to this country.

   2. States that 13 original colonies were established.

   3. States that colonists fought the Revolutionary War to gain independence from England.

   4. Tells some reasons why colonists wanted independence.

   5. States that the U.S. is rich with natural resources.

   6. Tells that the U.S. is in North America.

   7. States that the U.S. trades with many other countries.

   8. Explains the meaning of democracy.

   9. Tells that the country has a Constitution which is a written plan for running the federal government.

   10. Tells the basic rights guaranteed in the Constitution.

11. Gives basic information of role of president:

        a. Highest representative of nation.

        b. Four-year term.

        c. Elected by people.

        d. Can serve two terms.

        e. Lives in White House.

12. Explains basic information on role of legislature:

        a. Comprised of Senate and House of Representatives.

        b. Each state has two senators.

        c. Number of representatives depends upon population of each state.

        d. Senators serve a six-year term.

        e. Representatives serve a two-year term.

        f. Congressmen can run for reelection.

        g. Congress meets in the Capitol.

13. Tells basic information on role of Supreme Court:

        a. Is highest court in country.

        b. Interprets and reviews laws of nations.

        c. Meets in Supreme Court building in Washington, D.C.

_____d. Tells there is no appeal beyond Supreme Court.

_____e. President appoints justices.

_____14. Tells that the lower courts are called federal district courts.

_____15. States that people support the government by paying taxes.

VI. Understanding One's World

_____ 1. Tells that one-half of the earth is a hemisphere.

_____ 2. Tells that the U.S. is in the Northern Hemisphere.

_____ 3. Gives the names of the seven continents.

_____ 4. Locates the seven continents and five oceans on the globe.

_____ 5. Names the three countries which comprise North America.

_____ 6. Begins to speak about people of other countries and about their general customs.

_____ 7. States that Earth is one of nine planets that make up the solar system.

_____ 8. Explains that Earth revolves around the sun and that it takes one year to make a complete revolution.

_____ 9. States that the moon revolves around the earth.

_____10. Tells some of the major discoveries made through the space expeditions.

_____11. Explains that all places do not have daylight at the same time.

_____12. Tells that when we are having winter, many other countries are having summer.

_____13. Tells that when we are having our shortest days, many other countries are having their longest days.

_____14. Tells that an imaginary line called the equator divides the earth in half.

_____15. States that people who live near the equator get overhead sun the year round.

SOCIAL STUDIES—SENIOR HIGH LEVEL

I. Understanding One's Heritage

1. Reviews briefly the contributions of some famous Americans:

_____a. George Washington.

_____b. Abraham Lincoln.

_____c. Booker T. Washington.

_____d. George Washington Carver.

_____e. Franklin Delano Roosevelt.

_____f. John F. Kennedy.

_____g. Lyndon Johnson.

_____h. Richard Nixon.

_____i. Robert Kennedy.

_____ 2. Tells significance of all major holidays.

3. Tells the basic principles of the American way of life:

_____a. Shows acceptance of different races, religions, and social beliefs.

_____b. States that the Constitution guarantees basic rights to all citizens.

_____c. Explains that it is the duty of all citizens to protect these rights for all people.

4. Tells the impact of major historical and current events:

_____a. Revolutionary War.

_____b. Civil War.

_____c. World War I.

_____d. World War II.

_____e. Space program.

_____f. Vietnam war.

II. Understanding One's Rights, Responsibilities, and Privileges

1. Explains the basic principles associated with laws governing each of the following:

_____a. Ownership of property.

_____b. Driving cars.

_____c. Contracts.

_____d. Marriage.

_____e. Divorce.

_____ 2. States that laws protect all people.

_____ 3. States one has a moral responsibility for assisting in law enforcement, such as appearing as a witness or jury member.

4. Names the different types of taxes:
  _____a. Income—state and federal.
  _____b. Sales.
  _____c. Gasoline.
  _____d. Cigarette.
  _____e. Alcohol.
  _____f. Property.

_____ 5. Tells ways in which government is supported through taxes.

6. Tells the mechanics of voting:
  _____a. Tells how to use paper ballots and voting machines.
  _____b. Tells different kinds of elections such as primary, special, and regular.

_____ 7. Tells the obligations and benefits of serving in the armed forces.

_____ 8. Explains and participates in student government.

9. Uses various sources to gain information on condidates for public office:
  _____a. TV.
  _____b. Radio.
  _____c. Newspaper.
  _____d. Magazines.

III. *Understanding One's Community*

1. Tells the structure and function of city government:
  _____a. Executive—Mayor.
  _____b. Legislative—City Council.
  _____c. Judicial—Courts.

_____ 2. States that county officials serve community needs.

3. Explains the functions of county officials:
  _____a. County sheriff.
  _____b. County judge.
  _____c. County school superintendent.
  _____d. County court clerk.
  _____e. Tax assessor.
  _____f. Justice of the peace.

_____ 4. Tells the location of the courthouse.

_____ 5. Tells the method of paying bills for community utilities.

IV. *Understanding One's State*

1. Explains the structure and function of state government:
  _____a. Executive—Governor.
  _____b. Legislative—Senate and House of Representatives.
  _____c. Judicial—Supreme Court.

_____ 2. Tells how the three branches provide a system of checks and balances.

3. Tells the duties of the following state officers:
  _____a. Lieutenant Governor.
  _____b. Attorney General.
  _____c. Secretary of State.
  _____d. State Auditor.
  _____e. Treasurer.

4. Tells the services provided by various state departments:
  _____a. Public Health.
  _____b. Welfare.
  _____c. Highways.
  _____d. Police.

_____e. Agriculture.

_____f. Education.

_____g. Motor Vehicles.

_____ 5. Tells that court cases can be appealed to higher courts.

_____ 6. States that state senators and representatives are elected to represent the state in national government.

_____ 7. Tells functions of state Democratic and Republican parties.

V. Understanding One's Country

1. Tells the structure and function of federal government:

   _____a. Executive—President.

   _____b. Legislative—Senate and House of Representatives.

   _____c. Judicial—Supreme Court.

_____ 2. Explains how the three branches provide a system of checks and balances.

_____ 3. Tells the role and duties of the vice-president.

_____ 4. Tells the role of the president's cabinet.

5. Names the members and general duties of the cabinet:

   _____a. Secretary of State.

   _____b. Secretary of the Treasury.

   _____c. Secretary of Defense.

   _____d. Attorney General.

   _____e. Secretary of the Interior.

   _____f. Secretary of Agriculture.

   _____g. Postmaster General.

   _____h. Secretary of Health, Education, and Welfare.

   _____i. Secretary of Labor.

   _____j. Secretary of Commerce.

   _____k. Secretary of Housing and Urban Development.

   _____l. Secretary of Transportation.

_____ 6. Tells the purpose and the uses of the national census.

_____ 7. Tells the approximate population of the U.S.

_____ 8. Tells the basic differences between the Democratic and Republican parties.

VI. Understanding One's World

_____ 1. States that all countries do not have the same type of government.

_____ 2. Tells the basic differences between democracy and communism.

_____ 3. Associates communism with communistic countries.

_____ 4. Tells that leaders from all countries should strive for world peace.

SOCIAL COMPETENCE—PRIMARY LEVEL

I. Socialization

    1. Has good group relationships:

        ————a. Shares books, crayons, pencils, etc.

        ————b. Takes turns in group games, at water fountain, etc.

        ————c. Accepts limits set by teacher, principal, and janitor.

        ————d. Avoids unnecessary tattling.

        ————e. Avoids using physical force against others.

        ————f. Takes care of property.

        ————g. Begins to be aware of feelings of others.

        ————h. Has a friendly disposition.

        ————i. Obeys rules at home and school.

        ————j. Treats others as he would like to be treated.

        ————k. Begins to develop a sense of right and wrong.

    2. Engages in courteous behavior:

        ————a. Uses terms such as *please, thank you,* and *excuse me* at appropriate times.

        ————b. Demonstrates knowledge of when and where to place hands on others.

        ————c. Greets teacher and peers pleasantly in the morning.

II. Understanding and Accepting Oneself

    1. Understands self emotionally and physically:

        ————a. Recognizes and tells full name.

        ————b. Recognizes and tells address, birth date, age, and telephone number.

        ————c. Knows and tells race and religion.

        ————d. Verbalizes things he likes and dislikes.

        ————e. Engages in play activities appropriate to age and sex.

        ————f. Identifies times when he is happy and sad.

        ————g. Says people differ in appearance.

        ————h. Explains that his physical and emotional well-being affect the way he does school work.

        ————i. Begins to accept any physical limitation.

    2. Understands assets and limitations:

        ————a. Explains that everyone has strengths and weaknesses.

        ————b. Recognizes and tells about individual differences within class.

        ————c. Identifies his own major strengths and weaknesses.

    3. Establishes feelings of self-respect:

        ————a. Takes pride in accomplishment.

        ————b. Continues to try after experiencing failure.

SOCIAL COMPETENCE—INTERMEDIATE LEVEL

I. Socialization

    1. Has good group relationships:

        ————a. Practices sharing during play activities.

        ————b. Practices sharing during work activities.

        ————c. Explains rules of cooperation in such family activities as conversation, TV, family gatherings, etc.

        ————d. Shows respect for authority figures.

        ————e. Shows respect for property.

        ————f. Begins to develop self-control.

        ————g. States that one is responsible for his own actions and behavior.

_____h. Interacts with people from various backgrounds.

_____i. Accepts people of different races.

_____j. Accepts limitations and handicaps of others.

_____k. Avoids ridiculing others.

_____l. Accepts help from others.

_____m. Offers assistance to others.

_____n. Actively seeks friends.

_____o. Avoids fighting.

_____p. Practices honesty.

2. Engages in courteous behavior:

_____a. Explains and practices punctuality.

_____b. Practices good table manners.

_____c. Asks for things appropriately rather than demanding.

d. Explains about proper behavior:

_____(1) On the school bus.

_____(2) In the library.

_____(3) In downtown stores.

_____(4) At church.

3. Uses manners in communication:

_____a. Meets and greets friends in socially acceptable manner.

_____b. Uses telephone with proper courtesies.

_____c. Shows respect for authority by saying "Yes, Sir," "Yes, Ma'am," etc.

_____d. Uses simple expressions of courtesy.

_____e. Maintains eye contact when communicating.

_____f. Does not interrupt someone's conversation.

II. Understanding and Accepting Oneself

1. Understands self emotionally and physically:

_____a. Identifies times when he is happy or sad.

_____b. Identifies things that make him happy or sad.

_____c. Identifies things that make him angry.

_____d. Identifies various ways in which happiness, sadness, and anger can be expressed.

_____e. Identifies person he admires and states reasons.

_____f. Explains that children grow at different rates.

_____g. Tells that body will change in physical ways.

_____h. Begins to explain implications of physical disability.

_____i. Accepts responsibility for remediating physical disability such as wearing hearing aid or brace.

2. Can explain assets and limitations:

_____a. Identifies his strengths and weaknesses related to academic subjects and recreational activities.

_____b. Explains terminology he might hear around the school, which is associated with the special class (EMR, retarded, etc.).

_____c. Explains the importance of accepting limitations while at the same time working hard to remediate them.

_____d. Explains that everyone is retarded or limited in some way.

3. Establishes feelings of self-respect:

_____a. Associates feelings of self-gratification with successfully completing a task.

_____b. Approaches a new task with a positive attitude.

_____c. Does not feel personally threatened when he fails a particular test.

_____d. Shows respect for others and expects respect from others.

SOCIAL COMPETENCE—JUNIOR HIGH LEVEL

I. Socialization

   1. Has good group relationships:
- ——a. Participates in classroom, school, and community activities.
- ——b. Associates closely with peer group.
- ——c. Explains importance of group participation while maintaining one's individuality.
- ——d. Accepts responsibility in group whether as a leader or follower.
- ——e. Functions outside the group as an individual, as well as within the group.
- ——f. Makes attempts to resolve difficulties in a positive manner.
- ——g. Reacts appropriately with members of opposite sex.
- ——h. Accepts and carries out directions and orders.
- ——i. Realizes importance of maintaining good reputation.
- —— j. Explains importance of maintaining good reputation.
- ——k. Keeps an even disposition.
- ——l. Accepts individual differences of others.
- ——m. Practices loyalty to friends.
- ——n. Practices honesty and truthfulness.

   2. Engages in courteous behavior:
- ——a. Practices correct dating behavior.
-     b. Practices etiquette in following situations:
  - —— (1) On the street.
  - —— (2) In stores.
  - —— (3) Movies.
  - —— (4) Restaurant.
  - —— (5) Parties.
  - —— (6) Church.
  - —— (7) As a customer.
  - —— (8) As a guest.
  - —— (9) As a host.
  - ——(10) On the job.

   3. Uses manners in communication:
- ——a. Makes introductions appropriately.
- ——b. Uses socially acceptable language.
- ——c. Requests information from people appropriately.
- ——d. Continues to keep eye contact, speak distinctly, and not interrupt.
- ——e. Demonstrates knowledge of when slang terminology is acceptable and when it is unacceptable.

II. Understanding and Accepting Oneself

   1. Understands self emotionally and physically:
- ——a. Uses socially acceptable outlets for his emotions.
- ——b. Identifies various sources of anxieties and frustrations.
- ——c. Explains ways of dealing with anxieties and frustrations.
- ——d. Realizes need of maintaining self-control.
- ——e. Tells about emotional changes associated with puberty.
- ——f. Explains manner in which emotional problems impede academic achievement and job success.
- ——g. Can explain physical changes occurring during puberty.
- ——h. Shows concern for making most of his physical appearance.

   2. Explains assets and limitations:
- ——a. Tells the scope of the special education program.
- ——b. Tells that some people will ridicule or reject him since he is handicapped.
- ——c. Sets realistic goals for academic achievement.
- ——d. Begins to make appropriate vocational plans with consideration for assets and limitations.

3. Establishes feelings of self-respect:
  _____a. Feels capable of assuming personal responsibility within peer group.
  _____b. Takes pride in accomplishments.
  _____c. Feels that accomplishments are worthwhile and significant.

SOCIAL COMPETENCE—SENIOR HIGH LEVEL

I. Socialization

1. Has good group relationships:
  _____a. Distinguishes between right and wrong when faced with group pressure.
  _____b. Chooses and keeps worthwhile friends.
  _____c. Practices honesty in all dealings.
  _____d. Tells the necessary characteristics of good leadership.
  _____e. Assumes the responsibilities of an adult family member.
  _____f. Explains the responsibilities and benefits of neighborhood life.
  _____g. Obeys local and state laws.
  _____h. Explains the role of sharing and cooperation in maintaining good relationships with fellow employees.
  _____i. Explains the need for organizations, committees, and other groups.
  _____j. Gains acceptance as member of occupational group.
  _____k. Practices tolerance by accepting rights of others.
  _____l. Accepts total responsibility for behavior.
  _____m. Encourages others to respect authority and obey laws.

2. Engages in courteous behavior:
  _____a. Practices courtesy in all on-the-job situations.
  _____b. Encourages others to practice proper etiquette.

3. Uses manners in communication:
  _____a. Expresses appreciation and sympathy to others.
  _____b. Talks respectfully to employers and fellow workers.

II. Understanding and Accepting Oneself

1. Can explain self emotionally and physically:
  _____a. Has stable emotional adjustment.
  _____b. Maintains self-control.
  _____c. Realizes potential emotional problems and knows how to handle them.
  _____d. Tells about agencies and people within the community that offer emotional support and/or counseling.
  _____e. Makes the most of physical appearance.
  _____f. Accepts physical limitations and unattractive aspects of physical appearance.

2. Explains assets and limitations:
  _____a. Finds appropriate vocational placement in regard to abilities.
  _____b. Explains the long-range effects of his limitations on job opportunities.
  _____c. Tells about the standard of living that will be in line with his salary.

3. Establishes feelings of self-respect:
  _____a. Takes pride in job.
  _____b. Takes pride in home, community, and recreational activities.
  _____c. Realizes he is contributing member of society.
  _____d. States that he feels as if he can cope with most adult situations.

VOCATIONS—PRIMARY LEVEL

I. Vocationally Related Attitudes

———— 1. Begins to share toys and books.
———— 2. Begins to get along with others in the room, on the playground, and in group activities.
———— 3. Begins to use courtesy words such as *thank you, please, excuse me,* and *I'm sorry* at appropriate times.
———— 4. Follows rules in group activities.
———— 5. Knows the difference between his and other's belongings.
———— 6. Begins a task promptly when directed.
———— 7. Begins to accept correction.
———— 8. Begins to understand that children differ in work performance.

II. Vocationally Related Skills

———— 1. Demonstrates skills and concepts related to counting, money, telling time, and measurement (see Arithmetic —Primary Level for specific listing).
———— 2. Demonstrates gross-motor control.
———— 3. Speaks understandably and expresses complete thoughts.
———— 4. Recognizes and heeds signs of warning.
———— 5. Can tell the names and uses of common household and classroom objects.
———— 6. Follows directions with one or two directives.
———— 7. Works toward task completion.
———— 8. Begins to develop skills in using simple tools and equipment (scissors, paint, brushes, paste, etc.).
———— 9. Puts tools and supplies away after finishing a task.
      10. Performs routine jobs in the classroom:
          ———— a. Taking lunch report.
          ———— b. Straightening book shelves.
          ———— c. Keeping desks straight.
          ———— d. Emptying the trash.

III. Analysis of Occupations

———— 1. Explains the role of each family member at home.
      2. Explains the duties associated with jobs at school:
          ———— a. Janitor.
          ———— b. Principal.
          ———— c. Secretary.
          ———— d. Lunchroom worker.
          ———— e. Librarian.
          ———— f. Teacher.
      3. Names the titles and basic functions of community workers:
          ———— a. Police officer.
          ———— b. Firefighter.
          ———— c. Doctor.
          ———— d. Mail carrier.
          ———— e. Dentist.
———— 4. Explains that it takes many businesses and services to make up a functioning community.

IV. Getting a Job

      1. Verbally states personal data:
          ———— a. Full name.
          ———— b. Address, city, and state.
          ———— c. Age and birth date.
          ———— d. Father's and mother's name.

V. Understanding Responsibilities, Rights, and Benefits of the Worker

———— 1. States the various responsibilities of classroom jobs.

_____ 2. Explains the reasons that classroom jobs are necessary.

        3. Recognizes that consequences follow one's actions:

           _____a. When the job is performed well, praise is usually given.

           _____b. When the job is done poorly, punishment or scolding usually follows.

_____ 4. Explains how most adults are paid for their work.

_____ 5. Tells why, when one has a particular job to do, he must assume the responsibility of doing his best to complete it.

VOCATIONS—INTERMEDIATE LEVEL

I. Vocationally Directed Attitudes

_____ 1. Habitually uses courtesy words such as _please, thank you, excuse me,_ and _may I._

_____ 2. Evaluates his own efforts and production.

_____ 3. Names his own strengths and weaknesses.

_____ 4. Locates materials he needs to work with.

        5. Takes pride in accomplishments:

           _____a. Finishes a job that he starts.

           _____b. Recognizes importance of doing his best.

_____ 6. Demonstrates a good disposition.

_____ 7. Demonstrates a cooperative attitude.

_____ 8. Explains relationship between work in school and out of school.

_____ 9. Reacts positively to personal limitation and also the limitation of others.

_____10. Tells the importance of being alert while working.

II. Vocationally Related Skills

_____ 1. Demonstrates skills and concepts related to counting, money, telling time, and measurement (see Arithmetic —Intermediate Level).

_____ 2. Demonstrates fine-motor control.

_____ 3. Relates three or four events in chronological order.

_____ 4. Attends to a task for an extended period of time.

_____ 5. Remembers oral directions with one to three directives.

_____ 6. Can speak in sentences.

_____ 7. Speaks clearly.

_____ 8. Uses the telephone to make calls or to take messages.

_____ 9. Controls the pitch and volume of the voice.

_____10. Repeats information exactly as it is heard.

_____11. Writes legibly.

       12. Performs classroom cleaning jobs:

           _____a. Sweeps room.

           _____b. Dusts furniture.

           _____c. Cleans boards.

           _____d. Washes windows.

           _____e. Empties trash.

           _____f. Cleans lavatory and toilet.

III. Analysis of Occupations

_____ 1. States the duties of various community workers such as police officer, firefighter, storekeeper, farmer, janitor, and factory worker.

_____ 2. Lists many different kinds of jobs.

_____ 3. Explains that different skills and knowledges are required to perform different jobs.

_____ 4. States that different jobs require different types of training.

_____ 5. Explains the job at which parents work.

_____ 6. States the major areas of employment in the community.

IV. Getting a Job

      1. Spells personal data information:
          ———a. Full name.
          ———b. Address, city, and state.
          ———c. Birth date and birthplace.
          ———d. Father's and mother's full name.
   ———2. Introduces oneself and one's friends to others.
      3. Role plays proper interview behavior:
          ———a. States the importance of being polite and attentive.
          ———b. Knows how to shake hands.
          ———c. Maintains eye contact when spoken to or engaged in conversation.
          ———d. Is well groomed.
          ———e. Demonstrates knowledge of appropriate conversational topics by role playing.

V. Understanding Responsibilities, Rights, and Benefits of the Worker

      1. Begins to understand why people work:
          ———a. To get things they want.
          ———b. To make things for others.
          ———c. To find satisfaction.
          ———d. To get paid.
      2. Explains some of the responsibilities that are involved in assuming a job:
          ———a. To complete an assigned job.
          ———b. To do a job according to direction.
  ———3. Explains some of the causes and consequences of unemployment.
  ———4. Explains the benefits of salary and uses of salaries.
  ———5. Explains that people pay taxes to support government and to provide services.

VOCATIONS—JUNIOR HIGH LEVEL

I. Vocationally Related Attitudes

      1. Practices good work habits:
          ———a. Habitually gets to school on time.
          ———b. Asks for help and further instructions when necessary.
          ———c. Puts forth best effort in most tasks.
          ———d. Initiates tasks and carries them out with minimum supervision.
  ———2. Assumes responsibility in group projects.
  ———3. Practices common courtesies.
  ———4. Cooperates with others and acts upon opportunities to help them.
  ———5. Understands the importance of showing respect to those in authority.
  ———6. Accepts criticism.
  ———7. Practices safety precautions.
  ———8. Explains the importance of work experience.
  ———9. Explains that doing a good job at all times helps one to get good recommendations for other jobs.
  ———10. Understands that all jobs are important and that one should hold his job with honor and respect.

II. Vocationally Related Skills

  ———1. Demonstrates skills and concepts related to counting, money, telling time, and measurement (see Arithmetic —Junior High Level).
  ———2. Speaks clearly using proper and discrete language.
      3. Takes advantage of various transportation modes in getting around the community:
          ———a. Cars.
          ———b. Car pools.
          ———c. Bicycles.

_____d. Public transportation.

_____e. Walking.

_____ 4. Demonstrates ability in the manipulation of tools and materials.

_____ 5. Cares for and repairs tools and materials.

6. Can tell proper physical conditions leading to productive work:

_____a. Ventilation.

_____b. Temperature.

_____c. Light.

_____ 7. Accepts responsibility for keeping classroom clean.

8. Participates in a job training program in school situation:

_____a. Works with janitor.

_____b. Assists teacher, principal, or secretary as messenger.

_____c. Works in lunchroom.

III. Analysis of Occupations

_____ 1. Explains the role and potential benefit of vocational rehabilitation services for job information.

_____ 2. Makes contacts with vocational rehabilitation and other governmental agencies concerned with job information.

3. Makes survey of jobs in the community, compiling information on each of the following:

_____a. Name of job.

_____b. Location.

_____c. Pay.

_____d. Hours.

_____e. Duties.

_____f. Requirements.

_____g. Working conditions.

_____h. Advancement.

_____i. Transportation.

_____ 4. Evaluates each job in terms of personal placement.

_____ 5. Can list part-time jobs as well as full-time.

_____ 6. Can explain that personal strengths and weaknesses will determine the possibility of securing many jobs.

IV. Getting a Job

_____ 1. Practices filling out various application forms, reading, and spelling all words independently.

2. Can role play interview situation, engaging in proper behavior:

_____a. Gives introduction.

_____b. Engages in proper conversation.

_____c. Is courteous and polite.

_____d. Shows eye contact and general alertness.

_____e. Is well groomed.

_____f. Relates proper personal and vocational information.

_____g. "Sells" self in appropriate and positive manner.

_____ 3. Reads want ads in newspaper to locate jobs.

4. Makes contacts and takes advantage of services from following agencies:

_____a. Vocational Rehabilitation.

_____b. Public employment agencies.

_____c. Private employment agencies.

_____d. Personnel offices of plants and businesses.

_____ 5. Applies for and possesses social security card.

_____ 6. Writes letters of application.

_____ 7. Makes phone calls concerning job information and making job applications.

_____ 8. Knows the importance of having patience while looking for a job.

V. Responsibilities, Rights, and Benefits of the Worker

1. Explains some of the laws controlling employment:

_____a. Explains how and where to get a work certificate.

_____b. Explains some of the restrictions controlling employment for minors.

_____c. Tells where and how to get a birth certificate.

_____ 2. Tells the common causes of unemployment and firing.

_____ 3. Explains wage and hour laws.

4. Can explain the rights of the worker in terms of:

_____a. Right to fair wages.

_____b. Right to no discrimination on an unfair basis.

_____c. Right to be treated with dignity and respect.

_____d. Right to terminate employment.

5. Can explain responsibilities of the worker to the employer:

_____a. Tells why it is important to work at a competitive pace during work hours.

_____b. Tells why one should give appropriate notice before terminating a job.

VOCATIONS—SENIOR HIGH LEVEL

I. Vocationally Related Attitudes

_____ 1. Evaluates self realistically, recognizing own interests, abilities, and/or talents.

_____ 2. Appreciates and takes pride in personal work performance.

_____ 3. Explains the importance of maintaining good physical condition and personal appearance.

_____ 4. Explains the need for safety precautions for oneself and others.

_____ 5. Practices maintaining good working relations with peers and supervisors.

_____ 6. Explains the importance of being punctual and dependable.

_____ 7. Explains the importance of company loyalty.

_____ 8. Practices conservation of time and materials.

_____ 9. Evaluates own work.

II. Vocationally Related Skills

_____ 1. Demonstrates skills and concepts related to counting, money, telling time, and measurement (see Arithmetic—Senior High Level).

_____ 2. Works with minimum supervision.

_____ 3. Demonstrates specific and thorough skill training for chosen occupation.

_____ 4. Reads adequately for self-protection and welfare of others.

_____ 5. Converses appropriately with fellow workers and supervisors.

_____ 6. Assumes personal responsibility for care of materials and tools.

III. Analysis of Occupations

_____ 1. Knows specific information on jobs in own area.

_____ 2. Chooses most appropriate job with consideration of strengths and weaknesses.

_____ 3. Begins to get job experience.

_____ 4. Explains various positions of work—lay person, manager, supervisor, etc.

_____ 5. Explains funding source of his job and knows its relationship to job security.

IV. Getting a Job

_____ 1. Reads want ads daily.

_____ 2. Fills out job application forms with no problems.

_____ 3. Takes advantage of services of employment agencies.

4. Tells why:

_____a. Long-term employment is usually better than seasonal employment.

_____b. Wages are not always the most important factor in getting a job.

_____c. One should consider fringe benefits when choosing a job.

5. Carries out personal interview effectively.

6. Knows how to fill out the following forms:

_____a. Withholding tax.

_____b. Union forms.

_____ 7. Works closely with rehabilitation counselor.

V. Responsibilities, Rights, and Benefits

_____ 1. Can explain:

_____a. Straight salary.

_____b. Part-time work.

_____c. Commissions.

_____d. Time and a half.

_____e. Double time.

_____ 2. Names basic social security benefits.

3. Can explain the basic fringe benefits of:

_____a. Hospital and medical insurance.

_____b. Life insurance.

_____c. Sick pay.

_____d. Vacation pay.

_____e. Holiday pay.

_____f. Retirement program.

_____g. Disability payments.

_____h. Pensions.

_____i. Profit-sharing plans.

_____ 4. Demonstrates knowledge of unemployment compensation and how to apply for it.

5. Explains the following terms associated with unions:

_____a. Collective bargaining.

_____b. Strikes.

_____c. Picket.

_____d. Boycott.

_____e. Union contract.

_____ 6. Tells advantages and disadvantages of joining unions.

7. Explains the major responsibilities of the worker to the employer:

_____a. Why he should report to work regularly and on time.

_____b. What he should do in case he cannot report to work.

_____c. Why he should do a day's work with or without supervision.

LEISURE TIME—PRIMARY LEVEL

I. Participation in Organized Games

———— 1. Is eager to participate in games.
———— 2. Explains that games have rules.
———— 3. Plays simple games such as chase, hide-and-seek, jump rope, and marbles.

II. Enjoyment of Nature

———— 1. Takes walks to observe nature and observes flowers, trees, insects, etc.
———— 2. Collects rocks, flowers, leaves.
———— 3. Observes creeks and lakes.
———— 4. Helps take care of plants.
———— 5. Begins to demonstrate basic care of pets.
———— 6. Keeps classroom pet.

III. Develops Avocational Interests

———— 1. Plays with toys, puzzles, paints, and colors.
———— 2. Listens to stories.
———— 3. Watches television.
———— 4. Listens to records.
———— 5. Sings simple songs.
———— 6. Uses rhythm instruments.
———— 7. Listens to the radio.
———— 8. Makes craft projects.

LEISURE TIME—INTERMEDIATE LEVEL

I. Participation in Organized Games

———— 1. Defines the competitive nature of some games.
———— 2. Participates in team games such as baseball, football, and volleyball.
———— 3. Participates in simple games without adult leadership or supervision.
———— 4. Plays games cooperatively and by the rules.
———— 5. Plays quiet games such as checkers, dominos, and simple card games.
———— 6. Practices rules of good sportsmanship.
———— 7. Watches organized sporting events.

II. Enjoyment of Nature

———— 1. Expands interest in making flower, insect, rock, and leaf collections.
———— 2. Plants flowers and assumes responsibility for caring for them.
———— 3. Assumes responsibility for caring for pets.
———— 4. Names common flowers and trees.
———— 5. Names common pets and how to care for each.
———— 6. Names common insects.
———— 7. Makes a terrarium.
———— 8. Hikes.
———— 9. Observes small animal life such as fish, tadpoles, frogs, turtles, etc.
————10. Goes on nature walks and bicycle rides.
————11. Begins to notice different birds.
————12. Respects nature by not littering.

III. Develops Avocational Interests

_____ 1. Plays with toys appropriate to age level.
_____ 2. Sings songs from a variety of categories—folk, popular, spirituals, seasonal.
_____ 3. Marches to music.
_____ 4. Participates in folk dancing.
_____ 5. Listens to stories and records.
_____ 6. Reads books.
_____ 7. Begins to know schedule of favorite programs on television and the radio.
_____ 8. Watches television and listens to radio with regularity.
_____ 9. Attends movies appropriate to age.
_____10. Performs art and craft work.
_____11. Performs simple cooking.
_____12. Learns basic sewing skills.
_____13. Uses community recreation facilities such as swimming pool and playing fields.
_____14. Participates in the community public library program.

LEISURE TIME—JUNIOR HIGH LEVEL

I. Participation in Organized Games

_____ 1. Tells about rules of baseball, football, basketball, and volleyball.
_____ 2. Displays team spirit.
_____ 3. Participates in intramural or athletic teams.
_____ 4. Plays card games such as Gin Rummy and Hearts.
_____ 5. Plays board games such as Monopoly.
_____ 6. Learns to play pool.

II. Enjoyment of Nature

_____ 1. Takes hiking trips.
_____ 2. Goes on supervised camping trips.
_____ 3. Plants a flower and vegetable garden and assumes responsibility.
_____ 4. Identifies by name common birds, leaves, insects, etc.
_____ 5. Tells about pollution and helps to control it.
_____ 6. Does yard work such as cutting grass.
_____ 7. Goes on picnics.

III. Develops Avocational Interests

_____ 1. Visits with friends.
_____ 2. Watches television and listens to radio programs.
_____ 3. Cooks a variety of dishes.
_____ 4. Begins to develop sewing skills.
_____ 5. Listens to music from a variety of categories.
_____ 6. Develops skill in social dancing.
_____ 7. Attends movies.
_____ 8. Attends sporting events.
_____ 9. Reads newspaper, magazines, and books.
_____10. Begins to develop skill in wood working.
_____11. Broadens skill in art and craft activities.
_____12. Attends community sponsored entertainment activities.
_____13. Participates in community recreation program.
_____14. Takes company with the opposite sex.

LEISURE TIME—SENIOR HIGH LEVEL

I. Participation in Organized Games

———— 1. Practices skill development related to sports and organized games.
———— 2. Learns new games.
———— 3. Displays good sportsmanship.
———— 4. Recognizes outstanding individual achievement.

II. Enjoyment of Nature

———— 1. Participates in camping activities.
———— 2. Supervises younger children on picnics.
———— 3. Plants garden.
———— 4. Explains and appreciates seasonal changes of nature.
———— 5. Develops skill in fishing.
———— 6. Teaches younger children names of leaves, flowers, trees, birds, insects, etc.
———— 7. Builds a campfire and understands appropriate safety precautions.
———— 8. Prunes shrubbery.

III. Develops Avocational Interests

———— 1. Entertains friends.
———— 2. Broadens skills in cooking, sewing, and woodworking.
———— 3. Attends movies and community sponsored events.
———— 4. Follows television and radio schedule.
———— 5. Improves skill in social dancing.
———— 6. Plays simple musical instruments.
———— 7. Sings a variety of songs.
———— 8. Participates actively in public library program.
———— 9. Cares for younger children.
————10. Plans and carries out family leisure activities.

REFERENCES

Affleck, J. Q., Madge, S., Adams, A., & Lowenbraun, S. (1988). Integrated classroom versus resource model: Academic viability and effectiveness. *Exceptional Children, 54,* 339–348.

Agne, R. M., & Ducharme, E. R. (1977). Rearranging the parts: A modest proposal for continuing and inservice training. *Journal of Teacher Education, 28,* 16–19.

Algozzine, B., Christenson, S., & Ysseldyke, J. (1982). Probabilities associated with the referral to placement process. *Teacher Education and Special Education, 5,* 19–23.

Algozzine, B., Schmid, R., & Mercer, C. D. (1981). *Childhood behavior disorders: Applied research and educational practice.* Rockville, MD: Aspen Systems Corp.

Algozzine, B., & Ysseldyke, J. E. (1981). Special education services for normal children: Better safe than sorry? *Exceptional Children, 48,* 238–243.

Algozzine, B., & Ysseldyke, J. E. (1982). Classification decisions in learning disabilities. *Educational and Psychological Research, 2,* 117–129.

Algozzine, B., & Ysseldyke, J. E. (1983). Learning disabilities as a subset of school failure: The oversophistication of a concept. *Exceptional Children, 50,* 242–246.

Algozzine, B., & Ysseldyke, J. E. (1986). The future of the LD field: Screening and diagnosis. *Journal of Learning Disabilities, 19,* 394–98.

Allen, D. A., Hudd, S. S. (1987). Are we professionalizing parents? Weighing the benefits and pitfalls. *Mental Retardation, July,* 133–139.

Alper, S., & Noei, D. R. (1987). Extended school year services for students with severe handicaps: A national survey. *Journal of the Association for Persons with Severe Handicaps, 12,* 61–66.

American Occupational Therapy Association (1981). Related services and medical service requirements under current legal standards. *Focus, 1,* 26.

Ammer, J. J. (1984). The mechanics of mainstreaming: Considering the regular educator's perspective. *Remedial and Special Education, 5,* 15–20.

Armstrong v. Kline. 476 F. Supp. 583 (E.D. PA, 1979).

Bailey, D. B. (1984). A triaxial model of the interdisciplinary team and group process. *Exceptional Children, 51,* 17–25.

Barton, C. L. (1984). Parents and information: What they receive and what they need. *Mental Retardation and Learning Disabilities Bulletin, 12,* 98–104.

Battle v. Commonwealth, 79-2158, 79-2188-90, 79-2568-70. (3rd Cr., July 18, 1980).

Bennett, R. E. (1983). Research and evaluation priorities for special education assessment. *Exceptional Children, 50,* 110–117.

Benz, M. R., & Halpern, A. S. (1987). Transition services for secondary students with mild disabilities: A statewide perspective. *Exceptional Children, 53,* 507–514.

Berman, P., & McLaughlin, M. W. (1975). *Federal programs supporting education change* (Vol. 4). *The findings in review (R-1589/4-HEW).* Santa Monica, CA: The Rand Corporation.

Betts, E. A. (1957). *Foundations of reading instruction.* New York: American Book Company.

Birmingham and Lamphere School Districts v. Superintendent of Public Instruction for the State of Michigan, 328 N.W. 2d 59 (Ct. App. MI 1982).

Bloom, B. (1984). The search for methods of group instruction as effective as one-to-one tutoring. *Educational Leadership, May,* 4–17.

Bloom, B. S., Engelhart, M. D., Furst, E., Hill, W., & Krathwohl, D. R. (1956). *Taxonomy of educational objectives: Handbook I: Cognitive domain.* New York: David McKay.

Board of Education of the Hendrick Hudson Central School District v. Rowley, 102 S. Ct. 3034 (1982).

Braaten, S., Kauffman, J. E., Braaten, B., Polsgrove, L., & Nelson, C. (1988). The regular education initiative: Patent medicine for behavioral disorders. *Exceptional Children, 55,* 21–26.

Brigance, A. (1978). *Inventory of early development.* North Billerica MA: Curriculum Associates.

Brinkerhoff, J. L., & Vincent, L. J. (1986). Increasing parental decision-making at the individualized education program meeting. *Journal of the Division for Early Childhood, 11,* 46–58.

Brown, L., Rogan, P., Shiraga, B., Zanella Albright, K., Kossler, K., Bryson, F., Van Deventer, P., & Loomis, R. (1986). A vocational follow-up evaluation of the 1984–86 Madison Metropolitan School District graduates with severe intellectual disabilities. In L. Brown, R. Loomis, K.

Zanella Albright, P. Rogan, J. York, B. Shiraga, & E. Long (Eds.), *Educational programs for students with severe handicaps* (Vol. 16). Madison, WI: Madison Metropolitan School District.

Burlington School Committee of the Town of Burlington, Massachusetts v. Department of Education of the Commonwealth of Massachusetts, 105 S. Ct. 1996 (1985).

Campbell, P. H. (1987). The integrated programming team: An approach for coordinating professionals of various disciplines in programs for students with severe and multiple handicaps. *Journal of the Association for Persons with Severe Handicaps, 12,* 107–116.

Carlberg, C., & Kavale, K. (1980). The efficacy of special versus regular class placement for exceptional children: A meta analysis. *Journal of Special Education, 14,* 295–309.

Chalfant, J. C., Van Dusen, P. M., & Moultrie, R. (1979). Teacher assistance teams: A model for within building problem solving. *Learning Disability Quarterly, 2,* 85–96.

Christenson, S., Ysseldyke, J. E., Wang, J. J., & Algozzine, B. (1983). Teacher attributions for problems that result in referral for psychoeducational evaluation. *Journal of Educational Research, 76,* 174–180.

Cobb, B., & Phelps, A. (1983). Analyzing individualized education programs for vocational components: An exploratory study. *Exceptional Children, 50,* 62–64.

Cohen, R. A. (1969). Conceptual styles, culture conflict, and non-verbal tests of intelligence. *American Anthropologist, 71,* 828–856.

Council for Exceptional Children. (1987). Statement on the relationship between special education and general education. *Education for the Handicapped Law Report,* Supplement 194, 5A-156-57.

Dattilo, J., & Rusch, F. R. (1985). Effects of choice on leisure participation for persons with severe handicaps. *Journal of the Association for Persons with Severe Handicaps, 10*(4), 194–199.

Deno, S., Mirkin, P. K., & Chiang, B. (1982). Identifying valid measures of reading. *Exceptional Children, 49,* 36–45.

Deno, S. L. (1985). Curriculum-based measurement: The emerging alternative. *Exceptional Children, 52,* 219–232.

Diana v. State Board of Education, C-70-37 RFP, (N.D. Cal., 1970).

Dudley-Marling, C. (1985). Perceptions of the usefulness of the IEP by teachers of learning disabled and emotionally disturbed children. *Psychology in the Schools, 22,* 65–67.

Eaton, M. D., & Lovitt, T. C. (1972). Achievement tests vs. direct and daily measurement. In G. Semb (Ed.), *Behavior analysis and education.* Lawrence, KS: University of Kansas.

Edelfelt, R. (1977). The school of education and inservice education. *Journal of Teacher Education, 28,* 10–14.

Edmister, P., & Edstrand, R. E. (1987). Preschool programming: Legal and educational issues. *Exceptional Children, 54,* 130–136.

Education Turnkey Systems. (1981). *P.L. 94–142: A study of the implementation and impact at the state level* (Vol. 1). *Executive summary.* Falls Church, VA: Author.

Espino v. Besteiro, S20 F. Supp. 90S (1981).

Federal register (Vol. 42, pp. 42474–42515). Washington, DC: U.S. Government Printing Office, August 23, 1977.

Fiedler, J. F., & Knight, R. R. (1986). Congruence between assessed needs and IEP goals of identified behaviorally disabled students. *Behavior Disorders, 12,* 22–27.

Flanders, N. A. (1963). Teacher behavior and inservice programs. *Educational Leadership, 21,* 25–29.

Floden, R., Porter, A., Schmidt, W., & Freeman, D. (1980). Don't they all measure the same thing? In E. Baker & E. Quellnalz (Eds.), *Educational testing and evaluation.* Beverly Hills, CA: Sage.

Fordyce, W. (1981). On interdisciplinary peers. *Archives of Physical Medicine, 62,* 51–53.

Fraas, C. J. (1986). *Preschool programs for the education of handicapped children: Background, issues, and federal policy options* (Report No. 86-55 EPW. Publication HV750A). Washington, DC: Congressional Research Service, The Library of Congress.

Friend, M. (1984). Consultation skills for resource teachers. *Learning Disability Quarterly, 7,* 246–250.

Fuchs, D., & Fuchs, L. S. (1986). Test procedure bias: A meta analysis of examiner familiarity effects. *Review of Educational Research, 56,* 243–262.

Fuchs, D., & Fuchs, L. (1988). An evaluation of the adaptive learning environments model. *Exceptional Children, 55,* 115–127.

Fuchs, D., Fuchs, L. S., Benowitz, S., & Barringer, K. (1987). Norm-referenced tests: Are they valid for use with handicapped students? *Exceptional Children, 54,* 263–271.

Fuchs, L. S., & Fuchs, D. (1986). Curriculum-based assessment of progress toward long-term and short-term goals. *The Journal of Special Education, 20,* 69–80.

Fuqua, R. W., Hegland, S. M., & Karas, S. C. (1985). Processes influencing linkages between preschool handicap classrooms and homes. *Exceptional Children, 51,* 307–314.

Gartner, A., & Lipsky, D. K. (1987). Beyond special education: Toward a quality system for all students. *Harvard Educational Review, 57,* 367–394.

General Accounting Office. (1981). *Disparities still exist in who gets special education.* Washington, DC: Author.

Gerber, M. M., & Semmel, M. I. (1984). Teacher as imperfect test: Reconceptualizing the referral process. *Educational Psychologist, 19,* 137–148.

Gerber, P. J., Banbury, M. M., Miller, J. H., & Griffin, H. D. (1986). Special educator's perceptions of parental participation in the individual education plan process. *Psychology in the Schools, 23,* 158–163.

Godhu, R., Crosby, J., & Massey, S. (1977). Inservice: The professional development of educators. *Journal of Teacher Education, 28,* 24–30.

Goetz, L., Schuler, A., & Sailor, W. (1979). Teaching functional speech to the severely handicapped. *Journal of Autism and Developmental Disorders, 9,* 325–344.

Goldstein, S., Strickland, B., Turnbull, H. P., & Curry, L.

(1980). An observational analysis of the IEP conference. *Exceptional Children, 46,* 278–280.

Goldstein, S., & Turnbull, A. P. (1982). Strategies to increase parent participation in the IEP conference. *Exceptional Children, 46,* 278–286.

Goodlad, J. I. (1984). *A place called school: Prospects for the future.* New York: McGraw-Hill.

Graden, J. L., Casey, A., Bonstrom, O. (1985). Implementing a pre-referral system: Part II. The data. *Exceptional Children, 51,* 487–496.

Grossman, H. J. (1983). *Classification in mental retardation.* Washington, DC: American Association on Mental Deficiency.

Hagerty, G. J., & Abramson, M. (1987). Impediments to implementing national policy change for mildly handicapped students. *Exceptional Children, 53,* 315–324.

Hallahan, D. P., Keller, C. E., McKinney, J. D., Lloyd, J. W., & Bryan, T. (1988). Examining the research base of the regular education initiative: Efficacy studies and the ALEM. *Journal of Learning Disabilities, 21,* 29–35.

Halpern, A. S. (1985). Transition: A look at the foundation. *Exceptional Children, 51,* 479–483.

Hardman, M., & McDonnell, J. (1987). Implementing federal transition initiatives for youths with severe handicaps: The Utah community-based transition project. *Exceptional Children, 53,* 493–498.

Harrington, R. G., & Gibson, E. (1986). Preassessment procedures for learning disabled children: Are they effective. *Journal of Learning Disabilities, 19,* 538–541.

Hasazi, S. B., Gordon, L. R., & Roe, C. A. (1985). Factors associated with the employment status of handicapped youth exiting high school from 1975 to 1983. *Exceptional Children, 51,* 455–469.

Hawaii Department of Education v. Katherine D., No. 82:4096 (9th Cir., No. 7, 1983).

Hayek, R. A. (1987). The teacher assistance team: A pre-referral support system. *Focus on Exceptional Children, 20,* 1–8.

Heller, K. A., Holtzman, W. H., & Messick, S. (1982). *Placing children in special education.* Washington, DC: National Academy Press.

Houghton, J., Bronicki, G. J., & Guess, D. (1987). Opportunities to express preferences and make choices among students with severe disabilities in classroom setting. *Journal of the Association for Persons with Severe Handicaps, 12*(11), 18–27.

Hummel, J. W., & Degnan, S. C. (1986). Options for technology-assisted IEP's. *Journal of Learning Disabilities, 19,* 562–565.

Idol, L., Paolucci-Whitcomb, P., & Nevin, A. (1986). *Collaborative consultation.* Rockville, MD: Aspen.

Idol, L., & West, F. (1987). Consultation in special education (Part II): Training and practice. *Journal of Learning Disabilities, 20,* 474–488.

Idol-Maestas, L., & Ritter, S. (1985). A follow-up study of resource/consulting teachers: Factors that facilitate and inhibit teacher consultation. *Teacher Education and Special Education, 8,* 121–131.

Irving Independent School District v. Tatro, 104 S. Ct. 3371 (U.S. Sup. Ct. 1984).

Jenkins, J. R., & Pany, D. P. (1978). Standardized achievement tests: How useful for special education? *Exceptional Children, 44,* 448–453.

Jenkins, M. W. (1987). Effect of a computerized individual education program (IEP) writer on time savings and quality. *Journal of Special Education Technology, 8,* 55–66.

Lambert, N. M. (1988). Perspectives on eligibility for and placement in special education programs. *Exceptional Children, 54,* 297–301.

Larry P. v. Riles, 495 F. Supp. 96 (N.D. Cal. 1979).

Latham, G., & Burnham, J. (1985). Innovative methods for serving rural handicapped children. *School Psychology Review, 14,* 438–443.

Lawrence, G., Baker, D., Elzie, P., & Hansen, B. (1974). *Patterns of effective in-service education. A state-of-the-art summary of research on materials and procedures for changing teacher behaviors in in-service education.* Gainesville, FL: Florida State Department of Education.

Lewis, K. A., Schwartz, G. M., & Ianacone, R. N. (1988). Service coordination between correctional and public school systems for handicapped juvenile offenders. *Exceptional Children, 55,* 66–70.

Lipsky, D. K., & Gartner, A. (1987). Capable of achievement and worthy of respect: Education for the handicapped as if they were full fledged human beings. *Exceptional Children, 54,* 69–74.

Lora v. Board of Education of the City of New York, 1984: Final order, August 2, 1984, 587 F. Supp. 1572 (E.D. N.Y. 1984).

Lynch, E. W., Stein, R. C. (1987). Parent participation by ethnicity: A comparison of Hispanic, black, and anglo families. *Exceptional Children, 54,* 105–111.

Lyon, S., & Lyon, G. (1980). Team functioning and staff development: A role release approach to providing integrated educational services for severely handicapped students. *Journal of the Association for the Severely Handicapped, 5,* 250–263.

Madden, N. A., & Slavin, R. E. (1983). Effects of cooperative learning on the social acceptance of mainstreamed academically handicapped students. *The Journal of Special Education, 17,* 171–182.

Maher, C. A. (1985). Procedures for mainstreaming handicapped adolescents into regular education classrooms. *Techniques, 1,* 380–388.

Marshall v. McDaniel, Civil No. 482–233 (S.D. Ga. 1984).

Marver, J. D., & David, J. L. (1979). *Implementation of individualized education program requirements of P.L. 94–142.* Menlo Park, CA: SRI International.

Mattie T. v. Holliday, 3 EHLR 551:109 (N.D. Miss. 1979).

McCormick, L. P. (1985). Keeping up with language intervention trends. *Teaching Exceptional Children, Winter,* 123–128.

McGrady, H. J. (1985). Administrative support for mainstreaming learning disabled students. *Journal of Learning Disabilities, 18,* 464–466.

Minde, K. K., Hackett, J. D., Killon, D., & Silver, S. (1972). How they grow up: Physically handicapped children and their families. *American Journal of Rehabilitation Research, 5,* 235–237.

Morgan, D. P., & Rhode, G. (1983). Teachers' attitudes toward IEP's: A two-year follow-up. *Exceptional Children, 50,* 64–67.

Munson, S. (1986). Regular education teacher modification for mainstreamed mildly handicapped students. *Journal of Special Education, 20,* 489–502.

National Association of State Directors of Special Education. (1978). *The implementation of due process in Massachusetts.* Washington, DC: Author.

National Association of State Directors of Special Education (1985). *Opinions of state directors of special education and parent leaders on the implementation of procedural safeguards relative to the education of handicapped children and youth.* Washington, DC: Author.

Nevin, A., & Thousand, J. (1986). What the research says about limiting or avoiding referrals to special education. *Journal of Teacher Education and Special Education, 9,* 149–161.

Norman, C., & Zigmond, N. (1980). Characteristics of children labeled and served as learning disabled in school systems affiliated with Child Service Demonstration Centers. *Journal of Learning Disabilities, 13,* 16–21.

Office of Civil Rights. (1980). *Fall 1979 vocational education survey.* Washington, DC: Author.

Ortiz, A. A., Maldonado-Colon, E. (1986). Recognizing learning disabilities in bilingual children: How to lessen inappropriate referrals of language minority students to special education. *Journal of Reading, Writing & Learning Disabilities International, 2,* 43–56.

Osbourne, A. G. (1984). How the courts have interpreted the related services mandate. *Exceptional Children, 51,* 249–252.

Palfrey, J., DiPrete, L., Walker, D., Shannon, K., Maroney, E. (1987). *School children dependent on medical technology.* Washington, DC: D:ATA Institute: The Catholic University of America.

Palfrey, J. S., Sarro, L. J., Singer, J. D., & Wenger, M. (1987). Physician familiarity with the educational programs of their special needs patients. *Developmental and Behavioral Pediatrics, 8,* 198–202.

Palfrey, J. S., Singer, J. D., Raphael, E. S., & Walker, D. K. (1987). *Providing therapeutic services in various educational settings.* Boston, MA: The Children's Hospital.

Palfrey, J. S., Singer, J. D., Walker, D. K., & Butler, J. A. (1986). Health and special education: A study of new developments for handicapped children in five metropolitan communities. *Public Health Reports, 101,* 379–388.

Palfrey, J. S., Singer, J. D., Walker, D. K., & Butler, J. A. (1987). Early identification of children's special needs: A study in five metropolitan communities. *The Journal of Pediatrics, 3,* 651–659.

PASE v. Hannon, 506 F. Supp. 831 (N.D. Ill. 1980).

Peck, C. H. (1985). Increasing opportunities for social control by children with autism and severe handicaps: Effects on student behavior and perceived classroom climate. *The Journal of the Association for Persons with Severe Handicaps, 10*(4), 183–193.

Peterson, J., Heistad, D., Peterson, D., & Reynolds, M. (1985). Montevideo individualized prescriptive instructional management system. *Exceptional Children, 52,* 239–243.

Price, M., & Goodman, L. (1980). Individualized education programs: A cost study. *Exceptional Children, 46,* 446–458.

Public Law 94–142. The Education of All Handicapped Children Act.

Public Law 99–457. The Amendments to the Education of the Handicapped Act of 1986.

Pugach, M. (1982). Regular classroom teacher involvement in the development and utilization of IEPs. *Exceptional Children, 48,* 371–374.

Pugach, M. C. (1985). The limitations of federal special education policy: The role of classroom teachers in determining who is handicapped. *Journal of Special Education, 19,* 123–137.

Rainforth, B., & York, J. (1987). Integrating related services in community instruction. *The Journal of the Association for Persons with Severe Handicaps, 12,* 190–198.

Reilly, V. E., & Dembo, M. H. (1975). Teachers' views of inservice education: A question of confidence. *Phi Delta Kappan, 47,* 126.

Reschly, D. J. (1988). Learning characteristics of mildly handicapped students: Implications for classification, placement, and programming. In M. C. Wang, M. C. Reynolds, and H. J. Walberg, (Eds.), *The Handbook of Special Education: Research and Practice.* Oxford, England: Pergamon Press.

Ritchie, M. H. (1986). The influence of referral information on the diagnostic classification of exceptional children. *Exceptional Children, 33,* 181–186.

Ryan, L. B., & Rucker, C. N. (1986). Computerized vs. non-computerized individualized education programs: Teachers' attitudes, time, and cost. *Journal of Special Education Technology, 8,* 5–12.

Sabatino, D. A. (1981). Are appropriate educational programs operationally achievable under mandated promises of P.L. 94–142? *Journal of Special Education, 15,* 9–18.

Salend, S. (1987). Identifying school district policies for implementing mainstreaming. *Pointer, 32,* 34–37.

Salmon-Cox, L. (1981). Teachers and standardized achievement tests: What's really happening? *Phi Delta Kappan, 63,* 87–89.

Salvia, J., & Ysseldyke, J. E. (1978). *Assessment in special and remedial education.* Boston: Houghton Mifflin Company.

Sarason, S. B., & Doris, J. (1979). *Educational handicap, public policy, and social history.* New York: Free Press.

Schumaker, J. B., & Deshler, D. D. (1988). Implementing the regular education initiative in secondary schools. A different ballgame. *Journal of Learning Disabilities, 21,* 36–42.

Shepard, L. A., & Smith, M. L. (1983). An evaluation of the identification of learning disabled students in Colorado. *Learning Disability Quarterly, 6,* 115–127.

Shepard, L. A., Smith, L. A., & Vojir, C. P. (1983) Characteristics of pupils identified as learning disabled. *Journal of Special Education, 16,* 73–85.

Shevin, M., & Klein, N. (1984). Importance of choice-making skills for students with severe disabilities. *The Journal of the Association for Persons with Severe Handicaps,* 9(3), 159–166.

Shinn, M. R., Tindal, G. A., Spira, D. A. (1987). Special education referrals as an index of teacher tolerance: Are teachers imperfect tests? *Exceptional Children, 54,* 32–40.

Singer, J. D., & Butler, J. A. (1987). The education of all handicapped children act: Schools as agents of social reform. *Harvard Educational Review, 57,* 125–152.

Singer, J. D., Butler, J. A., Palfrey, J. S., & Walker, D. K. (1986). Characteristics of special education placements: Findings from probability. Samples in five metropolitan school districts. *Journal of Special Education, 20,* 319–337.

Skrtic, T. M. (1987). An organizational analysis of special education reform. *Counterpoint, 8,* 15–19.

Skrtic, T. M., Knowlton, H. E., & Clark, F. L. (1979). Action versus reaction: A curriculum development approach to inservice education. *Focus on Exceptional Children, 11,* 1–16.

Splitt, D. A. (1987). School law. *Executive Educator, 9,* 12.

Stainback, S., & Stainback, W. (1984). A rationale for the merger of special and regular education. *Exceptional Children, 51,* 102–111.

Stainback, S., & Stainback, W. (1987). Integration versus cooperation: A commentary on educating children with learning problems: A shared responsibility. *Exceptional Children, 54,* 66–68.

Stainback, W., Stainback, S., Courtnage, L., & Jaben, T. (1985). Facilitating mainstreaming by modifying the mainstream. *Exceptional Children, 52,* 144–152.

Stainback, W. C., Stainback, S. B., & Hatcher, C. W. (1983). Developing policies for extended year programs. *The Journal of the Association for Persons with Severe Handicaps, 8,* 5–9.

Strickland, B. (1982). *Perceptions of parents and school representatives regarding their relationship before, during, and after the due process hearing.* Unpublished doctoral dissertation, University of North Carolina at Chapel Hill.

Strickland, B. (1983). Legal issues that affect parents. In M. Seligman (Ed.), *The family with a handicapped child: Understanding and treatment* (pp. 27–59). Philadelphia: W. B. Saunders.

Turnbull, A. P., & Turnbull, H. R. (1982). Parent involvement in the education of handicapped children: A critique. *Mental Retardation, 20,* 115–122.

Turnbull, H. R. (1986). Appropriate education and Rowley. *Exceptional Children, 52,* 347–352.

Turnbull, H. R., Turnbull, A. P., Bronicki, G. J., Summers, J. A., & Roeder-Gordon, C. (1988). *Disability and the family.* Baltimore, MD: Paul Brooks Publishing.

Turnbull, H. R., Turnbull, A. P., & Wheat, M. J. (1982). Assumptions about parental participation: A legislative history. *Exceptional Education Quarterly, 3,* 1–8.

Turnbull, K. K., & Hughes, D. L. (1987). A pragmatic analysis of speech and language IEP conferences. *Language, Speech, and Hearing in the Schools, 18,* 275–286.

U.S. Department of Education. (1981). *Assistance to states for educating handicapped children: Interpretation of the individualized education program (IEP).* Washington, DC: U.S. Government Printing Office.

U.S. Department of Education. (1986). *Standards and guidelines for compliance with federal requirements for the education of the handicapped.* Washington, DC: Author.

U.S. Department of Education. (1988). *Tenth annual report to Congress on the implementation of the Education of the Handicapped Act.* Washington, DC: U.S. Government Printing Office.

U.S. Department of Education, Office of Special Education and Rehabilitative Services. (1987). *Ninth annual report to Congress on the implementation of the Education of the Handicapped Act.* Washington, DC: U.S. Government Printing Office.

U.S. Department of Education, Office of Special Education and Rehabilitative Services. (1985). *State EC/SE status and state participation in networks.* Unpublished matrix.

U.S. House of Representatives. (1986). *Education of the Handicapped Act Amendments of 1986* (Report 99–860). Washington, DC: U.S. Government Printing Office.

U.S. Library of Congress Congressional Research Service. (1986). *P.L. 94–142, The Education for All Handicapped Children Act: Its development, implementation and current issues. Special Report by Charlotte Jones Fraas.* Washington, DC: U.S. Department of Education.

Vaughn, S., Bos, C. S., Harrell, J. E., & Lasky, B. A. (1988). Parent participation in the initial placement/IEP conference ten years after mandated involvement. *Journal of Learning Disabilities, 21,* 82–89.

Vitello, S. J. (1986). The Tatro case: Who gets what and why. *Exceptional Children, 52,* 353–356.

Walker, H. (1984). *Teacher social behavior standards and expectations as determinants of classroom ecology, teacher behavior, and child outcomes. Final report.* Eugene, OR: University of Oregon, Center for Educational Policy and Analysis.

Walker, L. J. (1987). Procedural rights in the wrong system: Special education is not enough. In A. Gartner & T. Joe (Eds.), *Images of the Disabled/Disabling Images* (pp. 98–102). New York: Praeger.

Wang, M., & Reynolds, M. (1984). Avoiding the "Catch 22" in special education reform. *Exceptional Children, 51,* 497–502.

Wang, M. C., & Birch, J. W. (1984). Effective special education in regular classes. *Exceptional Children, 50,* 391–398.

Wang, M. C., Reynolds, M. C., & Walberg, H. J. (1986). Rethinking special education. *Educational Leadership, 44,* 26–34.

Weber, J., Stoneman, Z. (1986). Parental non-participation in program planning for the mentally retarded. *Applied Research in Mental Retardation, 7,* 359–369.

Wehman, P., Kregel, J., & Barcus, J. M. (1985). From school to work: A vocational transition model for handicapped students. In P. Wehman & J. W. Hill (Eds.), *Competitive employment for persons with moderate and severe mental retardation: From research to practice* (pp. 169–198). Richmond, VA: Commonwealth University, School of Education Rehabilitation Research and Training Center.

Wesson, C., King, R. P., & Deno, S. L. (1984). Direct and frequent measurement of student performance: If it's good for us, why don't we do it? *Learning Disability Quarterly, 7,* 45–48.

West, J. F., Idol, L. (1987). School consultation (Part I): An interdisciplinary perspective on theory, models, and research. *Journal of Learning Disabilities, 20,* 388–408.

White, R., & Calhoun, M. L. (1987). From referral to placement: Teachers' perceptions of their responsibilities. *Exceptional Children, 53,* 460–468.

Will, M. (1986). Educating children with learning problems: A shared responsibility. *Exceptional Children, 52,* 411–415.

Williams, R. L. (1970). Black pride, academic relevance, and individual achievement. *Counseling Psychologist, 2,* 18–22.

Witt, J. C., Miller, C. D., McIntyre, R. M., & Smith, D. (1984). Effects of variables on parental perceptions of staffing. *Exceptional Children, 51,* 27–32.

Yoshida, R. K., Fenton, K. S., Kaufman, M. J., & Maxwell, J. P. (1978). Parental involvement in special education pupil planning process: The school's perspective. *Exceptional Children, 44,* 531–534.

Ysseldyke, J. E. (1988). Classification of handicapped students. In M. C. Wang, M. C. Reynolds, & H. J. Walberg (Eds.), *Handbook of Special Education: Research and Practice.* Oxford, England: Pergamon Press.

Ysseldyke, J. E., Algozzine, B., & Allen, D. (1981). Participation of regular education teachers in special education team decision making: A naturalistic investigation. *Elementary School Journal, 82,* 160–165.

Ysseldyke, J. E., Algozzine, B., & Epps, S. (1983). Logical and empirical analysis of current practices in classifying students as handicapped. *Exceptional Children, 50,* 160–166.

Ysseldyke, J. E., Algozzine, B., Richey, L., & Graden, J. (1982). Declaring students eligible for learning disability services: Why bother with the data? *Learning Disability Quarterly, 5,* 37–44.

Ysseldyke, J. E., Algozzine, B., Shinn, M., & McGue, M. (1982). Similarities and differences between underachievers and students classified learning disabled. *Journal of Special Education, 16,* 73–85.

Ysseldyke, J. E., Algozzine, B., & Thurlow, M. (1980). *A naturalistic investigation of special education team meetings.* Minneapolis, MN: Institute for Research on Learning Disabilities, University of Minnesota.

Ysseldyke, J. E., Christenson, S., Pianta, B., & Algozzine, B. (1983). An analysis of teachers' reasons and desired outcomes for students referred for psychoeducational assessment. *Journal of Psychoeducational Assessment, 1,* 73–83.

Ysseldyke, J. E., Christenson, S., Pianta, B., Thurlow, M. L., & Algozzine, B. (October 1982). *An analysis of current practice in referring students for psychoeducational evaluation: Implications for change* (Research Report No. 91). Minneapolis, MN: Institute for Research on Learning Disabilities, University of Minnesota.

Ysseldyke, J. E., Pianta, B., Christenson, S., Wang, J., & Algozzine, B. (1983). An analysis of pre-referral intervention. *Psychology in the Schools, 20,* 194–196.

Ysseldyke, J. E., Thurlow, M., Graden, J., Wesson, C., Algozzine, B., & Deno, S. (1983). Generalizations from five years of research on assessment and decision making: The University of Minnesota Institute. *Exceptional Education Quarterly, 4,* 75–93.

Zigmond, N., Levin, E., & Laurie, T. E. (1985). Managing the mainstream: An analysis of teacher attitudes and student performance in mainstream high school programs. *Journal of Learning Disabilities, 18,* 535–541.

INDEX

WE VALUE YOUR OPINION—PLEASE SHARE IT WITH US

Merrill Publishing and our authors are most interested in your reactions to this textbook. Did it serve you well in the course? If it did, what aspects of the text were most helpful? If not, what didn't you like about it? Your comments will help us to write and develop better textbooks. We value your opinions and thank you for your help.

Text Title _____ Edition _____

Author(s) _____

Your Name (optional) _____

Address _____

City _____ State _____ Zip _____

School _____

Course Title _____

Instructor's Name _____

Your Major _____

Your Class Rank _____ Freshman _____ Sophomore _____ Junior _____ Senior

_____ Graduate Student

Were you required to take this course? _____ Required _____ Elective

Length of Course? _____ Quarter _____ Semester

1. Overall, how does this text compare to other texts you've used?

_____ Superior _____ Better Than Most _____ Average _____ Poor

2. Please rate the text in the following areas:

	Superior	Better Than Most	Average	Poor
Author's Writing Style	_____	_____	_____	_____
Readability	_____	_____	_____	_____
Organization	_____	_____	_____	_____
Accuracy	_____	_____	_____	_____
Layout and Design	_____	_____	_____	_____
Illustrations/Photos/Tables	_____	_____	_____	_____
Examples	_____	_____	_____	_____
Problems/Exercises	_____	_____	_____	_____
Topic Selection	_____	_____	_____	_____
Currentness of Coverage	_____	_____	_____	_____
Explanation of Difficult Concepts	_____	_____	_____	_____
Match-up with Course Coverage	_____	_____	_____	_____
Applications to Real Life	_____	_____	_____	_____

3. Circle those chapters you especially liked:
   1   2   3   4   5   6   7   8   9   10   11   12   13   14
   What was your favorite chapter? _____
   Comments:

4. Circle those chapters you liked least:
   1   2   3   4   5   6   7   8   9   10   11   12   13   14
   What was your least favorite chapter? _____
   Comments:

5. List any chapters your instructor did not assign. _____

6. What topics did your instructor discuss that were not covered in the text?_____

   _____

7. Were you required to buy this book? _____ Yes   _____ No

   Did you buy this book new or used? _____ New   _____ Used

   If used, how much did you pay? _____

   Do you plan to keep or sell this book? _____ Keep   _____ Sell

   If you plan to sell the book, how much do you expect to receive? _____

   Should the instructor continue to assign this book? _____ Yes   _____ No

8. Please list any other learning materials you purchased to help you in this course (e.g., study guide, lab manual).

   _____

9. What did you like most about this text? _____

   _____

10. What did you like least about this text? _____

   _____

11. General comments:

   May we quote you in our advertising? _____ Yes   _____ No

   Please mail to: Boyd Lane
                     College Division, Research Department
                     Box 508
                     1300 Alum Creek Drive
                     Columbus, Ohio 43216

   Thank you!